Theories at-a-Glance

The tables in this book compare theories over a range of topics, thereby providing you with the ability to easily compare, contrast, and grasp the practical aspects of each theory. These tables also serve as invaluable resources that can be used to review the key concepts, philosophies, limitations, contributions to multicultural counseling, applications, techniques, and goals of all the theories in this text.

The following chart provides a convenient guide to the tables in this text:

Pages

8-9	Table 1-1	Overview of Contemporary Counseling Models
74-76	Table 4-1	Comparison of Freud's Psychosexual Stages and Erikson's Psychosocial Stages
392-393	Table 13-1	A Comparison of Six Systemic Viewpoints in Family Therapy
435	Table 13-2	A Comparison of Four Approaches to Social Construction in Family Therapy
464-465	Table 14-1	The Basic Philosophies
466-467	Table 14-2	Key Concepts
469	Table 14-3	Goals of Therapy
472-473	Table 14-4	The Therapeutic Relationship
474-476	Table 14-5	Techniques of Therapy
476-477	Table 14-6	Applications of the Approaches
478-479	Table 14-7	Contributions to Multicultural Counseling
479-480	Table 14-8	Limitations in Multicultural Counseling
481-483	Table 14-9	Contributions of the Approaches
483-484	Table 14-10	Limitations of the Approaches
495-497	Table 15-1	Major Areas of Focus in Stan's Therapy

www.wadsworth.com

wadsworth.com is the World Wide Web site for Wadsworth and is your direct source to dozens of online resources.

At *wadsworth.com* you can find out about supplements, demonstration software, and student resources. You can also send email to many of our authors and preview new publications and exciting new technologies.

wadsworth.com
Changing the way the world learns®

G ERALD COREY is a professor of human services and counseling at California State University at Fullerton and a licensed psychologist. He recieved his doctorate in counseling from the University of Southern California. He is a Diplomate in Counseling Psychology, American Board of Professional Psychology; a National Certified Counselor; a Fellow of the American Psychological Association (Counseling Psychology); and a Fellow of the Association for Specialists in Group Work.

Jerry received the Outstanding Professor of the Year Award from California State University at Fullerton in 1991. He teaches both undergraduate and graduate courses in group counseling, as well as courses in experiential groups, the theory and practice of counseling, theories of counseling, and professional ethics. He is the author or co-author of 14 textbooks in counseling that are currently in print, 3 student videos with workbooks, and 50 articles in professional publications. *Theory and Practice of Counseling and Psychotherapy* has been translated into the Arabic, Indonesian, Portuguese, and Chinese languages. *Theory and Practice of Group Counseling* has been translated into Chinese and Spanish. In the past 20 years he has conducted workshops for mental health professionals with a special focus on training in group counseling at many universities in the United States as well as in Canada, Mexico, China, Germany, Belgium, Scotland, and Ireland.

Along with his wife, Marianne Schneider Corey, Jerry offers weeklong residential training workshops during the summer in Idyllwild, California. In his leisure time Jerry likes to travel, hike and bicycle in the mountains, and drive his 1931 Model A Ford.

Other textbooks, student manuals and workbooks, and educational videos by Gerald Corey from Brooks-Cole/Wadsworth include:

- *The Art of Integrative Counseling* (2001)
- *Student Video and Workbook for the Art of Integrative Counseling* (2001)
- *Case Approach to Counseling and Psychotherapy*, 5th Edition (2001)
- *Student Manual for Theory and Practice of Counseling and Psychotherapy,* 6th Edition (2001)
- *Theory and Practice of Group Counseling,* 5th Edition (and *Student Manual*) (2000)
- *Student Workbook for the Evolution of a Group* (2000, with Marianne Schneider Corey and Robert Haynes)
- *Student Workbook for Ethics in Action* (1998, with Marianne Schneider Corey and Robert Haynes)
- *Issues and Ethics in the Helping Professions,* 5th Edition (1998, with Marianne Schneider Corey and Patrick Callanan)
- *Becoming a Helper,* 3rd Edition (1998, with Marianne Schneider Corey)
- *I Never Knew I Had a Choice,* 6th Edition (1997, with Marianne Schneider Corey)
- *Groups: Process and Practice,* 5th Edition (1997, with Marianne Schneider Corey)
- *Group Techniques,* 2nd Edition (1992, with Marianne Schneider Corey, Patrick Callanan, and J. Michael Russell)

Jerry is co-author, with his daughters Cindy Corey and Heidi Jo Corey, of an orientation-to-college book entitled *Living and Learning* (1997), published by Wadsworth. He is also co-author (with Barbara Herlihy) of *Boundary Issues in Counseling: Multiple Roles and Responsibilities* (1997) and *ACA Ethical Standards Casebook,* 5th Edition (1996), both published by the American Counseling Association. He has also made three videos on various aspects of counseling practice: (1) *Student Video and Workbook for the Art of Integrative Counseling;* (2) *Ethics in Action* (student version and institutional version); and (3) *The Evolution of a Group.* Each of these student videos is accompanied by a student workbook. In the last two videos both Jerry and Marianne Schneider Corey co-present with a group. All of these student videos and accompanying student workbooks are available through Brooks-Cole/Wadsworth Publishing Company.

Bringing it all together . . .

Gerald Corey's BOOK AND VIDEO TEACHING PACKAGE FOR
Theory and Practice of Counseling and Psychotherapy,
Sixth Edition

Featuring the new edition of the widely-acclaimed, best-selling text!

Theory and Practice of Counseling and Psychotherapy, Sixth Edition
ISBN: 0-534-34823-8

Instructor's Edition for Theory and Practice of Counseling and Psychotherapy, Sixth Edition
ISBN: 0-534-37050-0

Student Manual for Theory and Practice of Counseling and Psychotherapy, Sixth Edition
ISBN: 0-534-34824-6

Case Approach to Counseling and Psychotherapy, Fifth Edition
ISBN: 0-534-34820-3

The Art of Integrative Counseling
ISBN: 0-534-57636-2

Student Video and Workbook for the Art of Integrative Counseling
ISBN: 0-534-57637-0

Brooks/Cole
Thomson Learning

In loving memory of my father and mother, both of whom continue to live within my spirit
Joseph Corey, who showed me that it is possible to overcome adversity
Josephine Corey, who inspired me to live a meaningful life

6th
Edition

Theory and Practice of Counseling and Psychotherapy

GERALD COREY

California State University, Fullerton
Diplomate in Counseling Psychology,
American Board of Professional Psychology

Brooks/Cole
Thomson Learning™

Australia • Canada • Mexico • Singapore • Spain • United Kingdom • United States

Counseling Editor: Julie Martinez
Assistant Editor: Annie Berterretche
Editorial Assistant: Marin Plank
Marketing Manager: Caroline Concilla
Project Editor: Tanya Nigh
Print Buyer: Karen Hunt
Permissions Editor: Bob Kauser
Production Service: Cecile Joyner /
   The Cooper Company

Text Designer: Terri Wright
Photo Researcher: Terri Wright
Copy Editor: Kay Mikel
Compositor: Thompson Type
Cover Designer: Harry Voigt
Cover Printer: Phoenix Color Corp.
Printer / Binder: Phoenix Color Corp.

For permission to use material from
this text, contact us by
   web: www.thomsonrights.com
   fax: 1-800-730-2215
   phone: 1-800-730-2214

**Library of Congress
Cataloging-in-Publication Data**

Corey, Gerald.
   Theory and practice of counseling
   and psychotherapy / Gerald Corey—
   6th ed.
      p. cm.
   Includes bibliographical references
   and index.
      ISBN 0-534-34823-8 (alk. paper)
      1. Counseling. 2. Psychotherapy.
   I. Title.

   BF637.C6 C574 2000
   158'.3—dc21   99-052087

 This book is printed on acid-free
recycled paper.

Photo credits: p. ii, Gerald Corey © Ed Young;
p. 67, courtesy National Library of Medicine;
p. 107, courtesy Alfred Adler Institute of Chicago;
p. 141, Harvard University Archives; p. 142,
Mark Kaufman; p. 169, courtesy Carl Rogers
Memorial Library; p. 193, courtesy The Gestalt
Journal Press, Hugh Wilkerson; p. 194, courtesy
The Gestalt Journal Press; p. 229, courtesy
William Glasser; p. 255, courtesy Arnold
Lazarus; p. 295, courtesy Dr. Albert Ellis; p. 296,
courtesy Aaron Beck; p. 341, courtesy Jean Baker
Miller; p. 341, courtesy Carolyn Zerbe Enns;
p. 342, Oliva M. Espin; p. 342, courtesy Laura
Brown; p. 384, courtesy Alfred Adler Institute
of Chicago; p. 384, courtesy Murray Bowen;
p. 384, Jackie Schwartz, Ph.D.; p. 385, courtesy
Carl Whitaker; p. 385, Anthony A. Buttone;
p. 386, courtesy Jay Haley; p. 386, courtesy
Cloé Madanes.

For more information, contact
Wadsworth/Thomson Learning
10 Davis Drive
Belmont, CA 94002-3098
USA
www.wadsworth.com

International Headquarters
Thomson Learning
290 Harbor Drive, 2nd Floor
Stamford, CT 06902-7477
USA

UK/Europe/Middle East/South Africa
Thomson Learning
Berkshire House
168-173 High Holborn
London WC1V 7AA
United Kingdom

Asia
Thomson Learning
60 Albert Street #15-01
Albert Complex
Singapore 189969

Canada
Nelson Thomson Learning
1120 Birchmount Road
Scarborough, Ontario M1K 5G4
Canada

CONTENTS

Preface   xiii

1 Basic Issues in Counseling Practice   1

1 Introduction and Overview   2
Introduction   3
Where I Stand   3
Suggestions for Using the Book   6
Overview of the Theory Chapters   7
Introduction to the Case of Stan   10

2 The Counselor: Person and Professional   14
Introduction   15
The Counselor as a Therapeutic Person   15
Personal Counseling for the Counselor   17
The Counselor's Values and the Therapeutic Process   19
Becoming an Effective Multicultural Counselor   25
Issues Faced by Beginning Therapists   29
Staying Alive as a Person and as a Professional   38
Summary   40

3 Ethical Issues in Counseling Practice   42
Introduction   43
Putting the Client's Needs Before Your Own   44
Ethical Decision Making   45
The Right of Informed Consent   47
Dimensions of Confidentiality   48
Ethical Issues in a Multicultural Perspective   50
Ethical Issues in the Assessment Process   52

Dual Relationships in Counseling Practice   55
Guidelines for Ethical Practice: A Review   57
Where to Go From Here   59

Recommended Supplementary Readings for Part 1   60
References and Suggested Readings for Part 1   62

 ## Theories and Techniques of Counseling   65

4   *Psychoanalytic Therapy*   *66*

Introduction   68
Key Concepts   68
The Therapeutic Process   87
Application: Therapeutic Techniques and Procedures   91
■ *Psychoanalytic Therapy Applied to the Case of Stan*   *95*
Summary and Evaluation   97
■ *Psychoanalytic Therapy From a Multicultural*
   Perspective   *102*
Where to Go From Here   103
Recommended Supplementary Readings   103
References and Suggested Readings   104

5   *Adlerian Therapy*   *106*

Introduction   108
Key Concepts   108
The Therapeutic Process   113
Application: Therapeutic Techniques and Procedures   117
■ *Adlerian Therapy Applied to the Case of Stan*   *128*
Summary and Evaluation   130
■ *Adlerian Therapy From a Multicultural Perspective*   *132*
Where to Go From Here   135
Recommended Supplementary Readings   137
References and Suggested Readings   137

6   *Existential Therapy*   *140*

Introduction   143
Key Concepts   145
The Therapeutic Process   153
Application: Therapeutic Techniques and Procedures   157
■ *Existental Therapy Applied to the Case of Stan*   *158*
Summary and Evaluation   159
■ *Existential Therapy From a Multicultural Perspective*   *163*

Where to Go From Here   165
Recommended Supplementary Readings   165
References and Suggested Readings   166

7   *Person-Centered Therapy*   *168*

Introduction   170
Key Concepts   172
The Therapeutic Process   174
Application: Therapeutic Techniques and Procedures   179
■ *Person-Centered Therapy Applied to the Case of Stan*   *181*
Summary and Evaluation   183
■ *Person-Centered Therapy From a Multicultural Perspective*   *187*
Where to Go From Here   189
Recommended Supplementary Readings   190
References and Suggested Readings   190

8   *Gestalt Therapy*   *192*

Introduction   195
Key Concepts   195
The Therapeutic Process   202
Application: Therapeutic Techniques and Procedures   208
■ *Gestalt Therapy Applied to the Case of Stan*   *217*
Summary and Evaluation   219
■ *Gestalt Therapy From a Multicultural Perspective*   *222*
Where to Go From Here   223
Recommended Supplementary Readings   225
References and Suggested Readings   226

9   *Reality Therapy*   *228*

Introduction   230
Key Concepts   231
The Therapeutic Process   235
Application: Therapeutic Techniques and Procedures   237
■ *Reality Therapy Applied to the Case of Stan*   *244*
Summary and Evaluation   246
■ *Reality Therapy From a Multicultural Perspective*   *249*
Where to Go From Here   251
Recommended Supplementary Readings   252
References and Suggested Readings   252

10   *Behavior Therapy*   *254*

Introduction   256
Key Concepts   259
The Therapeutic Process   261

Application: Therapeutic Techniques and Procedures   265
■ *Behavior Therapy Applied to the Case of Stan   280*
Summary and Evaluation   282
■ *Behavior Therapy From a Multicultural Perspective   286*
Where to Go From Here   288
Recommended Supplementary Readings   289
References and Suggested Readings   290

11   *Cognitive Behavior Therapy   294*

Introduction   297
Key Concepts   299
The Therapeutic Process   301
Application: Therapeutic Techniques and Procedures   304
Aaron Beck's Cognitive Therapy   309
Donald Meichenbaum's Cognitive Behavior Modification
   318
■ *Cognitive Behavior Therapy Applied to the Case
   of Stan   323*
Summary and Evaluation   326
■ *Cognitive Behavior Therapy From
   a Multicultural Perspective   331*
Where to Go From Here   333
Recommended Supplementary Readings   334
References and Suggested Readings   335

12   *Feminist Therapy   340*

Introduction   343
Key Concepts   347
The Therapeutic Process   353
Application: Therapeutic Techniques and Procedures   359
■ *Feminist Therapy Applied to the Case of Stan   364*
Summary and Evaluation   368
■ *Feminist Therapy From a Multicultural Perspective   373*
Where to Go From Here   375
Recommended Supplementary Readings   377
References and Suggested Readings   378

13   *Family Systems Therapy   382*

Introduction   387
Adlerian Family Therapy   391
Multigenerational Family Therapy   399
Human Validation Process Model   404
Experiential Family Therapy   412
Structural Family Therapy   416
Strategic Family Therapy   422

Social Constructionism and Family Therapy   427
Integration of Family Therapy Models   438
■ *Family Therapy Applied to the Case of Stan*   *439*
Summary and Evaluation   443
■ *Family Systems Therapy From a Multicultural Perspective*
    446
Where to Go From Here   448
Recommended Supplementary Readings   449
References and Suggested Readings   449

 # Integration
and Application   455

14 *An Integrative Perspective*   *456*

Introduction   457
The Trend Toward Psychotherapy Integration   457
Issues Related to the Therapeutic Process   468
The Place of Techniques and Evaluation
    in Counseling   474
Summary   487
Recommended Supplementary Readings   488
References and Suggested Readings   489

15 *Case Illustration: An Integration Approach in Working With Stan*   *493*

Introduction   494
■ *Working With Stan: Integration of Therapies*   *498*
Where to Go From Here   519

Author Index   521
Subject Index   525

PREFACE

This book is intended for counseling courses for undergraduate and graduate students in psychology, counselor education, and the human services and mental health professions. It surveys the major concepts and practices of the contemporary therapeutic systems and addresses some ethical and professional issues in counseling practice. The book aims at teaching students to select wisely from various theories and techniques, which will help them develop a personal style of counseling.

I have found that students appreciate an overview of the divergent contemporary approaches to counseling and psychotherapy. They also consistently say that the first course in counseling means more to them when it deals with them as people. Therefore, I stress the practical application of the material and encourage reflection. Using this book can be both a personal and an academic growth experience.

In this new sixth edition, every effort has been made to retain the major qualities that students and professors have found helpful in the previous editions: the succinct overview of the key concepts of each theory and their implications for practice, the straightforward and personal style, and the book's comprehensive scope. Care has been taken to present the theories in an accurate and fair way. I have also attempted to be simple, clear, and concise. Because many students want suggestions for supplementary reading as they study each therapy approach, I have included a reading list at the end of each chapter.

This edition updates the material and refines existing discussions. Part One deals with issues that are basic to the practice of counseling and psychotherapy. Chapter 1 puts the book into perspective, then students are introduced to the counselor—as a person and a professional—in Chapter 2. It is fitting that this material be dealt with before introducing theoretical concepts and counseling techniques because the role of the counselor as a person is highlighted throughout the text. Chapter 3 has been updated, rewritten, and shortened to focus on key ethical controversies in counseling practice.

Part Two is devoted to a consideration of 10 theories of counseling. Each of the theory chapters follows a common organizational pattern, and students can easily compare and contrast the various models. This pattern includes core topics such as key concepts, the therapeutic process, therapeutic techniques and procedures, and summary and evaluation. In this sixth edition six of the chapters in Part Two have been largely rewritten to reflect recent trends; other chapters were revised in relatively minor ways to bring the material up to date. Adlerian, Gestalt, reality, behavior, cognitive behavior, and family systems therapies have been extensively revised in this edition. The revisions were based on the recommendations of experts in each theory, and my thanks to them are contained in the acknowledgments. Both expert and general reviewers provided suggestions for adding and deleting material for this edition. Attention was given to current trends and recent developments in the practice of each theoretical approach.

An entirely new chapter on feminist therapy has been added to this edition (Chapter 12). This new chapter provides an alternative perspective to most of the other theories covered and also illustrates how ideas and strategies from feminist therapy can be incorporated into the various theoretical approaches. Feminist practitioners contend that to work effectively with either women or men it is essential to consider the influence society has on shaping gender roles. This approach puts a consideration of gender issues at the center of the therapeutic process.

Each of the 10 theory chapters summarizes key points and evaluates the contributions, strengths, limitations, and applications of these theories. Special attention is given to evaluating each theory from a multicultural perspective as well. The consistent organization of the summary and evaluation sections makes comparing theories easier. Students are given recommendations regarding where to look for further training for all of the approaches. Updated annotated lists of reading suggestions and extensive references at the end of these chapters are offered to stimulate students to expand on the material and broaden their learning through further reading.

In Part Three readers are helped to put the concepts together in a meaningful way through a discussion of the integrative perspective and consideration of a case study. Chapter 14 has been extensively revised and pulls together themes from all 10 theoretical orientations. This chapter develops the notion that an integrative approach to counseling practice is in keeping with meeting the needs of diverse client populations in many different settings. Numerous tables and other integrating material help students compare and contrast the 10 approaches. There is more emphasis in this edition on providing a framework for a creative synthesis among the therapeutic models, and students are given guidelines for beginning to formulate their own integration and personal philosophy of counseling.

The "Case of Stan" has been retained in Chapter 15 because it helps readers see the application of a variety of techniques at various stages in the counseling process with the same client. The focus is on an integrative approach that draws from all the therapies and uses a thinking, feeling, and behaving model. This chapter offers a good review of the various theories as applied to a case example.

This text can be used in a flexible way. Some instructors will prefer to follow my sequencing of chapters. Others will prefer to begin with the theory chapters (Part Two) and then deal later with the student's personal characteristics and ethical issues. The topics can be covered in whatever order makes the most sense. Readers are offered some suggestions for using this book at the end of Chapter 1.

In this edition I have made every effort to incorporate those aspects that have worked best in the courses on counseling theory and practice that

I regularly teach. To help readers apply theory to practice, I have also revised the student manual, which is designed for experiential work. The *Student Manual for Theory and Practice of Counseling and Psychotherapy* still contains open-ended questions and cases, structured exercises, self-inventories, and a variety of activities that can be done both in class and out of class. The sixth edition features a structured overview, as well as a glossary, for each of the theories and chapter quizzes for assessing the level of student mastery of basic concepts.

The newly revised and enlarged *Case Approach to Counseling and Psychotherapy* (Fifth Edition) features working with a case for each of the 10 therapeutic approaches. The casebook can either supplement this book or stand alone.

Accompanying this sixth edition of the text and student manual is a 2-hour videotape and workbook entitled *Student Video and Workbook for the Art of Integrative Counseling*, in which I demonstrate an integrative approach in counseling Ruth (the central character in the casebook). It contains mini-lectures on how I draw from key concepts and techniques from the 10 theories presented in the book. This video and workbook have been developed for student purchase and use as a self-study program and make an ideal learning package that can be used in conjunction with this text and manual. A new book, *The Art of Integrative Counseling,* is available for the first time this year. This book expands on the material in Chapter 14 of the textbook.

Some professors have found the textbook and the student manual to be ideal companions and realistic texts for a single course. Others like to use the textbook and the casebook as companions. With this revision it is now possible to have a complete learning package of four books, along with the *Student Video and Workbook for the Art of Integrative Counseling.* The *Case Approach to Counseling and Psychotherapy* and the new *Art of Integrative Counseling* book can also be used in a case-management practicum, in fieldwork courses, or in counseling techniques courses. The case examples include information extending from intake to termination. The integrated package affords instructors a great deal of flexibility to adapt the materials to their particular style of teaching and to the unique needs of their students.

Also available is a revised and updated *Instructor's Resource Manual,* which includes suggestions for teaching the course, class activities to stimulate interest, transparency masters, and a variety of test questions and final examinations. This instructor's manual is now geared for the following learning package: *Theory and Practice of Counseling and Psychotherapy, Student Manual for Theory and Practice of Counseling and Psychotherapy, Case Approach to Counseling and Psychotherapy, The Art of Integrative Counseling* (both the new book and the student video and workbook).

Acknowledgments

The suggestions I received from the many readers of prior editions who took the time to complete the survey at the end of the book have been most helpful. Many other people have contributed ideas that have found their way into this sixth edition. I especially appreciate the time and efforts of the manuscript reviewers, who offered constructive criticism and supportive commentaries, as well as those professors who have used this book and provided me with feedback that has been most useful in these revisions. Those who reviewed the manuscript of the sixth edition are: Philip Cooker, University of Mississippi; Mimi Lawson, graduate of the human services program, California State University at Fullerton; Barbara Herlihy, University of New Orleans; Walt Pawlovich, University of Saskatchewan; Pam Remer, University of Kentucky; and Betty Sims, doctoral student in counseling, Texas Southern University.

Special thanks are extended to the chapter reviewers, who provided consultation and detailed critiques. Their insightful and valuable comments have generally been incorporated into this edition:

- Chapter 4: William Blau, Copper Mountain College and Chapman University Academic Center; and J. Michael Russell of California State University, Fullerton
- Chapter 5: James Bitter, East Tennessee State University
- Chapter 6: Clemmont Vontress; and J. Michael Russell, California State University, Fullerton
- Chapter 7: David Cain, founder of the Person-Centered Association and a private practitioner in Carlsbad, California
- Chapter 8: Jon Frew, Private Practice, Vancouver, Washington
- Chapter 9: William Glasser, William Glasser Institute; and Robert Wubbolding, Xavier University and Center for Reality Therapy, Cincinnati, Ohio
- Chapter 10: David Guevremont, Blackstone Valley Psychological Institute; and Arnold A. Lazarus, Rutgers University
- Chapter 11: Albert Ellis, Albert Ellis Institute, New York; and Frank M. Dattilio, Center for Cognitive Therapy, University of Pennsylvania School of Medicine
- Chapter 12: Dana Comstock, St. Mary's University, San Antonio, Texas; Carolyn Zerbe Enns, Cornell College; Kathy Evans, University of South Carolina; Elizabeth Kincade, Indiana University of Pennsylvania; Pam Remer, University of Kentucky; and Susan Seem, SUNY—Brockport. Barbara Herlihy co-authored Chapter 12 with me.
- Chapter 13: Dorothy Stroh Becvar, Radford University; Jon Carlson of Lake Geneva Wellness Clinic, Lake Geneva, Wisconsin; and Frank M. Dattilio, Center for Cognitive Therapy, University of Pennsylvania School of Medicine. James Bitter co-authored Chapter 13 with me.

This book is the result of a team effort, which includes the combined talents of several people in the Brooks-Cole/Wadsworth family. I appreciate the opportunity to work with a dedicated and talented group of professionals in the publishing business. They include Eileen Murphy and Julie Martinez, editors in counseling; Tanya Nigh, senior project editor; Cecile Joyner of The Cooper Company, who coordinated the production of this book; and Kay Mikel, the manuscript editor of this edition, whose fine editorial assistance kept this book reader-friendly. I also want to recognize the work of the late Bill Waller, who edited previous editions of *Theory and Practice of Counseling and Psychotherapy* and whose influence has carried into this edition. I also appreciate the careful work that Mimi Lawson did in preparing the index and in assisting me with revisions to the *Instructor's Resource Manual*. Their talents, efforts, dedication, and extra time certainly have contributed to the quality of this text. With the professional assistance of these people, the ongoing task of revising this book continues to bring more joy than pain.

—Gerald Corey

PART 1

Basic Issues in Counseling Practice

1   *Introduction and Overview*

2   *The Counselor: Person and Professional*

3   *Ethical Issues in Counseling Practice*

Recommended Supplementary Readings for Part 1

References and Suggested Readings for Part 1

CHAPTER

Introduction and Overview

INTRODUCTION
WHERE I STAND
SUGGESTIONS FOR USING THE BOOK
OVERVIEW OF THE THEORY CHAPTERS
INTRODUCTION TO THE CASE OF STAN

INTRODUCTION

This book surveys 10 approaches to counseling and psychotherapy, presenting the basic concepts of each approach and discussing features such as the therapeutic process (including goals), the client/therapist relationship, and specific procedures used in the practice of counseling. This information will help you develop a balanced view of the major ideas of various therapists and the practical techniques they employ. I encourage you to keep an open mind and to seriously consider both the unique contributions and the particular limitations of each therapeutic system presented in Part Two.

Beginning students of counseling can start to acquire a counseling style tailored to their own personality by familiarizing themselves with the major approaches to therapeutic practice. I emphasize to my students that they will not gain the knowledge and experience needed to synthesize various approaches merely by completing an introductory course in counseling theory. This process will take many years of study, training, and practical counseling experience. Nevertheless, I recommend a personal synthesis as a framework for the professional education of counselors. The danger in presenting one model to which all students are expected to subscribe is that it could limit their effectiveness in working with future clients. Valuable dimensions of human behavior can be overlooked if the counselor is restricted to a single theory.

An undisciplined eclectic approach, however, can be an excuse for failing to develop a sound rationale for systematically adhering to certain concepts and to the techniques that are extensions of them. It is easy to pick and choose fragments from the various therapies that merely support one's biases and preconceptions. Nevertheless, a study of the various models presented here will show that some kind of integration of concepts and techniques from the various approaches is possible.

As I continue to develop the material for this book, I become increasingly aware that each therapeutic approach has useful dimensions. Accepting the validity of one model does not necessarily imply a rejection of seemingly divergent models. It is not a matter of a theory being "right" or "wrong," for every theory offers a unique contribution to understanding human behavior and has unique implications for counseling practice. There is a clear place for theoretical pluralism, especially in a society that is becoming increasingly pluralistic.

 ## WHERE I STAND

My own philosophical orientation is strongly influenced by the existential approach. Because this approach does not specify techniques and procedures, I draw techniques from the other models of therapy. I particularly like to use role-playing techniques. When people can reenact scenes from their lives, they often become far more involved than when they merely report anecdotes about themselves. In addition, many techniques I use are derived from cognitive behavior therapy.

I respect the psychoanalytic emphasis on early psychosexual and psychosocial development: One's past plays a crucial role in shaping one's current personality and behavior. Although I reject the deterministic notion that humans are the product of their early conditioning and, thus, are victims of their past, an exploration of the past is essential, particularly to the degree that the past is related to clients' present emotional or behavioral difficulties.

I value the cognitive behavioral focus on how our thinking affects the way we feel and behave. These therapies also give weight to current behavior. Although thinking and feeling are important dimensions, it can be a mistake to overemphasize them and not explore how clients are behaving. What people are doing often gives us a good clue to what they really want. I also value the emphasis on specific goals and on encouraging clients to formulate concrete aims for their own therapy sessions and in life. "Contracts" developed by clients are extremely useful, and I frequently either suggest specific "homework assignments" or ask my clients to devise their own.

More approaches have been developing methods that involve a collaboration between the therapist and client, making the therapeutic venture a sharing of responsibility. This collaborative relationship, coupled with teaching clients ways to use what they learn in therapy in their everyday lives, empowers clients to go into the world and take an active stance. Although I accept the value of increasing clients' insight and awareness, I consider it essential that they put into practice what they are learning in therapy.

A related assumption of mine is that clients can exercise increasing freedom to choose their future. Although we are surely influenced by our social environment and much of our behavior is a product of learning and conditioning, an increased awareness of these forces allows us to transcend them. Most of the contemporary models of counseling and therapy assume that clients are able to accept personal responsibility and that their failure to do so has largely resulted in their present emotional and behavioral difficulties.

This focus on acceptance of personal responsibility does not imply that we can be anything that we want. We need to recognize that social, environmental, cultural, and biological realities limit our freedom of choice. What seems crucial is learning how to cope with the external and internal forces that limit our decisions and behavior. Feminist therapy has contributed an awareness of how external conditions contribute to the problems of women and men and how gender-role socialization leads to a lack of gender equality. Family therapy teaches us that it is not possible to understand the individual apart from the context of the system. Both family therapy and feminist therapy are based on the premise that to understand the individual it is essential to take into consideration both the intrapsychic and the interpersonal dimensions. Thus, a comprehensive approach to counseling goes beyond focusing on our internal dynamics by addressing those environmental realities that influence us. Those therapies that focus exclusively on intrapsychic dimensions have limited utility in working with culturally diverse populations.

My philosophy of counseling does not include the assumption that therapy is exclusively for the "sick" and is aimed at "curing" psychological "ailments." Such a focus on psychopathology severely restricts therapeutic practice, mainly because it stresses deficits rather than strengths.

Psychotherapy is a process of engagement between two persons, both of whom are bound to change through the therapeutic venture. Perhaps one of the most significant characteristics of an effective therapist is the quality of *presence,* which is discussed in some detail in Chapters 6, 7, and 8.

Therapists are not in business to change clients, to give them quick advice, or to solve their problems for them. Therapists heal through a process of genuine dialogue with their clients. The kind of person a therapist is—the ways of being that he or she models—is the most critical factor affecting the client and promoting change. If practitioners possess wide knowledge, both theoretical and practical, yet lack human qualities of compassion, caring, good faith, honesty, realness, and sensitivity, they are merely technicians. In my judgment those who function exclusively as technicians do not make a significant difference in the lives of their clients. It seems essential to me that counselors explore their own values, attitudes, and beliefs in depth and that they work to increase their own awareness. Throughout the book I encourage you to find ways to personally relate to each of the therapies. By applying this material to yourself personally, you can go beyond a merely academic understanding.

Therapists must be willing to remain open to their own growth and to struggle in their lives if their clients are to believe in them and the therapeutic process. Why should clients seek therapists who are "finished products" and who do not do in their own lives what they expect clients to do in theirs? In short, practitioners teach clients by the behavior they model.

With respect to mastering the techniques of counseling and being able to apply them appropriately and effectively, it is my belief that, as a counselor, you are your very best technique. Your reactions to your clients, including sharing how you are affected in the relationship with them, can be the most useful catalyst in the therapeutic process. It is misleading to imbue students with the idea that counseling is a science that is distinct from the behavior and personality of the counselor. There is no substitute for developing techniques that are an expression of your personality and that work for you. It is impossible to separate the techniques you use from your personality and the relationship you have with your clients.

Administering techniques to clients without regard for the relationship variables is ineffective. Techniques cannot substitute for the hard work it takes to develop a constructive client/therapist relationship. Although counselors can learn attitudes and skills and acquire certain knowledge about personality dynamics and the therapeutic process, much of effective therapy is the product of artistry. Counseling entails far more than becoming a skilled technician. It implies that you are able to establish and maintain a good working relationship with your clients, that you can draw on your own experiences and reactions, and that you can identify techniques suited to the needs of your clients.

I encourage students and those with whom I consult to experience a wide variety of techniques themselves *as clients*. Reading about a technique in a book is one thing; actually experiencing it from the vantage point of a client is quite another. If you have practiced relaxation exercises, for example, you will have a much better feel for how to administer them and will know more about what to look for as you work with clients. If you have carried out real-life homework assignments as part of your own self-change program, you will have a lot more empathy for your clients and their potential problems. Your own anxiety over self-disclosing and confronting personal concerns can be a most useful anchoring point as you work with the anxieties of your clients. The courage you display in your therapy will help you appreciate how essential courage is for your clients.

The human qualities of a therapist are of primary importance, but it is not sufficient to be merely a good person with good intentions. To be effective, a therapist also must have supervised experiences in counseling and a knowledge of counseling theory and techniques. Further, it is essential to be well grounded in the various *theories of personality* and to learn how they are related to *theories of counseling*. Your conception of the person affects the interventions you make. Another factor, of course, are the individual characteristics of the client. Some practitioners make the mistake of relying on one type of intervention (supportive, confrontational, information giving) for most clients with whom they work. In reality, different clients may respond better to one type of intervention than another. Even during the course of an individual's therapy, he or she may need different interventions at different times. Practitioners should acquire a broad base of counseling techniques that are suitable for individual clients rather than forcing clients to fit one specialized form of intervention.

 ## SUGGESTIONS FOR USING THE BOOK

Here are some specific recommendations on how to get the fullest value from this book. The personal tone of the book invites you to relate what you are reading to your own experiences. As you read Chapter 2, "The Counselor: Person and Professional," begin the process of reflecting on your needs, motivations, values, and life experiences. Consider how you are likely to bring the person you are becoming into your professional work. You will assimilate much more knowledge about the various therapies if you make a conscious attempt to apply their key concepts and techniques to your own personal growth. Chapter 2 can also help you think about how to use yourself as your single most important therapeutic instrument. Chapter 3 deals with significant ethical issues in counseling practice, and it is useful to begin considering them early in the course.

Before you study each therapy in depth in Part Two, I suggest that you at least skim Chapter 14, which provides a comprehensive review of the key concepts from all 10 of the theories presented in this textbook. I attempt to show how an integration of these perspectives can form the basis for creating your own personal synthesis to counseling. In developing an integrative perspective, it is essential to think holistically. To understand human functioning, it is imperative to account for the physical, emotional, mental, social, cultural, political, and spiritual dimensions. If any of these facets of human experience is neglected, a theory is limited in explaining how we think, feel, and act.

To provide you with a consistent framework for comparing and contrasting the various therapies, the 10 theory chapters share a common format. This format includes a few notes on the personal history of the founder or another key figure; a brief historical sketch showing how and why each theory developed at the time it did; a discussion of the approach's key concepts; an overview of the therapeutic process, including the therapist's role and client's work; therapeutic techniques and procedures; a summary and evaluation; suggestions of how to continue your learning about each approach; and suggestions for further reading.

The *Student Manual for Theory and Practice of Counseling and Psychotherapy* is a most useful supplement to the text. Making full use of the manual will help you apply theory in practical situations. The manual features a glossary of key terms, prechapter self-inventories, comprehension tests for each chapter, summary outlines of key points, exercises and activities, and several case studies applied to each theory. The manual also contains a guide to *The Art of Integrative Counseling,* a new book that is an expansion of Chapter 14 in this text, as well as to the *Student Video and Workbook for the Art of Integrative Counseling.*

The newly revised and enlarged *Case Approach to Counseling and Psychotherapy* (Fifth Edition) features working with a case (Ruth) for each of the 10 therapeutic approaches. The casebook can either supplement this book or stand alone.

Accompanying this sixth edition of the text and student manual is the *Student Video and Workbook for the Art of Integrative Counseling.* In this 2-hour video, I demonstrate an integrative approach in counseling Ruth (the central character in the casebook). The video also contains commentary explaining how I draw from key concepts and techniques from the 10 theories presented in the textbook. This video has been developed for student use as a self-study program. It is an ideal complement to this textbook and the student manual.

OVERVIEW OF THE THEORY CHAPTERS

I have selected 10 therapeutic approaches for this book. Table 1-1 presents an overview of these approaches, which are explored in depth in Chapters 4 through 13. I have grouped these approaches into four general categories.

First are the *analytic approaches. Psychoanalytic therapy* is based largely on insight, unconscious motivation, and reconstruction of the personality. The reason for including the psychoanalytic model (and placing it first) is its major influence on all of the other formal systems of psychotherapy. Some of the therapeutic models are basically extensions of psychoanalysis, others are modifications of analytic concepts and procedures, and still

TABLE 1-1   ■   Overview of Contemporary Counseling Models

Psychoanalytic therapy	Key figure: Sigmund Freud. A theory of personality development, a philosophy of human nature, and a method of psychotherapy, it focuses on unconscious factors that motivate behavior. Attention is given to the events of the first 6 years of life as determinants of the later development of personality.
Adlerian therapy	Key figure: Alfred Adler. Following Adler, Rudolf Dreikurs is credited with popularizing this approach in the United States. A growth model, it stresses taking responsibility, creating one's own destiny, and finding meaning and goals to give life direction. Key concepts are used in most other current therapies.
Existential therapy	Key figures: Viktor Frankl, Rollo May, and Irvin Yalom. It reacts against the tendency to view therapy as a system of well-defined techniques. Instead, it stresses building therapy on the basic conditions of human existence, such as choice, the freedom and responsibility to shape one's life, and self-determination. It focuses on the quality of the person-to-person therapeutic relationship.
Person-centered therapy	Founder: Carl Rogers. This approach was developed during the 1940s as a nondirective reaction against psychoanalysis. Based on a subjective view of human experiencing, it places faith in and gives responsibility to the client in dealing with problems.
Gestalt therapy	Founders: Fritz and Laura Perls. An experiential therapy stressing awareness and integration, it grew as a reaction against analytic therapy. It integrates the functioning of body and mind.
Reality therapy	Founder: William Glasser. A short-term approach focusing on the present, it stresses a person's strengths. Clients learn more realistic behavior and thus achieve success.
Behavior therapy	Key figures: Arnold Lazarus and Albert Bandura. It applies the principles of learning to the resolution of specific behavioral disorders. Results are subject to continual experimentation. This technique is always in the process of refinement.
Cognitive behavior therapy	Key figures: Albert Ellis founded rational emotive behavior therapy, a highly didactic, cognitive, action-oriented model of therapy that stresses the role of thinking and belief systems as the root of personal problems. A. T. Beck founded cognitive therapy.
Feminist therapy	This approach grew out of the efforts of many women. A central concept is the concern for the psychological oppression of women. Focusing on the constraints imposed by the sociopolitical status to which women have been relegated, this approach explores women's identity development, self-concept, goals and aspirations, and emotional well-being.

(continued)

TABLE 1-1   ■   *(continued)*

Family systems therapy	A number of significant figures have been pioneers of the family systems approach. This systemic approach is based on the assumption that the key to changing the individual is understanding and working with the family.

others are positions that emerged as a reaction against psychoanalysis. Many of the other theories of counseling and psychotherapy have borrowed and integrated principles and techniques from psychoanalytic approaches.

Adlerian therapy differs from psychoanalytic theory in many respects, but it can broadly be considered an analytic perspective. Adlerians focus on meaning, goals, purposeful behavior, conscious action, belonging, and social interest. Although Adlerian theory accounts for present behavior by studying childhood experiences, it does not focus on unconscious dynamics.

The second category comprises the *experiential and relationship-oriented therapies:* the existential approach, the person-centered approach, and Gestalt therapy. The *existential approach* stresses a concern for what it means to be fully human. It suggests certain themes that are part of the human condition, such as freedom and responsibility, anxiety, guilt, awareness of being finite, creating meaning in the world, and shaping one's future by making active choices. This approach is not a unified school of therapy with a clear theory and a systematic set of techniques. Rather, it is a philosophy of counseling that stresses the divergent methods of understanding the subjective world of the person. The *person-centered approach,* which is rooted in a humanistic philosophy, places emphasis on the basic attitudes of the therapist. It maintains that the quality of the client/therapist relationship is the prime determinant of the outcomes of the therapeutic process. Philosophically, this approach assumes that clients have the capacity for self-direction without active intervention and direction on the therapist's part. It is in the context of a living and authentic relationship with the therapist that this growth force within the client is released. The final experiential approach is *Gestalt therapy,* which offers a range of experiments to help clients focus on what they are experiencing now.

Third are the *action therapies,* which include reality therapy, behavior therapy, rational emotive behavior therapy, and cognitive therapy. *Reality therapy* focuses on clients' current behavior. It stresses their personal responsibility for changing themselves by developing clear plans for new behaviors. Like reality therapy, *behavior therapy* puts a premium on doing and on taking steps to make concrete changes. A current trend in behavior therapy is toward paying increased attention to cognitive factors as an important determinant of behavior. *Rational emotive behavior therapy* and *cognitive therapy* highlight the necessity of learning how to challenge dysfunctional beliefs and automatic thoughts that lead to human misery. These approaches are used to help people undermine their faulty and self-defeating assumptions and to form a rational philosophy of life.

The fourth general approach is the *systems perspective,* of which feminist therapy and family therapy are a part. The systems orientation stresses the importance of understanding individuals in the context of the surroundings that influence their development. To bring about individual change, it is essential to pay attention to how the individual's personality has been affected by his or her gender-role socialization, culture, family, and other systems.

In my view, practitioners need to pay attention to what their clients are *thinking, feeling,* and *doing.* Thus, a complete therapy system must address all three of these facets. Some of the therapies included here highlight the role that cognitive factors play in counseling. Others place emphasis on the experiential aspects of counseling and the role of feelings. Still others emphasize putting plans into action and learning by doing. Combining all of these dimensions provides the basis for a powerful and comprehensive therapy. If any of these dimensions is excluded, the therapy approach is incomplete.

INTRODUCTION TO THE CASE OF STAN

Students learn a lot by seeing a theory in action, preferably in a live demonstration or as part of experiential activities in which they function in the alternating roles of client and counselor. Many students find the case history of a hypothetical client, Stan, helpful in understanding how various techniques are applied to the same person. Stan's case, which describes his life and struggles, is presented here to give you significant background material to draw from as you study the applications of the theories. Each of the 10 theory chapters in Part Two includes a discussion of how a therapist with the orientation under discussion is likely to proceed with Stan. We will examine the answers to questions such as these:

- What themes in Stan's life merit special attention in therapy?
- What concepts explain the nature of his problems?
- What are the general goals of his therapy?
- What possible techniques and methods would best meet these goals?
- What are some characteristics of the relationship between Stan and his therapist?
- How might the therapist proceed?

In Chapter 15 (which I recommend you read early) I present how I would work with Stan, suggesting concepts and techniques that I would draw on from many of the models (forming an integrative approach).

A single case can illustrate both contrasts and parallels among the approaches. It will also help you understand the practical applications of the 10 models and will provide some basis for integrating them. Try to sharpen your focus on certain attributes of each approach that can be incorporated into a personalized style of counseling.

The setting is a community mental health agency where both individual and group counseling by qualified staff are available. Stan is coming to counseling because of a court order as a stipulation of his probation. He was convicted of driving under the influence of alcohol. Although he does not think he has a serious drinking problem, the judge determined that he needed professional help. Stan arrives for an intake interview and provides the counselor with this information:

> At 25 years old I'm working in construction. I like building houses, but I'm pretty sure I don't want to stay in construction for the rest of my life. When it comes to my personal life, I've always had a rough time getting along with people. I suppose you could call me a "loner." I like having people in my life, but I just don't seem to know how to go about making friends or getting close to people. Probably the reason I sometimes drink a bit too much is because I'm so scared when it comes to mixing with people. Even though I hate to admit it, when I've been drinking, things don't seem quite so overwhelming. When I look at others, they seem to know the right things to say. Next to them I feel so dumb. I'm afraid that people will be bored with me and that if they really knew me they wouldn't want anything to do with me. Sure, I'd like to turn my life around, and I'm trying, but sometimes I just don't know where to begin. That's why I went back to school. Besides my work in construction, I'm also a part-time college student majoring in psychology. I want to better myself. In one of my classes, Psychology of Personal Adjustment, we talked about ourselves and how we wanted to change, and we also had to write an autobiographical paper. Should I bring it in?

That is the essence of Stan's introduction. The counselor says that she very much wants to read his autobiography. Stan hopes it will give her a better understanding of where he has been, where he is now, where he would like to go, and what he wants for himself. It reads as follows:

> Where I am currently in my life? At 25 I feel that I've wasted most of my life. By now I should be finished with college and into a good job, but instead I'm only a junior. I can't afford to really commit myself to pursuing college full time because I need to work to support myself. Even though construction work is hard, I like the satisfaction I get when I look at what I helped build.
>
> Although I'd like to build things as a hobby, I want to get into some profession where I could work with people, if I can ever get over my fears of what people think of me. Someday, I'm hoping to get a master's degree in counseling or in social work and eventually work as a counselor with kids who are in trouble. I feel I was helped by someone who cared about me, and I would like to have a similar influence on young people.
>
> At this time I live alone, have very few friends, and feel scared with people my own age or older. I feel good when I'm with kids, because they're so honest. But I worry a lot whether I'm smart enough to get through all the studies I'll need to do before I can become a counselor.
>
> One of my problems is that I drink heavily and frequently get drunk. This happens mostly when I feel alone and when I'm scared that I'll always feel as lonely and isolated as I do now. At first drinking makes me feel better, but later on I really feel rotten. I used to do drugs heavily, and once in a while I still get loaded.
>
> People really scare me, and I feel overwhelmed when I'm around strong and attractive women. I feel all cold, sweaty, and terribly uptight

when I'm with a woman. Maybe I think they're judging me, and I know they'll find out that I'm not much of a man. I'm afraid I won't measure up to being a *man*—always having to be strong, tough, and perfect. I'm not any of those, so I often wonder if I'm adequate as a man. I really have trouble seeing myself as sexually adequate. When I do have sex, I get uptight and worry that I won't be able to perform, and then I really feel terrible.

I feel anxiety much of the time, particularly at night. Sometimes I get so scared that I feel like running, but I just can't move. It's awful, because I often feel as if I'm dying at times like this. Then I fantasize about committing suicide, and I wonder who would care. Sometimes I see my family coming to my funeral feeling very sorry that they didn't treat me better. I even made a weak attempt to do myself in a couple of years ago. Much of the time I feel guilty that I haven't worked up to my potential, that I've been a failure, that I've wasted much of my time, and that I let people down a lot. I can really get down on myself and wallow in my guilt, and I feel *very depressed*. At times like this I think about how rotten I am, how I'll never be able to change, and how I'd be better off dead. Then I wouldn't have to hurt anymore, and I wouldn't want anything either. It's very difficult for me to get close to anyone. I can't say that I've ever loved a person, and I know that I've never felt fully loved or wanted.

Everything is not bleak. I did have enough guts to leave a lot of my shady past behind me, and I did get into college. I like my determination—I *want* to change. I'm tired of feeling like a loser, and I know that nobody is going to change my life for me. It's up to me to get what I want. Even though I feel scared a lot, I like it that I can *feel* my feelings and that I'm willing to take risks. I hate being a quitter.

What was my past like? What are some significant events and turning points in my life? A major turning point was the confidence my supervisor had in me at the youth camp where I worked the past few summers. He helped me get my job, and he also encouraged me to go to college. He said he saw a lot of potential in me for being able to work well with young people. That was hard for me to really believe, but his faith inspired me to begin to believe in myself. Another turning point was my marriage and divorce. This "relationship" didn't last long before my wife left me. Wow, that really made me wonder about what kind of man I was! She was a strong and dominant woman who was always telling me how worthless I was and how she couldn't stand to get near me. We met in a gambling casino in Las Vegas, and we tied the knot shortly after that. We had sex only a few times, and most of the time I was impotent. That was hard to take—a real downer! I'm so afraid to get close to a woman. I'm afraid she'll swallow me up. My parents never got a divorce, but I wish they had. They fought most of the time. I should say, my mother did most of the fighting. She was dominant and continually bitching at my father, whom I always saw as weak, passive, and mousy next to her. He would *never* stand up to her. There were four of us kids at home. My folks always compared me unfavorably with my older sister (Judy) and older brother (Frank). They were "perfect" children, successful honor students. My younger brother (Karl) and I fought a lot, and he was the one who was spoiled rotten by them. I really don't know what happened to me and how I turned out to be the failure of the bunch.

In high school I got involved with the wrong crowd and took a lot of drugs. I was thrown into a youth rehabilitation facility for stealing. Later I was expelled from regular school for fighting, and I landed in a continuation high school, where I would go to school in the mornings and have afternoons for on-the-job training. I got into auto mechanics and was fairly successful and even managed to keep myself employed for three years as a mechanic.

Back to my parents. I remember my father telling me: "You're really dumb. Why can't you be like your sister and brother? You'll never amount to a hill of beans! Why can't you ever do anything right?" And my mother treated me much the way she treated my father. She would say: "Why do you do so many things to hurt me? Why can't you grow up and be a man? You were a mistake. I wish I hadn't had you! Things are so much better around here when you're gone." I recall crying myself to sleep many nights, feeling so terribly alone and filled with anger and hate. And feeling so disgusted with myself. There was no talk of religion in my house, nor was there any talk about sex. In fact, I always find it hard to imagine my folks ever having sex.

Where would I like to be 5 years from now? What kind of person do I want to become, and what changes do I most want in my life? Most of all, I would just like to start feeling better about myself. I would really like to be able to stop drinking altogether and still feel good. I have an inferiority complex, and I know how to put myself down. I want to like myself much more than I do now. I hope I can learn to love at least a few other people, most of all, women. I want to lose my fear that women can destroy me. I would like to feel equal with others and not always have to feel apologetic for my existence. I don't want to suffer from this anxiety and guilt. And I hope that I can begin to think of myself as an OK person. I really want to become a good counselor with kids, and to do this I know I'm going to have to change. I'm not certain how I'll change or even what all the changes are I hope for. I do know that I want to get free of my self-destructive tendencies and learn to trust people more. Maybe when I begin to like myself more, I'll be able to trust that others might find something about me that is worth liking.

Effective therapists, regardless of their theoretical orientation, would pay attention to suicidal ideation. In his autobiography Stan says, "I fantasize about committing suicide, and I wonder who would care." At times he also doubts that he will ever change and wonders if he'd be better off dead. Before embarking on the therapeutic journey, the therapist would certainly make an assessment of Stan's current ego strength, which would include a discussion of his suicidal thoughts and feelings.

In Chapters 4 through 13, you can assume that a practitioner representing each of the theories has read Stan's case and is familiar with key themes in his life. Each therapist will illustrate the concepts and techniques of the particular approach as it applies to working with Stan. In addition, in these chapters you are asked to think about how you would continue counseling him from the different perspectives. In doing so, you may find it useful to refer to Stan's autobiography here and also to some of the material in Chapter 15.

CHAPTER

2

The Counselor: Person and Professional

INTRODUCTION

THE COUNSELOR AS A THERAPEUTIC PERSON
Personal Characteristics of Effective Counselors

PERSONAL COUNSELING FOR THE COUNSELOR

THE COUNSELOR'S VALUES AND THE THERAPEUTIC PROCESS
The Role of Values in Counseling
Dealing With Value Conflicts
The Role of Values in Developing Therapeutic Goals
Some Recommendations

BECOMING AN EFFECTIVE MULTICULTURAL COUNSELOR
Acquiring Competencies in Multicultural Counseling
Incorporating Culture Into Counseling Practice

ISSUES FACED BY BEGINNING THERAPISTS
Dealing With Our Anxieties
Being and Disclosing Ourselves
Avoiding Perfectionism
Being Honest About Our Limitations
Understanding Silence
Dealing With Demands From Clients
Dealing With Clients Who Lack Commitment
Tolerating Ambiguity
Avoiding Losing Ourselves in Our Clients
Developing a Sense of Humor
Sharing Responsibility With the Client
Declining to Give Advice
Defining Your Role as a Counselor
Learning to Use Techniques Appropriately
Developing Your Own Counseling Style

STAYING ALIVE AS A PERSON AND AS A PROFESSIONAL
Taking Responsibility
Preventing Burnout

SUMMARY

INTRODUCTION

In this chapter I ask you to examine my assumption that one of the most important instruments you have to work with as a counselor is yourself as a person. In preparing for counseling, you can acquire a knowledge of the theories of personality and psychotherapy, you can learn diagnostic and intervention techniques, and you can learn about the dynamics of human behavior. Such knowledge and skills are essential, but by themselves they are not sufficient for establishing and maintaining effective therapeutic relationships. To every therapy session we bring our human qualities and the experiences that have influenced us. In my judgment this human dimension is one of the most powerful determinants of the therapeutic encounter. If we hope to promote growth and change in our clients, we must be willing to promote growth in our own lives. Our most powerful source of influencing clients in a positive direction is our living example of who we are and how we continually make decisions about the kind of life we want to live.

A good way to begin your study of contemporary counseling theories is by reflecting on the personal issues that are raised in this chapter. Then, after you have studied the 10 theories of counseling, this chapter deserves another reading. I suggest that you reevaluate ways in which you can work on your development as a person, considering especially your needs, motivations, values, and personality traits that could either enhance or interfere with your effectiveness as a counselor. By remaining open to self-evaluation, you not only expand your awareness of self but also build the foundation for developing your abilities as a professional. The theme of this chapter is that the *person* and the *professional* are intertwined entities that cannot be separated in reality.

THE COUNSELOR AS A THERAPEUTIC PERSON

Because counseling is an intimate form of learning, it demands a practitioner who is willing to shed stereotyped roles and be a real person in a relationship. It is precisely within the context of such a person-to-person relationship that the client experiences growth. If as counselors we hide behind the safety of our professional role, our clients will keep themselves hidden from us. If we become merely technical experts and leave our own reactions, values, and self out of our work, the result will be sterile counseling. It is through our own genuineness and our aliveness that we can significantly touch our clients. If we make life-oriented choices, radiate a zest for life, and are real in our relationships with our clients, we can inspire and teach them in the best sense of the words. This does not mean that we are self-actualized persons who have "made it" or that we are without our problems. Rather, it implies that we are willing to look at our lives and make the changes we want. Because we affirm that changing is worth the risk and the effort, we hold out hope to our clients that they can become their own person and can like the person they are becoming.

In short, as therapists we serve as models for our clients. If we model incongruent behavior, low-risk activity, and deceit by remaining hidden and vague, we can expect our clients to imitate this behavior. If we model realness by engaging in appropriate self-disclosure, our clients will tend to be honest with us in the therapeutic relationship. To be sure, counseling can be for better or for worse. Clients can become more of what they are capable of becoming, or they can become less than they might be. In my judgment the degree of aliveness and psychological health of the counselor is the crucial variable that determines the outcome.

Personal Characteristics of Effective Counselors

How can counselors be therapeutic persons and model awareness and growth for their clients? In thinking about counselors who are therapeutic, I have isolated a cluster of personal qualities and characteristics. I do not expect any therapist to fully exemplify all these traits. Rather, for me the willingness to struggle to become a more therapeutic person is the crucial quality. This list is intended to stimulate you to examine your ideas of what kind of person can make a significant difference in the lives of others.

■ *Effective counselors have an identity.* They know who they are, what they are capable of becoming, what they want out of life, and what is essential.

■ *They respect and appreciate themselves.* They can give help and love out of their own sense of self-worth and strength.

■ *They are able to recognize and accept their own power.* They feel adequate with others and allow others to feel powerful with them.

■ *They are open to change.* They exhibit a willingness and courage to leave the security of the known if they are not satisfied with what they have. They make decisions about how they would like to change, and they work toward becoming the person they would like to become.

■ *They are making choices that shape their lives.* They are aware of early decisions they made about themselves, others, and the world. They are not the victims of these early decisions, for they are willing to revise them if necessary.

■ *They feel alive, and their choices are life-oriented.* They are committed to living fully rather than settling for mere existence.

■ *They are authentic, sincere, and honest.* They do not hide behind masks, defenses, sterile roles, and facades.

■ *They have a sense of humor.* They are able to put the events of life in perspective. They have not forgotten how to laugh, especially at their own foibles and contradictions.

■ *They make mistakes and are willing to admit them.* They do not dismiss their errors lightly, yet they do not choose to dwell on misery.

■ *They generally live in the present.* They are not riveted to the past, nor are they fixated on the future. They are able to experience the "now" and be present with others in the now.

■ *They appreciate the influence of culture.* They are aware of the ways in which their own culture affects them, and they respect the diversity of values espoused by other cultures. They are also sensitive to the unique differences arising out of social class, race, and gender.

■ *They have a sincere interest in the welfare of others.* This concern is based on respect, care, trust, and a real valuing of others.

■ *They become deeply involved in their work and derive meaning from it.* They can accept the rewards flowing from their work, yet they are not slaves to their work.

 ■ *They are able to maintain healthy boundaries.* Although they strive to be fully present for their clients, they don't carry the problems of their clients around with them during leisure hours. They know how to say no, which allows them to keep a balance in their lives.

This picture of the characteristics of effective counselors might appear monumental and unrealistic. Who could ever be all those things? Certainly I do not fit this bill! Do not think of these personal characteristics from an all-or-nothing perspective; rather, consider them on a continuum. A given trait may be highly characteristic of you, at one extreme, or it may be very uncharacteristic of you, at the other extreme. I have presented this picture of the therapeutic person with the hope that you will examine it and develop your own concept of what personality traits you think are essential to strive for to promote your own personal growth.

PERSONAL COUNSELING FOR THE COUNSELOR

Discussion of the counselor as a therapeutic person raises another issue debated in counselor education: whether people should participate in counseling or therapy before they become practitioners. My view is that counselors should have the experience of being clients at some time. Such self-exploration can increase their level of self-awareness. This experience can be obtained before their training, during it, or both, but I strongly support some form of personal exploration as a prerequisite to counseling others.

Such counseling should be viewed not as an end in itself but as a means to help a potential counselor become a more therapeutic person who will have a greater chance of having an impact on clients. Opportunities for self-exploration can be instrumental in helping counselors-in-training assess their motivations for pursuing this profession. Examining our values, needs, attitudes, and experiences can illuminate what we are getting from helping others. It is important that we know why we want to intervene in the lives of others. Self-exploration can help counselors avoid the pitfalls of continually giving to others yet finding little personal satisfaction from their efforts. There is value in continuing individual or group counseling as we begin to practice as professionals. At this time we often feel a sense of professional impotence, and we frequently feel like quitting. Student counselors would do well to recognize their helplessness and despair but to avoid deciding too soon that they are unsuited to be counselors. Personal counseling is an ideal place for beginning counselors to express and explore their concerns over whether they are able to help anyone.

Being therapists forces us to confront our unexplored blocks related to loneliness, power, death, sexuality, our parents, and so on. This does not mean that we need to be free of conflicts before we can counsel others, but we should be aware of what these conflicts are and how they are likely to affect us as counselors. For example, if we have great difficulty in dealing with anger and guilt in ourselves, chances are that we will do something to dilute these emotions when they occur in our clients. How can we be present for our clients and encourage them to express feelings that we are so intent on denying in ourselves?

When I began counseling others, old wounds were opened and feelings I had not explored in depth came to the surface. It was difficult for me to encounter a client's depression, because I had failed to come to terms with the way I had escaped from my own depression. Thus, I did my best to cheer up depressed clients by talking them out of what they were feeling, mainly because of my own inability to deal with such feelings. In the years when I began working as a counselor in a university counseling center, I frequently wondered what I could do for my clients. I often had no idea of what, if anything, my clients were getting from our sessions. I couldn't tell if they were getting better, staying the same, or getting worse. It was very important to me to note progress and see change in my clients. Because I did not see immediate results, I had many doubts about whether I could become an effective counselor. What I did not understand at the time was that my clients needed to struggle to find their own answers. It was *my need* to see them feel better quickly, for then I would know that I was helping them. It never occurred to me that clients often feel worse as they give up their defenses and open themselves to their pain. It took me some time to appreciate the courage involved in becoming fully engaged in the therapeutic venture.

Personal therapy can be instrumental in healing the healer. If student counselors are not actively involved in the pursuit of healing their own psychological wounds, they will probably have considerable difficulty entering the world of a client. As counselors we can take our clients no further than we have been willing to go in our own lives. If we are not committed personally to the value of struggling, we will not convince clients that they should pay the price of their struggle. Through being clients ourselves, we have an experiential frame of reference to view ourselves as we are. This provides a basis for compassion for our clients, for we can draw on our own memories of reaching impasses in our therapy, of both wanting to go further and at the same time wanting to stay where we are. Our own therapy can help us develop patience with our patients! We learn what it feels like to deal with anxieties that are aroused by self-disclosure and self-exploration. We may experience transference and thus know firsthand how it is to view our therapist as a parent figure. Being willing to participate in a process of self-exploration can reduce the chances of assuming an attitude of arrogance or of being convinced that we have "arrived" as a person. Indeed, experiencing counseling as a client is very different from merely reading about the counseling process.

The main reason for having students receive some form of psychotherapy is to help them learn to deal with countertransference (the process of seeing themselves in their clients, of overidentifying with their clients, or of meeting their needs through their clients). Recognizing the manifestations of their countertransference reactions is one of the most essential abilities of effective counselors. Unless counselors are aware of their own conflicts, needs, assets, and liabilities, they can use the therapy hour more for their own purposes than for being available for their clients, which becomes an ethical issue. Unaware counselors are in danger of being carried away on the client's emotional tidal wave, which is of no help to themselves or their client. It is unrealistic to think that counselors can completely rid themselves of any traces of countertransference or that they can ever fully resolve certain issues from the past. But they can become aware of the signs of these reactions and can deal with these feelings in their own therapy and supervision sessions.

THE COUNSELOR'S VALUES AND THE THERAPEUTIC PROCESS

As alluded to in the last section, the importance of self-exploration for counselors carries over to the values and beliefs they hold. My experience in teaching and supervising students of counseling shows me how crucial it is that students be aware of their values, of where and how they acquired them, and of how their values influence their interventions with clients. An excellent focus for the process of self-searching is examining how your values are likely to affect your work as a counselor. Counseling and therapy are not forms of indoctrination whereby practitioners persuade clients to act or feel in the "right way." Unfortunately, many well-intentioned counselors are overzealous in their mission of helping to "straighten people out." The implication is that by virtue of their greater wisdom they will provide answers for the troubled client. But counseling is not synonymous with preaching.

The Role of Values in Counseling

A core issue is the degree to which counselors' values should enter into a therapeutic relationship. As counselors we are often taught not to let our values show lest they bias the direction clients are likely to take. Yet we are simply not value-neutral, nor are we value-free; our therapeutic interventions rest on core values. Although our values do influence the way we practice, it is possible to maintain a sense of objectivity. Let me pose a series of questions designed to help you search yourself for your answers about the role of values in counseling:

- Is it best not to reveal your values to clients, lest you bias the directions your clients are likely to take?
- How can you become increasingly aware of the impact of your values on your clients?
- What are some ways that you can help clients clarify their own values?
- Is it possible for you to disagree with a client's values and still accept him or her as a person?
- Is the purpose of counseling to teach values to clients or to teach clients how to discover their own values?
- What is the difference between exposing or imposing your values on clients?
- Is it possible to separate a discussion of values from the therapeutic process?
- How can you retain your own sense of values and remain true to yourself, yet at the same time allow your clients the freedom to select values and behavior that differ sharply from yours?
- Is it ever justifiable for you to impose your values on clients? What about those situations in which you are convinced that the client's values will result in self-destructive behavior?
- What is the best course of action to take when you become aware of sharp value conflicts with certain clients?

From my perspective, the counselor's role is to create a climate in which clients can examine their thoughts, feelings, and actions and eventually arrive at solutions that are best for them. Your job is to assist individuals in finding answers that are most congruent with their own values. What seems critical is that you be aware of the nature of your values and how your beliefs and standards operate on the interventions you make with clients. Your function as a counselor is not to persuade or convince clients of the proper course to take but to help them assess their behavior so that they can determine the degree to which it is working for them. If clients acknowledge that what they are doing is not working, it is appropriate to challenge them to develop new ways of behaving to help them move closer to their goals. Of course, this process of challenging clients is done with full respect given to their right to decide which values they will use as a framework for living. Individuals seeking counseling are the ones who need to wrestle with clarifying their own values and goals, making informed decisions, choosing a course of action, and assuming the responsibility and accountability for the decisions they make. Because counseling is a process that involves teaching clients how to deal with their problems and find their own solutions based on their value system, it is essential that the counselor not short-circuit a client's exploration.

The question of the influence of the counselor's values on the client has ethical implications. Goals and therapeutic methods are expressions of the counselor's philosophy of life. Even though therapists should not directly teach the client or impose specific values, therapists do implement a philosophy of counseling, which is, in effect, a philosophy of life. Counselors communicate their values by the therapeutic goals to which they subscribe and by the procedures they employ to reach these goals.

Dealing With Value Conflicts

As an example of the influence that the counselor's philosophy of life can have on a client and of possible clashes over values between the client and the counselor, consider this case: The client, Joyce, is a married woman in her late 30s with three children. She has been in weekly individual therapy for 6 months. She is struggling to decide whether she wants to remain married to her husband, whom she perceives as boring, uninvolved with their children, complacent, and overly involved in his work. Although Joyce has urged him to join her in marriage counseling or undertake some form of therapy for himself, he has consistently refused. He maintains that he is fine and that she is the one with the problems. She tells the therapist that she would divorce him immediately "if it weren't for the kids" and that when the children finish high school, she will surely leave him. For now, however, she is ambivalent; she cannot decide whether she wants to accept the security she now has (along with the deadness of her relationship with her husband) or whether she is willing to leave this security and risk making a better life for herself. She has been contemplating having an affair so that someone other than her husband can meet her physical and emotional needs. She is also exploring the possibility of finding a job so that she will be less dependent on her husband. By getting a job, she could have outside opportunities for personal satisfaction and still remain in the marriage by deciding to accept what she has with him.

Consider these questions, and decide what value judgments can be made:

- One of Joyce's reasons for staying married is "for the sake of the children." What if you, as her therapist, accept this value and believe she should not challenge her marriage because children need both parents and a divorce is damaging? Might she be using the children as an excuse? What if your judgment is that she would be better off by divorcing now? What do your beliefs about divorce, marriage, and children have to do with her possible decisions?
- Joyce is talking about an affair as a possibility. What are your values concerning monogamy and extramarital sex? Do you believe having an affair would be helpful or destructive for your client?

Would you be able to allow her to make this decision? What influence might your views have on her? Could you objectively counsel her if your values differed from hers in this area?

In your practice you are likely to be faced with ethical issues involving sharp differences between your own values and certain values of your clients. In some situations these value conflicts do not become apparent until the therapeutic alliance is well established. Thus, it is not simply a matter of referring clients in cases of value clashes. Let's return to the case of Joyce and give her a new problem. Assume that she initially seeks counseling because of problems in her marriage. As you work with her, it becomes clear that she has a good deal of respect for you, that she wants to be liked by you, and that she seeks your acceptance and approval. One day she informs you that she has been having an affair, that she has not had sex with her husband for over a year, and that she has just found out that she is pregnant. Joyce is in a turmoil because none of her options appear satisfactory to her. She tells you that she is not in a financial or psychological position to support a child, especially if she decides to divorce her husband. She is becoming clearer that she does not want to remain in a relationship with him. Although she says that she is morally opposed to abortion, this is the path she is inclined to take.

Let's assume that you are personally opposed to abortion on moral or religious grounds. If so, would you be in a position to encourage her to explore all of her alternatives? Would you see it as your task to persuade her to accept another option besides abortion? Given the fact that you have been counseling her for several months, if you were to refer her to another counselor because of your beliefs and values on abortion, would this constitute abandonment? Would a referral be in her best interest? Can you respect your client's right to have a different value system from yours and help her decide what course to follow?

If you are morally opposed to abortion on the ground that it is taking the life of an innocent human being, it may be difficult for you to maintain objectivity. In discussions with students in my classes, I find that many of them say they have difficulty accepting the right of their clients to think differently from them with respect to moral beliefs and values in areas such as abortion, extramarital affairs, premarital sex, divorce, and a gay or lesbian sexual orientation. Some students say that if they see a behavior as being morally wrong they would not be able to condone it in clients. These students are likely to steer their clients in the direction of adopting the values they deem to be morally correct.

As a counselor, if you view it as your role to use your value system as the standard for decision making for your clients, ask yourself why you see it as your place to persuade your clients to live according to what you believe to be right and wrong. Let's examine some other scenarios in which the value systems of clients and counselors clash.

- Suzanne is single and engages in unprotected premarital sex with multiple partners. She tells you she met a guy in a bar and soon after had sex with him. She has no concern about either getting pregnant or contracting a sexually transmitted disease. If you were morally opposed to premarital sex or promiscuous behavior, would you attempt to change her behavior? If she were using preventive measures and restricting her sexual behavior to one man, would this make a difference in the way you might counsel her?
- Ruth is a lesbian. She is not coming to you to change her sexual orientation but to work out difficulties she is experiencing in being true to herself with members of her family. If you believe homosexuality is morally wrong, would you be able to respect her beliefs and her right to live differently? Would you accept her as a client?
- Maria wants to divorce her husband and marry another man whom she recently met. If you believe divorce would have a very negative impact on her children, could you work with her? What course might your counseling take with her?

It is easy to engage in self-deception when you attempt to convince yourself that your experiences and values do not enter into your therapeutic relationships. It is essential to clarify your position on a variety of controversial issues. Here are some examples.

- *Religion.* If therapists call themselves "Christian counselors" and see their beliefs about sin, salvation, and the client's relationship with Christ as a central part of the therapeutic process, how does their view influence clients who are nonreligious? Who are non-Christian? Who are Christian but do not accept the therapist's religious beliefs? What potential impact does a nonreligious therapist have on a client with a definite religious persuasion? Can the nonreligious therapist allow clients to maintain their religious values, or will the therapist confront these values as forms of "immature defenses"? What are your views on religion, and how do you think they will influence your work as a counselor?
- *Sexual orientation.* In working with gay or lesbian clients, how might your values influence what you say or do? If you see being gay as immoral or as a form of psychopathology, would you be able to encourage clients to retain their behavior and values? Would you encourage these clients to define their own goals, or would you be inclined to direct them toward the goals you think they should have? If a gay client accepted his sexual orientation, would you still be able to work with him on meeting his personal goals for therapy? Would you be inclined to refer him? Why or why not?
- *Right to die.* Your client recently learned that he is HIV-positive. He informs you that he does not want to die an agonizing death, as some of his friends have, and that he wants to do himself in before getting worse. What are your values pertaining to this person making the choice to end his life?

How would legal mandates influence you in following what you believe to be an ethical course?

The Role of Values in Developing Therapeutic Goals

Who should establish the goals of counseling? Almost all theories are in accord that it is largely the client's responsibility to decide these objectives, collaborating with the therapist as therapy proceeds. Counselors have general goals, which are reflected in their behavior during the therapy session, in their observations of the client's behavior, and in the interventions they make. It is critical that the general goals of counselors be congruent with the personal goals of the client.

In my view therapy ought to begin with an exploration of the client's expectations and goals. Clients initially tend to have vague ideas of what they expect from therapy. They may be seeking solutions to problems, they may want to stop hurting, they may want to change others so they can live with less anxiety, or they may seek to be different so that some significant persons in their lives will be more accepting of them. In some cases clients may have no goals; they are in the therapist's office simply because they were sent there by their parents, probation officer, or teacher. All they want is to be left alone. So where can a counselor begin? The intake session can be used most productively to focus on the client's goals or lack of them. The therapist may begin by asking questions such as these: What do you expect from counseling? Why are you here? What do you want? What do you hope to leave with? How is what you are presently doing working for you? What aspects of yourself or your life situation would you most like to change?

It is frustrating for therapists to hear clients make statements such as "I'd just like to understand myself more" or "I'd like to be happy." Counselors can bring these global and diffuse wishes into sharper focus by asking questions such as "What is keeping you from feeling happy?" "What do you understand about yourself now?" or "What would you like to understand about yourself that you don't now understand?" The main point is that setting goals seems unavoidable. The client and the counselor need to explore what they hope to obtain from the counseling relationship, whether they can work with each other, and whether their goals are compatible. Even more important, it is essential that the counselor be able to understand, respect, and work within the framework of the client's world rather than forcing the client to fit neatly into the therapist's scheme of values.

Some Recommendations

It is neither possible nor desirable for counselors to be scrupulously neutral with respect to values in the counseling relationship. Counselors should be willing to express their values openly when they are relevant to questions that come up in their sessions with clients. Counselors should guard against the tendency to assume either of two extreme positions. At one extreme are counselors who hold definite and absolute beliefs and see it as their job to exert influence on clients to adopt their values. These counselors tend to direct their clients toward the attitudes and values they judge to be "right." At the other extreme are counselors who maintain that they should keep their values out of their work and that the ideal is to strive for value-free counseling. Because these counselors are so intent on remaining "objective" and because they are so anxious not to influence their clients, they run the risk of immobilizing themselves.

Furthermore, clients often want and need to know where their therapist stands to critically examine their own thinking. Clients deserve honest involvement on the part of their counselor. It seems arrogant to me, and probably inaccurate, to assume that counselors know what is best for others. Therefore, counselors would do well to avoid equating therapy with pushing people to conform to certain "acceptable" standards. Counseling is a process whereby clients are challenged to honestly evaluate their values and decide for themselves in what ways they will modify those values and their behavior.

If you have definite values in certain areas and are intent on directing your clients toward your goals, ethical practice dictates that you inform potential clients of those values that will certainly influence your interventions with them. Through your professional disclosure statement, in which you describe your philosophy of the counseling relationship, it is a good idea to let potential clients know from the outset whether you are opposed to abortion or object to a gay or lesbian sexual orientation or any other values that are likely to influence your clients' decisions and behavior. Clients have a right to know your perspective before they get involved with you professionally.

I am not suggesting that you have to give up your values, for you do need to be true to yourself. Neither am I suggesting that you should be able to work with all clients or with all problems. If you are unable or unwilling to be objective in areas where there are value conflicts between you and a client, a referral is often the ethical alternative.

Many experienced counselors have resolved these and many other issues related to values and the therapeutic process. As a student counselor or beginning practitioner, you will probably have to address many previously unexamined issues to increase your effectiveness.

BECOMING AN EFFECTIVE MULTICULTURAL COUNSELOR

Part of the process of becoming an effective counselor involves learning how to recognize diversity and shaping your counseling practice to fit the client's world. It is essential for counselors to develop sensitivity to cultural differences if they hope to make interventions that are congruent with the values of their clients. Counselors bring their own heritage with them to their work, so they must know how cultural conditioning has influenced the directions they take with their clients. Moreover, unless the social and cultural context of clients is taken into consideration, it is most difficult to appreciate the nature of their struggles. Many counseling students have come to value characteristics such as making their own choices, expressing what they are feeling, being open and self-revealing, and striving for independence. Yet some clients may not share these goals. Certain cultures emphasize being emotionally reserved or being selective about sharing personal concerns. Counselors need to determine whether the assumptions they have made about the nature and functioning of therapy are appropriate for culturally diverse populations.

Clearly, effective counseling must take into account the impact of culture. Culture is, quite simply, the values and behaviors shared by a group of individuals. It is important to realize that culture does not refer just to an ethnic or racial heritage but includes age, gender, religion, sexual orientation, physical and mental ability, and socioeconomic status.

Acquiring Competencies in Multicultural Counseling

Effective counselors understand their own cultural conditioning, the conditioning of their clients, and the sociopolitical system of which they are a part. Acquiring this understanding begins with counselors' awareness of any cultural values, biases, and attitudes that may hinder their development of a positive view of pluralism.

Sue, Arredondo, and McDavis (1992), and Arredondo and her colleagues (1996), have developed a conceptual framework for competencies and standards in multicultural counseling. Their dimensions of competency involve three areas: beliefs and attitudes, knowledge, and skill. For a more in-depth treatment of multicultural counseling and therapy competence refer to D. W. Sue and Sue's (1999) excellent book *Counseling the Culturally Different: Theory and Practice.*

BELIEFS AND ATTITUDES OF CULTURALLY SKILLED COUNSELORS First, effective counselors have moved from being culturally unaware to ensuring that their personal biases, values, or problems will not interfere with their ability to work with clients who are culturally different from them. They believe cultural self-awareness and sensitivity to one's own cultural heritage are essential for any form of helping. They are aware of their positive and negative emotional reactions toward other racial and ethnic groups that may prove detrimental to establishing collaborative helping relationships. They seek to examine and understand the world from the vantage point of their clients. They respect clients' religious and spiritual beliefs and values. They are comfortable with differences between themselves and others in terms of race, ethnicity, culture, and beliefs. Rather than maintaining that their cultural heritage is superior, they are able to accept and value cultural diversity. They realize that traditional theories and techniques may not be appropriate for all clients or for all problems. They monitor their functioning through consultation, supervision, and further training or education.

KNOWLEDGE OF CULTURALLY SKILLED COUNSELORS   Second, culturally effective practitioners possess certain knowledge. They know specifically about their own racial and cultural heritage and how it affects them personally and professionally. Because they understand the dynamics of oppression, racism, discrimination, and stereotyping, they are in a position to detect their own racist attitudes, beliefs, and feelings. They understand the worldview of their clients, and they learn about their clients' cultural backgrounds. They do not impose their values and expectations on their clients from differing cultural backgrounds and avoid stereotyping clients. They understand that external sociopolitical forces influence all groups, and they know how these forces operate with respect to the treatment of minorities. These practitioners are aware of the institutional barriers that prevent minorities from utilizing the mental health services available in their communities. They possess knowledge about the historical background, traditions, and values of the client populations with whom they work. They know about minority family structures, hierarchies, values, and beliefs. Furthermore, they are knowledgeable about community characteristics and resources. Culturally skilled counselors know how to help clients make use of indigenous support systems. In areas where they are lacking in knowledge, they seek resources to assist them. The greater their depth and breadth of knowledge of culturally diverse groups, the more likely they are to be effective practitioners.

SKILLS AND INTERVENTION STRATEGIES OF CULTURALLY SKILLED COUNSELORS   Third, effective counselors have acquired certain skills in working with culturally diverse populations. Counselors take responsibility for educating their clients to the way the therapeutic process works, including matters such as goals, expectations, legal rights, and the counselor's orientation. Multicultural counseling is enhanced when practitioners use methods and strategies and define goals consistent with the life experiences and cultural values of their clients. Such practitioners modify and adapt their interventions to accommodate cultural differences. They do not force their clients to fit within one counseling approach, but they recognize that counseling techniques may be culture-bound. They are able to send and receive both verbal and nonverbal messages accurately and appropriately. They become actively involved with minority individuals outside the office (community events, celebrations, and neighborhood groups). They are willing to seek out educational, consultative, and training experiences to enhance their ability to work with culturally diverse client populations. They consult regularly with other professionals regarding issues of culture to determine whether or where referral may be necessary.

Incorporating Culture Into Counseling Practice

It is unrealistic to expect a counselor to know everything about the cultural background of a client. There is much to be said for letting clients teach counselors about relevant aspects of their culture. It is a good idea for counselors to ask clients to provide them with the information they will need to work effectively. It helps to assess the degree of acculturation and identity development that has taken place. This is especially true for individuals who have the experience of living in more than one culture. Clients often have allegiance to their own culture, and yet they may find certain characteristics of their new culture attractive. They may experience conflicts in integrating the two cultures in which they live. These core struggles can be productively explored in the therapeutic context if the counselor understands and respects this cultural conflict.

WELCOMING DIVERSITY   Counseling is by its very nature diverse in a multicultural society, so it is easy to see that there are no ideal therapeutic approaches. Instead, different theories have distinct features that have appeal for different cultural groups. Some theoretical approaches are limited when applied to certain populations. Effective multicultural practice demands an open stance on the part of the practitioner, flexibility, and a willingness to modify strategies to fit the needs and the situation of the individual client. Practitioners who truly respect their clients will be aware of clients' hesitations and will not be too quick to misinterpret this behavior. Instead, they will patiently attempt to enter the world of their clients as much as they can. It is not necessary for practitioners to have the same experiences as their clients, but they should be open to a similar set of feelings and struggles. It is not always by similarity but rather by differences that we are challenged to look at what we are doing.

SOME PRACTICAL GUIDELINES   Reflecting on the following guidelines may increase your effectiveness in serving diverse client populations:

■ Learn more about how your own cultural background has influenced your thinking and behaving. What specific steps can you take to broaden your base of understanding, both of your own culture and of other cultures?
■ Identify your basic assumptions, especially as they apply to diversity in culture, ethnicity, race, gender, class, religion, and sexual orientation. Think about how your assumptions are likely to affect your practice as a counselor.
■ Where did you obtain your knowledge about culture? Are your attitudes about diverse cultures your own, and have you carefully examined them?
■ Learn to pay attention to the common ground that exists among people of diverse backgrounds. What are some of the ways in which we all share universal concerns?

■ Spend time preparing clients for counseling. Teach them how to use their therapeutic experience to meet the challenges they face in their everyday lives.

■ Be flexible in applying the methods you use with clients. Don't be wedded to a specific technique if it is not appropriate for a given client.

■ Remember that practicing from a multicultural perspective can make your job easier and can be rewarding for both you and your clients.

It takes time, study, and experience to become an effective multicultural counselor. Multicultural competence cannot be reduced simply to cultural awareness and sensitivity, to a body of knowledge, or to a specific set of skills. Instead, it requires a combination of all of these areas.

ISSUES FACED BY BEGINNING THERAPISTS

This section is based on my observation and work with counselors-in-training and on my own struggles when I began practicing. I will identify some of the major issues that most of us typically face, particularly during the beginning stages of learning how to be therapists. Some of these recurring patterns of questions, conflicts, and issues provide the substance of seminars and practicum experiences in counseling. When counselor interns complete their formal course work and begin facing clients, they are put to the test of integrating and applying what they have learned. They soon realize that all they really have to work with is themselves—their own life experiences, values, and humanity. At that point some real concerns arise about their adequacies as counselors and as individuals and about what they can bring of themselves to the counseling relationship. Here are some useful guidelines for beginning counselors.

Dealing With Our Anxieties

Most beginning counselors, regardless of their academic and experiential backgrounds, anticipate meeting their initial clients with ambivalent feelings. As beginners, if we have enough sense, we are probably anxiety ridden and ask ourselves questions such as "What will I say?" "How will I say it?" "Will I be able to help?" "What if I make mistakes?" "Will my clients return, and if they do, what will I do next?"

A certain level of anxiety demonstrates that we are aware of the uncertainties of the future with our clients and of our abilities to really be there and stay with them. Our willingness to recognize and deal with these anxieties, as opposed to denying them by pretenses, is a mark of courage. That we have self-doubts seems perfectly normal; it is how we deal with them that counts. One way is to openly discuss them with a supervisor and peers. The possibilities are rich for meaningful exchanges and for gaining support from fellow interns who probably have many of the same concerns, fears, and anxieties.

Being and Disclosing Ourselves

Because we are typically self-conscious and anxious when we begin counseling, we tend to be overconcerned with what the books say and with the mechanics of how we should proceed. Inexperienced therapists too often fail to appreciate the values inherent in simply being themselves. It is possible to err by going to extremes in two different directions. At one end are counselors who lose themselves in their fixed role and hide behind a professional facade. At the other end are therapists who strive too hard to prove that they are human. At either end of these poles we are not being ourselves.

Take the first extreme. Here counselors are so bound up in maintaining stereotyped role expectations that little of them as a person shows through. Although counselors do have role functions, it is possible to responsibly perform them without blurring our identity and becoming lost in our role. I believe that the more insecure, frightened, and uncertain we are in our professional work, the more we will cling to the defense afforded by a role. The unrealistic expectation that we must be superhuman leads to becoming ossified in fixed roles.

At the other extreme counselors actively work at demonstrating their humanness. These counselors overreact and blur any distinction between the helper and the one who is helped. They tend to make the mistake of inappropriately burdening their clients with spontaneous impressions they are having toward them. Therapist disclosures should have the effect of encouraging clients to deepen their level of self-exploration or to enhance the therapeutic relationship. Excessive counselor disclosure often originates from the counselor's own needs, and in these cases clients' needs are secondary.

Avoiding Perfectionism

Both undergraduate students in human services and graduate students in counseling are prone to putting themselves under tremendous pressure. Do you recognize any of these self-talk statements?

- I have to be the perfect counselor, and if I'm not, I could do severe damage.
- I should know everything there is to know about my profession, and if I show that there is something I don't know, others will see me as incompetent.
- I ought to be able to help everybody who seeks my help. If there is someone I can't help, that just proves my incompetence.
- If a client doesn't get better, it must be my fault.
- Making a mistake is horrible, and failure is always fatal. If I were really professional, I wouldn't make mistakes.
- I should always radiate confidence; there is no room for self-doubt.

Perhaps one of the most common self-defeating beliefs with which we burden ourselves is that we must be perfect. Although we may well know *intellectually* that humans are not perfect, *emotionally* we often feel that there is little room for error. I attempt to teach counseling interns and students that they need not burden themselves with the idea that they must be perfect. They do not have to know everything, and there is no disgrace in revealing their lack of knowledge. Rather than trying to impress others and bluffing their way through difficult situations, they can always admit the truth and then set out to find information or answers (if indeed there is an answer). It takes courage to admit imperfections, but there is a value in being open about them.

To be sure, you *will* make mistakes, whether you are a beginning or a seasoned therapist. If our energies are tied up presenting an image of perfection, we will have little energy left to be present for our clients. What is more important than our mistakes is the lessons we learn from them. I tell students to challenge their notions that they should know everything and should be perfectly skilled. I encourage students to share their mistakes or what they perceive as errors. Students willing to risk making mistakes in supervised learning situations and willing to reveal their self-doubts will find a direction that leads to growth.

Being Honest About Our Limitations

A related fear that most of us have is of facing our limitations as counselors. We fear losing the client's respect if we say "I really feel that I can't help you on this point" or "I just don't have the kind of information or skill to help you with this problem." Clients' responses overwhelmingly confirm the value of honesty as opposed to an attempt to fake competence. Not only will we perhaps not lose our clients' respect, but we may gain their respect by frankly admitting our limitations.

We cannot realistically expect to succeed with every client. Even experienced counselors at times become glum and begin to doubt their value when forced to admit that there are clients whom they are not able to reach in a significant way. Be honest enough with yourself and with your client to admit that you cannot work successfully with everyone.

There is a delicate balance between learning our realistic limits and challenging what we sometimes think of as being "limits." For example, we may tell ourselves that we could never work with a specific client population because we cannot identify with them. Before deciding that we do not have the life experiences or the personal qualities to work with a given population, we might do well to try working in a setting with a population we do not intend to specialize in. This can be done through diversified field placements or visits to agencies.

Understanding Silence

Those silent moments during a therapeutic session may seem like silent hours to a beginning therapist. It is not uncommon to feel threatened by silences to the point of doing something counterproductive to break the silence and thus relieve our anxiety.

Silence can have many meanings. The client may be quietly thinking about some things that were discussed earlier or evaluating some insight just acquired. The client may be waiting for the therapist to take the lead and decide what to say next, or the therapist may be waiting for the client to do this. Either the client or the therapist may be bored, distracted, or preoccupied or may just not have anything to say for the moment. The client may be feeling hostile toward the therapist and thus be playing the game of "I'll just sit here like a stone and see if he [she] can get to me." The client and the therapist may be communicating without words. The silence may be refreshing, or the silence may say much more than words. Perhaps the interaction has been on a surface level, and both persons have some fear or hesitancy about getting to a deeper level. When silences occur, explore with your client what they mean. First, acknowledge the silence and your feelings about it. Then, rather than talking noisily simply to make each other comfortable, pursue its meanings.

Dealing With Demands From Clients

A major issue that puzzles many beginning counselors is how to deal with clients who seem to make constant demands. Because therapists feel that they should extend themselves in being helpful, they often burden themselves with the unrealistic standard that they should give unselfishly regardless of how great the demands on them are. The demands may manifest themselves in a variety of ways. Clients may call you frequently at home and expect you to talk at length; demand to see you more often or for a longer period than you can provide; want to see you socially; want you to adopt or in some other way take care of them and assume their responsibilities; expect you to manipulate another person (spouse, child, parent) to see and accept their point of view; demand that you not leave them and that you continually demonstrate how much you care; or demand that you tell them what to do and how to solve a problem. One way of heading off these demands is to make your expectations and boundaries clear during the initial counseling session or in the disclosure statement.

Dealing With Clients Who Lack Commitment

At the other extreme are clients who seem to have very little investment in counseling. Many clients are involuntary in that they are required by a court order to obtain therapy. In these cases you may well be challenged in your attempt to establish a working relationship. But it is possible to do effective work with clients who are sent to you.

Practitioners who work with involuntary clients must begin by openly discussing the nature of the relationship. They should not promise what they cannot or will not deliver. It is good practice to make clear the limits of confidentiality as well as any other factors that may affect the course of therapy. In working with involuntary clients it is especially important to prepare them for the process. Questions to take up include these:

- What is the therapy about?
- What are the joint responsibilities of the two parties?
- How might therapy help clients get what they want?
- What can clients do to increase the chances that the therapy experience will be positive?
- What are the potential risks and dangers?
- What can clients expect in the general course of treatment?

This kind of preparation can go a long way toward dealing with resistance. Often, in fact, resistance is brought about by a counselor who omits preparation and merely assumes that all clients are open and ready to benefit from therapy.

As a beginning counselor you can easily be drawn into unproductive games with clients who lack commitment if you expect yourself to have far greater investment in these clients than they have for themselves. It is possible to try too hard to be understanding and accepting, thereby making few demands on such clients. There are also situations in which a therapist completely blames "uncommitted clients" for a lack of progress in counseling. What appears to be a lack of commitment may be a lack of a client's understanding of the nature of counseling. Cultural and developmental variables play an important role in a client's readiness to participate in the therapeutic process.

Tolerating Ambiguity

Many beginning therapists experience the anxiety of not seeing the fruits of their labor. They ask themselves: "Am I really doing my client any good? Is the client perhaps getting worse? Is anything really occurring as a result of our sessions, or am I just deceiving myself into believing we're making progress?" I hope you will learn to tolerate the ambiguity of not knowing for sure whether your client is improving, at least during the initial sessions. Understand that clients may apparently "get worse" before they show therapeutic gains. After clients have decided to work toward self-honesty and drop their defenses and facades, they can be expected to experience an increase of personal pain and disorganization, which may result in depression or a panic reaction. Many a client has uttered: "My God, I was better off before I started therapy. Now I feel more vulnerable than before. Maybe I was happier when I was ignorant." Also, realize that the fruitful effects of the joint efforts of the therapist and the client may not be manifest for months (or even years) after the conclusion of therapy.

The year I began doing full-time individual and group counseling in a college counseling center was, professionally, the most trying year for me. I had been teaching a variety of psychology courses, and I could sense relatively quick results—or the lack of them. I found teaching gratifying, reinforcing, and many times exciting. In contrast, counseling seemed like a laborious and thankless task. The students who came to the counseling center did not evidence any miraculous cures, and some would come each week with the same complaints. They saw little progress, sought answers, wanted some formula for feeling better, or wanted a shot of motivation. I was plagued with self-doubts and skepticism. My need for reinforcement was so great that I was antitherapeutic for some. I needed them to need me, to tell me that I was effective, and to assure me that they were noticing positive changes.

My beginning experiences taught me that I needed to be able to tolerate not knowing whether a client was progressing or whether I was being instrumental in that person's growth or change. I learned that the only way to acquire self-trust as a therapist was to allow myself to feel my self-doubts, uncertainty about my effectiveness, and ambivalence over whether I wanted to continue as a counseling psychologist. As I became less anxious over my performance, I was able to pay increasing attention both to the client and to myself in the therapeutic relationship.

Avoiding Losing Ourselves in Our Clients

A common mistake for beginners is to worry too much about clients. There is a danger of incorporating clients' neuroses into our own personality. We lose sleep wondering what decisions they are making. We sometimes identify so closely with clients that we lose our own sense of identity and assume their identity. Empathy becomes distorted and militates against a therapeutic intervention. We need to learn how to "let clients go" and not carry around their problems until we see them again. The most therapeutic thing is to be as fully present as we are able to be (feeling with our clients and experiencing their struggles with them) but to let them assume the responsibility of their living and choosing outside of the session. If we become lost in clients' struggles and confusion, we cease being an effective agent in helping them find their way out of the darkness. If we accept the responsibility for our clients' decisions, we are blocking rather than fostering their growth.

This discussion relates to an issue that we all need to recognize and face in our work as counselors—namely, *countertransference,* which occurs when a counselor's own needs or unresolved personal conflicts become entangled in the therapeutic relationship. Because countertransference that is not recognized and not successfully dealt with has the effect of blurring therapist objectivity (and actually intruding in the counseling process), it is essential that counselor trainees focus on themselves in supervision sessions. By dealing with the reactions that are stirred up within themselves in their relationships with clients, they can learn a lot about how the needs and unfinished business in their own life can bog down clients' progress.

Because it may not be appropriate for us to use clients' time to work through our reactions to them, it is all the more important that we be willing to work on ourselves in our own sessions with another therapist, supervisor, or colleague. Although recognizing how our needs can intrude in our work as counselors is one beginning step, we need to be willing to continually explore what we are seeing in ourselves. If we do not, we increase the danger of losing ourselves in our clients and using them to meet our unfulfilled needs.

Developing a Sense of Humor

Therapy is a responsible matter, but it need not be deadly serious. Both clients and counselors can enrich a relationship by laughing. I have found that humor and tragedy are closely linked and that after allowing ourselves to feel some experiences that are painfully tragic, we can also genuinely laugh at how seriously we have taken our situation. We secretly delude ourselves into believing we are unique—that we are alone in our pain and we alone have experienced the tragic. What a welcome relief when we can admit that pain is not our exclusive domain. It is important to recognize that laughter or humor does not mean that work is not being accomplished. There are times, of course, when laughter is used to cover up anxiety or to escape from the experience of facing threatening material. The therapist needs to distinguish between humor that distracts and humor that enhances the situation.

Sharing Responsibility With the Client

The way in which counselors structure their sessions has implications for the balance of responsibility that will characterize the client/therapist relationship. In your work as a counselor it is essential that you become aware of the subtle ways your behavior can influence your clients. It is critical to monitor the impact of what you say and do. Frequently ask yourself: What am I doing? Whose needs are being met—my client's or my own? What is the effect of my behavior on my client?

You will probably struggle with finding the optimum balance in sharing responsibility with your clients. One mistake is to assume full responsibility for the direction and outcomes of therapy. This will lead to taking from your clients the rightful responsibility they need if they are to become empowered by making their own decisions. It could also increase the likelihood of your early burnout. Another mistake is for you to refuse to accept the responsibility for making accurate assessments and designing appropriate treatment plans for your clients. How responsibility will be shared should be addressed at the beginning of the therapeutic relationship. Early during the course of counseling, it is your responsibility to discuss specific matters such as length and overall duration of the sessions, confidentiality, general goals, and methods used to achieve goals. (Informed consent is discussed in Chapter 3.)

It is important to be alert to your clients' efforts to get you to assume responsibility for directing their lives. Many clients seek a "magic answer" as a way of escaping the anxiety of making their own decisions. Yet it is not your role to assume responsibility for directing your clients' lives. Client-initiated contracts and specific assignments are helpful in keeping the focus of responsibility on the client. Contracts can be changed, and new ones can be developed. Formulating contracts can continue during the entire counseling relationship. You might ask yourself, "Are my clients doing now what will move them toward greater independence and toward increasingly finding their answers within?" Perhaps the best measure of our general effectiveness as counselors is the degree to which clients are able to say to us, "I appreciate what you've been to me, and because of your faith in me, I feel I can now go it alone." Eventually, if we are good enough, we will be out of business!

Declining to Give Advice

A common mistaken notion is that giving advice is the same as counseling. It is not unusual to hear prospective students who are interviewing for admission to a graduate counseling program say, "I want a master's degree in counseling because my friends often come to me for advice. I've always been one who likes to help others." Quite often clients who are suffering come to a therapy session seeking and even demanding advice. They want more than direction; they want a wise counselor to make a decision or resolve a problem for them.

Counseling should not be confused with dispensing information. Therapists help clients discover their own solutions and recognize their own freedom to act. Therapists do not deprive clients of the opportunity to act freely. A common escape by many clients is not trusting themselves to find solutions, use their freedom, or discover their own direction. Even if we, as therapists, were able to resolve their struggles for them, we would be fostering their dependence on us. They would continually need to seek our counsel for every new twist in their difficulties. Instead of adopting the style of freely giving advice, ask clients questions such as "What possibilities do you see?" or "If I were able to solve this particular problem, how would that help you with future problems?" Our job is to help clients make independent choices and accept the consequences of their choices. The habitual practice of giving advice does not work toward this end.

Defining Your Role as a Counselor

One of your challenges as a counselor will be to define and clarify your professional role. As you read about the various theoretical orientations in Part Two, reflect on the counselor's role from each of these perspectives. Think about what role or roles you would most want to assume. At this point, how might you define the basic role of a therapist? Is the therapist a friend? An expert? A teacher? An advice giver? An information giver? A provider of alternatives? A confronter? As a counselor, might you have each of these functions at various times, and if so, what is your basic role in the counseling process? What influence might the setting in which you practice have on your role? What might you do when you are in conflict with the agency's view of what you should be doing?

The fact that a range of appropriate roles exists often confuses beginning counselors. There is no simple and universal answer to the question of the therapist's proper role. Factors such as the type of counseling, the counselor's level of training, the clientele to be served, and the therapeutic setting all need to be considered.

From my perspective the central function of counseling is to help clients recognize their own strengths, discover what is preventing them from using their strengths, and clarify what kind of person they want to be. Counseling is a process by which clients are invited to look honestly at their behavior and lifestyle and make certain decisions about how they want to modify the quality of their life. In this framework counselors provide support and warmth yet care enough to challenge and confront so that clients will be able to take the actions necessary to bring about significant change.

In your work as a counselor you would do well to make a critical evaluation of appropriate counseling functions. You can benefit from deciding in advance those functions that you feel are inconsistent with genuine counseling. It will help you to realize that the professional roles you assume are likely to be dependent on factors such as the client populations with whom you are working, the specific therapeutic services that you are providing, the particular stage of counseling, and the setting in which you work. Your role will not be defined once and for all. You will have to reassess the nature of your professional commitments and redefine your role at various times.

Learning to Use Techniques Appropriately

When counselors are at an impasse with clients, they sometimes have a tendency to look for the "right" techniques to get the sessions moving. As you saw in Chapter 1, relying on techniques too much can lead to mechanical counseling. Ideally, the techniques therapists use should evolve from the therapeutic relationship and should enhance the client's awareness or suggest possibilities for experimenting with new behavior. It is essential to understand the theoretical rationale for each technique used and to be sure the techniques are congruent with the goals of therapy. This does not mean that counselors need to restrict themselves to drawing on accepted techniques and procedures within a single model; quite the contrary. However, effective counselors avoid using techniques in a hit-or-miss fashion, to fill time, to meet their own needs, or to get things moving. Their methods are carefully chosen as a way to help clients make therapeutic progress.

Developing Your Own Counseling Style

Counselors-in-training need to be cautioned about the tendency to mimic the style of a supervisor, therapist, or some other model. It is important to accept that there is no "right" way to conduct therapy and that wide variations in approach can be effective. You will inhibit your potential effectiveness in reaching others if you attempt to imitate another therapist's style or if you fit most of your behavior during the session into the Procrustean bed of some expert's theory. Although I am fully aware that your style as a counselor will be influenced by teachers, therapists, and supervisors, I encourage you to be watchful of blurring your potential uniqueness by trying to imitate them. I advocate borrowing from others but, at the same time, finding a way that is distinctive to you.

STAYING ALIVE AS A PERSON AND AS A PROFESSIONAL

Ultimately, our single most important instrument is the person we are, and our most powerful technique is our ability to model aliveness and realness. We must take care of ourselves so that we remain fully alive. We need to work at dealing with those factors that threaten to drain life from us and render us helpless. I encourage you to consider how you can apply the theories you will be studying to enhance your life from both a personal and a professional standpoint. If you are aware of the factors that sap your vitality as a person, you are in a better position to prevent the condition known as *professional burnout*.

What is burnout? I have heard counselors complain that they are just going through the motions on their job. They feel that whatever they are doing makes no difference at all and that they have nothing left to give. Some of these practitioners have convinced themselves that this feeling of burnout is one of the inevitable hazards of the profession and that there is not much they can do to revitalize themselves. This assumption is lethal: it cements the feeling of impotence and leads to giving up hope. Equally bad are those practitioners who do not realize that they are burned out.

Burnout manifests itself in many ways. Those who experience this syndrome typically find that they are tired, drained, and without enthusiasm. They talk of feeling pulled by their many projects, most of which seem to have lost meaning. They feel that what they do have to offer is either not wanted or not received. They feel unappreciated, unrecognized, and unimportant, and they go about their jobs in a mechanical and routine way. They tend not to see any concrete results or fruits from their efforts. Often they feel oppressed by the "system" and by institutional demands, which, they contend, stifle any sense of personal initiative. A real danger is that the burnout syndrome can feed off of itself, so that practitioners feel more and more isolated. They may fail to reach out to one another and to develop a support system. Because burnout can rob us of the vitality we need personally and professionally, it is important to look at how we can prevent burnout.

Taking Responsibility

In my experience conducting training workshops, it has become almost standard to hear mental health workers blame the system and other external factors for their condition: the more they look outside of themselves for the reasons that they feel dead, the greater becomes their sense of impotence and hopelessness. At these workshops I often hear statements such as these:

- I'm failing as a counselor because my clients are highly resistant and don't really want to change. Besides, they're not capable of much change!
- The system here keeps us down. We're merely small cogs that need to keep functioning if this big machine is to continue working.
- I have far too many clients, and I also have too many demands on my time. All these demands make me feel useless, because I know I'll never be able to meet them.

Notice that these professionals are placing responsibility *outside* of themselves. This is the passive stance that so often contributes to general feelings of hopelessness and powerlessness. To the degree that professionals continue to blame external factors, they also surrender their own personal power. It is essential that counselors recognize that even though external realities do exert a toll on personal energy, they can be instrumental in bringing about changes, both in their environment and in themselves. Although bureaucratic obstacles can make it difficult to function effectively, it is possible to learn ways to survive with dignity within an institution and to engage in meaningful work.

Preventing Burnout

Learn to look within yourself to determine what choices you are making (and not making) to keep yourself alive. This can go a long way toward preventing what some people consider to be an inevitable condition associated with the helping professions. You have considerable control over whether you become burned out. Although you cannot always control stressful events, you do have a great deal of control over how you interpret and react to these events. It is important to realize that you cannot continue to give and give while getting little in return. There is a price to pay for always being available and for assuming that you are able to control the lives and destinies of others. Become attuned to the subtle signs of burnout rather than waiting for a full-blown condition of emotional and physical exhaustion to set in. Develop your own strategy for keeping yourself alive personally and professionally. Here are a few suggestions for preventing burnout:

- Evaluate your goals, priorities, and expectations to see if they are realistic and if they are getting you what you want.
- Recognize that you can be an active agent in your life.
- Find other interests besides work, especially if your work is not meeting your most important needs.
- Think of ways to bring variety into your work.
- Take the initiative to start new projects that have personal meaning, and do not wait for the system to sanction this initiative.

- Learn to monitor the impact of stress, on the job and at home.
- Attend to your health through adequate sleep, an exercise program, proper diet, meditation, and relaxation.
- Develop a few friendships that are characterized by a mutuality of giving and receiving.
- Learn how to ask for what you want, but don't expect always to get it.
- Learn how to work for self-confirmation and for self-rewards as opposed to looking externally for validation.
- Find meaning through play, travel, or new experiences.
- Take the time to evaluate the meaningfulness of your projects to determine where you should continue to invest time and energy.
- Avoid assuming burdens that are properly the responsibility of others. If you worry more about your clients than they do about themselves, for example, it would be well for you to reconsider this investment.
- Take classes and workshops, attend conferences, and read to gain new perspectives on old issues.
- Rearrange your schedule to reduce stress.
- Learn your limits, and learn to set limits with others.
- Learn to accept yourself with your imperfections, including being able to forgive yourself when you make a mistake or do not live up to your ideals.
- Exchange jobs with a colleague for a short period, or ask a colleague to join forces in a common work project.
- Form a support group with colleagues to share feelings of frustration and to find better ways of approaching the reality of difficult job situations.
- Cultivate some hobbies that bring pleasure.
- Make time for your spiritual growth.
- Become more active in your professional organization.
- Seek counseling as an avenue of personal development.

This is not an exhaustive list, but it does provide some direction for thinking about ways to keep yourself alive.

Make periodic assessments of the direction of your own life to determine if you are living the way you want. If not, decide what you are willing to actually *do* to *make* changes occur. By being in tune with yourself, by having the experience of centeredness and solidness, and by feeling a sense of personal power, you have the basis for integrating your life experiences with your professional experiences. Such a synthesis can provide the basis for being an effective professional.

 ## SUMMARY

One of the basic issues in the counseling profession concerns the significance of the counselor as a person in the therapeutic relationship. Counselors are asking people to take an honest look at themselves and to make choices concerning how they want to change, so it is critical that counselors themselves be searchers who hold their own lives open to the same kind of scrutiny. Counselors should repeatedly ask themselves questions such as "What do I personally have to offer others who are struggling to find their way?" and "Am I doing in my own life what I urge others to do?"

Counselors can acquire an extensive theoretical and practical knowledge and can make that knowledge available to their clients. But to every therapeutic session they also bring themselves as persons. They bring their human qualities and the life experiences that have molded them. It is my belief that professionals can be well versed in psychological theory and can learn diagnostic and interviewing skills and still be ineffective as helpers. If counselors are to promote growth and change in their clients, they must be willing to promote growth in their own lives by exploring their own choices and decisions and by striving to become aware of the ways in which they have ignored their own potential for growth. This willingness to attempt to live in accordance with what they teach and thus to be positive models for their clients is what makes counselors "therapeutic persons."

CHAPTER

Ethical Issues in Counseling Practice

INTRODUCTION

PUTTING CLIENTS' NEEDS BEFORE YOUR OWN

ETHICAL DECISION MAKING

   The Role of Ethical Codes as a Catalyst for Improving Practice
   Some Steps in Making Ethical Decisions

THE RIGHT OF INFORMED CONSENT

DIMENSIONS OF CONFIDENTIALITY

   General Guidelines on Confidentiality

ETHICAL ISSUES IN A MULTICULTURAL PERSPECTIVE

   Have Current Theories Outlived Their Usefulness?
   Are Counseling and Therapy Culture-Bound?
   Focusing on Both Individual and Environmental Factors

ETHICAL ISSUES IN THE ASSESSMENT PROCESS

   The Role of Diagnosis in Counseling
   Guidelines for the Use of Tests in Counseling

DUAL RELATIONSHIPS IN COUNSELING PRACTICE

   Ethics Codes and Dual Relationships
   Perspectives on Dual and Multiple Relationships

GUIDELINES FOR ETHICAL PRACTICE: A Review

WHERE TO GO FROM HERE

INTRODUCTION

This chapter introduces you to some of the ethical principles and issues that will be a basic part of your professional practice. Its purpose is to stimulate you to think further about these issues so that you can form a sound basis for making ethical decisions. Topics addressed include balancing clients' needs against your own needs, ways of making sound ethical decisions, educating clients about their rights, parameters of confidentiality, ethical concerns in counseling diverse client populations, ethical issues involving diagnosis and testing, and dealing with dual relationships.

As you become involved in counseling, you will find that interpreting the ethical guidelines of your professional organization and applying them to particular situations demand the utmost ethical sensitivity. Even responsible practitioners differ over how to apply established ethical principles to specific situations. It is clear that therapists are challenged to deal with questions that do not always have obvious answers. You will have to struggle with yourself to decide how to act in ways that will further the best interests of your clients. To help you make these decisions, consult with colleagues, keep yourself informed about laws affecting your practice, keep up to date in your specialty field, stay abreast of developments in ethical practice, reflect on the impact your values have on your practice, and be willing to engage in honest self-examination.

You will need to reexamine the ethical issues raised in this chapter periodically throughout your professional life. You can benefit from both formal and informal opportunities to discuss ethical dilemmas during your training program. Even if you resolve some ethical issues while completing a graduate program, there is no guarantee that they have been settled once and for all. These issues are bound to take on new dimensions as you gain more experience. I have found that students often burden themselves unnecessarily with the expectation that they should resolve all problem issues before they are ready to practice. Ethical decision making is an evolutionary process that requires you to be continually open and self-critical.

In recent years there has been an increased awareness of the ethical responsibility of counselors to alleviate human suffering on a broader scale. It is clear that practitioners cannot afford to confine themselves to their offices if they hope to reach a wide group of people who are in need of services. Many mental health professionals now emphasize social action by exerting their influence against such wrongs as discrimination against women and minority groups, the continuation of racism in society, the neglect of the aged, and inhumane practices against children. Seminars and workshops are conducted to awaken professionals to pressing needs in the community. In fact, many states now require continuing education in ethics as a condition for relicensure as a counselor or a psychologist. In sum, counselors are discovering that to bring about significant individual change they cannot ignore the major social ills that often create and exacerbate problems for individuals. Counselors must become active agents of constructive social change.

PUTTING CLIENTS' NEEDS BEFORE YOUR OWN

Issues pertaining to counselors meeting their needs through their professional work were examined in Chapter 2. The ethical dimensions of this topic are addressed here. I do not think that as counselors we can keep our personal needs completely separate from our relationships with clients. Ethically, it is essential that we become aware of our own needs, areas of unfinished business, potential personal conflicts, and defenses. We need to realize how such factors could interfere with helping our clients.

Our professional relationships with our clients exist for their benefit. A useful question to frequently ask yourself is, "Whose needs are being met in this relationship, my client's or my own?" It takes considerable professional maturity to make an honest appraisal of your behavior and its impact on clients. I do not think it is unethical for us to meet our personal needs through our professional work, yet it is essential that these needs be kept in perspective. For me, the ethical issue exists when we meet our needs, in either obvious or subtle ways, at the expense of our clients. The crux of the matter is to avoid exploiting clients.

What kind of awareness is crucial? We all have certain blind spots and distortions of reality. As helping professionals, we have responsibilities to work actively toward expanding our own self-awareness and to learn to recognize areas of prejudice and vulnerability. If we are aware of our personal problems and are willing to work them through, there is less chance that we will project them onto clients. If certain areas of struggle surface and old conflicts become reactivated, we have an ethical obligation to seek our own therapy so that we will be able to assist clients in confronting these same struggles.

We must also examine other, less obviously harmful, personal needs that can get in the way of creating growth-producing relationships. These other aspects of our personality include the need for control and power; the need to be nurturing and helpful; the need to change others in the direction of our own values; the need to persuade; the need for feeling adequate, particularly when it becomes overly important that the client confirm our competence; and the need to be respected and appreciated. I am not asserting that these needs are neurotic; on the contrary, it is essential that our needs be met if we are to be involved with helping others find satisfaction in their lives. Nor do I think that there is anything amiss in our deriving deep personal satisfaction from our work. And surely many of our needs for feeling worthwhile, important, respected, and adequate may enhance the quality of our work with others.

In summary, I believe many are motivated to enter the counseling profession because of their needs for power, for feeling useful and significant, and for reinforcing their feelings of adequacy. If helpers depend inordinately on others for their psychological gratification, they are likely to keep others in a dependent position. Because of their own emotional hunger they are unable to focus genuine attention on the client's deprivations. At the extreme, the helper is in greater need of the "helpee" than the other way around. For these reasons, ethical practice demands that counselors recognize the central importance of continuously evaluating in which direction their personality might influence clients—toward progress or stagnation.

 ## ETHICAL DECISION MAKING

As a practitioner you will ultimately have to apply the ethical codes of your profession to the many practical problems you face. You will not be able to rely on ready-made answers or prescriptions given by professional organizations, which typically provide only broad guidelines for responsible practice.

Part of the process of making ethical decisions involves learning about the resources from which you can draw when you are struggling with an ethical question. Although you are ultimately responsible for making ethical decisions, you do not have to do so in a vacuum. You should also be aware of the consequences of practicing in ways that are not sanctioned by organizations of which you are a member or the state in which you are licensed to practice.

The Role of Ethical Codes as a Catalyst for Improving Practice

Professional codes of ethics serve a number of purposes. They educate counseling practitioners and the general public about the responsibilities of the profession. They provide a basis for accountability, and through their enforcement, clients are protected from unethical practices. Perhaps most important, codes can provide a basis for reflecting on and improving one's professional practice. Self-monitoring is a better route for professionals to take than being policed by an outside agency (Herlihy & Corey, 1997b).

It should be emphasized that codes of ethics typically address a broad range of issues and behaviors. Thus, they describe minimal standards of behavior and identify and prohibit those behaviors that are unethical. There is a real difference between merely following the ethical codes and making a commitment to practicing with the highest ideals. *Mandatory ethics* entails a level of ethical functioning at which counselors simply act in compliance with minimal standards. *Aspirational ethics* pertains to striving for the optimum standards of conduct. Rather than merely focusing on ways to avoid a malpractice suit, therapists who are committed to aspirational ethics are primarily concerned with doing what is in the best interests of their clients.

From my perspective, one of the unfortunate trends is for ethics codes to increasingly take on legalistic dimensions. Many practitioners are so anxious about becoming embroiled in a lawsuit that they gear their practices mainly toward fulfilling legal minimums rather than thinking of what is right for their clients. In this era of litigation it makes sense to be aware of the legal aspects of practice and to do what is possible to reduce the chances of malpractice action, but it is a mistake to confuse legal behavior with being ethical. Although following the law is part of ethical behavior, being an ethical practitioner involves far more. One of the best ways to prevent being sued for malpractice rests in demonstrating respect for clients, having their welfare as a central concern, and practicing within the framework of professional codes.

Over time, most of the ethical codes of various mental health professions have evolved into lengthy documents, setting forth what is desired behavior and proscribing behavior that may not serve the client's welfare. Even though codes are becoming more specific, they do not convey ultimate truth, nor do they provide ready-made answers for the ethical dilemmas that practitioners will encounter. Ultimately, professionals are expected to exercise prudent judgment when it comes to interpreting and applying ethical principles to specific situations. In my view, ethical codes are best used as guidelines to formulate sound reasoning and serve practitioners in making the best judgments possible. Because ethics codes are creations of human beings, and because they are evolving documents that are modified over time, some degree of flexibility is essential in applying them. No code of ethics can delineate what would be the appropriate or best course of action in each problematic situation a professional will face.

Some Steps in Making Ethical Decisions

There are a number of different models for ethical decision making; most tend to focus on the application of principles to ethical dilemmas. After reviewing a few of these models, my colleagues and I have identified a series of procedural steps to help you think through ethical problems (see Corey, Corey, & Callanan, 1998; Corey, Corey, & Haynes, 1998):

- Identify the problem or dilemma. Gather information that will shed light on the nature of the problem. This will help you decide whether the problem is mainly ethical, legal, professional, clinical, or moral.
- Identify the potential issues. Evaluate the rights, responsibilities, and welfare of all those who are involved in the situation.
- Look at the relevant ethics codes for general guidance on the matter. Consider whether your own values and ethics are consistent with or in conflict with the relevant guidelines.
- Know the applicable laws and regulations. It is essential to determine whether any laws or regulations have a bearing on the ethical dilemma.

- Seek consultation from more than one source to obtain various perspectives on the dilemma. Obtain consultation with professionals who are knowledgeable about the issues involved in the situation under question.
- Brainstorm various possible courses of action. Continue discussing options with other professionals. Include the client in this process of considering options for action.
- Enumerate the consequences of various decisions, and reflect on the implications of each course of action for your client. Again, include the client in this process.
- Decide on what appears to be the best possible course of action. Once the course of action has been implemented, follow up to evaluate the outcomes and to determine if further action is necessary.

In reasoning through any ethical issue, there is rarely one ideal course of action to follow; different practitioners will make a variety of decisions. The more subtle the ethical dilemma, the more difficult the decision-making process will be.

Professional maturity implies that you are open to questioning and that you are willing to discuss your quandaries with colleagues. Because ethical codes do not make decisions for you, demonstrate a willingness to struggle, to raise questions, to discuss ethical concerns with others, and to continually clarify your values and examine your motivations. To the degree that it is possible, include the client at all phases of the ethical decision-making process.

 ## THE RIGHT OF INFORMED CONSENT

By educating your clients about their rights and responsibilities, you are both empowering them and building a trusting relationship with them. Assisting clients to make informed choices consists of providing them with the information they need to become active participants in the therapeutic relationship. Some aspects of the informed consent process include the general goals of counseling, the responsibilities of the counselor toward the client, the responsibilities of clients, limitations of and exceptions to confidentiality, legal and ethical parameters that could define the relationship, the qualifications and background of the practitioner, the fees involved, the services the client can expect, and the approximate length of the therapeutic process. Further areas might include the benefits of counseling, the risks involved, and the possibility that the client's case will be discussed with the therapist's colleagues or supervisors. This process of educating the client begins with the initial counseling session and continues for the duration of counseling.

The challenge of fulfilling the spirit of informed consent is to strike a balance between giving clients too much information and giving them too little. For example, it is too late to tell minors that you intend to consult with their parents *after* they have disclosed that they are considering an abortion. In such a case both the girlfriend and the boyfriend have a right to know about the limitations of confidentiality before they make such highly personal disclosures. Clients can be overwhelmed, however, if counselors go into too much detail initially about the interventions they are likely to make. It takes both intuition and skill for practitioners to strike a balance.

Providing for informed consent tends to promote the active cooperation of clients in their counseling plan. Clients often do not realize that they have any rights and do not think about their own responsibilities in solving their problems. Those who feel desperate for help may unquestioningly accept whatever their counselor says or does. They seek the expertise of a professional without realizing that the success of this relationship depends largely on their own investment in the process.

It is a good idea to have basic information about the therapy process in writing, as well as discussing with clients topics that will enable them to get the maximum benefit from their counseling experience. Clients can take this written information home and then bring up questions at the following session. (A sample "informed consent document" is reproduced in the student manual that accompanies this textbook.)

 ## DIMENSIONS OF CONFIDENTIALITY

Confidentiality, which is central to developing a trusting and productive client/therapist relationship, is both a legal and an ethical issue. State laws now address confidentiality in therapy, as do the ethical codes of all the mental health professions. Because no genuine therapy can occur unless clients trust in the privacy of their revelations to their therapists, professionals have the responsibility to define the degree of confidentiality that can be promised. Counselors have an ethical responsibility to discuss the nature and purpose of confidentiality with their clients early in the counseling process. In addition, clients have a right to know that their therapist may be discussing certain details of the relationship with a supervisor or a colleague.

Although most counselors agree on the essential value of confidentiality, they realize that it cannot be considered an absolute. There are times when confidential information must be divulged, and there are many instances in which whether to keep or to break confidentiality becomes a cloudy issue. In determining when to breach confidentiality, therapists must consider the requirements of the institution in which they work and the clientele they serve. Because these circumstances are frequently not clearly defined by accepted ethical codes, counselors must exercise professional judgment.

In general, confidentiality must be broken when it becomes clear that clients might do serious harm to either themselves or others. There is a legal requirement to break confidentiality in cases involving child abuse, abuse of the elderly, and danger to others. All mental health practitioners and interns need to be aware of their duty to report such abuse.

General Guidelines on Confidentiality

Here are some of the circumstances that dictate when information must legally be reported by counselors:

- When clients pose a danger to others or themselves
- When the therapist believes a client under the age of 16 is the victim of incest, rape, child abuse, or some other crime
- When the therapist determines that the client needs hospitalization
- When information is made an issue in a court action
- When clients request that their records be released to themselves or to a third party

In general, however, it is a counselor's primary obligation to protect client disclosures as a vital part of the therapeutic relationship. When assuring clients that what they reveal in sessions will generally be kept confidential, counselors should also tell them of any limitations on confidentiality. This practice does not necessarily inhibit successful counseling.

Therapists should discuss with their clients how certain information about them might be shared with others. It is generally accepted that therapists will have no professional contact with the family or friends of a client without first securing the client's permission. It is accepted, in addition, that information obtained in therapeutic relationships should be discussed with others for professional purposes only and limited to persons who are clearly related to the case.

The issue of confidentiality takes on added dimensions for students who are involved in a fieldwork placement or internship as part of their program. In most cases these counselor interns are required to keep notes on the proceedings with their individual clients or the members of their group. Also, group-supervision sessions at a clinic or university typically entail open discussions about the clients with whom these counselor interns are working. These discussions should always be conducted in a professional manner. If a particular individual client is being discussed, it is important that this person's identity be protected if at all possible. In many situations interns can actually show their clients what they are writing and discuss these notes with them. When clients receive this type of openness from their counselors, I have found they respond with greater frankness because they feel that information will be used *for* them, not *against* them.

Counselors must become familiar with local and state laws that govern their specialization. Yet this knowledge alone will not settle difficult situations. There are various and sometimes conflicting ways to interpret a law, and professional judgment plays a critical role in resolving most cases.

Legislators and judges seem inclined to bind all mental health practitioners to confidentiality while at the same time limiting its scope. They appear to believe confidentiality is necessary for a counseling relationship to be effective, but that it need not be absolute. For instance, practitioners have an obligation not only to warn and to protect others from the acts of dangerous people but also to protect suicidal clients. There are definite limitations to confidentiality when the counselor determines that a client is a suicide risk. The assessment and management of suicidal clients are typically stressful for counselors. The possibility of a client's suicide raises a number of difficult issues that practitioners must face, such as their degree of influence, competence, level of involvement with a client, responsibility, and legal obligations. Counselors need to demonstrate the ability to make appropriate interventions in critical situations.

 ## ETHICAL ISSUES IN A MULTICULTURAL PERSPECTIVE

Ethical practice requires that we take the client's cultural context into account in counseling practice. In this section we look at how it is possible for practitioners to practice unethically if they do not address cultural differences in counseling practice.

Have Current Theories Outlived Their Usefulness?

Some writers allege that current theories of counseling and psychotherapy—including some of the theories in Part Two of this textbook—are inadequate to describe, explain, predict, and deal with the richness and complexity of a culturally diverse population (Sue, Ivey, & Pedersen, 1996). It has also been asserted that contemporary theories cannot be easily adapted to a wide range of cultures and that the helping professions need to develop a theory of multicultural counseling and therapy.

I agree only to a point with this assertion. I believe current theories can be expanded to include a multicultural perspective. With respect to many of the traditional theories, assumptions made about mental health, optimum human development, the nature of psychopathology, and the nature of effective treatment often have little relevance for some clients. For traditional theories to be relevant in a multicultural society, they must incorporate an interactive person-in-the-environment focus. That is, individuals are best understood by taking into consideration salient cultural and environmental variables. It is essential for therapists to create therapeutic strategies that are congruent with the range of values and behaviors that are characteristic of a pluralistic society.

Are Counseling and Therapy Culture-Bound?

Multicultural specialists have asserted that theories of counseling and psychotherapy represent different worldviews, each with its own values, biases, and assumptions about human behavior. Some counselors have criticized traditional therapeutic practices as irrelevant for people of color and other special populations such as the elderly. Most techniques are derived from counseling approaches developed by and for White, male, middle-class, Western clients and therefore may not be applicable to clients from different racial, ethnic, and cultural backgrounds. Western models of counseling have major limitations when they are applied to certain special populations and minority groups such as Asian and Pacific Islanders, Latinos, Native Americans, and African Americans. Moreover, value assumptions made by culturally different counselors and clients have resulted in culturally biased counseling and have led to underuse of mental health services (D. W. Sue & Sue, 1999; Pedersen, 2000).

Some of the values implicit in contemporary counseling theories include an emphasis on individualism, the separate existence of the self, individuation as the foundation for maturity, and decision making and responsibility as resting with the individual rather than the group. In contrast, an Asian perspective would play down individuality and focus on interdependence and losing oneself in the totality of the cosmos.

It cannot be denied that the psychoanalytic, behavioral, cognitive behavioral, and existential approaches originated in the Euro-American culture and are grounded on a core set of values. I think it is a myth that these approaches are value-neutral and are applicable to all human beings. There is a danger of imposing these values as being the only right ones and as having universal applicability. The relationship-oriented therapies (person-centered theory, existential therapy, and Gestalt therapy) emphasize freedom of choice and self-actualization. Practitioners with such an orientation tend to focus on individual responsibility for making internal changes as a way to cope with problems, and they view individuation as the foundation for healthy functioning. In some cultures, however, the key values are collectivist. Rather than emphasizing the development of the individual, they focus on what is good for the group. Certainly, therapists who operate on the assumption that all clients should embrace individualism are in error. Regardless of the therapist's orientation, it is crucial to listen to clients and determine why they are seeking help and how best to deliver the help that is appropriate for them.

Focusing on Both Individual and Environmental Factors

A theoretical orientation provides practitioners with a map to guide them in a productive direction with their clients. It is hoped that the theory orients them but does not control what they attend to in the therapeutic venture. Counselors who operate from a multicultural framework also have certain assumptions and a focus that guides their practice. They view individuals in the context of the family and the culture, and their aim is to facilitate social action that will lead to change within the client's community rather than merely increasing the individual's insight. Both multicultural practitioners and feminist therapists maintain that therapeutic practice will be effective only to the extent that interventions are tailored toward social action aimed at changing those factors that are creating the client's problem rather than blaming the client for his or her condition.

An adequate theory of counseling *does* deal with the social and cultural factors of an individual's problems. However, there is something to be said for helping clients deal with their response to environmental realities. Counselors may well be at a loss in trying to bring about social change when they are sitting with a client who is in pain because of social injustice. By using techniques from many of the traditional therapies, counselors can help clients increase their awareness of their options in dealing with barriers and struggles. It is not a matter of focusing strictly on an individual's intrapsychic dynamics and forgetting about bringing about change in the environment; rather, it is a matter of aiding clients in clarifying how they are personally affected by external conditions and challenging them to make decisions about what they can do to change themselves if they cannot directly change the outside world. It is essential to focus on both individual and social factors if change is to occur, as both feminist therapy and family systems therapy teach us. Indeed, the person-in-the-environment perspective acknowledges this interactive reality. (For a more detailed treatment of the ethical issues in multicultural counseling, see D. W. Sue and Sue, 1999; Pedersen, 2000, and Chapter 10 of Corey, Corey, and Callanan, 1998.)

 # ETHICAL ISSUES IN THE ASSESSMENT PROCESS

Both clinical and ethical issues are associated with the use of diagnostic and testing procedures. As you will see when you study the various theories of counseling, some approaches place heavy emphasis on the role of assessment as a prelude to the treatment process. Other theories—mainly the relationship-oriented and experiential therapies—tend to view diagnosis and testing as an external frame of reference that can remove the therapist from understanding the deeply personal and subjective world of the client. These theories also have ethical implications for practitioners who focus too much on the client's history while failing to pay sufficient attention to present attitudes and behavior.

The Role of Diagnosis in Counseling

Psychodiagnosis is the analysis and explanation of a client's problems. It may include an explanation of the causes of the client's difficulties, an account of how these problems developed over time, a classification of any disorders, a specification of preferred treatment procedure, and an estimate of the chances for a successful resolution. The purpose of diagnosis in counseling and psychotherapy is to identify disruptions in a client's present behavior and lifestyle. Once problem areas are clearly identified, the counselor and client are able to establish the goals of the therapy process, and then a treatment plan can be tailored to the unique needs of the client. A diagnosis is not a final category; rather, it provides a working hypothesis that guides the practitioner in understanding the client. The therapy sessions provide useful clues about the nature of the client's problems. Thus, diagnosis begins with the intake interview and continues throughout the duration of therapy.

The "bible" for guiding practitioners in making diagnostic assessments is the fourth edition of the American Psychiatric Association's (1994) *Diagnostic and Statistical Manual of Mental Disorders* (DSM-IV). Clinicians who work in community mental health agencies, private practice, and other human service settings are generally expected to assess client problems within the framework of the DSM-IV. This manual advises practitioners that it represents only an initial step in a comprehensive evaluation. There is also a caution about the necessity of gaining additional information about the person being evaluated beyond that which is required to make a DSM-IV diagnosis.

Although some clinicians view diagnosis as central to the counseling process, others view it as unnecessary, as a detriment, or as discriminatory against ethnic minorities and women. As you will see in Chapter 12, feminist therapists contend that traditional diagnostic practices are often oppressive and that such practices are based on a White, male-centered, Western notion of mental health and mental illness. The feminist perspective also charges that these diagnoses ignore societal contexts. Feminists also challenge many DSM diagnoses. However, they do make assessments and draw conclusions about client problems and strengths.

CONSIDERING ETHNIC AND CULTURAL FACTORS IN ASSESSMENT AND DIAGNOSIS A danger of the diagnostic approach is the possible failure of counselors to consider ethnic and cultural factors in certain patterns of behavior. Unless cultural variables are considered, some clients may be subjected to an erroneous diagnosis. Certain behaviors and personality styles may be labeled neurotic or deviant simply because they are not characteristics of the dominant culture. Thus, counselors who work with African Americans, Asian Americans, Latinos, and Native Americans may erroneously conclude that a client is repressed, inhibited, passive, and unmotivated, all of which are seen as undesirable by Western standards.

In the *Code of Ethics and Standards of Practice,* the ACA (1995) recognizes that there are cultural implications of making proper diagnoses and of using tests. Furthermore, in assessments of clients with different backgrounds, the DSM-IV emphasizes the importance of being aware of unintentional bias and keeping an open mind to the presence of distinctive ethnic and cultural patterns that could influence the diagnostic process.

A COMMENTARY ON DIAGNOSIS Is there a way to bridge the gap between the extreme view that diagnosis is the essential core of therapy and the extreme view that it is a detrimental factor? Most practitioners and many writers in the field consider assessment and diagnosis to be a continuing process that focuses on understanding the client. The collaborative perspective that involves the client as an active participant in the therapy process implies that both the therapist and the client are engaged in a search-and-discovery process from the first session to the last. Even though some practitioners may avoid formal diagnostic procedures and terminology, it seems that they do raise certain questions, such as:

- What is going on in the client's life now, and what does the client want from therapy?
- What are the client's strengths and limitations?
- What is the client like in the counseling setting, and what does this behavior reveal about the client's actions outside of therapy?

■ How far should therapy go?
■ What is the client learning from therapy, and to what degree is he
or she applying this learning to daily living?

In dealing with these questions, the therapist is formulating some conception about what clients want and how they might best attain their goals.
Thus, diagnosis becomes a form of making tentative hypotheses, and these
hunches can be formed with clients and shared with them throughout the
process. This perspective on assessment and diagnosis is consistent with
the principles of feminist therapy, an approach that is critical of traditional
diagnostic procedures.

The process of assessment and diagnosis cannot be separated from
treatment, and ideally, this process helps the practitioner conceptualize a
case. Ethical dilemmas are created when diagnosis is done strictly for insurance purposes, which often entails arbitrarily assigning a client to a diagnostic classification. However, it is a clinical, legal, and ethical obligation
of therapists to screen clients for life-threatening problems such as organic
disorders, schizophrenia, bipolar disorder, and suicidal types of depression.
Students need to learn the clinical skills necessary to do this type of screening, which is a form of diagnostic thinking. To function in most mental health
agencies, practitioners need to become skilled in understanding and utilizing assessment and diagnostic procedures. For a more detail discussion of
assessment and diagnosis in counseling practice as it is applied to a single
case, consult *Case Approach to Counseling and Psychotherapy* (Corey, 2001c),
in which theorists in 10 different theoretical orientations share their diagnostic perspective on the case of Ruth.

Guidelines for the Use of Tests in Counseling

The place of testing in counseling and therapy is another controversial
issue. Models that emphasize the objective view of counseling are inclined
to use testing procedures to get information about clients or to provide them
with information so that they can make more realistic decisions. The person-
centered and existential orientations view testing much as they do diagnosis—as an external form of understanding that has little to do with effective
counseling.

A wide variety of tests can be used for counseling purposes, including
measures of interest, aptitude, achievement, attitudes and values, and personal characteristics. In my view tests can be used as an adjunct to counseling; valuable information, which can add to a client's capacity to make
decisions, can be gleaned from them. But some cautions and guidelines regarding the use of tests are worth noting:

■ Clients should be involved in the test-selection process. They should
decide which categories of tests, if any, they wish to take.
■ Clients' reasons for wanting tests, as well as their past experience
with tests, should be explored.

- A client needs to be aware that tests are only tools, and imperfect ones at that. As means to an end, tests do not provide "the answer." At best they provide additional information that can be explored in counseling and used in coming to certain decisions.
- The counselor should clarify the purposes of the tests and point out their limitations. This role implies that the counselor has a good grasp of what the test is about and that he or she has taken it.
- The test results, not simply scores, should be given to the client, and their meanings should be explored. In interpreting the results, the counselor should be tentative and neutral, refraining from judgments as much as possible and allowing clients to formulate their own meanings and conclusions.
- It is especially important to consider the ways in which socioeconomic, ethnic, gender, and cultural factors can affect test scores.

 # DUAL RELATIONSHIPS IN COUNSELING PRACTICE

Dual (or multiple) relationships, either sexual or nonsexual, occur when counselors assume two (or more) roles simultaneously or sequentially with a client. Some examples of dual relationships are combining the roles of teacher and therapist or of supervisor and therapist; bartering for goods or therapeutic services; borrowing money from a client; providing therapy to a friend, an employee, or a relative; engaging in a social relationship with a client; accepting an expensive gift from a client; becoming emotionally or sexually involved with a former client; and going into a business venture with a client.

Because dual relationships are necessarily complex and multidimensional, there are few simple and absolute answers to neatly resolve them. It is not always possible to play a single role in your work as a counselor, nor is it always desirable. You will probably have to wrestle with balancing more than one role, regardless of the setting in which you work or the client population you serve. Thus, it is critical that you give careful thought to the complexities of multiple relationships before embroiling yourself in ethically questionable situations.

Dual relationships are rarely a clear-cut matter, for ethical reasoning and judgment come into play when ethical codes are applied to specific situations (Corey & Herlihy, 1997; Herlihy & Corey, 1997a). Although dual relationships do carry inherent risks, they are not always harmful, unethical, and unprofessional. Some dual relationships are clearly exploitative and do serious harm both to the client and to the professional, but others may have more potential benefits to clients than potential risks.

Ethics Codes and Dual Relationships

What guidance do codes of ethics offer on handling dual relationships? Almost all of the codes of the professional organizations now advise against forming such relationships. These codes typically caution professionals against entering into those relationships "that could impair objectivity." The problem is that the codes are usually written in general terms, which demands that practitioners use their best judgment in each situation to determine if there is a potential for harm. The current focus of ethics codes is on keeping alert to the possibilities of damaging exploitation rather than a universal prohibition of all dual and multiple relationships.

Perspectives on Dual and Multiple Relationships

Some of the problematic aspects of engaging in dual relationships are that they are pervasive, they can be difficult to recognize, they are unavoidable at times, they are potentially harmful, and they are the subject of conflicting advice from various experts. A review of the literature reveals that dual and multiple relationships are hotly debated. Except for sexual intimacy with current clients, which is unequivocally considered unethical, there is not much consensus regarding the appropriate way to manage dual relationships.

A consensus of many writers is that dual and multiple relationships are inevitable in some situations and that a global prohibition does not seem to be a realistic answer. Because interpersonal boundaries are not static but undergo redefinition over time, the challenge for practitioners is to learn how to manage boundary fluctuations and to deal effectively with overlapping roles. One key to learning how to manage dual relationships is to think of ways to minimize the risks involved.

WAYS OF MINIMIZING RISK   In determining whether to proceed with a dual relationship, it is critical to consider whether the potential benefit of such a relationship outweighs the potential harm. It is your responsibility to develop safeguards aimed at reducing the potential for negative consequences. Herlihy and Corey (1997a) identify the following guidelines:

- Set healthy boundaries early in the therapeutic relationship. Informed consent is essential from the beginning and during the therapy process. Involve the client in ongoing discussions and in the decision-making process, and document your discussions.
- Consult with fellow professionals as a way to maintain objectivity and identify unanticipated difficulties. Realize that you don't need to make a decision alone.
- When dual relationships are potentially problematic, or when the risk for harm is high, it is always wise to work under supervision. It may be necessary to refer a client to another professional if problems develop or if harm seems likely. Document the nature of this supervision and any actions you take in your records.
- Throughout the process, self-monitoring is critical. It is a good idea to ask yourself whose needs are being met and to examine your motivations for becoming involved in a dual or multiple relationship.

A DECISION-MAKING MODEL   In working through a dual relationship concern, it is best to begin by ascertaining whether such a relationship can be avoided. Sometimes dual relationships are avoidable, and to get involved in them may be putting the client needlessly at risk. In other cases dual relationships are unavoidable. For instance, a counselor in a rural community may have as clients the local banker, merchant, and minister. In this setting, mental health practitioners may have to blend several professional roles and functions. They may also attend the same church or belong to the same community organization as their clients. These professionals are likely to find it more difficult to maintain clear boundaries than practitioners who work in a large city.

The decision-making model proposed by Herlihy and Corey (1997a) differentiates between unavoidable and avoidable relationships. In cases where a dual relationship is unavoidable, the guidelines for minimizing risks discussed in the previous section apply. If the dual relationship is avoidable, the counselor has a choice of what course of action to take. If the potential benefits outweigh the risks, it is still sound practice to follow all of the procedures listed earlier. If the risks outweigh the benefits, ethical practice demands that the counselor decline to enter into a conflicting relationship.

You are likely to encounter many forms of nonsexual dual relationships. One way of dealing with any potential problems is to do whatever is possible to completely avoid such relationships. Another alternative is to deal with each dilemma as it surfaces, making full use of informed consent and at the same time seeking consultation and supervision in dealing with the situation. This second alternative provides a professional challenge for self-monitoring. It is one of the hallmarks of professionalism to be willing to grapple with these ethical complexities of day-to-day practice.

 ## GUIDELINES FOR ETHICAL PRACTICE: A Review

Let me summarize this chapter by suggesting some guidelines for ethical practice. My hope is that you will spend some time reflecting on these as guidelines, apply them to yourself, and attempt to formulate your own views and positions on some of the topics raised in this chapter. The task of developing a sense of professional and ethical responsibility is never really finished, and new issues are constantly surfacing. Ethical issues demand periodic reflection and an openness to change.

1. Be aware of your personal needs, what you are getting from your work, and how your needs and behaviors influence your clients. It is essential that your own needs not be met at your clients' expense.
2. Exercise judgment in interpreting and applying the codes of ethics to particular cases. Remember that many problems have no clear-cut answers, and be ready to search for appropriate solutions.

3. Have a theoretical framework of behavior change to guide your practice.
4. Avoid any relationships with clients that are clearly a threat to therapy.
5. Inform clients of any circumstances that are likely to affect the confidentiality of their relationship and of any other matters that are likely to negatively influence the relationship.
6. Be aware of your values and attitudes, recognize the role your belief system plays in your relationships with your clients, and avoid imposing these beliefs, either subtly or directly.
7. Inform clients about the goals of counseling and the techniques and procedures that will be employed, possible risks associated with entering the relationship, and any other factors that are likely to affect their decision to establish a professional relationship with you. It is important to carefully document your approach to informed consent. Also, it is critical that you document your interventions in the client's record.
8. Realize that you teach your clients through a modeling process. Attempt to practice in your life what you encourage for your clients.
9. Counseling takes place in the context of the interaction of cultural backgrounds. You bring your culture to the counseling relationship, and your client's cultural values also operate in the process.
10. Learn a process for thinking about and dealing with ethical dilemmas, keeping in mind that most ethical issues are complex and defy simple solutions. The willingness to seek consultation is a sign of professional maturity.

Resolving the ethical dilemmas you will face requires a commitment to question your own behavior and motives. A sign of good faith is your willingness to share your struggles with colleagues. Such consultation can be of great help in clarifying issues by giving you another perspective on a situation. Being a professional counselor does not imply that you are perfect or superhuman. If you are willing to risk doing anything worthwhile in your work, you are bound to make some mistakes. What is crucial is your willingness to reflect on what you are doing and on whose needs are being given priority.

If there is one fundamental question that can serve to tie together all the issues discussed in this chapter, it is this: Who has the right to counsel another person? This question can be the focal point of your reflection on ethical and professional issues. It can also be the basis of your self-examination each day that you meet with clients. Continue to ask yourself: "What makes me think I have a right to counsel others?" "What do I have to offer the people I'm counseling?" "Am I doing in my own life what I'm encouraging my clients to do?" If you answer these questions honestly, you may be troubled. At times you may feel that you have no ethical right to counsel others, perhaps because your own life isn't always the model you would like it to be for your clients. More important than resolving all of life's issues is knowing what kinds of questions to ask and then remaining open to reflection.

WHERE TO GO FROM HERE

This chapter has introduced you to a number of ethical issues that you are bound to face at some point in your counseling practice. One chapter cannot begin to give in-depth coverage of these topics. Now that your interest has been piqued, you can continue by reading some of the ethics books listed in the Recommended Supplementary Readings. As a reference source, see the *ACA Ethical Standards Casebook* (Herlihy & Corey, 1996). I especially recommend our text in ethics, *Issues and Ethics in the Helping Professions* (Corey, Corey, & Callanan (1998); and, as well, a video that my colleagues and I did entitled *Ethics in Action* (Corey, Corey, & Haynes, 1998). *Ethics in Action* is available in a student version and is accompanied by a student workbook. In addition to reading, taking a separate course in ethical issues in the counseling profession would be most helpful in stimulating your thinking and giving you a framework for ethical decision making. As you read the rest of the chapters in this textbook, be alert for ethical issues as they relate to the various therapeutic approaches.

Familiarize Yourself With the Codes of Ethics

Each of the major mental health professional organizations has its own code of ethics. Although ethics codes do not provide answers to all ethical dilemmas you will encounter, they do offer general guidance on issues explored in this chapter, and it is essential that you know the basic content of the codes of your profession. All of the following codes of ethics are reprinted in the Appendices of *Issues and Ethics in the Helping Professions* (1998, Gerald Corey, Marianne Schneider Corey, and Patrick Callanan, Pacific Grove, CA: Brooks-Cole/Wadsworth.

- Codes of Ethics and Standards of Practice, *American Counseling Association* (ACA, 1995)
- Ethical Principles of Psychologists and Code of Conduct, *American Psychological Association* (APA, 1995)
- Code of Ethics, *National Association of Social Workers* (NASW, 1996)
- AAMFT Code of Ethics, *American Association for Marriage and Family Therapy* (AAMFT, 1998)
- Ethical Standards of Human Service Professionals, *National Organization of Human Service Education* (NOHSE, 1995)

Recommended Supplementary Readings for Part 1

Counseling the Culturally Different: Theory and Practice (D. W. Sue & Sue, 1999) is a classic in the field of multicultural counseling and therapy and is now a standard for most courses in minority mental health and treatment. The authors develop the thesis that becoming a competent multicultural practitioner involves freeing yourself from your cultural conditioning, understanding and accepting the legitimacy of alternative worldviews, and acquiring culturally appropriate intervention strategies in working with a diverse clientele.

Counseling American Minorities: A Cross-Cultural Perspective (Atkinson, Morten, & Sue, 1998) describes a minority-identity development model. This edited book has excellent sections dealing with counseling for Native Americans, Asian Americans, African Americans, and Latinos.

A Handbook for Developing Multicultural Awareness (Pedersen, 2000) is based on the assumption that all counseling is to some extent multicultural. In this useful handbook, the author deals with topics such as developing multicultural awareness, becoming aware of our culturally biased assumptions, acquiring knowledge for effective multicultural counseling, and learning skills to deal with cultural diversity.

A Theory of Multicultural Counseling and Psychotherapy (Sue, Ivey, & Pedersen, 1996) presents a rationale for a theory of multicultural counseling and sets forth a series of propositions and corollaries related to multicultural counseling that have implications for theory development, research, practice, and training. It also contains separate chapters dealing with specific populations.

Ethical Standards Casebook (Herlihy & Corey, 1996) contains a variety of useful cases that are geared to the *ACA Code of Ethics and Standards of Practice*. The examples illustrate and clarify the meaning and intent of the standards.

Boundary Issues in Counseling: Multiple Roles and Responsibilities (Herlihy & Corey, 1997a) puts the multiple-relationship controversy into perspective. It deals with issues in counselor preparation and focuses on dual relationships in a variety of work settings, including private practice, school counseling, rehabilitation counseling, consultation, and group counseling. (Both this book and the previous one can be purchased from the ACA, 5999 Stevenson Avenue, Alexandria, VA 22304; telephone: 703-823-9800.)

Ethics in Counseling and Psychotherapy: Standards, Research, and Emerging Issues (Welfel, 1998) presents a nine-step model of ethical decision making for analyzing complex ethical problems. The author focuses on ethical issues in diverse settings, managed care, and ethics in a multicultural setting. She also addresses legal and forensic issues.

The Virtuous Therapist: Ethical Practice of Counseling and Psychotherapy (Cohen & Cohen, 1999) offer a philosophical approach to mental health ethics. The authors deal with therapist responsibilities in suspected child abuse cases, domestic violence and abuse, pregnancy/abortion issues, confidentiality issues in HIV cases, and guidelines for multicultural counseling.

Issues and Ethics in the Helping Professions (Corey, Corey, & Callanan, 1998) is devoted entirely to the issues that were introduced briefly in Chapter 3. Some relevant chapters deal with the role of values in the client/counselor relationship, therapist responsibilities, therapist competence, factors influencing the client/

therapist relationship, and dual relationships. The book is designed to involve readers in a personal and active way, and many open-ended cases are presented to help readers formulate their thoughts on various issues.

Ethics in Action: Student Version (Corey, Corey, & Haynes, 1998) has a video and a workbook. The 60-minute video is divided into three parts: (1) ethical decision making, (2) values and the helping relationship, and (3) boundary issues and multiple relationships. The video and workbook emphasize the personal application of a problem-solving approach to a range of ethical dilemmas. The video includes vignettes demonstrating ethical situations and responses, commentary from the Coreys, and group interaction and discussion.

Student Manual for Theory and Practice of Counseling and Psychotherapy (Corey, 2001d) is designed to help you integrate theory with practice and to make the concepts covered in the book come alive. It consists of self-inventories, overview summaries of the theories, a glossary of key concepts, study questions, issues and questions for personal application, activities and exercises, comprehension checks and quizzes, case examples, a code of professional ethics, and a list of professional organizations to contact for resources. The manual is fully coordinated with the textbook to make it a personal study guide.

Case Approach to Counseling and Psychotherapy (Corey, 2001c) is structured along the same chapter lines as this textbook. Thus, if you want to focus more on case applications and see how each of the theories works in action, this casebook will be a handy supplement to the course. A hypothetical client, Ruth, experiences counseling from all of the therapeutic vantage points.

The Art of Integrative Counseling (Corey, 2001a) is a presentation of my own approach to integrating concepts and techniques from the various theories of counseling. My aim is to provide guidelines for readers in developing their own theoretical perspective.

Student Video and Workbook for the Art of Integrative Counseling (Corey, 2001b) is a 2-hour video with accompanying workbook designed to teach students ways of working with a client (Ruth) by drawing concepts and techniques from diverse theoretical approaches. The topics in this video parallel the topics in the book of the same name.

On Being a Therapist (Kottler, 1993) shows how the professional work in which therapists engage directly affects their personal lives. By becoming involved in the exploration of their clients' pain, therapists open up their own psychological wounds. Examples are given of the prices that therapists pay for working with high levels of stress.

I Never Knew I Had a Choice (Corey & Corey, 1997) is a good resource with which to continue a reading program on the counselor as a person. Topics include our struggle to achieve autonomy; the roles that work, love, sexuality, intimacy, and solitude play in our lives; the meaning of loneliness, death, and loss; and the ways in which we choose our values and philosophy of life.

Becoming a Helper (Corey & Corey, 1998) has chapters that expand on issues dealing with the personal and professional lives of helpers. Some of the topics emphasized include the motivations for becoming a helper, the helper in the helping process, value issues, common concerns facing counselors, dealing with life transitions, self-exploration and personal growth, understanding your family history, managing stress, the challenge of retaining your vitality, and dealing with professional burnout.

References and Suggested Readings for Part 1

AMERICAN ASSOCIATION FOR MARRIAGE AND FAMILY THERAPY. (1998). *AAMFT code of ethics.* Washington, DC: Author.

AMERICAN COUNSELING ASSOCIATION. (1995). *Code of ethics and standards of practice.* Alexandria, VA: Author.

AMERICAN PSYCHIATRIC ASSOCIATION. (1994). *Diagnostic and statistical manual of mental disorders* (4th ed.). Washington, DC: Author.

AMERICAN PSYCHOLOGICAL ASSOCIATION. (1995). *Ethical principles of psychologists and code of conduct.* Washington, DC: Author.

ARREDONDO, P., TOPOREK, R., BROWN, S., JONES, J., LOCKE, D., SANCHEZ, J., & STADLER, H. (1996). Operationalization of multicultural counseling competencies. *Journal of Multicultural Counseling and Development, 24*(1), 42–78.

*ATKINSON, D. R., MORTEN, G., & SUE, D. W. (Eds.). (1998). *Counseling American minorities: A cross-cultural perspective* (5th ed.). New York: McGraw Hill.

*BUGENTAL, J. F. T. (1987). *The art of the psychotherapist.* New York: Norton.

*COHEN, E. D., & COHEN, G. S. (1999). *The virtuous therapist: Ethical practice of counseling and psychotherapy.* Pacific Grove, CA: Brooks/Cole.

*COREY, G. (2001a). *The art of integrative counseling.* Pacific Grove, CA: Brooks-Cole/Wadsworth.

*COREY, G. (2001b). *Student video and workbook for the art of integrative counseling.* Pacific Grove, CA: Brooks-Cole/Wadsworth.

*COREY, G. (2001c). *Case approach to counseling and psychotherapy* (5th ed.). Pacific Grove, CA: Brooks-Cole/Wadsworth.

*COREY, G. (2001d). *Student manual for theory and practice of counseling and psychotherapy* (6th ed.). Pacific Grove, CA: Brooks-Cole/Wadsworth.

*COREY, G., & COREY, M. (1997). *I never knew I had a choice* (6th ed.). Pacific Grove, CA: Brooks/Cole.

*COREY, G., COREY, M., & CALLANAN, P. (1998). *Issues and ethics in the helping professions* (5th ed.). Pacific Grove, CA: Brooks/Cole.

*COREY, G., COREY, M., & HAYNES, R. (1998). *Ethics in action: Student version.* (Video and workbook). Pacific Grove, CA: Brooks/Cole.

COREY, G., & HERLIHY, B. (1997). Dual/multiple relationships: Toward a consensus of thinking. In *The Hatherleigh guide to ethics in therapy* (pp. 193–205). New York: Hatherleigh Press.

*COREY, M., & COREY, G. (1998). *Becoming a helper* (3rd ed.). Pacific Grove, CA: Brooks/Cole.

*GUY, J. D. (1987). *The personal life of the psychotherapist.* New York: Wiley.

*HERLIHY, B., & COREY, G. (1996). *ACA ethical standards casebook* (5th ed.). Alexandria, VA: American Counseling Association.

*HERLIHY, B., & COREY, G. (1997a). *Boundary issues in counseling: Multiple roles and responsibilities.* Alexandria, VA: American Counseling Association.

HERLIHY, B., & COREY, G. (1997b). Code of ethics as catalysts for improving practice. In *The Hatherleigh guide to ethics in therapy* (pp. 39–59). New York: Hatherleigh Press.

---

*Books and articles marked with an asterisk are suggested for further study.

*KENYON, P. (1999). *What would you do? An ethical case workbook for human service professionals.* Pacific Grove, CA: Brooks/Cole.

*KOTTLER, J. A. (1993). *On being a therapist* (Rev. ed.). San Francisco: Jossey-Bass.

KOTTLER, J. A., & BLAU, D. (1989). *The imperfect therapist: Learning from failure in therapeutic practice.* San Francisco: Jossey-Bass.

NATIONAL ASSOCIATION OF SOCIAL WORKERS. (1998). *Code of ethics.* Washington, DC: Author.

NATIONAL BOARD FOR CERTIFIED COUNSELORS. (1998). *Code of ethics.* Alexandria, VA: Author.

NATIONAL ORGANIZATION FOR HUMAN SERVICE EDUCATION. (1995). *Ethical standards of the National Organization for Human Service Education.* Philadelphia: Author.

*PEDERSEN, P. (2000). *A handbook for developing multicultural awareness* (3rd ed.). Alexandria, VA: American Counseling Association.

SUE, D. W., ARREDONDO, P., & McDAVIS, R. J. (1992). Multicultural counseling competencies and standards. A call to the profession. *Journal of Counseling and Development, 70*(4), 477–486.

*SUE, D. W., IVEY, A. E., & PEDERSEN, P. (1996). *A theory of multicultural counseling and therapy.* Pacific Grove, CA: Brooks/Cole.

*SUE, D. W., & SUE, D. (1999). *Counseling the culturally different: Theory and practice* (3rd ed.). New York: Wiley.

*WELFEL, E. R. (1998). *Ethics in counseling and psychotherapy: Standards, research, and emerging issues.* Pacific Grove, CA: Brooks/Cole.

PART 2

Theories and Techniques of Counseling

4 Psychoanalytic Therapy

5 Adlerian Therapy

6 Existential Therapy

7 Person-Centered Therapy

8 Gestalt Therapy

9 Reality Therapy

10 Behavior Therapy

11 Cognitive Behavior Therapy

12 Feminist Therapy

13 Family Systems Therapy

CHAPTER

Psychoanalytic Therapy

INTRODUCTION

KEY CONCEPTS
View of Human Nature
Structure of Personality
Consciousness and the Unconscious
Anxiety
Ego-Defense Mechanisms
Development of Personality
Jung's Perspective on the Development of Personality
Contemporary Trends: Self Psychology and Object-Relations Theory

THE THERAPEUTIC PROCESS
Therapeutic Goals
Therapist's Function and Role
Client's Experience in Therapy
Relationship Between Therapist and Client

APPLICATION: Therapeutic Techniques and Procedures
Maintaining the Analytic Framework
Free Association
Interpretation
Dream Analysis
Analysis and Interpretation of Resistance
Analysis and Interpretation of Transference

PSYCHOANALYTIC THERAPY APPLIED TO THE CASE OF STAN

SUMMARY AND EVALUATION
Contributions of the Psychoanalytic Approach
Limitations and Criticisms of the Psychoanalytic Approach

PSYCHOANALYTIC THERAPY FROM A MULTICULTURAL PERSPECTIVE
Contributions to Multicultural Counseling
Limitations for Multicultural Counseling

WHERE TO GO FROM HERE

RECOMMENDED SUPPLEMENTARY READINGS

REFERENCES AND SUGGESTED READINGS

SIGMUND FREUD

SIGMUND FREUD (1856-1939) was the firstborn in a Viennese family of three boys and five girls. His father, like many others of his time and place, was very authoritarian. Freud's family background is a factor to consider in understanding the development of his theory.

Even though Freud's family had limited finances and was forced to live in a crowded apartment, his parents made every effort to foster his obvious intellectual capacities. Freud had many interests, but his career choices were restricted because of his Jewish heritage. He finally settled on medicine. Only 4 years after earning his medical degree from the University of Vienna at the age of 26, he attained a prestigious position there as a lecturer.

Freud devoted most of his life to formulating and extending his theory of psychoanalysis. Interestingly, the most creative phase of his life corresponded to a period when he was experiencing severe emotional problems of his own.

When he was in his early 40s, he had numerous psychosomatic disorders as well as exaggerated fears of dying and other phobias. During this time, Freud was involved in the difficult task of self-analysis. By exploring the meaning of his own dreams he gained insights into the dynamics of personality development. He first examined his childhood memories and came to realize the intense hostility he had felt for his father. He also recalled his childhood sexual feelings for his mother, who was attractive, loving, and protective. He then clinically formulated his theory as he observed his patients work through their own problems in analysis.

Freud had very little tolerance for colleagues who diverged from his psychoanalytic doctrines. He attempted to keep control over the movement by expelling those who dared to disagree. Carl Jung and Alfred Adler, for example, worked closely with Freud, but each founded his own therapeutic school after repeated disagreements with Freud on theoretical and clinical issues.

Freud was highly creative and productive, frequently putting in 18-hour days. His collected works fill 24 volumes. Freud's productivity remained at this prolific level until late in his life when he contracted cancer of the jaw. During his last two decades, he underwent 33 operations and was in almost constant pain. He died in London in 1939.

As the originator of psychoanalysis, Freud distinguished himself as an intellectual giant. He pioneered new techniques for understanding human behavior, and his efforts resulted in the most comprehensive theory of personality and psychotherapy ever developed. ■

INTRODUCTION

Freud's views continue to influence contemporary practice. Many of his basic concepts are still part of the foundation on which other theorists build and develop. Indeed, most of the theories of counseling and psychotherapy discussed in this book have been influenced by psychoanalytic principles and techniques. Some of these therapeutic approaches extended the psychoanalytic model, others modified its concepts and procedures, and others emerged as a reaction against it.

Freud's psychoanalytic system is a model of personality development, a philosophy of human nature, and a method of psychotherapy. He gave psychotherapy a new look and new horizons, calling attention to psychodynamic factors that motivate behavior, focusing on the role of the unconscious, and developing the first therapeutic procedures for understanding and modifying the structure of one's basic character. Freud's theory is a benchmark against which many other theories are measured.

It is impossible to capture in one chapter the diversity of psychodynamic approaches that have arisen since Freud. The main focus of this chapter, rather, is on basic psychoanalytic concepts and practices, many of which originated with Freud. The chapter sketches therapies that apply classical psychoanalytic concepts to practice less rigorously than he did. The chapter also summarizes Erik Erikson's theory of psychosocial development, which extends Freudian theory in several ways. I also devote brief attention to Jung's approach and to contemporary psychoanalytic theory and practice, including some of the concepts of object-relations theory.*

KEY CONCEPTS

View of Human Nature

The Freudian view of human nature is basically deterministic. According to Freud, our behavior is determined by irrational forces, unconscious motivations, and biological and instinctual drives as these evolve through key psychosexual stages in the first 6 years of life. Kovel (1976) notes, however, that as the unconscious becomes conscious, blind habit is replaced by choice. This is an unusually liberated form of determinism.

Instincts are central to the Freudian approach. Although he originally used the term *libido* to refer to sexual energy, he later broadened it to include the energy of all the *life instincts*. These instincts serve the purpose of the survival of the individual and the human race; they are oriented to-

---

* I want to acknowledge the contributions of Dr. William Blau in updating and refining the ideas in this chapter for all the editions of this book.

ward growth, development, and creativity. Libido, then, should be understood as a source of motivation that encompasses sexual energy but goes beyond it. Freud includes all pleasurable acts in his concept of the life instincts; he sees the goal of much of life as gaining pleasure and avoiding pain.

Freud also postulates *death instincts,* which account for the aggressive drive. At times, people manifest through their behavior an unconscious wish to die or to hurt themselves or others. Managing this aggressive drive is a major challenge to the human race. In Freud's view, both sexual and aggressive drives are powerful determinants of why people act as they do.

Structure of Personality

According to the psychoanalytic view, the personality consists of three systems: the id, the ego, and the superego. These are names for psychological structures and should not be thought of as manikins that separately operate the personality; one's personality functions as a whole rather than as three discrete segments. The *id* is the biological component, the *ego* is the psychological component, and the *superego* is the social component.

From the orthodox Freudian perspective, humans are viewed as energy systems. The dynamics of personality consist of the ways in which psychic energy is distributed to the id, ego, and superego. Because the amount of energy is limited, one system gains control over the available energy at the expense of the other two systems. Behavior is determined by this psychic energy.

THE ID   The id is the original system of personality; at birth a person is all id. The id is the primary source of psychic energy and the seat of the instincts. It lacks organization and is blind, demanding, and insistent. A cauldron of seething excitement, the id cannot tolerate tension, and it functions to discharge tension immediately and return to a homeostatic condition. Ruled by the *pleasure principle,* which is aimed at reducing tension, avoiding pain, and gaining pleasure, the id is illogical, amoral, and driven to satisfy instinctual needs. The id never matures, remaining the spoiled brat of personality. It does not think but only wishes or acts. The id is largely unconscious, or out of awareness.

THE EGO   The ego has contact with the external world of reality. It is the "executive" that governs, controls, and regulates the personality. As a "traffic cop," it mediates between the instincts and the surrounding environment. The ego controls consciousness and exercises censorship. Ruled by the *reality principle,* the ego does realistic and logical thinking and formulates plans of action for satisfying needs. What is the relation of the ego to the id? The ego, as the seat of intelligence and rationality, checks and controls the blind impulses of the id. Whereas the id knows only subjective reality, the ego distinguishes between mental images and things in the external world.

THE SUPEREGO   The superego is the judicial branch of personality. It includes a person's moral code, the main concern being whether an action is good or bad, right or wrong. It represents the ideal rather than the real and strives not for pleasure but for perfection. The superego represents the traditional values and ideals of society as they are handed down from parents to children. It functions to inhibit the id impulses, to persuade the ego to substitute moralistic goals for realistic ones, and to strive for perfection. The superego, then, as the internalization of the standards of parents and society, is related to psychological rewards and punishments. The rewards are feelings of pride and self-love; the punishments are feelings of guilt and inferiority.

Consciousness and the Unconscious *or Evidence of the Unconscious*

Perhaps Freud's greatest contributions are his concepts of the unconscious and of the levels of consciousness, which are the keys to understanding behavior and the problems of personality. The unconscious cannot be studied directly but is inferred from behavior. Clinical evidence for postulating the unconscious includes the following: (1) dreams, which are symbolic representations of unconscious needs, wishes, and conflicts; (2) slips of the tongue and forgetting, for example, a familiar name; (3) posthypnotic suggestions; (4) material derived from free-association techniques; (5) material derived from projective techniques; and (6) the symbolic content of psychotic symptoms. *(wish)*

For Freud, consciousness is a thin slice of the total mind. Like the greater part of the iceberg that lies below the surface of the water, the larger part of the mind exists below the surface of awareness. The unconscious stores up all experiences, memories, and repressed material. Needs and motivations that are inaccessible—that is, out of awareness—are also outside the sphere of conscious control. Most psychological functioning exists in the out-of-awareness realm. The aim of psychoanalytic therapy, therefore, is to make the unconscious motives conscious, for only then can an individual exercise choice. Understanding the role of the unconscious is central to grasping the essence of the psychoanalytic model of behavior.

Unconscious processes are at the root of all forms of neurotic symptoms and behaviors. From this perspective, a "cure" is based on uncovering the meaning of symptoms, the causes of behavior, and the repressed materials that interfere with healthy functioning. It is to be noted, however, that intellectual insight alone does not resolve the symptom. The client's need to cling to old patterns (repetition) must be confronted by working through transference distortions, a process discussed later in this chapter.

Anxiety

Also essential to the psychoanalytic approach is its concept of anxiety. Anxiety is a state of tension that motivates us to do something. It develops out of a conflict among the id, ego, and superego over control of the available psychic energy. Its function is to warn of impending danger.

There are three kinds of anxiety: reality, neurotic, and moral. *Reality anxiety* is the fear of danger from the external world, and the level of such anxiety is proportionate to the degree of real threat. Neurotic and moral anxiety are evoked by threats to the "balance of power" within the person. They signal to the ego that unless appropriate measures are taken the danger may increase until the ego is overthrown. *Neurotic anxiety* is the fear that the instincts will get out of hand and cause one to do something for which one will be punished. *Moral anxiety* is the fear of one's own conscience. People with a well-developed conscience tend to feel guilty when they do something contrary to their moral code. When the ego cannot control anxiety by rational and direct methods, it relies on unrealistic ones—namely, ego-defense behavior.

Ego-Defense Mechanisms

coping mechanisms = do on purpose to deal w/ issues. conscious

Ego-defense mechanisms help the individual cope with anxiety and prevent the ego from being overwhelmed. Rather than being pathological, these ego defenses are normal behaviors. They can have adaptive value if they do not become a style of life to avoid facing reality. The defenses one uses depend on one's level of development and degree of anxiety. Defense mechanisms have two characteristics in common: They either deny or distort reality, and they operate on an unconscious level. Here are brief descriptions of some common ego defenses:

■ *Repression.* Repression is one of the most important Freudian processes, and it is the basis of many other ego defenses and of neurotic disorders. It is a means of defense through which threatening or painful thoughts and feelings are excluded from awareness. Freud explained repression as an involuntary removal of something from consciousness. It is assumed that most of the painful events of the first 5 years of life are so excluded, yet these events do influence later behavior.

■ *Denial.* Denial plays a defensive role similar to that of repression, yet it generally operates at preconscious and conscious levels. Denial of reality is perhaps the simplest of all self-defense mechanisms; it is a way of distorting what the individual thinks, feels, or perceives in a traumatic situation. It consists of defending against anxiety by "closing one's eyes" to the existence of threatening reality. In tragic events such as wars and other disasters, people often blind themselves to realities that would be too painful to accept.

■ *Reaction formation.* One defense against a threatening impulse is to actively express the opposite impulse. By developing conscious attitudes and behaviors that are diametrically opposed to disturbing desires, people do not have to face the anxiety that would result if they were to recognize these dimensions of themselves. Individuals may conceal hate with a facade

ex. looking @ soft porn on HBO and react in a extreme manner, but they like the soft porn

of love, be extremely nice when they harbor negative reactions, or mask cruelty with excessive kindness.

■ *Projection.* Another mechanism of self-deception consists of attributing to others one's own unacceptable desires and impulses. Lustful, aggressive, or other impulses are seen as being possessed by "those people out there, but not by me." For example, a man who is sexually attracted to his daughter may maintain that it is *she* who is behaving seductively with him. Thus, he does not have to recognize or deal with his own desires.

■ *Displacement.* One way to cope with anxiety is to discharge impulses by shifting from a threatening object to a "safer target." Displacement consists of directing energy toward another object or person when the original object or person is inaccessible. For example, the meek man who feels intimidated by his boss comes home and unloads inappropriate hostility onto his children.

■ *Rationalization.* Some people manufacture "good" reasons to explain away a bruised ego. Rationalization helps justify specific behaviors, and it aids in softening the blow connected with disappointments. When people do not get positions they have applied for in their work, they think of logical reasons they did not succeed, and they sometimes attempt to convince themselves that they really did not want the position anyway.

■ *Sublimation.* From the Freudian perspective, many of the great artistic contributions resulted from a redirection of sexual or aggressive energy into creative behaviors. Sublimation involves diverting sexual or aggressive energy into other channels, ones that are usually socially acceptable and sometimes even admirable. For example, aggressive impulses can be channeled into athletic activities, so that the person finds a way of expressing aggressive feelings and, as an added bonus, is often praised.

■ *Regression.* Some people revert to a form of behavior that they have outgrown. In this regression to an earlier phase of development, the demands are not so great. In the face of severe stress or extreme challenge, individuals may attempt to cope with their anxiety by clinging to immature and inappropriate behaviors. For example, children who are frightened in school may indulge in infantile behavior such as weeping, excessive dependence, thumbsucking, hiding, or clinging to the teacher. They are seeking to return to a time in their life when there was security.

■ *Introjection.* The mechanism of introjection consists of taking in and "swallowing" the values and standards of others. For example, in concentration camps some of the prisoners dealt with overwhelming anxiety by accepting the values of the enemy through an identification with the aggressor. Another example is the abused child, who assumes the abusing parent's way of handling stresses and thus continues the cycle of child beating. It should be noted that there are also positive forms of introjection, such as the incorporation of parental values or the attributes and values of the therapist (assuming that these are not merely uncritically accepted).

■ *Identification.* Although identification is part of the developmental process by which children learn sex-role behaviors, it can also be a defensive reaction. It can enhance self-worth and protect one from a sense of being

■ Undoing — taking it back

a failure. Thus, people who feel basically inferior may identify themselves with successful causes, organizations, or people in the hope that they will be perceived as worthwhile.

■ *Compensation.* Compensation consists of masking perceived weaknesses or developing certain positive traits to make up for limitations. Thus, children who do not receive positive attention and recognition may develop behaviors designed to at least get negative attention. This mechanism can have direct adjustive value, and it can also be an attempt by the person to say "Don't see the ways in which I am inferior, but see me in my accomplishments."

Development of Personality

IMPORTANCE OF EARLY DEVELOPMENT   A significant contribution of the psychoanalytic model is delineation of the stages of psychosocial and psychosexual development from birth through adulthood. This provides the counselor with the conceptual tools for understanding key developmental tasks characteristic of the various stages of life.

Understanding the psychoanalytic view of development is essential if a counselor is to work in depth with clients. I have found that the most typical problems people bring to counseling are (1) the inability to trust oneself and others, the fear of loving and forming close relationships, and low self-esteem; (2) the inability to recognize and express feelings of hostility, anger, rage, and hate, the denial of one's own power as a person, and the lack of feelings of autonomy; and (3) the inability to fully accept one's own sexuality and sexual feelings, difficulty in accepting oneself as a man or woman, and fear of sexuality. According to the Freudian psychoanalytic view, these three areas of personal and social development—love and trust, dealing with negative feelings, and developing a positive acceptance of sexuality—are all grounded in the first 6 years of life. This period is the foundation on which later personality development is built.

ERIKSON'S PSYCHOSOCIAL PERSPECTIVE   Erikson (1963) built on Freud's ideas and extended his theory by stressing the psychosocial aspects of development beyond early childhood. His theory of development holds that psychosexual growth and psychosocial growth take place together, and that at each stage of life we face the task of establishing an equilibrium between ourselves and our social world. He describes development in terms of the entire life span, divided by specific crises to be resolved. According to Erikson, a *crisis* is equivalent to a turning point in life, when we have the potential to move forward or to regress. At these turning points we can either resolve our conflicts or fail to master the developmental task. To a large extent, our life is the result of the choices we make at these stages. True

Erikson is often credited with bringing an emphasis on social factors to contemporary psychoanalysis. Classical psychoanalysis is grounded on *id psychology,* and it holds that instincts and intrapsychic conflicts are the basic factors shaping personality development (both normal and abnormal).

Contemporary psychoanalytic thinking tends to be based on *ego psychology,* which does not deny the role of intrapsychic conflicts but does emphasize the striving of the ego for mastery and competence throughout the human life span. Ego psychology deals with both the early and the later developmental stages, for the assumption is that current problems cannot simply be reduced to repetitions of unconscious conflicts from early childhood. The stages of adolescence, mid-adulthood, and later adulthood all involve particular crises that must be addressed. As one's past has meaning in terms of the future, there is a continuity in development, reflected by stages of growth; each stage is related to the other stages.

It is possible to view an individual's development from a combined perspective that includes both psychosexual and psychosocial factors. Erikson believed Freud did not go far enough in explaining the ego's place in development and did not give enough attention to social influences throughout the life span. Table 4-1 provides a comparison of these two views.

TABLE 4-1 ■ Comparison of Freud's Psychosexual Stages and Erikson's Psychosocial Stages

PERIOD OF LIFE	FREUD	ERIKSON
First year of life	*Oral stage* Sucking at mother's breasts satisfies need for food and pleasure. Infant needs to get basic nurturing, or later feelings of greediness and acquisitiveness may develop. Oral fixations result from deprivation of oral gratification in infancy. Later personality problems can include mistrust of others, rejecting others' love, and fear of or inability to form intimate relationships.	*Infancy: Trust versus mistrust* If significant others provide for basic physical and emotional needs, infant develops a sense of trust. If basic needs are not met, an attitude of mistrust toward the world, especially toward interpersonal relationships, is the result.
Ages 1–3	*Anal stage* Anal zone becomes of major significance in formation of personality. Main developmental tasks include learning independence, accepting personal power, and learning to express negative feelings such as rage and aggression. Parental discipline patterns and attitudes have significant consequences for child's later personality development.	*Early childhood: Autonomy versus shame and doubt* A time for developing autonomy. Basic struggle is between a sense of self-reliance and a sense of self-doubt. Child needs to explore and experiment, to make mistakes, and to test limits. If parents promote dependency, child's autonomy is inhibited and capacity to deal with world successfully is hampered.

TABLE 4-1   ■   *(continued)*

PERIOD OF LIFE	FREUD	ERIKSON
Ages 3–6	*Phallic stage* Basic conflict centers on unconscious incestuous desires that child develops for parent of opposite sex and that, because of their threatening nature, are repressed. Male phallic stage, known as *Oedipus complex,* involves mother as love object for boy. Female phallic stage, known as *Electra complex,* involves girl's strivings for father's love and approval. How parents respond, verbally and nonverbally, to child's emerging sexuality has an impact on sexual attitudes and feelings that child develops.	*Preschool age: Initiative versus guilt* Basic task is to achieve a sense of competence and initiative. If children are given freedom to select personally meaningful activities, they tend to develop a positive view of self and follow through with their projects. If they are not allowed to make own decisions, they tend to develop guilt over taking initiative. They then refrain from taking an active stance and allow others to choose for them.
Ages 6–12	*Latency stage* After the torment of sexual impulses of preceding years, this period is relatively quiescent. Sexual interests are replaced by interests in school, playmates, sports, and a range of new activities. This is a time of socialization as child turns outward and forms relationships with others.	*School age: Industry versus inferiority* Child needs to expand understanding of world, continue to develop appropriate gender-role identity, and learn the basic skills required for school success. Basic task is to achieve a sense of industry, which refers to setting and attaining personal goals. Failure to do so results in a sense of inadequacy.
Ages 12–18	*Genital stage* Old themes of phallic stage are revived. This stage begins with puberty and lasts until senility sets in. Even though there are societal restrictions and taboos, adolescents can deal with sexual energy by investing it in various socially acceptable activities such as forming friendships, engaging in art or in sports, and preparing for a career.	*Adolescence: Identity versus role confusion* A time of transition between childhood and adulthood. A time for testing limits, for breaking dependent ties, and for establishing a new identity. Major conflicts center on clarification of self-identity, life goals, and life's meaning. Failure to achieve a sense of identity results in role confusion.

(continued)

TABLE 4-1   ■   *(continued)*

PERIOD OF LIFE	FREUD	ERIKSON
Ages 18–35	*Genital stage continues* Core characteristic of mature adult is the freedom "to love and to work." This move toward adulthood involves freedom from parental influence and capacity to care for others.	*Young adulthood: Intimacy versus isolation* Developmental task at this time is to form intimate relationships. Failure to achieve intimacy can lead to alienation and isolation.
Ages 35–60	*Genital stage continues*	*Middle age: Generativity versus stagnation* There is a need to go beyond self and family and be involved in helping the next generation. This is a time of adjusting to the discrepancy between one's dreams and one's actual accomplishments. Failure to achieve a sense of productivity often leads to psychological stagnation.
Ages 60+	*Genital stage continues*	*Later life: Integrity versus despair* If one looks back on life with few regrets and feels personally worthwhile, ego integrity results. Failure to achieve ego integrity can lead to feelings of despair, hopelessness, guilt, resentment, and self-rejection.

THE FIRST YEAR OF LIFE   Freud labeled this first year of life the *oral stage*. As the mouth and lips are sensitive erogenous zones, sucking produces erotic pleasure for the infant. A lack of enough food or love during this life stage may lead to greediness and acquisitiveness. Material things that children seek become substitutes for what they really want—namely, food and love from the mother. Later personality problems that stem from the oral stage are the development of a view of the world based on mistrust, fear of reaching out to others, rejection of affection, fear of loving and trusting, low self-esteem, isolation and withdrawal, and an inability to form or maintain intense relationships.

In Erikson's psychosocial view infancy is characterized by a struggle between *trust and mistrust*. An infant's basic task is to develop a sense of trust in self, others, and the world. When love is absent, the result is a general sense of mistrust of others. Clearly, infants who feel accepted are in a more favorable position to successfully meet future developmental crises than are those who do not receive adequate nurturing.

AGES 1–3   The *anal stage* marks another step in development. The tasks to be mastered during this stage are learning independence, personal power, and autonomy and learning how to recognize and deal with negative feelings.

Beginning in the second year and extending into the third year, children continually face parental demands, experience frustrations when they handle objects and explore their environment, and are expected to master control of their bowels. When toilet training begins during the second year, children have their first major experience with discipline.

If strict toilet-training methods are used, children may express their anger by expelling their feces at inappropriate places and times. This behavior can lay the foundation for later adult characteristics such as cruelty, inappropriate displays of anger, and extreme disorderliness. Freud describes this as the *anal-aggressive* personality. In contrast, other parents might focus too much attention on their children's bowel movements by giving praise whenever they defecate, which can contribute to a child's exaggerated view of the importance of this activity. This focus might be associated with a person's need for being productive. Again, certain adults develop fixations revolving around extreme orderliness, hoarding, stubbornness, and stinginess. This is known as the *anal-retentive* personality. The important point is that later adult characteristics have their roots in the experiences of this period.

During the anal period of development, the child will surely experience so-called negative feelings such as hostility, destructiveness, anger, rage, hatred, and so on. It is important that children learn that these are acceptable feelings. Many clients in therapy have not yet learned to accept their anger and hatred toward those they love. Because they were either directly or indirectly taught that these feelings were bad and that parental acceptance would be withheld if they expressed them, they repressed them.

According to Erikson, early childhood is a time for developing *autonomy;* children who do not master the task of gaining some measure of self-control develop a sense of *shame and doubt* about their abilities. Parents who do too much for their children hamper their independence. Children who are encouraged to stay dependent will doubt their capacities for successfully dealing with the world.

It is important at this stage that children begin to acquire a sense of their own power. Children need to experiment, to make mistakes and feel that they are still acceptable persons, and to recognize some of their own power as separate and distinct individuals. So many clients are in counseling precisely because they have lost touch with their potential for power; they are struggling to define who they are and what they are capable of doing.

AGES 3–6   During the *phallic stage,* sexual activity becomes more intense, and the focus of attention is on the genitals—the boy's penis and the girl's clitoris. According to the orthodox Freudian view, the basic conflict of the phallic stage centers on the unconscious incestuous desires that children develop for the parent of the opposite sex. Because these feelings are of such a threatening nature, they are typically repressed; yet they are powerful determinants of later sexual development and adjustment. Along with the wish to possess the parent of the opposite sex comes the unconscious wish of the child to "do away with" the competition—the parent of the same sex.

dvpt of Superego

According to Freudian theory, boys and girls both experience sexual longings and conflicts, which they repress. Boys crave the attention of their mother, feel antagonistic toward father, and develop fears that father will punish them for incestuous feelings toward mother. This is known as the *Oedipus complex*. Mother becomes the love object both in fantasy and behavior, and boys exhibit sexual longings for mother.

At this time boys typically develop specific fears related to their penis, which Freud describes as *castration anxiety*. Fearing that father will retaliate by cutting off the offending organ, boys repress their sexual desire for mother. If the oedipal conflict is properly resolved, boys' sexual longings for mother are replaced with more acceptable forms of affection. At this time boys also develop a strong identification with father and may adopt many of his mannerisms.

The orthodox Freudian view of female development has stirred up considerable controversy and has met with negative reactions from many women. The *Electra complex* is the girls' counterpart to the Oedipus complex. Girls' first love object is mother, but love is transferred to father during this stage. Girls are said to develop negative feelings toward mother when they discover the absence of a penis, a condition known as *penis envy*. Girls try to compete with mother for their father's attention at this time. When girls realize they cannot replace mother, they begin an identification process by taking on some of the characteristics of mother's behavior.

The development of sexual attitudes assumes critical importance during this period of life. Perhaps one of the most frequently misunderstood terms in Freud's theory is *sexuality*. He uses it much more broadly than it is typically used. Sexuality refers to organ pleasure of any kind. The type of sexuality that becomes evident during the phallic stage does not necessarily refer to the child's desire for sexual intercourse with the opposite-sex parent. Although the boy's feelings toward his mother are erotically tinged, this kind of sexuality is more diffuse than sexual intercourse, and the child's concept of actual sexual intercourse is often undefined. It is during this period of psychosexual development that curiosity about sexual matters, sexual fantasies, masturbation, sex-role identification patterns, and sex play become increasingly evident.

From the psychosocial perspective, the core struggle of the preschool phase is between *initiative and guilt*. Erikson contends that the basic task of the preschool years is to establish a sense of competence and initiative. He places more stress on social development than on concerns relating to sexuality. During this time children are psychologically ready to pursue activities of their own choosing. If they are allowed the freedom to select meaningful activities, they tend to develop a positive outlook characterized by the ability to initiate and follow through. If they are not allowed to make some of their own decisions, however, or if their choices are ridiculed, they develop a sense of guilt over taking the initiative. Typically, they withdraw from taking an active stance and permit others to make decisions for them.

AGES 6–12   With the passing of the turbulence and the combined stresses of the oral, anal, and phallic stages of psychosexual development, the individual can enjoy a period of relative rest. The major structures of personality (id, ego, superego) are largely formed, as are the relationships between these subsystems. During this *latency period* new interests replace infantile sexual impulses. Socialization takes place, and children direct their interests to the larger world. The sexual drive is sublimated, to some extent, to activities in school, hobbies, sports, and friendships with members of the same sex.

The oral, anal, and phallic stages taken together are known as the pregenital period. A major characteristic of this period is a *narcissistic* orientation, or an inward and self-centered preoccupation. During the middle-childhood years, there is a turning outward toward relationships with others. Children of this age have an interest in the things of the external world as well as of their internal world. This period prevails until the onset of puberty.

Corresponding to the latency stage is Erikson's school-age stage, marked by a need to resolve the conflict between *industry and inferiority*. According to Erikson, the central task of middle childhood is to achieve a sense of industry, which is associated with creating goals that are personally meaningful and achieving them. If this is not done, feelings of inadequacy and inferiority will result and future developmental stages will be negatively influenced.

AGES 12–60+   Young adults move into the *genital stage* unless they become fixated at an earlier period of psychosexual development. The old themes of the phallic stage are revived and recapitulated, and adolescents typically develop interest in the opposite sex, engage in some sexual experimentation, and begin to assume adult responsibilities. As they move out of adolescence and into mature adulthood, they form intimate relationships, become free of parental influence, and develop the capacity to be interested in others. There is a trend away from narcissism and toward altruistic behavior and concern for others.

Freud was primarily concerned with the impact of resolving sexual issues during the first 6 years of life. He did not go into great detail in discussing the crises associated with adolescence or the stages of adulthood. For Freud, the genital stage continues throughout adulthood.

Erikson's view of development continues where Freud left off. It accounts for forces influencing adolescent development and various phases of adulthood. According to Erikson, the major developmental conflicts of the adolescent years are related to the formation of a *personal identity*. Adolescents struggle to define who they are, where they are going, and how to get there. If they fail to achieve a sense of identity, *role confusion* results. Adolescents have the task of integrating a system of values that will give their life direction. In the formation of a personal philosophy of life, they must make key decisions relating to religious beliefs, sexual ethics, values, and so forth. In this search for identity, models are especially important.

Erikson has delineated three stages that cover the adult period: young adulthood, middle age, and later life.

1. *Young adulthood.* In Erikson's view we approach adulthood after we master the adolescent conflicts over identity and role confusion. During young adulthood our sense of identity is tested again by the challenge of *intimacy versus isolation.* One key characteristic of the psychologically mature person is the ability to form intimate relationships. A prerequisite to establishing this intimacy with others is a confidence in our own identity. Intimacy involves an ability to share with others and to give to others from our own centeredness.

2. *Middle age.* This is a time for learning how to live creatively with both ourselves and others. On one hand, it can be one of the most productive periods of life. On the other hand, we may painfully experience the discrepancy between our dreams of young adulthood and the reality of what we have accomplished. Erikson sees the stimulus for continued growth in middle age as the crisis between *generativity and stagnation.* He considers generativity in the broad sense to include creating through a career, family, leisure-time activities, and so on. The main quality of productive adults is their ability to love well, to work well, and to play well. If adults fail to achieve a sense of productivity, they begin to stagnate and to die psychologically.

3. *Later life.* According to Erikson, the core crisis of the elderly is *integrity versus despair.* Ego integrity is achieved by those who feel few regrets; they have lived a productive and worthwhile life and have coped with their failures as well as their successes. They are not obsessed with what might have been, and they are able to derive satisfaction from what they have done. They are able to view death as a part of the life process, and they can still find meaning in how they are now living. The failure to achieve ego integrity tends to lead to feelings of despair, hopelessness, guilt, resentment, and self-disgust.

COUNSELING IMPLICATIONS   By taking a combined psychosexual and psychosocial perspective, counselors have a useful conceptual framework for understanding developmental issues as they appear in therapy. Regardless of a counselor's theoretical preference, relevant questions such as these can give direction to the therapeutic process:

- What are some major developmental tasks at each stage in life, and how are these tasks related to counseling?

- What are some themes that give continuity to this individual's life?
- What are some universal concerns of people at various points in life? How can people be challenged to make life-affirming choices at these points?
- What is the relationship between an individual's current problems and significant events from earlier years?
- What influential factors have shaped one's life?
- What choices were made at these critical periods, and how did the person deal with these various crises?

Counselors who work with a developmental perspective are able to see a continuity in life and to see certain directions their clients have taken. This perspective gives a broader picture of the individual's struggle, and clients are able to discover some significant connections among the various life stages.

Jung's Perspective on the Development of Personality

Carl Jung made monumental contributions to our deep understanding of the human personality. His pioneering work sheds light on human development, particularly during middle age. Jung places central importance on the psychological changes that are associated with midlife. He maintains that we need to let go of many of the values and behaviors that guided the first half of our life and confront our unconscious. We can best do this by paying attention to the messages of our dreams and by engaging in creative activities such as writing or painting. The task facing us during the midlife period is to be less influenced by rational thought and to instead give expression to these unconscious forces and integrate them into our conscious life (Schultz & Schultz, 1998).

Jung himself learned a great deal from his own midlife crisis. At age 81 he wrote about his recollections in his autobiography, *Memories, Dreams, Reflections* (1961), in which he also identified some of his major contributions. Jung made a choice to focus on the unconscious realm in his personal life, which also influenced the development of his theory of personality. However, he had a very different conception of the unconscious than did Freud. Although he was a colleague of Freud's and valued many of his contributions, he eventually came to the point of not being able to support some of his basic concepts, especially his theory of sexuality. Jung recalls Freud's words to him: "My dear Jung, promise me never to abandon the sexual theory. This is the most essential thing of all. You see, we must make a dogma of it, an unshakable bulwark" (Jung, 1961, p. 150). Jung became convinced that he could no longer collaborate with Freud because he believed Freud placed his own authority over truth. Freud had little tolerance for other theoreticians, such as Jung and Adler, who dared to challenge his theories. Although Jung had a lot to lose professionally by withdrawing from Freud, he saw no other choice. He subsequently developed a spiritual approach that places great emphasis on being impelled to find meaning in life in contrast to being driven by the psychological and biological forces described by Freud.

Jung maintains that humans are not merely shaped by past events (Freudian determinism) but that they also progress beyond their past. Part of the nature of humans is to be constantly developing, growing, and moving toward a balanced and complete level of development. For Jung, our present personality is determined both by who and what we have been and also by the person we hope to become. The process of self-actualization is oriented toward the future. His theory is based on the assumption that humans tend to move toward the fulfillment or realization of all of their capabilities. Achieving individuation—the harmonious integration of the conscious and unconscious aspects of personality—is an innate and primary goal. For Jung, we have both constructive and destructive forces, and to become integrated, it is essential to accept the dark side of our nature with its primitive impulses such as selfishness and greed. Acceptance of this dark side (or shadow) does not imply being dominated by this dimension of our being but simply recognizing that this is a part of our nature.

Jung teaches that many dreams contain messages from the deepest layer of the unconscious, which he describes as the source of creativity. He calls this deep layer the *collective unconscious,* the "powerful and controlling repository of ancestral experiences" (Schultz & Schultz, 1998, p. 92). Jung sees a connection between each person's personality and the past, not only childhood events but also the history of the species. Thus, dreams reflect both an individual's personal unconscious and the collective unconscious. This means that some dreams deal with an individual's relationship to a larger whole such as the family, universal humanity, or generations over time. The contents of the collective unconscious are called *archetypes.* Among the most important archetypes are the persona, the anima and animus, and the shadow. The *persona* is a mask, or public face, that we wear to protect ourselves. The *animus* and the *anima* represent both the biological and psychological aspects of masculinity and femininity, which are thought to coexist in both sexes. The *shadow* has the deepest roots and is the most dangerous and powerful of the archetypes. It represents our dark side, the thoughts, feelings, and actions that are socially reprehensible and that we tend to disown by projecting them outward. In a dream all of these parts can be considered manifestations of who and what we are.

Jung agrees with Freud that dreams provide a pathway into the unconscious, but he differs from Freud on their functions. Jung writes that dreams have two purposes. They are prospective, in that they help people prepare themselves for the experiences and events they anticipate in the near future. They also serve a compensatory function; that is, they work to bring about a balance between opposites within the person. They compensate for the overdevelopment of one facet of the individual's personality (Schultz & Schultz, 1998).

Jung views dreams more as an attempt to express than as an attempt to repress and disguise. Dreams are a creative effort of the dreamer in struggling with contradiction, complexity, and confusion. The aim of the dream is resolution and integration. According to Jung, each part of the dream can be understood as some projected quality of the dreamer. His method of interpretation draws on a series of dreams obtained from a person, during the course of which the meaning gradually unfolds. If you are interested in further reading, I suggest Jung (1961) and Harris (1996).

Contemporary Trends: Self Psychology and Object-Relations Theory

Psychoanalytic theory is continually evolving. Freud emphasized intrapsychic conflicts pertaining to the gratification of basic needs. Writers in the neo-Freudian school moved away from this orthodox position and contributed to the growth and expansion of the psychoanalytic movement by incorporating the cultural and social influences on personality. Then ego psychology, with its stress on psychosocial development throughout the life span, was developed largely by Erikson.

The more recent approaches are often classified under the labels *self psychology* or *object-relations theory*. "Object relations" are interpersonal relationships as they are represented intrapsychically. The term *object* was used by Freud to refer to that which satisfies a need, or to the significant person or thing that is the object, or target, of one's feelings or drives. It is used interchangeably with the term *other* to refer to an important person to whom the child, and later the adult, becomes attached. Rather than being individuals with separate identities, others are perceived by an infant as objects for gratifying needs. Object-relations theories have diverged from orthodox psychoanalysis, although some theorists attempt to integrate the increasingly varied ideas that characterize this school of thought (St. Clair, 2000).

SUMMARY OF STAGES OF DEVELOPMENT   These recent psychoanalytic theories center on predictable developmental sequences in which the early experiences of the self shift in relation to an expanding awareness of others. Once self/other patterns are established, it is assumed they influence later interpersonal relationships. Specifically, people search for relationships that match the patterns established by their earlier experiences. People who are either overly dependent or overly detached, for example, can be repeating patterns of relating they established with their mother when they were toddlers (Hedges, 1983). These newer theories provide insight into how an individual's inner world can cause difficulties in living in the actual world of people and relationships (St. Clair, 2000).

A central influence on contemporary object-relations theory is Margaret Mahler (1968), a pediatrician who emphasized the observation of children. In her view, the resolution of the Oedipus complex is less critical than the child's progression from a symbiotic relationship with a maternal figure toward separation and individuation. Her studies focus on the interactions between the child and the mother in the first 3 years of life. According to

Mahler, the self develops through four broad stages, which she conceptualizes somewhat differently from the traditional Freudian psychosexual stages. Her belief is that the individual begins in a state of psychological fusion with the mother and progresses gradually to separation. The unfinished crises and residues of the earlier state of fusion, as well as the process of separating and individuating, have a profound influence on later relationships. Object relations of later life build on the child's search for a reconnection with the mother (St. Clair, 2000). Psychological development can be thought of as the evolution of the way in which individuals separate and differentiate themselves from others.

The first phase of development of the self, in the first 3 or 4 weeks of life, Mahler calls *normal infantile autism.* Here the infant is presumed to be responding more to states of physiological tension than to psychological processes. The infant is, in many respects, unable to differentiate itself from its mother, and, according to Melanie Klein (1975), perceives parts—breasts, face, hands, and mouth—rather than a unified self. In this undifferentiated state there is no whole self, and there are no whole objects. When adults show the most extreme forms of lack of psychological organization and sense of self, they may be thought of as revealing fixations at this most primitive infantile stage.

Mahler's second phase, called *symbiosis,* is recognizable by the third month and extends roughly through the eighth month. Here, as with the first stage, the infant has a pronounced dependency on the mother. She (or the primary caregiver) is clearly a partner and not just an interchangeable part. The infant seems to expect a very high degree of emotional attunement with its mother.

Mahler's third phase starts by the fourth or fifth month, thus overlapping the second stage. This third phase she calls the *separation/individuation* process. It involves the child's moving through several subphases, away from symbiotic forms of relating. During this time of differentiation, the child experiences separation from significant others yet still turns to them for a sense of confirmation and comfort. The child may demonstrate ambivalence, torn between enjoying separate states of independence and dependence. The toddler who proudly steps away from the parents and then runs back to be swept up in approving arms illustrates some of the main issues of this period (Hedges, 1983, p. 109). Others are looked to as approving mirrors for the child's developing sense of self; optimally, these relationships can provide a healthy self-esteem.

Children who do not experience the opportunity to differentiate, and those who lack the opportunity to idealize others while also taking pride in themselves, may later suffer from *narcissistic* character disorders and problems of self-esteem. The narcissistic personality is characterized by a grandiose and exaggerated sense of self-importance and an exploitive attitude towards others, which serve the function of masking a frail self-concept. Such individuals seek attention and admiration from others. They unrealistically exaggerate their accomplishments, and they have a tendency toward extreme self-absorption. Kernberg (1975) characterizes narcissistic people as focusing on themselves in their interactions with others, having a great need to be admired, possessing shallow affect, and being exploitive and, at times, parasitic in their relationships with others. Kohut (1971) characterizes such people as perceiving threats to their self-esteem and as having feelings of emptiness and deadness.

"Borderline" conditions are also rooted in the period of separation/individuation. People with a *borderline personality disorder* have moved into the separation process but have been thwarted by maternal rejection of their individuation. In other words, a crisis ensues when the child does develop beyond the stage of symbiosis but the mother (or the mothering figure) is unable to tolerate this beginning individuation and withdraws emotional support. Borderline people are characterized by instability, irritability, self-destructive acts, impulsive anger, and extreme mood shifts. They typically experience extended periods of disillusionment, punctuated by occasional euphoria. Kernberg describes the syndrome as including a lack of clear identity, a lack of deep understanding of other people, poor impulse control, and the inability to tolerate anxiety (1975, pp. 161–162).

Mahler's fourth and final phase involves a move toward constancy of self and object. This development is typically pronounced by the 36th month (Hedges, 1983). By now others are more fully seen as separate from the self. Ideally, children can begin to relate without being overwhelmed with fears of losing their sense of individuality, and they may enter into the later psychosexual and psychosocial stages with a firm foundation of selfhood.

TREATING BORDERLINE AND NARCISSISTIC DISORDERS   Borderline and narcissistic disorders seem to be rooted in traumas and developmental disturbances during the separation/individuation phase. However, the full manifestations of the personality and behavioral symptoms tend to develop in early adulthood. Borderline and narcissistic symptoms such as splitting (a defensive process of keeping incompatible perceptions separate) and notions of grandiosity are behavioral manifestations of developmental tasks that were disturbed or not completed earlier (St. Clair, 2000).

Although this book does not emphasize diagnostic issues, a great deal of recent psychoanalytic writing deals with the nature and treatment of borderline and narcissistic personality disorders. To omit at least a brief discussion of these disorders would give an incomplete picture of the current thinking of object-relations theory, which sheds new light on the understanding of these disorders. Among the most significant theorists in this area are Kernberg (1975, 1976), Kohut (1971, 1977, 1984), and Masterson (1976). Kohut has maintained that people are their healthiest and best when they can feel both independence and attachment, taking joy in themselves and also being able to idealize others. Since mature adults feel a basic security grounded in a sense of freedom, self-sufficiency, and self-esteem, they are not compulsively dependent on others but also do not have to fear closeness.

INTEGRATION OF OBJECT-RELATIONS THEORY WITH COGNITIVE BEHAV-
IORAL TECHNIQUES   It is possible to combine the conceptual understanding of the contemporary psychoanalytic therapies with cognitive behavioral
therapies (which you will study in Chapter 11). Morgan and MacMillan
(1999) developed a three-phase integrated counseling model based on theoretical constructs of object-relations and attachment theory that incorpo-
rates cognitive behavioral techniques.

In the first phase, object-relations theory serves as the conceptual
basis for the assessment and relationship-building process. What children
learn from early interactions with parents clearly affects personality development and may result in problematic adult relationships. For meaningful
assessment to occur, it is essential that the counselor is able to hear the
stories of their clients, to grasp their phenomenological world, and to establish rapport with them. During this phase, therapists provide a supportive
holding environment that offers a safe place for clients to recall and explore
painful earlier memories. At this phase counseling includes an exploration
of clients' feelings regarding past and present circumstances and thought
patterns that influence clients' interpretation of the world.

In the second phase, the aim is to link insights gleaned from the initial assessment phase to the present to create an understanding of how
early relational patterns are related to present difficulties. This insight
often enables clients to acknowledge and express painful memories, feelings, and thoughts. As clients are able to process previously repressed and
dissociated memories and feelings in counseling, cognitive changes in perception of self and others often occurs. Both experiential and cognitive techniques are utilized in the second phase. As clients engage in the process of
cognitively restructuring life situations, they acquire new and adaptive
ways of thinking, feeling, and coping. They become increasingly able to take
active steps to improve their present existence. This process of cognitive restructuring fosters emotional growth and allows clients to assume personal
responsibility for their present decisions.

In the third and final phase of treatment, behavioral techniques with
goal setting and homework assignments are utilized to maximize change.
This is the action phase, a time for clients to attempt new behaviors based
on the insight, understanding, and cognitive restructuring achieved in the
prior phases of counseling. Clients take action, which leads to empowerment. Termination of counseling is a joint decision based on qualitative
changes in clients' relationships and lifestyle.

According to Morgan and MacMillan (1999), there is increasing support in the literature that integrating contemporary psychodynamic theory
with cognitive behavioral techniques can lead to observable, constructive
client changes. Establishing clear goals for each of the three phases of their
integrative model provides an efficient framework within which to structure the counseling interventions. Morgan and MacMillan claim that if these
treatment goals are well defined it is possible to work through all three
phases in a reasonable amount of time. Adapting the conceptual foundation

of psychoanalytic thinking to relatively brief therapy makes this approach useful in time-limited therapy.

This chapter permits only a brief treatment of the newer formulations in psychoanalytic theory. If you would like to pursue this emerging approach, an overview of this vast and growing literature can be found in Hedges (1983), Kaplan (1978), and St. Clair (2000).

 # THE THERAPEUTIC PROCESS

Therapeutic Goals

Two goals of Freudian psychoanalytic therapy are to make the unconscious conscious and to strengthen the ego so that behavior is based more on reality and less on instinctual cravings or irrational guilt. Successful analysis is believed to result in significant modification of the individual's personality and character structure. Using therapeutic methods to bring out unconscious material; childhood experiences are reconstructed, discussed, interpreted, and analyzed. It is clear that the process is not limited to solving problems and learning new behaviors. Rather, there is a deeper probing into the past to develop the level of self-understanding that is assumed to be necessary for a change in character. Analytic therapy is oriented toward achieving insight, but not just an intellectual understanding; it is essential that the feelings and memories associated with this self-understanding be experienced.

Therapist's Function and Role

Classical analysts typically assume an anonymous stance, which is sometimes called the "blank-screen" approach. They engage in very little self-disclosure and maintain a sense of neutrality to foster a *transference relationship,* in which their clients will make *projections* onto them. If therapists say little about themselves and rarely share their personal reactions, they believe whatever the client feels toward them will largely be the product of feelings associated with other significant figures from the past. These projections, which have their origins in unfinished and repressed situations, are considered "grist for the mill," and their analysis is the very essence of therapeutic work.

One of the central functions of analysis is to help clients acquire the freedom to love, work, and play. Other functions include assisting clients in achieving self-awareness, honesty, and more effective personal relationships; in dealing with anxiety in a realistic way; and in gaining control over impulsive and irrational behavior. The analyst must first establish a working relationship with the client and then do a lot of listening and interpreting. Particular attention is given to the client's resistances. The analyst listens, learns, and decides when to make appropriate interpretations. A major function of interpretation is to accelerate the process of uncovering unconscious material. The analyst listens for gaps and inconsistencies in the client's story, infers the meaning of reported dreams and free associations, and remains sensitive to clues concerning the client's feelings toward the analyst.

Organizing these therapeutic processes within the context of understanding personality structure and psychodynamics enables the analyst to formulate the nature of the client's problems. One of the central functions of the analyst is to teach clients the meaning of these processes so that they are able to achieve insight into their problems, increase their awareness of ways to change, and thus gain more rational control over their lives.

The process of psychoanalytic therapy is somewhat like putting the pieces of a puzzle together. Whether clients change depends considerably more on their readiness to change than on the accuracy of the therapist's interpretations. If the therapist pushes the client too rapidly or offers ill-timed interpretations, therapy is likely to become counterproductive.

Client's Experience in Therapy

Clients interested in psychoanalysis must be willing to commit themselves to an intensive and long-term therapy process. Typically, they come to therapy several times weekly for 3 to 5 years. After some face-to-face sessions with the analyst, clients lie on a couch and free-associate; that is, they say whatever comes to mind without self-censorship. This process of free association is known as the "fundamental rule." Clients report their feelings, experiences, associations, memories, and fantasies to the analyst. Lying on the couch encourages deep, uncensored reflections and reduces the stimuli that might interfere with getting in touch with their internal conflicts and productions. It also reduces their ability to "read" their analyst's face for reactions and, hence, fosters the projections characteristic of a regressive transference. At the same time, the analyst is freed from having to carefully monitor facial clues.

What has just been described is classical psychoanalysis. Many psychoanalytically oriented practitioners (as distinct from analysts) do not use all these techniques. Yet they do remain alert to transference manifestations and work with dreams and with unconscious material.

Clients in psychoanalytic therapy make a commitment with the therapist to stick with the procedures of an intensive therapeutic process. They agree to talk, because their verbal productions are the heart of psychoanalytic therapy. They are typically asked not to make any radical changes in their lifestyle during the period of analysis, such as getting a divorce or quitting their job.

Psychoanalytic clients are ready to terminate their sessions when they and their analyst agree that they have resolved those symptoms and conflicts that were amenable to resolution, have clarified and accepted their remaining emotional problems, have understood the historical roots of their difficulties, and can integrate their awareness of past problems with their present relationships. Successful analysis answers a client's "why" questions regarding his or her life. Clients who emerge successfully from analytic therapy report that they have achieved such things as an understanding of their symptoms and the functions they serve, an insight into how their environment affects them and how they affect the environment, and reduced defensiveness (Saretsky, 1978).

Relationship Between Therapist and Client

The client's relationship with the analyst is conceptualized in the transference process, which is the core of the psychoanalytic approach. Transference is the client's unconscious shifting to the analyst of feelings and fantasies that are reactions to significant others in the client's past. Transference allows clients to understand and resolve "unfinished business" from these past relationships. As therapy progresses, childhood feelings and conflicts begin to surface from the depths of the unconscious. Clients regress emotionally. Some of their feelings arise from conflicts such as trust versus mistrust, love versus hate, dependence versus independence, and autonomy versus shame and guilt. Transference takes place when clients resurrect from their early years intense conflicts relating to love, sexuality, hostility, anxiety, and resentment; bring them into the present; reexperience them; and attach them to the analyst. For example, clients may transfer unresolved feelings toward a stern and unloving father to the analyst, who, in their eyes, becomes stern and unloving. Hostile feelings are the product of negative transference, but clients may also develop a positive transference and, for example, fall in love with the analyst, wish to be adopted, or in many other ways seek the love, acceptance, and approval of an all-powerful therapist. In short, the analyst becomes a current substitute for significant others.

If therapy is to produce change, the transference relationship must be worked through. The *working-through* process consists of an exploration of unconscious material and defenses, most of which originated in early childhood. Working through is achieved by repeating interpretations and by exploring forms of resistance. It results in a resolution of old patterns and allows clients to make new choices. In the process of working through there is a constant going back to the raw data of the session in an attempt to gain new understandings of present experience. Clients have many opportunities to see the variety of ways in which their core conflicts and core defenses are manifested in their daily life. It is assumed that for clients to become psychologically independent they must not only become aware of this unconscious material but also achieve some level of freedom from behavior motivated by infantile strivings, such as the need for total love and acceptance from parental figures. If this demanding phase of the therapeutic relationship is not properly worked through, clients simply transfer their infantile wishes for universal love and acceptance to other figures they deem powerful. It is precisely in the client/therapist relationship that the manifestation of these childhood motivations becomes apparent. Because the transference relationship takes time to build in intensity and additional time to understand and resolve, working through requires a lengthy period in the total therapeutic process, ranging from 3 to 5 years or more.

However, even with long-term therapy all traces of our childhood needs and traumas will never be completely erased. Thus, our infantile conflicts may not be fully resolved, even though many aspects of transference are worked through with a therapist. We may need to struggle at times throughout our life with feelings that we project onto others as well as with unrealistic demands that we expect others to fulfill. In this sense we experience transference with many people, and our past is always a vital part of the person we are presently becoming.

It is a mistake to assume that all feelings clients have toward their therapists are manifestations of transference. Many of these reactions may have a reality base, and clients' feelings may well be directed to the here-and-now style the therapist exhibits. Every positive response (such as liking the therapist) should not be labeled "positive transference." Conversely, a client's anger toward the therapist may be a function of the therapist's behavior; it is a mistake to label all negative reactions as signs of "negative transference."

The notion of never becoming completely free of past experiences has significant implications for therapists who become intimately involved in the unresolved conflicts of their clients. Even if the conflicts of therapists have surfaced to awareness, and even if therapists have dealt with these personal issues in their own intensive therapy, they may still project distortions onto clients. The intense therapeutic relationship is bound to ignite some of the unconscious conflicts within therapists. Known as *countertransference*, this phenomenon occurs when there is inappropriate affect, when therapists respond in irrational ways, or when they lose their objectivity in a relationship because their own conflicts are triggered. Countertransference also refers to the reactions therapists have toward their clients that may interfere with their objectivity. For example, a male client may become excessively dependent on his female therapist. The client may look to her to direct him and tell him how to live, and he may look to her for the love and acceptance that he felt he was unable to secure from his mother. The therapist herself may have unresolved needs to nurture, to foster a dependent relationship, and to be told that she is significant, and she may be meeting her own needs by in some way keeping her client dependent. Unless she is aware of her own needs as well as her own dynamics, it is very likely that her dynamics will interfere with the progress of therapy.

All countertransference reactions should not be considered as detrimental to therapeutic progress. Searles (1979) suggests some positive outcomes to countertransference. A growing number of psychoanalysts are maintaining that countertransference reactions can provide an important means for understanding the world of the client. The analyst who notes a countertransference mood of irritability, for instance, may learn something about a client's pattern of being demanding. In this light countertransference can be seen as potentially useful, if it is explored in analysis. As the focus on the analytic process moves into material that is rooted in what Mahler (1968) calls symbiosis, issues emerge that deal with the early mother/infant partnership. Like this early relationship, the therapist/client relationship requires an especially high degree of emotional attunement. Viewed in this more positive way, countertransference becomes a key means of potentially helping the client. For a more detailed discussion of countertransference, see Searles (1979), who has done pioneering work in this area.

What is of paramount importance is that therapists develop some level of objectivity and not react irrationally and subjectively in the face of anger, love, adulation, criticism, and other intense feelings expressed by their clients. Most psychoanalytic training programs require that trainees undergo their own extensive analysis as a client. If psychotherapists become aware of symptoms (such as strong aversion to certain types of clients, strong attraction to other types of clients, developing psychosomatic reactions at definite times in therapeutic relationships, and the like), it behooves them to seek professional consultation or enter their own therapy for a time to work out unresolved personal issues that stand in the way of their being effective therapists.

It should be clear that the client/therapist relationship is of vital importance in psychoanalytic therapy. As a result of this relationship, particularly in working through the transference situation, clients acquire insights into their own unconscious psychodynamics. Awareness of and insights into repressed material are the bases of the analytic growth process. Clients are able to understand the association between their past experiences and their current behavior and character structure. The psychoanalytic approach assumes that without this dynamic self-understanding there can be no substantial personality change or resolution of present conflicts.

 ## APPLICATION: Therapeutic Techniques and Procedures

This section deals with the techniques most commonly used by psychoanalytically oriented therapists. Some features of psychoanalytic therapy (as opposed to traditional psychoanalysis) are:

- The therapy is geared more to limited objectives than to restructuring one's personality.
- The therapist is less likely to use the couch.
- There are probably fewer sessions.
- There is more frequent use of supportive interventions—such as reassurance, expressions of empathy and support, and suggestions—and more self-disclosure by the therapist.
- There is more focus on pressing practical issues than on working with fantasy material.

The techniques of psychoanalytic therapy are aimed at increasing awareness, fostering insights into the client's behavior, and understanding the meanings of symptoms. The therapy proceeds from the client's talk to catharsis to insight to working through unconscious material. This work is done to attain the goals of intellectual and emotional understanding and reeducation, which, it is hoped, lead to personality change. The six basic techniques of psychoanalytic therapy are (1) maintaining the analytic framework, (2) free association, (3) interpretation, (4) dream analysis, (5) analysis of resistance, and (6) analysis of transference.

Maintaining the Analytic Framework

The psychoanalytic process stresses maintaining a particular framework aimed at accomplishing the goals of this type of therapy. "Maintaining the analytic framework" refers to a whole range of procedural and stylistic factors, such as the analyst's relative anonymity, the regularity and consistency of meetings, and starting and ending the sessions on time. One of the most powerful features of psychoanalytically oriented therapy is that the consistent framework is itself a therapeutic factor, comparable on an emotional level to the regular feeding of an infant. Analysts attempt to minimize departures from this consistent pattern (such as vacations, changes in fees, or changes in the meeting environment).

Free Association

Free association plays a central role in the process of maintaining the analytic framework. Clients are encouraged to say whatever comes to mind, regardless of how painful, silly, trivial, illogical, or irrelevant it may be. Such *free association* is the central technique in psychoanalytic therapy. In essence, clients flow with any feelings or thoughts by reporting them immediately without censorship. As the analytic work progresses, most clients will occasionally depart from this basic rule, and these resistances will be interpreted by the therapist when it is timely to do so.

Free association is one of the basic tools used to open the doors to unconscious wishes, fantasies, conflicts, and motivations. This technique often leads to some recollection of past experiences and, at times, a release of intense feelings (catharsis) that have been blocked off. This release is not seen as crucial in itself, however. During the free-association process, the therapist's task is to identify the repressed material that is locked in the unconscious. The sequence of associations guides the therapist in understanding the connections clients make among events. Blockings or disruptions in associations serve as cues to anxiety-arousing material. The therapist interprets the material to clients, guiding them toward increased insight into the underlying dynamics.

As analytic therapists listen to their clients' free associations, they hear not only the surface content but also the hidden meaning. This awareness of the language of the unconscious has been termed "listening with the third ear" (Reik, 1948). Nothing the client says is taken at face value. For example, a slip of the tongue can suggest that an expressed affect is accompanied by a conflicting affect. Areas that clients do not talk about are as significant as the areas they do discuss. Although psychoanalytic theory offers guidelines, the individual client must determine the actual meanings of specific content through associations.

Interpretation

Interpretation consists of the analyst's pointing out, explaining, and even teaching the client the meanings of behavior that is manifested in dreams, free association, resistances, and the therapeutic relationship itself. The functions of interpretations are to allow the ego to assimilate new material and to speed up the process of uncovering further unconscious material.

Interpretation is grounded in the therapist's assessment of the client's personality and of what factors in the client's past contributed to his or her difficulties. Under contemporary definitions, interpretation includes identifying, clarifying, and translating the client's material.

In making an appropriate interpretation, the therapist must be guided by a sense of the client's readiness to consider it (Saretsky, 1978). The therapist uses the client's reactions as a gauge. It is important that interpretations be well timed; the client will reject ones that are inappropriately timed. A general rule is that interpretation should be presented when the phenomenon to be interpreted is close to conscious awareness. In other words, the analyst should interpret material that the client has not yet seen for him- or herself but is capable of tolerating and incorporating. Another general rule is that interpretation should always start from the surface and go only as deep as the client is able to go. A third general rule is that it is best to point out a resistance or defense before interpreting the emotion or conflict that lies beneath it.

✓ Dream Analysis

Dream analysis is an important procedure for uncovering unconscious material and giving the client insight into some areas of unresolved problems. During sleep, defenses are lowered and repressed feelings surface. Freud sees dreams as the "royal road to the unconscious;" for in them one's unconscious wishes, needs, and fears are expressed. Some motivations are so unacceptable to the person that they are expressed in disguised or symbolic form rather than being revealed directly.

Dreams have two levels of content: latent content and manifest content. *Latent content* consists of hidden, symbolic, and unconscious motives, wishes, and fears. Because they are so painful and threatening, the unconscious sexual and aggressive impulses that make up latent content are transformed into the more acceptable *manifest content,* which is the dream as it appears to the dreamer. The process by which the latent content of a dream is transformed into the less threatening manifest content is called *dream work.* The therapist's task is to uncover disguised meanings by studying the symbols in the manifest content of the dream.

During the session, therapists may ask clients to free associate to some aspect of the manifest content of a dream for the purpose of uncovering the latent meanings. Therapists participate in the process by exploring clients' associations with them. Interpreting the meanings of the dream elements helps clients unlock the repression that has kept the material from consciousness and relate the new insight to their present struggles. Rather than simply serving as a pathway to repressed material, dreams can also provide an understanding of clients' current functioning.

Analysis and Interpretation of Resistance

Resistance, a concept fundamental to the practice of psychoanalysis, is anything that works against the progress of therapy and prevents the client from producing previously unconscious material. Specifically, in analytic therapy resistance is the client's reluctance to bring to the surface of awareness unconscious material that has been repressed. Resistance refers to any idea, attitude, feeling, or action (conscious or unconscious) that fosters the status quo and gets in the way of change. During free association or association to dreams, the client may evidence an unwillingness to relate certain thoughts, feelings, and experiences. Freud views resistance as an unconscious dynamic that people use to defend against the intolerable anxiety and pain that would arise if they were to become aware of their repressed impulses and feelings.

As a defense against anxiety, resistance operates specifically in psychoanalytic therapy to prevent clients and therapists from succeeding in their joint effort to gain insights into the dynamics of the unconscious. Because resistance blocks threatening material from entering awareness, analytic therapists point it out, and clients must confront it if they hope to deal with conflicts realistically. The therapists' interpretation is aimed at helping clients become aware of the reasons for the resistance so that they can deal with them. As a general rule, therapists point out and interpret the most obvious resistances to lessen the possibility of clients' rejecting the interpretation and to increase the chance that they will begin to look at their resistive behavior.

Resistances are not just something to be overcome. Because they are representative of usual defensive approaches in daily life, they need to be recognized as devices that defend against anxiety but that interfere with the ability to accept change that could lead to experiencing a more gratifying life. It is extremely important that therapists respect the resistances of clients and assist them in working therapeutically with their defenses. If handled properly, resistance can be one of the most valuable tools in understanding the client.

Analysis and Interpretation of Transference

As was mentioned earlier, transference manifests itself in the therapeutic process at the point where clients' earlier relationships contribute to their distorting the present with the therapist. It makes sense that clients often react to their therapist as they did to a significant person. The transference situation is considered valuable because its manifestations provide clients with the opportunity to reexperience a variety of feelings that would otherwise be inaccessible. Through the relationship with the therapist, clients express feelings, beliefs, and desires that they have buried in their unconscious. Through appropriate interpretations and working through of these current expressions of early feelings, clients are able to change some of their long-standing patterns of behavior.

The analysis of transference is a central technique in psychoanalysis and psychoanalytically oriented therapy, for it allows clients to achieve here-and-now insight into the influence of the past on their present functioning. Interpretation of the transference relationship enables clients to work through old conflicts that are keeping them fixated and retarding their emotional growth. In essence, the effects of early relationships are counteracted by working through a similar emotional conflict in the therapeutic relationship. An example of utilizing transference is given in the next section on the case of Stan.

PSYCHOANALYTIC THERAPY APPLIED TO THE CASE OF STAN

In each of the chapters in Part 2, the case of Stan is used to demonstrate the practical applications of the theory in question. To give you a focus on Stan's central concerns, refer to the end of Chapter 1, where his biography is given. I also recommend that you at least skim Chapter 15, which deals with an integrative approach as applied to Stan.

In Chapters 4 through 13 you will notice that Stan is working with a female therapist. Given his feelings toward women, it may seem odd that he selected a woman for his therapist. However, knowing that he had difficulty with women, he deliberately made this choice as a way to challenge himself, both in his therapy and in his everyday life. As you will see, one of Stan's goals is to learn how to become less intimidated in the presence of women and to be more himself around them.

The psychoanalytic approach focuses on the unconscious psychodynamics of Stan's behavior. Considerable attention is given to material that he has repressed, such as his anxiety related to the threatened breakthrough of his sexual and aggressive impulses. In the past he had to rigidly control both these impulses, and when he did not, he got into trouble. He also developed a strong superego by in- *perfections* trojecting parental values and standards *swallowing values of others* and making them his own. These aspirations were unrealistic, for they were perfectionistic goals. He could be loved only if he became perfect; yet no matter what he attempted, it never seemed adequate. He internalized his anger and guilt, which became depression. At the extreme Stan demonstrated a self-destructive tendency, which is a way of inflicting punishment on himself. Instead of directing his hostility toward his parents and siblings, he turned it inward toward himself. Stan's preoccupation with drinking could be hypothesized as evidence of an oral fixation. Because he never received love and acceptance during his early childhood, he is still suffering from this deprivation and still desperately searching for approval and acceptance from others. Stan's sex-role identification was fraught with difficulties. He learned the basis of female/male relationships through his early experiences with his parents. What he saw was fighting, bickering, and discounting. His father was the weak one who always lost, and his mother was the strong, domineering force who could and did hurt men. Stan identified with his weak and impotent father; he generalized his fear of his mother to all women. It could be further hypothesized that he married a woman who was similar to his mother and who reinforced his feelings of impotence in her presence.

The opportunity to develop a transference relationship and work through it is the core of the therapy process. An assumption is that Stan will eventually relate to his therapist as he did to his mother and that the process will be a valuable means of gaining insight into the origin of his difficulties with women. The analytic process stresses an intensive exploration of his past. The goal is to make the unconscious conscious, so that he will no longer be determined by unconscious forces. Stan devotes much therapy time to reliving and exploring his early past. As he talks, he gains increased understanding of the dynamics of his behavior. He begins to see connections between his present problems and early experiences in his childhood. Thus, he explores memories of relationships with his siblings and with his mother and father and also explores how he has generalized his view of women and men from his view of these family members. It is expected that he will reexperience old feelings and uncover buried feelings related to traumatic events. Questions for Stan could include these: What did you do when you felt unloved? What did you have to do as a child with your negative feelings? Could you express your rage, hostility, hurt, and fears? What effects did your relationship with your mother have on you? What did this teach you about all women?

The analytic process focuses on key influences in Stan's developmental years. As he comes to understand how he has been shaped by these past experiences, he is increasingly able to exert control over his present functioning. Many of Stan's fears become conscious, and then his energy does not have to remain fixed on defending himself from unconscious feelings. Instead, he can make new decisions about his current life. He can do this only if he works through the transference relationship, however, for the depth of his endeavors in therapy largely determines the depth and extent of his personality changes. If the therapist is operating from a contemporary psychoanalytic orientation, her focus will be on Stan's developmental sequences. Particular attention is paid to understanding his current behavior in the world as largely a repetition of one of his earlier developmental phases. Because of his dependency, it is useful in understanding his behavior to see that he is now repeating patterns that he formed with his mother during his infancy. Viewed from this perspective, Stan has not accomplished the task of separation and individuation. He is still "stuck" in the symbiotic phase on some levels. He is unable to obtain his confirmation of worth from himself, and he has not resolved the dependence/independence struggle. Looking at his behavior from the viewpoint of self psychology can help the therapist deal with his difficulties in forming intimate relationships.

Follow-up: You Continue as Stan's Psychoanalytic Therapist

With each of the 10 theoretical orientations, you will be encouraged to try your hand at applying the principles and techniques you have just studied in the chapter to working with Stan from that particular perspective. The information presented about Stan from each of these theory chapters will provide you with some ideas of how you might continue work-ing with him if he were referred to you. Do your best to stay within the general spirit of each theory by identifying spe-cific concepts you would draw from and techniques that you might use in help-ing him explore the struggles he identi-fies. Here are a series of questions to pro-vide some structure in your thinking about his case:

- How much interest would you have in Stan's early childhood? What are some ways you'd help him see patterns be-tween his childhood issues and his cur-rent problems?

- Consider the transference relationship that is likely to be established between you and Stan. How might you react to his making you into a significant per-son in his life?

- In working with Stan, what counter-transference issues might arise for you?

- What resistances might you predict in your work with Stan? From a psychoan-alytic perspective, how would you inter-pret this resistance? What might it be like for you to encounter his resistance? ■

 ## SUMMARY AND EVALUATION

Some major concepts of psychoanalytic theory include the dynamics of the unconscious and its influence on behavior; the role of anxiety; and the de-velopment of personality at various life periods, including the oral, anal, phallic, latency, and genital stages.

Building on many of Freud's basic ideas, Erikson broadened the de-velopmental perspective by including psychosocial trends. In his model, each of the eight stages of human development is characterized by a crisis, or turning point. We can either master the developmental task or fail to re-solve the core struggle. These eight stages of the life span are infancy, early childhood, preschool age, school age, adolescence, young adulthood, middle age, and later life. (As a succinct review of these developmental turn-ing points, Table 4-1 compares Freud's and Erikson's views of growth and development.)

Unlike Freudian theory, Jungian theory is not reductionist. Jung views humans positively and focuses on individuation, the capacity of hu-mans to move toward wholeness and self-realization. To become what they are capable of becoming, individuals must explore the unconscious aspects of their personality, both the personal unconscious and the collective uncon-scious. In Jungian analytical therapy, the therapist assists the client in tap-ping his or her inner wisdom. The goal of therapy is not merely the resolution of immediate problems but the transformation of personality.

The contemporary trend in psychoanalytic theory is reflected in self psychology and object-relations theory. These approaches are based on the notion that at birth there is no differentiation between others and self and that others represent objects of need gratification for infants. Through the process of attachment, children enter the second stage of normal symbio-sis, during which there is still a lack of clarity between what is self and what is object. In the third stage children begin to draw away from this symbiosis and individuate, differentiating themselves as separate from the parents to whom they are attached. The fourth stage is one of integration.

Others are perceived as both separate and related. In normal development children are able to relate to their parents without fearing a loss of their sense of autonomy.

Psychoanalytic therapy consists largely of using methods to bring out unconscious material that can be worked through. It focuses primarily on childhood experiences, which are discussed, reconstructed, interpreted, and analyzed. The assumption is that this exploration of the past, which is typically accomplished by working through the transference relationship with the therapist, is necessary for character change. The most important techniques typically employed in psychoanalytic practice are maintaining the analytic framework, free association, interpretation, dream analysis, analysis of resistance, and analysis of transference.

Contributions of the Psychoanalytic Approach

I believe counselors can broaden their understanding of clients' struggles by appreciating Freud's many significant contributions. It must be emphasized that competent use of psychoanalytic techniques requires training beyond the scope of most counselors. Regardless of their theoretical orientation, however, it is well for counselors to be trained so that they will understand such psychoanalytic phenomena as transference, countertransference, resistance, and the use of ego-defense mechanisms as reactions to anxiety. The psychoanalytic approach provides counselors with a conceptual framework for looking at behavior and for understanding the origins and functions of symptoms. If counselors ignore the early history of the client, they are limiting their vision of the causes of the client's present suffering and the nature of the client's present functioning. Although there is little to be gained from blaming the past for the way a person is now or from dwelling on the past, it is very useful to understand and work with the past as it pertains to the client's current situation.

Some analysts are coming to accept that the past experienced by a client is not identical to the past of others who have shared or do share life with the client. Each person has constructed his or her own truth. This approach, which is prominent in family systems theory, is helping therapists avoid the pitfall of "blaming" parents and others for the client's woes while retaining the emerging truth as it unfolds in psychoanalytic therapy from the point of view of the client.

For therapeutic practice the psychoanalytic point of view is particularly useful in (1) understanding resistances that take the form of canceling appointments, fleeing from therapy prematurely, and refusing to look at oneself; (2) understanding that unfinished business can be worked through, so that clients can provide a new ending to some of the events that have crippled them emotionally; (3) understanding the value and role of transference; and (4) understanding how the overuse of ego defenses, both in the counseling relationship and in daily life, can keep clients from functioning effectively.

You may have a difficult time understanding and accepting some of the Freudian notions about the stages of development. The Oedipus complex, penis envy, castration anxiety, incestuous feelings, and connections between past situations and current character may seem rather obscure on initial presentation. I recall that I had many doubts about the validity of these concepts when I first studied them in my undergraduate days. However, my professional work has given me a wider perspective on the Freudian view of psychosexual development. It is essential to keep in mind that this view must be understood from the vantage point of the time in which Freud wrote, during the Victorian era of the authoritarian father. Much of what he described makes sense when it is seen in historical and cultural perspective.

The psychoanalytic approach provides a framework for a dynamic understanding of the role of early childhood events and the impact of these experiences on the contemporary struggles faced by clients. Without completely accepting the orthodox Freudian position, we can still draw on many of these analytic concepts as a framework for understanding clients and for helping them achieve a deeper understanding of the roots of their conflicts.

If the psychoanalytic approach is considered in a broader context than its initial Freudian perspective, it becomes a more powerful model for understanding human behavior. Although I find Freud's psychosexual concepts of great value, I think that adding Erikson's stress on psychosocial factors gives a more complete picture of the critical turning points at each stage of development. Integrating these two perspectives is, in my view, most useful for understanding key themes in the development of personality. Erikson's developmental schema does not avoid the psychosexual issues and stages postulated by Freud; rather, Erikson extended the stages of psychosexual development throughout life. His perspective integrates psychosexual and psychosocial concepts without diminishing the import of either.

Sociocultural factors provide practitioners with a framework for understanding the major tasks and crises of each stage of development. According to Hamachek (1988), the principal strength of psychosocial theory is that it acknowledges that humans are biological, psychological, and social beings and that an interactive mix of these inner and outer forces shapes humans. The key needs and developmental tasks, along with the challenges inherent at each stage of life, provide a model for understanding some of the core conflicts clients explore in their therapy sessions. This approach gives special weight to childhood and adolescent factors that are significant in later stages of development while recognizing that the later stages also have their significant crises. Themes and threads can be found running through clients' lives.

Contributions of Modern Analytic Theorists

The contemporary trends in psychoanalytic thinking have contributed to the understanding of how our current behavior in the world is largely a repetition of patterns set during one of the early phases of development. Object-relations theory helps us see the ways in which clients interacted with significant others in the past and how they are superimposing these early experiences on present relationships. For the many clients in therapy who are struggling with issues such as separation and individuation, intimacy, dependence versus independence, and identity, these newer formulations can provide a framework for understanding how and where aspects of development have been fixated. They have significant implications for many areas of human interaction such as intimate relationships, the family and child rearing, and the therapeutic relationship. There are some analytic therapists who demonstrate an openness toward integrating various methods. For example, Marmor (1997) states: "I try to avoid putting every patient on a Procrustean bed of a singular therapeutic method but rather adapt my approach to the patient's own unique needs" (p. 32).

In my opinion it is possible to have an analytic framework that gives structure and direction to a counseling practice and at the same time to draw on other therapeutic techniques. I find value in the contributions of those writers who have built on the basic ideas of Freud and have added an emphasis on the social forces affecting personality development. In contemporary psychoanalytic practice more latitude is given to the therapist in using techniques and in developing the therapeutic relationship. The newer psychoanalytic theorists have enhanced, extended, and refocused classical analytic techniques. They are concentrating on the development of the ego and are paying attention to the social factors that influence the differentiation of an individual from others.

In a critique of long-term psychodynamic therapy, Strupp (1992) assumes that this approach will remain a luxury for most people in our society. But he contends that the various contemporary modifications of psychoanalysis have infused psychodynamic psychotherapy with renewed vitality and vigor.

Although contemporary psychodynamic forms diverge considerably in many respects from the original Freudian emphasis on drives, the basic Freudian concepts of unconscious motivation, the influence of early development, transference, countertransference, and resistance are still central to the newer modifications. Strupp notes a decline in practices based on the classical analytic model due to reasons such as time commitment, expense, limited applications to diverse client populations, and questionable benefits. He acknowledges that the realities stemming from managed care will mean increasing emphasis on short-term treatments for specific disorders, limited goals, and containment of costs.

Some of the current trends and directions in psychodynamic theory and practice that Strupp (1992) identifies are summarized here:

- The emphasis on treatment has shifted from the "classical" interest in curing neurotic disorders to the problems of dealing therapeutically with chronic personality disorders, borderline conditions, and narcissistic personality disorders. There is also a movement toward devising specific treatments for specific disorders.
- Increased attention is being paid to establishing a good therapeutic alliance early in therapy. A collaborative working relationship is now viewed as a key factor in a positive therapeutic outcome.
- There is a renewed interest in the development of briefer forms of psychodynamic therapy, largely due to societal pressures for ac-

countability and cost-effectiveness. The indications are that time-limited therapy will be used more in the future.

■ Psychodynamic group therapy is becoming more popular. It has received widespread acceptance for a number of reasons: it is more economical, it provides clients with opportunities to learn how they function in groups, and it offers a unique perspective on understanding problems and working them through therapeutically.

Limitations and Criticisms of the Psychoanalytic Approach

In general, considering factors such as time, expense, and availability of trained psychoanalytic therapists, the practical applications of many psychoanalytic techniques are limited. This is especially true of methods such as free association on the couch, dream analysis, and analysis of the transference relationship. A major limitation of psychoanalysis as a practical technique is that many severely disturbed clients lack the level of ego strength needed for this treatment.

The anonymous role of the therapist can be justified on theoretical grounds, but in therapy situations other than classical psychoanalysis this stance is unduly restrictive. The classical technique of nondisclosure can be misused in short-term individual therapy and assessment. Therapists in these situations who adopt the blank-screen aloofness that is called for theoretically only in the "pure" context of classical psychoanalysis may actually be keeping themselves hidden as persons in the guise of "being professional."

From a feminist perspective there are distinct limitations to a number of Freudian concepts, especially the Oedipus and Electra complexes. In her review of feminist counseling and therapy, Enns (1993) also notes that the object-relations approach has been criticized for its emphasis on the role of the mother/child relationship in determining later interpersonal functioning. The approach gives great responsibility to mothers for deficiencies and distortions in development. Fathers are conspicuously absent from the hypothesis about patterns of early development; only mothers are blamed for inadequate parenting.

A major limitation of psychoanalytic therapy is the relatively long time commitment required to accomplish analytic goals. Indeed, Alperin (1997) raises the question "Is psychoanalytically oriented psychotherapy compatible with managed care?" He persuasively argues that managed care violates many of the basic premises upon which psychoanalytic therapy rests. He argues that analytic therapists who offer services under managed care cannot provide their clients with privacy and confidentiality and that the requirements and justifications for treatment under managed care plans negatively affect the therapeutic relationship and are injurious to the client. Psychodynamic therapy is a comprehensive approach to treating symptoms. It focuses on the resolution of conflicts within the underlying character structure. The basic principles of the psychodynamic approach are both different from and incompatible with the philosophy of managed care.

It should be noted that psychoanalysts are attempting to creatively meet modern challenges while retaining their original focus on depth and inner life (DeAngelis, 1996). Many psychoanalytically oriented therapists support the move to the use of briefer therapy when this is indicated by the client's needs rather than by arbitrary limits set by third party payors. Unfortunately, the reality has been not a belt-tightening by the therapeutic disciplines but a demolition of the concept that treatment should be based on client needs and the likeliness of client benefit. Analysts tend to be skeptical of "quick fix" techniques and simplistic solutions to complex psychodynamic problems. Hence, it is understandable that many psychoanalytically oriented group therapists resist pressures to limit their work to short-term, managed care therapy. They view the economic pressures as a way to promote superficial therapy, the benefit of which is only illusionary.

 # PSYCHOANALYTIC THERAPY FROM A MULTICULTURAL PERSPECTIVE

Contributions to Multicultural Counseling

Psychoanalytically oriented therapy can be appropriate for culturally diverse populations. Comas-Diaz and Minrath (1985) recommend that the diffused sense of identity prevalent among borderline clients from ethnic minorities be examined from both a sociocultural and a developmental perspective. One aid to helping clients rebuild their identity is to emphasize strengths rather than deficiencies among ethnically different groups. Racial and ethnic minorities must simultaneously develop two sets of identity: a general overall ego identity as well as a cultural identity. Minority youths have a more complex adolescent experience because of this dual identity. Erikson's psychosocial approach, with its emphasis on critical issues in stages of development, has particular application to people of color. Counselors can help these clients review environmental situations at the various critical turning points in their lives to determine how certain events have affected them either positively or negatively.

Psychotherapists need to recognize and confront their own potential sources of bias and how countertransference could be conveyed unintentionally through their interventions. To the credit of the psychoanalytic approach, it stresses the value of intensive psychotherapy as part of the training of therapists, which helps them become aware of their own sources of countertransference.

Limitations for Multicultural Counseling

Traditional psychoanalytic approaches are costly, and psychoanalytic therapy is generally perceived as being based on upper- and middle-class values. Ethnic minority clients may not share these values, and for many the cost of treatment is prohibitive. Another limitation pertains to the ambiguity inherent in most psychoanalytic approaches. This can be problematic for ethnic minority clients, particularly Asian Americans, who may prefer a more structured, problem-oriented approach to counseling.

Furthermore, intrapsychic analysis may be in direct conflict with some clients' social framework and environmental perspective. This is especially true in working within the framework of long-term, in-depth analysis. Psychoanalytic therapy is more concerned with long-term personality reconstruction than with short-term problem solving.

Atkinson, Thompson, and Grant (1993) underscore the need for therapists to consider possible external sources of clients' problems, especially if clients have experienced an oppressive environment. The psychoanalytic approach can be criticized for failing to adequately address the social, cultural, and political factors that result in an individual's problems. If there is no balance between the external and internal perspectives, clients will be blamed for their condition.

There are likely to be some difficulties in applying a psychoanalytic approach with low-income clients. If these clients seek professional help, they are generally concerned with dealing with a crisis situation and with finding answers to concrete problems, or at least some direction, in addressing survival needs pertaining to housing, employment, and child care. This does not imply that low-income ethnic minority clients are unable to profit from analytic therapy but, rather, that this particular orientation could be more beneficial *after* more pressing issues and concerns have been resolved.

 # WHERE TO GO FROM HERE

If this chapter has provided the impetus for you to learn more about the psychoanalytic approach or the contemporary offshoots of psychoanalysis, select a few books from the Recommended Supplementary Readings and References and Suggested Readings. Various colleges and universities offer special workshops or short courses through continuing education on topics such as therapeutic considerations in working with borderline and narcissistic personalities. These workshops could give you a new perspective on the range of applications of contemporary psychoanalytic therapy. For further information about training programs, workshops, and graduate programs in various states, contact:

> *American Psychoanalytic Association (Apsa)*
> 309 East 49th Street, New York, NY 10017
> Telephone: (212) 752-0450, Fax: (212) 593–0571
> Website: *http://www.apsa.org*

Recommended Supplementary Readings

Psychoanalytic Theory: An Introduction (Elliott, 1994) provides a thorough coverage of the psychoanalytic implications for "postmodern" theories, systems approaches, and feminist thought.

Techniques of Brief Psychotherapy (Flegenheimer, 1982) is useful in describing the processes of client selection, therapist training, and modifications of techniques used in brief psychoanalytic therapy.

The Psychoanalytic Conspiracy (Langs, 1982) is a good description of the search for truth in analytic therapy. Criticism of other schools is somewhat extreme in its severity, but the book provides a useful admonition to counselors to be self-aware.

Object Relations and Self Psychology: An Introduction (St. Clair, 2000) provides an overview and critical assessment of two streams of psychoanalytic theory and practice: object-relations theory and self psychology. An introductory chapter describes the basic concepts and deals with some core issues. Especially useful are the chapters discussing the approaches of Margaret Mahler, Otto Kernberg, and Heinz Kohut. The book looks at how these different theorists vary from one another and how they depart from the classical Freudian model. This is a good place to start if you want an update on the contemporary trends in psychoanalysis.

References and Suggested Readings*

*ALPERIN, R. M. (1997). Is psychoanalytically oriented psychotherapy compatible with managed care? In R. M. Alperin & D. G. Phillips (Eds.), *The impact of managed care on the practice of psychotherapy: Innovation, implementation, and controversy* (pp. 185–198). New York: Brunner/Mazel.

ATKINSON, D. R., THOMPSON, C. E., & GRANT, S. K. (1993). A three-dimensional model for counseling racial/ethnic minorities. *The Counseling Psychologist, 2*(2), 257–277.

COMAS-DIAZ, L., & MINRATH, M. (1985). Psychotherapy with ethnic minority borderline clients. *Psychotherapy, 22*(25), 418–426.

COREY, G. (2000). *Theory and practice of group counseling* (5th ed.). Pacific Grove, CA: Brooks-Cole/Wadsworth.

*COREY, G. (2001). *Case approach to counseling and psychotherapy* (5th ed.). Pacific Grove, CA: Brooks-Cole/Wadsworth.

*DeANGELIS, T. (1996). Psychoanalysis adapts to the 1990s. *APA Monitor, 27*(9), 1, 43.

*ELLIOT, A. (1994). *Psychoanalytic theory: An introduction.* Oxford UK & Cambridge USA: Blackwell.

ENNS, C. Z. (1993). Twenty years of feminist counseling and therapy: From naming biases to implementing multifaceted practice. *The Counseling Psychologist, 21*(1), 3–87.

*ERIKSON, E. H. (1963). *Childhood and society* (2nd ed.). New York: Norton.

*FLEGENHEIMER, W. V. (1982). *Techniques of brief psychotherapy.* New York: Aronson.

FREUD, S. (1949). *An outline of psychoanalysis.* New York: Norton.

*FREUD, S. (1955). *The interpretation of dreams.* London: Hogarth Press.

HAMACHEK, D. F. (1988). Evaluating self-concept and ego development within Erikson's psychosocial framework: A formulation. *Journal of Counseling and Development, 66*(8), 354–360.

---

*Books marked with an asterisk are recommended for further reading.

*HARRIS, A. S. (1996). *Living with paradox: An introduction to Jungian psychology.* Pacific Grove, CA: Brooks/Cole.

*HEDGES, L. E. (1983). *Listening perspectives in psychotherapy.* New York: Aronson.

*JUNG, C. G. (1961). *Memories, dreams, reflections.* New York: Vintage.

KAPLAN, L. (1978). *Oneness and separateness.* New York: Simon & Schuster.

KERNBERG, O. F. (1975). *Borderline conditions and pathological narcissism.* New York: Aronson.

KERNBERG, O. F. (1976). *Object-relations theory and clinical psychoanalysis.* New York: Aronson.

KERNBERG, O. F. (1997). Convergences and divergences in contemporary psychoanalytic technique and psychoanalytic psychotherapy. In J. K. Zeig (Ed.), *The evolution of psychotherapy: The third conference* (pp. 3–22). New York: Brunner/Mazel.

KLEIN, M. (1975). *The psychoanalysis of children.* New York: Dell.

KOHUT, H. (1971). *The analysis of self.* New York: International Universities Press.

KOHUT, H. (1977). *Restoration of the self.* New York: International Universities Press.

KOHUT, H. (1984). *How does psychoanalysis cure?* Chicago: University of Chicago Press.

KOVEL, J. (1976). *A complete guide to therapy.* New York: Pantheon.

*LANGS, R. (1982). *The psychotherapeutic conspiracy.* New York: Aronson.

MAHLER, M. S. (1968). *On human symbiosis or the vicissitudes of individuation.* New York: International Universities Press.

MARMOR, J. (1997). The evolution of an analytic psychotherapist: A sixty-year search for conceptual clarity in the tower of Babel. In J. K. Zeig (Ed.), *The evolution of psychotherapy: The third conference* (pp. 23–36). New York: Brunner/Mazel.

MASTERSON, J. F. (1976). *Psychotherapy of the borderline adult: A developmental approach.* New York: Brunner/Mazel.

MORGAN, B., & MacMILLAN, P. (1999). Helping clients move toward constructive change: A three-phase integrative counseling model. *Journal of Counseling and Development, 77*(2), 153–159.

REIK, T. (1948). *Listening with the third ear.* New York: Pyramid.

*ST. CLAIR, M. (2000). *Object relations and self psychology: An introduction* (3rd ed.). Pacific Grove, CA: Brooks-Cole/Wadsworth.

SARETSKY, T. (1978). The middle phase of treatment. In G. D. Goldman & D. S. Milman (Eds.), *Psychoanalytic psychotherapy* (pp. 91–110). Reading, MA: Addison-Wesley.

*SCHULTZ, D., & SCHULTZ, S. E. (1998). *Theories of personality* (6th ed.). Pacific Grove, CA: Brooks/Cole.

*SEARLES, H. F. (1979). *Countertransference and related subjects. Selected papers.* New York: International Universities Press.

STRUPP, H. H. (1992). The future of psychodynamic psychotherapy. *Psychotherapy, 29*(1), 21–27.

*WOLITZKY, D. L., & Eagle, M. N. (1997). Psychoanalytic theories of psychotherapy. In P. L. Wachtel & S. B. Messer (Eds.), *Theories of psychotherapy: Origins and evolution* (pp. 39–96). Washington, DC: American Psychological Association.

CHAPTER

5

Adlerian Therapy

INTRODUCTION

KEY CONCEPTS
View of Human Nature
Subjective Perception of Reality
Unity and Patterns of Human Personality
Social Interest and Community Feeling
Birth Order and Sibling Relationships

THE THERAPEUTIC PROCESS
Therapeutic Goals
Therapist's Function and Role
Client's Experience in Therapy
Relationship Between Therapist and Client

APPLICATION: Therapeutic Techniques and Procedures
Phase 1: Establishing the Relationship
Phase 2: Exploring the Individual's Dynamics
Phase 3: Encouraging Self-Understanding and Insight
Phase 4: Helping With Reorientation
Areas of Application

ADLERIAN THERAPY APPLIED TO THE CASE OF STAN

SUMMARY AND EVALUATION
Summary
Contributions of the Adlerian Approach
Limitations and Criticisms of the Adlerian Approach

ALDERIAN THERAPY FROM A MULTICULTURAL PERSPECTIVE
Contributions to Multicultural Counseling
Limitations for Multicultural Counseling

WHERE TO GO FROM HERE

RECOMMENDED SUPPLEMENTARY READINGS

REFERENCES AND SUGGESTED READINGS

ALFRED ADLER

ALFRED ADLER (1870-1937) was the third child in a Vienna family of six boys and two girls. His brother Rudolf died as a young boy. Adler's early childhood was not a happy time, for he was sickly and very much aware of death. At age 4 he almost died of pneumonia. Adler associated this time with his decision to become a doctor.

Because he was ill so much during the first few years of his life, Adler was pampered by his mother. Later he was "dethroned" by a younger brother. It appears that he developed a trusting relationship with his father and that he did not feel very close to his mother. He was jealous of his older brother, Sigmund, which led to strained relationships between the two during childhood and adolescence. His early years were characterized by struggling to overcome childhood weaknesses and feelings of inferiority. It is clear that these family experiences had an impact on the formation of his theory. Nevertheless, he is an example of a person who shaped his own life as opposed to having it determined by fate.

Adler was a poor student, and his teacher advised his father that Adler was fit to be a shoemaker but not much else. With determined effort Adler eventually rose to the top of his class. He went on to study medicine at the University of Vienna, entered private practice as an ophthalmologist, and then shifted to general medicine. He eventually specialized in neurology and psychiatry, and he had a keen interest in incurable childhood diseases.

Adler had a passionate concern for the common person and was outspoken about child-rearing practices, school reforms, and prejudices that resulted in conflict. He spoke and wrote in simple and nontechnical language so that the public could understand and apply the principles of his Individual Psychology. After serving in World War I as a medical officer, Adler created 32 child guidance clinics in the Vienna public schools and began training teachers, social workers, physicians, and other professionals. He pioneered the practice of teaching professionals through live demonstrations with parents and children before large audiences. The clinics he founded grew in number and in popularity, and he was indefatigable in lecturing and demonstrating his work.

Adler lived by this overcrowded work schedule, yet he still took some time to sing, enjoy music, and be with friends. In the mid-1920s he began lecturing in the United States, and he later made frequent visits and tours. He ignored the warning of his friends to slow down, and his packed schedule continued. On May 28, 1937, while taking a walk before a scheduled lecture in Aberdeen, Scotland, Adler collapsed and died of heart failure. ∎

INTRODUCTION

Along with Freud and Jung, Alfred Adler was a major contributor to the development of the psychodynamic approach to therapy. After 8 to 10 years of collaboration, Freud and Adler parted company, with Freud taking the position that Adler was a heretic who had deserted him. Adler resigned as president of the Vienna Psychoanalytic Society in 1911 and founded the Society for Individual Psychology in 1912. Freud then asserted that it was not possible to support Adlerian concepts and still remain in good standing as a psychoanalyst.

Later, a number of other psychoanalysts deviated from Freud's orthodox position (see Chapter 4). These Freudian revisionists, who included Karen Horney, Erich Fromm, and Harry Stack Sullivan, agreed that social and cultural factors were of great significance in shaping personality. Even though these three therapists are typically called neo-Freudians, it would be more appropriate, as Heinz Ansbacher (1979) has suggested, to refer to them as neo-Adlerians because they moved away from Freud's biological and deterministic point of view and toward Adler's social-psychological and teleological (or goal-oriented) view of human nature.

Adler stresses the unity of personality, contending that people can only be understood as integrated and complete beings. This view espouses the purposeful nature of behavior, emphasizing that where we are striving to go is more important than where we have come from. Adler saw humans as both the creators and the creations of their own lives; that is, people develop a unique style of living that is both a movement toward and an expression of their selected goals. In this sense, we create ourselves rather than merely being shaped by our childhood experiences.*

After Adler's death in 1937, Rudolf Dreikurs was the most significant figure in bringing Adlerian psychology to the United States, especially as its principles applied to education, individual and group therapy, and family counseling. Dreikurs is credited with giving impetus to the idea of child guidance centers and to training professionals to work with a wide range of clients.

 KEY CONCEPTS

View of Human Nature

Adler abandoned Freud's basic theories because he believed Freud was excessively narrow in his stress on biological and instinctual determination. Adler holds that the individual begins to form an approach to life some-

---

* I want to acknowledge the diligent efforts and contributions of Dr. James Bitter of East Tennessee State University in bringing this chapter up to date and for expanding the section dealing with the therapeutic process and practical applications.

where in the first 6 years of living. Adler's focus is on how the person's perception of the past and his or her interpretation of early events has a continuing influence. On many theoretical grounds Adler was in opposition to Freud. According to Adler, for example, humans are motivated primarily by social relatedness rather than by sexual urges; behavior is purposeful and goal-directed; and consciousness, more than unconsciousness, is the focus of therapy. Unlike Freud, Adler stresses choice and responsibility, meaning in life, and the striving for success, completion, and perfection.

Adler's theory focuses on inferiority feelings, which he sees as a normal condition of all people and as a source of all human striving. Rather than being considered a sign of weakness or abnormality, feelings of inferiority can be the wellspring of creativity. They motivate us to strive for mastery, success (superiority), and completion. We are driven to overcome our sense of inferiority and strive for increasingly higher levels of development (Schultz & Schultz, 1998). Indeed, at around 6 years of age our fictional vision of ourselves as perfect or complete begins to form into a life goal. The life goal unifies the personality and becomes the source of human motivation; every striving and every effort to overcome inferiority is now in line with this goal.

From the Adlerian perspective human behavior is not determined solely by heredity and environment. Instead, we have the capacity to interpret, influence, and create events. Adler asserts that *what* we were born with is not as important as what we *do* with the abilities we possess. Although Adlerians reject the deterministic stance of Freud, they do not go to the other extreme and maintain that individuals can become whatever they want to be. Adlerians recognize that biological and environmental conditions limit our capacity to choose and to create.

Adlerians put the focus on reeducating individuals and reshaping society. Adler was the forerunner of a subjective approach to psychology that focuses on internal determinants of behavior such as values, beliefs, attitudes, goals, interests, and the individual perception of reality. He was a pioneer of an approach that is holistic, social, goal-oriented, and humanistic.

Subjective Perception of Reality

Adlerians attempt to view the world from the client's subjective frame of reference, an orientation described as phenomenological. It is phenomenological in that it pays attention to the individual way in which people perceive their world. This "subjective reality" includes the individual's perceptions, thoughts, feelings, values, beliefs, convictions, and conclusions. Behavior is understood from the vantage point of this subjective perspective. How life is in reality is less important than how the individual believes life to be.

As you will see in chapters that follow, many contemporary theories have incorporated this notion of the client's subjective worldview as a basic factor explaining behavior. Some of the other approaches that have a phenomenological perspective are existential therapy, person-centered therapy, Gestalt therapy, the cognitive behavioral therapies, reality therapy, and some of the systemic and constructivist approaches.

Unity and Patterns of Human Personality

A basic premise of Adlerian *Individual Psychology* is that personality can only be understood holistically and systemically; that is, the individual is seen as an indivisible whole, born, reared, and living in specific familial, social, and cultural contexts. People are social, creative, decision-making beings who act with purpose and cannot be fully known outside the contexts that have meaning in their lives (Sherman & Dinkmeyer, 1987).

The human personality becomes unified through development of a life goal. An individual's thoughts, feelings, beliefs, convictions, attitudes, character, and actions are expressions of his or her uniqueness, and all reflect a plan of life that allows for movement toward a self-selected life goal. An implication of this holistic view of personality is that the client is an integral part of a social system. There is more focus on interpersonal relationships than on the individual's internal psychodynamics.

BEHAVIOR AS PURPOSEFUL AND GOAL-ORIENTED   Individual Psychology assumes that all human behavior has a purpose. Humans set goals for themselves, and behavior becomes unified in the context of these goals. Adler replaced deterministic explanations with teleological (purposive, goal-oriented) ones. A basic assumption of Individual Psychology is that what we are striving for is crucial. Thus, Adlerians are interested in the future, without minimizing the importance of past influences. They assume that decisions are based on the person's experiences, on the present situation, and on the direction in which the person is moving. They look for continuity by paying attention to themes running through a person's life.

Adlerians use the term *fictional finalism* to refer to an imagined central goal that guides a person's behavior. Adler was influenced by the philosopher Hans Vaihinger's (1965) view that people live by fictions (or views of how the world should be). Applied to human motivation, a guiding fiction might be expressed as: "Only when I am perfect can I be secure" or "Only when I am important can I be accepted." The fictional goal represents an individual's image of a perfected position, for which he or she strives in any given situation. The term *finalism* refers to the ultimate nature of the person's goal and the ever-present tendency to move in a certain direction. Because of this ultimate goal, we have the creative power to choose what we will accept as truth, how we will behave, and how we will interpret events.

STRIVING FOR SIGNIFICANCE AND SUPERIORITY   Adler stresses that striving for perfection and coping with inferiority by seeking mastery are innate (Ansbacher & Ansbacher, 1979). To understand human behavior, it is essential to grasp the ideas of basic inferiority and compensation. According to Adler, the second we experience inferiority, we are pulled by the striving for superiority. He maintains that the goal of success pulls people forward toward mastery and enables them to overcome obstacles. The goal of superiority contributes to the development of human community. However, it is important to note that "superiority," as used by Adler, does not necessarily mean being superior to others. Rather, it means moving from a perceived lower position to a perceived higher position, from a felt minus to a felt plus. People cope with feelings of helplessness by striving for competence, mastery, and perfection. They can seek to change a weakness into a strength, for example, or strive to excel in one area of concentration to compensate for defects in other areas. The unique way in which people develop a style of striving for competence is what constitutes individuality.

LIFESTYLE   The term *lifestyle* refers to an individual's basic orientation to life, or one's personality, and includes the themes that characterize the person's existence. Synonyms are plan of life, life movement, strategy for living, and road map of life. Our lifestyle is the characteristic way we move toward our life goal. Adler saw us as actors, creators, and artists. In striving for goals that have meaning to us, we develop a unique style of life (Ansbacher, 1974). This concept accounts for why all of our behaviors fit together to provide consistency to our actions. Understanding one's lifestyle is somewhat like understanding the style of a composer: "We can begin wherever we choose: every expression will lead us in the same direction—toward the one motive, the one melody, around which the personality is built" (Adler, as cited in Ansbacher & Ansbacher, 1964, p. 332).

No two people develop exactly the same lifestyle. In striving for the goal of superiority, some develop their intellect; others, their artistic talent; others, athletic skills; and so on. These styles of life consist of people's views about themselves and the world and their distinctive behaviors and habits as they pursue personal goals. Everything we do is influenced by this unique lifestyle. Experiences within the family and relationships between siblings contribute to development of this lifestyle (Sherman & Dinkmeyer, 1987).

Social Interest and Community Feeling

Social interest and *community feeling (Gemeinschaftsgefühl)* are probably Adler's most significant and distinctive concepts (Ansbacher, 1992). These terms refer to individuals' awareness of being part of the human community and to individuals' attitudes in dealing with the social world. Social interest includes striving for a better future for humanity. The socialization process, which begins in childhood, involves finding a place in society and acquiring a sense of belonging and of contributing (Kefir, 1981). Social interest is taught, learned, and used. Adler equated social interest with a sense of identification and empathy with others: "to see with the eyes of another, to hear with the ears of another, to feel with the heart of another" (as cited in Ansbacher & Ansbacher, 1979, p. 42). The degree to which we successfully share with others and are concerned with the welfare of others is a measure of our mental health (Sherman & Dinkmeyer, 1987). From the Adlerian perspective, as social interest develops, feelings of inferiority and alienation diminish. People express social interest through shared activity and mutual respect. Those without community feeling and social interest become discouraged and end up on the useless side of life.

Individual Psychology rests on a central belief that our happiness and success are largely related to this social connectedness. Because we are part of a society, we cannot be understood in isolation from the social context. Humans seek a place in the family and in society to fulfill a basic need to feel secure, accepted, and worthwhile. Many of the problems we experience are related to the fear of not being accepted by the groups we value. If our sense of belonging is not fulfilled, anxiety is the result. Only when we have a sense of belonging are we able to act with courage in facing and dealing with our problems.

Mosak (1977) contends that we must face and master five life tasks: (1) relating to others (friendship), (2) making a contribution (work), (3) achieving intimacy (love and family relationships), (4) getting along with ourselves (self-acceptance), and (5) developing our spiritual dimension (including values, meaning, life goals, and our relationship with the universe, or cosmos). Furthermore, it is essential that we define our sex roles and learn to relate to others. Because we are not self-sufficient, we need to learn to become interdependent. Work is basic to survival, and therefore it is important that we create meaning in work and that we accept our part in this social enterprise. Our feelings about ourselves and our level of self-acceptance are determinants of how effectively we are able to form interpersonal relationships.

Birth Order and Sibling Relationships

The Adlerian approach is unique in giving special attention to the relationships between siblings and the psychological birth position in one's family. Adler identified five psychological positions: oldest, second of only two, middle, youngest, and only. (Actual birth order itself is less important than the individual's interpretation of his or her place in the family.) Because Adlerians view most human problems as social in nature, they emphasize intrafamily relationships.

Adler (1958) observes that many people wonder why children in the same family often differ so widely. Adler states that it is a fallacy to assume that children of the same family are formed in the same environment. Although siblings share aspects in common in the family constellation, the psychological situation of each child is different from that of the others because of the order of their birth. The following description of the influence of birth order is based on Ansbacher and Ansbacher (1964), Dreikurs (1953), and Adler (1958).

1. The *oldest child* generally receives a good deal of attention, and during the time she is the only child, she is typically somewhat spoiled as the center of attention. She tends to be dependable and hard working and strives to keep ahead. When a new brother or sister arrives on the scene, however, she finds herself ousted from her favored position. She is no longer unique or special. She may readily believe that the newcomer (or intruder) will rob her of the love to which she is accustomed.

2. The *second child* is in a different position. From the time he is born, he shares the attention with another child. The typical second child behaves as if he were in a race and is generally under full steam at all times. It is as though this second child were in training to surpass the older brother or sister. This competitive struggle between the first two children influences the later course of their lives. The younger child develops a knack for finding out the elder child's weak spots and proceeds to win praise from both parents and teachers by achieving successes where the older sibling has failed. If one is talented in a given area, the other strives for recognition by developing other abilities. The second-born is often opposite to the firstborn.

3. The *middle child* often feels squeezed out. She may become convinced of the unfairness of life and feel cheated. This person can assume a "poor me" attitude and can become a problem child. However, especially in families characterized by conflict, the middle child may become the switchboard and the peacemaker, the person who holds things together. If there are four children in a family, the second child will often feel like a middle child and the third will be more easygoing, more social, and may align with the firstborn.

4. The *youngest child* is always the baby of the family and tends to be the most pampered one. He has a special role to play, for all the other children are ahead of him. Youngest children tend to go their own way. They often develop in ways no others in the family have thought about.

5. The *only child* has a problem of her own. Although she shares some of the characteristics of the oldest child (namely, high achievement drive), she may not learn to share or cooperate with other children. She will learn to deal with adults well, as they make up her original familial world. Often, the only child is pampered by her parents and may become dependently tied to one or both of them. She may want to have center stage all of the time, and if her position is challenged, she will feel it is unfair.

Birth order and the interpretation of one's position in the family have a great deal to do with how adults interact in the world. Individuals acquire a certain style of relating to others in childhood and form a definite picture of themselves that they carry into their adult interactions. In Adlerian therapy, working with family dynamics, especially relationships among siblings, assumes a key role. Although it is important to avoid stereotyping individuals, it does help to see how certain personality trends that began in childhood as a result of sibling rivalry influence individuals throughout life.

THE THERAPEUTIC PROCESS

Therapeutic Goals

Adlerian counseling rests on a collaborative arrangement between the client and the counselor. In general, the therapeutic process includes forming a relationship based on mutual respect and identifying, exploring, and disclosing *mistaken goals* and *faulty assumptions* within the person's style of living. This is followed by a reeducation of the client toward the useful side of life. The main aim of therapy is to develop the client's sense of belonging and to assist in the adoption of behaviors and processes characterized by community feeling and social interest. This is accomplished by increasing the client's self-awareness and challenging and modifying his or her fundamental premises, life goals, and basic concepts (Dreikurs, 1967, 1997).

Adlerians do not see clients as being "sick" and in need of being "cured." Rather, the goal is to reeducate clients so that they can live in society as equals, both giving to society and receiving from others (Mosak, 1995). Therefore, the counseling process focuses on providing information, teaching, guiding, and offering encouragement to discouraged clients. Encouragement is the most powerful method available for changing a person's beliefs. It helps clients build self-confidence and stimulates courage. Courage is the willingness to act *even when fearful* in ways that are consistent with social interest. Fear and courage go hand in hand; without fear, there would be no need for courage. The loss of courage, or discouragement, results in mistaken and dysfunctional behavior. Discouraged people do not act in line with social interest on the useful side of life.

Adlerian counselors educate clients in new ways of looking at themselves, others, and life. Through the process of providing clients with a new "cognitive map," a fundamental understanding of the purpose of their behavior, counselors assist them in changing their perceptions. Mosak (1995) lists these goals for the educational process of therapy:

- Fostering social interest
- Helping clients overcome feelings of discouragement and inferiority
- Modifying clients' views and goals—that is, changing their lifestyle
- Changing faulty motivation
- Assisting clients to feel a sense of equality with others
- Helping clients become contributing members of society

Therapist's Function and Role

Adlerian counselors realize that clients can become discouraged and function ineffectively because of mistaken beliefs, faulty values, and goals in the useless side of life. They operate on the assumption that clients will feel and behave better if they discover and correct their basic mistakes. Therapists tend to look for major mistakes in thinking and valuing such as mistrust, selfishness, unrealistic ambitions, and lack of confidence.

A major function of the therapist is to make a comprehensive assessment of the client's functioning. Therapists gather information on the client's *family constellation,* which includes parents, siblings, and others living in the home, by means of a questionnaire. When summarized and interpreted, this questionnaire gives a picture of the individual's early social world. From this information the therapist is able to get a perspective on the client's major areas of success and failure and on the critical influences that have had a bearing on the role the client has decided to assume in the world. The counselor also uses *early recollections* as a diagnostic tool. These recollections are of single incidents from childhood that we are able to reexperience. They reflect our current convictions, evaluations, attitudes, and biases (Griffith & Powers, 1984). These memories provide a brief picture of how we see ourselves and others and what we anticipate for our future. After these early recollections are summarized and interpreted, the therapist identifies some of the major successes and mistakes in the client's life. The aim is to provide a point of departure for the therapeutic venture. This process is called a *lifestyle assessment.* When this process is completed, the counselor and the client have targets for therapy.

Client's Experience in Therapy

How do clients maintain their lifestyle, and why do they resist changing it? Generally, people fail to change because they do not recognize the errors in their thinking or the purposes of their behaviors, do not know what to do differently, and are fearful of leaving old patterns for new and unpredictable outcomes. Thus, even though their ways of thinking and behaving are not successful, they tend to cling to the familiar patterns (Manaster & Corsini, 1982; Sweeney, 1998). Clients in Adlerian counseling focus their work on desired outcomes and lifestyle, which will provide a blueprint for their actions.

In therapy clients explore what Adlerians call *private logic,* the concepts about self, others, and life that constitute the philosophy on which an individual's lifestyle is based. Clients' problems arise because the conclusions based on their private logic often do not conform to the requirements of social living. The core of the therapy experience consists of clients' discovering the purposes of behavior or symptoms and the basic mistakes associated with their coping. Learning how to correct faulty assumptions and conclusions is central to therapy.

To provide a concrete example, think of a chronically depressed middle-aged man who begins therapy. After a lifestyle assessment is completed, these basic mistakes are identified:

- He has convinced himself that nobody could really care about him.
- He rejects people before they have a chance to reject him.
- He is harshly critical of himself, expecting perfection.
- He has expectations that things will rarely work out well.
- He burdens himself with guilt because he is convinced he is letting everyone down.

Even though this man may have developed these mistaken ideas about life when he was young, he is still clinging to them as rules for living. His expectations, most of which are pessimistic, tend to be fulfilled because on some level he is seeking to validate his beliefs. Indeed, his depression will eventually serve the purpose of helping him avoid contact with others, a life task at which he expects to fail. In therapy this man will learn how to challenge the structure of his private logic. In his case the syllogism goes as follows:

- "I am basically unlovable."
- "The world is filled with people who are likely to be rejecting."
- "Therefore, I must keep to myself so I won't be hurt."

This person has held onto several basic mistakes. His private logic declares a psychological focus for him. Mosak (1977) would say that there are central themes or convictions in this client's life, some of which may be: "I must get what I want in life." "I must control everything in my life." "I must know everything there is to know, and a mistake would be catastrophic." "I must be perfect in everything I do."

It is easy to see how depression might follow from this thinking, but Adlerians also know that the depression serves as an excuse for this man's retreat from life. It is important for the therapist to listen for the underlying purposes of this client's behavior. Adlerians see feelings as being aligned with thinking and as the fuel for behaving. First we think, then feel, and then act. Because emotions and cognitions serve a purpose and aim at a goal, much therapy time is spent discovering and understanding that purpose and reorienting the client in a useful way. Because the client is not perceived by the therapist to be "sick," but as mainly discouraged, the therapist will give the client much encouragement that change is possible. Through the therapeutic process, the client will discover that he has resources and options to draw on in dealing with significant life issues and life tasks.

Relationship Between Therapist and Client

Adlerians consider a good client/therapist relationship to be one between equals that is based on cooperation, mutual trust, respect, confidence, and alignment of goals. They place special value on the counselor's modeling of communication and acting in good faith. From the beginning of therapy the relationship is a collaborative one, characterized by two persons working equally toward specific, agreed-on goals. Dinkmeyer, Dinkmeyer, and Sperry (1987) maintain that at the outset of counseling clients should begin to formulate a plan, or contract, detailing what they want, how they plan to get where they are heading, what is preventing them from successfully attaining their goals, how they can change nonproductive behavior into constructive behavior, and how they can make full use of their assets in achieving their purposes. This therapeutic contract sets forth the goals of the counseling process and specifies the responsibilities of both therapist and client. Developing a contract is not a requirement of Adlerian therapy, but it brings a tight focus to therapy.

Clients are not viewed as passive recipients; rather, they are active parties in a relationship between equals. Through this *collaborative part-*

nership, clients recognize that they are responsible for their behavior. Although Adlerians view the quality of the therapeutic relationship as relevant to the outcomes of therapy, they do not assume that this relationship alone will bring about change. However, without initial trust and rapport, the difficult work of changing one's style of living is not likely to occur.

APPLICATION: Therapeutic Techniques and Procedures

Adlerian counseling is structured around four central objectives that correspond to the four phases of the therapeutic process (Dreikurs, 1967). These phases are not linear and do not progress in rigid steps; rather, they can best be understood as a weaving that leads to a tapestry. These stages are:

1. Establishing the proper therapeutic relationship
2. Exploring the psychological dynamics operating in the client (an assessment)
3. Encouraging the development of self-understanding (insight into purpose)
4. Helping the client make new choices (reorientation and reeducation)

Dreikurs (1997) incorporated these stages into what he called *minor psychotherapy* in the context and service of holistic medicine. His approach to therapy has been elaborated in what is now called *Adlerian brief therapy* (ABT) (Bitter, Christensen, Hawes, & Nicoll, 1998).

Phase 1: Establishing the Relationship

The Adlerian counselor works in a collaborative way with clients, and this relationship is based on a sense of deep caring, involvement, and friendship. Therapeutic progress is possible only when there is an alignment of clearly defined goals between therapist and client. The counseling process, to be effective, must deal with the personal issues the client recognizes as significant and is willing to discuss and change.

Many counselors receive information about clients before they meet clients for the first time. This information may have been gathered in an intake or as part of a referral process. It may even be part of earlier agency records related to previous therapy. If this database contains enough useful information, Adlerian counselors start to orient themselves to the client by forming initial hypotheses that will have to be checked, considered, and reconsidered in therapy sessions. Even if initial hypotheses prove incorrect, the act of orienting the therapist's mind toward the client's psychological life is always a useful beginning.

Adlerian counselors seek to make person-to-person contact with clients rather than starting with "the problem." Clients surface their concerns in therapy rather quickly, but the initial focus should be on the person, not the problem. Adlerian counselors train themselves to gather as much information as possible from their five senses in the first few minutes of therapy. How does the person present him- or herself? What can be known from how the client greets the therapist, orients him- or herself, talks about him- or herself and others, and handles the new situation of therapy? Attending and listening to the client involves paying close attention to the messages conveyed by the client's tone of voice, posture, facial expressions, gestures, and even hesitations in speech. A focus on what the counselor is sensing or experiencing often leads to a show of genuine interest and fascination. Such an interest facilitates expression of the client's stories and concerns.

> We often start an interview with "What do you want me to know about you?", rather than "What brought you in?" or "What did you want to talk about today?" Meeting and valuing the person is essential to positive change; the relationship may not be everything that matters, but [it] is *almost* everything that matters. (Bitter et al., 1998, p. 98)

One way to create a working therapeutic relationship is for counselors to help clients become aware of their assets and strengths, rather than dealing continually with their deficits and liabilities. During the initial phase, a positive relationship is created by listening, responding, demonstrating respect for clients' capacity to understand purpose and seek change, and exhibiting faith, hope, and caring. When clients enter therapy, they typically have a diminished sense of self-worth and self-respect. They lack faith in their ability to cope with the tasks of life. Therapists provide support, which is an antidote to despair and discouragement. For some people, therapy may be one of the few times in which they have truly experienced a caring human relationship. Encouragement starts from faith in clients and proceeds toward helping them use all of their personal and external resources (Dinkmeyer & Losoncy, 1980).

Adlerians pay more attention to the subjective experiences of the client than they do to using techniques. They fit their techniques to the needs of each client. During the initial phase of counseling, the main techniques are attending and listening with empathy, following the subjective experience of the client as closely as possible, identifying and clarifying goals, and suggesting initial hunches about purpose in client symptoms, actions, and interactions. Adlerians attempt to grasp both the verbal and nonverbal messages of the client; they want to access the core patterns in the client's life. If the client feels deeply understood and accepted, the client is likely to focus on what he or she wants from therapy and thus establish goals. At this stage the counselor's function is to provide a wide-angle perspective that will eventually help the client view his or her world differently.

Phase 2: Exploring the Individual's Dynamics

The second phase of Adlerian counseling proceeds from two interview forms: the subjective interview and the objective interview (Dreikurs, 1997). In the *subjective interview* the counselor helps the client to tell his or her story as completely as possible. This process is facilitated by a generous use of empathic listening and responding. Active listening, however, is not enough. The subjective interview must follow from a sense of wonder, fascination, and interest. What the client says will spark an interest in the counselor and lead, naturally, to the next most significant question or inquiry about the client and his or her life story. Indeed, the best subjective interviews treat clients as experts in their own lives, allowing clients to feel completely heard. Throughout the subjective interview, the Adlerian counselor is listening for clues to the purposive aspects of the client's coping and approaches to life. "The subjective interview should extract patterns in the person's life, develop hypotheses about what works for the person, and determine what accounts for the various concerns in the client's life" (Bitter et al., 1998, p. 98).

An initial assessment of the purpose symptoms, actions, or difficulties have in a person's life can be gained from what Dreikurs (1997) calls "The Question." Adlerians often end a subjective interview with this question: "How would your life be different, and what would you do differently, if you did not have this symptom or problem?" Adlerians use this question to help with differential diagnosis. If nothing would be different, especially with physical symptoms, Adlerians suspect that the problem may be organic and require medical intervention. More often the symptoms or problems experienced by the client help the client avoid something that is perceived as necessary but from which the person wishes to retreat, usually a life task: "If it weren't for this depression, I would get out more and see my friends." Such a statement betrays the client's concern about the possibility of being a good friend or being welcomed by his or her friends. "I need to get married, but how can I with these panic attacks?" indicates the person's worry about being a partner in a marriage.

The *objective interview* seeks to discover information about (a) how problems in the client's life began; (b) any precipitating events; (c) a medical history, including current and past medications; (d) a social history; (e) the reasons the client chose therapy at this time; (f) the person's coping with life tasks; and (g) a lifestyle assessment. Mozdzierz and his colleagues (1984) describe the counselor as a "lifestyle investigator" during this phase of therapy. Based on interview approaches developed by Adler and Dreikurs, the lifestyle assessment starts with an investigation of the person's family constellation and early childhood history (Powers & Griffith, 1987; Shulman & Mosak, 1988). Counselors also interpret the person's early memories, seeking to understand the whole person as he or she grew up in a social setting. They operate on the assumption that it is the interpretations people develop about themselves, others, the world, and life that govern what they do. Lifestyle assessment seeks to develop a holistic narrative of the person's life, to make sense of the way the person copes with life tasks, and to uncover the private interpretations and logic involved in that coping. For example, if Jenny has lived most of her life in a critical environment, and now she believes she must be perfect to avoid even the appearance of failure, the assessment process will highlight the restricted living that follows from this perspective.

THE FAMILY CONSTELLATION   Adlerian assessment relies heavily on an exploration of the client's family constellation or family system, including the client's evaluation of conditions that prevailed in the family when the person was a young child (family atmosphere), birth order, parental relationship and family values, and extended family and culture. Some of these questions are almost always explored:

- Who was the favorite child?
- What was your father's relationship with the children? Your mother's?
- Which child was most like the father? The mother? In what respects?
- Who among the siblings was most different from you? In what ways?
- Who among the siblings was most like you? In what ways?
- What were you like as a child?
- How did your parents get along? In what did they both agree? How did they handle disagreements? How did they discipline the children?

An investigation of family constellation is far more comprehensive than these few questions, but these questions give an idea of the type of information the counselor is seeking. The questions are always tailored to the individual client with the goal of eliciting the client's perceptions of self and others, of development, and of the experiences that have affected that development.

EARLY RECOLLECTIONS   Another assessment procedure used by Adlerians is to ask the client to provide his or her earliest memories, including the age of the person at the time of the remembered events and the feelings or reactions associated with the recollections. Early recollections are one-time occurrences pictured by the client in clear detail. Adler reasoned that out of the millions of early memories we might have we select those special memories that project the essential convictions and even the basic mistakes of our lives.

To tap such recollections, the counselor might proceed as follows: "I would like to hear about your early memories. Think back to when you were very young, as early as you can remember, and *tell me something that happened one time.*" After receiving each memory, the counselor might also ask: "What part stands out to you? If you played the whole memory like a movie and stopped it at one frame, what would be happening? Putting yourself in that moment, what are you feeling? What's your reaction?" Three memories are usually considered a minimum to assess a pattern, and some counselors ask for as many as a dozen memories.

Adlerian therapists use early recollections for many different purposes. These include (a) assessment of the person's convictions about self, others, life, and ethics; (b) assessment of the client's stance in relation to the counseling session and the counseling relationship; (c) verification of coping patterns; and (d) assessment of individual strengths, assets, and interfering ideas (Bitter et al., 1998, p. 99).

In interpreting these early recollections, Adlerians may consider questions such as these:

- What part does the person take in the memory? Is the person an observer or a participant?
- Who else is in the memory? What position do others take in relation to the person?
- What are the dominant themes and overall patterns of the memories?
- What feelings are expressed in the memories?
- Why does the person choose to remember this event? What is the person trying to convey?

PERSONALITY PRIORITIES   For the last two decades, an assessment of personality priorities has become an important road to understanding interactional coping. An Adlerian psychologist from Israel, Nira Kefir (1981), originally designated four priorities: superiority (or significance), control, comfort, and pleasing. Personality priorities are similar to what Adler called safeguarding tendencies. Unless challenged, people rely on a number-one priority, a first line of defense that they use as an immediate response to perceived stress or difficulty. Each priority involves a dominant behavior pattern with supporting convictions that an individual uses to cope. Priorities become pathways for relating to others and for attaining a sense of significance. Kefir describes four behavioral patterns that reflect these priorities:

1. People using *superiority* (significance) strive for significance through leadership or accomplishment or through any other avenue to make them feel superior. They seek to avoid meaninglessness in life but often complain of being overworked or overburdened.
2. People who *control* look for guarantees against ridicule. They feel a need for complete mastery of situations so that they will not be humiliated. They do not want to behave in a socially unsuccessful way, and they are willing to pay the price of social distance to achieve this safety.
3. People seeking *comfort* want to avoid stress or pain at all costs. They tend to delay dealing with problems and making decisions, and they do their best to avoid anything that implies stress or pain. The price they pay is low productivity.
4. People who aim to *please* want to avoid rejection by seeking constant approval and acceptance. Out of their fear of not being liked, they go to great lengths to win approval.

It is not the therapist's job to work toward changing a client's main priority. Instead, the goal is to enable the client to recognize the feelings he or she evokes in others and the price the client pays for clinging to a number-one priority. Kefir (1981) asserts that to increase our self-awareness we must learn what our priority, or condition for feeling significant, is. We also need to find alternative ways to gain significance by using a wider range of behaviors. (See Kefir, 1981, pp. 403–407, for further discussion of working with priorities in counseling.)

INTEGRATION AND SUMMARY   Once material has been gathered from both subjective and objective interviews with the client, integrated summaries of the data are developed. Different summaries are prepared for different clients, but common ones are a narrative summary of the person's subjective experience and life story; a summary of family constellation and developmental data; a summary of early recollections, personal strengths or assets, and interfering ideas; and a summary of coping strategies. The summaries are presented to the client and discussed in the session, with the client and the counselor together refining specific points. Dinkmeyer, Dinkmeyer, and Sperry (1987) suggest that it is useful for the counselor to have the client read the summaries aloud. In this way the client has the chance to discuss specific topics and to raise questions. Also, the counselor can learn much about the client from hearing the client read and observing his or her nonverbal reactions.

Mosak (1995) includes an analysis of common basic mistakes. He believes lifestyle can be conceived of as a personal mythology. People behave *as if* the myths were true because, for them, they *are true.* Mosak lists five basic mistakes:

1. *Overgeneralizations:* "There is no fairness in the world."
2. *False or impossible goals:* "I must please everyone if I am to feel loved."
3. *Misperceptions of life and life's demands:* "Life is so very difficult for me."
4. *Denial of one's basic worth:* "I'm basically stupid, so why would anyone want anything to do with me?"
5. *Faulty values:* "I must get to the top, regardless of who gets hurt in the process."

As another example of a summary of basic mistakes, consider this list of mistaken notions that are evident in Stan's autobiography (see Chapter 1):

- "Don't get close to people, especially women, because they will suffocate and control you if they can." (overgeneralization)
- "I was not really wanted by my parents, and therefore it is best for me to become invisible." (denial of one's basic worth)
- "It is extremely important that people like me and approve of me; I'll bend over backwards to do what people expect." (false or impossible goals)

To get a clearer idea of the assessment procedures Adlerians typically use, consult *Understanding Lifestyle: The Psycho-Clarity Process* (Powers &

Griffith, 1987), which contains a detailed presentation of an initial interview, guidelines for lifestyle assessment, suggestions for making summaries, and notes for the course of therapy. This book delineates an assessment process that is probably fairly close to the process Alfred Adler originally used. *IPCW: The Individual Psychology Client Workbook With Supplements* (Powers & Griffith, 1995) contains a detailed and comprehensive initial interview protocol and an excellent form for a lifestyle assessment. Also the *Manual for Life Style Assessment* (Shulman & Mosak, 1988) presents a comprehensive guide for the initial interview and for establishing the lifestyle. This book contains the approach that has come to be known (among Adlerians) as the "Chicago method." The student manual that accompanies this textbook gives a concrete example of the lifestyle assessment as it is applied to the case of Stan. In *Case Approach to Counseling and Psychotherapy* (Corey, 2001), Jim Bitter presents a detailed lifestyle assessment of another hypothetical client, Ruth, based on the form by Powers and Griffith (1995). Consulting these references will help you get a concrete grasp of how Adlerian concepts come to life in practice.

Phase 3: Encouraging Self-Understanding and Insight

Adlerians believe almost everything in human life has a purpose. Self-understanding is only possible when hidden purposes and goals of behavior are made conscious. When Adlerians speak of insight, they are referring to an understanding of the motivations that operate in a client's life.

Disclosure and well-timed interpretations are techniques that facilitate the process of gaining insight. They are focused on here-and-now behavior and on the expectations and anticipations that arise from one's intentions. Adlerian disclosures and interpretations are concerned with creating awareness of one's direction in life, one's goals and purposes, one's private logic and how it works, and one's current behavior.

In practice, goal disclosure tends to be continuous throughout therapy. It can happen within minutes of the start of the first meeting or at any time during the process. It is used for a multitude of purposes, among them (a) making unconscious processes conscious; (b) confronting "resistance," so that client and therapist goals can align; and (c) exploring the purposes of symptoms, feelings, behaviors, and human difficulties or blocks. Because human behavior is social behavior, assessing the *social* (interactive) *results* of an individual's actions is the easiest way to discover goals and purposes and to formulate a hypothesis for interpretation.

Adlerian interpretations are suggestions presented tentatively in the form of open-ended sharings that can be explored in the sessions. They are hunches or guesses, and they are often stated thusly: "It seems to me that . . . ," "Could it be that . . . ," or "This is how it appears to me . . ." Because interpretations are presented in this manner, clients are not led to defend themselves, and they feel free to discuss and even argue with the counselor's hunches and impressions. Through this process, clients eventually come to understand their motivations, the ways in which they are now contributing to the maintenance of the problem, and what they can do to correct the situation.

Powers and Griffith (1987) maintain that learning how to make interpretations is more a matter of virtue than of technique. It is important that practitioners have the courage to extend themselves in empathic and intuitive guessing. As practitioners gain increased confidence in what they have to offer, they become increasingly capable of empathy and develop more courage to make guesses. They add that it is crucial for counselors to have the humility to acknowledge wrong guesses when they are corrected or when interpretations are rejected by their clients.

Phase 4: Helping With Reorientation

The final stage of the therapeutic process is the action-oriented phase known as reorientation and reeducation: putting insights into practice. This phase focuses on helping people discover new and more functional alternatives. Clients are both encouraged and challenged to develop the courage to take risks and make changes in their lives.

In some cases significant changes are needed if clients are to overcome discouragement and find a place for themselves in this life. More often, however, people merely need to be reoriented toward the useful side of life. The useful side involves a sense of belonging and being valued, having an interest in others and their welfare, courage, the acceptance of imperfection, confidence, a sense of humor, a willingness to contribute, and an outgoing friendliness. The useless side of life is characterized by self-absorption, withdrawal from life tasks, self-protection, or acts against one's fellow human beings. People on the useless side of life become less functional and are more susceptible to psychopathology. Adlerian counseling stands in opposition to self-depreciation, isolation, and retreat, and it seeks to help clients gain courage and to connect to strengths within themselves, to others, and to life. Throughout this phase, no intervention is more important than encouragement.

THE ENCOURAGEMENT PROCESS   Encouragement is the most distinctive Adlerian procedure, and it is central to all phases of counseling and therapy. It is especially important as people consider change in their lives. Encouragement literally means "to build courage" (Bitter et al., 1998). Courage develops when people become aware of their strengths, when they feel they belong and are not alone, and when they have a sense of hope and can see new possibilities for themselves and their daily living. Adlerians seize every opportunity the client provides to introduce and reinforce encouragement (Powers & Griffith, 1987). Because clients often do not recognize or accept their positive qualities, strengths, or internal resources, one of the counselor's tasks is to help them do so.

Adlerians believe discouragement is the basic condition that prevents people from functioning, and they see encouragement as the antidote. Encouragement takes many forms, depending on the phase of the counseling process. In the relationship phase, encouragement results from the mutual respect the counselor seeks to engender. In the assessment phase, which is partially designed to illuminate personal strengths, clients are encouraged to recognize that they are in charge of their own lives and can make different choices based on new understandings. Even disclosure is encouraging, because it helps to make sense out of what has previously been unknown or unclear. During reorientation, encouragement comes when new possibilities are generated and when people are acknowledged and affirmed for taking positive steps to change their lives for the better. Indeed, counseling often becomes one of the few places where a celebration of personal growth is seen as essential to positive change.

CHANGE AND THE SEARCH FOR NEW POSSIBILITIES   During the reorientation phase of counseling, clients make decisions and modify their goals. They are encouraged to act *as if* they were the people they want to be, which can serve to challenge self-limiting assumptions. Clients are asked to catch themselves in the process of repeating old patterns that have led to ineffective behavior. Commitment is an essential part of reorientation. If clients hope to change, they must be willing to set tasks for themselves and do something specific about their problems. In this way, clients translate their new insights into concrete actions.

This action-oriented phase is a time for solving problems and making decisions. The counselor and the client consider possible alternatives and their consequences, evaluate how these alternatives will meet the client's goals, and decide on a specific course of action. The best alternatives and new possibilities are those generated by the client, and the counselor must offer the client a great deal of support and encouragement during this stage of the process.

MAKING A DIFFERENCE   Adlerian counselors seek to make a difference in the lives of their clients. That difference may be manifested by a change in behavior or attitude or perception. Adlerians use many different techniques to promote change, some of which have become common interventions in other therapeutic models. Techniques that go by the names of immediacy, advice, humor, silence, paradoxical intention, acting as if, spitting in the client's soup, catching oneself, the push-button technique, externalization, re-authoring, avoiding the traps, confrontation, use of stories and fables, early recollection analysis, task setting and commitment, giving homework, and terminating and summarizing have all been used (Carlson & Slavik, 1997; Dinkmeyer, Dinkmeyer, & Sperry, 1987; Disque & Bitter, 1998; Manaster & Corsini 1982; Mosak, 1995). Indeed, some Adlerians have recently attempted to associate specific techniques to given problems and concerns

(Mosak & Maniacci, 1998; Sperry & Carlson, 1996). Adlerians are pragmatic when it comes to using techniques that are appropriate for a given
client. In general, however, Adlerian counselors still focus on motivation
modification more than behavior change and encourage clients to make
holistic changes on the useful side of living. All counseling is a cooperative
effort, and making a difference depends on the counselor's ability to win the
client's cooperation.

Areas of Application

Because Individual Psychology is based on a growth model, not a medical model, it is applicable to such varied spheres of life as child guidance,
parent/child counseling, marital counseling, family therapy, group counseling,
individual counseling with children, adolescents, and adults, cultural conflicts, correctional and rehabilitation counseling, and mental health institutions. Its principles have been widely applied to substance abuse programs,
social problems to combat poverty and crime, problems of the aged, school
systems, religion, and business.

APPLICATION TO EDUCATION   Adler had a keen interest in applying his
ideas to education, especially in finding ways to remedy faulty lifestyles of
school children. He initiated a process to work with students in groups and
to educate parents and teachers. By providing teachers with ways to prevent and correct basic mistakes of children, he sought to promote social interest and mental health. Besides Adler, the main proponent of Individual
Psychology as a foundation for the teaching/learning process was Dreikurs
(1968, 1971). Major teacher education models are based on Adlerian/Drei-
kursian principles (see Albert, 1996).

APPLICATION TO PARENT EDUCATION   Parent education to improve the
relationship between parent and child by promoting greater understanding
and acceptance has been a major Adlerian contribution. Parents are taught
simple Adlerian principles of behavior that can be applied in the home. Initial topics include understanding the purpose of a child's misbehavior, learning to listen, helping children accept the consequences of their behavior,
applying emotion coaching, holding family meetings, and using encouragement. The book considered to be the mainstay of many Adlerian parent-
study groups is *Children: The Challenge,* by Dreikurs and Soltz (1964).
Other books that present Adlerian parent education materials are *STEP:
The Parent Handbook* (Dinkmeyer, McKay, Dinkmeyer, & McKay, 1987) and
Active Parenting Today (Popkin, 1993).

APPLICATION TO MARRIAGE COUNSELING   Adlerian marital therapy is
designed to assess a couple's beliefs and behaviors while educating them in
more effective ways of meeting their goals. Clair Hawes has developed an
approach to couples counseling within the Adlerian brief therapy model. In

addition to addressing the compatibility of lifestyles, Hawes looks at the early recollections of the marriage and each partner's relationship to a broad set of life tasks, including occupation, social relationships, intimate relationships, kinkeeping, spirituality, self-care, and self-worth (Bitter et al., 1998; Hawes, 1993; Hawes & Blanchard, 1993).

The full range of techniques applicable to other forms of counseling can be used in working with couples. In marriage counseling and marriage education, couples are taught specific techniques that enhance communication and cooperation. Some of these techniques are listening, paraphrasing, giving feedback, having marriage conferences, listing expectations, doing homework, and enacting problem solving.

Adlerians will sometimes see married people as a couple, sometimes individually, and then alternately as a couple and as individuals. Rather than looking for who is at fault in the relationship, the therapist considers the lifestyles of the partners and the interaction of the two lifestyles. Emphasis is given to helping them decide if they want to maintain their marriage and, if so, what changes they are willing to make.

APPLICATION TO FAMILY COUNSELING   With its emphasis on the family constellation, holism, and the freedom of the therapist to improvise, Adler's approach contributed to the foundation of the family therapy perspective. Adlerians working with families focus on the family atmosphere, the family constellation, and the interactive goals of each member. The family atmosphere is the climate characterizing the relationship between the parents and their attitudes toward life, sex roles, decision making, competition, cooperation, dealing with conflict, responsibility, and so forth. This atmosphere, including the role models the parents provide, influences the children as they grow up. The therapeutic process seeks to increase awareness of the interaction of the individuals within the family system. Those who practice Adlerian family therapy strive to understand the goals, beliefs, and behaviors of each family member and the family as an entity in its own right. The Adlerian approach to family counseling is dealt with in more detail in Chapter 13.

APPLICATION TO GROUP WORK   Adler and his coworkers used a group approach in their child guidance centers in Vienna as early as 1921 (Dreikurs, 1969). Dreikurs, a colleague, extended and popularized Adler's work with groups and used group psychotherapy in his private practice for over 40 years. Although he introduced group therapy into his psychiatric practice as a way to save time, he quickly discovered some unique characteristics of groups that made them an effective way of helping people change. Dreikurs' (1969) rationale for groups is as follows: "Since man's [sic] problems and conflicts are recognized in their social nature, the group is ideally suited not only to highlight and reveal the nature of a person's conflicts and maladjustments but to offer corrective influences" (p. 43). Inferiority feelings can be challenged and counteracted effectively in groups, and the mistaken concepts and values that are at the root of social and emotional problems can be deeply influenced because the group is a value-forming agent (Sonstegard, 1998a).

The group provides the social context in which members can develop a sense of belonging and a sense of community. Sonstegard (1998b) writes that group participants come to see that many of their problems are interpersonal in nature, that their behavior has social meaning, and that their goals can best be understood in the framework of social purposes.

 # ADLERIAN THERAPY APPLIED TO THE CASE OF STAN

The basic aims of an Adlerian therapist working with Stan are fourfold and correspond to the four stages of counseling: (1) establishing and maintaining a good working relationship with Stan, (2) exploring Stan's dynamics, (3) encouraging Stan to develop insight and understanding, and (4) helping Stan see new alternatives and make new choices.

To develop mutual trust and respect, the therapist pays close attention to Stan's subjective experience and attempts to get a sense of how he has reacted to the turning points in his life. During the initial session, Stan reacts to his counselor as the expert who has the answers. Stan is convinced he has made a mess of his life and that when he attempts to make decisions he generally ends up regretting the results. Thus, Stan approaches his counselor out of desperation and almost pleads for a prescription for coping with his problems. Because his counselor views counseling as a relationship between equals, she initially focuses on his feeling of being unequal to most other people. A good place to begin is exploring his feelings of inferiority, which he says he feels in most situations. The goals of counseling are developed mutually, and the counselor avoids deciding for Stan what his goals should be. She also resists giving Stan the simple formula he is requesting.

Stan's counselor prepares a lifestyle assessment based on a questionnaire that taps information about Stan's early years, especially his experiences in his family. (See the student manual for this text for a complete description of this lifestyle assessment form as it is applied to Stan.) This assessment includes a determination of whether he poses a danger to himself because Stan did mention suicidal inclinations. During this assessment phase, which might take a few sessions, the Adlerian counselor explores Stan's social relationships, his relationships with members of his family, his work responsibilities, his role as a man, and his feelings about himself. She places considerable emphasis on Stan's goals in life and his priorities. She does not pay a great deal of attention to his past, except to show him the consistency between his past and present as he is moving toward the future.

Adlerian therapists assume that they can learn a great deal about the individual's dynamics from early recollections. Because Stan's counselor places value on exploring early recollections as a source of understanding his goals, motivations, and values, she asks Stan to report his earliest memories. He replies as follows:

I was about 6, I went to school, and I was scared of the other kids and the teacher. When I came home, I cried and told my mother I didn't want to go back to school. She yelled at me and called me a baby. After that I felt horrible and even more scared.

Another of Stan's early recollections was at age 8:

My family was visiting my grandparents. I was playing outside, and some neighborhood kid hit me for no reason. We got in a big fight, and my mother came out and scolded me for being such a rough kid. She wouldn't believe me when I told her he had started the fight. I felt angry and hurt that she didn't believe me.

Based on these early recollections, Stan's counselor suggests that Stan sees life as frightening and unpredictably hostile and that he feels he cannot count on women; they are likely to be harsh, unbelieving, and uncaring.

Stan talks about his priorities during several therapy sessions. Initially he tentatively identifies one of his priorities as *superiority*. He tends to overstress the value of being competent, of accomplishing one feat after another, of winning, of being right at all costs, and of moving ahead in most situations. He tends to weigh himself down with the responsibility of constantly trying to prove himself, and he experiences a high level of stress in working so hard at being competent. Of course, his striving for superiority grows out of the pervasive feelings of inferiority that he has experienced for most of his life.

Eventually, Stan pinpoints *control* as his number-one priority. He often encounters situations that embarrass or humiliate him. He believes that if he can control his world he can also control his painful feelings. Some of the methods Stan uses to gain control over these feelings are escaping through alcohol, avoiding interpersonal situations that are threatening to him, keeping to himself, and deciding that he can't really count on others for psychological support. Stan begins to realize that although his style of seeking control apparently reduces his anxiety he is paying a steep price for his behavior. The feelings he evokes in others are frustration

and a lack of interest; for himself, the price he pays is distance from others and diminished spontaneity and creativity.

Having gathered the data based on the lifestyle assessment about his family constellation, his early recollections, and his priorities, the therapist assists Stan in the process of summarizing and interpreting this information. Particular attention is given by the therapist to identifying basic mistakes, which are faulty conclusions about life and self-defeating perceptions. Some of the mistaken conclusions Stan has reached are:

- "I must not get close to people, because they will surely hurt me."
- "Because my own parents didn't want me and didn't love me, I'll never be desired or loved by anybody."
- "If only I could become perfect, maybe people would acknowledge and accept me."
- "Being a man means not showing emotions."

The information the counselor summarizes and interprets leads to insight and increased self-understanding on Stan's part. He becomes more aware of how he is functioning. He learns that he is not "sick" and in need of being "cured"; rather, he is discouraged and needs to be encouraged to reorient his life. Through continued emphasis on his beliefs, goals, and intentions, Stan comes to see how his private logic is inaccurate. In his case, a syllogism for his style of life can be explained in this way: (1) "I am unloved, insignificant, and do not count;" (2) "the world is a threatening place to be, and life is unfair;" (3) "therefore, I must find ways to protect myself and keep safe." During this phase of the process, Stan's counselor makes interpretations centering on his lifestyle, his current direction, his goals and purposes, and how his private logic works. Of course,

Stan is expected to carry out homework assignments that assist him in translating his insights into new behavior. In this way he is an active participant in his therapy.

In the reorientation phase of therapy, Stan and his counselor work together to consider alternative attitudes, beliefs, and actions. By now Stan sees that he does not have to be locked into past patterns, feels encouraged, and realizes that he does have the power to change his life. He accepts that he will not change merely by gaining insights and knows that he will have to make use of these insights by carrying out an action-oriented plan. Stan begins to feel that he can create a new life for himself and not remain the victim of circumstances.

Follow-Up: You Continue as Stan's Adlerian Therapist

Use these questions to help you think about how you would counsel Stan:

- What are some ways you would attempt to establish a relationship with Stan based on trust and mutual respect? Can you imagine any difficulties you might have in developing this relationship?
- What aspects of Stan's lifestyle particularly interest you? In counseling him, how might these be explored?
- The Adlerian therapist identified four of Stan's mistaken conclusions. Can you identify with any of these basic mistakes? If so, do you think this would help or hinder your therapeutic effectiveness with him?
- Working from an Adlerian perspective, how might you assist Stan in discovering his social interest and going beyond a preoccupation with his own problems?
- What strengths and resources in Stan might you draw on to support his determination and commitment to change? ■

SUMMARY AND EVALUATION

Summary

Adler was far ahead of his time, and most contemporary therapies have incorporated at least some of his ideas. Individual Psychology assumes that people are motivated by social factors; are responsible for their own thoughts, feelings, and actions; are the creators of their own lives, as opposed to being helpless victims; and are impelled by purposes and goals, looking more toward the future than to the past.

The basic goal of the Adlerian approach is to help clients identify and change their mistaken beliefs about, self, others, and life and thus participate more fully in a social world. Clients are not viewed as mentally sick but as discouraged. The therapeutic process helps clients become aware of their patterns and make some basic changes in their style of living, which lead to changes in the way they feel and behave. The role of the family in the development of the individual is emphasized. Therapy is a cooperative venture, sometimes structured by a contract, and geared toward challenging clients to translate their insights into action in the real world.

Adlerian therapists are resourceful in drawing on many methods. The Adlerian viewpoint is applicable to a wide range of human relations, including but not limited to individual and group counseling, marital and family therapy, and the alleviation of social problems.

Contributions of the Adlerian Approach

The Adlerian approach gives practitioners a great deal of freedom in working with clients. Adlerian counselors are not bound to follow a specific procedure. Instead, they use their clinical judgment in applying a wide range of techniques that they think will work best for a particular client.

The Adlerian concepts I draw on most in my work with clients are (1) the importance of looking to one's life goals, including assessing how these goals influence an individual; (2) the focus on the individual's interpretation of early experiences in the family, with special emphasis on their current impact; (3) the clinical use of early recollections; (4) the need to understand and confront basic mistakes; (5) the cognitive emphasis, which holds that emotions and behaviors are largely influenced by one's beliefs and thinking processes; (6) the idea of working out an action plan designed to help clients make changes; (7) the collaborative relationship, whereby the client and therapist work toward mutually agreed-on goals; and (8) the emphasis given to encouragement during the entire counseling process. Several Adlerian concepts have implications for personal development. One of these notions that has helped me to understand the direction of my life is the assumption that feelings of inferiority are linked to a striving for superiority (Corey, as cited in Nystul, 1999a).

The Adlerian approach to social factors in personality lends itself exceptionally well to working with individuals in groups. Major Adlerian contributions have been made in the following areas: elementary education, consultation groups with teachers, parent education groups, marriage counseling, family counseling, and group counseling. A strength of the Adlerian approach is that it is based on technical eclecticism; that is, a variety of cognitive, behavioral, and experiential techniques are used. This lends itself to versatility in meeting the needs of a diverse range of clients (Watts, 1999).

It is difficult to overestimate the contributions of Adler to contemporary therapeutic practice. Many of his ideas were revolutionary and far ahead of his time. His influence went beyond counseling individuals, extending into the community mental health movement (Ansbacher, 1974). Abraham Maslow, Viktor Frankl, Rollo May, and Albert Ellis have all acknowledged their debt to Adler. Both Frankl and May see him as a forerunner of the existential movement because of his position that human beings are free to choose and are entirely responsible for what they make of themselves. This view makes him also a forerunner of the subjective approach to psychology, which focuses on the internal determinants of behavior: values, beliefs, attitudes, goals, interests, personal meanings, subjective perceptions of reality, and strivings toward self-realization.

In my opinion, one of Adler's most important contributions is his influence on other therapy systems. Many of his basic ideas have found their way into other psychological schools, such as family systems approaches, Gestalt therapy, learning theory, reality therapy, rational emotive behavior therapy, cognitive therapy, person-centered therapy, and existentialism (Corey, 1999). All these approaches are based on a similar concept of the person as purposive and self-determining and as always striving for growth, value, and meaning in this world (Terner & Pew, 1978). In several important respects, Adler seems to have paved the way for current developments in the cognitive therapies. Adlerians' basic premise is that if clients can change their thinking then they can change their feelings and behavior. A study of contemporary counseling theories reveals that many of Adler's notions have reappeared in these modern approaches with different nomenclature, and often without giving Adler the credit that is due to him (Watts, 1999).

Contemporary Adlerian theory is an integrative approach, combining cognitive, psychodynamic, and systems perspectives. In many respects it resembles contemporary social constructionist theories, or constructive therapies. Some of these common characteristics include an emphasis on establishing a respectful client/therapist relationship, an emphasis on clients' strengths and resources, and an optimistic and future orientation (Watts, 1999; Watts & Carlson, 1999).

Limitations and Criticisms of the Adlerian Approach

Adler had to choose between devoting his time to formalizing his theory and teaching others the basic concepts of Individual Psychology. He placed practicing and teaching before organizing and presenting a well-defined and systematic theory. Thus, his written presentations are often difficult to follow, many of them coming from transcripts of lectures he gave. Initially, many people considered his ideas somewhat loose and too simplistic.

Although writing and research on Adlerian theory has improved over the last 20 years, a large part of the theory still requires empirical testing and comparative analysis. This is especially true in the conceptual areas that Adlerians accept as axiomatic: for example, the development of lifestyle; the unity of the personality and an acceptance of a singular view of self; the rejection of the prominence of heredity in determining behavior, especially pathological behavior; and the usefulness of the multiple interventions used by various Adlerians.

 # ADLERIAN THERAPY FROM A MULTICULTURAL PERSPECTIVE

Contributions to Multicultural Counseling

Although the Adlerian approach is called Individual Psychology, its focus is on the person in a social context. Adlerians' interest in helping others, in social interest, in belonging, and in the collective spirit fits well with the value systems of many ethnic groups. Cultures that stress the welfare of the social group and emphasize the role of the family will find the Adlerian focus on social interest to be congruent with their values. According to Mozdzierz and his colleagues (1984), Adlerians operate on the assumption that people are basically social, goal-seeking decision makers who live at their best when they cooperate, contribute to the common good, and face the demands of life. Therapists aim at increasing the individual's social interest and helping him or her contribute within an interpersonal framework.

Native American clients, for example, tend to value cooperation over competition. One such client told a story about a group of boys who were in a race. When one boy got ahead of the others, he would slow down and allow the others to catch up, and they all made it to the finish line at the same time. Although the coach tried to explain that the point of the race was for an individual to finish first, these boys were socialized to work together cooperatively as a group. Adlerian therapy is easily adaptable to cultural values that emphasize community.

Clients who enter therapy are often locked into rigid ways of perceiving, interpreting, and behaving. It is likely that they have not questioned how their culture has influenced them. Thus, they may feel resigned to "the way things are." Mozdzierz and his colleagues (1984) characterize these clients as myopic and contend that one of the therapist's functions is to provide them with another pair of glasses that will allow them to see things more clearly. The Adlerian emphasis on the subjective fashion in which people view and interpret their world leads to a respect for clients' unique values and perceptions. Adlerian counselors use interpretations as an opportunity for clients to view things from a different perspective, yet it is up to the clients to decide whether to open their eyes and use these glasses. Adlerians do not decide for clients what they should change or what their goals should be; rather, they work collaboratively with their clients in ways that enable them to reach their self-defined goals.

Not only is Adlerian theory congruent with the values of many cultural groups, but the approach offers flexibility in applying a range of cognitive and action-oriented techniques to helping clients explore their practical problems. Adlerian practitioners are not wedded to any particular set of procedures. Instead, they are conscious of the value of fitting their techniques to the needs of their clients. Although they utilize a diverse range of methods, most of them do conduct an assessment of each client's lifestyle. This assessment is heavily focused on the structure and dynamics within the client's family. Because of their cultural background, many clients have been conditioned to respect their family heritage and to appreciate the impact of their family on their own personal development. It is essential that counselors be sensitive to the conflicting feelings and struggles of their clients. If counselors demonstrate an understanding of these cultural values, it is likely that these clients will be receptive to an exploration of their lifestyle. Such an exploration will involve a detailed discussion of their own place within their family.

If "culture" is defined as a broad concept (to include age, roles, lifestyle, and gender differences), there can be cultural differences even within a family. The Adlerian approach emphasizes the value of subjectively understanding the unique world of an individual. Culture is one significant dimension for grasping the subjective and experiential perspective of an individual. Pedersen (1990) expresses this idea well:

> Culture provides a metaphor to better understand the different perspectives within each of us as our different social roles compete, complement, and cooperate with one another in our decisions. It also provides an alternative for better understanding others whose culturally learned assumptions are different from our own. (p. 94)

Adler introduced notions with implications toward multiculturalism that have as much or more relevance today as they did during Adler's time (Pedersen, as cited in Nystul, 1999b). Some of these ideas include (1) the importance of the cultural context, (2) the emphasis on health as opposed to pathology, (3) a holistic perspective on life, (4) the value of understanding individuals in terms of their core goals and purposes, (5) the ability to exercise freedom within the context of societal constraints, and (6) the focus on prevention and the development of a proactive approach in dealing with problems. Adler's holistic perspective is an articulate expression of what Pedersen calls a "culture-centered" or multicultural approach to counseling.

Adlerians view a client's cultural heritage in the same way that they address birth order. Indeed, both birth order and culture are vantage points, contexts from which one views self, others, and life. Vantage points can be generally described, but they are not the same for all individuals. Culture influences each person, but it is expressed within each individual differently, according to the perception, evaluation, and interpretation of culture that the person holds.

Adlerian counselors seek to be sensitive to cultural and gender issues. Adler was one of the first psychologists at the turn of the century to advocate equality for women. He recognized that men and women were different in many ways, but he felt that the two genders were deserving of equal value and respect. This respect and appreciation for difference extends to culture as well as gender. Adlerians find in different cultures opportunities for viewing the self, others, and the world in multidimensional ways. Indeed, the strengths of one culture can often help correct the mistakes in another culture.

Limitations for Multicultural Counseling

As is true of most Western models, the Adlerian approach tends to focus on the self as the locus of change and responsibility. Because other cultures have different conceptions, this primary emphasis on changing the autonomous self may be problematic for many clients.

Another limitation of Adlerian therapy involves its detailed explorations of one's early childhood, early memories, and dynamics within the family. Many clients who have pressing problems are likely to resent intrusions into areas of their lives that they may not see as connected to the struggles that bring them into therapy. In addition, revealing family information may be considered inappropriate by members of some cultures.

Finally, although therapists have expertise in the problems of living, they are not experts in solving other people's problems. Instead, they view it as their function to teach people alternative methods of coping with life concerns. However, the culture of some clients may contribute to their viewing the counselor as the "expert" and expecting that the counselor will provide them with solutions to their problems.

 WHERE TO GO FROM HERE

If you find that your thinking is allied with the Adlerian approach, you might consider seeking training in Individual Psychology or becoming a member of the North American Society of Adlerian Psychology (NASAP). After attending the 1998 NASAP convention and meeting many of the attendees, I was motivated to become a member. This annual convention provides a good introduction to the current applications of Adlerian principles for many of the helping professions. To obtain information on NASAP and a list of Adlerian organizations and institutes, contact:

> *North American Society of Adlerian Psychology (NASAP)*
> 65 East Wacker Place, Suite 1710
> Chicago, IL 60601-7298
> Telephone: (312) 629-8801
> Fax: (312) 629-8859
> E-mail: *nasap@msn.com*
> Website: *www.alfredadler.org*

The society publishes a newsletter and a quarterly journal and maintains a list of institutes, training programs, and workshops in Adlerian psychology. *The Journal of Individual Psychology* presents current scholarly and professional research. Columns on counseling, education, and parent and family education are regular features. Information about subscriptions is available by contacting the society.

If you are interested in pursuing training, postgraduate study, continuing education, or a degree, contact NASAP for a list of 58 Adlerian organizations and institutes. A few of these training institutes, some of which grant degrees, are listed here:

> *Adler School of Professional Psychology*
> 65 East Wacker Place, Suite 2100
> Chicago, IL 60601-7298
> Telephone: (312) 201-5900
> Fax: (312) 201-5917
> E-mail: *information@adler.edu*
> Website: *www.adler.edu*

Satellites of the Adler School of Professional Psychology are:

> *Adlerian Graduate School of Ontario, Inc.*
> 48 St. Clair Ave. West, Suite 1000
> Toronto, Ontario, M4V 3B6, Canada
> Telephone: (416) 923-4419

Adlerian Psychology Association of British Columbia
1193 Kingsway, Suite 101
Vancouver, British Columbia V5V 3C9, Canada
Telephone: (604) 874-4614
Fax: (604) 874-4834

Alfred Adler Institute of Fort Wayne
1720 Beacon Street
Fort Wayne, IN 46805
Telephone: (219) 424-6443

Adler-Dreikurs Institute of Human Relations
Room 0313, MLK Building
Bowie State University
Bowie, MD 20715
Telephone: (301) 464-7715
Website: *www.bowiestate.edu/academics/profess/adi/index.html*

Alfred Adler Institute of Minnesota
1001 Highway 7, Suite 344
Hopkins, MN 55305
Telephone: (612) 988-4170
Fax: (612) 988-4171
E-mail: *Admin@AlfredAdler.edu*

Adlerian Training Institute
Dr. Bill Nicoll, Coordinator
P. O. Box 276358
Boca Raton, FL 33427-6358
Telephone: (954) 757-2845

The Alfred Adler Institute of San Francisco
7 Cameo Way
San Francisco, CA 94131
Telephone: (415) 282-1661
E-mail: *HTStein@att.net*
Website: *http://ourworld.compuserv.com/homepages/hstein/*

*The International Committee for Adlerian Summer Schools and
    Institutes (ICASSI)**
Betty Haeussler
9212 Morley Road
Lanham, MD 20706
Fax: (301) 595-0669
E-mail: *PeteHMSU64@aol.com*

---

* ICASSI was founded by Rudolf Dreikurs to promote international awareness and understanding of the teachings of Alfred Adler, his psychological method of treatment, and his
philosophy of life. This Summer Institute offers a wide range of courses (from introductory
to advanced levels) dealing with the teachings of Alfred Adler and Rudolf Dreikurs. Opportunities for personal growth, professional development, special interest sessions, recreation,
and multicultural exchanges are integral parts of the ICASSI program.

Recommended Supplementary Readings

Interventions and Strategies in Counseling and Psychotherapy (Watts & Carlson, 1999) acknowledges the important contributions of Alfred Adler and illustrates the many ways Adlerian ideas have influenced the development of contemporary theories.

Adlerian Counseling: A Practitioner's Approach (4th ed.) (Sweeney, 1998) is the most comprehensive source on Adlerian counseling. It includes Adler's life and work, an explanation of many key Adlerian concepts, and an overview of the counseling process as it is applied to individuals, couples, families, and groups.

Techniques in Adlerian Psychology (Carlson & Slavik, 1997) is an edited volume containing techniques for individual therapy with adults, child counseling, and couples and families counseling. Techniques described include lifestyle assessment, use of birth order, early recollection analysis, questioning and confrontation techniques, use of stories and fables, acting "as if," humor, paradoxical approaches, and the push-button technique.

Understanding Life-Style: The Psycho-Clarity Process (Powers & Griffith, 1987) is one of the best sources of information for doing a lifestyle assessment. This book comes alive with many good clinical examples. Separate chapters deal with interview techniques, lifestyle assessment, early recollections, the family constellation, and methods of summarizing and interpreting information.

References and Suggested Readings*

ADLER, A. (1958). *What life should mean to you.* New York: Capricorn. (Original work published 1931)

ADLER, A. (1964). *Social interest. A challenge to mankind.* New York: Capricorn. (Original work published 1938)

ALBERT, L. (1996). *Cooperative discipline.* Circle Pines, MN: American Guidance Service.

ANSBACHER, H. L. (1974). Goal-oriented individual psychology: Alfred Adler's theory. In A. Burton (Ed.), *Operational theories of personality* (pp. 99–142). New York: Brunner/Mazel.

*ANSBACHER, H. L. (1979). The increasing recognition of Adler. In. H. L. Ansbacher & R. R. Ansbacher (Eds.), *Superiority and social interest. Alfred Adler, A collection of his later writings* (3rd rev. ed., pp. 3–20). New York: Norton.

*ANSBACHER, H. L. (1992). Alfred Adler's concepts of community feeling and social interest and the relevance of community feeling for old age. *Individual Psychology, 48*(4), 402–412.

*ANSBACHER, H. L., & ANSBACHER, R. R. (Eds.). (1964). *The individual psychology of Alfred Adler.* New York: Harper & Row/Torchbooks. (Original work published 1956)

*ANSBACHER, H. L., & ANSBACHER, R. R. (Eds.). (1979). *Superiority and social interest. Alfred Adler, A collection of his later writings* (3rd rev. ed.). New York: Norton.

*BITTER, J. R., CHRISTENSEN, O. C., HAWES, C., & NICOLL, W. G. (1998). Adlerian brief therapy with individuals, couples, and families. *Directions in Clinical and Counseling Psychology, 8*(8), 95–111.

---

* Books and articles marked with an asterisk are suggested for further study.

*CARLSON, J., & SLAVIK, S. (Eds.). (1997). *Techniques in Adlerian psychology.* Bristol, PA: Accelerated Development.

*CHRISTENSEN, O. C. (Ed.). (1993). *Adlerian family counseling* (rev. ed.). Minneapolis, MN: Educational Media Corp.

*COREY, G. (1999). Adlerian contributions to the practice of group counseling: A personal perspective. *Journal of Individual Psychology, 55*(1), 4–14.

COREY, G. (2000). *Theory and practice of group counseling* (5th ed.). Pacific Grove, CA: Brooks-Cole/Wadsworth.

*COREY, G. (Ed.). (2001). *Case approach to counseling and psychotherapy* (5th ed.). Pacific Grove, CA: Brooks-Cole/Wadsworth.

DINKMEYER, D. C., DINKMEYER JR., D. C., & SPERRY, L. (1987). *Adlerian counseling and psychotherapy* (2nd ed.). Columbus, OH: Merrill.

DINKMEYER, D., MC KAY, G., DINKMEYER JR., D., & MC KAY, J. (1997). *STEP: The parent handbook.* Circle Pines, MN: American Guidance Service.

DINKMEYER, D., & LOSONCY, L. E. (1980). *The encouragement book: Becoming a positive person.* Englewood Cliffs, NJ: Prentice-Hall.

*DISQUE, J. G., & BITTER, J. R. (1998). Integrating narrative therapy with Adlerian lifestyle assessment: A case study. *Journal of Individual Psychology, 54*(4), 431–450.

*DREIKURS, R. (1953). *Fundamentals of Adlerian psychology.* Chicago: Alfred Adler Institute.

*DREIKURS, R. (1967). *Psychodynamics, psychotherapy, and counseling. Collected papers.* Chicago: Alfred Adler Institute.

DREIKURS, R. (1968). *Psychology in the classroom* (2nd ed.). New York: Harper & Row.

DREIKURS, R. (1969). Group psychotherapy from the point of view of Adlerian psychology. In H. M. Ruitenbeck (Ed.), *Group therapy today: Styles, methods, and techniques* (pp. 37–48). New York: Aldine-Atherton. (Original work published 1957)

*DREIKURS, R. (1971). *Social equality: The challenge of today.* Chicago: Regnery.

*DREIKURS, R. (1997). Holistic medicine. *Individual Psychology, 53*(2), 127–205.

DREIKURS, R., & MOSAK, H. H. (1966). The tasks of life: I. Adler's three tasks. *The Individual Psychologist, 4,* 18–22.

DREIKURS, R., & MOSAK, H. H. (1967). The tasks of life: II. The fourth task. *The Individual Psychologist, 4,* 51–55.

DREIKURS, R., & SOLTZ, V. (1964). *Children: The challenge.* New York: Hawthorn.

ECKSTEIN, D. (1995). *The encouragement process in life-span development.* Dubuque, IA: Kendall/Hunt.

ECKSTEIN, D., & BARUTH, L. (1996). *The theory and practice of lifestyle assessment.* Dubuque, IA: Kendall/Hunt.

GRIFFITH, J., & POWERS, R. L. (1984). *An Adlerian lexicon.* Chicago: Americas Institute of Adlerian Studies.

HAWES, E. C. (1993). Marriage counseling and enrichment. In O. C. Christensen (Ed.), *Adlerian family counseling* (rev. ed., pp. 125–163). Minneapolis, MN: Educational Media Corp.

HAWES, C., & BLANCHARD, L. M. (1993). Life tasks as an assessment technique in marital counseling. *Individual Psychology, 49,* 306–317.

KEFIR, N. (1981). Impasse/priority therapy. In R. J. Corsini (Ed.), *Handbook of innovative psychotherapies* (pp. 401–415). New York: Wiley.

*MANASTER, G. J., & CORSINI, R. J. (1982). *Individual psychology. Theory and practice.* Itasca, IL: F. E. Peacock.

MOSAK, H. H. (1995). Adlerian psychotherapy. In R. J. Corsini & D. Wedding (Eds.), *Current psychotherapies* (5th ed., pp. 51–94). Itasca, IL: F. E. Peacock.

MOSAK, H. H., & MANIACCI, M. P. (1998). *Tactics in counseling and psychotherapy.* Itasca, IL: F. E. Peacock.

MOSAK, H. H., & SHULMAN, B. H. (1988). *Lifestyle inventory.* Muncie, IN: Accelerated Development.

MOZDZIERZ, G. J., LISIECKI, J., BITTER, J. R., & WILLIAMS, A. L. (1984). Role-functions for Adlerian therapists. *Individual Psychology, 42*(2), 154–177.

NYSTUL, M. S. (1999a). An interview with Gerald Corey. *Journal of Individual Psychology, 55*(1), 15–25.

NYSTUL, M. (1999b). An interview with Paul Pedersen. *Journal of Individual Psychology, 55*(2), 216–224.

PEDERSEN, P. (1990). The multicultural perspective as a fourth force in counseling. *Journal of Mental Health Counseling, 12*(1), 93–95.

POPKIN, M. (1993). *Active parenting today.* Atlanta, GA: Active Parenting.

*POWERS, R. L., & GRIFFITH, J. (1987). *Understanding life-style. The psycho-clarity process.* Chicago: Americas Institute of Adlerian Studies.

*POWERS, R. L., & GRIFFITH, J. (1995). *IPCW: The individual psychology client workbook with supplements.* Chicago: Americas Institute of Adlerian Studies. (Original work published 1986)

SCHULTZ, D., & SCHULTZ, S. E. (1998). *Theories of personality* (6th ed.). Pacific Grove, CA: Brooks/Cole.

*SHERMAN, R., & DINKMEYER, D. (1987). *Systems of family therapy. An Adlerian integration.* New York: Brunner/Mazel.

*SHULMAN, B. H., & MOSAK, H. H. (1988). *Manual for life style assessment.* Muncie, IN: Accelerated Development.

*SONSTEGARD, M. A. (1998a). A rationale for group counseling. *Journal of Individual Psychology, 54*(2), 164–175.

*SONSTEGARD, M. A. (1998b). The theory and practice of Adlerian group counseling and psychotherapy. *Journal of Individual Psychology, 54*(2), 217–250.

*SPERRY, L., & CARLSON, J. (1996). *Psychopathology and psychotherapy. From DSM-IV diagnosis to treatment.* Washington, DC: Accelerated Development.

*SWEENEY, T. J. (1998). *Adlerian counseling: A practitioner's approach* (4th ed.). Philadelphia, PA: Accelerated Development/Taylor & Francis Group.

*TERNER, J., & PEW, W. L. (1978). *The courage to be imperfect: The life and work of Rudolf Dreikurs.* New York: Hawthorn.

VAIHINGER, H. (1965). *The philosophy of "as if."* London: Routledge & Kegan Paul.

* WATTS, R. E. (1999). The vision of Adler: An introduction. In R. E. Watts, & J. Carlson (Eds.), *Interventions and strategies in counseling and psychotherapy* (pp. 1–13). Philadelphia, PA: Accelerated Development/Taylor & Francis Group.

* WATTS, R. E., & CARLSON, J. (Eds.). (1999). *Interventions and strategies in counseling and psychotherapy.* Philadelphia, PA: Accelerated Development/Taylor & Francis Group.

CHAPTER

6

Existential Therapy

INTRODUCTION
Historical Background

KEY CONCEPTS
View of Human Nature
Proposition 1: The Capacity for Self-Awareness
Proposition 2: Freedom and Responsibility
Proposition 3: Striving for Identity and Relationship to Others
Proposition 4: The Search for Meaning
Proposition 5: Anxiety as a Condition of Living
Proposition 6: Awareness of Death and Nonbeing

THE THERAPEUTIC PROCESS
Therapeutic Goals
Therapist's Function and Role
Client's Experience in Therapy
Relationship Between Therapist and Client

APPLICATION: Therapeutic Techniques and Procedures

EXISTENTIAL THERAPY APPLIED TO THE CASE OF STAN

SUMMARY AND EVALUATION
Summary
Contributions of the Existential Approach
Limitations and Criticisms of the Existential Approach

EXISTENTIAL THERAPY FROM A MULTICULTURAL PERSPECTIVE
Contributions to Multicultural Counseling
Limitations for Multicultural Counseling

WHERE TO GO FROM HERE

RECOMMENDED SUPPLEMENTARY READINGS

REFERENCES AND SUGGESTED READINGS

VIKTOR FRANKL

VIKTOR FRANKL (1905-1997) was born and educated in Vienna. He founded the Youth Advisement Centers there in 1928 and directed them until 1938. From 1942 to 1945 Frankl was a prisoner in the Nazi concentration camps at Auschwitz and Dachau, where his parents, brother, wife, and children died. He vividly remembered his horrible experiences in these camps, yet he was able to use them in a constructive way and did not allow them to dampen his love and enthusiasm for life. He traveled all around the world, giving lectures in Europe, Latin America, Southeast Asia, and the United States.

Frankl received his M.D. in 1930 and his Ph.D. in 1949, both from the University of Vienna. He became an associate professor at the University of Vienna and later was a distinguished speaker at the United States International University in San Diego. He was a visiting professor at Harvard, Stanford, and Southern Methodist universities. Frankl's works have been translated into more than 20 languages, and his ideas continue to have a major impact on the development of existential therapy. His compelling book *Man's Search for Meaning* (1963) has been a best-seller around the world.

Although Frankl had begun to develop an existential approach to clinical practice before his grim years in the Nazi death camps, his experiences there confirmed his views. Frankl (1963) observed and personally experienced the truths expressed by existential philosophers and writers, including the view that love is the highest goal to which humans can aspire and that our salvation is through love. That we have choices in every situation is another notion confirmed by his experiences in the concentration camps. Even in terrible situations, he believed, we could preserve a vestige of spiritual freedom and independence of mind. He learned experientially that everything could be taken from a person but one thing: "the last of human freedoms—to choose one's attitude in any given set of circumstances, to choose one's own way" (p. 104). Frankl believed that the essence of being human lies in searching for meaning and purpose. We can discover this meaning through our actions and deeds, by experiencing a value (such as love or achievements through work), and by suffering.

I have selected Frankl as one of the key figures of the existential approach because of the dramatic way in which his theories were tested by the tragedies of his life. His life was an illustration of his theory, for he lived what his theory espouses. Although others have written about existential concepts, they have not met with the popularity of Frankl. ■

ROLLO MAY

ROLLO MAY (1909-1994) first lived in Ohio and then moved to Michigan as a young child with his five brothers and a sister. He remembered his home life as being unhappy, a situation that had something to do with his interest in psychology and counseling. In his personal life May struggled with his own existential concerns and the failure of two marriages.

During his youth, May spent some time studying ancient Greek civilization, which he believed gave him a perspective on human nature. He later traveled to Vienna and studied with Alfred Adler. While he was pursuing his doctoral program, he came down with tuberculosis, which resulted in a 2-year stay in a sanitarium. During his recovery period, May spent much time reading and learning firsthand about the nature of anxiety. This study resulted in his book *The Meaning of Anxiety* (1950). His popular book *Love and Will* (1969) reflects his own personal struggles with love and intimate relationships and mirrors Western society's questioning of its values pertaining to sex and marriage.

The greatest personal influence on May was the German philosopher Paul Tillich (author of *The Courage to Be,* 1952), who spent much time with him discussing philosophical, religious, and psychological topics. Most of May's writings reflect a concern with the nature of human experience, such as recognizing and dealing with power, accepting freedom and responsibility, and discovering one's identity. He draws from his rich knowledge based on the classics and his existential perspective.

May was one of the main proponents of humanistic approaches to psychotherapy, and he was the principal American spokesman of European existential thinking as it is applied to psychotherapy. His view is that psychotherapy should be aimed at helping people discover the meaning of their lives and should be concerned with the problems of *being* rather than with problem solving. Questions of being include learning to deal with issues such as sex and intimacy, growing old, and facing death. According to May, the real challenge is for people to be able to live in a world where they are alone and where they will eventually have to face death. He contends that our individualism should be balanced by what Adler refers to as social interest. Therapists need to help individuals find ways to contribute to the betterment of the society in which they live. If individuals in society were grounded on these higher values, therapists might well be out of business. ■

INTRODUCTION

Existential therapy can best be described as a *philosophical approach* that influences a counselor's therapeutic practice. As such it is not a separate school of therapy or a neatly defined model with specific techniques. Thus, this chapter will focus on some of the existential ideas and themes that have significant implications for the existentially oriented practitioner.

The existential approach rejects the deterministic view of human nature espoused by orthodox psychoanalysis and radical behaviorism. Psychoanalysis sees freedom as restricted by unconscious forces, irrational drives, and past events; behaviorists see freedom as restricted by sociocultural conditioning. In contrast, existential therapists acknowledge some of these facts about the human situation but emphasize our freedom to choose what to make of our circumstances. This approach is grounded on the assumption that we are free and therefore responsible for our choices and actions. We are the authors of our lives, and we draw up the blueprints for their design.

A basic existential premise is that we are not victims of circumstance, because to a large extent we are what we choose to be. A major aim of therapy is to encourage clients to reflect on life, to recognize their range of alternatives, and to decide among them. Once clients begin the process of recognizing the ways in which they have passively accepted circumstances and surrendered control, they can start on a path of consciously shaping their own lives.

Van Deurzen-Smith (1988, 1997) writes that existential counseling is not designed to "cure" people in the tradition of the medical model. Rather, clients are viewed as being sick of life or awkward at living. They need help in surveying the terrain and in deciding on the best route to take, so that they can ultimately discover their own way. Existential therapy is a process of searching for the value and meaning in life. The therapist's basic task is to encourage clients to explore their options for creating a meaningful existence. We can begin by recognizing that we do not have to remain passive victims of our circumstances but instead can consciously become the architect of our life.

Historical Background

There are many streams in the existential therapy movement. It was not founded by any particular person or group. Rather, drawing from a major orientation in philosophy, it arose spontaneously in different parts of Europe and among different schools of psychology and psychiatry in the 1940s and 1950s. It grew out of an effort to help people resolve the dilemmas of contemporary life, such as isolation, alienation, and meaninglessness. Early writers focused on the individual's experience of being alone in the world and facing the anxiety of this situation. Rather than trying to develop sets of rules for therapy, they focused on understanding these deep human experiences (May & Yalom, 1995).

Viktor Frankl was a central figure in developing existential therapy. As a student of Freud, he began his career in psychiatry with a psychoanalytic orientation. Later, he was influenced by the writings of existential philosophers, and he began developing his own existential philosophy and psychotherapy. He was fond of quoting Nietzsche: "He who has a *why* to live for can bear with almost any *how*" (as cited in Frankl, 1963, pp. 121, 164). Frankl contended that those words could be the motto for all psychotherapeutic practice. Another quotation from Nietzsche seems to capture the essence of his own experience and his writings: "That which does not kill me, makes me stronger" (as cited in Frankl, 1963, p. 130).

Frankl reacted against most of Freud's deterministic notions and built his theory and practice of psychotherapy on such basic concepts as freedom, responsibility, meaning, and the search for values. He developed *logotherapy,* which means "therapy through meaning." The central theme running through his works is the *will to meaning.* According to Frankl, the modern person has the means to live but often has no meaning to live for. The malady of our time is meaninglessness, or the "existential vacuum," which is often experienced when people do not busy themselves with routine and with work. The therapeutic process is aimed at challenging individuals to find meaning and purpose through, among other things, suffering, work, and love (Frankl, 1965).

Rollo May was one of the key figures responsible for bringing existentialism from Europe to the United States and for translating key concepts into psychotherapeutic practice. His writings have had a significant impact on existentially oriented practitioners. Of primary importance in introducing existential therapy to the United States was the book *Existence: A New Dimension in Psychiatry and Psychology* (May, Angel, & Ellenberger, 1958). According to May, it takes courage to "be," and our choices determine the kind of person we become. There is a constant struggle within us. Although we want to grow toward maturity and independence, we realize that expansion is often a painful process. Hence, the struggle is between the security of dependence and the delights and pains of growth.

Along with May, two other significant existential therapists in the United States are James Bugental and Irvin Yalom. In *The Art of the Psychotherapist* (1987), Bugental describes a life-changing approach to therapy. He views therapy as a journey taken by the therapist and the client that delves deeply into the client's subjective world. He emphasizes that this quest demands the willingness of the therapist to be in contact with his or her own phenomenological world. According to Bugental, the central concern of therapy is to help clients examine how they have answered life's existential questions and to challenge them to revise their answers to begin living authentically.

Yalom acknowledges the contributions of both European and American psychologists and psychiatrists who have influenced the development of existential thinking and practice. Drawing on his clinical experience and on empirical research, philosophy, and literature, Yalom has developed an existential approach to therapy that focuses on four ultimate human concerns:

death, freedom, existential isolation, and meaninglessness. His comprehensive textbook, *Existential Psychotherapy* (1980), is considered a pioneering accomplishment. He acknowledges Frankl as an eminently pragmatic thinker who has had an impact on his writing and practice. Yalom believes the vast majority of experienced therapists, regardless of their theoretical orientation, employ many of the existential themes discussed in his book. He contends that the four ultimate concerns that constitute the heart of existential psychodynamics have enormous relevance to clinical work.

 # KEY CONCEPTS

View of Human Nature

The crucial significance of the existential movement is that it reacts against the tendency to identify therapy with a set of techniques. Instead, it bases therapeutic practice on an understanding of what it means to be human. The existential movement stands for respect for the person, for exploring new aspects of human behavior, and for divergent methods of understanding people. It uses numerous approaches to therapy based on its assumptions about human nature. The current focus of the existential approach is on clients who feel alone in the world and are facing the anxiety of this isolation. Rather than trying to develop rules for therapy, existential practitioners strive to understand these deep human experiences (May & Yalom, 1995).

The existential view of human nature is captured, in part, by the notion that the significance of our existence is never fixed once and for all; rather, we continually re-create ourselves through our projects. Humans are in a constant state of transition, emerging, evolving, and becoming. Being a person implies that we are discovering and making sense of our existence. We continually question ourselves, others, and the world. Although the specific questions we raise vary in accordance with our developmental stage in life, the fundamental themes do not vary. We pose questions such as "Who am I? Who have I been? Where am I going?"

The basic dimensions of the human condition, according to the existential approach, include (1) the capacity for self-awareness; (2) freedom and responsibility; (3) creating one's identity and establishing meaningful relationships with others; (4) the search for meaning, purpose, values, and goals; (5) anxiety as a condition of living; and (6) awareness of death and nonbeing. I develop these propositions in the following sections by summarizing themes that emerge in the writings of existential therapists, and I also discuss the implications for counseling practice of each of these propositions.

Proposition 1: The Capacity for Self-Awareness

As human beings, we can reflect and make choices because we are capable of self-awareness. The greater our awareness, the greater our possibilities for freedom (see Proposition 2). Thus, to expand our awareness is to increase our capacity to live fully. We become aware that:

- We are finite, and we do not have an unlimited time to do what we want with our life.
- We have the potential to take action or not to act; inaction is a decision.
- We choose our actions, and therefore we can partially create our own destiny.
- Meaning is not automatically bestowed on us but is the product of our searching and of our discovering a unique purpose.
- Existential anxiety, which is basically a consciousness of our own freedom, is an essential part of living; as we increase our awareness of the choices available to us, we also increase our sense of responsibility for the consequences of these choices.
- We are subject to loneliness, meaninglessness, emptiness, guilt, and isolation.
- We are basically alone, yet we have an opportunity to relate to other beings.

We can choose either to expand or to restrict our consciousness. Because self-awareness is at the root of most other human capacities, the decision to expand it is fundamental to human growth. Here are some dawning awarenesses that individuals may experience in the counseling process:

- They see how they are trading the security of dependence for the anxieties that accompany choosing for themselves.
- They begin to see that their identity is anchored in someone else's definition of them; that is, they are seeking approval and confirmation of their being in others instead of looking to themselves for affirmation.
- They learn that in many ways they are keeping themselves prisoner by some of their past decisions, and they realize that they can make new decisions.
- They learn that although they cannot change certain events in their lives they can change the way they view and react to these events.
- They learn that they are not condemned to a future similar to the past, for they can learn from their past and thereby reshape their future.
- They realize that they are so preoccupied with death and dying that they are not appreciating living.
- They are able to accept their limitations yet still feel worthwhile, for they understand that they do not need to be perfect to feel worthy.
- They come to realize that they are failing to live in the present moment because of preoccupation with the past, planning for the future, or trying to do too many things at once.

Increasing self-awareness, which includes awareness of alternatives, motivations, factors influencing the person, and personal goals, is an aim of all counseling. It is the therapist's task to indicate to the client that a price must be paid for increased awareness. As we become more aware, it is more difficult to "go home again." Ignorance of our condition may have brought contentment along with a feeling of partial deadness, but as we open the doors in our world, we can expect more struggle as well as the potential for more fulfillment.

Proposition 2: Freedom and Responsibility

A characteristic existential theme is that people are free to choose among alternatives and therefore have a large role in shaping their destinies. Even though we have no choice about being thrust into the world, the manner in which we live and what we become are the result of our choices. Because of the reality of this essential freedom, we must accept responsibility for directing our lives. However, it is possible to avoid this reality by making excuses. In speaking about "bad faith," the existentialist philosopher Jean-Paul Sartre (1971) refers to the inauthenticity of not accepting personal responsibility. Examples of statements of bad faith are: "Since that's the way I'm made, I couldn't help what I did" or "Naturally I'm this way, because I grew up in an alcoholic family." Sartre claims we are constantly confronted with the choice of what kind of person we are becoming, and to exist is never to be finished with this kind of choosing.

We are responsible for our lives, for our actions, and for our failures to take action. From Sartre's perspective people are condemned to freedom. He calls for a *commitment* to choosing for ourselves. Existential guilt is being aware of having evaded a commitment, or having chosen not to choose. This is the guilt we experience when we do not live authentically. It results from allowing others to define us or to make our choices for us. Sartre said, "We are our choices." An inauthentic mode of existence consists of lacking awareness of personal responsibility for our lives and passively assuming that our existence is largely controlled by external forces. In contrast, living authentically implies being true to our own evaluation of what is a valuable existence for ourselves.

For existentialists, then, being free and being human are identical. Freedom and responsibility go hand in hand. We are the authors of our lives in the sense that we create our destiny, our life situation, and our problems (Russell, 1978). Assuming responsibility is a basic condition for change. Clients who refuse to accept responsibility by persistently blaming others for their problems will not profit from therapy.

Frankl (1978) also links freedom with responsibility. He suggested that the Statue of Liberty on the East Coast be supplemented by a Statue of Responsibility on the West Coast. His basic premise is that freedom is bound by certain limitations. We are not free from conditions, but we are free to take a stand against these restrictions. Ultimately, these conditions are subject to our decisions. We are responsible.

The therapist assists clients in discovering how they are avoiding freedom and encourages them to learn to risk using it. Not to do so is to cripple clients and make them neurotically dependent on the therapist. Therapists need to teach clients that they can explicitly accept that they have choices, even though they may have devoted most of their life to evading them.

People often come to counselors because they feel that they have lost control of how they are living. They may look to the counselor to direct them, give them advice, or produce magical cures. They may also need to be heard and understood. Two central tasks of the therapist are inviting clients to recognize how they have allowed others to decide for them and encouraging them to take steps toward autonomy. In challenging clients to explore other ways of being that are more fulfilling than their present restricted existence, some existential counselors ask, "Although you have lived in a certain pattern, now that you recognize the price of some of your ways, are you willing to consider creating new patterns?" Others may have a vested interest in keeping the client in an old pattern, so the initiative for changing it will have to come from the client.

Proposition 3: Striving for Identity and Relationship to Others

People are concerned about preserving their uniqueness and centeredness, yet at the same time they have an interest in going outside of themselves to relate to other beings and to nature. Each of us would like to discover a self—that is, to find (or create) our personal identity. This is not an automatic process, and it takes courage. As relational beings, we also strive for connectedness with others. We must give of ourselves to others and be concerned with them. Many existential writers discuss loneliness, uprootedness, and alienation, which can be seen as the failure to develop ties with others and with nature.

The trouble with so many of us is that we have sought directions, answers, values, and beliefs from the important people in our world. Rather than trusting ourselves to search within and find our own answers to the conflicts in our life, we sell out by becoming what others expect of us. Our being becomes rooted in their expectations, and we become strangers to ourselves.

THE COURAGE TO BE   It does take courage to learn how to live from the inside (Tillich, 1952). We struggle to discover, to create, and to maintain the core deep within our being. One of the greatest fears of clients is that they will discover that there is no core, no self, no substance and that they are merely reflections of everyone's expectations of them. A client may say: "My fear is that I'll discover I'm nobody, that there really is nothing to me. I'll find out that I'm an empty shell, hollow inside, and nothing will exist if I shed my masks."

Existential therapists may begin by asking their clients to allow themselves to intensify the feeling that they are nothing more than the sum of others' expectations and that they are merely the introjects of parents and parent substitutes. How do they feel now? Are they condemned to stay this way forever? Is there a way out? Can they create a self if they find that they are without one? Where can they begin? Once clients have demonstrated the courage to recognize this fear, to put it into words and share it, it does not seem so overwhelming. I find that it is best to begin work by inviting clients to accept the ways in which they have lived outside themselves and to explore ways in which they are out of contact with themselves.

THE EXPERIENCE OF ALONENESS   The existentialists postulate that part of the human condition is the experience of aloneness. But they add that we can derive strength from the experience of looking to ourselves and sensing our separation. The sense of isolation comes when we recognize that we cannot depend on anyone else for our own confirmation; that is, we alone must give a sense of meaning to life, and we alone must decide how we will live. If we are unable to tolerate ourselves when we are alone, how can we expect anyone else to be enriched by our company? Before we can have any solid relationship with another, we must have a relationship with ourselves. We must learn to listen to ourselves. We have to be able to stand alone before we can truly stand beside another.

There is a paradox in the proposition that humans are existentially both alone and related, but this very paradox describes the human condition. To think that we can cure the condition, or that it should be cured, is a mistake. Ultimately we are alone.

THE EXPERIENCE OF RELATEDNESS   We humans depend on relationships with others. We want to be significant in another's world, and we want to feel that another's presence is important in our world. When we are able to stand alone and dip within ourselves for our own strength, our relationships with others are based on our fulfillment, not our deprivation. If we feel personally deprived, however, we can expect little but a clinging, parasitic, symbiotic relationship with someone else.

Perhaps one of the functions of therapy is to help clients distinguish between a neurotically dependent attachment to another and a life-affirming relationship in which both persons are enhanced. The therapist can challenge clients to examine what they get from their relationships, how they avoid intimate contact, how they prevent themselves from having equal relationships, and how they might create therapeutic, healthy, and mature human relationships.

STRUGGLING WITH OUR IDENTITY   The awareness of our ultimate aloneness can be frightening, and some clients may attempt to avoid accepting their aloneness and isolation. Because of our fear of dealing with our aloneness, Farha (1994) points out that some of us get caught up in ritualistic behavior patterns that cement us to an image or identity we acquired in early childhood. He writes that some of us become trapped in a *doing* mode to avoid the experience of *being*.

Part of the therapeutic journey consists of the therapist challenging clients to begin to examine the ways in which they have lost touch with their identity, especially by letting others design their life for them. The therapy process itself is often frightening for clients when they realize that they have surrendered their freedom to others and that in the therapy relationship they will have to assume their freedom again. By refusing to give easy solutions or answers, existential therapists confront clients with the reality that they alone must find their own answers.

Proposition 4: The Search for Meaning

A distinctly human characteristic is the struggle for a sense of significance and purpose in life. In my experience the underlying conflicts that bring people into counseling and therapy are centered in these existential questions: Why am I here? What do I want from life? What gives my life purpose? Where is the source of meaning for me in life?

Existential therapy can provide the conceptual framework for helping clients challenge the meaning in their lives. Questions that the therapist might ask are, "Do you like the direction of your life? Are you pleased with what you now are and what you are becoming? If you are confused about who you are and what you want for yourself, what are you doing to get some clarity?"

THE PROBLEM OF DISCARDING OLD VALUES   One of the problems in therapy is that clients may discard traditional (and imposed) values without finding other, suitable ones to replace them. What does the therapist do when clients no longer cling to values that they never really challenged or internalized and now experience a vacuum? Clients report that they feel like a boat without a rudder. They seek new guidelines and values that are appropriate for the newly discovered facets of themselves, and yet for a time they are without them. Perhaps the task of the therapeutic process is to help clients create a value system based on a way of living that is consistent with their way of being.

The therapist's job might well be to trust the capacity of clients to eventually discover an internally derived value system that does provide a meaningful life. They will no doubt flounder for a time and experience anxiety as a result of the absence of clear-cut values. The therapist's trust is important in teaching clients to trust their own capacity to discover a new source of values.

MEANINGLESSNESS   When the world they live in seems meaningless, clients may wonder whether it is worth it to continue struggling or even living. Faced with the prospect of our mortality, we might ask: "Is there any point to what I do now, since I will eventually die? Will what I do be forgotten once I am gone? Given the fact of mortality, why should I busy myself with anything?" A man in one of my groups captured precisely the idea of personal significance when he said, "I feel like another page in a book that has been turned quickly, and nobody bothered to read the page." For Frankl (1978) such a feeling of meaninglessness is the major existential neurosis of modern life.

Meaninglessness in life leads to emptiness and hollowness, or a condition that Frankl calls the *existential vacuum*. Because there is no preordained design for living, people are faced with the task of creating their own meaning. At times people who feel trapped by the emptiness of life withdraw from the struggle of creating a life with purpose. Experiencing meaninglessness and establishing values that are part of a meaningful life are issues that may well be taken up in counseling.

Related to the concept of meaninglessness is what existential practitioners call *existential guilt*. This is a condition that grows out of a sense of incompleteness, or a realization that we are not what we might have become. It is the awareness that our actions and choices express less than our full range as a person. This guilt is not viewed as neurotic, nor is it seen as a symptom that needs to be cured. Instead, the existential therapist explores it to see what clients can learn about the ways in which they are living their life.

CREATING NEW MEANING   Logotherapy is designed to help clients find a meaning in life. The therapist's function is not to tell clients what their particular meaning in life should be but to point out that they can discover meaning even in suffering (Frankl, 1978). This view does not share the pessimistic flavor that some people find in existential philosophy. It holds that human suffering (the tragic and negative aspects of life) can be turned into human achievement by the stand an individual takes in the face of it. Frankl also contends that people who confront pain, guilt, despair, and death can challenge their despair and thus triumph. Yet meaning is not something that we can directly search for and obtain. Paradoxically, the more rationally we seek it, the more we are likely to miss it. Yalom (1980) and Frankl are in basic agreement on the point that, like pleasure, meaning must be pursued obliquely. Finding meaning in life is a by-product of *engagement*, which is a commitment to creating, loving, working, and building.

Proposition 5: Anxiety as a Condition of Living

Anxiety, arising from one's personal strivings to survive and to maintain and assert one's being, must be confronted as an inevitable part of the human condition. Existential therapists differentiate between normal and neurotic anxiety, and they see anxiety as a potential source of growth. Normal anxiety is an appropriate response to an event being faced. Further, this kind of anxiety does not have to be repressed, and it can be used as a motivation to change. Neurotic anxiety, in contrast, is out of proportion to the situation. It is typically out of awareness, and it tends to immobilize the person. Because we could not survive without some anxiety, it is not a therapeutic goal to eliminate normal anxiety. Being psychologically healthy entails living with as little neurotic anxiety as possible while accepting and struggling with normal anxiety that is a part of living. Life cannot be lived, nor can death be faced, without anxiety (May & Yalom, 1995).

Existential anxiety is a constructive form of normal anxiety and can be a stimulus for growth. We experience this anxiety as we become increasingly aware of our freedom and the consequences of accepting or rejecting that freedom. In fact, when we make a decision that involves reconstruction of our life, the accompanying anxiety can be a signal that we are ready for personal change. If we learn to listen to the subtle messages of anxiety, we can dare to take the steps necessary to change the direction of our lives.

Many clients who seek counseling want solutions that will enable them to eliminate anxiety. Although attempts to avoid anxiety by creating the illusion that there is security in life may help us cope with the unknown, we really know on some level that we are deceiving ourselves when we think we have found fixed security. We can blunt anxiety by constricting our life and thus reducing choices. Opening up to new life, however, means opening up to anxiety. We pay a steep price when we short-circuit anxiety.

People who have the courage to face themselves are, nonetheless, frightened. I am convinced that those who are willing to live with their anxiety for a time are the ones who profit from personal therapy. Those who flee too quickly into comfortable patterns might experience a temporary relief but in the long run seem to experience the frustration of being stuck in their old ways.

According to May (1981), freedom and anxiety are two sides of the same coin; anxiety is associated with the excitement accompanying the birth of a new idea. Thus, we experience anxiety when we use our freedom to move out of the known into the realm of the unknown. Out of fear, many of us try to avoid taking such a leap into the unknown.

Existential therapy helps clients come to terms with the paradoxes of existence—life and death, success and failure, freedom and limitations, and certainty and doubt. As people recognize the realities of their confrontation with pain and suffering, their need to struggle for survival, and their basic fallibility, anxiety surfaces. Van Deurzen-Smith (1991) contends that an essential aim of existential therapy is not to make life seem easier or safer but to encourage clients to recognize and deal with the sources of their insecurity and anxiety. Facing existential anxiety involves viewing life as an adventure rather than hiding behind securities that seem to offer protection. As she puts it, "We need to question and scrape away at the easy answers and expose ourselves to some of the anxiety that can bring us back to life in a real and deep way" (p. 46).

It is essential that therapists recognize existential anxiety and guide clients in finding ways of dealing with it constructively. Existential therapy does not aim at eliminating anxiety, for to do so would be to cut off a source of vitality. Counselors have the task of encouraging clients to develop the courage to face life squarely, largely by taking a stance, performing an action, or making a decision (Van Deurzen-Smith, 1988).

The existential therapist can help clients recognize that learning how to tolerate ambiguity and uncertainty and how to live without props can be a necessary phase in the journey from dependence to autonomy. The therapist and client can explore the possibility that although breaking away from crippling patterns and building new lifestyles will be fraught with anxiety for a while, anxiety will diminish as the client experiences more satisfaction with newer ways of being. When a client becomes more self-confident, the anxiety that results from an expectation of catastrophe will decrease.

Proposition 6: Awareness of Death and Nonbeing

The existentialist does not view death negatively but holds that awareness of death as a basic human condition gives significance to living. A distinguishing human characteristic is the ability to grasp the reality of the future and the inevitability of death. It is necessary to think about death if we are to think significantly about life. If we defend ourselves against the reality of our eventual death, life becomes insipid and meaningless. But if we realize that we are mortal, we know that we do not have an eternity to complete our projects and that each present moment is crucial. Our awareness of death is the source of zest for life and creativity. Death and life are interdependent, and though physical death destroys us, the idea of death saves us (Yalom, 1980).

The recognition of death plays a significant role in psychotherapy, for it can be the factor that helps us transform a stale mode of living into a more authentic one (Yalom, 1980). Thus, one focus in existential therapy is on exploring the degree to which clients are doing the things they value. Without being morbidly preoccupied by the ever-present threat of nonbeing, clients can develop a healthy awareness of death as a way to evaluate how well they are living and what changes they want to make in their lives. Those who fear death also fear life. If we affirm life and live in the present as fully as possible, however, we will not be obsessed with the end of life.

 # THE THERAPEUTIC PROCESS

Therapeutic Goals

A basic goal of many therapeutic systems is enabling individuals to accept the awesome freedom and responsibility to act. Existential therapy is best considered as an invitation to clients to recognize the ways in which they are not living fully authentic lives and to make choices that will lead to their becoming what they are capable of being. The existential orientation holds that there is no escape from freedom, in the sense that we can always be held responsible. We can relinquish our freedom, however, which is the ultimate inauthenticity.

Existential therapy seeks to take clients out of their rigid grooves and to challenge their narrow and compulsive trends, which are blocking their freedom. Although this process gives individuals a sense of release and increased autonomy, the new freedom does bring about anxiety. Freedom is a venture down new pathways, and there is no certainty about where these paths will lead. The "dizziness" and dread of freedom must be confronted if growth is to occur (May, 1981). The lack of guarantees in life is precisely what generates anxiety. Thus, existential therapy aims at helping clients face this anxiety and engage in action that is based on the authentic purpose of creating a worthy existence.

May (1981) contends that people come to therapy with the self-serving illusion that they are inwardly enslaved and that someone else (the therapist) can free them. Thus, "the purpose of psychotherapy is not to 'cure' the clients in the conventional sense, but to help them become aware of what they are doing and to get them out of the victim role" (p. 210). The task of existential therapy is to teach clients to listen to what they already know about themselves, even though they may not be attending to what they know. Therapy is a process of bringing out the latent aliveness in the client (Bugental, 1986).

Bugental (1990) identifies three main tasks of therapy: (1) to assist clients in recognizing that they are not fully present in the therapy process itself and in seeing how this pattern may limit them outside of therapy; (2) to support clients in confronting the anxieties that they have so long sought to avoid; and (3) to help clients redefine themselves and their world in ways that foster greater genuineness of contact with life. In short, increased awareness is the central goal of existential therapy. According to Bugental, it allows clients to discover that alternative possibilities exist where none were recognized before and that they are able to make changes in their way of being in the world.

Therapist's Function and Role

Existential therapists are primarily concerned with understanding the subjective world of clients to help them come to new understandings and options. The focus is on clients' current life situations, not on helping clients recover a personal past (May & Yalom, 1995). Typically, existential therapists show wide latitude in the methods they employ, varying not only from client to client but also with the same client at different phases of the therapeutic process. On one hand, they may make use of techniques that grow from diverse theoretical orientation, yet no set of techniques is considered essential. On the other hand, some existential therapists abhor techniques, seeing them as rigid, routine, and manipulative. They do not use a bag of techniques to get their clients to explore their existence. Instead, their main interest is in the unique struggle of each client. Existential therapists assist individuals in discovering the reason for their "stuckness" (Vontress,

Johnson, & Epp, 1999). Throughout the therapeutic process, techniques are secondary to establishing a relationship that will enable the counselor to effectively challenge and understand the client. Existential therapists are especially concerned about clients avoiding responsibility; they invite clients to accept personal responsibility. When clients complain about the predicaments they are in and blame others, the therapist is likely to ask them how they contributed to the situation.

Therapists with an existential orientation usually deal with people who have what could be called a *restricted existence*. These clients have a limited awareness of themselves and are often vague about the nature of their problems. They may see few, if any, options for dealing with life situations, and they tend to feel trapped or helpless. A central task of the therapist is to confront these clients with the ways they are living a restricted existence, or how they are stuck, and to help them become aware of their own part in creating this condition. The therapist may hold up a mirror, so to speak, so that clients can gradually engage in self-confrontation. In this way clients can see how they became the way they are and how they might enlarge the way they live. Once clients are aware of factors in their past and of stifling modes of their present existence, they can begin to accept responsibility for changing their future.

Client's Experience in Therapy

Clients in existential therapy are clearly encouraged to take seriously their own subjective experience of their world. They are challenged to take responsibility for how they *now* choose to be in their world. Effective therapy does not stop with this awareness itself, for the therapist encourages clients to take action on the basis of the insights they develop through the therapeutic process. Clients are expected to go out into the world and decide *how* they will live differently. Further, they must be active in the therapeutic process, for during the sessions they must decide what fears, guilts, and anxieties they will explore.

Merely deciding to enter psychotherapy is itself a scary prospect for most clients. The experience of opening the doors to oneself is often frightening, exciting, joyful, depressing, or a combination of all of these. As clients wedge open the closed doors, they also begin to loosen the deterministic shackles that have kept them psychologically bound. Gradually, they become aware of what they have been and who they are now, and they are better able to decide what kind of future they want. Through the process of their therapy, clients can explore alternatives for making their visions real.

When clients plead helplessness and attempt to convince themselves that they are powerless, May (1981) reminds them that their journey toward freedom began by putting one foot in front of the other to get to his office. As minute as their range of freedom may be, they can begin building and augmenting that range by taking small steps.

Another aspect of the experience of being a client in existential therapy is confronting ultimate concerns rather than coping with immediate problems. Some major themes of therapy sessions are anxiety, freedom and responsibility, isolation, alienation, death and its implications for living, and the continual search for meaning. Existential therapists assist clients in facing life with courage, hope, and a willingness to find meaning in life.

Relationship Between Therapist and Client

Existential therapists give central prominence to their relationship with the client. The relationship is important in itself because the quality of this person-to-person encounter in the therapeutic situation is the stimulus for positive change. Therapists with this orientation believe their basic attitudes toward the client and their own personal characteristics of honesty, integrity, and courage are what they have to offer. Therapy is a journey taken by therapist and client, a journey that delves deeply into the world as perceived and experienced by the client. But this type of quest demands that therapists also be in contact with their own phenomenological world. As Vontress and colleagues (1999) state, existential counseling is a voyage into self-discovery for both client and therapist. In achieving the goal of assisting clients to confront ways they are experiencing "stuckness" in their lives, it is essential for the counselor to adopt a flexible style and to draw from different theoretical approaches with different clients.

Buber's (1970) conception of the I/Thou relationship has significant implications here. Relating in an I/Thou fashion means that there is direct, mutual, and present interaction. Rather than prizing therapeutic objectivity and professional distance, existential therapists strive to create caring and intimate relationships with clients. It is all too easy for counselors to smile and nod without really listening and attending. Many clients will sense this absence, or lack of presence, and it will negatively affect the relationship.

Existential therapists share their reactions to clients with genuine concern and empathy as one way of deepening the therapeutic relationship. Bugental (1987) emphasizes the crucial role that the *presence* of the therapist plays in this relationship. In his view many therapists and therapeutic systems overlook its fundamental importance. He contends that therapists are too often so concerned with the content of what is being said that they are not aware of the distance between themselves and their clients. "The therapeutic alliance is the powerful joining of forces which energizes and supports the long, difficult, and frequently painful work of life-changing psychotherapy. The conception of the therapist here is not of a disinterested observer-technician but of a fully alive human companion for the client" (p. 49).

The core of the therapeutic relationship is respect, which implies faith in clients' potential to cope authentically with their troubles and in their ability to discover alternative ways of being. Clients eventually come to view themselves as active and responsible for their own existence, whereas before therapy they were likely to see themselves as helpless. They develop an increased ability to accept and confront the freedom they possess.

Therapists invite clients to grow by modeling authentic behavior. If therapists keep themselves hidden during the therapeutic session or if they engage in inauthentic behavior, clients will also remain guarded and persist in their inauthentic ways. Thus, therapists can help clients become less of a stranger to themselves by selectively disclosing their own responses at appropriate times. Of course, this disclosure does not mean an uncensored sharing of every fleeting feeling or thought. Rather, it entails a willingness to share persistent reactions with clients, especially when this sharing is likely to be facilitative.

APPLICATION: Theraputic Techniques and Procedures

The existential approach is unlike most other therapies in that it is not technique-oriented. The interventions existential practitioners employ are based on philosophical views about the essential nature of human existence. Existential therapists are free to draw from techniques that flow from many other orientations. However, they do not employ an array of unintegrated techniques; they have a set of assumptions and attitudes that guide their interventions with clients.

In a discussion of therapeutic techniques, Van Deurzen-Smith (1990a) points out that the existential approach is well known for its deemphasis of techniques. She stresses the importance of therapists reaching sufficient depth and openness in their own lives to allow them to venture into clients' murky waters without getting lost. She asserts that therapists who are fully available while their clients explore their deepest issues are implying that their own being is subject to change. Van Deurzen-Smith reminds us that existential therapy is a collaborative adventure in which both the client and the therapist will be transformed if they allow themselves to be touched by life.

The use of the therapist's self is the core of therapy (Baldwin, 1987). It is in the I/Thou encounter, when the deepest self of the therapist meets the deepest part of the client, that the counseling process is at its best. Therapy is a creative, evolving process of discovery that can be conceptualized in three general phases.

During the initial phase, counselors assist clients in identifying and clarifying their assumptions about the world. Clients are invited to define and question the ways in which they perceive and make sense of their existence. They examine their values, beliefs, and assumptions to determine their validity. This is a difficult task for many clients because they may initially present their problems as resulting almost entirely from external causes. They may focus on what other people "make them feel" or on how others are largely responsible for their actions or inaction. The counselor teaches them how to reflect on their own existence and to examine their role in creating their problems in living.

During the middle phase of existential counseling, clients are encouraged to more fully examine the source and authority of their present value system. This process of self-exploration typically leads to new insights and some restructuring of their values and attitudes. Clients get a better idea of what kind of life they consider worthy to live and develop a clearer sense of their internal valuing process.

The final phase of existential counseling focuses on helping clients take what they are learning about themselves and put it into action. The aim of therapy is to enable clients to find ways of implementing their examined and internalized values in a concrete way. Clients typically discover their strengths and find ways to put them to the service of living a purposeful existence.

 # EXISTENTIAL THERAPY APPLIED TO THE CASE OF STAN

The counselor with an existential orientation approaches Stan with the view that he has the capacity to increase his self-awareness and decide for himself the future direction of his life. She wants him to realize more than anything else that he does not have to be the victim of his past conditioning but can be the architect in redesigning his future. He can free himself of his deterministic shackles and accept the responsibility that comes with directing his own life. This approach does not stress techniques but emphasizes the importance of the therapist's understanding of Stan's world, primarily by establishing an authentic relationship as a means to a fuller degree of self-understanding.

Stan is demonstrating what Sartre would call "bad faith," which refers to his not accepting personal responsibility. Examples of his implicit statements of bad faith include: "My family never really cared for me; this is why I feel unworthy most of the time." "That's the way I am; I can't help what I do." "Naturally I'm a loser, because I've been rejected so many times." The therapist confronts Stan with the ways in which he is attempting to escape from his freedom through alcohol and drugs. Eventually, she confronts him with the passivity that is keeping him unfree. She reaffirms that he is now entirely re-

sponsible for his life, for his actions, and for his failure to take action. She does this in a kind manner, but she is still firm in challenging Stan.

The counselor does not see Stan's anxiety as something that needs to be cured; rather, he needs to learn that realistic anxiety is a vital part of living with uncertainty and freedom. Because there are no guarantees and because the individual is ultimately alone, Stan can expect to experience some degree of healthy anxiety, aloneness, guilt, and even despair. These conditions are not neurotic in themselves, but the way in which Stan orients himself to these conditions and how he copes with his anxiety are critical.

Stan talks about feeling so low at times that he fantasizes about suicide. Certainly, the therapist investigates further to determine if he poses an immediate threat to himself. In addition to this assessment to determine lethality, the existential therapist may view his thoughts of "being better off dead" as symbolic. Could it be that he feels that Stan is dying as a person? Is Stan using his human potential? Is he choosing a dead way of merely existing instead of affirming life? Is Stan mainly trying to elicit sympathy from his family? The existentially oriented therapist confronts Stan with the meaning and purpose in his life. Is there any reason for Stan to want to continue living? What are some of the projects that enrich his life? What can Stan do to find a sense of purpose that will make him feel more significant and more alive?

Stan needs to accept the reality that he may at times feel alone. Choosing for oneself and living from one's own center accentuates the experience of aloneness. He is not, however, condemned to a life of isolation, alienation from others, and loneliness. The therapist helps Stan discover his own centeredness and live by the values he chooses and creates for himself. By doing so, Stan can become a more substantial person and learn to appreciate himself more. When he does, the chances are lessened that he will have a clinging need to secure approval from others, particularly his parents and parental substitutes. Instead of forming a dependent relationship, Stan could choose to relate to others out of his strength. Only then would

there be the possibility of overcoming his feelings of separateness and isolation.

Follow-Up: You Continue as Stan's Existential Therapist

Use these questions to help you think about how you would counsel Stan:

- If Stan resisted your attempts to help him see that he was responsible for the direction of his life, what interventions might you make?
- Stan experiences a great deal of anxiety. From an existential perspective, how do you view his anxiety? How might you work with his anxiety in creative ways?
- If Stan talks with you about suicide as a way out of despair and a life without meaning, how will you be inclined to work with him? Can you think of any ways Stan could find more meaning and purpose in his life? ■

 ## SUMMARY AND EVALUATION

Summary

As humans, according to the existentialist view, we are capable of self-awareness, which is the distinctive capacity that allows us to reflect and to decide. With this awareness we become free beings who are responsible for choosing the way we live, and we thus influence our own destiny. This awareness of freedom and responsibility gives rise to existential anxiety, which is another basic human characteristic. Whether we like it or not, we are free, even though we may seek to avoid reflecting on this freedom. The knowledge that we must choose, even though the outcome is not certain, leads to anxiety. This anxiety is heightened when we reflect on the reality that we are mortal beings. Facing the inevitable prospect of eventual death gives the present moment significance, for we become aware that we do not have forever to accomplish our projects. Our task is to create a life that has *GOAL* meaning and purpose. As humans we are unique in that we strive toward fashioning purposes and values that give meaning to living. Whatever meaning our life has is developed through freedom and a commitment to make choices in the face of uncertainty.

Existential therapy places central prominence on the person-to-person relationship. It assumes that client growth occurs through this genuine encounter. It is not the techniques a therapist uses that make a therapeutic difference; rather, it is the quality of the client/therapist relationship that heals.

Because this approach is basically concerned with matters such as the goals of therapy, basic conditions of being human, and therapy as a shared journey, practitioners are not bound by specific techniques. Although existential therapists may apply techniques from other orientations, their interventions are guided by a philosophical framework about what it means to be human.

Contributions of the Existential Approach

The existential approach has helped bring the person back into central focus. It has concentrated on the central facts of human existence: self-consciousness and our consequent freedom. To the existentialist goes the credit for providing a new view of death as a positive force, not a morbid prospect to fear, for death gives life its meaning. The existentialist has contributed a new dimension to the understanding of anxiety, guilt, frustration, loneliness, and alienation. I particularly appreciate the way in which Vontress and colleagues (1999) capture the essence of an existential therapist's aim: "Ultimately, the existential counselor wishes to explore concertedly with the client all of life, not simply the random issues that emerge in session, whose transient importance may only fade into the background of the larger scheme of life that went unexplored" (p. 58).

In my own work I've found that an existential view does provide the framework for understanding universal human concerns. These themes that come up in counseling sessions include wrestling with the problem of personal freedom, dealing with self-alienation and estrangement from others, facing the fear of death and nonbeing, finding the courage to live from within one's center, searching for a meaningful life, discovering a personal set of values, being able to deal constructively with anxiety and guilt, and making choices that lead to a fullness of personal expression.

One of the major contributions of the existential approach is its emphasis on the human quality of the therapeutic relationship. This aspect lessens the chances of dehumanizing psychotherapy by making it a mechanical process. Existential counselors reject the notions of therapeutic objectivity and professional distance, viewing them as being unhelpful. This is put quite nicely in these words: "Being an existential counselor would seem to mean having the courage to be a caring human being in an insensitive world (Vontress et al., 1999, p. 44).

I very much value the existential emphasis on freedom and responsibility and the person's capacity to redesign his or her life by choosing with awareness. This perspective provides a sound philosophical base on which to build a personal and unique therapeutic style because it addresses itself to the core struggles of the contemporary person.

AREAS OF APPLICATION   What problems are most amenable to an existential approach? For which populations is existential therapy particularly useful? A strength of the perspective is its focus on available choices and pathways toward personal growth. Even for brief counseling, existential therapy can focus clients on significant areas such as assuming personal responsibility, making a commitment to deciding and acting, and expanding their awareness of their current situation. For clients who are struggling with developmental crises, existential therapy is especially appropriate (May & Yalom, 1995). Some examples of these critical turning points that mark passages from one stage of life into another are the struggle for identity in adolescence, coping with possible disappointments in middle age, adjusting to children leaving home, coping with failures in marriage and work, and dealing with increased physical limitations as one ages. These developmental challenges involve both dangers and opportunities. Uncertainty, anxiety, and struggling with decisions are all part of this process.

Van Deurzen-Smith (1990a) suggests that this form of therapy is best suited for clients who are committed to dealing with their problems about living. The approach has particular relevance for people who feel alienated from the current expectations of society or for those who are searching for meaning in their lives. It tends to work well with people who are at a crossroads, for example, with those coping with changes of personal circumstances such as bereavement or loss of employment. Van Deurzen-Smith believes that existential therapy works better with individuals who question the state of affairs in the world and are willing to challenge the status quo. It can be useful for people who are on the edge of existence, such as those who are dying, who are working through a developmental or situational crisis, or who are starting a new phase of life.

Bugental and Bracke (1992) assert that the value and vitality of a psychotherapy approach depend on its ability to assist clients in dealing with the sources of pain and dissatisfaction in their lives. They contend that the existential orientation is particularly suited to individuals who are experiencing a lack of a sense of identity. The approach offers promise for individuals who are struggling to find meaning or who complain of feelings of emptiness.

CONTRIBUTIONS TO THE INTEGRATION OF PSYCHOTHERAPIES   According to May and Yalom (1995, p. 290), the main aim of the founders of existential therapy is that its key concepts and themes will become integrated into all therapeutic schools rather than existential therapy being a separate school. They think that this integration is clearly occurring. Although Bugental and Bracke (1992) are interested in the infusion of existential notions into other therapy approaches, they have some concerns. They call for a careful examination of areas of confluence and of divergence among the theoretical perspectives. They offer these postulates for maintaining the integrity of the existential perspective as efforts toward integration proceed:

- The subjectivity of the client is a key focus in understanding significant life changes.
- A full presence and commitment of both the therapist and client are essential to life-changing therapy.

- The main aim of therapy is to help clients recognize the ways in which they are constricting their awareness and action.
- A key focus of therapy is on how clients actually use the opportunities in therapy for examining and changing their lives.
- As clients become more aware of the ways in which they define themselves and their world, they can also see new alternatives for choice and action.
- In situations involving transference and countertransference, therapists have an opportunity to model taking responsibility for themselves while inviting their clients to do the same.

Bugental and Bracke (1992) say that experienced clinicians of contrasting orientations often accept some existential concepts and thus operate implicitly within an existential framework. Bugental and Bracke see the possibility of a creative integration of the conceptual propositions of existential therapy with psychodynamic or cognitive approaches.

Limitations and Criticisms of the Existential Approach

A major criticism often aimed at this approach is that it lacks a systematic statement of the principles and practices of psychotherapy. Some practitioners have trouble with what they perceive as its mystical language and concepts. Those who prefer a counseling practice based on research contend that the concepts should be empirically sound, that definitions should be operational, that the hypotheses should be testable, and that therapeutic practice should be based on the results of research into both the process and outcomes of counseling.

Some therapists who claim adherence to an existential orientation describe their therapeutic style in vague and global terms such as *self-actualization, dialogic encounter, authenticity,* and *being in the world.* This lack of precision causes confusion at times and makes it difficult to conduct research on the process or outcomes of existential therapy.

Both beginning and advanced practitioners who are not of a philosophical turn of mind tend to find many of the existential concepts lofty and elusive. And those counselors who do find themselves close to this philosophy are often at a loss when they attempt to apply it to practice. As we have seen, this approach places primary emphasis on understanding the world of clients. It is assumed that techniques follow understanding. The fact that few techniques are generated by this approach makes it essential for practitioners to develop their own innovative procedures or to borrow from other schools of therapy

Philosophical insight may not be appropriate for some clients. For example, the existential approach may be ineffective in working with the seriously disturbed. However, R. D. Laing (1965, 1967) has used an existential point of view in successfully treating schizophrenic patients. Laing's positive results suggest that existential practitioners may work well with all sorts of populations, treating people in humane ways that are in keeping with this approach while at the same time drawing on some of the more active and directive intervention methods to meet the unique needs of their clients.

EXISTENTIAL THERAPY FROM A MULTICULTURAL PERSPECTIVE

Contributions to Multicultural Counseling

Vontress and colleagues (1999) write about the existential foundation of cross-cultural counseling. Because the existential approach is grounded in the universal characteristics of human beings, they maintain that it is perhaps the most applicable of all approaches when working with culturally diverse clients. They write: "Existential counseling is probably the most useful approach to helping clients of all cultures find meaning and harmony in their lives, because it focuses on the sober issues each of us must inevitably face: love, anxiety, suffering, and death" (p. 32). These are the human experiences that transcend the boundaries that separate cultures.

Vontress (1996) points out that all people are multicultural in the sense that they are all products of many cultures. He encourages counselors in training to focus on the universal commonalities of clients first and secondarily on areas of differences. Thus, in working with cultural diversity it is essential to recognize simultaneously the commonalities and differences of human beings. He notes: "Cross-cultural counseling, in short, does not intend to teach specific interventions for each culture, but to infuse the counselor with a cultural sensitivity and tolerant philosophical outlook that will befit all cultures" (p. 164).

A strength of the existential approach is that it enables clients to examine the degree to which their behavior is being influenced by social and cultural conditioning. Clients can be challenged to look at the price they are paying for the decisions they have made. Although it is true that some clients may not feel a sense of freedom, their freedom can be increased by recognizing the social limits they are facing. Their freedom can be hindered by institutions and limited by their family. In fact, it may be difficult to separate individual freedom from the context of their family structure.

A client who is struggling with feeling limited by her family situation can be invited to look at her part in this process. For example, Meta, a Norwegian American, is working to attain a professional identity as a social worker, but her family thinks she is being selfish and neglecting her primary duties. The family is likely to exert pressure on her to give up her personal interests in favor of what they feel is best for the welfare of the entire family. Meta may feel trapped in the situation and see no way out unless she rejects what her family wants. In cases such as this, it is useful to explore the client's underlying values and to help her determine whether her values are working for her and for her family. Clients such as Meta have the challenge of weighing values and balancing behaviors between two cultures. Ultimately, Meta must decide in what ways she might change her situation. The existential therapist will invite Meta to begin to explore what she *can* do. She can begin to reclaim her personal power by considering her own part in the difficulties she is having and in what direction she is inclined to move.

It is essential to respect the purpose that clients have in mind when they initiate therapy. If we pay careful attention to what our clients tell us about what they want, we can operate within an existential framework. We can encourage clients to weigh the alternatives and to explore the consequences of what they are doing with their lives. Even though oppressive forces may be severely limiting the quality of their lives, we can help clients see that they are not merely the victims of circumstances beyond their control. At the same time that these clients are learning how to change their external environment, they can also be challenged to look within themselves to recognize their own contributions to their plight. Through the therapy experience, they may be able to discover new courses of action that will lead to a change in their situation.

Limitations for Multicultural Counseling

There are some limitations of the existential approach as it is applied to multicultural populations. For those who hold a systemic perspective, the existentialists can be criticized on the grounds that they are excessively individualistic and that they ignore the social factors that cause human problems. Some culturally different clients may operate on the assumption that they have very little choice. They often feel that environmental circumstances severely restrict their ability to influence the direction of their lives. Even if they change internally, they see little hope that the external realities of racism, discrimination, and oppression will change. They are likely to experience a deep sense of frustration and feelings of powerlessness when it comes to making changes outside of themselves. As you will see in Chapter 12, feminist therapists maintain that therapeutic practice will be effective only to the extent that therapists intervene with some form of social action to change those factors that are creating clients' problems. In working with people of color who come from the barrio or ghetto, for example, it is important to take up their survival issues. If a counselor consistently tells these clients that they have a choice in making their life better, they may feel patronized and misunderstood. These real-life issues can provide a good focus for counseling, assuming the therapist is willing to deal with them.

A limitation within existential theory is that it is highly focused on the philosophical assumption of self-determination, which does not take into account the complex social identities in which many racial and ethnic minorities find themselves embedded. In many cultures it is not possible to talk about the self and self-determination apart from the context of the social network.

Another problem with this approach is the lack of direction that clients may get from the counselor. Although clients may feel better if they have an opportunity to talk and to be understood, they are likely to expect the counselor to do something to bring about a change in their life situation. Many clients expect a structured and problem-oriented approach to counseling that is not found in the existential approach, which places the responsibility on the client for providing the direction of therapy. A major challenge facing the counselor is to provide enough concrete direction for these clients without taking the responsibility away from them.

 WHERE TO GO FROM HERE

The Society for Existential Analysis is a professional organization devoted to exploring issues pertaining to an existential/phenomenological approach to counseling and therapy. Membership is open to anyone interested in this approach and includes students, trainees, psychotherapists, philosophers, psychiatrists, counselors, and psychologists. Members receive a regular newsletter and an annual copy of the *Journal of the Society for Existential Analysis*. The society provides a list of existentially oriented psychotherapists for referral purposes. The School of Psychotherapy and Counselling at Regent's College in London offers an advanced diploma in existential psychotherapy as well as short courses in the field. For information on any of the above, contact:

> *Society for Existential Analysis*
> School of Psychotherapy and Counselling, Regent's College
> Inner Circle, Regent's Park
> London, England NWI 4NS United Kingdom
> Telephone: +44(0)20 7487 7406
> Fax: +44(0) 20 7487 7446
> E-mail: *spc@regents.ac.uk*

Recommended Supplementary Readings

Existential Counselling in Practice (Van Deurzen-Smith, 1988) develops a practical method of counseling based on the application of concepts of existential philosophy. The author puts into clear perspective topics such as anxiety, authentic living, clarifying one's worldview, determining values, discovering meaning, and coming to terms with life. She draws on her experience as an existential psychotherapist in describing numerous case illustrations.

Everyday Mysteries: Existential Dimensions of Psychotherapy (Van Deurzen-Smith, 1997) deals with the philosophical contributions to existential therapy and discusses the existential world view.

Existential Psychotherapy (Yalom, 1980) is a superb treatment of ultimate human concerns of death, freedom, isolation, and meaninglessness as these issues relate to therapy. This book has depth and clarity, and it is rich with clinical examples that illustrate existential themes.

The Art of the Psychotherapist (Bugental, 1987) is an outstanding book that bridges the art and science of psychotherapy, making places for both. The author is an insightful and sensitive clinician who writes about the psychotherapist/client journey in depth from an existential perspective.

I Never Knew I Had a Choice (Corey & Corey, 1997) is a self-help book written from an existential perspective. Topics include our struggle to achieve autonomy; the meaning of loneliness, death, and loss; and how we choose our values and philosophy of life.

Cross-Cultural Counseling: A Casebook (Vontress, Johnson, & Epp, 1999) contains case studies of culturally diverse clients. These cases are explored within three frameworks: from a conceptual perspective, from an existential perspective, and from the vantage point of the DSM-IV diagnostic model. There is a marvelous chapter on the existential foundations of cross-cultural counseling.

References and Suggested Readings*

BALDWIN, D. C., Jr. (1987). Some philosophical and psychological contributions to the use of self in therapy. In M. Baldwin & V. Satir (Eds.), *The use of self in therapy* (pp. 27–44). New York: Haworth Press.

BUBER, M. (1970). *I and thou* (W. Kaufmann, trans.). New York: Scribner's.

BUGENTAL, J. F. T. (1981). *The search for authenticity: An existential-analytic approach to psychotherapy* (rev. ed.). New York: Holt, Rinehart & Winston.

BUGENTAL, J. F. T. (1986). Existential-humanistic psychotherapy. In I. L. Kutash & A. Wolf (Eds.), *Psychotherapist's casebook* (pp. 222–236). San Francisco: Jossey-Bass.

*BUGENTAL, J. F. T. (1987). *The art of the psychotherapist.* New York: Norton.

BUGENTAL, J. F. T. (1990). Existential-humanistic psychotherapy. In J. K. Zeig & W. M. Munion (Eds.), *What is psychotherapy? Contemporary perspectives* (pp. 189–193). San Francisco: Jossey-Bass.

BUGENTAL, J. F. T., & BRACKE, P. E. (1992). The future of existential-humanistic psychotherapy. *Psychotherapy, 29*(1), 28–33.

COREY, G. (2000). *Theory and practice of group counseling* (5th ed.). Pacific Grove, CA: Brooks-Cole/Wadsworth.

*COREY, G. (2001). *Case approach to counseling and psychotherapy* (5th ed.). Pacific Grove, CA: Brooks-Cole/Wadsworth.

*COREY, G., & COREY, M. (1997). *I never knew I had a choice* (6th ed.). Pacific Grove, CA: Brooks/Cole.

*VAN DEURZEN-SMITH, E. (1988). *Existential counselling in practice.* London: Sage.

*VAN DEURZEN-SMITH, E. (1990a). *Existential therapy.* London: Society for Existential Analysis Publications.

VAN DEURZEN-SMITH, E. (1990b). What is existential analysis? *Journal of the Society for Existential Analysis, 1,* 6–14.

VAN DEURZEN-SMITH, E. (1991). Ontological insecurity revisited. *Journal of the Society for Existential Analysis, 2,* 38–48.

VAN DEURZEN-SMITH, E. (1992). Dialogue as therapy. *Journal of the Society for Existential Analysis, 3,* 15–23.

---

*Books and articles marked with an asterisk are suggested for further study.

VAN DEURZEN-SMITH, E. (1997). *Everyday mysteries: Existential dimensions of psychotherapy*. London: Routledge.

FARHA, B. (1994). Ontological awareness: An existential/cosmological epistemology. *The Person-Centered Periodical, 1*(I), 15–29.

*FRANKL, V. (1963). *Man's search for meaning*. Boston: Beacon.

FRANKL, V. (1965). *The doctor and the soul*. New York: Bantam Books.

FRANKL, V. (1969). *The will to meaning: Foundations and applications of logotherapy*. New York: New American Library.

FRANKL, V. (1978). *The unheard cry for meaning*. New York: Simon & Schuster/ Touchstone.

GOULD, W. B. (1993). *Viktor E. Frankl: Life with meaning*. Pacific Grove, CA: Brooks/Cole.

LAING, R. D. (1965). *The divided self*. Baltimore: Pelican.

LAING, R. D. (1967). *The politics of experience*. New York: Ballantine.

MAY, R. (1950). *The meaning of anxiety*. New York: Ronald Press.

*MAY, R. (1953). *Man's search for himself*. New York: Dell.

MAY, R. (1958). The origins and significance of the existential movement in psychology. In R. May, E. Angel, & H. R. Ellenberger (Eds.), *Existence: A new dimension in psychiatry and psychology*. New York: Basic Books.

MAY, R. (Ed.). (1961). *Existential psychology*. New York: Random House.

MAY, R. (1969). *Love and will*. New York: Norton.

MAY, R. (1975). *The courage to create*. New York: Norton.

MAY, R. (1981). *Freedom and destiny*. New York: Norton.

*MAY, R. (1983). *The discovery of being: Writings in existential psychology*. New York: Norton.

MAY, R., ANGEL, E., & ELLENBERGER, H. F. (Eds.). (1958). *Existence: A new dimension in psychiatry and psychology*. New York: Basic Books.

*MAY, R., & YALOM, I. (1995). Existential psychotherapy. In R. J. Corsini & D. Wedding (Eds.), *Current psychotherapies* (5th ed., pp. 262–292). Itasca, IL: F. E. Peacock.

PROCHASKA, J. O., & NORCROSS, J. C. (1999). *Systems of psychotherapy: A transtheoretical analysis* (4th ed.). Pacific Grove, CA: Brooks/Cole.

RUSSELL, J. M. (1978). Sartre, therapy, and expanding the concept of responsibility. *American Journal of Psychoanalysis, 38,* 259–269.

SARTRE, J. P. (1971). *Being and nothingness*. New York: Bantam Books.

*SCHNEIDER, K. J., & ROLLO, M. (1995). *The psychology of existence: An integrative, clinical perspective*. New York: McGraw-Hill.

TILLICH, P. (1952). *The courage to be*. New Haven, CT: Yale University Press.

*VONTRESS, C. E. (1986). Existential anxiety: Implications for counseling. *Journal of Mental Health Counseling, 8,* 100–109.

VONTRESS, C. E. (1988). An existential approach to cross-cultural counseling. *Journal of Multicultural Counseling and Development, 16*(2), 73–83.

*VONTRESS, C. E. (1996). A personal retrospective on cross-cultural counseling. *Journal of Multicultural Counseling and Development, 24*(3), 156–166.

*VONTRESS, C. E., JOHNSON, J. A., & EPP, L. R. (1999). *Cross-cultural counseling: A casebook*. Alexandria, VA: American Counseling Association.

*YALOM, I. D. (1980). *Existential psychotherapy*. New York: Basic Books.

YALOM, I. D. (1989). *Love's executioner: And other tales of psychotherapy*. New York: Harper Perennial.

YALOM, I. D. (1991). *When Nietzsche wept*. New York: Basic Books.

CHAPTER

7

Person-Centered Therapy

INTRODUCTION
  Historical Background
  Existentialism and Humanism
KEY CONCEPTS
  View of Human Nature
  Basic Characteristics
THE THERAPEUTIC PROCESS
  Therapeutic Goals
  Therapist's Function and Role
  Client's Experience in Therapy
  Relationship Between Therapist and Client
APPLICATION: Therapeutic Techniques and Procedures
  Evolution of Person-Centered Methods
  The Role of Assessment
  Areas of Application
PERSON-CENTERED THERAPY APPLIED TO THE CASE OF STAN
SUMMARY AND EVALUATION
  Summary
  Contributions of the Person-Centered Approach
  Limitations and Criticisms of the Person-Centered Approach
PERSON-CENTERED THERAPY FROM A MULTICULTURAL PERSPECTIVE
  Contributions to Multicultural Counseling
  Limitations for Multicultural Counseling
WHERE TO GO FROM HERE
RECOMMENDED SUPPLEMENTARY READINGS
REFERENCES AND SUGGESTED READINGS

CARL ROGERS

C ARL ROGERS (1902-1987), a major spokesperson for humanistic psychology, led a life that reflected the ideas he developed for half a century. He showed a questioning stance, a deep openness to change, and a courage to forge into unknown territory, both as a person and as a professional. In writing about his early years, Rogers (1961) recalls his family atmosphere as characterized by close and warm relationships but also by strict religious standards. Play was discouraged, and the virtues of the Protestant ethic were extolled. His boyhood was somewhat lonely, and he pursued scholarly interests instead of social ones. During his college years his interests and academic major changed from agriculture to history, then to religion, and finally to clinical psychology.

In 1964 Rogers joined the staff at the Western Behavioral Sciences Institute in La Jolla, California, where he worked with groups of people who were seeking to improve their abilities in human relations. In 1968 he and his colleagues established the Center for the Studies of the Person in La Jolla.

Dr. Rogers earned recognition around the world for originating and developing the humanistic movement in psychotherapy, pioneering in research, and influencing all fields related to psychology. In an interview Rogers was asked what he would want his parents to know about his contributions if he could communicate with them. He replied that he could not imagine talking to his mother about anything of significance because he was sure she would have some negative judgment. Interestingly, a core theme in his theory is the necessity for nonjudgmental listening and acceptance if clients are to change (Heppner, Rogers, & Lee, 1984).

During the last 15 years of his life, Rogers applied the person-centered approach to politics by training policymakers, leaders, and groups in conflict. Perhaps his greatest passion was directed toward the reduction of interracial tensions and the effort to achieve world peace, for which he was nominated for the Nobel Peace Prize. After a fall in 1987 that resulted in a fractured hip, he successfully underwent an operation. During the night following his surgery, however, his heart failed, and he died a few days later as he had hoped to—"with his boots on and, as always, looking forward" (Cain, 1987a). In writing some reflections, Rogers said that his life at 85 was better than anything he could have dreamed of or expected. He added: "I do not know when I will die, but I do know that I will have lived a full and exciting 85 years!" (1987b, p. 152).

In an assessment of Rogers's impact, Cain (1987b) writes that the therapist, author, and person were the same man. Rogers lived his life in accordance with his theory in his dealings with a wide variety of people in diverse settings. His faith in people deeply affected the development of his theories and the way that he related to all those with whom he came in contact. Rogers knew who he was, felt comfortable with his beliefs, and was without pretense. According to Cain, Rogers embodied the characteristics of the fully functioning person. He was not afraid to take a strong position and challenge the status quo throughout his professional career. ■

INTRODUCTION

Historical Background

The person-centered approach is based on concepts from humanistic psychology, and it shares many concepts and values with the existential perspective presented in Chapter 6. Rogers's basic assumptions are that people are essentially trustworthy, that they have a vast potential for understanding themselves and resolving their own problems without direct intervention on the therapist's part, and that they are capable of self-directed growth if they are involved in a specific kind of therapeutic relationship. From the beginning, he emphasized the attitudes and personal characteristics of the therapist and the quality of the client/therapist relationship as the prime determinants of the outcome of the therapeutic process. He consistently relegated to a secondary position matters such as the therapist's knowledge of theory and techniques.

In tracing the major turning points in Rogers's approach, Zimring and Raskin (1992) have identified four periods of development. The first period was during the 1940s, a time when he developed what was known as *nondirective counseling* as a reaction against the directive and traditional psychoanalytic approaches to individual therapy. His theory emphasized the counselor's creation of a permissive and nondirective climate. He caused a great furor when he challenged the basic assumption that "the counselor knows best." He also challenged the validity of commonly accepted therapeutic procedures such as advice, suggestion, direction, persuasion, teaching, diagnosis, and interpretation. Based on his conviction that diagnostic concepts and procedures were inadequate, prejudicial, and often misused, he omitted them from his approach. Nondirective counselors avoided sharing a great deal about themselves with clients and instead focused mainly on reflecting and clarifying the clients' verbal and nonverbal communications with the aim of gaining insight into those feelings.

In the second period, during the 1950s, Rogers (1951) renamed his approach *client-centered therapy* to reflect its focus on the client rather than on nondirective methods. Central importance was given to the phenomenological world of the client. Rogers assumed that the best vantage point for understanding how people behave was from their own internal frame of reference. He focused more explicitly on the actualizing tendency as the basic motivational force that leads to client change.

The third period, during the 1960s, began with the publication of *On Becoming a Person* (Rogers, 1961). The focus of the approach was on the nature of "becoming the self that one truly is." The process of "becoming one's experience" is characterized by an openness to experience, a trust in one's experience, an internal locus of evaluation, and the willingness to be in process. During the 1960s, Rogers and his associates continued to test the underlying hypotheses of the client-centered approach by conducting extensive research on both the process and the outcomes of psychotherapy.

He was interested in how people best progress in psychotherapy, and he studied the qualities of the client/therapist relationship as a catalyst leading to personality change. On the basis of this research the approach was further refined (Rogers, 1961). For example, client-centered philosophy was applied to education and was called student-centered teaching. It was also applied to encounter groups, which were led by laypersons in the 1960s (Rogers, 1970).

The fourth phase, during the 1970s and 1980s, was marked by considerable expansion to education, industry, groups, conflict resolution, and the search for world peace. Because of Rogers's ever-widening scope of influence, including his interest in how people obtain, possess, share, or surrender power and control over others and themselves, his theory became known as the *person-centered approach*. This shift in terms reflected the broadening application of the approach. Although the person-centered approach has been applied mainly to individual and group counseling, important areas of further application include education, family life, leadership and administration, organizational development, health care, cross-cultural and interracial activity, and international relations. It was during the late 1970s and most of the 1980s that Rogers directed his efforts toward applying the person-centered approach to politics, especially to the achievement of world peace.

Existentialism and Humanism

In the 1960s and 1970s there was a growing interest among counselors in a "third force" in therapy as an alternative to the psychoanalytic and behavioral approaches. Under this heading fall existential therapy, the person-centered approach, and Gestalt therapy, developed by Fritz and Laura Perls (the subjects of Chapter 8). Both person-centered therapy and Gestalt therapy are experiential and relationship-oriented.

Partly because of this historical connection and partly because representatives of existentialist thinking and humanistic thinking have not always clearly sorted out their views, the connections between the terms *existentialism* and *humanism* have tended to be confusing for students and theorists alike. The two viewpoints have much in common, yet there are also significant philosophical differences between them. They share a respect for the client's subjective experience and a trust in the capacity of the client to make positive and constructive conscious choices. They have in common an emphasis on concepts such as freedom, choice, values, personal responsibility, autonomy, purpose, and meaning. They differ in that existentialists take the position that we are faced with the anxiety of choosing to create an identity in a world that lacks intrinsic meaning. The humanists, in contrast, take the somewhat less anxiety-evoking position that each of us has a natural potential that we can actualize and through which we can find meaning.

The underlying vision of humanistic philosophy is captured by the metaphor of how an acorn, if provided with the appropriate conditions, will "automatically" grow in positive ways, pushed naturally toward its actualization as an oak. In contrast, for the existentialist there is nothing that we "are"; no internal "nature" we can count on, and we are faced at every moment with a choice about what to make of this condition. The humanistic philosophy on which the person-centered approach rests is expressed in attitudes and behaviors that create a growth-producing climate. According to Rogers (1986b), when this philosophy is lived, it helps people develop their capacities and stimulates constructive change in others. Individuals are empowered, and they are able to use this power for personal and social transformation.

As will become evident in this chapter, the existential and person-centered approaches have a number of parallel concepts, especially as they apply to the client/therapist relationship at the core of therapy. The phenomenology that is basic to the existentialist approach is also fundamental to person-centered theory. Both approaches focus on the client's perceptions and call for the therapist to enter the client's subjective world.

 ## KEY CONCEPTS

View of Human Nature

A common theme originating in Rogers's early writing and continuing to permeate all of his works is a basic sense of trust in the client's ability to move forward in a constructive manner if the appropriate conditions fostering growth are present. His professional experience taught him that if one is able to get to the core of an individual, one finds a trustworthy, positive center (Rogers, 1987c). He firmly maintains that people are trustworthy, resourceful, capable of self-understanding and self-direction, able to make constructive changes, and able to live effective and productive lives (Cain, 1987b). When therapists are able to experience and communicate their realness, caring, and nonjudgmental understanding, significant changes in the client are most likely to occur.

Rogers expresses little sympathy for approaches based on the assumption that the individual cannot be trusted and instead needs to be directed, motivated, instructed, punished, rewarded, controlled, and managed by others who are in a superior and "expert" position. He maintains that three therapist attributes create a growth-promoting climate in which individuals can move forward and become what they are capable of becoming. These attributes are (1) congruence (genuineness, or realness), (2) unconditional positive regard (acceptance and caring), and (3) accurate empathic understanding (an ability to deeply grasp the subjective world of another person). According to Rogers, if these attitudes are communicated by the helper, those being helped will become less defensive and more open to themselves and their world, and they will behave in prosocial and constructive ways. The basic drive to fulfillment implies that people will move toward health if the way seems open for them to do so. Thus, the goals of counseling are to set clients free and to create those conditions that will enable them to engage in meaningful self-exploration. When people are free, they will be able to find their own way (Combs, 1989).

This positive view of human nature has significant implications for the practice of therapy. Because of the belief that the individual has an inherent capacity to move away from maladjustment and toward psychological health, the therapist places the primary responsibility on the client. The person-centered approach rejects the role of the therapist as the authority who knows best and of the passive client who merely follows the dictates of the therapist. Therapy is thus rooted in the client's capacity for awareness and self-directed change in attitudes and behavior.

Seeing people in this light means that the therapist focuses on the constructive side of human nature, on what is right with the person, and on the assets that people bring with them to therapy. The emphasis is on how clients act in their world with others, how they can move forward in constructive directions, and how they can successfully encounter obstacles (both from within themselves and outside of themselves) that are blocking their growth. Practitioners with a humanistic orientation aim at challenging their clients to make changes that will lead to living fully and authentically, with the realization that this kind of existence demands a continuing struggle. People never arrive at a final or a static state of being self-actualized; rather, they are continually involved in the process of actualizing themselves.

Basic Characteristics

Rogers did not present the person-centered theory as a fixed and completed approach to therapy. He hoped that others would view his theory as a set of tentative principles relating to how the therapy process develops, not as dogma. Rogers and Wood (1974, pp. 213–214) describe the characteristics that distinguish the person-centered approach from other models. An adaptation of this description follows.

The person-centered approach focuses on the client's responsibility and capacity to discover ways to more fully encounter reality. Clients, who know themselves best, are the ones to discover more appropriate behavior for themselves based on a growing self-awareness. The approach emphasizes the phenomenal world of the client. With an attempt to apprehend the client's internal frame of reference, therapists concern themselves mainly with the client's perception of self and of the world.

According to the person-centered approach, psychotherapy is only one example of a constructive personal relationship. People experience psychotherapeutic growth in and through a relationship with another person who is caring, understanding, and real. It is the relationship with a counselor who is congruent (matching external behavior and expression with internal feelings and thoughts), accepting, and empathic that facilitates therapeutic change for the client. Person-centered theory holds that the therapist's function is to be present and accessible to the client and to focus on the here-and-now experience.

This approach is perhaps best characterized as a way of being and as a shared journey in which therapist and client reveal their humanness and participate in a growth experience. The therapist can be a guide on this journey because he or she is usually more experienced and more psychologically mature than the client. However, it is important to realize that the therapeutic relationship involves two people, both of whom are fallible. Both of them can get better at what they are doing, yet they have limits. It is not realistic to expect that any therapist can be real, caring, understanding, and accepting all of the time with all clients (Sanford, 1990).

 # THE THERAPEUTIC PROCESS

Therapeutic Goals

The goals of person-centered therapy are different from those of traditional approaches. The person-centered approach aims toward a greater degree of independence and integration of the individual. Its focus is on the person, not on the person's presenting problem. In Rogers's view (1977) the aim of therapy is not merely to solve problems. Rather, it is to assist clients in their growth process, so that they can better cope with problems they are now facing and with future problems.

Rogers (1961) writes that people who enter psychotherapy often ask: "How can I discover my real self? How can I become what I deeply wish to become? How can I get behind my facades and become myself?" The underlying aim of therapy is to provide a climate conducive to helping the individual become a fully functioning person. Before clients are able to work toward that goal, they must first get behind the masks they wear, which they develop through the process of socialization. Clients come to recognize that they have lost contact with themselves by using these facades. In a climate of safety in the therapeutic session, they also come to realize that there are other possibilities.

When the facades are worn away during the therapeutic process, what kind of person emerges from behind the pretenses? Rogers (1961) describes people who are becoming increasingly actualized as having (1) an openness to experience, (2) a trust in themselves, (3) an internal source of evaluation, and (4) a willingness to continue growing. Encouraging these characteristics is the basic goal of person-centered therapy.

These four characteristics provide a general framework for understanding the direction of therapeutic movement. The therapist does not choose specific goals for the client. The cornerstone of person-centered theory is the view that clients in a relationship with a facilitating therapist have the capacity to define and clarify their own goals. Many counselors, however, experience difficulty in allowing clients to decide for themselves their specific goals in therapy. Although it is easy to give lip service to the concept of clients' finding their own way, it takes considerable respect for clients and faith on the therapist's part to encourage clients to listen to themselves and follow their own directions, particularly when they make choices that are not what the therapist hoped for.

Therapist's Function and Role

The role of person-centered therapists is rooted in their ways of being and attitudes, not in techniques designed to get the client to "do something." Research on person-centered therapy seems to indicate that the attitudes of therapists, rather than their knowledge, theories, or techniques, facilitate personality change in the client. Basically, therapists use themselves as an instrument of change. When they encounter the client on a person-to-person level, their "role" is to be without roles. Their function is to establish a therapeutic climate that helps the client grow.

The person-centered therapist thus creates a helping relationship in which clients experience the necessary freedom to explore areas of their life that are now either denied to awareness or distorted. They become less defensive and more open to possibilities within themselves and in the world. First and foremost, the therapist must be willing to be real in the relationship with clients. Instead of viewing clients in preconceived diagnostic categories, the therapist meets them on a moment-to-moment experiential basis and enters their world. Through the therapist's attitudes of genuine caring, respect, acceptance, and understanding, clients are able to loosen their defenses and rigid perceptions and move to a higher level of personal functioning.

Client's Experience in Therapy

Therapeutic change depends on clients' perceptions both of their own experience in therapy and of the counselor's basic attitudes. If the counselor creates a climate conducive to self-exploration, clients have the opportunity to explore the full range of their experience, which includes their feelings, beliefs, behavior, and worldview. What follows is a general sketch of clients' experiences in therapy.

Clients come to the counselor in a state of incongruence; that is, a discrepancy exists between their self-perception and their experience in reality. For example, Leon, a college student, may see himself as a future physician, yet his below-average grades might exclude him from medical school. The discrepancy between how Leon sees himself (self-concept) or how he would *like* to view himself (ideal self-concept) and the reality of his poor academic performance may result in anxiety and personal vulnerability, which can provide the necessary motivation to enter therapy. Leon must perceive that a problem exists or, at least, that he is uncomfortable enough with his present psychological adjustment to want to explore possibilities for change.

One reason clients seek therapy is a feeling of basic helplessness, powerlessness, and an inability to make decisions or effectively direct their own lives. They may hope to find "the way" through the guidance of the therapist. Within the person-centered framework, however, clients soon learn that they can be responsible for themselves in the relationship and that they can learn to be freer by using the relationship to gain greater self-understanding.

As counseling progresses, clients are able to explore a wider range of beliefs and feelings (Rogers, 1987e). They can express their fears, anxiety, guilt, shame, hatred, anger, and other emotions that they had deemed too negative to accept and incorporate into their self-structure. With therapy, people distort less and move to a greater acceptance and integration of conflicting and confusing feelings. They increasingly discover aspects within themselves that had been kept hidden. As clients feel understood and accepted, their defensiveness is less necessary, and they become more open to their experience. Because they are not as threatened, feel safer, and are less vulnerable, they become more realistic, perceive others with greater accuracy, and become better able to understand and accept others. They come to appreciate themselves more as they are, and their behavior shows more flexibility and creativity. They become less oriented to meeting others' expectations, and thus they begin to behave in ways that are truer to themselves. These individuals empower themselves to direct their own lives instead of looking outside of themselves for answers. They move in the direction of being more in contact with what they are experiencing at the present moment, less bound by the past, less determined, freer to make decisions, and increasingly trusting in themselves to manage their own lives. In short, their experience in therapy is like throwing off the self-imposed shackles that had kept them in a psychological prison. With increased freedom they tend to become more mature psychologically and more actualized.

Relationship Between Therapist and Client

Rogers (1957) formulated his hypothesis of the necessary and sufficient conditions for change, which dealt with the core conditions promoting therapeutic progress. The basic hypothesis of person-centered therapy is summarized in this sentence: "If I can provide a certain type of relationship, the other person will discover within himself or herself the capacity to use that relationship for growth and change, and personal development will occur" (Rogers, 1961, p. 33). Rogers hypothesizes further that "significant positive personality change does not occur except in a relationship" (1967, p. 73).

What are the characteristics of the therapeutic relationship that are conducive to creating a suitable psychological climate in which the client will experience the freedom necessary to initiate personality change? According to Rogers (1957, 1987e), these are necessary and sufficient conditions for personality change to occur:

1. Two people are in psychological contact.
2. The first, whom we shall term the client, is experiencing incongruency or is anxious.
3. The second person, whom we shall term the therapist, is congruent or integrated in the relationship.

4. The therapist experiences unconditional positive regard and acceptance for the client.
5. The therapist experiences an empathic understanding of the client's internal frame of reference and strives to communicate this experience to the client.
6. The communication to the client of the therapist's empathic understanding and acceptance is to a minimal degree achieved.

Rogers hypothesizes that no other conditions are necessary. If the six conditions exist over some period of time, constructive personality change will occur. The conditions do not vary according to client type. Further, they are necessary and sufficient for all approaches to therapy and apply to all personal relationships, not just to psychotherapy. The therapist need not have any specialized knowledge. Accurate psychological diagnosis is not necessary and more often than not may interfere with effective therapy. Rogers admitted that his theory was striking and radical. His formulation has generated considerable controversy, for he asserts that many conditions other therapists commonly regard as necessary for effective psychotherapy are nonessential.

From Rogers's perspective the client/therapist relationship is characterized by equality. Therapists do not keep their knowledge a secret or attempt to mystify the therapeutic process. The process of change in the client depends to a large degree on the quality of this equal relationship. As clients experience the therapist listening in an accepting way to them, they gradually learn how to listen acceptingly to themselves. As they find the therapist caring for and valuing them (even the aspects that have been hidden and regarded as negative), clients begin to see worth and value in themselves. As they experience the realness of the therapist, clients drop many of their pretenses and are real with both themselves and the therapist.

As noted earlier, three personal attitudes of the therapist form a central part of the therapeutic relationship: (1) congruence, or genuineness, (2) unconditional positive regard and acceptance, and (3) accurate empathic understanding.

CONGRUENCE, OR GENUINENESS   Of the three characteristics, congruence is the most important. Congruence implies that therapists are real; that is, they are genuine, integrated, and authentic during the therapy hour. They are without a false front, their inner experience and outer expression of that experience match, and they can openly express feelings, thoughts, reactions, and attitudes that are present in the relationship with the client.

Through authenticity the therapist serves as a model of a human being struggling toward greater realness. Being congruent might necessitate the expression of anger, frustration, liking, attraction, concern, boredom, annoyance, and a range of other feelings in the relationship. This does not mean that therapists should impulsively share all their reactions, for self-disclosure must also be appropriate and well timed. A pitfall is that counselors can try too hard to be genuine. Sharing because one thinks it will be good for the client, without being genuinely moved to express something regarded as personal, can be incongruent. Person-centered therapy stresses that counseling will be inhibited if the counselor feels one way about the client but acts in a different way. Hence, if the counselor either dislikes or disapproves of the client but feigns acceptance, therapy will not work.

Rogers's concept of congruence does not imply that only a fully self-actualized therapist can be effective in counseling. Because therapists are human, they cannot be expected to be fully authentic. If therapists are congruent in their relationships with clients, however, the process of therapy will get under way. Congruence exists on a continuum rather than on an all-or-nothing basis, as is true of all three characteristics.

UNCONDITIONAL POSITIVE REGARD AND ACCEPTANCE   The second attitude therapists need to communicate is a deep and genuine caring for the client as a person. The caring is unconditional; it is not contaminated by evaluation or judgment of the client's feelings, thoughts, and behavior as good or bad. It is important that therapists' caring be nonpossessive. If the caring stems from their own need to be liked and appreciated, constructive change in the client is inhibited. Therapists value and warmly accept clients without placing stipulations on their acceptance. It is not an attitude of "I'll accept you when . . ."; rather, it is one of "I'll accept you as you are." Therapists communicate through their behavior that they value their clients as they are and that clients are free to have feelings and experiences without risking the loss of their therapists' acceptance. Acceptance is the recognition of clients' rights to have their own beliefs and feelings; it is not the approval of all behavior. All overt behavior need not be approved of or accepted.

According to Rogers's (1977) research, the greater the degree of caring, prizing, accepting, and valuing of the client in a nonpossessive way, the greater the chance that therapy will be successful. He also makes it clear that it is not possible for therapists to genuinely feel acceptance and unconditional caring at all times. However, if therapists have little respect for their clients, or an active dislike or disgust, it is not likely that the therapeutic work will be fruitful.

ACCURATE EMPATHIC UNDERSTANDING   One of the main tasks of the therapist is to understand clients' experience and feelings sensitively and accurately as they are revealed in the moment-to-moment interaction during the therapy session. The therapist strives to sense clients' subjective experience, particularly in the here and now. The aim is to encourage clients to get closer to themselves, to feel more deeply and intensely, and to recognize and resolve the incongruity that exists within them.

Empathic understanding implies that the therapist will sense clients' feelings *as if* they were his or her own without becoming lost in those feelings. It is important to understand that accurate empathy goes beyond recognition of obvious feelings to a sense of the less clearly experienced feelings of clients. Part of empathic understanding is the therapist's ability to reflect the experiencing of clients. One of the functions of therapist reflection is to encourage and enable clients to become more reflective themselves. Therapist empathy results in clients' self-understanding and clarification of their beliefs and worldviews.

Empathy is not an artificial technique that therapists routinely use. Rather, empathy is a deep and subjective understanding of the client *with* the client. Therapists are able to share the client's subjective world by tuning in to their own feelings that are like the client's feelings. Yet therapists must not lose their own separateness. Rogers asserts that when therapists can grasp the client's private world as the client sees and feels it—without losing the separateness of their own identity—constructive change is likely to occur. According to David Cain (personal communication, July 15, 1997), empathy, especially emotionally focused empathy, helps clients (1) pay attention and value their experiencing, (2) process their experience cognitively and bodily, (3) see old experience in new ways, (4) modify their self-perceptions and their worldview, and (5) increase their confidence in their perceptions, in making decisions, and in following a course of action.

APPLICATION: Therapeutic Techniques and Procedures

Evolution of Person-Centered Methods

Contemporary person-centered therapy is best considered as the result of an evolutionary process that continues to remain open to change and refinement. Certain trends go back more than 55 years. Rogers's original emphasis was on methods of reflecting feelings. As his view of psychotherapy developed, its focus shifted away from therapeutic techniques and toward the therapist's personal qualities, beliefs, and attitudes and toward the relationship with the client. Thorne (1992) points out that Rogers was committed to "the task of demystifying therapeutic relationships so that they could be studied and experienced as vibrant interactions between real human beings rather than as private, hermetic and essentially mysterious treatment processes between distressed patients and omniscient professionals" (pp. 46–47).

One of Rogers's main contributions to the counseling field is the notion that the quality of the therapeutic relationship, as opposed to administering techniques, is the primary agent of growth in the client. The therapeutic relationship is the critical variable. Techniques do not function separately from the person of the counselor. As was discussed in Chapter 2, counselors need to evolve as persons, not just acquire a repertoire of therapeutic strategies.

In the person-centered framework the "techniques" are listening, accepting, respecting, understanding, and responding. A preoccupation with using techniques will depersonalize the relationship. The techniques must be an honest expression of the therapist; they cannot be used self-consciously, for then the counselor is not genuine. Although person-centered therapists subscribe to a set of basic beliefs about human beings and the desirable characteristics of a client/therapist relationship, they may differ widely in their therapeutic style or the manner in which they implement these beliefs in their counseling practice (Thorne, 1992).

As this approach has developed, counselors have been allowed greater freedom in participating more actively in the relationship. This change encourages the use of a wider variety of methods and allows for considerable diversity in personal style. Rather than restricting themselves by emulating the style of Carl Rogers, counselor trainees need to find their own way by developing a personal style.

The Role of Assessment

Assessment is frequently viewed as a prerequisite to the treatment process. Many mental health agencies utilize a variety of assessment procedures, including diagnostic screening, identification of clients' strengths and liabilities, and various tests. It may seem that assessment techniques are foreign to the spirit of the person-centered approach. What matters, however, is not how the counselor assesses the client but the client's self-assessment. From a person-centered perspective, the best source of knowledge about the client is the individual client. For example, some clients may request certain tests as a part of the counseling process. It is important for the counselor to follow the client's lead in the therapeutic dance (Ward, 1994).

In the early development of nondirective therapy, Rogers (1942) recommended caution in using tests or in taking a complete case history at the outset of counseling. If a counseling relationship began with a battery of tests, he believed clients could get the impression that the counselor would be providing the solutions to their problems. But Rogers admitted that tests might have a place, especially if they were used toward the conclusion of counseling and if the client requested them.

Assessment seems to be gaining in importance in short-term treatments in most counseling agencies, and it is imperative that clients be involved in a collaborative process in making decisions that are central to their therapy. Thus, it may not be a question of whether to incorporate assessment into therapeutic practice but of how to involve clients as fully as possible in their assessment and treatment process.

Areas of Application

The person-centered approach is used extensively in training professionals and paraprofessionals who work with people in a variety of settings. This approach emphasizes staying with clients as opposed to getting ahead of them with interpretations. Hence, it is safer than models of therapy that put the therapist in the directive position of making interpretations, forming diagnoses, probing the unconscious, analyzing dreams, and working toward more radical personality changes.

People without advanced psychological education are able to benefit by translating the therapeutic conditions of genuineness, empathic understanding, and unconditional positive regard into both their personal and professional lives. The basic concepts are straightforward and easy to comprehend, and they encourage locating power in the person rather than fostering an authoritarian structure in which control and power are denied to the person. The core skills can be used by many people in the helping professions. These skills are also essential as a foundation for virtually all of the other therapy systems covered in this book. If counselors are lacking in these relationship and communication skills, they will not be effective in carrying out a treatment program for their clients.

An area where I see the person-centered approach as being especially applicable is crisis intervention. Many people in the helping professions (nursing, medicine, education, the ministry) are the first on the scene in a variety of crises. Consider specific life events that can lead to crises, such as an unwanted pregnancy, an illness, or the loss of a loved one. Even if the helping person is not a trained mental health professional, he or she can do much if the basic attitudes described in this chapter are present. When people are in crisis, one of the first steps is to give them an opportunity to fully express themselves. Sensitive listening, hearing, and understanding are essential at this point. Although a person's crisis is not likely to be resolved by one or two contacts with a helper, such contacts can pave the way for an openness to receiving help later. If the person in crisis does not feel understood and accepted, the situation will probably become aggravated, so that the person may lose hope of "returning to normal" and may not seek help in the future. Genuine support, caring, and nonpossessive warmth can go a long way in building bridges that can motivate people to *do* something to work through and resolve a crisis. People in trouble do not need false reassurances that "everything will be all right." Yet the presence of and psychological contact with a caring person can do much to bring about healing.

 ## PERSON-CENTERED THERAPY APPLIED TO THE CASE OF STAN

Stan's autobiography indicates that he has a fairly clear idea of what he wants for his life. The person-centered therapist relies on his self-report of the way he views himself rather than on a formal assessment and diagnosis. She is concerned with understanding him from his internal frame of reference. Stan has stated goals that are meaningful for him. He is motivated to change and seems to have sufficient anxiety to work toward these desired changes.

The person-centered counselor thus has faith in his ability to find his own way and trusts that he has within himself the necessary resources for personal growth. She encourages Stan to speak freely about the discrepancy between the person he sees himself as being and the person he would like to become; about his feelings of being a failure, being inadequate, or being unmanly; about his fears and uncertainties; and about his hopelessness at times. She strives to create an atmosphere of freedom and security that will encourage Stan to explore the threatening aspects of himself. To do this, the counselor listens intently not only to Stan's words but also to the manner in which he delivers his message. She attempts to understand what it must be like to live in his world. She conveys to him the basic attitudes of understanding and accepting, and through this positive regard he may well be able to drop his pretenses and more fully and freely explore his personal concerns.

Stan has a low evaluation of his self-worth. Although he finds it difficult to believe that others really like him, he wants to feel loved ("I hope I can learn to love at least a few people, most of all, women"). He wants to feel equal to others and not have to apologize for his existence, yet most of the time he is keenly aware that he feels inferior. If his therapist can create a supportive, trusting, and encouraging atmosphere, Stan is likely to feel that she is genuinely interested in him. He can use the relationship to learn to be more accepting of himself, with both his strengths and limitations. He has the opportunity to openly express his fears of women, of not being able to work with people, and of feeling inadequate and stupid. He can explore how he feels judged by his parents and by authorities. He has an opportunity to express his guilt—that is, his feelings that he has not lived up to his parents' expectations and that he has let them and himself down. He can also relate his feelings of hurt over not having ever felt loved and wanted. He can express the loneliness and isolation that he so often feels, as well as the need to dull these feelings with alcohol or drugs.

In relating his feelings, Stan is no longer totally alone, for he is taking the risk of letting his therapist into his private world. In doing so, how will he be helped?

Through the relationship with her, Stan gradually gets a sharper focus on his experiencing and is able to clarify his own feelings and attitudes. He sees that he has the capacity to muster his own strengths and make his own decisions. In short, the therapeutic relationship tends to free him from his self-defeating ways. Because of the caring and faith he experiences from his therapist, Stan is able to increase his own faith and confidence in his ability to resolve his difficulties and discover a new way of being.

Therapy will be successful if Stan comes to view himself in a more positive light. He will be more sensitive to messages within himself and less dependent on confirmation from others around him. He will gradually discover that there is someone in his life whom he can depend on—himself.

Follow-Up: You Continue as Stan's Person-Centered Therapist

Use these questions to help you think about how you would counsel Stan:

- Knowing what you do of Stan, how much faith do you have that he has the capacity to find his own way without active intervention on your part as a therapist?
- How would you describe Stan's deeper struggles? What is his world like from his vantage point?
- In working with Stan from the person-centered perspective, how do you imagine you would function without relying on structured techniques?
- To what extent do you think that the relationship you could develop with Stan would help him move forward in a positive direction? What, if anything, might get in your way—either with him or in yourself—in establishing a therapeutic relationship?   ■

SUMMARY AND EVALUATION

Summary

Person-centered therapy is based on a philosophy of human nature that postulates an innate striving for self-actualization. Further, Rogers's view of human nature is phenomenological; that is, we structure ourselves according to our perceptions of reality. We are motivated to actualize ourselves in the reality that we perceive.

Rogers's theory rests on the assumption that clients can understand the factors in their lives that are causing them to be unhappy. They also have the capacity for self-direction and constructive personal change. Change will occur if a congruent therapist is able to establish with the client a relationship that he or she perceives as genuine, accepting, and understanding. Therapeutic counseling is based on an I/Thou, or person-to-person, relationship in the safety and acceptance of which clients drop their defenses and come to accept and integrate aspects that they have denied or distorted. The person-centered approach emphasizes this personal relationship between client and therapist; the therapist's attitudes are more critical than are knowledge, theory, or techniques. Clients are encouraged to use this relationship to unleash their growth potential and become more of the person they choose to become.

This approach places primary responsibility for the direction of therapy on the client. Clients are confronted with the opportunity to decide for themselves and come to terms with their own personal power. The general goals of therapy are becoming more open to experience, achieving self-trust, developing an internal source of evaluation, and being willing to continue growing. Specific goals are not imposed on clients; rather, clients choose their own values and goals. Current applications of the theory emphasize more active participation by the therapist or facilitator than was the case earlier. More latitude is given for them to express values, reactions, and feelings as they are appropriate to what is occurring in therapy. Counselors can be fully involved as persons in the relationship.

Contributions of the Person-Centered Approach

In assessing the merits and significance of the person-centered approach, Cain (1990a) points out that when Rogers founded nondirective counseling over 50 years ago there were very few other therapeutic approaches. He notes: "At a point in time when there are well over 200 therapeutic approaches, it is worth noting that the client-centered approach continues to have a significant place and role among the major therapeutic systems" (p. 5). The longevity of this approach is certainly a factor to consider in assessing its influence.

Rogers had a major impact on the field of counseling and psychotherapy. When he introduced his revolutionary ideas in the 1940s, he provided a powerful and radical alternative to psychoanalysis and to the directive approaches then practiced. Rogers was a pioneer in shifting the therapeutic focus from an emphasis on technique to that of relationship. According to Farber (1996), Rogers's notions regarding empathy, egalitarianism, the primacy of the therapeutic relationship, and the value of research are commonly accepted by many practitioners and have been incorporated into other theoretical orientations with little acknowledgment of their origin. In spite of Rogers's enormous influence on the practice of psychotherapy, his contributions have been overlooked in clinical psychology programs. With the exception of counselor education and counseling psychology programs, Rogers's work has not been given the respect it deserves (Farber, 1996), and there are few person-centered graduate programs in the United States today.

Rogers consistently opposed the institutionalization of a client-centered "school." Likewise, he reacted negatively to the idea of founding institutes, granting certificates, and setting standards for membership. He feared this institutionalization would lead to an increasingly narrow, rigid, and dogmatic perspective. Rogers (1987c) warned that too much loyalty to a method, a school of thought, or a technique could have a counterproductive effect on the counseling process. The advice he often gave to students-in-training and followed in his own life was this: "There is one *best* school of therapy. It is the school of therapy you develop for yourself based on a continuing critical examination of the effects of your way of being in the relationship" (p. 185).

To its credit, this approach allows for diversity and does not foster practitioners who become mere followers of a guru. It is unfortunate that many followers of Rogers simply imitated his reflective style and equated that with the approach. It is unduly restricting for practitioners to limit themselves to the use of reflection as their primary response. Counselors can be person-centered and practice in a diversity of ways, so long as they demonstrate a belief in the core therapeutic conditions and so long as their practices do not undercut the capacity of clients to discover the best path for themselves. In their edited book, *The Psychotherapy of Carl Rogers,* Farber, Brink, and Raskin (1996) present critical reviews of Rogers's therapeutic style and offer some illuminating commentary on alternative styles.

EMPHASIS ON RESEARCH   One of Rogers's contributions to the field of psychotherapy was his willingness to state his concepts as testable hypotheses and to submit them to research. He literally opened the field to research. He was truly a pioneer in his insistence on subjecting the transcripts of therapy sessions to critical examination and applying research technology to counselor/client dialogues (Combs, 1988). Even his critics give Rogers credit for having conducted and inspired others to conduct extensive studies of counseling process and outcome. He presented a challenge to psychology to design new models of scientific investigation capable of dealing with the inner, subjective experiences of the person. His theories of therapy and personality change have had a tremendous heuristic effect, and though much controversy surrounds this approach, his work has challenged practitioners and theoreticians to examine their own therapeutic styles and beliefs.

Person-centered research has been conducted predominantly on the hypothesized necessary and sufficient conditions of therapeutic personality change (Cain, 1986, 1987b). Most of the other counseling approaches covered in this book have incorporated the importance of the therapist's attitude and behavior in creating a therapeutic relationship that is conducive to the use of their techniques. For instance, the cognitive behavioral approaches have developed a wide range of strategies designed to help clients deal with specific problems. These approaches are based on the assumption that a trusting and accepting client/therapist relationship is necessary for successful application of these procedures. Yet these practitioners contend that the working relationship is not sufficient to produce change. Active procedures are needed to bring it about.

I believe the therapeutic core conditions are necessary for therapy to succeed, yet I do not see them as being sufficient conditions for change for all clients at all times. These basic attitudes are the foundation on which counselors must then build the *skills* of therapeutic intervention. The appropriate use of techniques and the application of skills in counseling are important, but there is a tendency to place too much emphasis on counseling skills to the neglect of the development of the personal characteristics and attitudes of the counselor.

Limitations and Criticisms of the Person-Centered Approach

Some students-in-training and practitioners with a person-centered orientation have a tendency to be very supportive of clients without being challenging. Out of their misunderstanding of the basic concepts of the approach, some have limited the range of their responses and counseling styles to reflections and empathic listening. Although there is value in really hearing a client and in reflecting and communicating understanding, counseling entails more than this. One limitation of the approach is the way some practitioners become "client-centered" to the extent that they diminish the value of their own power as a person and thus lose the impact of their personality on the client.

More than any other quality, the therapist's genuineness determines the power of the therapeutic relationship. If therapists submerge their unique identity and style in a passive and nondirective way, they may not be harming many clients, but they may not be powerfully affecting clients. Therapist authenticity and congruence are so vital to this approach that those who practice within this framework must feel natural in doing so and must find a way to express their own reactions to clients. If not, a real possibility is that person-centered therapy will be reduced to a bland, safe, and ineffectual pabulum.

Cain (1988) organized a "roundtable" discussion on the issue "Why do you think there are so few person-centered practitioners or scholars considering that literally thousands of persons throughout the world attest to the enormous impact Carl Rogers has had on their personal and professional lives?" The responses of participants reflect some of the sources of criticisms of this approach. These responses include:

- Person-centered therapy is too simple.
- It is limited to techniques of attending and reflecting.
- The approach is ineffective and leads to undirected rambling by the client.
- Rather than emphasizing the counselor as a person, it would be better to focus on developing a variety of techniques that can be applied to solving specific problems.
- More emphasis should be placed on systematic training of counseling skills and less on the attitudes of the counselor.
- It is not necessarily true that individuals have within them a growth potential, or actualizing tendency.
- Not all clients have the capacity to trust their own inner direction and find their own answers.

According to Combs (1988), the person-centered approach has been somewhat resistant of the idea that the counselor should function as a teacher, seeing such a role as indicating that the counselor knows what is best for the client. Combs, in contrast, describes counseling as a process to help clients learn better and more satisfying ways of being in the world. He adds that counselors cannot help teaching and influencing their clients by their verbal and nonverbal behavior. He contends that they should recognize and accept their teaching role and use it to help clients attain their goals. I think counselors can carry out both therapeutic and educative functions. They can teach clients, yet they can also encourage clients to move toward independence.

CRITICISMS OF RESEARCH AND THEORY   Although I have applauded person-centered therapists for their willingness to subject their hypotheses and procedures to empirical scrutiny, some researchers have been critical of methodological errors contained in some of these studies. Accusations of scientific shortcomings involve using control subjects who are not candidates for therapy, failing to use an untreated control group, failing to account for placebo effects, reliance on self-reports as a major way to assess the outcomes of therapy, and using inappropriate statistical procedures.

Rogers (1986a) saw that solid research would be essential to the future development of the person-centered approach. He acknowledged that there was relatively little new knowledge being developed in the field, and he expressed concern that the approach could become dogmatic and restrictive. For him, the way to avoid such regression was through "studies—simultaneously hardheaded and tender minded—which open new vistas, bring new insights, challenge our hypotheses, enrich our theory, expand our knowledge, and involve us more deeply in an understanding of the phenomena of human change" (p. 259).

David Cain, the person-centered therapist who reviewed this chapter, comments that although Rogers valued research neither he nor his colleagues have conducted much significant research in over 20 years. There has been little evolution of concepts or methods in person-centered theory since the 1960s. According to Cain (1993), the major reason person-centered counseling is not now thriving is this lack of evolution. He contends that Rogers and the client-centered community in general have remained rather insulated from and unaffected by advances in the fields of human development, clinical psychology, psychiatry, psychopathology, and other approaches to counseling and psychotherapy. The potential of this approach is severely limited because of the relative paucity of information that is being incorporated. In addition, he argues, person-centered therapy is limited by a strong and conservative group committed to preserving the approach in its traditional form. Cain asserts that clients will not receive optimal help from traditional therapists who are practicing in limited and constricted ways. He concludes that the person-centered approach seems to be on the decline in the United States.

PERSON-CENTERED THERAPY FROM A MULTICULTURAL PERSPECTIVE

Contributions to Multicultural Counseling

Person-centered therapy has made significant contributions to the field of human relations with diverse cultural groups. Rogers has had a global impact. His work has reached over 30 countries, and his writings have been translated into 12 languages. Person-centered philosophy and practice can now be studied in several European countries, South America, and Japan. Here are some examples of ways in which this approach has been incorporated in various cultures:

- In several European countries person-centered concepts have had a significant impact on the practice of counseling as well as on education, cross-cultural communication, and reduction of racial and political tensions. In the 1980s Rogers (1987d) elaborated on a theory of reducing tension among antagonistic groups that he began developing in 1948.
- In the 1970s Rogers and his associates began conducting workshops promoting cross-cultural communication. Well into the 1980s he led large workshops in many parts of the world. International encounter groups have provided participants with multicultural experiences.
- Japan, Australia, South America, and Mexico have all been receptive to person-centered concepts and have adapted these practices to fit their cultures.
- Shortly before his death, Rogers conducted intensive workshops with professionals in both Moscow and Thilisi in the former Soviet Union.

Cain (1987c) sums up the far-reaching extent of the person-centered approach to cultural diversity: "Our international family consists of millions of persons worldwide whose lives have been affected by Carl Rogers's writings and personal efforts as well as his many colleagues who have brought his and their own innovative thinking and programs to many corners of the earth" (p. 149).

Limitations for Multicultural Counseling

Although the person-centered approach has made significant contributions to counseling people with diverse social, political, and cultural backgrounds, there are some limitations to practicing exclusively within this framework. Many clients who come to community mental health clinics or who are involved in outpatient treatment tend to want more structure than is provided by this approach. Some ethnic minority clients seek professional help to deal with a crisis, to alleviate psychosomatic symptoms, or to learn coping skills in dealing with everyday problems. When these clients do seek professional help, it may be as a last resort. They expect a directive counselor and can be put off by one who does not provide some structuring.

A second limitation of the person-centered approach is that it is difficult to translate the core conditions into actual practice in certain cultures. Communication of these core conditions must be consistent with the client's cultural framework. Consider, for example, the expression of therapist congruence. Clients accustomed to indirect communication may be uncomfortable with the openness and directness of the person-centered counselor.

A third limitation in applying the person-centered approach with diverse clients pertains to the fact that this approach extols the value of an *internal* locus of evaluation. Yet some ethnic groups value an *external* locus of evaluation. In these cultures, clients are likely to be highly influenced by societal expectations and not simply motivated by their own personal preference. Also, the focus on the development of the individual is often at odds with the cultural value that stresses the common good. It may be viewed as selfish to think about one's personal growth rather than being primarily concerned with what is best for the group.

Consider the example of Lupe, a Latina client, who might well consider the interests of her family over her self-interests. From a person-centered perspective she could be viewed as being in danger of "losing her own identity" by being primarily concerned with her role in taking care of others in the family. A counselor could make a mistake by pushing her to make her personal wants a priority. The context of her cultural values and her level of commitment to these values must be considered in working with her. The counselor may well encourage Lupe to explore how well her values are working for her, but it would be inappropriate for the counselor to impose a vision of the kind of woman she should be. (This topic is discussed more extensively in Chapter 12.)

Although there may be distinct limitations in working exclusively within a person-centered perspective with certain clients because of their cultural background, it should not be concluded that this approach is unsuitable for these clients. There is great diversity among any group of people, and therefore, there is room for a variety of therapeutic styles. More activity and structuring may be called for than is usually the case in a person-centered framework, but the potential positive impact of a counselor who responds empathically to a culturally different client cannot be underestimated. Often, a client has never met someone like the counselor who is able to truly listen and understand. Counselors will certainly find it challenging to empathize with clients who have had a vastly different life experience.

 WHERE TO GO FROM HERE

The Association for Humanistic Psychology (AHP) is an organization devoted to promoting personal integrity, creative learning, and active responsibility in embracing the challenges of being human in these times. For information, contact:

> *Association for Humanistic Psychology*
> 45 Franklin St. #315
> San Francisco, CA 94102
> Telephone: (415) 864-8850
> Fax: (415) 864-8853
> Website: *http://www.ahpweb.org/*

If you are interested in obtaining training and supervised experience in the person-centered approach, or if you want information about workshops, experiential groups, community meetings, or exchanges between individuals as ways of learning about person-centered therapy, contact:

> *Linda Reed, Director*
> Center for Studies of the Person
> 1150 Silverado, Suite #112
> La Jolla, CA 92037
> Telephone: (858) 459-3861
> E-mail: *stillwell@cari.net*
> Website: *www.centerfortheperson.org*

You might also consider joining the Association for the Development of the Person-Centered Approach, an interdisciplinary international organization with more than 250 members. Membership includes a subscription to the *Person-Centered Journal,* the association's newsletter, a membership directory, and information about the annual meeting. It also provides information about continuing education and supervision and training in the person-centered approach. General membership is $65 a year; student membership is $25 a year. For more information, contact:

> *Julie Rabin*
> P. O. Box 396
> Orange, MA 01364
> Telephone: (978) 544-6512
> E-mail: *jlrabin@aol.com*

Recommended Supplementary Readings

One of the best primary sources for further reading is Rogers's *On Becoming a Person* (1961), a collection of his articles on the process of psychotherapy, its outcomes, the therapeutic relationship, education, family life, communication, and the nature of the healthy person.

A Way of Being (Rogers, 1980) contains a series of writings on Rogers's personal experiences and perspectives, as well as chapters on the foundations and applications of the person-centered approach.

The Psychotherapy of Carl Rogers: Cases and Commentary (Farber, Brink, & Raskin, 1996) describes the evolution of person-centered therapy, compares the views of person-centered therapists with those of other orientations, and explores the contributions that Rogers made to contemporary practice.

Facilitating Emotional Change: The Moment-by-Moment Process (Greenberg, Rice, & Elliott, 1996) is based on an experiential therapy framework and describes refinements to person-centered therapy. While strongly identifying the importance of the therapeutic relationship, the authors also point to the importance of responding to "markers" of a client's troubled reaction to a specific situation.

Focusing-Oriented Psychotherapy: A Manual of the Experiential Method (Gendlin, 1996) describes how to encourage therapeutic progress when clients keep repeating the same emotional and behavioral patterns. Gendlin demonstrates how the body has its own way of knowing and how this experience needs to be processed for change to occur.

References and Suggested Readings*

CAIN, D. J. (1986). Editorial: A call for the "write stuff." *Person-Centered Review, 1*(2), 117–124.

CAIN, D. J. (1987a). Carl Rogers' life in review. *Person-Centered Review, 2*(4), 476–506.

CAIN, D. J. (1987b). Carl R. Rogers: The man, his vision, his impact. *Person-Centered Review, 2*(3), 283–288.

CAIN, D. J. (1987c). Our international family. *Person-Centered Review, 2*(2), 139–149.

CAIN, D. J. (Ed.). (1988). Roundtable discussion: Why do you think there are so few person-centered practitioners or scholars considering that literally thousands of persons throughout the world attest to the enormous impact Carl Rogers has had on their personal and professional lives? *Person-Centered Review, 3*(3), 353–390.

CAIN, D. J. (1990a). Fifty years of client-centered therapy and the person-centered approach. *Person-Centered Review, 5*(1), 3–7.

CAIN, D. J. (1990b). Further thoughts about nondirectiveness and client-centered therapy. *Person-Centered Review, 5*(1), 89–99.

CAIN, D. J. (1993). The uncertain future of client-centered counseling. *Journal of Humanistic Education and Development, 31*(3), 133–138.

COMBS, A. W. (1988). Some current issues for person-centered therapy. *Person-Centered Review, 3*(3), 263–276.

COMBS, A. W. (1989). *A theory of therapy: Guidelines for counseling practice.* Newbury Park, CA: Sage.

COREY, G. (2000). *Theory and practice of group counseling* (5th ed.). Pacific Grove, CA: Brooks-Cole/Wadsworth.

---

*Books and articles marked with an asterisk are suggested for further study

COREY, G. (2001). *Case approach to counseling and psychotherapy* (5th ed.). Pacific Grove, CA: Brooks-Cole/Wadsworth.

FARBER, B. A. (1996). Introduction. In B. A. Farber, D. C. Brink, & P. M. Raskin (Eds.), *The psychotherapy of Carl Rogers: Cases and commentary* (pp. 1–14). New York: Guilford Press.

*FARBER, B. A., BRINK, D. C., & RASKIN, P. M. (Eds.). (1996). *The psychotherapy of Carl Rogers: Cases and commentary.* New York: Guilford Press.

*GENDLIN, E. T. (1996). *Focusing-oriented psychotherapy: A manual of the experiential method.* New York: Guilford Press.

*GREENBERG, L. S., RICE, L. N., & ELLIOTT, R. (1996). *Facilitating emotional change: The moment-by-moment process.* New York: Guilford Press.

HEPPNER, R. R., ROGERS, M. E., & LEE, L. A. (1984). Carl Rogers: Reflections on his life. *Journal of Counseling and Development, 63*(1), 14–20.

ROGERS, C. (1942). *Counseling and psychotherapy.* Boston: Houghton Mifflin.

ROGERS, C. (1951). *Client-centered therapy.* Boston: Houghton Mifflin.

ROGERS, C. (1957). The necessary and sufficient conditions of therapeutic personality change. *Journal of Consulting Psychology, 21,* 95–103.

*ROGERS, C. (1961). *On becoming a person.* Boston: Houghton Mifflin.

ROGERS, C. (1967). The conditions of change from a client-centered viewpoint. In B. Berenson & R. Carkhuff (Eds.), *Sources of gain in counseling and psychotherapy.* New York: Holt, Rinehart & Winston.

ROGERS, C. (1970). *Carl Rogers on encounter groups.* New York: Harper & Row.

ROGERS, C. (1977). *Carl Rogers on personal power: Inner strength and its revolutionary impact.* New York: Delacorte Press.

*ROGERS, C. (1980). *A way of being.* Boston: Houghton Mifflin.

ROGERS, C. (1983). *Freedom to learn in the 80's.* Columbus, OH: Merrill.

ROGERS, C. (1986a). Carl Rogers on the development of the person-centered approach. *Person-Centered Review, 1*(3), 257–259.

ROGERS, C. (1986b). Client-centered therapy. In I. L. Kutash & A. Wolf (Eds.), *Psychotherapists casebook* (pp. 197–208). San Francisco: Jossey-Bass.

ROGERS, C. R. (1987a). Inside the world of the Soviet professional. *Counseling and Values, 32*(1), 46–66.

ROGERS, C. R. (1987b). Carl Rogers's column: On reaching 85. *Person-Centered Review, 2*(2), 150–152.

ROGERS, C. R. (1987c). Rogers, Kohut, and Erickson: A personal perspective on some similarities and differences. In J. K. Zeig (Ed.), *The evolution of psychotherapy* (pp. 179–187). New York: Brunner/Mazel.

ROGERS, C. R. (1987d). Steps toward world peace, 1948–1986: Tension reduction in theory and practice. *Counseling and Values, 32*(1), 12–16.

ROGERS, C. R. (1987e). The underlying theory: Drawn from experiences with individuals and groups. *Counseling and Values, 32*(1), 38–45.

ROGERS, C., & WOOD, J. (1974). Client-centered theory: Carl Rogers. In A. Burton (Ed.), *Operational theories of personality.* New York: Brunner/Mazel.

SANFORD, R. (1990). Client-centered psychotherapy. In J. K. Zeig & W. M. Munion (Eds.), *What is psychotherapy? Contemporary perspectives* (pp. 81–86). San Francisco: Jossey-Bass.

THORNE, B. (1992). *Carl Rogers.* Newbury Park, CA: Sage.

WARD, F. L. (1994). Client-centered assessment. *The Person-Centered Periodical, 1*(1), 31–38.

ZIMRING, F. M., & RASKIN, N. J. (1992). Carl Rogers and client/person-centered therapy. In D. K. Freedheim (Ed.), *History of psychotherapy: A century of change* (pp. 629–656). Washington, DC: American Psychological Association.

CHAPTER

8

Gestalt Therapy

INTRODUCTION

KEY CONCEPTS
View of Human Nature
Some Principles of Gestalt Therapy Theory
The Now
Unfinished Business
Personality as Peeling an Onion
Contact and Resistances to Contact
Energy and Blocks to Energy

THE THERAPEUTIC PROCESS
Therapeutic Goals
Therapist's Function and Role
Client's Experience in Therapy
Relationship Between Therapist and Client

APPLICATION: Therapeutic Techniques and Procedures
The Experiment in Gestalt Therapy
Preparing Clients for Gestalt Experiments
The Role of Confrontation
Techniques of Gestalt Therapy

GESTALT THERAPY APPLIED TO THE CASE OF STAN

SUMMARY AND EVALUATION
Summary
Contributions of Gestalt Therapy
Limitations and Criticisms of Gestalt Therapy

GESTALT THERAPY FROM A MULTICULTURAL PERSPECTIVE
Contributions to Multicultural Counseling
Limitations for Multicultural Counseling

WHERE TO GO FROM HERE

RECOMMENDED SUPPLEMENTARY READINGS

REFERENCES AND SUGGESTED READINGS

FRITZ PERLS

Wilhelm Reich, a psychoanalyst who pioneered methods of self-understanding and personality change by working with the body. He was also supervised by several other key figures in the psychoanalytic movement, including Karen Horney.

Perls broke away from the psychoanalytic tradition around the time that he emigrated to the United States in 1946. He later established the New York Institute for Gestalt Therapy in 1952. Eventually, he settled in Big Sur, California, and gave workshops and seminars at the Esalen Institute, carving out his reputation as an innovator in psychotherapy. Here he had a great impact on people, partly through his professional writings but mainly through personal contact in his workshops.

Personally, Perls was both vital and perplexing. People typically either responded to him in awe or found him harshly confrontive and saw him as meeting his own needs through showmanship. He was viewed variously as insightful, witty, bright, provocative, manipulative, hostile, demanding, and inspirational. Unfortunately, some of the people who attended his workshops became followers of the "guru" and went out to spread the gospel of Gestalt therapy. Even though Perls mentioned in one of his books his concerns over those who mechanically functioned as Gestalt therapists and promoted phoniness, it appeared to many that he did little to discourage this kind of cult.

Readers who want a first hand account of the life of Perls should read his autobiography, *In and Out of the Garbage Pail* (1969b). ■

FREDERICK S. ("FRITZ") PERLS (1893–1970) was the main originator and developer of Gestalt therapy. Born in Berlin in a lower-middle-class Jewish family, he later identified himself as a source of much trouble for his parents. Although he failed the seventh grade twice and was expelled from school because of difficulties with the authorities, he still managed to complete his schooling and receive an M.D. with a specialization in psychiatry. In 1916 he joined the German Army and served as a medic in World War I.

After the war Perls worked with Kurt Goldstein at the Goldstein Institute for Brain-Damaged Soldiers in Frankfurt. It was through this association that he came to see the importance of viewing humans as a whole rather than as a sum of discretely functioning parts. Later he moved to Vienna and began his psychoanalytic training. Perls was analyzed by

LAURA PERLS

LAURA POSNER PERLS (1905–1990) was born in Pforzheim, Germany. She began playing the piano at the age of 5 and played with professional skill by the time she was 18. From the age of 8 she was involved in modern dance, and both music and modern dance remained a vital part of her adult life. By the time Laura began her practice as a psychoanalyst, she had prepared for a career as a concert pianist, had attended law school, achieved a graduate degree in Gestalt psychology, and made an intensive study of philosophy. Clearly, Laura already had a rich background when she met Fritz in 1926 and they began their collaboration, which resulted in Gestalt therapy. Laura and Fritz were married in 1930. They founded the New York Institute for Gestalt Therapy and did a great deal of training in this approach. As a team, they made significant contributions to the development and maintenance of the Gestalt therapy movement in the United States from the late 1940s until her death in 1990. Laura Perls's own words make it clear that Fritz was a generator, not a developer or organizer. At the 25th anniversary of the New York Institute for Gestalt Therapy, Laura stated: "Without the constant support from his friends, and from me, without the constant encouragement and collaboration, Fritz would never have written a line, nor founded anything" (Perls, 1990, p. 18).

Laura paid a great deal of attention to contact and support, which differed from Fritz's concern with awareness. Her emphasis on contact underscored the role of the interpersonal and of being responsive to the environment at a time when the popular notion of Gestalt therapy was that it fostered responsibility only to oneself. She corrected some of the excesses committed in the name of Gestalt therapy and adhered to the basic principles of Gestalt therapy theory. She taught that every Gestalt therapist needs to develop his or her own therapeutic style. From her perspective, whatever is integrated in our personality becomes support for what we use technically (Humphrey, 1986). ■

INTRODUCTION

Gestalt therapy, developed by Fritz Perls and his wife, Laura, in the 1940s, is an existential/phenomenological approach based on the premise that individuals must be understood in the context of their ongoing relationship with the environment. The initial goal is for clients to gain *awareness* of what they are experiencing and doing. Through this awareness, change automatically occurs. The approach is *phenomenological* because it focuses on the client's perceptions of reality and *existential* because it is grounded in the notion that people are always in the process of becoming, remaking, and rediscovering themselves. Gestalt therapy is lively and promotes direct experiencing rather than the abstractness of talking about situations. The approach is *experiential* in that clients come to grips with *what* and *how* they are thinking, feeling, and doing as they interact with the therapist. Gestalt counselors value being fully present during the therapeutic encounter, and growth occurs out of genuine contact between client and therapist.

Although Perls was influenced by psychoanalytic concepts, he took issue with Freud's theory on a number of grounds. Whereas Freud's view of human beings is basically mechanistic, Perls stresses a holistic approach to personality. Freud focused on repressed intrapsychic conflicts from early childhood, whereas Perls valued examining the present situation. This approach focuses much more on process than on content. It emphasizes what is being presently experienced rather than the content of what clients reveal. Perls asserts that how individuals behave in the present moment is far more crucial to self-understanding than *why* they behave as they do.

One of the therapist's roles is to devise *experiments* designed to increase clients' self-awareness of what they are doing and how they are doing it. Awareness includes insight, self-acceptance, knowledge of the environment, responsibility for choices, and the ability to make contact with others. It is based on a here-and-now experiencing that is always changing. Clients are expected to do their own seeing, feeling, sensing, and interpreting, as opposed to waiting passively for the therapist to give them insight and answers.

KEY CONCEPTS

View of Human Nature

Fritz Perls's conception of human nature is that clients are manipulative and avoid self-reliance and responsibility. Given this basic assumption, the Gestalt therapist's function is to confront and frustrate the client's escape from responsibility. Perls (1969a) practiced Gestalt therapy paternalistically. Clients have to grow up, stand on their own two feet, and "deal with their life problems themselves" (p. 225). His style of doing therapy involved two personal agendas: moving the client from environmental support to self-support and reintegrating the disowned parts of personality. Perls's conception of human nature and agendas toward self-reliance and reintegration set the stage for a variety of techniques and for a confrontive, frustrating style of conducting therapy.

In contrast to Perls's way of working, contemporary Gestalt therapy stresses dialogue between the client and therapist. The therapist has no agenda, no desire to get anywhere, and understands that the essential nature of the individual's relationship with the environment is interdependence, not independence. This approach creates the ground for contact and experiments that are spontaneous and organic to the moment-to-moment experience of the therapeutic engagement.

The Gestalt view of human nature is rooted in existential philosophy, phenomenology, and field theory. Genuine knowledge is the product of what is immediately evident in the experience of the perceiver. Therapy aims not at analysis but at awareness and contact with the environment. The environment or "field" consists of both the external and internal world. The quality of contact with aspects of the external world (for example, other people) and the internal world (for example, parts of the self that are disowned) is monitored. The process of "reowning" parts of oneself that have been disowned and the unification process proceed step by step until clients become strong enough to carry on with their own personal growth. By becoming aware, clients become able to make informed choices and thus to live a meaningful existence.

A basic assumption of Gestalt therapy is that individuals have the capacity to "self-regulate" in their environment if they are fully aware of what is happening in and around them. Therapy provides the setting and opportunity for that awareness and contacting process to be supported and restored.

The Gestalt theory of change posits that the more we attempt to be who or what we are not, the more we remain the same. Beisser (1970) suggests that it is not possible to change something about ourselves by trying to be different. According to his paradoxical theory of change, we change when we become aware of what we are as opposed to trying to become what we are not. It is important for clients *to be* as fully as possible in their current position, rather than striving to become what they "should be." Rather than being a change agent, Beisser sees the role of the therapist as assisting the client to increase awareness, which will allow re-identification with the part of the self from which he or she is alienated (Breshgold, 1989).

Some Principles of Gestalt Therapy Theory

Several basic principles underlying the theory of Gestalt therapy are briefly described in this section: holism, field theory, the figure-formation process, and organismic self-regulation. Other key concepts of Gestalt therapy are developed in more detail in the sections that follow.

HOLISM   According to Latner (1986), holism is one of the foundational principles of Gestalt therapy. All of nature is seen as a unified and coherent whole, and the whole is different from the sum of its parts. We can only be understood to the extent that we take into consideration all dimensions of human functioning. Because Gestalt therapists are interested in the whole person, they place no superior value on a particular aspect of the individual. Gestalt practice attends to a client's thoughts, feelings, behaviors, body, and dreams. The emphasis is on integration, how the parts fit together, and how the individual makes contact with the environment.

FIELD THEORY   Gestalt therapy is based on field theory, which is grounded on the principle that the organism must be seen in its environment, or in its context, as part of the constantly changing field. Gestalt therapy rests on the principle that everything is relational, in flux, interrelated, and in process. Gestalt therapists pay attention to and explore what is occurring at the boundary between the person and the environment.

THE FIGURE-FORMATION PROCESS   Derived from the field of visual perception by a group of Gestalt psychologists, the figure-formation process describes how the individual organizes the environment from moment to moment. In Gestalt therapy the undifferentiated field is called the background, or ground, and the emerging focus of attention is called the figure (Latner, 1986). The figure-formation process tracks how some aspect of the environmental field emerges from the background and becomes the focal point of the individual's attention and interest. The dominant needs of an individual at a given moment influence this process (Frew, 1997).

ORGANISMIC SELF-REGULATION   The figure-formation process is intertwined with the principle of "organismic self-regulation," a process by which equilibrium is "disturbed" by the emergence of a need, a sensation, or an interest. Organisms will do their best to regulate themselves, given their own capabilities and the resources of their environment (Latner, 1986). Individuals can take actions and make contacts that will restore equilibrium or contribute to growth and change. In therapeutic work what emerges for the client is associated with what is of interest or what the client needs to be able to regain a sense of equilibrium. Gestalt therapists direct the client's awareness to the figures that emerge from the background during a therapy session and use the figure-formation process as a guide for the focus of therapeutic work.

The Now

The present is the most significant tense in Gestalt therapy. One of the main contributions of the Gestalt approach is its emphasis on learning to appreciate and fully experience the present moment. Focusing on the past can be a way to avoid coming to terms with the present.

In speaking of the "now ethos," E. Polster and Polster (1973) develop the thesis that "power is in the present." Many people invest their energies in bemoaning their past mistakes and ruminating about how life could and should have been different, or they engage in endless resolutions and plans for the future. As they direct their energy toward what was or what might have been, the power of the present diminishes.

To help the client make contact with the present moment, the Gestalt therapist asks "what" and "how" questions but rarely asks "why" questions. To promote "now" awareness, the therapist encourages a dialogue in the present tense by asking questions such as "What is happening now? What is going on now? What are you experiencing as you sit there and attempt to talk? What is your awareness at this moment? How are you experiencing your fear? How are you attempting to withdraw at this moment?"

Most people can stay in the present for only a short while and are inclined to find ways of interrupting the flow of the present. Instead of experiencing their feelings in the here and now, clients often *talk about* their feelings, almost as if their feelings were detached from their present experiencing. A Gestalt therapist's aim is to help clients make contact with their experience with vividness and immediacy. Thus, if a client begins to talk about sadness, pain, or confusion, the therapist makes every attempt to have the client experience that sadness, pain, or confusion *now*. As the client attends to the present experience, the therapist gauges how much anxiety or discomfort is present and chooses further interventions accordingly. The therapist might choose to allow the client to flee from the present moment, only to extend another invitation several minutes later. If a feeling emerges, the therapist might suggest an experiment that would allow the client to become more aware of the feeling.

Gestalt therapists recognize that the past will make regular appearances in the present moment, usually because of some lack of completion of that past experience. When the past seems to have a significant bearing on clients' present attitudes or behavior, it is dealt with by bringing it into the present as much as possible. Thus, when clients speak about their past, the therapist may ask them to reenact it as though they were living it now. The therapist directs clients to "bring the fantasy here" and strive to relive the feelings they experienced earlier. For example, rather than talking about a past childhood trauma with her father, a client *becomes* the hurt child and talks directly to her father in fantasy.

Unfinished Business

When figures emerge from the background but are not completed and resolved, individuals are left with unfinished business, which can be manifest in unexpressed feelings such as resentment, rage, hatred, pain, anxiety, grief, guilt, and abandonment. Because the feelings are not fully experienced in awareness, they linger in the background and are carried into present life in ways that interfere with effective contact with oneself and others. Unfinished business persists until the individual faces and deals with the unexpressed feelings. In speaking of the effects of unfinished business, E. Polster and Polster (1973) maintain that "these incomplete directions *do seek* completion and when they get powerful enough, the individual is beset with preoccupation, compulsive behavior, wariness, oppressive energy and much self-defeating behavior" (p. 36). The effects of unfinished business often show up in some blockage within the body. Gestalt therapists emphasize paying attention to the bodily experience on the assumption that if feelings are unexpressed they tend to result in some physical symptom.

Unacknowledged feelings create unnecessary emotional debris that clutters present-centered awareness. For example, consider a man who never really felt loved and accepted by his mother. No matter how he sought her approval, he was always left feeling that he was not adequate. In an attempt to deflect the direction of this need for maternal approval in the present, he may look to women for his confirmation of worth as a man. In developing a variety of games to get women to approve of him, he reports that he is still not satisfied. The unfinished business is preventing him from authentic intimacy with women, because his need is that of a child rather than an adult. He needs to return to the old business and express his unacknowledged feelings of disappointment to achieve closure. He will have to tolerate the uncomfortable feelings that accompany recognizing and working through this impasse.

The impasse, or *stuck point,* is a situation in which individuals believe they are unable to support themselves and thus seek external support. The therapist's task is to help clients get through the impasse so that growth is possible. The counselor assists clients by providing situations that encourage them to fully experience their condition of being stuck. By completely experiencing the impasse, they are able to get into contact with their frustrations and accept whatever is, rather than wishing they were different. Gestalt therapy is based on the notion that individuals have a striving toward actualization and growth and that if they accept all aspects of themselves without judging these dimensions they can begin to think, feel, and act differently.

Personality as Peeling an Onion

Perls (1970) likens the unfolding of adult personality to peeling an onion. To achieve psychological maturity, individuals must strip off five layers of neurosis. These superimposed growth disorders are (1) the phony, (2) the phobic, (3) the impasse, (4) the implosive, and (5) the explosive. The first layer we encounter, the *phony layer,* consists of reacting to others in stereotypical and inauthentic ways. This is the level where we play games and get lost in roles. By behaving *as if* we were a person that we are not, we are trying to live up to a fantasy that we or others have created. Once we become aware of the phoniness of game playing and become more honest, we experience unpleasantness and pain.

The next layer we encounter is the *phobic layer*. At this level we attempt to avoid the emotional pain associated with seeing aspects of ourselves that we would prefer to deny. Our resistances to accepting ourselves the way we actually are pop up. We have catastrophic fears that if we recognize who we really are and present that side of ourselves to others they will surely reject us.

Beneath the phobic layer is the *impasse,* or the point where we are stuck in our own maturation. Typically, this is the time when we attempt to manipulate the environment to do our seeing, hearing, feeling, thinking, and deciding for us. At the impasse we often feel a sense of deadness and feel that we are nothing. If we hope to feel alive, it is essential that we get through the impasse.

If we allow ourselves to fully experience our deadness, rather than denying it or running away, the *implosive level* comes into being. Perls (1970) writes that it is necessary to go through this implosive layer to get to the authentic self. By getting into contact with this layer we expose our defenses and begin to make contact with our genuine self. Perls contends that peeling back the implosive layer creates an explosive state. When we contact the *explosive layer,* we let go of phony roles and pretenses, and we release a tremendous amount of energy that we have been holding in by pretending to be who we are not. To become alive and authentic, it is necessary to achieve this explosion into pain and into joy.

Contact and Resistances to Contact

In Gestalt therapy contact is necessary if change and growth are to occur. When we make contact with the environment, change is inevitable. Contact is made by seeing, hearing, smelling, touching, and moving. Effective contact means interacting with nature and with other people without losing one's sense of individuality. It is the continually renewed creative adjustment of individuals to their environment (M. Polster, 1987). Prerequisites for good contact are clear awareness, full energy, and the ability to express oneself (Zinker, 1978). Miriam Polster claims that contact is the lifeblood of growth. It entails zest, imagination, and creativity. There are only moments of this type of contact, so it is most accurate to think of levels of contact rather than a final state to achieve. After a contact experience there is typically a withdrawal to integrate what has been learned.

The Gestalt therapist also focuses on resistances to contact, which are defenses we develop to prevent us from experiencing the present in a full and real way. E. Polster and Polster (1973) describe five major channels of resistance that are challenged in Gestalt therapy: introjection, projection, retroflection, deflection, and confluence.

Introjection is the tendency to uncritically accept others' beliefs and standards without assimilating them to make them congruent with who we are. These introjects remain alien to us because we have not analyzed and restructured them. When we introject, we passively incorporate what the environment provides, spending little time on becoming clear about what we want or need. If we remain in this stage, our energy is bound up in taking things as we find them.

Projection is the reverse of introjection. In projection we disown certain aspects of ourselves by assigning them to the environment. When we are projecting, we have trouble distinguishing between the inside world and the outside world. Those attributes of our personality that are inconsistent with our self-image are disowned and put onto other people. By seeing in others the very qualities that we refuse to acknowledge in ourselves, we avoid taking responsibility for our own feelings and the person who we are, and this keeps us powerless to initiate change.

Retroflection consists of turning back to ourselves what we would like to do to someone else or doing to ourselves what we would like someone else to do to us. If we lash out and injure ourselves, for example, we are often directing aggression inward that we are fearful of directing toward others. This process seriously restricts engagement between the person and his or her environment. Typically, these maladaptive styles of functioning are adopted out of our awareness; part of the process of Gestalt therapy is to help us discover a self-regulatory system so that we can deal realistically with the world.

Deflection is the process of distraction so that it is difficult to maintain a sustained sense of contact. People who deflect attempt to diffuse contact through the overuse of humor, abstract generalizations, and questions rather than statements (Frew, 1986). They engage their environment on an inconsistent basis, which results in their feeling a sense of emotional depletion. Deflection involves a diminished emotional experience. People who deflect speak through and for others.

Confluence involves a blurring of the differentiation between the self and the environment. For people who are oriented toward blending in, there is no clear demarcation between internal experience and outer reality. Confluence in relationships involves an absence of conflicts, or a belief that all parties experience the same feelings and thoughts. It is a style of contact characteristic of clients who have a high need to be accepted and liked. It is a way of staying safe by going along with others and not expressing one's true feelings and opinions. This condition makes genuine contact extremely difficult. A therapist might assist clients who use this channel of resistance by asking questions such as "What are you doing now? What are you experiencing at this moment? What do you want right now?"

Introjection, projection, retroflection, deflection, and confluence represent styles of resisting contact. The concern of Gestalt therapists is the interruption of contact with the environment when the individual is unaware of this process. Terms such as *resistance to contact* or *boundary disturbance* refer to the characteristic styles people employ in their attempts to control their environment. The premise in Gestalt therapy is that contact is both normal and healthy, and clients are encouraged to become increasingly aware of their dominant style of blocking contact.

Energy and Blocks to Energy

In Gestalt therapy special attention is given to where energy is located, how it is used, and how it can be blocked. Blocked energy is another form of resistance. It can be manifested by tension in some part of the body, by posture, by keeping one's body tight and closed, by not breathing deeply, by looking away from people when speaking as a way to avoid contact, by choking off sensations, by numbing feelings, and by speaking with a restricted voice, to mention only a few.

The Gestalt therapist is especially interested in interruptions between sensation and awareness, interruptions between awareness and mobilization of energy, and interruptions between mobilization of energy and action (Zinker, 1978). Much of the therapeutic endeavor involves finding the focus of interrupted energy and bringing these sensations to the client's awareness. Clients may not be aware of their energy or where it is located, and they may experience it in a negative way. Zinker believes therapy at its best involves a dynamic relationship that awakens and nourishes the client without sapping the therapist of his or her own energy. He maintains that it is the therapist's job to help clients locate the ways in which they are blocking energy and transform this blocked energy into more adaptive behaviors. Clients can be encouraged to recognize how their resistance is being expressed in their body. Rather than trying to rid themselves of certain bodily symptoms, clients can be encouraged to delve fully into tension states. By allowing themselves to exaggerate their tight mouth and shaking legs, they can discover for themselves how they are diverting energy and keeping themselves from a full expression of aliveness.

 ## THE THERAPEUTIC PROCESS

Therapeutic Goals

The basic goal of Gestalt therapy is attaining awareness and, with it, greater choice. Awareness includes knowing the environment, knowing oneself, accepting oneself, and being able to make contact. Increased and enriched awareness, by itself, is seen as curative. Without awareness clients do not possess the tools for personality change. With awareness they have the capacity to face and accept denied parts as well as to fully experience their subjectivity. They can become unified and whole. When clients stay with their awareness, important unfinished business will always emerge so that it can be dealt with in therapy. The Gestalt approach helps clients note their own awareness process so that they can be responsible and can selectively and discriminatingly make choices. Awareness emerges within the context of a genuine meeting between the client and therapist, or within the context of I/Thou relating (Jacobs, 1989; Yontef, 1993).

The existential view (see Chapter 6) is that we are continually engaged in a process of remaking and discovering ourselves. We do not have a static identity but discover new facets of our being as we face new challenges. Gestalt therapy is basically an existential encounter out of which clients tend to move in certain directions. Through a creative involvement in Gestalt process, Zinker (1978) expects clients will:

- Move toward increased awareness of themselves
- Gradually assume ownership of their experience (as opposed to making others responsible for what they are thinking, feeling, and doing)
- Develop skills and acquire values that will allow them to satisfy their needs without violating the rights of others
- Become more aware of all of their senses
- Learn to accept responsibility for what they do, including accepting the consequences of their actions
- Move from outside support toward increasing internal support
- Be able to ask for and get help from others and be able to give to others

Therapist's Function and Role

Beisser's (1970) paradoxical theory of change contends that when we face and fully become what we are, rather than what we think we *should be,* we open rich possibilities for change. Through engagement with clients, Gestalt therapists assist clients in developing their own awareness and experiencing how they *are* in the present moment. According to Perls, Hefferline, and Goodman (1951), the therapist's job is to invite clients into an active partnership where they can learn about themselves by adopting an experimental attitude toward life in which they try out new behaviors and notice what happens.

Gestalt therapists notice what is in both the foreground and the background. The therapist's job is to encourage clients to attend to their sensory awareness in the present moment. According to Yontef (1993), although the therapist functions as a guide and a catalyst, presents experiments, and shares observations, the basic work of therapy is done by the client. Yontef stresses that the therapist's job is to create a climate in which clients are likely to try out new ways of being. Gestalt therapists do not force change on clients through confrontation. Instead, they work within a context of I/Thou dialogue in a here-and-now framework.

An important function of Gestalt therapists is paying attention to clients' body language. These nonverbal cues provide rich information as they often represent feelings of which the client is unaware. The therapist needs to be alert for gaps in attention and awareness and for incongruities between verbalizations and what clients are doing with their bodies. For example, therapists might direct clients to speak for and become their gestures or body parts. Gestalt therapists often ask: "What do your eyes say?" "If your hands could speak at this moment, what would they say?" "Can you carry on a conversation between your right and left hands?" Clients may verbally express anger and at the same time smile. Or they may say they are in pain and at the same time laugh. Therapists can ask clients to become aware of how they are using their laughter to mask feelings of anger or pain.

In addition to calling attention to clients' nonverbal language, the Gestalt counselor places emphasis on the relationship between language patterns and personality. Clients' speech patterns are often an expression of their feelings, thoughts, and attitudes. The Gestalt approach focuses on overt speaking habits as a way to increase clients' awareness of themselves, especially by asking them to notice whether their words are congruent with what they are experiencing or instead are distancing them from their emotions.

The Gestalt counselor gently challenges clients by interventions that help them become aware of the effects of their language patterns. Language can both describe and conceal. By focusing on language, clients are able to increase their awareness of what they are experiencing in the present moment and of how they are avoiding coming into contact with this here-and-now experience. Here are some examples of the aspects of language that Gestalt therapists might focus on:

- *"It" talk.* When clients say "it" instead of "I," they are using depersonalizing language. The counselor may ask them to substitute personal pronouns for impersonal ones so that they will assume an increased sense of responsibility. For example, a client says, "It is difficult to make friends." She could be asked to restate this by making an "I" statement—"I have trouble making friends."

- *"You" talk.* Global and impersonal language tends to keep the person hidden. It takes some degree of art to get clients to describe what is going on within them in a manner that reveals their experience. The counselor often points out generalized uses of "you" and asks the client to substitute "I" when this is what is meant. When a client says, "You feel sort of hurt when people don't accept you," he can be asked to look at how he is distancing himself from intense feelings by using a generalized "you." Again, the client can be encouraged to change this impersonal "you" into an "I" statement, such as "I feel hurt when I'm not accepted."

- *Questions.* Questions have a tendency to keep the questioner hidden, safe, and unknown. Gestalt counselors often ask clients to change their questions into statements. In making personal statements, clients begin to assume responsibility for what they say. They may become aware of how they are keeping themselves mysterious through a barrage of questions and how this serves to prevent them from making declarations that express themselves.

- *Language that denies power.* Some clients have a tendency to deny their personal power by adding qualifiers or disclaimers to their statements. For example, a client might say, "I want to stop feeling like a victim, but I feel powerless to change." Often what follows a "but" serves to discount the first part of the statement. The counselor may also point out to clients how certain qualifiers subtract from their effectiveness. Experimenting with omitting qualifiers such as "maybe," "perhaps," "sort of," "I guess," "possibly," and "I suppose" can help clients change ambivalent messages into clear and direct statements. Likewise, when clients say "I can't," they are really implying "I won't." Asking clients to substitute "won't" for "can't" often assists them in owning and accepting their power by taking responsibility for their decisions. Other words that deny power are the "shoulds" and "oughts" that some people habitually use. By changing these "I shoulds" to "I choose to" or "I want to," clients begin to take active steps to reduce the feeling of being driven and not in control of their lives. The counselor must be careful in intervening so that clients do not feel that everything they say is subject to scrutiny. Rather than fostering a morbid kind of introspection, the counselor hopes to foster awareness of what is really being expressed through words.

■ *Listening to clients' metaphors.* In his workshops, Erv Polster emphasizes the importance of a therapist learning how to listen to the metaphors of clients. By tuning into metaphors, the therapist gets rich clues to clients' internal struggles. Examples of metaphors that can be amplified include client statements such as "It's hard for me to spill my guts in here." "At times I feel that I don't have a leg to stand on." "I feel like I have a hole in my soul." "I need to be prepared in case someone blasts me." "I felt ripped to shreds after you confronted me last week." "After this session, I feel as though I've been put through a meat grinder." Beneath the metaphor may lie a suppressed internal dialogue that represents critical unfinished business or reactions to a present interaction. For example, to the client who says she feels that she has been put through a meat grinder, the therapist could ask: "What is your experience of being ground meat?" or "Who is doing the grinding?" It is essential to encourage this client to say more about what she is experiencing. The art of therapy consists of translating the meaning of these metaphors into manifest content so that they can be dealt with in therapy.

■ *Listening for language that uncovers a story.* Polster (1995) also teaches the value of what he calls "fleshing out a flash." He reports that clients often use language that is elusive yet gives significant clues to a story that illustrates their life struggles. Effective therapists learn to pick out a small part of what someone says and then to focus on and develop this element. Clients are likely to slide over pregnant phrases, but the alert therapist can ask questions that will help them flesh out their story line. It is essential for therapists to pay attention to what is fascinating about the person who is sitting before them and get that person to tell a story.

In a workshop I observed Erv Polster's magnificent style in challenging a person (Joe) who had volunteered for a demonstration of an individual session. Although Joe had a fascinating story to reveal about a particular facet of his life, he was presenting himself in a lifeless manner, and the energy was going flat. Eventually, Polster asked him, "Are you keeping my interest right now? Does it matter to you whether I am engaged with you?" Joe looked shocked, but he soon got the point. He accepted Polster's challenge to make sure that he not only kept the therapist interested but also presented himself in a way to keep those in the audience interested. It was clear that Polster was directing Joe's attention to a process of *how* he was expressing his feelings and life experiences rather than being concerned with *what* he was talking about.

Polster believes storytelling is not always a form of resistance. Instead, it can be the heart of the therapeutic process. He maintains that people are storytelling beings. The therapist's task is to assist clients in telling their story in a lively way. Polster has mentioned that many people come to therapy to change the titles of their stories rather than to transform their life stories.

Client's Experience in Therapy

The general orientation of Gestalt therapy is toward dialogue. Whereas Fritz Perls would have said that clients must be confronted about how they avoid accepting responsibility, the dialogic attitude carried into Gestalt therapy originally by Laura Perls creates the ground for a meeting place between client and therapist. Other issues that can become the focal point of therapy include the client/therapist relationship and the similarities in the ways clients relate to the therapist and to others in their environment. Clients in Gestalt therapy are active participants who make their own interpretations and meanings. It is they who increase awareness and decide what they will or will not do with their personal meaning.

Miriam Polster (1987) describes a three-stage integration sequence that characterizes client growth in therapy. The first part of this sequence consists of *discovery*. Clients are likely to reach a new realization about themselves or to acquire a novel view of an old situation, or they may take a new look at some significant person in their lives. Such discoveries often come as a surprise to them.

The second stage of the integration sequence is *accommodation,* which involves clients' recognizing that they have a choice. Clients begin by trying out new behaviors in the supportive environment of the therapy office, and then they expand their awareness of the world. Making new choices is often done awkwardly, but with support clients can gain skill in coping with difficult situations. Clients are likely to carry out homework assignments that are aimed at achieving success. If an out-of-office experiment does not go well, the client and therapist can explore what went wrong and why. The discussion can move forward into new action by asking what can be done differently next time.

The third stage of the integration sequence is *assimilation,* which involves clients' learning how to influence their environment. At this phase clients feel capable of dealing with the surprises they encounter in everyday living. They are now beginning to do more than passively accept the environment. Behavior at this stage may include taking a stand on a critical issue. Eventually, clients develop confidence in their ability to improve and improvise. Improvisation is the confidence that comes from knowledge and skills. Clients are able to make choices that will result in getting what they want. The therapist points out that something has been accomplished and acknowledges the changes that have taken place within the client. At this phase clients have learned what they can do to maximize their chances of getting what is needed from their environment.

Relationship Between Therapist and Client

As an existential brand of therapy, Gestalt practice involves a person-to-person relationship between therapist and client. Therapists are responsible for the quality of their presence, for knowing themselves and the client, and for remaining open to the client. They are also responsible for establishing and maintaining a therapeutic atmosphere that will foster a spirit of work on the client's part. The therapist's experiences, awareness, and perceptions provide the background of the therapy process, and the client's awareness and reactions constitute the foreground. It is important that therapists allow themselves to be affected by their clients and that they actively share their own present perceptions and experiences as they encounter clients in the here and now.

Gestalt therapists not only allow their clients to be who they are but also remain themselves and do not get lost in a role. They are willing to express their reactions and observations, they share their personal experience and stories in relevant and appropriate ways, and they do not manipulate clients. Further, they give feedback that allows clients to develop an awareness of what they are actually doing. The therapist must encounter clients with honest and immediate reactions and explore with them their fears, catastrophic expectations, blockages, and resistances.

A number of writers have given central importance to the I/Thou relationship and the quality of the therapist's presence, as opposed to technical skills. They warn of the dangers of becoming technique-bound and losing sight of their own being as they engage the client. The therapist's attitudes and behavior and the relationship that is established are what really count (Jacobs, 1989; E. Polster, 1987a, 1987b; M. Polster, 1987; Yontef, 1993). These writers point out that current Gestalt therapy has moved beyond earlier therapeutic practices. Many contemporary therapists place increasing emphasis on factors such as presence, authentic dialogue, gentleness, more direct self-expression by the therapist, decreased use of stereotypic exercises, and a greater trust in the client's experiencing. Laura Perls (1976) expresses well this notion that the person of the therapist is more important than the techniques he or she uses. She writes:

> A Gestalt therapist does not use techniques; he applies *himself in* and *to* a situation with whatever professional skill and life experience he has accumulated and integrated. There are as many styles as there are therapists and clients who discover themselves and each other and together invent their relationship. (p. 223)

E. Polster and Polster (1973) emphasize the importance of therapists knowing themselves and being therapeutic instruments. Like artists who need to be in touch with what they are painting, therapists are artistic participants in the creation of new life. The Polsters implore therapists to use their own experiences as essential ingredients in the therapy process. According to them, therapists are more than mere responders or catalysts. If they are to function effectively, therapists must be in tune with both their clients and themselves. Therapy is a two-way engagement that changes both the client and the therapist. If therapists are not sensitively tuned to their own qualities of tenderness, toughness, and compassion and to their reactions to the client, they become technicians.

In a seminal article, "Dialogue in Gestalt Theory and Therapy," Jacobs (1989) explores the role of the therapeutic relationship as a factor in healing and the extent to which the client/therapist relationship is the focus of therapy. She shows how Martin Buber's philosophy of dialogue, which involves a genuine and loving meeting, is congruent with Gestalt concepts of contact, awareness, and the paradoxical theory of change. Jacobs asserts that a current trend in Gestalt practice is toward greater emphasis on the client/therapist relationship rather than on techniques divorced from the context of this encounter. She believes therapists who operate from this orientation establish a present-centered, nonjudgmental dialogue that allows clients to deepen their awareness and to find contact with another person.

The techniques that therapists employ evolve out of this process. Experiments should be aimed at awareness, not at simple solutions to a client's problem. Jacobs maintains that if therapists use experiments when they are frustrated with a client and want to change the person, they are misusing the experiments and will probably thwart rather than foster growth and change.

 # APPLICATION: Therapeutic Techniques and Procedures

The Experiment in Gestalt Therapy

Although the Gestalt approach is concerned with the obvious, its simplicity should not be taken to mean that the therapist's job is easy. Developing a variety of interventions is simple, but employing these methods in a mechanical fashion allows clients to continue inauthentic living. If clients are to become authentic, they need contact with an authentic therapist. In *Creative Process in Gestalt Therapy* Zinker (1978) emphasizes the role of the therapist as a creative agent of change, an inventor, and a compassionate and caring human being. Although borrowing from Perls, Zinker has carried Gestalt therapy beyond the Perlsian style.

Before discussing the variety of Gestalt methods you could include in your repertoire of counseling procedures, it is helpful to differentiate between exercises (or techniques) and experiments. *Exercises* are ready-made techniques that are sometimes used to evoke certain emotions (such as the expression of anger) in clients. Exercises or techniques can be used in many situations to make something happen or to achieve a goal. They can be catalysts for individual work or for promoting interaction among members of a therapy group. Techniques were fundamental to the kind of therapy Perls carried out, as well as for some early Gestalt practitioners who were trained by him. *Experiments,* in contrast, grow out of the interaction between client and therapist. They can be considered the very cornerstone of experiential learning. The experiment is fundamental to modern Gestalt therapy. Zinker (1978) sees therapy sessions as a series of experiments, which are the avenues for clients to learn experientially. What is learned from an experiment is a surprise to both the client and the counselor. Gestalt experiments are a creative adventure and a way in which clients can express themselves behaviorally. Experiments are spontaneous, one-of-a-kind, and relevant to a particular moment and a particular development of a figure-formation process. They are not designed to achieve a particular goal but occur in the context of a moment-to-moment contacting process between therapist and client. Polster (1995) indicates that experiments are designed by the therapist and evolve from the theme already developing through therapeutic engagement, such as the client's report of needs, dreams, fantasies, and body awareness. Yontef (1993) states that experimentation is an attitude inherent in all Gestalt therapy and is a collaborative process with full participation of the client.

Miriam Polster (1987) says that an experiment is a way to bring out some kind of internal conflict by making this struggle an actual process. It is aimed at facilitating a client's ability to work through the stuck points of his or her life. Experiments encourage spontaneity and inventiveness by bringing the possibilities for action directly into the therapy session. By dramatizing or playing out problem situations or relationships in the relative safety of the therapy context, clients increase their range of flexibility of behavior. According to Polster, Gestalt experiments can take many forms: imagining a threatening future encounter; setting up a dialogue between a client and some significant person in his or her life; dramatizing the memory of a painful event; reliving a particularly profound early experience in the present; assuming the identity of one's mother or father through role playing; focusing on gestures, posture, and other nonverbal signs of inner expression; or carrying on a dialogue between two conflicting aspects within the person. Through these experiments, clients actually experience the feelings associated with their conflicts. Experiments bring struggles to life by inviting clients to enact them in the present. It is crucial that experiments be tailored to each individual and used in a timely manner; they also need to be carried out in a context that offers a balance between support and risk. Sensitivity and careful attention on the therapist's part is essential so that clients are "neither blasted into experiences that are too threatening nor allowed to stay in safe but infertile territory" (M. Polster & Polster, 1990, p. 104).

Preparing Clients for Gestalt Experiments

If students-in-training limit their understanding of Gestalt therapy to simply reading about the approach, Gestalt methods are likely to seem abstract and the notion of experiments may seem strange. Asking clients to "become" an object in one of their dreams, for instance, may seem silly and pointless. It is important for counselors to *personally* experience the power of Gestalt experiments and to feel comfortable suggesting them to clients.

It is also essential that counselors establish a relationship with their clients, so that the clients will feel trusting enough to participate in the learning that can result from Gestalt experiments. Clients will get more from Gestalt experiments if they are oriented and prepared for them. Through a trusting relationship with the therapist, clients are likely to recognize their resistance and allow themselves to participate in these experiments.

If clients are to cooperate, counselors must avoid directing them in a commanding fashion to carry out an experiment. Typically, I ask clients if they are willing to try out an experiment to see what they might learn from it, and I take care to emphasize that no specific result is expected. I also tell clients that they can stop when they choose to, so the power is with them. Clients at times say that they feel silly or self-conscious or that the task feels artificial or unreal. At such times I am likely to respond: "Oh, why not go ahead and be silly? Will the roof cave in if you act foolish? Are you willing to give it a try and see what happens?" I cannot overemphasize the power of the therapeutic relationship and the necessity for trust as the foundation for implementing any technique. If I meet with resistance, I tend to be interested in exploring the client's reluctance. It is helpful to know the reason the client is stopping. Reluctance to become emotionally involved often is a function of the client's cultural background. Some clients have been conditioned to work hard to maintain emotional control. They may have reservations about expressing intense feelings openly, even if they are in an emotional state. This can well be due to their socialization and to cultural norms they abide by. In some cultures it is considered rude to express emotions openly, and there are certain cultural injunctions against showing one's vulnerability or psychological pain. If clients have had a long history of containing their feelings, it is understandable that they will be reluctant to participate in experiments that are likely to bring their emotions to the surface. Of course, many men have been socialized not to express intense feelings. Their reluctance to allow themselves to be emotional needs to be dealt with in a respectful manner.

Other clients may resist becoming emotionally involved because of their fear, lack of trust, concern over being foolish, or some other concern. The *way* in which clients resist doing an experiment reveals a great deal about their personality and their way of being in the world. Therefore, Gestalt therapists expect and respect the emergence of resistance. The therapist's aim is not to eliminate clients' defenses but to meet clients wherever they are.

One way of conceptualizing resistance from a Gestalt perspective is to view it as a resistance to awareness of aspects of self or aspects of the environment. This may take the form of resistance to awareness of a part of the personality which was originally alienated because the painful feelings could not be tolerated. The Gestalt approach brings resistance into awareness so that more direct expression becomes possible. Through this process clients are able to re-identify with previously disowned thoughts, feelings, or impulses (Perls, Hefferline, & Goodman, 1951). The current thinking in Gestalt therapy places much less emphasis on resistance than the early version of Gestalt therapy. In fact, the current view proposes that the term "resistance" is actually incompatible with the philosophical and theoretical tenets of Gestalt therapy (Breshgold, 1989). Although it is possible to look at "resistance to awareness" and "resistance to contact," the idea of resistance is unnecessary to the Gestalt perspective. In their article, "Therapy Without Resistance," Polster and Polster (1976) suggest that instead of attempting to make something happen it is best for therapists to observe what is actually and presently happening. This gets away from the notion that clients are resisting and thus behaving wrongly. According to the Polsters, change occurs through contact and awareness—one does not have to try to change.

It is well to remember that Gestalt experiments are designed to expand clients' awareness and to help them try out new modes of behavior. Within the safety of the therapeutic situation, clients are given opportunities to "try on" a new behavior and, thus, heighten the awareness of a particular aspect of functioning or experience (Breshgold, 1989). Experiments are only means to the end of helping people change, not ends in themselves. The following guidelines, largely taken from Passons (1975) and Zinker (1978), are suggestions I find useful both in preparing clients for Gestalt experiments and in carrying them out in the course of therapy:

- It is important for the counselor to be sensitive enough to know when to leave the client alone.
- To derive maximum benefit from Gestalt experiments, the counselor must be sensitive to introducing them at the right time.
- The nature of the experiment depends on the individual's problems, what the person is experiencing, and the life experiences that both the client and the therapist bring to the session.
- Experiments require the client's active role in self-exploration.
- Gestalt experiments work best when the therapist is respectful of the client's cultural background and is in good contact with the person.
- If the counselor meets with hesitation, it is a good idea to explore its meaning for the client.
- It is important that the counselor be flexible in using techniques, paying particular attention to how the client is responding.
- The counselor should be ready to scale down tasks so that the client has a good chance to succeed in his or her efforts. It is not helpful to suggest experiments that are too advanced for a client.

■ The counselor should learn which experiments can best be practiced in the session itself and which can best be performed outside.

The Role of Confrontation

Students are sometimes put off by their perception that a Gestalt counselor's style is direct and confrontational. I tell my students that it is a mistake to equate the practice of any theory with its founder. Indeed, the contemporary practice of Gestalt therapy has progressed beyond the style exhibited by Perls. Yontef (1993) refers to the Perlsian style as a "boom-boom-boom therapy" characterized by theatrics, abrasive confrontation, and intense catharsis. He implies that the charismatic style of Perls probably met more of his own narcissistic needs than the needs of his clients. Yontef is critical of the anti-intellectual, individualistic, dramatic, and confrontive flavor that characterized Gestalt therapy in the "anything goes environment" of the 1960s. Although there is now less emphasis on confrontation in Gestalt practice, this should not be taken to mean that confrontation is absent.

The style of the therapist and the environment that he or she creates has a great deal to do with a client's willingness to participate in experiments. Frew (1992) talks of three therapy styles—the imposing, competing, and confirming stances. He describes both the imposing stance and the competing stance as being confrontational. Using the *imposing stance,* the therapist is less concerned with understanding and respecting the client's experience than in meeting his or her own agenda for the client. The therapist is the expert who evaluates, diagnoses, confronts, interprets, and dominates the relationship. It is a position of power and control, with little attention paid to what the client wants from the therapist. Using the *competing stance,* the therapist promotes the ethos of rugged individualism. In the competing environment there is a dance of negotiation, compromise, and a process of give and take. In contrast, in the *confirming stance* the therapist is interested in acknowledging the whole being of the client. At the moment of confirmation, the client's needs and experience become the center of the relationship. Frew states that the confirming posture demands curiosity and patience, restraint and trust, and compassion and confidence. The therapist attends to the client's experience without forcing the client to be other than he or she is. By staying with the client's awareness, the therapist provides the ground for freer functioning and change.

Confrontation is a part of many Gestalt techniques, yet it does not have to be viewed as a harsh attack. Confrontation can be done in such a way that clients cooperate, especially when they are *invited* to examine their behaviors, attitudes, and thoughts. Counselors can encourage clients to look at certain incongruities, especially gaps between their verbal and nonverbal expression. Further, confrontation does not have to be aimed at weaknesses or negative traits; clients can be challenged to recognize how they are blocking their strengths and are not living as fully as they might.

An essential ingredient in effective confrontation is respect for the client. Counselors who care enough to make demands on their clients are telling them, in effect, that they could be in fuller contact with themselves and others. Ultimately, however, clients must decide for themselves if they want to accept this invitation to learn more about themselves. This caveat needs to be kept in mind with all of the experiments that are to be described.

Techniques of Gestalt Therapy

Experiments can be useful tools to help the client gain fuller awareness, experience internal conflicts, resolve inconsistencies and dichotomies, and work through an impasse that is preventing completion of unfinished business.

Levitsky and Perls (1970) provide a brief description of a number of interventions used by Gestalt therapists, some of which I will describe here. I have modified this material and added suggestions for implementing these methods. As mentioned earlier, these techniques can be used to elicit emotion, produce action, or achieve a specific goal. When used at their best, these techniques fit the therapeutic situation and highlight whatever the client is experiencing.

THE INTERNAL DIALOGUE EXERCISE   One goal of Gestalt therapy is to bring about integrated functioning and acceptance of aspects of one's personality that have been disowned and denied. Gestalt therapists pay close attention to splits in personality function. A main division is between the "top dog" and the "underdog," and therapy often focuses on the war between the two.

The top dog is righteous, authoritarian, moralistic, demanding, bossy, and manipulative. This is the "critical parent" that badgers with "shoulds" and "oughts" and manipulates with threats of catastrophe. The underdog manipulates by playing the role of victim: by being defensive, apologetic, helpless, and weak and by feigning powerlessness. This is the passive side, the one without responsibility, and the one that finds excuses. The top dog and the underdog are engaged in a constant struggle for control. The struggle helps to explain why one's resolutions and promises often go unfulfilled and why one's procrastination persists. The tyrannical top dog demands that one be thus-and-so, whereas the underdog defiantly plays the role of disobedient child. As a result of this struggle for control, the individual becomes fragmented into controller and controlled. The civil war between the two sides continues, with both sides fighting for their existence.

The conflict between the two opposing poles in the personality is rooted in the mechanism of introjection, which involves incorporating aspects of others, usually parents, into one's ego system. It is essential that clients become aware of their introjects, especially the toxic introjects that poison the system and prevent personality integration.

The empty-chair technique is one way of getting the client to externalize the introject, a technique Perls used a great deal. Using two chairs, the therapist asks the client to sit in one chair and be fully the top dog and then shift to the other chair and become the underdog. The dialogue can continue between both sides of the client. Essentially, this is a role-playing technique in which all the parts are played by the client. In this way the introjects can surface, and the client can experience the conflict more fully. The conflict can be resolved by the client's acceptance and integration of both sides. This exercise helps clients get in touch with a feeling or a side of themselves that they may be denying; rather than merely talking about a conflicted feeling, they intensify the feeling and experience it fully. Further, by helping clients realize that the feeling is a very real part of themselves, the intervention discourages them from disassociating the feeling.

The goal of this exercise is to promote a higher level of integration between the polarities and conflicts that exist in everyone. The aim is not to rid oneself of certain traits but to learn to accept and live with the polarities. Many common conflicts lend themselves to the game of dialogue. Some that I find applicable include (1) the parent inside versus the child inside, (2) the responsible one versus the impulsive one, (3) the puritanical side versus the sexual side, (4) the "good side" versus the "bad side," (5) the aggressive self versus the passive self, (6) the autonomous side versus the resentful side, and (7) the hard worker versus the goof-off.

MAKING THE ROUNDS   Making the rounds is a Gestalt exercise that involves asking a person in a group to go up to others in the group and either speak to or do something with each person. The purpose is to confront, to risk, to disclose the self, to experiment with new behavior, and to grow and change. I have experimented with "making the rounds" when I sensed that a participant needed to face each person in the group with some theme. For example, a group member might say: "I've been sitting here for a long time wanting to participate but holding back because I'm afraid of trusting people in here. And besides, I don't think I'm worth the time of the group anyway." I might counter with "Are you willing to do something right now to get yourself more invested and to begin to work on gaining trust and self-confidence?" If the person answers affirmatively, my suggestion could well be: "Go around to each person and finish this sentence: 'I don't trust you because . . .'" Any number of exercises could be invented to help individuals involve themselves and choose to work on the things that keep them frozen in fear.

Some other related illustrations and examples that I find appropriate for the making-the-rounds intervention are reflected in clients' comments such as these: "I would like to reach out to people more often." "Nobody in here seems to care very much." "I'd like to make contact with you, but I'm afraid of being rejected [or accepted]." "It's hard for me to accept good stuff; I always discount good things people say to me." "It's hard for me to say negative things to people; I always want to be nice." "I'd like to feel more comfortable in touching and getting close."

THE REVERSAL TECHNIQUE   Certain symptoms and behaviors often represent reversals of underlying or latent impulses. Thus, the therapist could ask a person who claims to suffer from severe inhibitions and excessive timidity to play the role of an exhibitionist. I remember a client in one of our groups who had difficulty being anything but sugary sweet. I asked her to reverse her typical style and be as negative as she could be. The reversal worked well; soon she was playing her part with real gusto, and later she was able to recognize and accept her "negative side" as well as her "positive side."

The theory underlying the reversal technique is that clients take the plunge into the very thing that is fraught with anxiety and make contact with those parts of themselves that have been submerged and denied. This technique can help clients begin to accept certain personal attributes that they have tried to deny.

THE REHEARSAL EXERCISE   Oftentimes we get stuck rehearsing silently to ourselves so that we will gain acceptance. When it comes to the performance, we experience stage fright, or anxiety, because we fear that we will not play our role well. Internal rehearsal consumes much energy and frequently inhibits our spontaneity and willingness to experiment with new behavior. When clients share their rehearsals out loud with a therapist, they become more aware of the many preparatory means they use in bolstering their social roles. They also become increasingly aware of how they try to meet the expectations of others, of the degree to which they want to be approved, accepted, and liked, and of the extent to which they go to attain acceptance.

THE EXAGGERATION EXERCISE   One aim of Gestalt therapy is for clients to become more aware of the subtle signals and cues they are sending through body language. Movements, postures, and gestures may communicate significant meanings, yet the cues may be incomplete. In this exercise the person is asked to exaggerate the movement or gesture repeatedly, which usually intensifies the feeling attached to the behavior and makes the inner meaning clearer. Some examples of behaviors that lend themselves to the exaggeration technique are trembling (shaking hands, legs), slouched posture and bent shoulders, clenched fists, tight frowning, facial grimacing, crossed arms, and so forth. If a client reports that his or her legs are shaking, for instance, the therapist may ask the client to stand up and exaggerate the shaking. Then the therapist may ask the client to put words to the shaking limbs.

STAYING WITH THE FEELING   Most clients desire to escape from fearful stimuli and to avoid unpleasant feelings. At key moments when clients refer to a feeling or a mood that is unpleasant and from which they have a great urge to flee, the therapist may urge the clients to stay with their feeling. The therapist may encourage them to go deeper into the feeling or behavior they wish to avoid. Facing, confronting, and experiencing feelings not only takes courage but also is a mark of a willingness to endure the pain necessary for unblocking and making way for newer levels of growth.

THE GESTALT APPROACH TO DREAM WORK   In psychoanalysis dreams are interpreted, intellectual insight is stressed, and free association is used to explore the unconscious meanings of dreams. The Gestalt approach does not interpret and analyze dreams. Instead, the intent is to bring dreams back to life and relive them as though they were happening now. The dream is acted out in the present, and the dreamer becomes a part of his or her dream. The suggested format for working with dreams includes making a list of all the details of the dream, remembering each person, event, and mood in it, and then becoming each of these parts by transforming oneself, acting as fully as possible and inventing dialogue. Each part of the dream is assumed to be a projection of the self, and the client creates scripts for encounters between the various characters or parts. All of the different parts of a dream are expressions of the client's own contradictory and inconsistent sides, and, by engaging in a dialogue between these opposing sides, the client gradually becomes more aware of the range of his or her own feelings.

Perls's concept of projection is central in his theory of dream formation. According to him, every person and every object in the dream represents a projected aspect of the dreamer. Perls (1969a) suggests that "we start with the impossible assumption that whatever we believe we see in another person or in the world is nothing but a projection" (p. 67). He writes that the recognition of the senses and the understanding of projections go hand in hand. Clients do not think about or analyze the dream but use it as a script and experiment with the dialogue among the various parts of the dream. Because clients can act out a fight between opposing sides, eventually they can appreciate and accept their inner differences and integrate the opposing forces. Freud called the dream the royal road to the unconscious, but to Perls (1969a) dreams are the "royal road to integration" (p. 66).

According to Perls, the dream is the most spontaneous expression of the existence of the human being. It represents an unfinished situation, but every dream also contains an existential message regarding oneself and one's current struggle. Everything can be found in dreams if all the parts are understood and assimilated. Perls asserts that if dreams are property worked with, the existential message becomes clearer. According to him, dreams serve as an excellent way to discover personality voids by revealing missing parts and clients' methods of avoidance. If people do not remember dreams, they may be refusing to face what is wrong with their life. At the very least, the Gestalt counselor asks clients to talk to their missing dreams. For example, as directed by her therapist, a client reported the following dream in the present tense, as though she were still dreaming:

> I have three monkeys in a cage. One big monkey and two little ones! I feel very attached to these monkeys, although they are creating a lot of chaos in a cage that is divided into three separate spaces. They are fighting with one another—the big monkey is fighting with the little monkey. They are getting out of the cage, and they are clinging onto me. I feel like pushing them away from me. I feel totally overwhelmed by the chaos that they are creating around me. I turn to my mother and tell her that I need help, that I can no longer handle these monkeys because they are driving me crazy. I feel very sad and very tired, and I feel discouraged. I am walking away from the cage, thinking that I really love these monkeys, yet I have to get rid of them. I am telling myself that I am like every-

body else. I get pets, and then when things get rough, I want to get rid of them. I am trying very hard to find a solution to keeping these monkeys and not allowing them to have such a terrible effect on me. Before I wake up from my dream, I am making the decision to put each monkey in a separate cage, and maybe that is the way to keep them.

The therapist then asked his client, Brenda, to "become" different parts of her dream. Thus, she became the cage, and she became and had a dialogue with each monkey, and then she became her mother, and so forth. One of the most powerful aspects of this technique was Brenda's reporting her dream as though it were still happening. She quickly perceived that her dream expressed a struggle she was having with her husband and her two children. From her dialogue work, Brenda discovered that she both appreciated and resented her family. She learned that she needed to let them know about her feelings and that together they might work on improving an intensely difficult lifestyle. She did not need an interpretation from her therapist to understand the clear message of her dream.

 ## GESTALT THERAPY APPLIED TO THE CASE OF STAN

The Gestalt-oriented therapist will focus on the unfinished business that Stan has with his parents, siblings, and ex-wife. It appears that this unfinished business consists mainly of feelings of resentment, yet he turns this resentment inward toward himself. His present life situation will be spotlighted, but he may also need to re-experience past feelings that could be interfering with his present attempts to develop intimacy with others.

Although the focus is on Stan's present behavior, his therapist is likely to guide him toward becoming aware of how he is carrying old baggage around and how it interferes with his life today. Her task is to assist him in re-creating the context in which he made earlier decisions that are no longer serving him well. Essentially, Stan needs to learn that his decision about the way he had to be to survive during his childhood years may no longer be appropriate. One of his cardinal decisions was: "I'm stupid, and it would be better if I were not here. I'm a loser."

Stan has been influenced by cultural messages that he has accepted. His counselor is interested in exploring his cultural background, including his values and the values characteristic of his culture. With this focus, it is likely that the counselor may help Stan identify some of the following cultural injunctions: "Don't talk about your family with strangers, and don't hang out your dirty linen in public." "Don't confront your parents, because they deserve respect." "Don't be too concerned about yourself." "Don't show your vulnerabilities; hide your feelings and weaknesses." Stan's counselor may challenge Stan to examine those injunctions that are no longer functional. Although he can decide to retain those aspects of his cultural background that he prizes, he is also in a position to modify certain cultural expectations. Of course, this will be done when these issues emerge in the foreground of his work.

Stan's therapist encourages him to attend to what becomes figural as the session begins. She may make interventions such as "What are you experiencing as we are getting started today?" The main point is that as she encourages Stan to tune into his present experience and selectively makes observations, it is likely that a number of figures will emerge. The goal is to focus on a figure of interest that seems to hold the most energy or relevance for Stan. When a figure is identified, the task becomes heightening Stan's awareness of this thought, feeling, body sensation, or insight through related experiments. The therapist designs these experiments to create awareness or to create contact possibilities between Stan and herself. Stan's therapist places value on practicing Gestalt therapy dialogically, which means that she aims to be as fully present as possible and is interested in understanding Stan's world. She will make decisions about how much self-disclosure to make, which will be done for Stan's benefit and to strengthen the therapeutic relationship.

In typical Gestalt fashion, Stan deals with his present struggles within the context of the relationship with his therapist, not simply by talking about his past or by analyzing his insights. She may ask him to "become" some of those individuals who told him how to think, feel, and behave as a child. He can then become the child that he was and respond to them from the place where he feels the most confusion or pain. He experiences in new ways the feelings that accompany his beliefs about himself, and he comes to a deeper appreciation of how his feelings and thoughts influence what he is doing today.

Stan has learned to hide his emotions rather than to reveal them. Understanding this about him, his counselor explores his hesitations and concerns about "getting into feelings." She recognizes that he is hesitant in expressing his emotions and helps him assess whether he would like to experience them more fully and express them more freely.

When Stan decides that he does want to experience his emotions rather than deny them, the therapist asks: "What are you aware of now having said what you did?" Stan says that he can't get his ex-wife out of his mind. He tells the therapist how he feels so much pain over that relationship and how he is frightened of getting involved again lest he be hurt another time. The therapist continues to ask Stan to focus inward and get a better sense of what is standing out for him at this very moment. Stan replies: "I'm hurt and angry over all the pain that I've allowed her to inflict on me." She asks him to imagine himself in earlier scenes with his ex-wife, as though the painful situation were occurring in the here and now. He symbolically relives and reexperiences the situation, perhaps by talking "directly" to his wife. He tells her of his resentments and hurts and eventually moves toward completing his unfinished business with her. By participating in this experiment, Stan is attaining more awareness of what he is now doing and how he keeps himself locked into his past.

Once an experiment is agreed on, it is enacted and debriefed. At this point, depending on time constraints, the session ends or Stan is invited to attend to the next prominent figure that emerges. The art of practicing Gestalt therapy consists of blending the therapist's figure formation with the client's. Stan's figure should be the sovereign one, with the therapist bringing her own ideas, observations, and feelings into contact with Stan to influence his process. The therapist's disclosures can add to and deepen Stan's exploration of key issues, but to make appropriate choices, the therapist's experience, timing, and attunement are crucial.

Follow-Up: You Continue as Stan's Gestalt Therapist

Use these questions to help you think about how to counsel Stan:

- How might you begin a session with Stan? As a Gestalt therapist, would you suggest a direction he pursue? Would you wait for him to initiate work? Would you ask him to continue from where he left off in the previous session? Would you attend to whatever theme or issue becomes figural to him?
- What unfinished business can you identify in Stan's case? Does any of his experience of being stuck remind you of aspects within yourself? As his Gestalt therapist, how might you work with Stan if he did bring up your own unfinished business?

- Stan's Gestalt therapist created an experiment to assist Stan in dealing with pain, resentment, and hurt over situations with his ex-wife. How might you have worked with the material Stan brought up? What kind of experiment might you design? How would you decide what kind of experiment to create?
- How might you work with Stan's cultural messages? Would you be able to respect his cultural values and still encourage him to make an assessment of some of the ways in which his culture is affecting him today? ■

 SUMMARY AND EVALUATION

Summary

Gestalt therapy is an experiential approach that stresses present awareness and the quality of contact between the individual and the environment. The major focus is on assisting the client to become aware of how behaviors once part of creatively adjusting to past environments may be interfering with effective functioning and living in the present. The goal of the approach is, first and foremost, awareness.

Another therapeutic aim is to assist clients in exploring how they make contact with elements of their environment. Change occurs through the heightened awareness of "what is." Because the Gestalt therapist has no agenda beyond assisting clients to increase their awareness, there is no need to label a client's behavior as "resistance." Instead, the therapist simply follows this new process as it emerges. The therapist has faith that self-regulation is a naturally unfolding process that does not have to be controlled (Breshgold, 1989). With awareness, clients are able to reconcile polarities and dichotomies within themselves and proceed toward the reintegration of all aspects of themselves.

The therapist works with the client to identify the "figures," or most salient aspects of the individual/environmental field, as they emerge from the background. The Gestalt therapist believes each client is capable of self-regulating if those figures are engaged and resolved so others can replace them. The role of the Gestalt therapist is to help clients identify the most pressing issues, needs, and interests and to design experiments that carry those figures into contact or that explore resistances to contact and awareness.

Contributions of Gestalt Therapy

Gestalt methods bring conflicts and human struggles to life. With this approach, people actually experience their struggles, as opposed to merely talking about problems endlessly in a detached manner. I especially like the range of experiments a therapist can suggest to help clients discover new facets of themselves.

Another of Gestalt therapy's contributions is the exciting way in which the past is dealt with in a lively manner by bringing relevant aspects into the present. Therapists challenge clients in creative ways to become aware of and work with issues that are obstructing current functioning. Further, paying attention to the obvious verbal and nonverbal leads provided by clients is a useful way to approach a counseling session. Through the skillful and sensitive use of Gestalt interventions, practitioners can assist clients in heightening their present-centered awareness of what they are thinking and feeling as well as what they are doing. Clients are provided with a wide range of tools—in the form of Gestalt experiments—for making decisions about changing the course of living.

The Gestalt approach to working with dreams is a unique pathway for people to increase their awareness of key themes in their lives. By seeing each aspect of a dream as a projection of themselves, clients are able to bring the dream to life, to interpret its personal meaning, and to assume responsibility for it.

Some other contributions of Gestalt therapy include:

- Gestalt therapy is a holistic approach that values each aspect of the individual's experience equally. Therapists allow the figure-formation process to guide them. They do not approach clients with a preconceived set of biases or a set agenda. Instead, they place emphasis on what occurs at the boundary between the individual and the environment.
- Gestalt therapy operates with a unique notion about change. The therapist does not try to move the client anywhere. The main goal is to increase the client's awareness of "what is." Instead of trying to make something happen, the therapist's role is assisting the client to increase awareness which will allow re-identification with the part of the self from which he or she is alienated.
- Gestalt therapy is a creative approach that utilizes experiments to move clients from talk to action and experience. The focus is on growth and enhancement rather than being a system of techniques to treat disorders.

Limitations and Criticisms of Gestalt Therapy

Most of my criticisms of Gestalt therapy pertain to the older version, or the style of Fritz Perls, that emphasized confrontation and deemphasized the cognitive factors of personality. This style of Gestalt therapy placed more attention on using techniques to confront clients and getting them to experience their feelings. Contemporary Gestalt therapy has come a long way, and more attention is being given to theoretical instruction, theoretical exposition, and cognitive factors in general (Yontef, 1993).

Although Gestalt therapy discourages interrupting the process of immediate experiencing and integration by focusing on cognitive explanations, clients do clarify their thinking, explore beliefs, and put meaning to experiences they are reliving in therapy. Gestalt therapy also discourages the therapist from *teaching* clients, as opposed to *facilitating* the clients' own process of self-discovery and learning. This is based on the fundamental belief in organismic self-regulation, which implies that clients arrive at their own truths through awareness and improved contact with the environment. It seems to me, however, that clients can engage in self-discovery and at the same time benefit from appropriate teaching by the therapist. Why should therapy exclude giving information, making suggestions, cognitive processing, explanations, interpretations, and coaching on the therapist's part? As you will see, I favor blending the emotional and experiential work of Gestalt therapy with concepts and techniques of the cognitive and behavioral approaches (especially behavior therapy, rational emotive behavior therapy, and reality therapy).

Current Gestalt practice places a high value on the contact and dialogue between the therapist and client. For Gestalt therapy to be effective, the therapist must have a high level of personal development. Being aware of one's own needs and seeing that they do not interfere with the client's process, being present in the moment, and being willing to be nondefensive and self-revealing all demand a lot of the therapist. There is a danger that therapists who are inadequately trained will be primarily concerned with impressing clients.

SOME CAUTIONS   A major concern I have about Gestalt therapy is the potential danger for abusing power. Typically, Gestalt therapists are highly active and directive, and if they do not have the characteristics mentioned by Zinker (1978)—sensitivity, timing, inventiveness, empathy, and respect for the client— their experiments can easily boomerang.

The techniques utilized by Fritz Perls have been incorporated by many therapists who do not have a solid grounding in the theory and practice of Gestalt therapy. Therapists who rely on ready-made techniques, rather than experiments that grow out of dialogue in the therapeutic relationship, can actually damage this relationship. An ethical issue is raised by inept therapists who use powerful techniques to stir up feelings and open up problems that clients have kept from full awareness, only to abandon the clients once they have managed to have a dramatic catharsis. Such a failure to stay with clients, helping them work through what they have experienced and bring some closure to the experience, can be detrimental.

Ethical practice depends on the level of training and supervision of therapists, and the most immediate limitation of Gestalt, or any other therapy, is the skill, training, experience, and judgment of the therapist. Proper training in Gestalt therapy involves reading and learning the theory, hours of supervised practice, observing Gestalt therapists at work, and experiencing one's own personal therapy. Therapists who are trained in the theory and method of Gestalt therapy are far less likely to do poor work. Such therapists have learned to blend a phenomenological and dialogic approach, which is inherently respectful to the client, with well-timed experiments.

 GESTALT THERAPY FROM A MULTICULTURAL PERSPECTIVE

Contributions to Multicultural Counseling

There are opportunities to sensitively and creatively use Gestalt methods, if they are timed appropriately, with culturally diverse populations. One of the advantages of drawing on Gestalt experiments is that they can be tailored to fit the unique way in which an individual perceives and interprets his or her culture. Gestalt therapists approach each client in an open way and without preconceptions. This is particularly important in working with clients from other cultures.

Gestalt therapy is particularly effective in helping people integrate the polarities within themselves. Many bicultural clients experience an ongoing struggle to reconcile what appear to be diverse aspects of the two cultures in which they live. In one of my weeklong groups, a dynamic piece of work was done by a woman with European roots. Her struggle consisted of integrating her American side with her experiences in Germany as a child. I asked her to "bring her family into this group" by talking to selected members in the group as though they were members of her family. She was asked to imagine that she was 8 years old and that she could now say to her parents and siblings things that she had never expressed. I asked her to speak in German (since this was her primary language as a child). The combined factors of her trust in the group, her willingness to re-create an early scene by reliving it in the present moment, and her symbolic work with fantasy helped her achieve a significant breakthrough. She was able to put a new ending to an old and unfinished situation through her participation in this Gestalt experiment.

There are many opportunities to apply Gestalt experiments in creative ways with diverse client populations. In cultures where indirect speech is the norm, nonverbal behaviors may emphasize the unspoken content of verbal communication. These clients may express themselves nonverbally more expressively than they do with words. Gestalt therapists may ask clients to focus on their gestures, facial expressions, and what they are experiencing within their own body. One of the advantages of drawing on Gestalt experiments is that they can be tailored to fit the unique way in which an individual perceives and interprets his or her culture. Gestalt therapists approach their clients with an open mind and without preconceptions. This is essential in working with clients from other cultures. Moreover, Gestalt therapists attempt to fully understand the background of their clients' culture. They are concerned about how and which aspects of this background become central or figural for them and what meaning clients place on these figures.

Limitations for Multicultural Counseling

To a greater extent than is true of most other approaches, there are definite hazards in too quickly utilizing some Gestalt experiments with ethnic minority clients. Gestalt methods tend to produce a high level of intense feelings. This focus on affect has some clear limitations with those clients who have been culturally conditioned to be emotionally reserved. As mentioned earlier, some clients believe expressing feelings openly is a sign of weakness and a display of one's vulnerability. Counselors who operate on the assumption that catharsis is necessary for any change to occur are likely to find certain clients becoming increasingly resistant, and such clients may prematurely terminate counseling. Other clients have strong cultural injunctions prohibiting them from directly expressing their emotions to their parents (such as "Never show your parents that you are angry at them" or "Strive for peace and harmony, and avoid conflicts"). I recall a client from India who was asked by his counselor to "bring your father into the room." The client was very reluctant to even symbolically tell his father of his disappointment with their relationship. In his culture the accepted way to deal with his father was to use his uncle as a go-between, and it was considered highly inappropriate to express any negative feelings toward one's father. The client later said that he would have felt very guilty if he had symbolically told his father what he sometimes thought and felt.

Gestalt therapists who have truly integrated their approach are sensitive enough to practice in a flexible way. They consider the client's cultural framework and are able to adapt methods that are likely to be well received. They strive to help clients experience themselves as fully as possible in the present, yet they are not rigidly bound by dictates, nor do they routinely intervene whenever clients stray from the present. Sensitively staying in contact with a client's flow of experiencing entails the ability to focus on the person and not on the mechanical use of techniques for a certain effect.

 # WHERE TO GO FROM HERE

If you are interested in furthering your knowledge and skill in the area of Gestalt therapy, you might consider pursuing Gestalt training, which would include attending workshops, seeking out personal therapy from a Gestalt therapist, and enrolling in a Gestalt training program that would involve reading, practice, and supervision. A few resources for training in Gestalt therapy are:

Gestalt Institute of Cleveland
1588 Hazel Drive
Cleveland, OH 44106
Telephone: (216) 421-0468
Fax: (216) 421-1729
E-mail: *104032.2164@compuserve.com*

Gestalt Training Center in San Diego
P.O. Box 2189
La Jolla, CA 92038
Telephone: (619) 454-9139

Gestalt Associates Training, Los Angeles
1460 7th Street, Suite 300
Santa Monica, CA 90401
Telephone: (310) 395-6844
Fax: (310) 319-1663
E-mail: *ritaresnick@gatla.org*

Gestalt Center for Psychotherapy and Training
26 West 9th Street
New York, NY 10011
Telephone: (212) 387-9429

The New York Institute for Gestalt Therapy
P.O. Box 238, Old Chelsea Station
New York, NY 10011
Telephone: (212) 864-8277
E-mail: *GestalSing@aol.com*

The Center for Gestalt Development, Inc.
P.O. Box 990
Highland, New York 12528-0990
Telephone: (914) 691-7192
Fax: (914) 691-6530
E-mail: *tgjournal@gestalt.org*
Website: *http://www.gestalt.org*

The Center for Gestalt Development, Inc., publishes *The Gestalt Directory* on a yearly basis. It includes information about Gestalt practitioners and training programs throughout the world. The training center's program is described in detail, including admission requirements, costs, length of program, certifications, and other pertinent data. Single copies of *The Gestalt Directory* are free of charge. Requests for copies must be in writing. Also available are books, audiotapes, and videotapes dealing with Gestalt practice.

The Gestalt Journal, which is devoted to the theory and practice of Gestalt therapy, is available from the Center for Gestalt Development, Inc. Published twice yearly, it offers articles, reviews, and commentaries of interest to the practitioner, theoretician, academician, and student; the current subscription fee is $35.

Some other journals devoted to Gestalt therapy are:

British Gestalt Journal
P.O. Box 2994
London N5 1U6
England, 0171-359-3000

Gestalt Review Journals
The Analytic Press, Inc.
810 E. 10th Street
P.O. Box 1897
Lawrence, KS 66044-8897
Telephone: (800) 627-0629
Fax: (913) 843-1274
Website: *http://www.analyticpress.com/ordering.html*

Australian Gestalt Journal
24 Sundowner Court
Mermaid Waters, Qld. 4218
Australia
(02)9876 6018
E-mail: *justbruno@bigpond.com*

Recommended Supplementary Readings

Gestalt Therapy Verbatim (Perls, 1969a) is one of the best places to get a firsthand account of the style in which Perls worked. If you like that book and want to know more about Perls as a person, I recommend *In and Out of the Garbage Pail* (Perls, 1969b).

Fritz Perls (Clarkson & Mackewn, 1993) provides a detailed overview of Perls's life and his contributions to the theory and practice of Gestalt therapy. The authors have excellent chapters on the criticisms and rebuttals of this approach and an assessment of his overall influence.

Gestalt Therapy Integrated: Contours of Theory and Practice (E. Polster & Polster, 1973) is a superb source for those who want a more advanced and theoretical treatment of this model.

Creative Process in Gestalt Therapy (Zinker, 1978) is a beautifully written book that is a delight to read. Zinker captures the essence of Gestalt therapy as a combination of phenomenology and behavior modification by showing how the therapist functions much like an artist in creating experiments that encourage clients to expand their boundaries. His concepts are fleshed out with rich clinical examples. The book shows how Gestalt can be practiced in a creative, eclectic, and integrative style.

Body Process: Working With the Body in Psychotherapy (Kepner, 1993) is a well-written book that deals with many basic principles of Gestalt therapy, emphasizing the role of the body as an integral part of Gestalt practice.

Awareness, Dialogue and Process: Essays on Gestalt Therapy (Yontef, 1993) is an excellent collection that develops the message that much of Gestalt therapy theory and practice consists of dialogue. This book brings the reader up to date with some current trends in the practice of Gestalt counseling.

The Healing Relationship in Gestalt Therapy: A Dialogic / Self Psychology Approach (Hycner & Jacobs, 1995) is highly recommended as a source to understand contemporary Gestalt therapy that is based on a meaningful dialogic relationship between client and therapist. The authors address issues that are at the core of the therapeutic relationship.

References and Suggested Readings*

BEISSER, A. R. (1970). The paradoxical theory of change. In J. Fagan & I. L. Shepherd (Eds.), *Gestalt therapy now* (pp. 77–80). New York: Harper & Row (Colophon).

BRESHGOLD, E. (1989). Resistance in Gestalt therapy: An historical theoretical perspective. *The Gestalt Journal, 12*(2), 73–102.

*CLARKSON, P., & MACKEWN, J. (1993). *Fritz Perls*. London: Sage.

COREY, G. (2000). *Theory and practice of group counseling* (5th ed.). Pacific Grove, CA: Brooks-Cole/Wadsworth.

*COREY, G. (2001). *Case approach to counseling and psychotherapy* (5th ed.). Pacific Grove, CA: Brooks-Cole/Wadsworth.

*FEDER, B., & RONALL, R. (Eds.). (1994). *Beyond the hot seat: Gestalt approaches to group*. Highland, NY: The Gestalt Journal Press.

FREW, J. E. (1986). The functions and patterns of occurrence of individual contact styles during the development phase of the Gestalt group. *The Gestalt Journal, 9*(1), 55–70.

FREW, J. E. (1992). From the perspective of the environment. *The Gestalt Journal, 15*(1), 39–60.

FREW, J. E. (1997). A Gestalt therapy theory application to the practice of group leadership. *Gestalt Review, 1*(2), 131–149.

HUMPHREY, K. (1986). Laura Perls: A biographical sketch. *The Gestalt Journal, 9*(1), 5–11.

*HYCNER, R., & JACOBS, L. (1995). *The healing relationship in Gestalt therapy*. Highland, NY: Gestalt Journal Press.

JACOBS, L. (1989). Dialogue in Gestalt theory and therapy. *The Gestalt Journal, 12*(1), 25–67.

*KEPNER, J. I. (1993). *Body process: Working with the body in psychotherapy*. San Francisco: Jossey-Bass.

*LATNER, J. (1986). *The Gestalt therapy book*. Highland, NY: Center for Gestalt Development.

LEVITSKY, A., & PERLS, F. (1970). The rules and games of Gestalt therapy. In J. Fagan & I. Shepherd (Eds.), *Gestalt therapy now* (pp. 140–149). New York:

---

*Books and articles marked with an asterisk are suggested for further study
Harper & Row (Colophon).

PASSONS, W. R. (1975). *Gestalt approaches in counseling.* New York: Holt, Rinehart & Winston.

*PERLS, F. (1969a). *Gestalt therapy verbatim.* Moab, UT: Real People Press.

PERLS, F. (1969b). *In and out of the garbage pail.* Moab, UT: Real People Press.

PERLS, F., HEFFERLINE, R., & GOODMAN, R. (1951). *Gestalt therapy integrated: Excitement and growth in the human personality.* New York: Dell.

PERLS, L. (1970). One Gestalt therapist's approach. In J. Fagan & I. Shepherd (Eds.), *Gestalt therapy now* (pp. 125–129). New York: Harper & Row (Colophon).

PERLS, L. (1976). Comments on new directions. In E. W. L. Smith (Ed.), *The growing edge of Gestalt therapy* (pp. 221–226). New York: Brunner/Mazel.

PERLS, L. (1986). Opening address: 8th annual conference on the theory and practice of Gestalt therapy—May 17, 1985. *The Gestalt Journal, 9*(1), 12–15.

PERLS, L. (1990). A talk for the 25th anniversary. *The Gestalt Journal, 13*(2), 15–22.

POLSTER, E. (1987a). Escape from the present: Transition and storyline. In J. K. Zeig (Ed.), *The evolution of psychotherapy* (pp. 326–340). New York: Brunner/Mazel.

POLSTER, E. (1987b). *Every person's life is worth a novel.* New York: Norton.

*POLSTER, E. (1995). *A population of selves: A therapeutic exploration of personality diversity.* San Francisco: Jossey-Bass.

*POLSTER, E. (1997). The therapeutic power of attention: Theory and technique. In J. K. Zeig (Ed.), *The evolution of psychotherapy: The third conference* (pp. 221–229). New York: Brunner/Mazel.

*POLSTER, E., & POLSTER, M. (1973). *Gestalt therapy integrated: Contours of theory and practice.* New York: Brunner/Mazel.

POLSTER, E., & POLSTER, M. (1976). Therapy without resistance: Gestalt therapy. In A. Burton (Ed.), *What makes behavior change possible?* (pp. 259–277). New York: Brunner/Mazel.

POLSTER, M. (1987). Gestalt therapy: Evolution and application. In J. K. Zeig (Ed.), *The evolution of psychotherapy* (pp. 312–325). New York: Brunner/Mazel.

*POLSTER, M. (1992). *Eve's daughters: The forbidden heroism of women.* San Francisco: Jossey-Bass.

POLSTER, M., & POLSTER, E. (1990). Gestalt therapy. In J. K. Zeig & W. M. Munion (Eds.), *What is psychotherapy? Contemporary perspectives* (pp. 103–107). San Francisco: Jossey-Bass.

*YONTEF, G. M. (1993). *Awareness, dialogue and process: Essays on Gestalt therapy.* Highland, NY: Gestalt Journal Press.

*ZINKER, J. (1978). *Creative process in Gestalt therapy.* New York: Random House (Vintage).

*ZINKER, J. (1994). *In search of good form: Gestalt therapy with couples and families.* San Francisco: Jossey-Bass.

CHAPTER

9

Reality Therapy

INTRODUCTION

KEY CONCEPTS
>   *View of Human Nature*
>   *A Choice Theory Explanation of Behavior*
>   *Characteristics of Reality Therapy*

THE THERAPEUTIC PROCESS
>   *Therapeutic Goals*
>   *Therapist's Function and Role*
>   *Client's Experience in Therapy*
>   *Relationship Between Therapist and Client*

APPLICATION: Therapeutic Techniques and Procedures
>   *The Practice of Reality Therapy*
>   *The Counseling Environment*
>   *Procedures That Lead to Change*
>   *The "WDEP" System*
>   *Applications of Reality Therapy*

REALITY THERAPY APPLIED TO THE CASE OF STAN

SUMMARY AND EVALUATION
>   *Summary*
>   *Contributions of Reality Therapy*
>   *Limitations and Criticisms of Reality Therapy*

REALITY THERAPY FROM A MULTICULTURAL PERSPECTIVE
>   *Contributions to Multicultural Counseling*
>   *Limitations for Multicultural Counseling*

WHERE TO GO FROM HERE

RECOMMENDED SUPPLEMENTARY READINGS

REFERENCES AND SUGGESTED READINGS

WILLIAM GLASSER

WILLIAM GLASSER (b. 1925) was educated at Case Western Reserve University in Cleveland, Ohio. Initially a chemical engineer, he turned to psychology (M.A., Clinical Psychology, 1948) and then to psychiatry, attending medical school (M.D., 1953) with the intention of becoming a psychiatrist. By 1957 he had completed his psychiatric training at the Veterans Administration and UCLA in Los Angeles and in 1961 was board certified in psychiatry.

Very early he rejected the Freudian model, and by the end of his residency he began to put together what by 1962 became known as reality therapy. The essence of reality therapy, now taught all over the world, is that we are all responsible for what we choose to do. We may be the product of our past, but we are not victims of the past unless we choose to be. All problems are in the present; thus, reality therapy spends very little time in the past.

Dr. Glasser has used reality therapy successfully in every area of psychiatry except with very young children. In these instances, he suggests that working with their parents is more effective. Very early Glasser began to work in schools, teaching the core idea that success in school can overcome unsatisfying family relationships and that a good education is the best road to a successful life. His school work and, recently, his community work focus on mental health and preventing problems rather than on counseling.

By the late 1970s Glasser was looking for a theory that could explain all his work. Glasser learned about *control theory* from William Powers, and he believed this theory had great potential. He spent the next 20 years expanding, revising, and clarifying what he was initially taught. By 1996 Glasser had become convinced that these revisions had so changed the theory that it was misleading to continue to call it control theory, and he changed the name to *choice theory* to reflect all that he had developed.

Choice theory is at the heart of all Glasser does. In *Choice Theory, A New Psychology of Personal Freedom* (1998) Glasser explains how choice theory has become a part of reality therapy. ■

INTRODUCTION

Reality therapy is based on choice theory as it is explained in Glasser's (1998, 2000) most recent books.* (Glasser's ideas as presented in this chapter pertain to his 1998 and 2000 works unless otherwise specified.) Reality therapists believe the underlying problem of all clients is the same: they are either involved in a present unsatisfying relationship or lack what could even be called a relationship. If therapy is to be successful, the therapist must guide the client to a satisfying relationship and literally teach the client to behave in more effective ways than he or she is presently behaving.

Few clients have any clear understanding that their problem is the way they are choosing to behave. What they do know is that they feel a great deal of pain or that they are unhappy because they have been sent for counseling by someone with authority who is not satisfied with their behavior—typically a court official, a school administrator, or a spouse or parent. Reality therapists recognize that clients choose their behaviors as a way to deal with the frustration caused by the unsatisfying relationship. All of these behavior choices—ranging from profound psychosis to mild depression—are described in detail in the DSM-IV (APA, 1994).

Glasser (1998, 2000) believes clients should not be labeled with a diagnosis except when it is necessary for insurance purposes. In Glasser's view, all diagnoses are descriptions of the behaviors people choose to deal with the pain and frustration that is endemic to unsatisfying present relationships. They are not mental illnesses. He believes mental illnesses are conditions such as Alzheimer's disease, epilepsy, head trauma, and brain infections—conditions associated with tangible brain damage. Because these people are suffering from a brain abnormality, they should be treated primarily by neurologists (Glasser, 2000).

It is not yet known why one client will choose one "mental illness" over another, but certainly being exposed to people who make such choices—and learning from them—may be an important factor. Knowing why the specific behavior is chosen is not necessary for successful therapy. Therapy consists mainly of teaching clients to make more effective choices as they deal with the people they need in their lives. Because choice theory explains how to choose to behave in ways that improve relationships, teaching choice theory to clients is part of reality therapy. If clients are successful, they will begin to choose more effective behaviors. For example, if they are "choosing to depress," they don't have to continue telling themselves and others "I'm depressed." Instead, they can say, "I've been choosing to depress because

---

*Initially I asked William Glasser to review this chapter for this sixth edition. He cheerfully agreed not only to review the chapter but to rewrite much of it. Dr. Glasser told me that he had drastically changed his approach in 1996 and that it would be necessary to do a major rewrite to ensure that this chapter would reflect his current thinking. This completely revised chapter explains how choice theory has been integrated into reality therapy.

that was the best way I could deal with a situation. I'm going to look for better choices."

It is essential for reality therapists to establish a satisfying relationship with clients. It is from this relationship that clients learn to trust the therapist, and from this trust clients learn to stop making the destructive or self-destructive choices that are currently mislabeled "mental illnesses." Once this trust is established, the skill of the therapist as a teacher becomes paramount. This skill—really an art based on choice theory plus a lot of experience—is a lifelong learning process. Good therapists are always engaged in the process of becoming, and they themselves are in healthy relationships. Reality therapy, in its association with choice theory, raises the fundamental question "What is a successful life?" It partially answers that question by stating that we must have at least one satisfying relationship, that is, a relationship that enables us to satisfy the instructions written into our genes. Choice theory describes these as basic needs. How these needs are included in therapy will be explained shortly.

 ## KEY CONCEPTS

View of Human Nature

Choice theory posits that we are not born blank slates waiting to be *externally motivated* by forces in the world around us. Rather, we are born with five genetically encoded needs—survival, love and belonging, power, freedom, and fun—that drive us all our lives. Each of us has all five needs, but they vary in strength. For example, we all have a need for love and belonging, but some of us need more love than others.

Our brain functions as a control system. It continually monitors our feelings to determine how well we are doing in our lifelong effort to satisfy these needs. Whenever we feel bad, one or more of these five needs is unsatisfied. Although we may not be aware of our needs, we know that we want to feel better. Driven by pain, we try to figure out how to feel better. Reality therapists teach clients choice theory so clients can identify the frustrated need and try to satisfy it. If clients succeed, they are rewarded with good feelings. Glasser (2000) believes the need to *love and to belong* is the primary need because we need people to satisfy the other needs.

Choice theory explains that we do not satisfy our needs directly. What we do, beginning shortly after birth and continuing all our lives, is to keep close track of anything we do that feels very good. We store this knowledge in a special place in our brain called our *quality world.* It is not large, but it contains the people we are closest to and most enjoy being with. It may also contain people we don't know but whom we imagine it would be very pleasurable to know. It also contains things we own or would like to own and even things like a beautiful sunset that we couldn't own but may be important to us. Also included are systems of belief that give us pleasure, such as our religious, political, or personal beliefs.

The quality world is at the core of our lives. It is our personal Shangri-la—the world we would like to live in if we could. It is completely based on our needs, but unlike the needs, which are general, it is very specific. We need love, but we put the *actual people* we want to love in our quality world. People are, by far, the most important component of this world, and these are the people we most want to connect with.

People who enter therapy typically have no one in their quality world or, more often, have someone there whom they are unable to relate to in a satisfying way. For therapy to have a chance of success, therapists must be people clients would consider putting in their quality worlds. Getting into the clients' quality world is the art of therapy. It is from this relationship with the therapist that clients begin to learn how to get close to the people they need.

Choice Theory Explanation of Behavior

Choice theory asserts that all we ever do from birth to death is behave and that our behavior is internally motivated and chosen. Every total behavior is always our best attempt to get what we want to satisfy our needs. Behavior is purposeful because it is designed to close the gap between what we want and what we perceive we are getting. Specific behaviors are always generated from this discrepancy. Our behaviors come from the inside, and thus we choose our destiny.

Total behavior teaches that all behavior is made up of four inseparable but distinct components—*acting, thinking, feeling,* and *physiology*—that must accompany all of our actions, thoughts, and feelings. If we think of our behavioral choices as a car, the *motor* is the basic needs, the *steering wheel* allows us to steer the car in the direction of our quality world, and acting, thinking, feeling, and physiology are the *wheels*. Acting and thinking, both obviously chosen, are the front wheels; they steer the car. Feeling and physiology are the back wheels, which have to follow the front wheels. They can't be independently or directly steered any more than we can directly choose how we feel or our physiology.

We can't directly choose our feelings and physiology, but we can indirectly choose many feelings and some of our physiology. For example, if we choose to hit our head against a wall (front wheels) we will suffer pain in the rear *feeling* wheel. If we choose to run on a hot day, we will perspire, our rear *physiology* wheel. We would neither have a painful head nor a sweaty body if we didn't choose actions and thoughts that led to these occurrences.

Glasser says that to speak of being depressed, having a headache, being angry, or being anxious implies passivity and lack of personal responsibility, and it is inaccurate. It is more accurate to think of these as parts of total behaviors and to use the verb forms *depressing, headaching, angering,* and *anxietying* to describe them. He speaks of people depressing or angering themselves rather than being depressed or being angry. When people choose misery by developing a range of "paining" behaviors, it is because these are the best behaviors they are able to devise at the time, and these behaviors often get them what they want.

When a reality therapist starts teaching choice theory, the client will often protest and say, "I'm suffering, don't tell me I'm choosing to suffer like this." A reality therapist's answer is that the suffering is not *directly* chosen. Rather, it is part of a total behavior that the therapist can explain to the client. But the client will likely persist and ask "Why?" Glasser offers three explanations for why we choose to suffer.

First, whenever anyone is involved in a frustrating relationship, it is normal to choose anger. From this angering, it is easy to lash out and hurt someone. Depressing and many other chosen symptoms immobilize us and provide a way to restrain this anger.

Second, depressing is the most common way people have discovered to ask for help without begging. When we suffer, people reach out to us. It is important to our need for power that we not beg, and depressing is the perfect way to get attention and even help without begging.

Third, depressing, and all other forms of what are commonly called mental illnesses, allows us to *avoid* doing what we are afraid to do. For example, when we lose a good job we may quickly depress. Friends may tell us, "Look, don't wait around, get out your resume. The longer you wait the harder it is to get work." We may say, "You're right, but I'm just too depressed to do it, maybe next week." This is because we are afraid there may be no good jobs, we don't want any more rejection, and the choice to depress gets us off the hook.

Characteristics of Reality Therapy

Reality therapy focuses quickly on the unsatisfying relationship or the lack of a relationship, which is the cause of the problem. It doesn't take much time or much skill to find out which it is, as the client will almost always bring it up. But what is characteristic is that the client will blame the other party for the failure of the relationship or for the misery he or she is suffering.

Reality therapy does not get involved with finding fault. It focuses on what the client *can* control in the relationship. Glasser teaches that there is no sense talking about what the client can't control. When clients point out correctly that this is unfair, the therapist may agree and say, "There is no guarantee that life is fair. The only guarantee is that you are the only person whom you know you can change. Complaining may feel good for a short time, but it is a completely ineffective behavior. If complaining were effective, there would be a lot more happy people in the world."

There is no shortage of people who spend their lives complaining and getting nowhere, but reality therapists do not listen very long to complaining, blaming, and criticizing. These are the three most ineffective behaviors in our behavioral repertoire. Clients tend to be expert complainers, blamers, and criticizers. Because reality therapists give short attention to these three self-defeating total behaviors, they tend to disappear from therapy.

EMPHASIS ON RESPONSIBILITY   If we choose all we do, we must be responsible for what we choose. This does not mean we should be blamed or punished, unless we break the law, but it does mean the therapist should never lose sight of the fact that clients are responsible for what they do. Clients may reject the idea that they are choosing to be sick or to behave in "crazy" ways. Therapists are wise not to engage in a debate with these clients. Doing so gives clients an excuse to choose to behave in even more self-defeating ways in an attempt to convince the therapist that they can't do much for themselves.

Instead, therapists should focus on what clients can choose, for doing so gets them closer to the people they need. For example, being involved in meaningful activities, such as work, is a good way to gain the respect of other people. It is very difficult for adults to feel good about themselves if they don't engage in some form of meaningful activity. All programs for the "mentally ill" should include some work or meaningful activity. As clients begin to feel good about themselves, it is less necessary for them to continue to choose irresponsible behaviors.

REJECTION OF TRANSFERENCE   Since the inception of reality therapy, Glasser has consistently maintained that reality therapists should make no effort to be anyone but themselves. Transference is a way that both therapist and client avoid taking responsibility for whom they are now. It is unrealistic for therapists to go along with the idea that they are anyone but themselves. Assume the client claims, "I see you as my father or mother and this is why I'm behaving the way I am." In such a situation Glasser advises therapists to say clearly and firmly, "I am not your mother, father, or anyone but myself." The reason this is called reality therapy is that most clients are all too willing to avoid taking responsibility for what they are doing and tend to leap at anything the therapist offers that will help them avoid behaving responsibly.

Glasser contends that transference was created by Freud to avoid getting personally involved in clients' lives. The reality therapist welcomes responsible involvement. It is the best and quickest way, and often the only way, to teach clients how to relate to the people they need. By being themselves, therapists can use the relationship to teach clients how to relate to others in their lives.

KEEPING THE THERAPY IN THE PRESENT   Most clients come to counseling convinced that their problems started in the past and that they must revisit the past if they are to be helped. Glasser (2000) grants that we are products of our past but argues that we are not able to change our past. Still, many therapeutic methods continue to teach that to function well in the present we must understand our past and, unless we revisit it, we can't understand it. Although this seems reasonable, Glasser maintains that it is incorrect. It is an attractive opportunity that many clients grasp to avoid dealing with their real problems, which are always associated with an unsatisfying *present* relationship.

When we have had an unsatisfying relationship in the past—perhaps we were abused as a child—it doesn't make any difference whether it was our fault or someone else's fault. What occurred can't be changed or erased.

We can neither change what we did to others, nor what others did to us. Although we may have been traumatized by past events, Glasser (2000) believes we are not victims of the past unless we presently choose to be. We generally do not discover solutions to our problems through explorations of the past. A theme of Glasser's writings is that the past is over and that revisiting it extensively is a waste of time. All we can do is try to change our present behavior so that we can get along with people we now need.

The reality therapist does not totally reject the past, but the therapist devotes only enough time to past failures to assure clients that they are not being rejected. As soon as possible, therapists tell clients: "It's over, it can't be changed. The more time we spend back there, the more we avoid facing your real problem: gaining a satisfying relationship now." In Glasser's (2000) experience, most clients are more than ready to face the present. They go back to the past because they have been led to believe this is what the therapist wants.

AVOID FOCUSING ON THE SYMPTOMS   In traditional therapy a great deal of time is spent focusing on symptoms by asking clients how they feel and why they are obsessing or phobicking. In the same way that focusing on the past "protects" clients from facing the reality of unsatisfying present relationships, focusing on symptoms does the same thing. The pain or the symptom that clients choose is not important to the counseling process. Reality therapists spend little time on symptoms because they cannot be improved until clients' significant relationships are improved.

Glasser (2000) contends that clients will complain forever about their symptoms if the therapist will listen. Coupling this with long journeys into the past is what results in lengthy therapy. Getting rid of these two impediments to therapy and focusing on present problems can shorten most therapy considerably. Something can be accomplished in one or two sessions, and much can be done in 10 sessions.

 ## THE THERAPEUTIC PROCESS

Therapeutic Goals

The goals of therapy are to help clients get connected or reconnected with the people they have chosen to put in their quality world and to teach clients choice theory. In most instances clients come voluntarily for therapy, and these clients are the easiest to help.

But there is a further goal of reality therapy, which many experts in the field would not call therapy. This involves working with the large group of people who are so resistant to psychotherapy that it seems impossible to get them involved. Characteristically, these people do not want to see the therapist and actively resist therapy. They often engage in violent behavior, addictions, and other kinds of antisocial behaviors. If they once had responsible people in their quality world, they have removed them.

Many people, some as young as 10 years of age, have given up on responsible caring adults because they have not been able to relate to them successfully. They have no responsible adults in their quality world. These people can't give up on pleasure, as that is impossible, but they have given up on love and belonging. Some seek pleasure by destroying things or hurting people. Others seek pleasure directly through addicting drugs or sexual pleasure that has nothing to do with satisfying another person. Such people scoff at the idea that they need others. As soon as a counselor recognizes that he or she is dealing with a disconnected, pleasure-seeking person, it is best to give up all the usual goals of counseling and focus on just one thing—doing whatever is possible to get connected with this person. If the counselor can't make a connection, there is no possibility of providing significant help. If the counselor *can* make a connection with this client, then the goal of teaching the client how to create other satisfying relationships can slowly begin.

Therapist's Function and Role

One primary function of reality therapists is to assist clients in dealing with the present. From the beginning, the practice of reality therapy takes place in the present. A reality therapist asks, "Are the total behaviors you are choosing getting you what you need? Is this choice realistic? Is it getting you closer to the people you need or want to get to know?"

It is from the satisfying client/therapist relationship that therapists are able to engage clients in an evaluation of all their relationships, exploring what they want and how effective they are at getting what they want. From this clients can decide what they can do to improve the relationships they have or how to find new ones. It is important that clients see therapists as people who know what life is all about, who are successful in dealing with it, and who are not afraid to discuss any subject with their clients.

Client's Experience in Therapy

According to Glasser (2000), clients may feel that just being with the reality therapist is a good experience. Clients are likely to think, "Therapy is safe, this therapist won't hurt me. She isn't afraid to talk to me about any part of my life and many parts of her life." Ideally, clients will learn that therapy is more than just talk as they are exposed to behaviors that have worked in the lives of their therapists. Clients will most likely find therapy to be gently, but firmly, confronting. Clients are constantly being asked if what they are choosing to do is bringing them closer to the people they need or getting them in touch with new people, if they have no one now.

Clients can expect to experience some urgency in therapy. Time is important, as each session may be the last. This need not be a long, drawn-out process. They should be able to think, "I can begin to use what we talked about today in my life. I am able to bring my present experiences to the therapy as my problems are in the present and my therapist will not let me escape from that fact. I see the therapist as a strong, active, positive force in my life, not a mirror or as a tape recorder that plays back what I just said."

Relationship Between Therapist and Client

Before effective therapy can occur, an involvement between client and counselor must be established. Clients need to know that the helping person cares enough about them to accept them and to help them fulfill their needs in the real world. Reality therapy emphasizes an understanding and supportive relationship. An important factor is the willingness of counselors to develop their own individual therapeutic style. Sincerity and being comfortable with one's style are crucial traits in being able to carry out therapeutic functions.

For involvement between the therapist and the client to occur, the counselor must have certain personal qualities, including warmth, understanding, acceptance, concern, respect for the client, openness, and the willingness to be challenged by others. One of the best ways to develop this goodwill and therapeutic friendship is simply by listening to clients. Involvement is also promoted by talking about a wide range of topics that have relevance for clients. Once involvement has been established, the counselor confronts clients with the reality and consequences of their current behavior.

Wubbolding and Brickell (1998) identify the following personal qualities of the reality therapist: empathy, congruence, energy, and having a positive view of human nature. They list as professional characteristics a sense of paradox and the ability to reframe, an ability to communicate hope, an ability to define a problem in solvable terms, an ability to use metaphors, being ethical, and being culturally sensitive.

From Glasser's perspective, the art of reality therapy is to be able to establish a therapeutic relationship with almost every client the therapist is asked to help. This implies that the therapist has the ability to feel comfortable with a wide variety of people who, under most circumstances, would not be a part of his or her life.

The therapist is committed to demystifying the therapeutic process. The client can ask for and expect to get an explanation for anything that is going on. Therapy is always a mentoring process in which the therapist is the teacher and the client is the student. From their good relationship with their therapist, who has a large repertoire of successful life experiences, clients learn to satisfy their own needs, especially, how to relate to the important people in their lives.

 ## APPLICATION: Therapeutic Techniques and Prodedures

The Practice of Reality Therapy

The practice of reality therapy can best be conceptualized as the *cycle of counseling,* which consists of two major components: (1) creating the counseling environment and (2) implementing specific procedures that lead to changes in behavior. The art of counseling is to weave these components together in ways that lead clients to evaluate their lives and decide to move in more effective directions.

How do these components blend in the counseling process? The cycle of counseling begins with establishing a working relationship with clients. The process proceeds through an exploration of clients' wants, needs, and perceptions. Clients then explore their total behavior and make their own evaluation of how effective they are in getting what they want. If clients decide to try new behavior, they make plans that will lead to change, and they commit themselves to their plan. The cycle of counseling includes following up on how well clients are doing and offering further consultation as needed.

It is important to keep in mind that although the concepts may seem simple as they are presented here, being able to translate them into actual therapeutic practice takes considerable skill and creativity. Although the principles will be the same when used by any counselor who is certified in reality therapy, the manner in which they are applied does vary depending on the counselor's style and personal characteristics. Just because the principles are applied in a progressive manner, they should not be thought of as discrete and rigid categories. The art of practicing reality therapy involves far more than following procedures in a step-by-step fashion.

In this section I draw heavily from the writings of Robert Wubbolding, a reality therapist who developed a set of procedures (WDEP system) for both practicing and teaching reality therapy. This material renders choice theory practical and useable by counselors, and it provides a basis for conceptualizing and applying the theory. As is true of all the theories presented in this book, there are various ways of putting these theories into actual practice. Many reality therapists operate within the spirit of choice theory, yet practice in their own unique ways. I especially value Wubbolding's contributions to teaching reality therapy and to conceptualizing therapeutic procedures, which are discussed in this section. The discussion that follows is best considered as an aid for teaching reality therapy, but it should not be thought of as a replacement for the extensive training that is needed to counsel effectively. It is an integrated summary and adaptation of material from various sources (Glasser, 1965, 1980, 1984a, 1984b, 1992, 1997, 1998; Glasser & Wubbolding, 1995; Wubbolding, 1988, 1991, 1996, 2000; Wubbolding & Associates, 1998).

The Counseling Environment

The counseling environment should be a living example of choice theory in action. Counselors use no external control behaviors. If a client attempts in any way to control the therapist, the therapist uses this as an opportunity to explain the difference between external control and choice theory. Counselors will no more let the clients control them than they will try to control their clients. In choice theory there is no attempt at coercion by the therapist and no successful coercion by the client. In this coercion-free atmosphere clients feel free to be creative and to begin to try new behaviors or past successful behaviors they haven't used in a long time.

For most clients, this choice theory atmosphere is a new experience. Many will distrust it and try to replace it with the more coercive atmosphere they are used to, but the counselor resists all these self-destructive attempts. In a short period of time the client will begin to enjoy the caring, accepting, noncoercive choice theory environment. It is from this confronting yet always noncriticizing, nonblaming, noncomplaining, caring environment that the client learns to create the satisfying environment that leads to successful relationships.

Procedures That Lead to Change

Change is always a choice. Reality therapists begin by asking clients what they want from therapy. They also inquire about the choices clients are making in their relationships. Glasser maintains there is always a major unsatisfied relationship, although in the beginning the client may deny this is the case. For example, the client might say, "I'm depressed. My depression is the problem. Why are you talking about my relationships? They're fine." Or the client will say something like, "Of course it's my relationship, if you were married to a jerk like him, you'd be depressed too. But I'm not getting a divorce, just help me to feel better; that's what I came here for." In both examples the client avoids talking about the real problem, which is the unsatisfying or missing relationship.

In the first session a skilled therapist looks for and defines the wants of the client. The therapist also looks for a key unsatisfying present relationship—usually with a spouse, a child, a parent, or an employer. Glasser advises therapists to help the client see how an unsatisfying present relationship is at the core of his or her problem. When it is obvious to the client that this is where the problem is, the therapist might ask, "Whose behavior can you control?" This question may need to be asked several times during the next few sessions to deal with the client's resistance to looking at his or her own behavior.

There is a tendency for clients to blame the other person in the relationship. When clients begin to realize that they can control only their own behavior, therapy is under way. The rest of therapy focuses on how clients can make better choices.

More choices are available than clients may realize, and the therapist explores these possible choices. Clients may be stuck in misery, blaming, and the past, but they can choose to change—even if the other person in the relationship does not change. Any change in a relationship causes the whole relationship to change, and clients can choose to change what they *do*. When the relationship changes, clients can choose to give up the symptomatic behavior or behaviors. Depressing is the most common, but problem behaviors can range through the whole gamut of psychological complaints and psychosomatic diseases.

Reality therapists explore the tenets of choice theory with clients, helping clients identify basic needs, discovering clients' quality world, and finally, helping clients understand that they are choosing the total behaviors that are their symptoms. In every instance when clients make a change, it is their choice. With the therapist's help, clients learn to make better choices than they did when they were on their own.

Through this process, clients learn that things don't just happen. With planning, clients are able to take much more effective control of their lives. We are not at the mercy of others, and we are not victims. Using choice theory to gain and maintain successful relationships is a skill that can be learned. Clients will learn to ask themselves before they act, "Will doing or saying what I am about to do or say bring us closer together? If it won't, then I won't do or say it." According to Glasser (1992), the procedures that lead to change are based on the assumption that human beings are motivated to change (1) when they are convinced that their present behavior is not getting them what they want and (2) when they believe they can choose other behaviors that will get them closer to what they want.

The "WDEP" System

Glasser and Wubbolding (1995) and Wubbolding (1991, 2000; Wubbolding & Associates, 1998) use an acronym, WDEP, to describe key procedures that can be used in the practice of reality therapy. Each of the letters refers to a cluster of strategies: W = wants and needs; D = direction and doing; E = evaluation; and P = planning and commitment. These strategies are designed to promote change. Let's look at each one in more detail.

WANTS (EXPLORING WANTS, NEEDS, AND PERCEPTIONS)   Reality therapists ask, "What do you want?" Through the therapist's skillful questioning, clients are encouraged to recognize, define, and refine how they wish to meet their needs. Part of counseling consists of exploring the "picture album," or "quality world," of clients and how their behavior is aimed at moving their perception of the external world closer to their inner world of wants.

The skilled reality therapist counsels in a noncritical and accepting way so that clients will reveal what is in their special world. Clients are given the opportunity to explore every facet of their lives, including what they want from their family, friends, and work. Furthermore, it is useful for clients to define what they expect and want from the counselor and from themselves (Wubbolding, 1988, 1991; Wubbolding & Associates, 1998). This exploration of wants, needs, and perceptions should continue throughout the counseling process as clients' pictures change.

Some useful questions to help clients pinpoint what they want include: "If you were the person that you wish you were, what kind of person would you be?" "What would your family be like if your wants and their wants matched?" "What would you be doing if you were living as you want to?" "Do you really want to change your life?" "What is it you want that you don't seem to be getting from life?" "What do you think stops you from making the changes you would like?" This line of questioning sets the stage for applying other procedures in reality therapy.

DIRECTION AND DOING   Reality therapy stresses current behavior and is concerned with past events only insofar as they influence how clients are behaving now. The focus on the present is characterized by the question so often asked by the reality therapist: "What are you doing?" Even though problems may be rooted in the past, clients need to learn how to deal with them in the present by learning better ways of getting what they want. The past may be discussed if doing so will help clients plan for a better tomorrow. The therapist's challenge is to help clients make more need-satisfying choices.

Early in counseling it is essential to discuss with clients the overall direction of their lives, including where they are going and where their behavior is taking them. This exploration is preliminary to the subsequent evaluation of whether it is a desirable direction. The therapist holds a mirror before the client and asks, "What do you see for yourself now and in the future?" It often takes some time for this reflection to become clear to clients so they can verbally express their perceptions (Wubbolding, 1988).

Reality therapy concentrates on changing current total behavior, not merely attitudes and feelings. To accomplish this, reality therapists focus on questions like these: "What are you doing now?" "What did you actually do this past week?" "What did you want to do differently this past week?" "What stopped you from doing what you say you want to do?" "What will you do tomorrow?"

Listening to clients talk about feelings can be productive, but only if it is linked to what they are doing. When an emergency light on the car dashboard lights up, the driver is alerted that something is wrong and that immediate action is necessary to remedy a problem. In a similar way, when clients talk about problematic feelings, rather than focusing on these feelings, counselors encourage clients to take action by changing what they are doing and thinking. According to Glasser (1980, 1992), what we are doing is easy to see and impossible to deny; thus, it serves as the proper focus in therapy. Discussions centering on feelings, without strongly relating them to what people are doing, are counterproductive. Reality therapy focuses on gaining awareness of current total behavior. This process helps clients get what they want and helps them develop a positive self-image.

EVALUATION   The core of reality therapy, as we have seen, is to ask clients to make the following evaluation: "Does your present behavior have a reasonable chance of getting you what you want now, and will it take you in the direction you want to go?" Through skillful questioning, the counselor helps clients evaluate their behavior. These questions include "Is what you are doing helping or hurting you?" "Is what you are doing now what you want to be doing?" "Is your behavior working for you?" "Is there a healthy congruence between what you are doing and what you believe?" "Is what you are doing against the rules?" "Is what you want realistic or attainable?" "Does it help you to look at it that way?" "How committed are you to the therapeutic process and to changing your life?" "After you examine what you want carefully, does it appear to be in your best interests and in the best interest of others?" (Wubbolding, 1988, 2000; Wubbolding & Associates, 1998).

Asking clients to evaluate each component of their total behavior is a major task in reality therapy. It is the counselor's task to confront clients with the consequences of their behavior, to get clients to judge the quality of their actions, and to help them make effective choices. Individuals will not change until they first decide that a change would be more advantageous. Without an honest self-assessment, it is unlikely that clients will change. Thus, reality therapists are relentless in their efforts to help clients conduct explicit self-evaluations of each behavioral component. When therapists ask a depressing client if this behavior is helping in the long run, they introduce the idea of choice to the client. The process of evaluation of the doing, thinking, feeling, and physiological components of total behavior is within the scope of the client's responsibility.

Reality therapists may be directive with certain clients at the beginning of treatment. This is done to help clients recognize that some behaviors are not effective. In working with clients who are in crisis, for example, it is sometimes necessary to suggest straightforwardly what will work and what will not. Other clients, such as alcoholics and children of alcoholics, need direction early in the course of treatment, for they often do not have the thinking behaviors in their control system to be able to make consistent evaluations of when their lives are seriously out of effective control. These clients are likely to have blurred pictures and, at times, to be unaware of what they want or whether their wants are realistic. As they grow and continually interact with the counselor, they learn to make the evaluations with less help from the counselor (Wubbolding, 1988).

PLANNING AND COMMITMENT   Much of the significant work of the counseling process involves helping clients identify specific ways to fulfill their wants and needs. Once clients determine what they want to change, they are generally ready to explore other possible behaviors and formulate an action plan. The process of creating and carrying out plans enables people to gain effective control over their lives. If the plan does not work, for whatever reason, counselor and client work together to devise a different plan. There is no rigidity in reality therapy. The plan gives the client a starting point, a toehold on life, but plans can be modified as needed. Throughout this planning phase, the counselor continually urges the client to assume responsibility for his or her own choices and actions.

Wubbolding (1988, 1991, 1996, 2000) discusses the central role of planning and commitment. The culmination of the cycle of counseling rests with a plan of action. He uses the acronym SAMIC[3] to capture the essence of a good plan: simple, attainable, measurable, immediate, involved, controlled by the planner, committed to, and continuously done. He writes that clients gain more effective control over their lives with plans that have these characteristics:

■ The plan should be within the limits of the motivation and capacities of each client. Skillful counselors help clients identify plans that involve greater need-fulfilling payoffs. Clients may be asked, "What plans could you make now that would result in a more satisfying life?"

- Good plans are simple and easy to understand. Although they need to be specific, concrete, and measurable, plans should be flexible and open to modification as clients gain a deeper understanding of the specific behaviors they want to change. It is important to realize that there is no perfect plan, which means that plans are subject to revision.
- The plan should involve a positive course of action, and it should be stated in terms of what the client is willing to do. Counselors can help clients recognize that even small plans can help them take significant steps toward their desired changes.
- Counselors should encourage clients to develop plans that they can carry out independently of what others do. Plans that are contingent on others lead clients to sense that they are not steering their own ship but are at the mercy of the ocean.
- Effective plans are repetitive and, ideally, are performed daily.
- Plans should be carried out as soon as possible. Counselors can ask questions such as "What are you willing to do today to begin to change your life?" "You say you would like to stop depressing. What are you going to do now to attain this goal?"
- Effective planning involves process-centered activities. For example, clients may plan to do any of the following: apply for a job, write a letter to a friend, take a yoga class, substitute nutritious food for junk food, devote two hours a week to volunteer work, or take a vacation that they have been wanting.
- Before clients carry out their plan, it is a good idea for them to evaluate it with their therapist to determine if it is realistic and attainable and if it relates to what they need and want. After the plan has been carried out in real life, it is useful to evaluate it again. The counselor needs to ask, "Is your plan helpful?" If a plan does not work, it can be reevaluated and alternatives can be considered.
- To help clients commit themselves to their plan, it is useful for them to firm it up in writing.

Resolutions and plans are empty unless there is a commitment to carry them out. It is up to clients to determine how to take their plans outside the restricted world of therapy and into the everyday world. Effective therapy can be the catalyst that leads to self-directed, responsible living.

Clients who are filled with negativity *expect* others to give up on them. It is important that counselors not easily give up their belief in their clients' ability to find a more responsible life, even if clients make little effort to follow through. If counselors give up, it tends to confirm clients' beliefs that no one cares enough to help.

In addition to counselors' attitudes that create an environment conducive to client change, Wubbolding (1988) emphasizes the importance of practitioners' being willing to seek consultation with others who are trained in reality therapy. Regardless of how well a person practices reality therapy, Wubbolding contends, there is room for improvement. This can be achieved both by consultation and by developing an ongoing plan for professional development.

Applications of Reality Therapy

Reality therapy is applicable to counseling, social work, education, crisis intervention, corrections and rehabilitation, institutional management, and community development. It is a popular approach in schools, correctional institutions, general hospitals, state mental hospitals, halfway houses, and substance abuse centers. Most of the military clinics that treat drug and alcohol abusers use reality therapy as their preferred therapeutic approach.

Experienced reality therapists have successfully counseled clients who refused to talk or even to look at the therapist. The only criterion for this therapy is that the client be in the same room with the counselor and that the counselor be protected from being attacked by the client. Glasser has counseled in a mental hospital where an aide was in the room to protect him from attack. In counseling a client who would not talk, Glasser told the client: "I will talk to you and ask questions and then if you do not answer I will answer for you." After doing this for about 10 minutes, the client spoke up and said, "I wouldn't have said that, I would have said. . . ." Therapy proceeded normally from that point.

It is impossible to describe all the techniques that reality therapists have used over the years. Many of them are created on the spot with therapists asking themselves "How can I reach this person?" There are two ways to reach anyone: (1) say something that moves the therapist and the client closer or (2) say something that drives the therapist and the client further apart. Obviously, the first way is the goal of reality therapy.

REALITY THERAPY APPLIED TO THE CASE OF STAN

The reality therapist is guided by the key concepts of choice theory to identify Stan's behavioral dynamics, to provide a direction for him to work toward, and to teach him about better alternatives for getting what he wants. Stan has chosen a variety of painful symptoms that have not been effective in getting him what he needs—a satisfying relationship. Stan's choices "help" him to restrain his anger, to ask for help, and to avoid facing his real problem—the lack of a satisfying relationship. Stan has chosen to be a victim of his past and to blame his present misery on what has happened to him. Stan has been living the life of a victim, blaming others and looking backward instead of forward. Stan's reality therapist shows him that he does not have to be a victim of his past unless he chooses to be. Although she has compassion for his suffering and the difficulties he continues to face, she wants Stan to realize that if he decides to change he has many options. She has a hunch that he wants to focus on talking about his past because that is easier than facing the present, which will involve considerable work. She grants that all of his behavior is his best attempt to get what he wants, yet she also helps Stan see that what he is doing is not working very well. As counseling progresses, Stan learns that even though most of his problems did indeed begin in childhood there is little he can now do to undo what happened. He eventually realizes that he has little control over changing others but has a great deal of control over what he can do now.

Initially, Stan wants to tell his counselor how miserable he feels. He does this by attempting to focus on his major symptoms: depression, anxiety, inability to sleep, and other psychosomatic symptoms, He very much needs someone who is willing to listen to him and not criticize him for what he says. For most of Stan's life people have criticized him. As Stan presents his story to his therapist, he expects criticism and invites it. During the early phase of counseling, the therapist listens to him and continues to reinforce the idea that she will not criticize him. She works at establishing involvement with him to provide a good foundation on which to support future therapy. Over time Stan will learn that he can make a satisfying relationship with the therapist and from this relationship begin to face the fact that he needs a good relationship now in his life. He will learn that all his symptoms and avoidance keep him from getting what he needs. His symptoms interfere with any chance he has to gain and maintain a successful present relationship.

Although the counselor listens, she also challenges Stan, especially as he focuses on his misery and his symptoms. She explains to him that he has an ideal picture of what he wants his life to be, yet he does not possess effective behaviors for meeting his needs. The counselor talks to him about his needs and how this type of therapy will teach him to satisfy them in effective ways. She also explains that his total behavior is made up of acting, thinking, feeling, and physiology. Even though he says he hates feeling anxious most of the time, Stan learns that much of what he is doing and thinking is directly leading to his unwanted feelings and physio-

logical reactions. When Stan complains of feeling depressed much of the time, anxious at night, and overcome by panic attacks, she lets him know that she is more interested in what he is doing and thinking. These are the components that can be directly changed.

Without being critical, she teaches Stan that his *depressing* is the action part of his choice. Although he may feel he has little control over how he feels, over his bodily sensations, and over his thoughts, the therapist wants Stan to understand that he can begin to take different action, which is likely to change his depressing experience.

If Stan is allowed to talk more than briefly about his symptoms and complain that he is a victim, he will not be able to make the satisfying relationship with the therapist that he needs. Therefore, Stan's therapist will continually ask this question: "Is what you are choosing to do getting you what you want?" When he complains he isn't choosing what's happening, that it's all happening to him, he will be asked: "If this is so, why isn't it happening here?"

Stan tells his counselor about the pictures in his head, a few of which are becoming a counselor, acting confident in meeting people, thinking of himself as a worthwhile person, and enjoying life. Through therapy he makes the evaluation that much of what he is doing is not getting him closer to these pictures or getting him what he wants. After he decides that he is willing to work on himself to be different, the majority of time in the sessions is devoted to making plans and discussing their implementation. Together he and the therapist focus on the steps he can take right now to bring about the changes he would like. Instead of waiting for others to initiate contacts, Stan practices seeking out those people he would like to get to know better. He might get involved in volunteer work with young people at a community agency, especially since this is the kind of activity he finds meaningful. Stan is encouraged to actually do more of the things he wants to do rather than focusing on what he perceives to be his deficits. As Stan continues to carry out plans in the real world, he gradually begins to experience success. When he does backslide, his counselor does not put him down but helps him do better. Together they develop a new plan that they feel more confident about. She is not willing to give up on him, which is a source of real inspiration for him to keep working on himself.

Stan's therapist will teach him choice theory, and, if he is willing to engage in some reading, she might suggest that he read and reflect on the book, *Choice Theory* (Glasser, 1998). He may bring into his sessions some of what he is learning from his reading, and eventually Stan will be able to take effective control over his own life. The combination of working with a reality therapist, reading, and his willingness to put what he is learning into practice by engaging in new behaviors in the world will assist Stan in replacing self-destructive choices with life-affirming choices. Stan will come to increasingly accept that he is the only person who can control his own behavior. He will come to

the realization that if he wants a better life he must choose to do things that get him closer to other people. In less than a year the combination of reality therapy and learning choice theory is highly likely to substantially change the way Stan chooses to live his life. It will take this long because he has a lot to learn!

Follow-Up: You Continue as Stan's Reality Therapist

Use these questions to help you think about how to counsel Stan:

- If Stan complains of feeling depressed most of the time and wants you to "cure" him, how might you proceed?
- If Stan persists, telling you that his mood is getting the best of him and that he wants you to work with his physician in getting him on an antidepressant drug, what might you say or do?
- What are some of Stan's basic needs that are not being met? What action plans can you think of to help Stan find better ways of getting what he wants?
- In working with Stan as a reality therapist, what interventions might you make to help him explore his total behavior? ■

 ## SUMMARY AND EVALUATION

Summary

The reality therapist functions as a teacher and a model, confronting clients in ways that help them evaluate what they are doing and whether their behavior is fulfilling their basic needs without harming themselves or others. The heart of reality therapy is learning how to make better and more effective choices and gain more effective control. People take charge of their lives rather than being the victims of circumstances beyond their control. Thus, practitioners of reality therapy focus on what clients are *able and willing to do in the present* to change their behavior. Practitioners teach clients how to make significant connections with others. Therapists continue to ask clients to evaluate the effectiveness of what they are choosing to do to determine if better choices are possible.

The practice of reality therapy weaves together two components, the counseling environment and specific procedures that lead to changes in behavior. This process enables clients to move in the direction of getting what they want. The goals of reality therapy include behavioral change, better decision making, improved significant relationships, enhanced living, and more effective satisfaction of the psychological needs.

Contributions of Reality Therapy

Among the advantages of reality therapy are its relatively short-term focus and the fact that it deals with conscious behavioral problems. Insight and awareness are not enough; the client's self-evaluation, a plan of action, and a commitment to following through are the core of the therapeutic process. I like the focus on strongly encouraging clients to evaluate their life situation, to decide if what they are doing is working or not, and to commit themselves to make changes. The existential underpinnings of choice theory are a major strength of this approach. People are not viewed as victims of depression or as being hopelessly and helplessly depressed. Rather, they are choosing to depress. People are personally responsible for who they are and what they are becoming. Clients are viewed as doing the best they can, or making the choices they hope will result in fulfilling their needs.

One of the aspects of choice theory that I especially value is the emphasis placed on guiding clients in the self-evaluation process. Too often counseling fails because therapists have an agenda for clients. The reality therapist helps clients conduct a searching inner inventory of their own actions, cognitions, and feelings. Once clients decide for themselves that their present behavior is not working, they are then much more likely to consider acquiring a new behavioral repertoire.

Limitations and Criticisms of Reality Therapy

One of the main limitations of reality therapy is that it does not give adequate emphasis to the role of these aspects of the counseling process: the unconscious, the power of the past and the effect of traumatic experiences in early childhood, the therapeutic value of dreams, and the place of transference. Because reality therapy focuses almost exclusively on consciousness, it does not take into account factors such as repressed conflicts and the power of the unconscious in influencing how we think, feel, behave, and choose.

I believe dreams are powerful tools in helping people recognize their internal conflicts, yet the analysis of dreams is not part of the reality therapist's repertoire. According to Glasser (2000), it is not therapeutically useful to mention or explore dreams; spending time discussing dreams is time wasted. Glasser (1984a) claims there is virtually no evidence to indicate that working with dreams is of any therapeutic value, and he holds that such work can be used as a defense to avoid talking about one's behavior. My colleagues and I continue to be impressed by the richness of dreams, which can be a shorthand message of clients' central struggles, hopes, and visions of the future. Asking clients to recall, report, share, and relive their dreams in the here and now of the therapeutic session can help unblock them and has paved the way for clients to take a different course of action.

Similarly, I have a difficult time accepting Glasser's view of transference as a misleading concept, for I find that clients are able to learn that significant people in their lives have a present influence on how they perceive and react to others. True, a focus on transference can be an avoidance on the part of both therapist and client, yet to rule out an exploration of this special type of projection that distorts accurate perception of others seems narrow in my view.

Glasser makes the generalization that the DSM-IV is incorrect in its categorization of various forms of mental illness. I am also critical of the way the DSM-IV is sometimes used, and I have trouble with the concept of labeling people. However, Glasser's views are rather extreme. As you will recall, Glasser (2000) contends that chronic depression, profound psychosis, and alcoholism are all chosen behaviors. Apart from specific brain pathology, Glasser argues that mental illness is the result of an individual's unsatisfying present relationships. It seems simplistic to me to view all psychological disorders as behavioral choices to deal with the pain and frustration associated with unsatisfying relationships. Biochemical and genetic factors are associated with certain forms of behavioral disorders, and I have trouble accepting the notion that all mental illness is chosen behavior. Also, Glasser's views on this subject can lead to blaming the victim. People suffering from chronic depression or schizophrenia are struggling with coping with a real illness. In reality therapy these people have additional guilt to carry if they accept the premise that they are *choosing* their condition.

Finally, I believe reality therapy is vulnerable to the practitioner who assumes the role of an expert in deciding for others such questions as how life should be lived, what is realistic or unrealistic, and what constitutes responsible behavior. Therapists who make evaluations for their clients are really imposing their values on them. It is not the therapist's role to evaluate the behavior of clients. Rather, clients need to engage in the process of self-evaluation to determine how well certain behaviors are working and what changes they may want to make. Reality therapists need to monitor their tendency to judge clients' behavior and tell clients how to behave differently. Counselors who are unaware of their own need to give abundant and frequent advice can stunt clients' growth and autonomy by strongly influencing clients to accept their view of reality. If counselors do this, however, they are perverting the basic concepts inherent in reality therapy/choice theory, for the approach calls on clients to make their own evaluation of their behavior.

REALITY THERAPY FROM A MULTICULTURAL
PERSPECTIVE

Contributions to Multicultural Counseling

The core principles of choice theory/reality therapy have much to offer in
the area of multicultural counseling. In cross-cultural therapy it is essential that counselors respect the differences in worldview between themselves and their clients. Counselors demonstrate their respect for the
cultural values of their clients by helping them explore how satisfying their
current behavior is both to themselves and to others. Once clients make
this assessment, they can formulate realistic plans that are consistent with
their cultural values. It is a further sign of respect that the counselor re-
frains from deciding what behavior should be changed. Through skillful
questioning on the counselor's part, ethnic minority clients can be helped to
determine the degree to which they have acculturated into the dominant
society. It is possible for them to find a balance, retaining their ethnic identity and values while integrating some of the values and practices of the
dominant group. Again, the counselor does not determine this balance for
clients but challenges them to arrive at their own answer. With this focus
on acting and thinking rather than on identifying and exploring feelings,
many clients are less likely to display resistance to counseling.

Glasser (1998) contends that reality therapy can be applied both individually and in groups to anyone with any psychological problem in any
cultural context. We are all members of the same species and have the same
genetic structure; therefore, relationships are the problem in all cultures.

Wubbolding (1990b, 2000) has expanded the practice of reality therapy
to multicultural situations. He believes reality therapy must be modified to
fit the cultural context of people other than North Americans. Wubbolding's
experience in conducting reality therapy workshops in Japan, Taiwan, Hong
Kong, Singapore, Korea, India, and countries in Europe has taught him about
the difficulty in making generalizations about other cultures. Based on
these multicultural experiences, he has adapted the cycle of counseling to
working with Japanese clients. He points to some basic language differences between Japanese and Western cultures. North Americans are inclined to say what they mean, to be assertive, and to be clear and direct in
asking for what they want. In Japanese culture, assertive language is not
appropriate between a child and a parent or between an employee and a
supervisor. Ways of communicating are more indirect. Because of these
style differences, adaptations such as these are needed to make the practice of reality therapy relevant to Japanese clients:

- The reality therapist's tendency to ask direct questions may need
  to be softened, with questions being raised more elaborately and

indirectly. It may be a mistake to ask individualistic questions built around whether specific behaviors meet the client's need. Confrontation should be avoided in working with Japanese clients.

■ There is no exact Japanese translation for the word "plan," nor is there an exact word for "accountability," yet both of these are key dimensions in the practice of reality therapy.

■ In asking clients to make plans and commit to them, Western counselors do not settle for a response of "I'll try." Instead, they tend to push for an explicit pledge to follow through. In Japanese culture, however, the counselor is likely to accept an "I'll try" as a firm commitment.

These are but a few illustrations of ways in which reality therapy might be adapted to non-Western clients. Although this approach assumes that all people have the same basic needs (survival, love and belonging, power, fun, and freedom), the way these needs are expressed depends largely on the cultural context. Reality therapists cannot work in exactly the same manner with all clients. In working with culturally diverse clients, the therapist must allow latitude for a wide range of acceptable behaviors to satisfy these needs. As with other theories and the techniques that flow from them, flexibility is a foremost requirement.

Reality therapy does provide clients with tools to make the desired changes. This is especially true during the planning phase, which is so central to the process of reality therapy. The focus is on positive steps that can be taken, not on what cannot be done. Clients identify those problems that are causing them difficulty, and these problems become the targets for change. This type of specificity and the direction that is provided by an effective plan are certainly assets in working with diverse client groups.

Limitations for Multicultural Counseling

One of the shortcomings in working with ethnic minority clients is that this approach does not take into account some very real environmental forces that operate against them in their everyday lives. Discrimination and racism are unfortunate realities, and these forces do limit many minority clients in getting what they want from life. If counselors do not accept these environmental restrictions, such clients are likely to feel misunderstood. There is a danger that some reality therapists will too quickly or too forcefully stress the ability of these clients to take charge of their lives.

Another problem with this style of therapy is that some clients are very reluctant to say what they need. Their cultural values and norms may not reinforce them in assertively asking for what they want. In fact, they may be socialized to think more of what is good for the social group than of their individual wants. In working with people with these values, counselors must "soften" reality therapy somewhat. Such clients should not be pushed to assertively declare their wants. If this method is not applied sensitively, these clients are likely to leave therapy. If reality therapy is to be used effectively with clients from other cultures, the procedures must be adapted to the life experiences and values of members from various cultures (Glasser & Wubbolding, 1995).

Reality therapy should be used artfully and not blindly. Many of its principles and concepts can be incorporated in a dynamic and personal way in the style of counselors, and there is a basis for integrating these concepts with most of the other therapeutic approaches covered in this book.

 WHERE TO GO FROM HERE

More than 1,000 therapists have completed the training in reality therapy and choice theory offered by the William Glasser Institute. They have been awarded a Certificate of Completion, and many have gone on to become instructors. The training process takes at least 18 months to complete and is offered all over the United States and Canada. It consists of a Basic Intensive Week (all weeks are 4 1/2 days) and a follow-up Basic Practicum (all practicums are 30 hours), an Advanced Intensive Week, an Advanced Practicum, and a final Certification Week in which trainees demonstrate their skills. To assure personal attention, no more than 13 people are assigned to a group. Dr. Glasser is personally involved in all certification weeks. Complete information on this popular program can be obtained directly from the Institute.

> *The William Glasser Institute*
> William Glasser, M.D., President and Founder
> 22024 Lassen Street, Suite 118
> Chatsworth, CA 91311
> Telephone: (818) 700-8000 or (800) 899-0688
> Fax: (818) 700-0555
> E-mail: *wginst@earthlink.net*
> Website: *http://www.wglasserinst.com*

> *Center for Reality Therapy*
> Dr. Robert E. Wubbolding, Director
> PMB 383
> 7672 Montgomery Road
> Cincinnati, OH 45236-4258
> Telephone: (513) 561-1911
> Fax: (513) 561-3568
> E-mail: *wubsrt@fuse.net*

The *International Journal of Reality Therapy* publishes manuscripts covering both the research and practice of reality therapy and choice theory, as well as many articles using William Glasser's ideas in education. To subscribe, contact:

Dr. Lawrence Litwack, Editor
International Journal of Reality Therapy
203 Lake Hall
Northeastern University
360 Huntington Ave.
Boston, MA 02115

Recommended Supplementary Readings

Choice Theory: A New Psychology of Personal Freedom (Glasser, 1998) deals with a range of topics including love and marriage, family, workplace, schooling and education, and community. In this popular and easy-to-read book, the author outlines a theory of personal freedom.

Reality Therapy in Action (Glasser, 2000) represents the author's latest thinking about choice theory. He uses many cases to give readers a sense of how choice theory principles can actually be applied in helping people establish better relationships. He develops the existential theme that we choose all of our total behaviors. Because we are responsible for our behavior, we are capable of acquiring more effective coping styles.

Using Reality Therapy (Wubbolding, 1988) presents reality therapy as a philosophy of life rather than a doctrinaire theory or set of prescriptions. Practical and clearly written, this book extends the scope of reality therapy to include paradoxical techniques, humor, skillful questioning, self-help, and supervision.

Reality Therapy for the 21st Century (Wubbolding, 2000) is a comprehensive and practical book that represents major extensions and developments of reality therapy. The practical formulation of the WDEP system of reality therapy is highlighted. Included are multicultural adaptations and summaries of research studies validating the theory and practice of reality therapy.

References and Suggested Readings*

AMERICAN PSYCHIATRIC ASSOCIATION. (1994). *Diagnostic and statistical manual of mental disorders* (4th ed.). Washington, DC: Author.

COREY, G. (2000). *Theory and practice of group counseling* (5th ed.). Pacific Grove, CA: Brooks-Cole/Wadsworth.

*COREY, G. (2001). *Case approach to counseling and psychotherapy* (5th ed.). Pacific Grove, CA: Brooks-Cole/Wadsworth.

GLASSER, N. (Ed.). (1980). *What are you doing? How people are helped through reality therapy.* New York: Harper & Row.

GLASSER, N. (Ed.). (1989). *Control theory in the practice of reality therapy: Case studies.* New York: Harper & Row.

*GLASSER, W. (1965). *Reality therapy: A new approach to psychiatry.* New York: Harper & Row.

GLASSER, W. (1976). *Positive addiction.* New York: Harper & Row.

---

*Books and articles marked with an asterisk are suggested for further study.

GLASSER, W. (1980). Reality therapy: An explanation of the steps of reality therapy. In N. Glasser (Ed.), *What are you doing? How people are helped through reality therapy* (pp. 48–60). New York: Harper & Row.

GLASSER, W. (1984a). Reality therapy. In R. Corsini (Ed.), *Current psychotherapies* (3rd ed., pp. 320–353). Itasca, IL: F. E. Peacock.

GLASSER, W. (1984b). *Take effective control of your life.* New York: Harper & Row.

*GLASSER, W. (1992). Reality therapy. *New York State Journal for Counseling and Development, 7*(1), 5–13.

*GLASSER, W. (1997). Teaching and learning reality therapy. In J. K. Zeig (Ed.), *The evolution of psychotherapy: The third conference* (pp. 123–133). New York: Brunner/Mazel.

*GLASSER, W. (1998). *Choice theory: A new psychology of personal freedom.* New York: HarperCollins.

GLASSER, W., GLASSER, C. (1999). *The language of choice theory.* New York: HarperCollins.

*GLASSER, W. (2000). *Reality therapy in action.* New York: HarperCollins.

GLASSER, W., & WUBBOLDING, R. (1995). Reality therapy. In R. Corsini & D. Wedding (Eds.), *Current psychotherapies* (5th ed., pp. 293–321). Itasca, IL: F. E. Peacock.

*WUBBOLDING, R. E. (1988). *Using reality therapy.* New York: Harper & Row (Perennial Library).

WUBBOLDING, R. E. (1990a). *Evaluation: The cornerstone in the practice of reality therapy.* Alexandria, Egypt: Omar Center for Psychological and Academic Consultations, Studies, and Services.

WUBBOLDING, R. E. (1990b). *Expanding reality therapy: Group counseling and multicultural dimensions.* Cincinnati, OH: Real World Publications.

*WUBBOLDING, R. E. (1991). *Understanding reality therapy.* New York: Harper & Row (Perennial Library).

*WUBBOLDING, R. E. (1996). Reality therapy: Theoretical underpinnings and implementation in practice. *Directions in Mental Health Counseling, 6*(9), 4–16.

*WUBBOLDING, R. E. (1999). *Cycle of managing, supervising, counseling and coaching (chart)* (11th revision). Cincinnati, OH: Center for Reality Therapy.

*WUBBOLDING, R. E. (2000). *Reality therapy for the 21st century.* Muncie, IN: Accelerated Development (Taylor & Francis).

WUBBOLDING, R. E., & ASSOCIATES. (1998). Multicultural awareness: Implications for reality therapy and choice theory. *International Journal of Reality Therapy, 17*(2), 4–6.

WUBBOLDING, R. E., & BRICKELL, J. (1998). Qualities of the reality therapist. *International Journal of Reality Therapy, 17*(2), 47–49.

CHAPTER

10

Behavior Therapy

INTRODUCTION
Historical Background
Four Areas of Development

KEY CONCEPTS
View of Human Nature
Basic Characteristics and Assumptions

THE THERAPEUTIC PROCESS
Therapeutic Goals
Therapist's Function and Role
Client's Experience in Therapy
Relationship Between Therapist and Client

APPLICATION: Therapeutic Techniques and Procedures
Relaxation Training and Related Methods
Systematic Desensitization
Exposure Therapies
Eye Movement Desensitization and Reprocessing
Assertion Training
Self-Management Programs and Self-Directed Behavior
Multimodal Therapy

BEHAVIOR THERAPY APPLIED TO THE CASE OF STAN

SUMMARY AND EVALUATION
Summary
Contributions of Behavior Therapy
Limitations and Criticisms of Behavior Therapy

BEHAVIOR THERAPY FROM A MULTICULTURAL PERSPECTIVE
Contributions to Multicultural Counseling
Limitations for Multicultural Counseling

WHERE TO GO FROM HERE

RECOMMENDED SUPPLEMENTARY READINGS

REFERENCES AND SUGGESTED READINGS

ARNOLD LAZARUS

ARNOLD A. LAZARUS (b. 1932) was born and educated in Johannesburg, South Africa. The youngest of four children (his sisters were 17 and 14 when he was born, and his brother was 9), he grew up in a neighborhood where there were very few children, and he remembers being lonely and frightened. He learned to play the piano at an early age and performed on Saturday mornings at a movie theater during intermission, for which he received the equivalent of one dollar. "When I was 7," he says, "I used to play like a talented 12-year-old, but when I turned 14 and still played like a 12-year-old, I decided to quit!" At that time his interests changed to bodybuilding, weight lifting, boxing, and wrestling. He adds, "I was a pathetically skinny kid, often beaten up and bullied, so I started training rather frantically." Through sheer determination he ended up winning boxing and weight-lifting competitions and planned to own and operate a gym or health center.

Although Dr. Lazarus grew up in South Africa, he strongly identified with the United States. At an early age he felt that racism and discrimination were totally unacceptable. These views got him into lots of fights, which was another reason he took up boxing and weight lifting. He entered college intending to major in English with a view to journalism as a career but soon switched majors to psychology and sociology. He obtained a master's degree in experimental psychology in 1957 and a Ph.D. in clinical psychology in 1960, and then he went into full-time private practice in Johannesburg. In 1963 he was invited by Albert Bandura to teach at Stanford University. Later he held teaching positions at Temple University Medical School and Yale University.

He is a Fellow of the Academy of Clinical Psychology, a Distinguished Professor Emeritus at Rutgers University, and is President of the Center for Multimodal Psychological Services in Princeton, New Jersey. He also gives lectures and workshops in the United States and abroad.

Lazarus has received many honors and has won numerous awards. These include the Distinguished Service Award from the American Board of Professional Psychology, and two Distinguished Professional Contributions Awards from the American Psychological Association. He is also the first recipient of the prestigious First Annual Cummings PSYCHE Award for his innovative and enduring contributions to time-effective psychotherapy. He has written 16 books and over 200 professional articles. He is widely recognized as an international authority on brief, efficient, and effective psychotherapy. ■

INTRODUCTION

Behavior therapy offers various action-oriented methods to help people change what they are doing and thinking. Many techniques, particularly those developed within the last three decades, emphasize cognitive processes. Writers in the field often make the case that because this orientation is so diverse it is difficult to clearly agree on a definition of behavior therapy. Recent definitions focus on the application of principles broadly derived from psychological research, the rejection of a traditional intrapsychic or medical model of behavior, and the empirical evaluation of treatment effectiveness (Glass & Arnkoff, 1992).

Historical Background

The behavioral approach had its origin in the 1950s and early 1960s as a radical departure from the dominant psychoanalytic perspective. At this time the behavior therapy movement differed from other therapeutic approaches in its application of principles of classical and operant conditioning (which will be explained shortly) to the treatment of a variety of problem behaviors. Today, behavior therapy can no longer be defined so simply. The summary of key developments presented here is based on Spiegler and Guevremont's (1998) description of the approach's historical roots.

Contemporary behavior therapy arose simultaneously in the United States, South Africa, and Great Britain in the 1950s. In spite of harsh criticism and resistance from traditional psychotherapists, the approach was able to survive. Its focus was on demonstrating that behavioral conditioning techniques were effective and were a viable alternative to traditional psychotherapy.

In the 1960s Albert Bandura developed social learning theory, which combined classical and operant conditioning with observational learning. He made cognition, which had been ruled out by B. F. Skinner's radical behaviorism, a legitimate focus for behavior therapy. During the 1960s a number of cognitive behavioral approaches sprang up, and they still have a significant impact on therapeutic practice. Albert Ellis created rational emotive behavior therapy, Aaron Beck developed cognitive therapy, and Donald Meichenbaum devised treatments such as stress inoculation and self-instructional training.

It was during the 1970s that behavior therapy emerged as a major force in psychology and made a significant impact on education, psychotherapy, psychiatry, and social work. Behavioral techniques were developed and expanded, and they were also applied to fields such as business, industry, and child rearing. This approach was now viewed as the treatment of choice for certain psychological problems.

The 1980s were characterized by a search for new horizons in concepts and methods that went beyond traditional learning theory. Behavior therapists continued to subject their methods to empirical scrutiny and to consider the impact of the practice of therapy on both their clients and the larger society. Increased attention was given to the role of affect in therapeutic change, as well as to the role of biological factors in psychological disorders. Two of the most significant developments in the field were (1) the continued emergence of cognitive behavior therapy as a major force and (2) the application of behavioral techniques to the prevention and treatment of medical disorders.

By the late 1990s the Association for Advancement of Behavior Therapy claimed a membership of about 5,000. Behavior therapy has prospered throughout the world, and currently there are scores of behavior therapy societies in existence. There are at least 50 journals devoted mainly to behavior therapy and its many offshoots (Fishman & Franks, 1997). Behavior therapy today is marked by a diversity of views and procedures. The central characteristics that unite this heterogeneous movement are an orientation toward treatment, a focus on behavior, an emphasis on learning, and rigorous assessment and evaluation (Kazdin, 1994).

Four Areas of Development

Behavior therapy began to emerge into distinct streams in the 1970s, all of which shared a common methodological and learning theory core (Fishman & Franks, 1997). Contemporary behavior therapy can be understood by considering four major areas of development: classical conditioning, operant conditioning, social learning theory, and cognitive behavior therapy.

In *classical conditioning* certain respondent behaviors, such as knee jerks and salivation, are elicited from a passive organism. In the 1950s Wolpe and Lazarus of South Africa and Hans Eysenck of England began using the findings of experimental research with animals to help treat phobias in clinical settings. They based their work on Hullian learning theory and Pavlovian (or classical) conditioning. An underlying characteristic of the work of these pioneers was the focus on experimental analysis and evaluation of therapeutic procedures. Wolpe's contribution to the development of the technique of systematic desensitization, which is described later in this chapter, is based on the classical conditioning model, and it illustrates how principles of learning derived from the experimental laboratory can be applied clinically.

Operant conditioning focuses on actions that operate on the environment to produce consequences. Examples of operant behaviors include reading, writing, driving a car, and eating with utensils. Such behaviors include most of the significant responses we make in everyday life. If the environmental changes brought about by the behavior are reinforcing—that is, if they provide some reward to the organism or eliminate aversive stimuli—the chances are strengthened that the behavior will occur again. If the environmental changes produce no reinforcement, the chances are lessened that the behavior will recur.

At the same time that Wolpe, Lazarus, and Eysenck were carrying out their experiments in the 1950s, Skinner was studying the use of the principles of operant conditioning with psychotic patients in the United States. Skinner's view of controlling behavior is based on the principles of operant conditioning, which rest on the assumption that changes in behavior are brought about when that behavior is followed by a particular kind of consequence. Skinner contends that learning cannot occur in the absence of some kind of reinforcement, either positive or negative. For him actions that are reinforced tend to be repeated, and those that are discouraged tend to be extinguished. His general writings apply concepts of operant conditioning to society. His model is based on reinforcement principles and has the goal of identifying and controlling environmental factors that lead to behavioral change.

Positive reinforcement is a process in which a response is followed by the presentation of a stimulus. It involves the addition of something (such as praise or money or food) as a consequence of certain behavior. This stimulus is the positive reinforcer. For example, a child may whine when she wants candy. If her father gives her the candy each time she whines, to quiet her, her whining is positively reinforced. Negative reinforcement involves the removal of unpleasant stimuli from a situation once a certain behavior has occurred. Negative reinforcers are generally unpleasant, and the individual is motivated to exhibit a desired behavior to avoid the unpleasant condition. For example, I will eventually go to the woodpile and bring in logs for the stove because I have learned that if I don't my wife will tell me how lazy I am or the house will get cold. I am gradually learning to interrupt my work long enough to fetch wood, because if I don't, there are some unpleasant consequences!

The *social learning approach* was developed by Albert Bandura (1977). The behaviorists of both the classical and operant conditioning models excluded any reference to mediational concepts (such as the role of thinking processes, attitudes, and values), perhaps as a reaction against the insight-oriented psychodynamic approaches. Social learning theory, in its most advanced form, is interactional, interdisciplinary, and multimodal (Bandura, 1982). Behavior is influenced by stimulus events, by external reinforcement, and by cognitive mediational processes. Social learning theory gives prominence to the reciprocal interactions between an individual's behavior and the environment. A basic assumption is that people are capable of self-directed behavior change. For Bandura (1982) self-efficacy is the individual's belief or expectation that he or she can master a situation and bring about desired change. The theory of self-efficacy represents one of the first major attempts to provide a unified theoretical explanation of how behavior therapy and other psychotherapy procedures work (Fishman & Franks, 1997).

Cognitive behavior therapy, along with social learning theory, now represent the mainstream of contemporary behavior therapy. Since the early 1970s, the behavioral movement has conceded a legitimate place to thinking, even to the extent of giving cognitive factors a central role in understanding and treating behavioral problems. Cognitive behavior therapists emphasize cognitive processes and private events (such as the client's self-talk) as mediators of behavior change (see Bandura, 1969, 1986; Beck, 1976; Beck & Weishaar, 1995; Fishman & Franks, 1997; Goldfried & Davison, 1976; Lazarus, 1989; London, 1986; Mahoney, 1977, 1979, 1991; Meichenbaum, 1977, 1985).

With the rising costs of health care, the emergence of national health programs, and the increasing involvement of psychologists in health issues, there will be a need for even greater integration of behavioral self-help, coping skills training, relaxation training, and self-management programs (Glass & Arnkoff, 1992). Furthermore, it has been predicted that the importance of cognitive and affective processes in behavior change will attract increasing attention. Treatment procedures may well be refined and applied to an ever-broader range of psychiatric disorders and health problems (Wilson & Agras, 1992).

In this chapter I will describe some of the basic behavior therapy principles and will clarify important characteristics of traditional behavior therapy. The bulk of the material describes the application of therapeutic techniques to many different populations. Chapter 11 will be devoted to the cognitive behavioral approaches, which focus on changing clients' cognitions that maintain psychological disorders. The key figures associated with this approach include Ellis, Beck, and Meichenbaum.

 # KEY CONCEPTS

View of Human Nature

Modern behavior therapy is grounded on a scientific view of human behavior that implies a systematic and structured approach to counseling. This view does not rest on a deterministic assumption that humans are a mere product of their sociocultural conditioning. Rather, the current view is that the person is the producer *and* the product of his or her environment.

Whereas radical behaviorists such as Skinner (1948, 1971) ruled out the possibility of self-determination and freedom, the current trend is toward developing procedures that actually give control to clients and thus increase their range of freedom. Behavior modification aims to increase people's skills so that they have more options for responding. By overcoming debilitating behaviors that restrict choices, people are freer to select from possibilities that were not available earlier. Thus, as behavior modification is typically applied, it will increase rather than stifle individual freedom (Kazdin, 1978).

Philosophically, the behavioristic and the humanistic approaches have often been viewed as polar opposites. The writings of contemporary behavior therapists suggest that bridges are being built, allowing the possibility of a fruitful synthesis. The strict environmental view of human nature that is based on a stimulus/response model of behavior has been criticized by Bandura (1974, 1977, 1986), the pioneer of social learning theory. He rejects the mechanistic and deterministic model of human behavior because of its exclusive reliance on environmental determinants. He contends that this view, which holds that we are passive agents subjected to the influences of our surroundings, does indeed fail to take into account our capacity to actually affect our environment.

Other writers have made a case for using behavioristic methods to attain humanistic ends (Kazdin, 1994; Meichenbaum, 1977; Thoresen & Coates, 1980; Watson & Tharp, 1997). According to Thoresen and Coates (1980), greater attention is being given to the emerging similarities among theories. They identify three interrelated themes that characterize this convergence. First is the focus on therapy as an action-oriented approach. Clients are being asked to act rather than to reflect passively and introspect at length on their problems. They are being helped to take specific actions to change their lives. Second is the increasing concern of behavior therapists with how stimulus events are mediated by cognitive processes and private or subjective meanings. Third is the increasing emphasis on the role of responsibility for one's behavior. Given the techniques and skills of self-change, people have the capacity to improve their lives by altering one or more of the various factors influencing their behavior. These three converging themes provide a conceptual framework for a bridge between the behavioral and humanistic approaches.

Basic Characteristics and Assumptions

Spiegler and Guevremont (1998) list seven recurrent themes that characterize behavior therapy.

1. Behavior therapy is based on the principles and procedures of the scientific method. Experimentally derived principles of learning are systematically applied to help people change their maladaptive behaviors. Conclusions are based on what has been observed rather than on personal beliefs. The distinguishing characteristic of behavioral practitioners is their systematic adherence to specification and measurement. They state treatment goals in concrete and objective terms to make replication of their interventions possible. Throughout the course of therapy, they assess problem behaviors and the conditions that are maintaining them. Research methods are used to evaluate the effectiveness of both assessment and treatment procedures. Thus, behavioral concepts and procedures are stated explicitly, tested empirically, and revised continually.

2. Behavior therapy deals with the client's current problems and the factors influencing them, as opposed to historical determinants. Counselors assume that a client's problems are influenced by present conditions. They then use behavioral techniques to change the relevant current factors that are influencing the client's behaviors.

3. In behavior therapy clients are expected to be active by engaging in specific actions to deal with their problems. Rather than simply talking

about their condition, they *do* something to bring about change. They monitor their behaviors both during and outside the therapy sessions, learn and practice coping skills, and role-play new behavior.

4. Behavior therapy is generally carried out in the client's natural environment, as much as possible. The approach is largely educational in that learning is viewed as being at the core of therapy. It emphasizes teaching clients skills of self-management, with the expectation that they will be responsible for transferring what they learn in the therapist's office to their everyday lives. Homework assignments are an integral part of behavior therapy.

5. Behavior therapy emphasizes a self-control approach. Therapists frequently train clients to initiate, conduct, and evaluate their own therapy. Clients are empowered through this process of being responsible for their changes.

6. Behavioral procedures are tailored to fit the unique needs of each client. Several therapy techniques may be used to treat an individual client's problems. An important question that serves as a guide for this choice is *"What* treatment, by *whom,* is the most effective for *this* individual with *that* specific problem and under *which* set of circumstances?" (Paul, 1967, p. 111).

7. The practice of behavior therapy is based on a collaborative partnership between therapist and client, and every attempt is made to inform clients about the nature and course of treatment.

These assumptions represent a basis for unity within the heterogeneity of the behavioral approaches. The basic assumption is that disorders commonly treated in therapy are best understood from the perspective of experimental psychology (Wilson, 1978). In addition, the behavioral therapies have these characteristics in common:

- Behavior therapy moves from the simple to the complex, from easier to harder, and from less threatening to more threatening.
- The behavioral approach is relatively brief, often involving fewer therapy sessions and less overall time than many other approaches to therapy.
- Several behavioral techniques are often combined in a treatment package in an attempt to increase the effectiveness of therapy.

 # THE THERAPEUTIC PROCESS

Therapeutic Goals

Goals occupy a place of central importance in behavior therapy. The general goal is to create new conditions for learning on the assumption that learning can ameliorate problem behaviors. The client usually formulates

improve

the goals, which are specifically defined at the outset of the therapeutic process. Continual assessment throughout therapy determines the degree to which these goals are being met. Assessment and treatment occur together.

Contemporary behavior therapy stresses clients' active role in deciding about their treatment. The therapist assists clients in formulating goals that are specific, unambiguous, and measurable. A number of characteristics of behavior therapy ensure that the rights of clients are protected. These include the detailed specification of goals and target behaviors, a reliance on empirically tested procedures, the brief nature of treatment, and the collaborative relationship between client and therapist (Spiegler & Guevremont, 1998). The goals of therapy must be refined to the point that they are clear, concrete, understood, and agreed on by the client and the counselor. This process of determining therapeutic goals entails a negotiation between client and counselor, which results in a contract that guides the course of therapy. Behavior therapists and clients alter goals throughout the therapeutic process as needed.

The sequence of selecting and defining goals is described by Cormier and Cormier (1998, pp. 228–231). This process demonstrates the essential nature of a collaborative relationship:

- The counselor provides a rationale for goals, explaining the role of goals in therapy, the purpose of goals, and the client's participation in the goal-setting process.
- The client specifies the positive changes he or she wants from counseling. Focus is on what the client wants to do rather than on what the client does not want to do.
- The client and counselor determine whether the stated goals are changes "owned" by the client.
- Together the client and the counselor explore whether the goals are realistic.
- The cost-benefit effect of all identified goals are explored, with counselor and client discussing the possible advantages and disadvantages of the goals.
- Client and counselor then decide (1) to continue seeking the stated goals, (2) to reconsider the client's goals, or (3) to seek a referral.
- Once goals have been agreed upon, a process of defining them begins. The counselor and client discuss the behaviors associated with the goals, the circumstances required for change, the nature of subgoals, and a plan of action to work toward these goals.

Behavioral strategies can be used to accomplish societal goals as well as individual goals. For example, behavior modification programs in hospitals and other institutions have established goals endorsed by society. These aims include returning an individual to the community, fostering self-help, increasing social skills, and alleviating bizarre behaviors. The general goals of behavior therapy are to increase personal choice and effective living. Relieving people from behaviors that interfere with living fully is consistent with the democratic value that individuals should be able to pursue their own goals freely as long as these goals are consistent with the general social good (Kazdin, 1978, 1994).

Therapist's Function and Role

Behaviorally oriented practitioners pay attention to the clues given by clients, and they are willing to follow their clinical hunches. They use some techniques common to other approaches, such as summarizing, reflection, clarification, and open-ended questioning. But other functions distinguish behavioral clinicians from their counterparts (Spiegler & Guevremont, 1998). For example, behavior therapists:

- Systematically attempt to get information about situational antecedents, the dimensions of the problem behavior, and the consequences of the problem
- Clarify the client's problem (with the client)
- Design a target behavior
- Formulate the goals for therapy (with the client)
- Identify the maintaining conditions
- Implement a change plan
- Evaluate the success of the change plan
- Conduct follow-up assessments

As an example of how a behavior therapist might perform these functions, assume that a client comes to therapy to reduce her anxiety, which is preventing her from leaving the house. The therapist is likely to begin with a specific analysis of the nature of her anxiety. The therapist will ask how she experiences the anxiety of leaving her house, including what she actually *does* in these situations. Systematically, the therapist gathers information about this anxiety. When did it begin? In what situations does it arise? What does she do at these times? What are her feelings and thoughts in these situations? How do her present fears interfere with living effectively? What are the consequences of her behaviors in threatening situations? After this assessment, specific behavioral goals will be developed and strategies will be designed to help the client reduce her anxiety to a manageable level. The therapist will get a commitment from her to work toward the specified goals, and the two of them will evaluate her progress toward meeting these goals throughout the duration of therapy.

Another important function of the therapist is role modeling for the client. Bandura (1969, 1971a, 1971b, 1977, 1986) maintains that most of the learning that occurs through direct experiences can also be acquired through observation of others' behavior. One of the fundamental processes by which clients learn new behavior is through imitation. The therapist, as a person, becomes a significant model. Because clients often view the therapist as worthy of emulation, they pattern attitudes, values, beliefs, and behavior after him or her. Thus, therapists should be aware of the crucial role that they play. To be unaware of the power they have in influencing the client's way of thinking and behaving is to deny the central importance of their own personhood in the therapeutic process.

Client's Experience in Therapy

One of the unique contributions of behavior therapy is that it provides the therapist with a well-defined system of procedures to employ within the context of a well-defined role. It also provides the client with a clear role, and it stresses the importance of client awareness and participation in the therapeutic process. Behavior therapy is characterized by an active role for both therapist and client. A large part of the therapist's role is to teach concrete skills through role playing, modeling, behavior rehearsal, and feedback. Likewise, the client engages in modeling, role playing, rehearsal, and other active behaviors as part of therapy and generally receives active homework assignments (such as self-monitoring of problem behaviors) to complete between therapy sessions. Clients must be motivated to change and must be willing to cooperate in carrying out therapeutic activities, both during therapy sessions and in everyday life. If clients are not involved in this way, the chances are slim that therapy will be successful.

Clients are encouraged to experiment for the purpose of enlarging their repertoire of adaptive behaviors. They are helped to generalize and to transfer the learning acquired within the therapeutic situation to situations outside therapy. Counseling is not complete unless actions follow verbalizations. Indeed, it is only when the transfer of changes is made from the sessions to everyday life and when the effects of therapy are extended beyond termination that treatment can be considered successful (Granvold & Wodarski, 1994). It is clear that clients are expected to do more than merely gather insights; they need to be willing to make changes and continue implementing new behavior once formal treatment has ended.

Treatment goals are stated in concrete and measurable terms, which provides clients with a frame of reference for assessing their progress in accomplishing their goals. Clients are as aware as the therapist when the goals have been accomplished and when it is appropriate to terminate treatment. After successful behavior therapy, clients experience an increase of options for behaving, which broadens their range of personal freedom (Spiegler & Guevremont, 1998).

Relationship Between Therapist and Client

Some clinical and research evidence suggests that a therapeutic relationship, even in the context of a behavioral orientation, can contribute significantly to the process of behavior change (Granvold & Wodarski, 1994). A good therapeutic relationship increases the chances that the client will be receptive to therapy. Not only is it important that the client cooperate with the therapeutic procedures, but the client's positive expectations and hope for success about the effectiveness of therapy often contribute to successful outcomes. The skilled behavior therapist conceptualizes problems behaviorally and makes use of the client/therapist relationship in facilitating change.

As you will recall, the experiential therapies (existential therapy, person-centered therapy, and Gestalt therapy) place primary emphasis on the nature of the engagement between counselor and client. In psychoanalysis the transference relationship serves as the stage on which therapy is played. In contrast, most behavioral practitioners do not assign an all-important role to relationship variables. Instead, they contend that factors such as warmth, empathy, authenticity, permissiveness, and acceptance are necessary, but not sufficient, for behavior change to occur. The client/therapist relationship is a foundation on which therapeutic strategies are built to help clients change in the direction they wish. Lazarus (1989) maintains that unless clients respect their therapist it will be difficult to develop the trust necessary for clients to engage in significant self-disclosure. But, he adds, counselors need an array of clinical skills and techniques to employ once an effective client/therapist relationship has been established. Behavior therapists tend to be active and directive and to function as consultants and problem solvers. Because they use a coping model in instigating behavioral change in the client's natural environment, it is important that they be personally supportive.

APPLICATION: Therapeutic Techniques and Procedures

A major part of behavior therapy involves behavioral assessment. Assessment begins with the client's complaint, which is then analyzed to determine its antecedents and consequences. The client keeps a record of the frequency and intensity of occurrences, and this becomes the tool in devising a therapeutic plan and in deciding whether the therapy is working. There are numerous practical and easy-to-use assessment instruments, including countless self-report inventories, behavior rating scales, self-monitoring forms, and simple observational techniques for collecting useful information on clients' problems. Simple behavioral assessment methods can be usefully applied to working with clients with a diverse range of problems. Two resources that review current behavioral methods and instruments for major client problems are *Clinical Handbook of Psychological Disorders: A Step-by-Step Manual* (Barlow, 1993) and *Assessment of Childhood Disorders* (Mash & Terdal, 1997).

Assessment is an ongoing process in behavior therapy and is an integral part of the treatment program. One strength of the behavioral approaches to counseling and psychotherapy is development of specific therapeutic procedures that lend themselves to refinement through the scientific method. Behavioral techniques must be shown to be effective through objective means, and there is a constant effort to improve them. Although behavior therapists may make mistakes in analysis or in applying therapeutic procedures, the results of their mistakes are obvious to them because they receive continual direct feedback from their clients. The main finding produced by research in the behavioral therapies is that treatment outcomes are multifaceted. Changes are not all or nothing. Improvements are likely to occur in some areas but not in others. All improvements do not emerge at one time, and gains in some areas may be associated with problems emerging in other areas (Kazdin, 1982; Voltz & Evans, 1982).

In contemporary behavior therapy any technique that can be demonstrated to change behavior may be incorporated in a treatment plan. Lazarus (1989, 1992b, 1996b, 1997a) advocates the use of diverse techniques, regardless of their theoretical origin. In his view, the more extensive the range of therapy techniques, the more potentially effective the therapist is. It is clear that behavior therapists do not have to restrict themselves strictly to methods derived from learning theory. Likewise, behavioral techniques can be incorporated into other approaches.

The therapeutic procedures used by behavior therapists are specifically designed for a particular client rather than being randomly selected from a "bag of techniques." Therapists are often quite creative in their interventions. In the following sections I will describe a range of behavioral techniques available to the practitioner: relaxation training, systematic desensitization, exposure therapies, eye movement desensitization and reprocessing, assertion training, self-management programs, and multimodal therapy. These techniques do not encompass the full spectrum of behavioral procedures, but they do represent a sample of the approaches used in behavior therapy. For a comprehensive discussion of behavioral methods, I highly recommend *Contemporary Behavior Therapy* (Spiegler & Guevremont, 1998).

Relaxation Training and Related Methods

Relaxation training has become increasingly popular as a method of teaching people to cope with the stresses produced by daily living. It is aimed at achieving muscle and mental relaxation and is easily learned. After clients learn the basics of relaxation procedures, it is essential that they practice these exercises daily to obtain maximum results.

Jacobson (1938) is credited with initially developing the progressive relaxation procedure. It has since been refined and modified, and relaxation procedures are frequently used in combination with a number of other behavioral techniques. These include systematic desensitization, assertion training, self-management programs, tape-recorded instruction, biofeedback-induced relaxation, hypnosis, meditation, and autogenic training (teaching control of bodily and imaginal functions through autosuggestion).

Relaxation training involves several components that typically require from 4 to 8 hours of instruction. Clients are given a set of instructions that asks them to relax. They assume a passive and relaxed position in a quiet environment while alternately contracting and relaxing muscles. Deep and regular breathing is also associated with producing relaxation. At the same time clients learn to mentally "let go," perhaps by focusing on pleasant thoughts or images. Relaxation becomes a well-learned response, which can become a habitual pattern if practiced daily for 20 or 25 minutes. Clients are encouraged to actually feel and experience the tension building up, to notice their muscles getting tighter and study this tension, and to hold and fully experience the tension. Also, it is useful for clients to experience the difference between a tense and a relaxed state.

Until the last few years relaxation training was used primarily as a part of systematic desensitization procedures (discussed in the next section). Recently, relaxation procedures have been applied to a variety of clinical problems, either as a separate technique or in conjunction with related methods. The most common use has been with problems related to stress and anxiety, which are often manifested in psychosomatic symptoms. Other ailments for which relaxation training is helpful include high blood pressure and other cardiovascular problems, migraine headaches, asthma, and insomnia.

Systematic Desensitization

Systematic desensitization is a basic behavioral procedure developed by Joseph Wolpe, one of the pioneers of behavior therapy. Clients imagine successively more anxiety-arousing situations at the same time that they engage in a behavior that competes with anxiety. Gradually, or systematically, clients become less sensitive (desensitized) to the anxiety-arousing situation. This procedure can be considered a form of exposure therapy because clients are required to expose themselves to anxiety-arousing images as a way to reduce anxiety.

Systematic desensitization, which is based on the principle of classical conditioning, is one of the most widely employed and empirically researched behavior therapy procedures. It was the first major behavioral treatment for anxiety-related disorders and is currently used to treat anxiety and avoidance reactions. Systematic desensitization is both an effective and efficient treatment (Spiegler & Guevremont, 1998).

The therapist first conducts an initial interview to identify specific information about the anxiety and to gather relevant background information about the client. This interview, which may last several sessions, gives the therapist a good understanding of who the client is. The therapist questions the client about the particular circumstances that elicit the conditioned fears. For instance, under what circumstances does the client feel anxious? If the client is anxious in social situations, does the anxiety vary with the number of people present? Is the client more anxious with women or men? The client is asked to begin a self-monitoring process consisting of observing and recording situations during the week that elicit anxiety responses. Some therapists also administer a questionnaire to gather additional data about situations leading to anxiety.

If the decision is made to use the desensitization procedure, the therapist gives the client a rationale for the procedure and briefly describes what is involved. Morris (1986) outlines three steps in the use of systematic desensitization: (1) relaxation training, (2) development of the anxiety hierarchy, and (3) systematic desensitization proper.

The steps in *relaxation training* are based on a modified version of the technique developed by Jacobson (1938) and described in detail by Wolpe (1990). The therapist uses a very quiet, soft, and pleasant voice to teach progressive muscular relaxation. The client is asked to create imagery of previously relaxing situations, such as sitting by a lake or wandering through a beautiful field. It is important that the client reach a state of calm and peacefulness. The client is then taught how to relax all the muscles while visualizing the various parts of the body, with emphasis on the facial muscles. The arm muscles are relaxed first, followed by the head, the neck and shoulders, the back, abdomen, and thorax, and then the lower limbs. The client is instructed to practice relaxation outside the session for about 30 minutes each day.

The therapist then works with the client to develop an *anxiety hierarchy* for each of the identified areas. Stimuli that elicit anxiety in a particular area, such as rejection, jealousy, criticism, disapproval, or any phobia, are analyzed. The therapist constructs a ranked list of situations that elicit increasing degrees of anxiety or avoidance. The hierarchy is arranged in order from the worst situation the client can imagine down to the situation that evokes the least anxiety. If it has been determined that the client has anxiety related to fear of rejection, for example, the highest anxiety-producing situation might be rejection by the spouse, next, rejection by a close friend, and then rejection by a coworker. The least disturbing situation might be a stranger's indifference toward the client at a party.

Desensitization does not begin until several sessions after the initial interview has been completed. Enough time is allowed for clients to learn relaxation in therapy sessions, to practice it at home, and to construct their anxiety hierarchy. The desensitization process begins with the client reaching complete relaxation with eyes closed. A neutral scene is presented, and the client is asked to imagine it. If the client remains relaxed, he or she is asked to imagine the least anxiety-arousing scene on the hierarchy of situations that has been developed. The therapist moves progressively up the hierarchy until the client signals that he or she is experiencing anxiety, at which time the scene is terminated. Relaxation is then induced again, and the client continues up the hierarchy. Treatment ends when the client is able to remain in a relaxed state while imagining the scene that was formerly the most disturbing and anxiety-producing. The core of systematic desensitization is repeated exposure to anxiety-evoking situations without experiencing any negative consequences.

Homework and follow-up are essential components of successful desensitization (Cormier & Cormier, 1998). Clients can practice selected relaxation procedures daily, at which time they visualize scenes completed in the previous session. Gradually, they also expose themselves to daily-life situations as a further way to manage their anxieties.

Systematic desensitization is an appropriate technique for treating phobias, but it is a misconception that it can be applied only to the treatment of anxiety. It has also been used effectively in dealing with nightmares, anorexia nervosa, obsessions, compulsions, stuttering, body image disturbances, and depression. Cormier and Cormier (1998) indicate that, historically, desensitization probably has the longest track record of any behavioral technique in dealing with fears, and its positive results have been documented repeatedly. Systematic desensitization is often acceptable to clients because they are gradually and symbolically exposed to anxiety-evoking situations. A safeguard is that clients are in control of the process by going at their own pace and terminating exposure when they begin to experience more anxiety than they want to tolerate (Spiegler & Guevremont, 1998).

Exposure Therapies

Desensitization is one type of exposure therapy, but there are others. Two variations of traditional systematic desensitization are *in vivo* desensitization and flooding.

IN VIVO DESENSITIZATION   *In vivo* desensitization involves client exposure to the actual feared situations in the hierarchy in real life rather than simply imagining situations. Clients engage in brief and graduated series of exposures to feared events. Clients can terminate exposure if they experience a high level of anxiety. As is the case with systematic desensitization, clients learn competing responses involving muscular relaxation. In some cases the therapist may accompany clients as they encounter feared situations. For example, a therapist could go with clients in an elevator if they had phobias of using elevators. People who have extreme fears of certain animals could be exposed to these animals in real life in a safe setting with a therapist. Self-managed *in vivo* desensitization is an alternative when it is not practical for a therapist to be with clients in real-life situations. If it is appropriate and possible for clients to be exposed to the feared situations, *in vivo* desensitization is the treatment of choice because it will foster greater generalization and will yield results more effectively than imaginal desensitization procedures.

FLOODING   Another form of exposure therapy is flooding, which refers to either *in vivo* or imaginal exposure to anxiety-evoking stimuli for a prolonged period of time. As is characteristic of all exposure therapies, even though the client experiences anxiety during the exposure, the feared consequences do not occur.

In vivo flooding consists of intense and prolonged exposure to the actual anxiety-producing stimuli. Remaining exposed to feared stimuli for a prolonged period without engaging in any anxiety-reducing behaviors allows the anxiety to decrease on its own. Generally, highly fearful clients tend to curb their anxiety through the use of maladaptive behaviors. In flooding, clients are prevented from engaging in their usual maladaptive responses to anxiety-arousing situations. Flooding shares with systematic desensitization the advantages linked with gradual and brief exposure without the potential limitation of clients being unable to imagine scenes clearly. *In vivo* flooding tends to reduce anxiety rapidly.

Imaginal flooding is based on similar principles and follows the same procedures except the exposure occurs in the client's imagination instead of in daily life. An advantage of using imaginal flooding over *in vivo* flooding is that there are no restrictions on the nature of the anxiety-arousing situations that can be treated. *In vivo* exposure to actual traumatic events (airplane crash, rape, fire, flood) is often not possible nor is it appropriate for both ethical and practical reasons. Imaginal flooding can re-create the circumstances of the trauma in a way that does not bring about adverse consequences to the client. Survivors of an airplane crash, for example, may suffer from a range of debilitating symptoms. They are likely to have nightmares and flashbacks to the disaster, they may avoid travel by air or have anxiety about travel by any means, and they probably have a variety of distressing symptoms such as guilt, anxiety, and depression.

The exposure technique of flooding can be fruitfully applied to a range of intense fears, such as fears of flying, riding in a subway or a train, fears of riding on escalators or elevators, and phobic reactions to certain animals. Flooding is frequently used in the behavioral treatment for anxiety-related disorders, phobias, obsessive-compulsive disorder, posttraumatic stress disorder, and agoraphobia. flooding + meds.

In their evaluation of flooding, Spiegler and Guevremont (1998) state that both *in vivo* flooding and imaginal flooding have a key role in treating anxiety-related disorders. Prolonged/intense exposure can be both an effective and efficient way to reduce clients' anxiety. However, because of the discomfort associated with prolonged/intense exposure, some clients may not elect these exposure treatments. Furthermore, prolonged and intense exposure to the anxiety-provoking situation can result in the client feeling more fearful than before treatment.

From an ethical perspective, clients should have adequate information about prolonged/intense exposure therapy before agreeing to participate. It is important that they understand that anxiety will be induced as a way to reduce it. Clients need to make informed decisions after considering the pros and cons of subjecting themselves to temporarily stressful aspects of treatment.

Spiegler and Guevremont (1998) conclude that exposure therapies are the single most potent behavioral procedures available for anxiety-related disorders, and they can have long-lasting effects. However, they add, using exposure as a sole treatment procedure is not always sufficient. In cases involving severe and multifaceted disorders, more than one behavioral intervention is often required.

Eye Movement Desensitization and Reprocessing

Since the mid-1990s, much attention has been given in both the popular and research press to eye movement desensitization and reprocessing (EMDR). This approach has become both popular and controversial in the United States, Canada, Europe, and Australia. Developed by Francine Shapiro (1995), this therapeutic procedure involves integrating a wide range of procedural elements along with the use of rhythmic eye movements and other bilateral stimulation to treat traumatic stress and memories of clients. EMDR is a form of exposure therapy designed to assist clients in dealing with traumatic memories, and it has been applied to a variety of populations including children, couples, sexual abuse victims, combat veterans, victims of crime, rape survivors, accident victims, and individuals dealing with anxiety, panic, depression, grief, addictions, and phobias (Shapiro, 1995). The most commonly researched and reported use of this procedure is with posttraumatic stress disorders.

EMDR consists of eight essential phases, and it draws from many of the procedures used in behavior therapy. A more complete discussion of these phases can be found in Shapiro (1995); only a brief explanation is provided here.

1. EMDR is used to help clients restructure their cognitions or to reprocess information. The first phase of treatment involves obtaining a client's history. Once the practitioner has completed a full evaluation of the client, a detailed treatment plan is designed. As is typical of behavior therapy, this initial phase involves conceptualizing and defining the client's problem and identifying and evaluating specific outcome goals. Additionally, specific targets are selected, such as (1) dysfunctional memories that set the groundwork for the pathology, (2) present situations that trigger the disturbance, and (3) specific skills and behaviors necessary for adaptive future action.

2. The preparation phase involves establishing a therapeutic alliance. The therapist explains the EMDR process and its effects, discusses any concerns or expectations the client may have, initiates relaxation procedures, and creates a safe climate where the client is able to engage in emotive imagery.

3. In the assessment phase the therapist identifies the components of the target and establishes a baseline response before processing begins. This assessment includes identifying a traumatic memory that results in anxiety, identifying the emotion and physical sensations associated with the traumatic event, evaluating the subjective unit of disturbance (SUD) scale of images, identifying a negative cognition that is associated with the disturbing event, and finding an adaptive belief (or positive cognition) that would lessen the anxiety surrounding the traumatic event.

4. In the desensitization phase, the client visualizes the traumatic image, verbalizes the maladaptive belief (or negative cognition), and pays attention to the physical sensations. Exposure is limited, and the client may have direct exposure to the most disturbing element for less than one minute per session. Then other associations arise. During this process, the client is instructed to visually track the therapist's index finger as it is moved rapidly and rhythmically back and forth across the client's line of vision from 12 to 24 times. The client is instructed (1) to block out the negative experience momentarily and breathe deeply and (2) to report what he or she is imagining, feeling, and thinking.

5. The installation phase consists of installing and increasing the strength of the positive cognition the client has identified as the replacement

for the original negative cognition. For example, a rape victim may have a negative cognition such as "I should have fought harder or run away." This negative cognition will be replaced with a functional statement such as "Now, I am in control" or "Under the circumstances, I did the very best I could have done." The objective is to associate the traumatic event with an adaptive belief so that the memory no longer has the power to result in anxiety and negative thinking. The focus is on the strength of the client's positive self-assessment, which is pivotal for therapeutic gains to be maintained.

6. After the positive cognition has been installed, the client is asked to visualize the traumatic event and the positive cognition and to scan his or her body mentally from top to bottom and identify any bodily tension states. The body scan is completed when the client is able to visualize the target event and, at the same time, experience little bodily tension and be able to experience the positive cognition.

7. It is essential that adequate closure be brought to the end of each session. The therapist reminds the client that he or she may experience disturbing images, emotions, and thoughts between the sessions. The client is asked to keep a log or journal and record any disturbing material. The use of the log and relaxation or visualization techniques are crucial for client stability between sessions. Instructions are typically given to the client in the form of homework to be completed. Some interventions clients are expected to make use of during this phase of treatment include relaxation, guided imagery, meditation, self-monitoring, and breathing exercises.

8. Reevaluation is the last phase of treatment, which should be implemented at the beginning of each new session. Much as behavior therapists review homework with their clients at a new session, the clinician using EMDR assists the client in reaccessing previously reprocessed targets and reviews the client's responses to determine if the treatment is progressing. This last phase of EMDR includes several behavioral processes: reconceptualization of the client's problems, establishing new therapeutic goals, engaging in further desensitization, continuing the work of cognitive restructuring, continuing the self-monitoring process, and collaboratively evaluating the outcome of treatment.

RECENT EMDR STUDIES   Although Spiegler & Guevremont (1998) believe many of the studies on EMDR are methodologically flawed, EMDR has more controlled outcome research to support it than any other method used in the treatment of posttraumatic stress disorder (PTSD). In 1995 the APA Division 12 (Clinical Psychology) initiated a project to determine the degree to which extant therapeutic methods were supported by solid empirical evidence. Independent reviewers (Chambless et al., 1998) recently placed EMDR on a list of "empirically validated treatments" as "probably efficacious for civilian PTSD." In addition, exposure therapy (e.g., flooding) and stress inoculation therapy were described as "probably efficacious for PTSD." No other therapy techniques were judged to be empirically supported by controlled research for any posttraumatic stress disorder population. A meta-analysis of all psychological and drug treatments for PTSD reported: "The results of the present study suggest that EMDR is effective for PTSD, and that it is more efficient than other treatments" (Van Etten & Taylor, 1998).

Controlled outcome studies with civilian trauma victims showed that after three EMDR sessions 84% to 90% of the subjects no longer met the criteria for PTSD. The Rothbaum (1997) study found that after three EMDR sessions 90% of the rape victims no longer met the full criteria for PTSD. In a test of subjects whose responses to EMDR were reported, it was found that 84% of the participants initially diagnosed with PTSD still failed to meet the criteria at the 15-month follow-up (Wilson, Becker, & Tinker, 1995, 1997). In a controlled study by Marcus, Marquis, and Sakai (1997), which was funded by Kaiser Permanente, 100% of single trauma victims and 80% of multiple trauma victims no longer had PTSD after 5 hours of EMDR treatment. In a recent systematically evaluated case series by Lazrove et al. (in press), only one subject dropped out very early in the study. Of the seven subjects who completed treatment (including mothers who had lost their children to drunken drivers), none met PTSD criteria at follow-up. In a study of traumatized adolescent women (Scheck, Schaeffer & Gillette, 1998) after only two sessions of EMDR approximately 77% no longer had PTSD.

Barker and Hawes (1999) claim that, used appropriately and effectively, EMDR tends to speed up the Adlerian Individual Psychology process of challenging negative lifestyle convictions that block an individual from achieving a goal of significance and belonging. Their article summarizes the efficacy of EMDR as it is applied to Adlerian theory:

> Not only does EMDR bring about change in clients at a rate that is unprecedented, but it deals with very painful episodes so quickly that clients do not have to subject themselves to lengthy abreactions or reliving of their traumatic histories. We have found EMDR to be in harmony with Individual Psychology theory, from the mutual respect inherent in the process and the congruence with lifestyle assessment. The research findings of EMDR outcome studies provide support for its efficacy and permanence of change. Our own experience has seen EMDR effective with individuals from different cultures and with a variety of problems. (p. 158)

TRAINING IN EMDR Eye movement desensitization and reprocessing draws from a wide range of behavioral interventions, all of which contribute to the complexity and therapeutic power of this approach. Shapiro (1995) emphasizes the ethical parameters of using this approach, stressing the importance of the safety and welfare of the client. Shapiro points out that EMDR may appear simple to some, yet the ethical use of the procedure demands training and clinical supervision. Because of the powerful reactions from clients, it is essential that practitioners know how to safely and effectively manage these occurrences. Therapists should not use this procedure unless they receive proper training and supervision from an EMDR-authorized instructor. Information regarding training can be obtained by contacting the EMDR Institute, P. O. Box 51010, Pacific Grove, CA 93950.

Assertion Training

Assertion training is one form of social skills training. At each developmental stage in life important social skills must be mastered. Children need to learn how to make friends, adolescents need to learn how to interact with the opposite sex, and adults must learn how to effectively relate to mates, peers, and supervisors. People who lack social skills frequently experience interpersonal difficulties at home, at work, at school, and during leisure time. Many people have difficulty feeling that it is appropriate or right to assert themselves. Assertion training can be useful for those (1) who cannot express anger or irritation, (2) who have difficulty saying no, (3) who are overly polite and allow others to take advantage of them, (4) who find it difficult to express affection and other positive responses, or (5) who feel they do not have a right to express their thoughts, beliefs, and feelings.

The basic assumption underlying assertion training is that people have the right (but not the obligation) to express themselves. One goal of assertion training is to increase people's behavioral repertoire so that they can make the _choice_ of whether to behave assertively in certain situations. Another goal is teaching people to express themselves in ways that reflect sensitivity to the feelings and rights of others. Assertion does not mean aggression; thus, truly assertive people do not stand up for their rights at all costs, ignoring the feelings of others.

Many assertion training methods are based on principles of the cognitive behavioral therapies (Chapter 11). Most assertion training programs focus on clients' negative self-statements, self-defeating beliefs, and faulty thinking. People often behave in unassertive ways because they don't think they have a right to state a viewpoint or ask for what they want or deserve. Thus, their thinking leads to passive behavior. Effective assertion training programs do more than give people skills and techniques for dealing with difficult situations. These programs challenge people's beliefs that accompany their lack of assertiveness and teach them to make constructive self-statements and to adopt a new set of beliefs that will result in assertive behavior.

Assertion training is not a panacea, but it is a treatment of choice for most clients with interpersonal difficulties. Although counselors can adapt assertion training procedures to suit their own style, it is important to include behavioral rehearsal and continual assessment as basic aspects of the program. According to Alberti and Emmons (1995a), there are many advantages to conducting assertiveness training in a group setting. The group provides a laboratory for members to work on common problems and goals. It offers the support and guidance that is necessary to experiment with new behaviors. There are also diverse perspectives for feedback on interpersonal issues. Because the assertion training group focuses on social situations that involve anxiety, it offers a realistic opportunity for people to face and challenge their difficulties in a structured and safe environment. As members are learning new skills, they have the advantage of social reinforcement.

Alberti and Emmons indicate that assertiveness training groups are not appropriate for all people. Individual clients should be assessed before assigning them to a group. Furthermore, they recommend that members be prepared for the group experience. They stress the importance of a trusting atmosphere for productive work to occur. If you are interested in learning more about the issues involved in assertion training and how to set up such a program, consult *Your Perfect Right: A Guide to Assertive Behavior* (Alberti & Emmons, 1995a).

Self-Management Programs and Self-Directed Behavior

There is a growing trend toward integrating cognitive and behavioral methods to help clients manage their own problems (Kanfer & Goldstein, 1986). A related trend, toward "giving psychology away," involves psychologists' sharing their knowledge so that "consumers" can increasingly lead self-directed lives and not be dependent on experts to deal with their problems. Psychologists who share this perspective are primarily concerned with teaching people the skills they will need to manage their own lives effectively.

Self-management is a relatively recent phenomenon in counseling and therapy, with reports of clinical applications increasing since the 1970s. Self-management strategies include, but are not limited to, self-monitoring, self-reward, self-contracting, and stimulus control. The basic idea of self-management assessments and interventions is that change can be brought about by teaching people to use coping skills in problematic situations. Generalization and maintenance of the outcomes are enhanced by encouraging clients to accept the responsibility for carrying out these strategies in daily life. Self-management strategies have been applied to many populations and many problems, including anxiety, depression, and pain.

In self-management programs people make decisions concerning specific behaviors they want to control or change. Some common examples are control of smoking, drinking, and drugs; learning study and time-management skills; and dealing with obesity and overeating. People frequently discover that a major reason that they do not attain their goals is the lack of certain skills. It is in such areas that a self-directed approach can provide the guidelines for change and a plan that will lead to change.

Five characteristics of an effective self-management program are identified by Cormier and Cormier (1998):

1. A combination of self-management strategies is usually more useful than a single strategy.
2. Self-management efforts need to be employed regularly over a sustained period or their effectiveness may be too limited to produce any significant change.
3. Clients should set realistic goals and then evaluate the degree to which they are being met.
4. The use of self-reinforcement is an important component of self-management programs.
5. Some degree of environmental support is necessary to maintain changes that result from a self-management program.

Watson and Tharp (1997) offer a four-stage model designed for self-directed change:

1. *Selecting goals.* The initial stage begins with specifying what changes are desired. Goals should be established one at a time, and they should be measurable, attainable, positive, and significant for the person.

2. *Translating goals into target behaviors.* Next, the goals selected are translated into target behaviors. A key question is, "What specific behaviors do I want to increase or decrease?"

3. *Self-monitoring.* A major first step in self-directed change is the process of self-monitoring, in which clients deliberately and systematically observe their own behavior. One of the simplest methods for observing behavior is keeping a *behavioral diary.* The occurrence of a particular behavior is recorded by the client, along with comments about the relevant antecedent cues and consequences.

4. *Working out a plan for change.* This stage begins with a comparison between the information obtained from self-monitoring and clients' standards for a specific behavior. After clients make the evaluation of behavioral changes they want to acquire, they devise an action program to bring about actual change. Some type of self-reinforcement system is necessary in this plan because reinforcement is the cornerstone of modern behavior therapy. Self-reinforcement is a temporary strategy clients use until they successfully implement the new behaviors in everyday life.

To determine the degree to which clients are achieving their goals, it is essential to *evaluate the plan for change.* The plan of action is continually adjusted and revised as clients learn other ways to meet their goals. Evaluation is an ongoing process rather than a one-time occurrence, and self-direction is a lifelong practice.

Multimodal Therapy

Multimodal therapy is a comprehensive, systematic, holistic approach to behavior therapy developed by Lazarus (1971, 1986, 1987b, 1989, 1992a, 1992b, 1995, 1997a). It is an open system that encourages *technical eclecticism.* New techniques are constantly being introduced and existing techniques are refined, but they are never used in a shotgun manner. Multimodal therapists take great pains not to try to fit the client to a predetermined treatment. Instead, they make a careful attempt to determine precisely what relationship and what treatment strategies will work best with each client and under which particular circumstances. The underlying assumption of this approach is that because individuals are troubled by a variety of specific problems it is appropriate that a multitude of treatment strategies be used in bringing about change. Therapeutic flexibility and versatility, along with breadth over depth, are valued highly in the multimodal orientation. Multimodal therapists are constantly adjusting their procedures to achieve the client's goals in therapy (Lazarus, 1995, 1997a).

TECHNICAL ECLECTICISM   Multimodal therapists recognize that many clients come to therapy needing to learn skills, and therapists are willing to teach, coach, train, model, and direct their clients. They typically function directively by providing information, instruction, and reactions. They challenge self-defeating beliefs, offer constructive feedback, provide positive reinforcement, and are appropriately self-disclosing. It is essential that therapists start where the client is and then move into other productive areas for exploration. Failure to apprehend the client's situation can easily leave the client feeling alienated and misunderstood (Lazarus, 1995).

Multimodal therapists borrow techniques from many other therapy systems. Some techniques they employ in individual psychotherapy are anxiety-management training, behavior rehearsal, bibliotherapy, biofeedback, communication training, contingency contracting, hypnosis, meditation, modeling, paradoxical strategies, positive imagery, positive reinforcement, relaxation training, self-instruction training, sensate-focus training, social skills and assertiveness training, the empty chair, time projection, and thought stopping. (See Lazarus, 1987a for a detailed description of these methods.) Most of these techniques are standard behavioral procedures drawn from the four major thrusts of the behavioral approach: classical, operant, social learning, and cognitive behavioral.

In espousing technical (or systematic) eclecticism, Lazarus is not arguing in favor of theoretical eclecticism, because blending bits and pieces of different theories is likely to obfuscate matters. By remaining theoretically consistent but technically eclectic, however, practitioners can spell out precisely what interventions they will employ with various clients, as well as the means by which they select these procedures. Systematic eclecticism borrows techniques from diverse sources without necessarily subscribing to the theories that spawned them (Lazarus, 1992b, 1995, 1996b, 1997a; Lazarus & Beutler, 1993; Lazarus, Beutler, & Norcross, 1992). The purpose of technical eclecticism is not to produce another separate school of therapy but to "engender an open system of empirically grounded clinical practice, an interdisciplinary and collaborative cadre of researchers building on each other's work" (Lazarus et al., 1992, p. 17). They hope that in the future therapists will think and practice eclectically and integratively—but critically.

THE BASIC I.D.   The essence of Lazarus's multimodal approach is the premise that the complex personality of human beings can be divided into seven major areas of functioning: B = behavior; A = affective responses; S = sensations; I = images; C = cognitions; I = interpersonal relationships; and D = drugs, biological functions, nutrition, and exercise (Lazarus, 1989, 1992a, 1992b, 1995, 1997a, 1997b). Although these modalities are interactive, they can be considered discrete functions. This model implies that we are social beings who move, feel, sense, imagine, and think.

A complete assessment and treatment program must account for each modality of the BASIC I.D., which is the cognitive map linking each aspect of personality. Comprehensive brief therapy involves correcting irrational beliefs, deviant behaviors, unpleasant feelings, bothersome images, stressful relationships, negative sensations, and possible biochemical imbalances. Multimodal therapists believe that the more clients learn in therapy the less likely it is that old problems will reoccur. They view enduring change as a function of combined strategies and modalities.

Four principles embody the essence of the multimodal perspective (Lazarus, 1997a): (1) Humans act and interact across the seven areas of the BASIC I.D.; (2) these modalities are interconnected and must be treated as an interactive system; (3) accurate evaluation (diagnosis) is best accomplished by systematically assessing each of the seven modalities and the interaction among them; and (4) a comprehensive approach to treatment involves the specific correction of significant problems across the BASIC I.D.

Multimodal therapy begins with a comprehensive assessment of the seven modalities of human functioning. Clients are asked questions pertaining to the BASIC I.D. What follows is a modification of this assessment process based on questions Lazarus typically asks (1989, 1995, 1997a):

1. *Behavior.* This modality refers primarily to overt behaviors, including acts, habits, and reactions that are observable and measurable. Some questions asked are: "What would you like to change?" "How active are you?" "What would you like to start doing?" "What would you like to stop doing?" "What are some of your main strengths?" "What specific behaviors keep you from getting what you want?"

2. *Affect.* This modality refers to emotions, moods, and strong feelings. Questions sometimes asked include: "What emotions do you experience most often?" "What makes you laugh?" "What makes you cry?" "What makes you sad, mad, glad, scared?" "What emotions are problematic for you?"

3. *Sensation.* This area refers to the five basic senses of touch, taste, smell, sight, and hearing. Examples of questions asked are: "Do you suffer from unpleasant sensations, such as pains, aches, dizziness, and so forth?" "What do you particularly like or dislike in the way of seeing, smelling, hearing, touching, and tasting?"

4. *Imagery.* This modality pertains to ways in which we picture ourselves, and it includes memories, dreams, and fantasies. Some questions asked are: "What are some bothersome recurring dreams and vivid memories?" "Do you have a vivid imagination?" "How do you view your body?" "How do you see yourself now?" "How would you like to be able to see yourself in the future?"

5. *Cognition.* This modality refers to insights, philosophies, ideas, opinions, self-talk, and judgments that constitute one's fundamental values, attitudes, and beliefs. Questions include: "What are some ways in which you meet your intellectual needs?" "How do your thoughts affect your emotions?" "What are the values and beliefs you most cherish?" "What are some negative things you say to yourself?" "What are some of your central faulty be-

liefs?" "What are the main 'shoulds,' 'oughts,' and 'musts' in your life? How do they get in the way of effective living?"

6. *Interpersonal relationships.* This modality refers to interactions with other people. Examples of questions include: "How much of a social being are you?" "To what degree do you desire intimacy with others?" "What do you expect from the significant people in your life?" "What do they expect from you?" "Are there any relationships with others that you would hope to change?" "If so, what kinds of changes do you want?"

7. *Drugs/biology.* This modality includes more than drugs, encompassing consideration of clients' nutritional habits and exercise patterns as well. Some questions asked are: "Are you healthy and health conscious?" "Do you have any concerns about your health?" "Do you take any prescribed drugs?" "What are your habits pertaining to diet, exercise, and physical fitness?"

This preliminary investigation brings out some central and significant themes that can then be productively explored using a detailed life-history questionnaire. (See Lazarus and Lazarus, 1991, for the multimodal life-history inventory.) Once the main profile of a person's BASIC I.D. has been established, the next step consists of an examination of the interactions among the different modalities. This second phase of work intensifies specific facets of the client's problem areas and allows the therapist to understand the person more fully as well as to devise effective coping and treatment strategies.

BRIEF AND COMPREHENSIVE THERAPY   Lazarus (1997a, 1997b) advocates for short-term and comprehensive treatment. In this era wherein brief therapy is in vogue, Lazarus (1997b, p. 85) maintains that "[V]irtually anyone can be brief, but can they also be effective and achieve durable results?" For therapy to be short-term, comprehensive, and effective, therapists must examine these eight issues (Lazarus, 1997a, 1997b):

- Conflicting or ambivalent feelings
- Maladaptive behaviors
- Misinformation
- Missing information
- Interpersonal pressures and demands
- External stressors outside the immediate interpersonal network
- Severe traumatic experiences
- Biological dysfunctions

A major premise of multimodal therapy is that *breadth* is often more important than *depth*. The more coping responses a client learns in therapy, the less are the chances for a relapse (Lazarus, 1996a). Therapists identify one specific issue from each aspect of the BASIC I.D. framework as a target for change and teach clients a range of techniques they can use to combat faulty thinking, to learn to relax in stressful situations, and to acquire effective interpersonal skills. Clients can then apply these skills to a broad range of problems in their everyday lives.

ROLE OF THE MULTIMODAL THERAPIST Multimodal therapists tend to be very active during therapy sessions, functioning as trainers, educators, consultants, and role models. They provide information, instruction, and feedback as well as modeling assertive behaviors, challenging self-defeating beliefs, offering constructive criticism and suggestions, offering positive reinforcements, and being appropriately self-disclosing.

Effective therapy calls for counselors to be "authentic chameleons" (Lazarus, 1993), meaning that a flexible repertoire of relationship styles is as important as a wide range of techniques in enhancing treatment outcomes. Therapists need to make choices regarding different styles of relating to clients. They will have to decide when and how to be directive or supportive, cold or warm, formal or informal, and tough or tender. Lazarus (1996a) states that one of his major accomplishments as a therapist over the years has been learning to blend appropriate and effective techniques with the most suitable relationship style.

BEHAVIOR THERAPY APPLIED TO THE CASE OF STAN

Working with Stan from a behavioral perspective, the therapist begins with a comprehensive assessment utilizing the categories that are part of the multimodal approach. In Stan's case many specific and interrelated problems can be identified using the BASIC I.D. diagnosis:

Behavior

- Is defensive, avoids eye contact, speaks hesitantly
- Uses alcohol excessively
- Has a poor sleep pattern
- Displays various avoidance behaviors

Affect

- Feels anxiety
- Panics (especially at night when trying to sleep)
- Experiences depression
- Fears criticism and rejection
- Feels worthless and stupid
- Feels isolated and alienated

Sensation

- Feels dizziness
- Suffers from impotence
- Has palpitations
- Gets headaches

Imagery

- Receives ongoing negative parental messages
- Has an unfavorable body image and poor self-image
- Has suicidal fantasies at times
- Fantasizes being shunned by others, especially women

Cognition

- Has worrying thoughts (death and dying)
- Has many self-defeating thoughts and beliefs
- Is governed by categorical imperatives ("shoulds," "oughts," "musts")
- Seeks new values
- Compares himself negatively with others
- Engages in fatalistic thinking

Interpersonal Characteristics

- Is unassertive
- Has an unsatisfactory relationship with his parents
- Has very few friends
- Is afraid of contact with women and fears intimacy
- Feels socially inferior

Drugs and Biological Factors

- Abuses alcohol
- Has used illegal drugs
- Lacks an exercise program
- Has various physical complaints
- Shows no organic pathology

After completing this assessment, Stan's therapist focuses on helping him define the specific areas where he would like to make changes. They talk about how the therapy sessions (and his work outside of them) can help him reach his goals. Early during treatment the therapist helps Stan translate some of his general goals into concrete and measurable ones. Thus, when he says "I want to feel better about myself," she helps him define more specific goals. When he says "I want to get rid of my inferiority complex," she replies: "What are some situations in which you feel inferior?" "What do you actually do that leads to feelings of inferiority?" Stan's concrete aims include his desire to function without drugs or alcohol. She asks him to keep a record of when he drinks and what events lead to drinking.

Stan indicates that he does not want to feel apologetic for his existence. His therapist asks him to engage in some assertiveness-training exercises. Because he has trouble talking with his boss or coworkers, she demonstrates how to approach them more directly and confidently. This procedure includes modeling, role playing, and behavior rehearsal. He then tries more effective behaviors with his therapist, who plays the role of the boss and then gives feedback on how strong or apologetic he seemed.

Stan's anxiety about women can also be explored using behavior rehearsal. The therapist plays the role of a woman Stan wants to date. He practices being the way he would like to be with his date and says the things to his therapist that he might be afraid to say to his date. During this rehearsal, Stan can explore his fears,

get feedback on the effects o ior, and experiment with m behavior.

Systematic desensitization is appr⌐ priate in working with Stan's fear of failing. He first learns relaxation procedures during the sessions and then practices them daily at home. Next, he lists his specific fears relating to failure. Stan identifies his greatest fear as sexual impotence with a woman. The least fearful situation he identifies is being with a female student for whom he does not feel an attraction. He then imagines a pleasant scene and begins a desensitization process focusing first on his lesser fears and working up to the anxiety associated with his greatest fear.

The goal of therapy is to help Stan modify the behavior that results in his feelings of guilt and anxiety. This approach does not place importance on his past except to the extent necessary to modify his faulty learning. The therapist does not explore his childhood experiences but works directly with the present behaviors that are causing his difficulties. Insight is not seen as important, nor is having Stan experience or reexperience his feelings. By learning more appropriate coping behaviors, eliminating unrealistic anxiety and guilt, and acquiring more adaptive responses, Stan's presenting symptoms will decrease, and he will report a greater degree of satisfaction.

Follow-Up: You Continue as Stan's Behavior Therapist

Use these questions to help you think about how to counsel Stan:

- What is your impression of Stan's characteristics as defined using the multimodal perspective? What are some areas you might be inclined to pursue?
- How would you collaboratively work with Stan in identifying specific behavioral goals to give a direction to your therapy?

- As a behavior therapist, you are far more interested in Stan's current struggles than in his early childhood issues. How might you deal with Stan if he indicated that he wanted to talk about what happened to him as a child?
- What behavioral techniques might be most appropriate in helping Stan with his problems?

- Stan indicates that he does not want to feel apologetic for his existence. How might you help him translate this wish into a specific behavioral goal? What behavioral techniques might you draw on in helping him in this area?
- What homework assignments are you likely to suggest for Stan? ■

 SUMMARY AND EVALUATION

Summary

Contemporary behavior therapy (unlike traditional behaviorism and radical behaviorism) places emphasis on the interplay between the individual and the environment. Because cognitive factors have a place in the practice of behavior therapy, techniques from this approach can be used to attain humanistic ends. It is clear that bridges can connect the humanistic and the behavioristic therapies, especially with the current focus of attention on self-directed approaches and multimodal therapy.

Behavior therapy is diverse with respect not only to basic concepts but also to techniques that can be applied in coping with specific problems. The behavioral movement includes four major areas of development: classical conditioning, operant conditioning, social learning theory, and increasing attention to the cognitive factors influencing behavior (the subject of Chapter 11). A unique characteristic of behavior therapy is its strict reliance on the principles of the scientific method. Concepts and procedures are stated explicitly, tested empirically, and revised continually. Treatment and assessment are interrelated and occur simultaneously. Research is considered to be a basic aspect of the approach, and therapeutic techniques are continually refined.

A hallmark of behavior therapy is the identification of specific goals at the outset of the therapeutic process. In helping clients achieve their goals, behavior therapists typically assume an active and directive role. Although the client generally determines *what* behavior will be changed, the therapist typically determines *how* this behavior can best be modified. In designing a treatment plan, behavior therapists employ techniques and procedures from a wide variety of therapeutic systems and apply them to the unique needs of each client.

Contributions of Behavior Therapy

Behavior therapy challenges us to reconsider our global approach to counseling. Some may assume they know what a client means by the statement,

"I feel unloved; life has no meaning." A humanist might nod in acceptance to such a statement, but the behaviorist will retort: "Who specifically is not loving you?" "What is going on in your life to bring about this meaninglessness?" "What are some specific things you might be doing that contribute to the state you are in?" "What would you most like to change?" Behavior therapy focuses on specifics.

Another contribution is the wide variety of specific behavioral techniques at the disposal of the therapist. Because behavior therapy stresses *doing,* as opposed to merely talking about problems and gathering insights, practitioners use many behavioral strategies to assist clients in formulating a plan of action for changing behavior. Behavioral techniques have been extended to more areas of human functioning than have any of the other therapeutic approaches (Kazdin, 1994). Behavior therapy is deeply enmeshed in medicine, geriatrics, pediatrics, rehabilitation programs, and stress management. This approach has made significant contributions to health psychology, especially in the areas of helping people maintain a healthy lifestyle and in managing illness. Behavioral methods have been effectively used in combating cigarette smoking, overeating, and overdrinking. They are of value in helping people stick to an exercise plan and in managing stress and hypertension. In fact, behavioral medicine, the wellness movement, and approaches to holistic health incorporate behavioral strategies as part of their practice.

The APA's Task Force on Promotion and Dissemination of Psychological Procedures (APA, 1995) has compiled a report on recommendations and resources for the treatment of a wide range of specific problems. The report is intended as a growing resource for clinicians and researchers interested in bulimia, chronic headache, chronic pain, chronically mentally ill, depression, discordant couples, enuresis, generalized anxiety disorder, obsessive compulsive disorder, panic disorder, posttraumatic stress disorder, social phobia, and specific phobia.

Another major contribution of behavior therapy is its emphasis on research into and assessment of treatment outcomes. It is up to practitioners to demonstrate that therapy is working. If progress is not being made, therapists look carefully at the original analysis and treatment plan. Of all the therapies presented in this book, this approach and its techniques have been subjected to the highest degree of empirical research. This scrutiny may account for the fact that this model has changed so dramatically since its origin. In the early years of research, investigators framed questions in terms of global outcomes. Now they ask specific questions such as "Which type of client, meeting with which type of counselor, using which type of treatment, will yield what outcome?" It is recognized that some techniques and therapists are appropriate for certain clients but not for others. Furthermore, almost no procedure can be expected to lead to behavior change in all clients or to correct all the problems of any client (Kanfer & Goldstein, 1986). This kind of focused research is characteristic of behavior therapy.

A contribution of behavior therapists is their willingness to examine the effectiveness of their procedures in terms of the generalizability, meaningfulness, and durability of change. Most studies show that behavior therapy methods are more effective than no treatment. Moreover, a number of behavioral procedures are currently the best treatment strategies available for a range of specific problems. Compared with alternative approaches, behavioral techniques have generally been shown to be at least as effective and frequently more effective in changing target behaviors (Spiegler & Guevremont, 1998).

A related strength of the behavioral approach is the emphasis on ethical accountability. Behavior therapists, in general, have been particularly concerned with the ethical aspects of practice. Although they have powerful means of modifying behavior at their disposal, their willingness to involve clients in the various stages of the therapy process seems to serve as a good safeguard. At the outset of therapy clients learn about the nature of counseling, the procedures that may be employed, and the benefits and risks. Clients are given information about the specific therapy procedures appropriate for their particular problems. Clients also participate in the choice of techniques that will be used in dealing with their problems. With this information clients become informed, fully enfranchised partners in the therapeutic venture.

Behavior therapy is ethically neutral in that it does not dictate whose behavior or what behavior should be changed. At least in cases of voluntary counseling, the behavioral practitioner only specifies *how* to change those behaviors the client targets for change. Clients have a good deal of control and freedom in deciding *what* the goals of therapy will be. Furthermore, behavior therapists use empirically tested techniques, assuring that clients are receiving both effective and relatively brief treatment. This emphasis on brief and effective therapy is a key aspect of ethical practice (Spiegler & Guevremont, 1998).

Limitations and Criticisms of Behavior Therapy

Behavior therapists need to listen very carefully to their clients and to allow them to express and explore their feelings before implementing a treatment plan. The basic therapeutic conditions stressed by person-centered therapists—active listening, accurate empathy, positive regard, genuineness, respect, and immediacy—can be integrated in a behavioral framework. However, too often counselors are so anxious to work toward resolving problems that they are not fully present with their clients. A mistake some counselors make is focusing on the presenting issue instead of listening to the client's deeper message.

Behavior therapy has been criticized for a variety of reasons. Let's examine five common criticisms and misconceptions people often have about behavior therapy, together with my reactions.

1. *Behavior therapy may change behaviors, but it does not change feelings.* Some critics argue that feelings must change before behavior can change.

Behavioral practitioners generally contend that if clients can change their behavior their feelings are also likely to change. They hold that empirical evidence has not shown that feelings must be changed first, and behavioral clinicians do in actual practice deal with feelings as an overall part of the treatment process.

I do not think behavior therapy deals with emotional processes as fully or as adequately as do the experiential therapies. A general criticism of both the behavioral and the cognitive approaches is that clients are not encouraged to experience their emotions. In concentrating on how clients are behaving or thinking, counselors play down the working through of emotional issues. Generally, I favor initially focusing on what clients are feeling and then working with the behavioral and cognitive dimensions.

2. *Behavior therapy ignores the important relational factors in therapy.* The charge is often made that the importance of the relationship between client and therapist is discounted in behavior therapy. Although it appears to be true that behavior therapists do not place primary weight on the relationship variable, this does not mean the approach is condemned to a mechanical and nonhumanistic level of functioning. Behavior therapists acknowledge that a good working relationship with their clients is a basic foundation necessary for the effective use of techniques. As Lazarus (1996b) states, "The relationship is the soil that enables the techniques to take root" (p. 61).

Research has not shown the behavioral therapies to be any different from other therapeutic orientations in the relationship variables that emerge (Sloane, Staples, Cristol, Yorkston, & Whipple, 1975). Some therapists may be attracted to behavior therapy because they can be directive, can play the role of expert, or can avoid the anxieties and ambiguities of establishing a more personal relationship. But this is not an intrinsic characteristic of the approach, and many behavior therapists are more humanistic in practice than some therapists who profess to practice humanistic therapy.

3. *Behavior therapy does not provide insight.* If this assertion is indeed true, behavior modification theorists would probably respond that insight isn't necessary. They do not focus on insight because of the absence of clear evidence that insight is critical to outcome. Behavior is changed directly. If the goal of achieving insight is an eventual change of behavior, then behavior therapy, which has proven results, has the same effect. Moreover, a change in behavior often leads to a change in understanding; it is a two-way street.

Nevertheless, many people want not just to change their behavior but also to gain an understanding of why they behave the way they do. These answers are often buried deep in past learning and in historical events. Although it is possible for behavior therapists to give explanations in this realm, in fact they usually do not.

4. *Behavior therapy treats symptoms rather than causes.* The psychoanalytic assumption is that early traumatic events are at the root of present dysfunction. Behavior therapists may acknowledge that deviant responses

have historical origins, but they contend that history is seldom important in the maintenance of current problems. Thus, behavior therapy focuses on providing the client with opportunities to acquire the new learning needed for effectively coping with problem situations.

Related to this criticism is the notion that unless historical causes of present behavior are therapeutically explored new symptoms will soon take the place of those that were "cured." Behaviorists rebut this assertion on both theoretical and empirical grounds. They do not accept the assumption that symptoms are manifestations of underlying intrapsychic conflicts. Instead, they contend that behavior therapy directly changes the maintaining conditions, which are the causes, of problem behaviors (symptoms). Furthermore, they assert that there is no empirical evidence that symptom substitution occurs after behavior therapy has successfully eliminated unwanted behavior (Kazdin & Wilson, 1978; Sloane et al., 1975; Spiegler & Guevremont, 1998).

5. *Behavior therapy involves control and manipulation by the therapist.* Some writers in behavior therapy clearly acknowledge that therapists do have control, but they contend that this capacity to manipulate relevant variables is not necessarily undesirable or unethical. Kazdin (1994) believes no issues of control and manipulation are associated with behavioral strategies that are not also raised by other therapeutic approaches. He maintains that behavior therapy does not embrace particular goals or argue for a particular lifestyle, nor does it have an agenda for changing society.

Surely, in all therapeutic approaches there is control by the therapist, who hopes to change behavior in some way. This does not mean, however, that clients are helpless victims at the mercy of the whims and values of the therapist. Contemporary behavior therapists employ techniques aimed at increased self-direction and self-control, which are skills clients actually learn in the therapy process.

 ## BEHAVIOR THERAPY FROM A MULTICULTURAL PERSPECTIVE

Contributions to Multicultural Counseling

Behavior therapy has some clear advantages over many other theories in working with multicultural populations. Because of their cultural and ethnic backgrounds, some clients hold values that are contrary to the free expression of feelings and the sharing of personal concerns. Behavioral counseling does not place emphasis on experiencing catharsis. Rather, it stresses changing specific behaviors and developing problem-solving skills. Clients who are looking for action plans and behavioral change are likely to cooperate with this approach; they can see that it offers them concrete methods for dealing with their problems of living.

Behavior therapy focuses on environmental conditions that contribute to a client's problems. Social and political influences can play a significant role in the lives of people of color through discriminatory practices and economic problems. A strength of behavioral procedures is that they take into consideration the social and cultural dimensions of the client's life. Kanfer and Goldstein (1986) emphasize the need to give careful consideration to the client's life setting, personal values, and biological and sociopsychological characteristics. They also point out that various sociocultural developments contribute to psychological problems and to violence and abuse in personal relationships.

The behavioral approach has moved beyond treating clients for a specific symptom or behavioral problem. Instead, it stresses a thorough evaluation of the person's life circumstances to ascertain not only whether the target behavior is amenable to change but also whether such a change is likely to lead to a significant improvement in the client's total life situation.

In designing a change program for clients from diverse backgrounds, effective behavioral practitioners conduct a functional analysis of the problem situation. This assessment includes the cultural context in which the problem behavior occurs, the consequences both to the client and to the client's sociocultural environment, the resources within the environment that can promote change, and the impact that change is likely to have on others in the client's surroundings. According to Spiegler and Guevremont (1998), assessment methods should be chosen with the client's cultural background in mind. Counselors must be knowledgeable as well as open and sensitive to issues such as: What is considered normal and abnormal behavior in the client's culture? What are the clients' culturally based conceptions of their problems? What kind of information about the client is essential in making an accurate assessment?

Limitations for Multicultural Counseling

According to Spiegler and Guevremont (1998), a future challenge for behavior therapists is to develop empirically based recommendations for how behavior therapy can optimally serve diverse clients. They state that although behavior therapy is sensitive to differences among clients in a broad sense, there is a need for behavior therapists to become more responsive to *specific* issues of ethnic and cultural diversity. Behavior therapists have paid little attention to issues of race, gender, ethnicity, and sexual orientation (Iwamasa & Smith, 1996; Purcell, Campos, & Perilla, 1996). For example, some African American clients are slow to trust a European American therapist, which may be a healthy response to racism. However, a culturally insensitive therapist may misinterpret this "cultural paranoia" as clinical paranoia (Ridley, 1995).

Some behavioral counselors focus on using a variety of techniques in narrowly treating specific behavioral problems. Instead of viewing clients in the context of their sociocultural environment, these practitioners concentrate too much on problems within the individual. In doing so they may overlook significant issues in the lives of clients. Such practitioners are not likely to bring about beneficial changes for ethnically diverse clients.

The fact that behavioral interventions often work well raises an interesting issue in multicultural counseling. When clients make significant personal changes, it is very likely that others in their environment will react to these people differently. Before deciding too quickly on goals for therapy, counselor and client need to discuss the advantages and disadvantages of change. It is essential for therapists to conduct a thorough assessment of the interpersonal and cultural dimensions of the problem. Clients should be helped in assessing the possible consequences of some of their newly acquired social skills. Once goals are determined and therapy is under way, clients should have opportunities to talk about the problems they encounter as they become different people in their home and work settings. For example, a client may want to become more assertive with her husband and children and may strive for increased independence. It is conceivable that as she becomes more assertive and independent divorce may result. Her culture may place a premium on compliance with tradition, and being assertive can lead to problems if she decides to stay within that culture. As a divorced woman, she could find herself without any support from relatives and friends, and she might eventually regret having made the changes she did.

 ## WHERE TO GO FROM HERE

Because the literature in this field is so extensive and diverse, it is not possible in one brief survey chapter to present a comprehensive in-depth discussion of behavioral techniques. I hope you will be challenged to examine any misconceptions you may hold about behavior therapy and be stimulated to do some further reading of selected sources.

If you have an interest in further training in behavior therapy, the Association for Advancement of Behavior Therapy (AABT) is an excellent source. AABT is a membership organization of more than 4,500 mental health professionals and students who are interested in behavior therapy, cognitive behavior therapy, behavioral assessment, and applied behavioral analysis. If you are interested in becoming a member of this organization, contact:

> *Association for Advancement of Behavior Therapy*
> 305 Seventh Avenue, 16th Floor
> New York, NY 10001-6008
> Telephone: (212) 647-1890 or (800) 685-AABT
> Fax: (212) 647-1865
> E-mail: *membership@aabt.org*
> Website: *www.aabt.org*

Full and associate memberships are $142 and include one journal subscription (to either *Behavior Therapy* or *Cognitive and Behavioral Practice*), AABT's Membership Directory, and a subscription to the *Behavior Thera-*

pist (a newsletter with feature articles, training updates, and association news). Membership also includes reduced registration and continuing education course fees for AABT's annual convention, which features workshops, master clinician programs, symposia, and other educational presentations. Student memberships are $30. Members receive discounts on all AABT publications, some of which are:

- *Directory of Graduate Training in Behavior Therapy and Experimental-Clinical Psychology.* An excellent source for students and job seekers who want information on programs with an emphasis on behavioral training.
- *Directory of Psychology Internships: Programs Offering Behavioral Training.* Describes training programs having a behavioral component.
- *Behavior Therapy.* An international quarterly journal focusing on original experimental and clinical research, theory, and practice.
- *Cognitive and Behavioral Practice.* A quarterly journal that features clinically oriented articles.

You can keep up with this ever-expanding field by consulting these journals devoted exclusively to behavior therapy: *Advances in Behaviour Research and Therapy, Behaviour Research and Therapy, Behavioural Assessment, Behavior Modification, Behavioural Psychotherapy, Journal of Behavior Therapy and Experimental Psychiatry, Child and Family Behavior Therapy, Cognitive Therapy and Research,* and *Journal of Applied Behavior Analysis.* The last listed can be reached at:

Journal of Applied Behavior Analysis
Mary Louise Wright
Department of Human Development
University of Kansas
Lawrence, KS 66045-2133
Telephone: (785) 843-0008
Fax: (785) 843-5909
E-mail: *jabamlw@idir.net*

Recommended Supplementary Readings

Contemporary Behavior Therapy (Spiegler & Guevremont, 1998) is a comprehensive and up-to-date treatment of basic principles and applications of the behavior therapies, as well as a fine discussion of ethical issues. Specific chapters deal with procedures that can be usefully applied to a range of client populations: behavioral assessment, modeling therapy, systematic desensitization, exposure therapies, cognitive restructuring, and cognitive coping skills.

Interviewing Strategies for Helpers: Fundamental Skills and Cognitive Behavioral Interventions (Cormier & Cormier, 1998) is a comprehensive and clearly written textbook dealing with training experiences and skill development. Its excellent documentation offers practitioners a wealth of material on a variety of topics, such as assessment procedures, selection of goals, development of appropriate treatment programs, and methods of evaluating outcomes.

Brief But Comprehensive Psychotherapy: The Multimodal Way (Lazarus, 1997a) is an excellent source of techniques and procedures for brief interventions that can be applied with diverse client populations in various settings. It represents an attempt to deal with the whole person by developing assessments and treatment interventions for all the modalities of human experience.

Self-Directed Behavior: Self-Modification for Personal Adjustment (Watson & Tharp, 1997) provides readers with specific steps for carrying out self-modification programs. The authors deal with selecting a goal, developing a plan, keeping progress notes, and recognizing and coping with obstacles to following through with a self-directed program.

References and Suggested Readings*

*ALBERTI, R. E., & EMMONS, M. L. (1995a). *Your perfect right: A guide to assertive behavior* (6th ed.). San Luis Obispo, CA: Impact.

ALBERTI, R. E., & EMMONS, M. L. (1995b). *Your perfect right: A manual for assertiveness trainers.* San Luis Obispo, CA: Impact.

AMERICAN PSYCHOLOGICAL ASSOCIATION, Division 12. (1995). *Manuals for empirically validated treatments: A project of the task force on psychological interventions.* Washington, DC: Author.

BANDURA, A. (1969). *Principles of behavior modification.* New York: Holt, Rinehart & Winston.

BANDURA, A. (Ed.). (1971a). *Psychological modeling: Conflicting theories.* Chicago: Aldine-Atherton.

BANDURA, A. (1971b). Psychotherapy based upon modeling principles. In A. E. Bergin & S. L. Garfield (Eds.), *Handbook of psychotherapy and behavior change.* New York: Wiley.

BANDURA, A. (1974). Behavior therapy and the models of man. *American Psychologist, 29,* 859–869.

BANDURA, A. (1977). *Social learning theory.* Englewood Cliffs, NJ: Prentice-Hall.

BANDURA, A. (1982). Self-efficacy mechanisms in human agency. *American Psychologist, 37,* 122–147.

BANDURA, A. (1986). *Social foundations of thought and action: A social cognitive theory.* Englewood Cliffs, NJ: Prentice-Hall.

BARKER, S. B., & HAWES, E. C. (1999). Eye movement desensitization and reprocessing in Individual Psychology. *Journal of Individual Psychology, 55*(2), 146–161.

BARLOW, D. H. (Ed.). (1993). *Clinical handbook of psychological disorders: A step-by-step manual* (2nd ed.). New York: Guilford Press.

*BECK, A. T. (1976). *Cognitive therapy and emotional disorders.* New York: New American Library.

BECK, A. T., & WEISHAAR, M. E. (1995). Cognitive therapy. In R. J. Corsini & D. Wedding (Eds.), *Current psychotherapies* (4th ed., pp. 285–320). Itasca, IL: F. E. Peacock.

CHAMBLESS, D. L., Baker, M. J., Baucom, D. H., Beutler, L. E., Calhoun, K. S., Crits-Christoph, P., Daluto, A., DeRubeis, R., Detweiler, J., Haaga, D. A. F., Bennett Johnson, S., McCurry, S., Mueser, K. T., Pope, K. S., Sanderson, W. C., Shoham, V., Stickle, T., Williams, D. A., & Woody, S. R. (1998). Update on empirically validated therapies, II. *Clinical Psychologist, 51*(1), 3–16.

-----

*Books and articles marked with an asterisk are suggested for further study.

COREY, G. (2000). *Theory and practice of group counseling* (5th ed.). Pacific Grove, CA: Brooks-Cole/Wadsworth.

*COREY, G. (2001). *Case approach to counseling and psychotherapy* (5th ed.). Pacific Grove, CA: Brooks-Cole/Wadsworth.

*CORMIER, W. H., & CORMIER, L. S. (1998). *Interviewing strategies for helpers: Fundamental skills and cognitive behavioral interventions* (4th ed.). Pacific Grove, CA: Brooks/Cole.

*FISHMAN, D. B., & FRANKS, C. M. (1997). The conceptual evolution of behavior therapy. In P. L. Wachtel & S. B. Messer (Eds.), *Theories of psychotherapy: Origins and evolution* (pp. 131–180). Washington, DC: American Psychological Association.

*GLASS, C. R., & ARNKOFF, D. B. (1992). Behavior therapy. In D. K. Freedheim (Ed.), *History of psychotherapy: A century of change* (pp. 587–628). Washington, DC: American Psychological Association.

GOLDFRIED, M. R., & DAVISON, G. C. (1976). *Clinical behavior therapy.* New York: Holt, Rinehart & Winston.

GRANVOLD, D. K., & WODARSKI, J. S. (1994). Cognitive and behavioral treatment: Clinical issues, transfer of training, and relapse prevention. In D. K. Granvold (Ed.), *Cognitive and behavioral treatment: Method and applications* (pp. 353–375). Pacific Grove, CA: Brooks/Cole.

IWAMASA, G. Y., & SMITH, S. K. (1996). Ethnic diversity in behavioral psychology. *Behavior modification, 20,* 45–59.

JACOBSON, E. (1938). *Progressive relaxation.* Chicago: University of Chicago Press.

KANFER, E. H., & GOLDSTEIN, A. P. (1986). Introduction. In F. H. Kanfer & A. R. Goldstein (Eds.), *Helping people change: A textbook of methods* (3rd ed., pp. 1–18). New York: Pergamon Press.

KAZDIN, A. E. (1978). *History of behavior modification: Experimental foundations of contemporary research.* Baltimore: University Park Press.

KAZDIN, A. E. (1982). Symptom substitution, generalization, and response covariation: Implications for psychotherapy outcome. *Psychological Bulletin, 91,* 349–365.

KAZDIN, A. E. (1994). *Behavior modification in applied settings* (5th ed.). Pacific Grove, CA: Brooks/Cole.

KAZDIN, A. E., & WILSON, G. T. (1978). *Evaluation of behavior therapy: Issues, evidence, and research strategies.* Cambridge, MA: Ballinger.

LAZARUS, A. A. (1971). *Behavior therapy and beyond.* New York: McGraw-Hill.

LAZARUS, A. A. (1986). Multimodal therapy. In J. C. Norcross (Ed.), *Handbook of eclectic psychotherapy* (pp. 65–93). New York: Brunner/Mazel.

LAZARUS, A. A. (1987a). The multimodal approach with adult outpatients. In N. S. Jacobson (Ed.), *Psychotherapists in clinical practice.* New York: Guilford Press.

LAZARUS, A. A. (1987b). The need for technical eclecticism: Science, breadth, depth, and specificity In J. K. Zeig (Ed.), *The evolution of psychotherapy* (pp. 164–178). New York: Brunner/Mazel.

LAZARUS, A. A. (1989). *The practice of multimodal therapy.* Baltimore: Johns Hopkins University Press.

LAZARUS, A. A. (1992a). The multimodal approach to the treatment of minor depression. *American Journal of Psychotherapy, 46*(1), 50–57.

LAZARUS, A. A. (1992b). Multimodal therapy: Technical eclecticism with minimal integration. In J. C. Norcross & M. R. Goldfried (Eds.), *Handbook of psychotherapy integration* (pp. 231–263). New York: Basic Books.

*LAZARUS, A. A. (1993). Tailoring the therapeutic relationship, or being an authentic chameleon. *Psychotherapy, 30,* 404–407.

LAZARUS, A. A. (1995). Multimodal therapy. In R. Corsini & D. Wedding (Eds.), *Current psychotherapies* (5th ed., pp. 322–355). Itasca, IL: F. E. Peacock.

*LAZARUS, A. A. (1996a). Some reflections after 40 years of trying to be an effective psychotherapist. *Psychotherapy, 33*(1), 142–145.

*LAZARUS, A. A. (1996b). The utility and futility of combining treatments in psychotherapy. *Clinical Psychology: Science and Practice, 3*(1), 59–68.

*LAZARUS, A. A. (1997a). *Brief but comprehensive psychotherapy: The multimodal way.* New York: Springer.

*LAZARUS, A. A. (1997b). Can psychotherapy be brief, focused, solution-oriented, and yet comprehensive? A personal evolutionary perspective. In J. K. Zeig (Ed.), *The evolution of psychotherapy: The third conference* (pp. 83–94). New York: Brunner/Mazel.

LAZARUS, A. A., & BEUTLER, L. E. (1993). On technical eclecticism. *Journal of Counseling and Development, 71*(4), 381–385.

LAZARUS, A. A., BEUTLER, L. E., & NORCROSS, J. C. (1992). The future of technical eclecticism. *Psychotherapy, 29*(1), 11–20.

LAZARUS, A. A., & LAZARUS, C. N. (1991). *Multimodal life-history inventory.* Champaign, IL: Research Press.

LAZARUS, A. A., & LAZARUS, C. N. (1997). *The 60-second shrink: 101 strategies for staying sane in a crazy world.* San Luis Obispo, CA: Impact.

LAZROVE, S., KITE, L., TRIFFLEMAN, E., MCGLASHAN, T., & ROUNSAVILLE, B. (in press). The use of EMDR as a treatment for chronic PTSD—encouraging results of an open trial. *American Journal of Orthopsychiatry.*

LONDON, P. (1986). *The modes and morals of psychotherapy* (2nd ed.). Washington, DC: Hemisphere.

MAHONEY, M. J. (1977). Reflections on the cognitive-learning trend in psychotherapy. *American Psychologist, 32,* 5–13.

MAHONEY, M. J. (1979). *Self-change: Strategies for solving personal problems.* New York: Norton.

MAHONEY, M. J. (1991). *Human change processes: The scientific foundations of psychotherapy.* New York: Basic Books.

MARCUS, S. V., MARQUIS, P., & SAKAI, C. (1997). Controlled study of treatment of PTSD using EMDR in an HMO setting. *Psychotherapy, 34*(3), 307–315.

MASH, E. J., & TERDAL, L. G. (Eds.). (1997). *Assessment of childhood disorders* (3rd ed.). New York: Guilford Press.

*MEICHENBAUM, D. (1977). *Cognitive behavior modification: An integrative approach.* New York: Plenum.

MEICHENBAUM, D. (1985). *Stress inoculation training.* New York: Pergamon Press.

MORRIS, R. J. (1986). Fear reduction methods. In F. H. Kanfer & A. P. Goldstein (Eds.), *Helping people change: A textbook of methods* (3rd ed., pp. 145–190). New York: Pergamon Press.

PAUL, G. L. (1967). Outcome research in psychotherapy. *Journal of Consulting Psychology, 31,* 109–188.

PURCELL, D. W., CAMPOS, P. E., & PERILLA, J. L. (1996). Therapy with lesbians and gay men: A cognitive behavioral perspective. *Cognitive and Behavioral Practice, 3,* 391–415.

RIDLEY, C. R. (1995). *Overcoming unintentional racism in counseling and therapy: A practitioner's guide to intentional intervention.* Thousand Oaks, CA: Sage.

ROTHBAUM, B. O. (1997). A controlled study of eye movement desensitization and reprocessing for posttraumatic stress disordered sexual assault victims. *Bulletin of the Menninger Clinic, 61*(3), 317–334.

SCHECK, M. M., SCHAEFFER, J. A., & GILLETTE, C. S. (1998). Brief psychological intervention with traumatized young women: The efficacy of eye movement desensitization and reprocessing. *Journal of Traumatic Stress, 11*(1), 25–44.

*SHAPIRO, F. (1995). *Eye movement desensitization and reprocessing: Basic principles, protocols, and procedures.* New York: Guilford Press.

*SHAPIRO, F. (1997). *EMDR: The breakthrough therapy for overcoming anxiety, stress and trauma.* New York: Basic Books.

SHAPIRO, F. (1998). Eye movement desensitization and reprocessing (EMDR): Historical context, recent research, and future directions. In L. Vandecreek, S. Knapp, & T. L. Jackson (Eds.), *Innovations in Clinical Practice: A Source Book* (Vol. 16, pp. 143–162). Sarasota, FL: Professional Resource Press.

SKINNER, B. F. (1948). *Walden II.* New York: Macmillan.

SKINNER, B. F. (1971). *Beyond freedom and dignity.* New York: Knopf.

SLOANE, R. B., STAPLES, E. R., CRISTOL, A. H., YORKSTON, N. J., & WHIPPLE, K. (1975). *Psychotherapy versus behavior therapy.* Cambridge, MA: Harvard University Press.

*SPIEGLER, M. D., & GUEVREMONT, D. C. (1998). *Contemporary behavior therapy* (3rd ed.). Pacific Grove, CA: Brooks/Cole.

THORESEN, C. E., & COATES, T. J. (1980). What does it mean to be a behavior therapist? In C. E. Thoresen (Ed.), *The behavior therapist.* Pacific Grove, CA: Brooks/Cole.

VAN ETTEN, M. L., & TAYLOR, S. (1998). Comparative efficacy of treatments for posttraumatic stress disorder: A meta-analysis. *Clinical Psychology and Psychotherapy, 5,* 126–144.

VOLTZ, L. M., & EVANS, I. M. (1982). The assessment of behavioral interrelationships in child behavior therapy. *Behavioral Assessment, 4,* 131–165.

*WATSON, D. L., & THARP, R. G. (1997). *Self-directed behavior: Self-modification for personal adjustment* (7th ed.). Pacific Grove, CA: Brooks/Cole.

WILSON, G. T. (1978). Cognitive behavior therapy: Paradigm shift or passing phase? In J. P. Foreyt & D. P. Rathjen (Eds.), *Cognitive behavior therapy: Research and applications.* New York: Plenum.

WILSON, G. T., & AGRAS, W. S. (1992). The future of behavior therapy. *Psychotherapy, 29*(1), 39–43.

WILSON, S. A., BECKER, L. A., & TINKER, R. H. (1995). Eye movement desensitization and reprocessing (EMDR) treatment for psychologically traumatized individuals. *Journal of Consulting and Clinical Psychology, 63*(6), 928–937.

WILSON, S. A., BECKER, L. A., & TINKER, R. H. (1997). Fifteen-month follow-up of eye movement desensitization and reprocessing (EMDR) treatment for posttraumatic stress disorder and psychological trauma. *Journal of Consulting and Clinical Psychology, 65*(6), 1047–1056.

WOLPE, J. (1958). *Psychotherapy by reciprocal inhibition.* Stanford, CA: Stanford University Press.

WOLPE, J. (1990). *The practice of behavior therapy* (4th ed.). Elmsford, NY: Pergamon Press.

CHAPTER

11

Cognitive Behavior Therapy

INTRODUCTION
  Development of Rational Emotive Behavior Therapy
KEY CONCEPTS
  View of Human Nature
  View of Emotional Disturbance
  A-B-C Theory of Personality
THE THERAPEUTIC PROCESS
  Therapeutic Goals
  Therapist's Function and Role
  Client's Experience in Therapy
  Relationship Between Therapist and Client
APPLICATION: Therapeutic Techniques and Procedures
  The Practice of Rational Emotive Behavior Therapy
  Applications of REBT to Client Populations
AARON BECK'S COGNITIVE THERAPY
  Introduction
  Basic Principles of Cognitive Therapy
  The Client / Therapist Relationship
  Applications of Cognitive Therapy
DONALD MEICHENBAUM'S COGNITIVE BEHAVIOR MODIFICATION
  Introduction
  How Behavior Changes
  Coping Skills Programs
  Constructivism as a Trend in Cognitive Behavior Therapy
COGNITIVE BEHAVIOR THERAPY APPLIED TO THE CASE OF STAN
SUMMARY AND EVALUATION
  Summary
  Contributions of the Cognitive Behavioral Approaches
  Limitations and Criticisms of the Cognitive Behavioral Approaches
COGNITIVE BEHAVIOR THERAPY FROM A MULTICULTURAL PERSPECTIVE
  Contributions to Multicultural Counseling
  Limitations for Multicultural Counseling
WHERE TO GO FROM HERE
RECOMMENDED SUPPLEMENTARY READINGS
REFERENCES AND SUGGESTED READINGS

ALBERT ELLIS

ALBERT ELLIS (b. 1913) was born in Pittsburgh but escaped to the wilds of New York at the age of 4 and has lived there (except for a year in New Jersey) ever since. He was hospitalized nine times as a child, mainly with nephritis, and developed renal glycosuria at the age of 19 and diabetes at the age of 40. By rigorously taking care of his health and stubbornly refusing to make himself miserable about it, he has lived an unusually robust and energetic life.

Realizing that he could counsel people skillfully and that he greatly enjoyed doing so, Ellis decided to become a psychologist. Believing psychoanalysis to be the deepest form of psychotherapy, Ellis was analyzed and supervised by a training analyst. From 1947 to 1953 he practiced classical analysis and analytically oriented psychotherapy.

After coming to the conclusion that psychoanalysis was a relatively superficial and unscientific form of treatment, he experimented with several other systems. Early in 1955 he combined humanistic, philosophical, and behavioral therapy to form rational-emotive therapy (now known as rational emotive behavior therapy, or REBT). Ellis is rightly known as the grandfather of cognitive behavior therapy.

To some extent Dr. Ellis developed his approach as a method of dealing with his own problems during his youth. At one point in his life, for example, he had exaggerated fears of speaking in public. During his adolescence he was extremely shy around young women. At age 19 he forced himself to talk to 100 women in the Bronx Botanical Gardens over a period of one month. Although he never managed to get a date from these brief encounters, he does report that he desensitized himself to his fear of rejection by women. By applying cognitive behavioral methods, he has managed to conquer some of his worst blocks (Ellis, 1994, 1997). Moreover, he has learned to actually enjoy public speaking and other activities about which he was once highly anxious.

People who hear Ellis lecture often comment on his abrasive, humorous, and flamboyant style (Dryden, 1989). He does see himself as more abrasive than most in his workshops, and he also considers himself humorous and startling in some ways. In his workshops it seems that he takes delight in giving vent to his eccentric side. He enjoys his work, which is his primary commitment in life.

Ellis is highly energetic and productive and is surely one of the most prolific writers in the field of counseling and psychotherapy. He has practiced psychotherapy, group therapy, marriage and family counseling, and sex therapy for more than 50 years. In his busy professional life he sees as many as 80 clients a week for individual sessions, conducts 5 group therapy sessions weekly, and gives about 200 talks and workshops to professionals and the public each year.

Ellis has published over 60 books and more than 700 articles, mostly on the theory and applications of REBT. He is a Diplomate in Clinical Psychology of the American Board of Professional Psychology, in Clinical Hypnosis of the American Board of Psychological Hypnosis, and of the American Board of Medical Psychotherapists. ■

AARON T. BECK

AARON TEMKIN BECK (b. 1921) was born in Providence, Rhode Island. His childhood was characterized by adversity, and his early schooling was interrupted by a life-threatening illness, yet he overcame this problem and ended up a year ahead of his peer group (Weishaar, 1993). Throughout his life he struggled with a variety of fears: blood injury fears, fear of suffocation, tunnel phobia, anxiety about his health, and public speaking anxiety. Beck used his personal problems as a basis for understanding others and developing his theory.

A graduate of Brown University and Yale School of Medicine, Beck was initially attracted to neurology but switched to psychiatry during his residency. Dr. Beck is the pioneering figure in cognitive therapy, one of the most influential and empirically validated approaches to psychotherapy. Cognitive therapy is also the most comprehensive theory of depression in the world.

Beck attempted to validate Freud's theory of depression, but his research resulted in his parting company with Freud's motivational model and the explanation of depression as self-directed anger. As a result of this decision, Beck endured isolation and rejection from many in the psychiatric community for many years. Through his research, Beck developed a cognitive theory of depression. He found the cognitions of depressed persons to be characterized by errors in logic that he called "cognitive distortions." For Beck, negative thoughts reflect underlying, dysfunctional beliefs and assumptions. When these beliefs are triggered by situational events, a depressive pattern is put in motion. Beck believes clients can assume an active role in modifying their dysfunctional thinking and thereby gain relief from a range of psychiatric conditions. His continuous research in the areas of psychopathology and the utility of cognitive therapy has earned him a place of prominence in the scientific community in the United States.

Beck joined the Department of Psychiatry of the University of Pennsylvania in 1954, where he currently holds the position of Professor (Emeritus) of Psychiatry. Beck's pioneering research established the efficacy of cognitive therapy for depression. He has successfully applied cognitive therapy to depression, generalized anxiety and panic disorders, alcoholism and drug abuse, eating disorders, marital and relationship problems, and personality disorders. He has developed assessment scales for depression, suicide risk, anxiety, self-concept, and personality.

He is the founder of the Beck Institute, which is a research and training center directed by one of his four children, Dr. Judith Beck. He has eight grandchildren and has been married for 46 years. To his credit, Aaron Beck has focused on developing the cognitive therapy skills of hundreds of clinicians. In turn, they have established their own cognitive therapy centers. ■

INTRODUCTION

Rational emotive behavior therapy (REBT) is a challenging perspective that has little in common with the psychoanalytic, person-centered, and Gestalt approaches. REBT has more in common with the therapies that are oriented toward cognition and behavior in that it stresses thinking, judging, deciding, analyzing, and doing. This approach is based on the assumption that cognitions, emotions, and behaviors interact significantly and have a reciprocal cause-and-effect relationship. REBT has consistently emphasized all three of these modalities and their interactions, thus qualifying it as a multimodal and integrative approach (Ellis, 1994, 1997, 1998, 1999; Ellis & Dryden, 1997).

The basic assumption of REBT is that people contribute to their own psychological problems, as well as to specific symptoms, by the way they interpret events and situations. To a large degree cognitive behavior therapy is based on the assumption that a reorganization of one's self-statements will result in a corresponding reorganization of one's behavior. Meichenbaum (1977) writes that within a learning theory framework clients' cognitions are explicit behaviors that can be modified in their own right, just as are overt behaviors that can be directly observed. Thus, behavioral techniques such as operant conditioning, modeling, and behavioral rehearsal can also be applied to the more covert and subjective processes of thinking and internal dialogue. All of the cognitive behavioral approaches include a variety of behavioral strategies as a part of their integrative repertoire.

Several of the more prominent cognitive behavioral approaches are featured here, including Ellis's rational emotive behavior therapy (REBT), Beck's cognitive therapy (CT), and Meichenbaum's cognitive behavior therapy (CBT). More than 20 different therapies have been labeled "cognitive" or "cognitive behavioral" (Dattilio & Padesky, 1990; Mahoney & Lyddon, 1988).

As is true of behavior therapy, the cognitive behavioral approaches are quite diverse, but they do share these attributes: (1) a collaborative relationship between client and therapist, (2) the premise that psychological distress is largely a function of disturbances in cognitive processes, (3) a focus on changing cognitions to produce desired changes in affect and behavior, and (4) a generally time-limited and educational treatment focusing on specific and structured target problems (Arnkoff & Glass, 1992; Dobson & Block, 1988; Weishaar, 1993). All of the cognitive behavioral approaches are based on a structured psychoeducational model, and they all emphasize the role of homework, place responsibility on the client to assume an active role both during and outside of the therapy sessions, and draw from a variety of cognitive and behavioral strategies to bring about change.

Development of Rational Emotive Behavior Therapy

Ellis argued that the psychoanalytic approach is more than inefficient because people often seem to get worse instead of better (Ellis, 1988, 1999).

He began to persuade and encourage his clients to do the very things they were most afraid of doing, such as risking rejection by significant others. Gradually, he became much more eclectic and more active and directive as a therapist, and REBT became a general school of psychotherapy aimed at providing clients with the tools to restructure their philosophic and behavioral styles (Ellis & Yeager, 1989).

Although REBT is generally conceded to be the parent of today's cognitive behavioral approaches, it was preceded by earlier schools of thought. Ellis acknowledges his debt to the ancient Greeks, especially the Stoic philosopher Epictetus, who said, in the first century A.D., "People are disturbed not by things, but by the view which they take of them" (as cited in Ellis, 1995). Horney's (1950) ideas on the "tyranny of the shoulds" are also apparent in the conceptual framework of REBT. Ellis also gives credit to Adler as an influential precursor. As you will recall, Adler writes that our emotional reactions and lifestyle are associated with our basic beliefs and are therefore cognitively created. Like the Adlerian approach, REBT emphasizes the role of social interest in determining psychological health. There are other Adlerian influences on REBT, such as the importance of goals, purposes, values, and meanings in human existence; the focus on active teaching; the use of persuasive methods; and the giving of live demonstrations before an audience (Dryden & Ellis, 1988; Ellis, Gordon, Neenan, & Palmer, 1997; Yankura & Dryden, 1994).

REBT's basic hypothesis is that our emotions stem mainly from our beliefs, evaluations, interpretations, and reactions to life situations. Through the therapeutic process, clients learn skills that give them the tools to identify and dispute irrational beliefs that have been acquired and self-constructed and are now maintained by self-indoctrination. They learn how to replace such ineffective ways of thinking with effective and rational cognitions, and as a result they change their emotional reactions to situations. The therapeutic process allows clients to apply REBT principles of change not only to a particular presenting problem but also to many other problems in life or future problems they might encounter (Ellis, 1999).

Several therapeutic implications flow from these assumptions: The focus is on working with *thinking* and *acting* rather than primarily with expressing feelings. Therapy is seen as an *educational process*. The therapist functions in many ways like a teacher, especially in collaborating with a client on homework assignments and in teaching strategies for straight thinking; and the client is a learner, who practices the skills discussed in therapy in everyday life.

The concepts of cognitive behavior therapy raise several key questions that you would do well to keep in mind as you read this chapter: Is psychotherapy essentially a process of reeducation? Is it appropriate for therapists to use persuasion and highly directive methods? How effective is it to attempt to help clients reduce their faulty thinking by using questions, logic, advice, information, and interpretations? Will changing one's thoughts often lead to changing how one feels and acts? What are the advantages of a collaborative client/therapist relationship?

KEY CONCEPTS

View of Human Nature

Rational emotive behavior therapy is based on the assumption that human beings are born with a potential for both rational, or "straight," thinking and irrational, or "crooked," thinking. People have predispositions for self-preservation, happiness, thinking and verbalizing, loving, communion with others, and growth and self-actualization. They also have propensities for self-destruction, avoidance of thought, procrastination, endless repetition of mistakes, superstition, intolerance, perfectionism and self-blame, and avoidance of actualizing growth potentials. Taking for granted that humans are fallible, REBT attempts to help them accept themselves as creatures who will continue to make mistakes yet at the same time learn to live more at peace with themselves.

Ellis has concluded that humans are *self-talking, self-evaluating,* and *self-sustaining.* They develop emotional and behavioral difficulties when they mistake *simple preferences* (desires for love, approval, success) for dire needs. Ellis also affirms that humans have an inborn tendency toward growth and actualization, yet they often sabotage their movement toward growth due to their inborn tendency toward crooked thinking and self-defeating patterns they have learned (Ellis, 1998, 1999; Ellis & Blau, 1998; Ellis & Dryden, 1997; Ellis & Tafrate, 1997).

View of Emotional Disturbance

We originally learn irrational beliefs from significant others during child-hood. Additionally, we create irrational dogmas and superstitions by our-selves. Then we actively reinstill self-defeating beliefs by the processes of autosuggestion and self-repetition and by behaving as if they are useful. Hence, it is largely our own repetition of early-indoctrinated irrational thoughts, rather than a parent's repetition, that keeps dysfunctional atti-tudes alive and operative within us.

REBT contends that people do not *need* to be accepted and loved, even though this may be highly desirable. The therapist teaches clients how to feel undepressed even when they are unaccepted and unloved by signifi-cant others. Although REBT encourages people to experience sadness over being unaccepted, it attempts to help them find ways of overcoming depres-sion, anxiety, hurt, loss of self-worth, and hatred.

REBT insists that blame is the core of most emotional disturbances. Therefore, if we are to recover from a neurosis or a personality disorder, we had better stop blaming ourselves and others. Instead, it is important that we learn to accept ourselves despite our imperfections. Ellis (1987b; Ellis & Blau, 1998; Ellis & Harper, 1997) hypothesizes that we have strong tenden-cies to escalate our desires and preferences into dogmatic "shoulds," "musts," "oughts," demands, and commands. Ellis suggests that when we are upset it is a good idea to look to our hidden dogmatic "musts" and absolutistic "shoulds." Such demands create disruptive feelings and dysfunctional behaviors (Ellis, 1987b; Ellis & Dryden, 1997).

Here are some irrational ideas that we internalize and that inevitably lead to self-defeat (Ellis, 1994, 1997, 1998; Ellis & Dryden, 1997; Ellis & Harper, 1997):

- "I *must* have love or approval from all the significant people in my life."
- "I *must* perform important tasks competently and perfectly well."
- "Because I strongly desire that people treat me considerately and fairly, they *absolutely must* do so!"
- "If I don't get what I want, it's terrible, and I can't stand it."
- "It's easier to avoid facing life's difficulties and responsibilities than to undertake more rewarding forms of self-discipline."

We have a strong tendency to make and keep ourselves emotionally disturbed by internalizing self-defeating beliefs such as these, making it virtually impossible to achieve and maintain good mental health (Ellis, 1987b).

A-B-C Theory of Personality

The A-B-C theory of personality is central to REBT theory and practice. A is the existence of a fact, an event, or the behavior or attitude of an individual. C is the emotional and behavioral consequence or reaction of the individual; the reaction can be either healthy or unhealthy. A (the activating event) does not cause C (the emotional consequence). Instead, B, which is the person's belief about A, largely causes C, the emotional reaction.

The interaction of the various components can be diagrammed like this:

A (activating event) ← B (belief) → C (emotional and behavioral consequence)
                          ↑
              D (disputing intervention) → E (effect) → F (new feeling)

If a person experiences depression after a divorce, for example, it may not be the divorce itself that causes the depressive reaction but the person's *beliefs* about being a failure, being rejected, or losing a mate. Ellis would maintain that the beliefs about the rejection and failure (at point B) are what mainly cause the depression (at point C)—not the actual event of the divorce (at point A). Thus, human beings are largely responsible for creating their own emotional reactions and disturbances. Showing people how they can change the irrational beliefs that directly "cause" their disturbed emotional consequences is the heart of REBT (Ellis, 1998, 1999; Ellis & Dryden, 1997; Ellis, Gordon, Neenan, & Palmer, 1997; Ellis & Harper, 1997).

How is an emotional disturbance fostered? It is fed by the illogical sentences clients continually repeat to themselves, such as "I am totally to blame for the divorce," "I am a miserable failure, and everything I did was wrong," "I am a worthless person." Ellis repeatedly makes the point that "you mainly feel the way you think." Disturbed emotional reactions such as depression and anxiety are initiated and perpetuated by clients' self-defeating belief systems, which are based on irrational ideas clients have incorporated and invented.

After A, B, and C comes D (disputing). Essentially, D is the application of the scientific method to help clients challenge their irrational beliefs. Because the principles of logic can be taught, they can be used to destroy any unrealistic, unverifiable hypothesis. There are three components of this disputing process: detecting, debating, and discriminating. First, clients learn how to *detect* their irrational beliefs, particularly their absolutistic "shoulds" and "I musts," their "awfulizing," and their "self-downing." Then clients *debate* their dysfunctional beliefs by learning how to logically and empirically question them and to vigorously argue themselves out of and act against believing them. Finally, clients learn to *discriminate* irrational (self-defeating) beliefs from rational (self-helping) beliefs (Ellis, 1994, 1996).

Although REBT uses many other cognitive, emotive, and behavioral methods to help clients minimize their irrational beliefs, it stresses this process of disputing both during therapy sessions and in everyday life. Eventually clients arrive at E, an effective philosophy, which has a practical side. A new and effective rational philosophy consists of replacing unhealthy thoughts with healthy ones. If we are successful in doing this, we also create F, or a new set of feelings. Instead of feeling seriously anxious or depressed, we feel appropriately in accord with a situation. The best way to begin to feel better is to develop an effective and rational philosophy. Thus, instead of berating oneself and punishing oneself with depression over the divorce, one would reach a rational and empirically based conclusion: "Well, I'm genuinely sorry our marriage didn't work out and that we divorced. Although I wish we could have worked things out, we didn't, and that isn't the end of the world. Because our marriage failed doesn't mean I'm a failure in life, and it's foolish for me to continue blaming myself and making myself wholly responsible for the breakup." According to REBT theory, the ultimate effect is minimizing feelings of depression and self-condemnation.

In sum, philosophical restructuring to change our dysfunctional personality involves these steps: (1) fully acknowledging that we are largely responsible for creating our own emotional problems; (2) accepting the notion that we have the ability to change these disturbances significantly; (3) recognizing that our emotional problems largely stem from irrational beliefs; (4) clearly perceiving these beliefs; (5) seeing the value of disputing such self-defeating beliefs; (6) accepting the fact that if we expect to change we had better work hard in emotive and behavioral ways to counteract our beliefs and the dysfunctional feelings and actions that follow; and (7) practicing REBT methods of uprooting or changing disturbed consequences for the rest of our life (Ellis, 1998, 1999).

 # THE THERAPEUTIC PROCESS

Therapeutic Goals

The many roads taken in rational emotive behavior therapy lead toward the one destination of clients minimizing their emotional disturbances and

self-defeating behaviors by acquiring a more realistic and workable philosophy of life. Other important therapeutic goals include reducing a tendency
for blaming oneself or others for what goes wrong in life and learning ways
to deal with future difficulties. REBT is designed to induce people to examine and change some of their most basic values that keep them disturbed.
For example, if a client's fear is of failing in her marriage, the aim is not
merely to reduce that specific fear but to work with her exaggerated fears of
failing in general.

Therapist's Function and Role

The therapist has specific tasks, and the first step is to show clients that
they have incorporated many irrational "shoulds," "oughts," and "musts."
Clients learn to separate their rational beliefs from their irrational ones.
The therapist encourages and persuades clients to engage in activities that
will counter their self-defeating beliefs.

A second step in the therapeutic process is to demonstrate that clients
are keeping their emotional disturbances active by continuing to think il-
logically. In other words, because clients keep reindoctrinating themselves,
they are largely responsible for their own neuroses.

Merely showing clients that they have illogical processes is not enough,
however, for a client is likely to say, "Now I understand that I have fears of
failing and that these fears are exaggerated and unrealistic. But I'm still
afraid of failing!" To get beyond client's mere recognition of irrational
thoughts, the therapist takes a third step—helping clients modify their
thinking and abandon their irrational ideas. The therapist assists clients
in understanding the vicious circle of the self-blaming process.

The fourth step in the therapeutic process is to challenge clients to develop a rational philosophy of life so that in the future they can avoid becoming the victim of other irrational beliefs. Tackling only specific problems
or symptoms can give no assurance that new illogical fears will not emerge.
What is desirable, then, is for the therapist to dispute the core of the irrational thinking and to teach clients how to substitute rational beliefs and
attitudes for irrational ones.

A therapist who works within this framework functions differently
from most other practitioners. Because REBT is essentially a cognitive and
directive behavioral process, it often minimizes the intense relationship between therapist and client. The therapist mainly employs a persuasive
methodology that emphasizes education. Ellis outlines what the REBT practitioner does (1994, 1995, 1998, 1999; Ellis & Dryden, 1997; Ellis & MacLaren,
1998; Ellis & Velten, 1992, 1998):

- Encourages clients to discover a few basic irrational ideas that mo-
  tivate much disturbed behavior
- Challenges clients to validate their ideas
- Demonstrates to clients the illogical nature of their thinking
- Uses humor to confront the irrationality of clients' thinking

- Uses a logical analysis to minimize these irrational beliefs
✖ ■ Shows how these beliefs are inoperative and how they will lead to future emotional and behavioral disturbances ✖
- Explains how these ideas can be replaced with more rational ideas that are empirically grounded
- Teaches clients how to apply the scientific approach to thinking so that they can observe and minimize present or future irrational ideas and illogical deductions that foster self-destructive ways of feeling and behaving
- Uses several cognitive, emotive, and behavioral methods to help clients work directly on their feelings and to act against their disturbances

The therapist takes the mystery out of the therapeutic process, teaching clients about the cognitive hypothesis of disturbance and showing how irrational beliefs lead to negative consequences. When clients understand that certain irrational beliefs lead to dysfunctional emotions and behaviors, the therapist challenges clients to examine why they are clinging to the old misconceptions instead of letting go of them. Insight alone does not typically lead to personality change, but it can help clients see how they are continuing to sabotage themselves and what they can do to change. REBT therapists actively *teach* clients that by hard work and by carrying out behavioral homework assignments they can minimize irrational thinking that leads to disturbances in feeling and behaving.

Client's Experience in Therapy

Once clients begin to accept that their beliefs are the primary cause of their emotions and behaviors, they are able to participate effectively in the cognitive restructuring process (Ellis, Gordon, Neenan, & Palmer, 1997; Ellis & MacLaren, 1998). In large measure, the client's role in REBT is that of a learner. Psychotherapy is viewed as a reeducative process whereby the client learns how to apply logical thought to problem solving and emotional change.

The therapeutic process focuses on clients' experiences in the present. Like the person-centered and existential approaches to therapy, REBT mainly emphasizes here-and-now experiences and clients' present ability to change the patterns of thinking and emoting that they constructed earlier. The therapist does not devote much time to exploring clients' early history and making connections between their past and present behavior. Nor does the therapist usually explore in depth clients' early relationships with their parents or siblings. Instead, the therapeutic process stresses that regardless of clients' basic, irrational philosophies of life they are presently disturbed because they still believe in their self-defeating view of themselves and their world. Questions of where, why, or how they acquired their irrational philosophy are of secondary importance to REBT. The other cognitive behavior therapies place more emphasis on this, however.

Clients are expected to actively work outside the therapy sessions. Homework is carefully designed and agreed on and is aimed at getting clients to carry out positive actions that induce emotional and attitudinal change. These assignments are checked in later sessions, and clients learn effective ways to dispute self-defeating thinking. Toward the end of therapy, clients review their progress, make plans, and identify strategies for dealing with continuing or potential problems.

Relationship Between Therapist and Client

In close agreement with the person-centered concept of unconditional positive regard is REBT's concept of *full acceptance,* or *tolerance.* Therapists show their full acceptance by refusing to evaluate their clients as persons while at the same time being willing to honestly confront clients' nonsensical thinking and self-destructive behaviors. Unlike the relationship-oriented therapies, REBT does not place a premium on personal warmth and empathic understanding. Too much warmth and understanding can be counterproductive, fostering a sense of dependence for approval from the therapist. REBT therapists accept their clients as imperfect beings without giving personal warmth, instead using a variety of impersonal techniques such as teaching, bibliotherapy, and behavior modification (Ellis, 1995; Ellis & Blau, 1998; Ellis & Harper, 1997), but always modeling as well as teaching unconditional full acceptance. (Some REBT practitioners do give more emphasis to the importance of building rapport than does Ellis.)

Rational emotive behavior therapists are often open and direct in disclosing their own beliefs and values. Some are willing to share their own imperfections as a way of disputing clients' unrealistic notions that therapists are "completely put together" persons. Transference is not encouraged, and when it does occur, the therapist is likely to confront it. The therapist wants to show that a transference relationship is based on the irrational belief that the client must be liked and loved by the therapist, or parent figure (Ellis, 1995).

REBT differs from many other therapeutic approaches in that it does not place much value on free association, working with dreams, focusing on the client's past history, endlessly expressing and exploring feelings, or dealing with transference phenomena. Ellis (1995) believes devoting any length of time to these factors is "indulgence therapy," which might result in clients *feeling* better but will rarely aid them in *getting* better.

◤ APPLICATION: Therapeutic Techniques and Procedures

The Practice of Rational Emotive Behavior Therapy

Rational emotive behavior therapists are multimodal and integrative. They use a variety of cognitive, affective, and behavioral techniques, tailoring them to individual clients (Kwee & Ellis, 1997), however, the emphasis is placed on cognition and behavior as opposed to affect. These techniques are applied to the treatment of a range of common clinical problems such as anxiety, depression, anger, marital difficulties, poor interpersonal skills, parenting failures, personality disorders, obsessive-compulsive disorders, eating disorders, psychosomatic disorders, addictions, and psychotic disorders (Warren & McLellarn, 1987). What follows is a brief summary of the major cognitive, emotive, and behavioral techniques Ellis describes (Ellis, 1994, 1998, 1999; Ellis & Dryden, 1997; Ellis & MacLaren, 1998; Ellis & Velten, 1992, 1998).

COGNITIVE METHODS   REBT practitioners usually incorporate a forceful cognitive methodology in the therapeutic process. They demonstrate to clients in a quick and direct manner what it is that they are continuing to tell themselves. Then they teach clients how to deal with these self-statements so that they no longer believe them, encouraging them to acquire a philosophy based on reality. REBT relies heavily on thinking, disputing, debating, challenging, interpreting, explaining, and teaching. Here are some cognitive techniques available to the therapist.

■ *Disputing irrational beliefs.* The most common cognitive method of REBT consists of the therapist actively disputing clients' irrational beliefs and teaching them how to do this challenging on their own. Clients go over a particular "must," "should," or "ought" until they no longer hold that irrational belief, or at least until it is diminished in strength. Here are some examples of questions or statements clients learn to tell themselves: "Why *must* people treat me fairly?" "How do I become a total flop if I don't succeed at important tasks I try?" "If I don't get the job I want, it may be disappointing, but I can certainly stand it." "If life doesn't always go the way I would like it to, it isn't *awful,* just inconvenient."

■ *Doing cognitive homework.* REBT clients are expected to make lists of their problems, look for their absolutistic beliefs, and dispute these beliefs. Homework assignments are a way of tracking down the absolutist "shoulds" and "musts" that are part of their internalized self-messages. Part of homework consists of applying the A-B-C theory to many of the problems clients encounter in daily life. They often fill out the REBT Self-Help Form (which is reproduced in the student manual of this text). The REBT therapist actually teaches the client how to think differently, or models for them, as opposed to the other forms of cognitive behavior therapy.

In carrying out homework in REBT, clients are encouraged to put themselves in risk-taking situations that will allow them to challenge their self-limiting beliefs. For example, a client with a talent for acting who is afraid to act in front of an audience because of fear of failure may be asked to take a small part in a stage play. The client is instructed to replace negative self-statements such as "I will fail," "I will look foolish," or "No one will like me" with more positive messages such as "Even if I do behave foolishly at times, this does not make me a foolish *person.* I can act. I will do the best I can. It's nice to be liked, but not everybody will like me, and that isn't the end of the world." The theory behind this and similar assignments is that clients often create a negative, self-fulfilling prophecy and actually fail because they told themselves in advance that they would. Clients are encouraged to carry out specific assignments during the sessions and, especially, in everyday situations between sessions. In this way clients gradually learn to deal with anxiety and challenge basic irrational thinking. Because therapy is seen as an educational process, clients are also encouraged to read REBT self-help books, such as Ellis's *How to Stubbornly Refuse to Make Yourself Miserable About Anything—Yes, Anything!* (1988) and *How to Be Happy and Remarkably Less Disturbable* (1999). They also listen to and criticize tapes of their own therapy sessions. Making changes is hard work, and doing work outside the sessions is of real value in revising clients' thinking, feeling, and behaving.

■ *Changing one's language.* REBT contends that imprecise language is one of the causes of distorted thinking processes. Clients learn that "musts," "oughts," and "shoulds," can be replaced by *preferences.* Instead of saying, "It would be absolutely awful if . . . ," they can learn to say "it would be inconvenient if . . ." Clients who use language patterns that reflect helplessness and self-condemnation can learn to employ new self-statements. They can assume personal power by replacing their "shoulds" and "musts" with nonabsolute preferences. Through the process of changing their language patterns and making new self-statements, clients come to think and behave differently. As a consequence, they also begin to feel differently.

■ *Using humor.* REBT contends that emotional disturbances often result from taking oneself too seriously and losing one's sense of perspective and humor over the events of life. Consequently, counselors employ humor to counterattack the overserious side of individuals and to assist them in disputing their "musturbatory" philosophy of life. Ellis himself tends to use a good deal of humor to combat exaggerated thinking that leads clients into trouble (1986). In his workshops and therapy sessions Ellis typically uses humorous songs, and he encourages people to sing to themselves or in groups when they feel depressed or anxious (Ellis, 1998, 1999). Humor shows the absurdity of certain ideas that clients steadfastly maintain, and it can be of value in helping clients take themselves much less seriously.

EMOTIVE TECHNIQUES   REBT practitioners use a variety of emotive procedures, including unconditional acceptance, rational-emotive role playing, modeling, rational-emotive imagery, and shame-attacking exercises. Clients are taught the value of unconditional acceptance. Even though their behavior may be difficult to accept, they can decide to see themselves as worthwhile persons. Clients are taught how destructive it is to engage in "putting oneself down" for perceived deficiencies.

REBT practitioners do not necessarily focus on all the details of the presenting problem, nor do they attempt to get the client to extensively express feelings surrounding the problem. Although REBT employs a variety of emotive and forceful therapeutic strategies, it does so in a selective and discriminating manner. These strategies are used both during the therapy sessions and as homework assignments in daily life. Their purpose is not simply to provide a cathartic experience but to help clients *change* some of their thoughts, emotions, and behaviors (Ellis, 1996, 1998, 1999; Ellis & Dryden, 1997). Let's look at some of these evocative and emotive therapeutic techniques in more detail.

■ *Rational-emotive imagery.* This technique is a form of intense mental practice designed to establish new emotional patterns. Clients imagine themselves thinking, feeling, and behaving exactly the way they would like to think, feel, and behave in real life (Maultsby, 1984). They can also be shown how to imagine one of the worst things that could happen to them, how to feel inappropriately upset about this situation, how to intensely experience their feelings, and then how to change the experience to an appropriate feeling (Ellis, 1998, 1999; Ellis & Yeager, 1989). Once clients are able to change their feelings to appropriate ones, they stand a better chance of changing their behavior in the situation. Such a technique can be usefully applied to interpersonal and other situations that are problematic for the individual. Ellis (1988) maintains that if we keep practicing rational-emotive imagery several times a week for a few weeks, we will reach the point that we no longer feel upset over such events. (If you are interested in an illustration of rational-emotive imagery, see Ellis, 1979a; see also Ellis's therapeutic work with a hypothetical patient, Ruth, in Corey, 2001.)

■ *Role playing.* There are both emotional and behavioral components in role playing. The therapist often interrupts to show clients what they are telling themselves to create their disturbances and what they can do to change their inappropriate feelings to appropriate ones. Clients can rehearse certain behaviors to bring out what they feel in a situation. The focus is on working through the underlying irrational beliefs that are related to unpleasant feelings. For example, a woman may put off applying to a graduate school because of her fears of not being accepted. Just the thought of not being accepted to the school of her choice brings out her feelings of "being stupid." She role-plays an interview with the dean of graduate students, notes her anxiety and the irrational beliefs leading to it, and challenges the irrational thoughts that she absolutely must be accepted and that not gaining such acceptance means that she is a stupid and incompetent person.

■ *Shame-attacking exercises.* Ellis (1988, 1998, 1999) has developed exercises to help people reduce irrational shame over behaving in certain ways. He thinks that we can stubbornly refuse to feel ashamed by telling ourselves that it is not catastrophic if someone thinks we are foolish. The main point of these exercises is that clients work to feel unashamed even when others clearly disapprove of them. This procedure typically involves both emotive and behavioral components. Clients may accept a homework assignment to take the risk of doing something that they are ordinarily afraid to do because of what others might think. Minor infractions of social conventions often serve as useful catalysts. For example, clients may shout out the stops on a bus or a train, wear "loud" clothes designed to attract attention, sing at the top of their lungs, ask a silly question at a lecture, ask for a left-handed monkey wrench in a grocery store, or refuse to tip a waitress or waiter who gives them poor service. By carrying out such assignments, clients are likely to find out that other people are not really that interested in their behavior. They work on themselves so that they do not feel ashamed or humiliated. They continue practicing these exercises until they realize that their feelings of shame are self-created and until they are able to behave in less inhibited ways. Clients eventually learn that they often have no reason for continuing to let others' reactions or possible disapproval stop them from doing the things they would like to do.

■ *Use of force and vigor.* Ellis has suggested the use of force and energy as a way to help clients go from intellectual to emotional insight. Clients are also shown how to conduct forceful dialogues with themselves in which they express their irrational beliefs and then powerfully dispute them. Sometimes the therapist will engage in reverse role playing by strongly clinging to the client's self-defeating philosophy; the client is asked to vigorously debate with the therapist in an attempt to persuade him or her to give up these dysfunctional ideas. Force and energy are a basic part of shame-attacking exercises.

BEHAVIORAL TECHNIQUES   REBT practitioners use most of the regular behavior therapy procedures, especially operant conditioning, self-management principles, systematic desensitization, relaxation techniques, and modeling. Behavioral homework assignments to be carried out in real-life situations are particularly important. These assignments are done systematically and are recorded and analyzed on a form. Many involve desensitization, skill training, and assertiveness training. REBT clients are encouraged to desensitize themselves gradually and also, at times, to perform the very things they dread doing. For example, a person with a fear of elevators may decrease his or her fears by going up and down in an elevator 20 or 30 times in a day. Clients actually do new and difficult things, and in this way they put their insights to use in the form of concrete action. By acting differently, they also tend to incorporate functional beliefs.

RESEARCH EFFORTS   REBT is characterized by a growing collection of therapeutic strategies for assisting people in changing their maladaptive cognitions. Therapists typically use a combination of cognitive, emotive, and behavioral methods within a single session with a given client. If a particular technique does not seem to be producing results, the therapist is likely to switch to another. This technical eclecticism and therapeutic flexibility make controlled research difficult (Wessler, 1986). As enthusiastic as he is about cognitive behavior therapy, Ellis admits that practically all therapy outcome studies are flawed (personal communication, July 17, 1997). According to him, these studies mainly test how people *feel better* but not how they have made a profound philosophical-behavioral change and thereby *get better* (Ellis, 1998, 1999). Most REBT studies focus on cognitive, not emotive and behavioral, methods.

Applications of REBT to Client Populations

REBT has been widely applied to the treatment of anxiety, hostility, character disorders, psychotic disorders, and depression; to problems of sex, love, and marriage (Ellis & Blau, 1998); to child rearing and adolescence; and to social skills training and self-management (Ellis, 1979b; Ellis, Gordon, Neenan, & Palmer, 1997). However, Ellis does not assert that all clients can be helped through logical analysis and philosophical reconstruction.

In one-to-one work REBT tends to be focused on a specific problem. Ellis (1994) writes that most clients who are seen for individual therapy have 1 session weekly for anywhere from 5 to 50 sessions. REBT is also suitable for group therapy, because the members are taught to apply its principles to one another in the group setting. Ellis recommends that most clients experience group therapy as well as individual therapy at some point.

REBT is also applied to couples counseling and family therapy. In working with couples the partners are taught the principles of REBT so that they can work out their differences or at least become less disturbed about them. In family therapy, individual family members are encouraged to consider letting go of the demand that others in the family behave in ways they would like them to. Instead, REBT teaches family members that they are primarily responsible for their own actions and for changing their own reactions to the family situation.

REBT is well suited as a brief form of therapy, whether it is applied to individuals, groups, couples, or families. Ellis originally developed REBT to try to make psychotherapy shorter and more efficient than most other systems of therapy—hence, it is a brief therapy. The A-B-C approach to changing basic disturbance-creating attitudes can be learned in 1 to 10 sessions. Ellis has used REBT successfully in 1- and 2-day marathons and in 9-hour REBT intensives (Ellis, 1996; Ellis & Dryden, 1997). People with specific problems, such as coping with the loss of a job or dealing with retirement, are taught how to apply REBT principles to treat themselves, often with supplementary didactic materials (books, tapes, self-help forms, and the like). REBT is also a useful perspective for helping people who are experiencing a crisis. In most crises our cognitive perspective has a lot to do with how a particular event affects us. REBT can help victims in their search for understanding.

 ## AARON BECK'S COGNITIVE THERAPY

Introduction

Aaron Beck developed an approach known as *cognitive therapy* (CT), which has a number of similarities to rational emotive behavior therapy. Both are active, directive, time-limited, present-centered, and structured approaches (Beck, Rush, Shaw, & Emery, 1979). CT is an insight-focused therapy that emphasizes recognizing and changing negative thoughts and maladaptive beliefs. Beck's approach is based on the theoretical rationale that the way people feel and behave is determined by how they perceive and structure their experience. The theoretical assumptions of cognitive therapy are (1) that people's internal communication is accessible to introspection, (2) that clients' beliefs have highly personal meanings, and (3) that these meanings can be discovered by the client rather than being taught or interpreted by the therapist (Weishaar, 1993).

Beck developed his theory independently of Ellis, but they exchanged ideas. Beck credits Ellis with introducing the fundamental concept of focusing on cognitive factors as a route to changing feelings and behaviors. Ellis sees Beck as an extremely clear thinker who has made major contributions to psychotherapy through his research (Weishaar, 1993).

The basic theory of CT holds that to understand the nature of an emotional episode or disturbance it is essential to focus on the cognitive content of an individual's reaction to the upsetting event or stream of thoughts (DeRubeis & Beck, 1988). The goal is to change the way clients think by using their automatic thoughts to reach the core schemata and begin to introduce the idea of schema restructuring. This is done by encouraging clients to gather and weigh the evidence in support of their beliefs. Clinical studies indicate the value of cognitive therapy in a wide variety of disorders, particularly depression and the anxiety disorders (Beck, 1991b). It has been successfully applied in treating phobias, psychosomatic disorders, eating disorders, anger, panic disorders (Dattilio & Salas-Auvert, 1998), substance abuse (Beck, Wright, Newman, & Liese, 1993), and chronic pain (Beck, 1987), and has been used in crisis intervention (Dattilio & Freeman, 1994).

Basic Principles of Cognitive Therapy

Beck, as a practicing psychoanalytic therapist for many years, grew interested in his clients' "automatic thoughts" (personalized notions that are triggered by particular stimuli that lead to emotional responses). As a part of his psychoanalytic study, he was looking at the dream content of depressed clients for anger that they were turning back on themselves. He began to notice that more than retroflected anger, as Freud theorized with depression, there was a bias in their interpretation or thinking. Beck asked clients to observe negative automatic thoughts that persisted even though they were contrary to objective evidence, and from this he developed the most comprehensive theory on depression in the world.

Beck contends that people with emotional difficulties tend to commit characteristic "logical errors" that tilt objective reality in the direction of self-deprecation. Cognitive therapy perceives psychological problems as stemming from commonplace processes such as faulty thinking, making incorrect inferences on the basis of inadequate or incorrect information, and failing to distinguish between fantasy and reality. Let's examine some of the systematic errors in reasoning that lead to faulty assumptions and misconceptions, which are termed *cognitive distortions* (Beck et al., 1979; Beck & Weishaar, 1995; Dattilio & Freeman, 1992).

■ *Arbitrary inferences* refer to making conclusions without supporting and relevant evidence. This includes "catastrophizing," or thinking of the absolute worst scenario and outcomes for most situations. You might begin your first job as a counselor with the conviction that you will not be liked or valued by either your colleagues or your clients. You are convinced that you fooled your professors and somehow just managed to get your degree, but now people will certainly see through you!

■ *Selective abstraction* consists of forming conclusions based on an isolated detail of an event. In this process other information is ignored, and the significance of the total context is missed. The assumption is that the events that matter are those dealing with failure and deprivation. As a counselor, you might measure your worth by your errors and weaknesses, not by your successes.

■ *Overgeneralization* is a process of holding extreme beliefs on the basis of a single incident and applying them inappropriately to dissimilar events or settings. If you have difficulty working with one adolescent, for example, you might conclude that you will not be effective counseling any adolescents. You might also conclude that you will not be effective working with *any* clients!

■ *Magnification and minimization* consist of perceiving a case or situation in a greater or lesser light than it truly deserves. You might make this cognitive error by assuming that even minor mistakes in counseling a client could easily create a crisis for the individual and might result in psychological damage.

■ *Personalization* is a tendency for individuals to relate external events to themselves, even when there is no basis for making this connection. If a client does not return for a second counseling session, you might be absolutely convinced that this absence is due to your terrible performance during the initial session. You might tell yourself, "This situation proves that I really let that client down, and now she may never seek help again."

■ *Labeling and mislabeling* involve portraying one's identity on the basis of imperfections and mistakes made in the past and allowing them to define one's true identity. Thus, if you are not able to live up to all of a client's expectations, you might say to yourself, "I'm totally worthless and should turn my professional license in right away."

■ *Polarized thinking* involves thinking and interpreting in all-or-nothing terms, or categorizing experiences in either-or extremes. With such dichotomous thinking, events are labeled in black or white terms. You might give yourself no latitude for being an imperfect person and imperfect counselor. You might view yourself as either being the perfectly competent counselor (which means you always succeed with all clients) or as a total flop if you are not fully competent (which means there is no room for any mistakes).

Beck (1976) writes that, in the broadest sense, "cognitive therapy consists of all of the approaches that alleviate psychological distress through the medium of correcting faulty conceptions and self-signals" (p. 214). For him the most direct way to change dysfunctional emotions and behaviors is to modify inaccurate and dysfunctional thinking. The cognitive therapist teaches clients how to identify these distorted and dysfunctional cognitions through a process of evaluation. Through a collaborative effort, clients learn to discriminate between their own thoughts and events that occur in reality. They learn the influence that cognition has on their feelings and behaviors and even on environmental events. Clients are taught to recognize, observe, and monitor their own thoughts and assumptions, especially their negative automatic thoughts.

After they have gained insight into how their unrealistically negative thoughts are affecting them, clients are trained to test these automatic thoughts against reality by examining and weighing the evidence for and against them. This process involves empirically testing their beliefs by actively engaging in a Socratic dialogue with the therapist, carrying out homework assignments, gathering data on assumptions they make, keeping a record of activities, and forming alternative interpretations (Freeman & Dattilio, 1994). Clients form hypotheses about their behavior and eventually learn to employ specific problem-solving and coping skills. Through a process of guided discovery, clients acquire insight about the connection between their thinking and the ways they feel and act.

Cognitive therapy emphasizes the present and aims to be time limited. Therapy is focused on current problems, regardless of diagnosis, although the past may be brought into therapy under certain circumstances, such as when the client expresses a strong desire to talk about a past situation; when work on current problems results in little or no cognitive, behavioral, and emotional change; or when the therapist considers it essential to understand how and when certain dysfunctional beliefs originated and how these ideas have a current impact on the client. With this present-centered focus, cognitive therapy tends to be brief. The therapy goals include providing symptom relief, assisting clients in resolving their most pressing problems, and teaching clients relapse prevention strategies.

SOME DIFFERENCES BETWEEN CT AND REBT   In both Beck's cognitive therapy and REBT, reality testing is highly organized. Clients come to realize on an experiential level that they have misconstrued situations. Yet there are some important differences between REBT and CT, especially with respect to therapeutic methods and style.

REBT is often highly directive, persuasive, and confrontive; it also focuses on the teaching role of the therapist. In contrast, Beck uses a Socratic dialogue by posing open-ended questions to clients with the aim of getting clients to reflect on personal issues and arrive at their own conclusions. The CT therapist places more emphasis on helping clients discover their misconceptions for themselves and generally applies more structure than REBT. Through this reflective questioning process, the therapist attempts to collaborate with clients in testing the validity of their cognitions (a process termed *collaborative empiricism*). Therapeutic change is the result of clients confronting faulty beliefs with contradictory evidence that they have gathered and evaluated.

The REBT therapist works to persuade clients that certain of their beliefs are irrational, showing them that such beliefs simply won't work, largely through a process of rational disputation. Beck (1976) takes exception to REBT's concept of irrational beliefs, asserting that telling clients they are "thinking irrationally" can be detrimental because many clients believe they are "seeing things as they really are" (p. 246). CT therapists view dysfunctional beliefs as being problematic because they interfere with normal cognitive processing, not because they are irrational (Beck & Weishaar, 1995). Instead of irrational beliefs, Beck maintains that some ideas are too absolute, broad, and extreme. For him, people live by *rules* (premises or formulas); they get into trouble when they label, interpret, and evaluate by a set of rules that are unrealistic or when they use the rules inappropriately or excessively. If clients make the determination that they are living by rules that are likely to lead to misery, the therapist may suggest alternative rules for them to consider, without indoctrinating them. Although cognitive therapy often begins by recognizing the client's frame of reference, the therapist continues to ask for evidence for a belief system.

The Client/Therapist Relationship

One of the main ways the practice of cognitive therapy differs from the practice of rational emotive behavior therapy is its emphasis on the therapeutic relationship. As you will recall, Ellis views the therapist largely as a teacher and does *not* think that a warm personal relationship with clients is essential. In contrast, Beck (1987) emphasizes that the quality of the therapeutic relationship is basic to the application of cognitive therapy. Successful counseling rests on a number of desirable characteristics of therapists, such as genuine warmth, accurate empathy, nonjudgmental acceptance, and the ability to establish trust and rapport with clients. The core therapeutic conditions described by Rogers in his person-centered approach are viewed by cognitive therapists as being necessary, but not sufficient, to produce optimum therapeutic effect. Therapists must also have a cognitive conceptualization of cases, be creative and active, be able to engage clients through a process of Socratic questioning, and be knowledgeable and skilled in the use of cognitive and behavioral strategies aimed at guiding clients in significant self-discoveries that will lead to change (Weishaar, 1993). The therapist functions as a catalyst and a guide who helps clients understand how their beliefs and attitudes influence the way they feel and act. Therapists promote corrective experiences that lead to cognitive change and acquiring new skills (Beck et al., 1979; Beck & Weishaar, 1995).

Cognitive therapists encourage clients to take an active role in the therapy process. Clients are expected to bring up topics to explore, identify the distortions in their thinking, summarize important points in the session, and collaboratively devise homework assignments that they agree to carry out (J. Beck, 1995; Meichenbaum, 1997).

Cognitive therapists are continuously active and deliberately interactive with clients; they also strive to engage clients' active participation and collaboration throughout all phases of therapy. The therapist and client work together to frame the client's conclusions in the form of a testable hypothesis. Beck conceptualizes a partnership to devise personally meaningful evaluations of the client's negative assumptions, as opposed to the therapist directly suggesting alternative cognitions (Beck & Haaga, 1992; J. Beck,

1995). The assumption is that lasting changes in the client's thinking and behavior will be most likely to occur with the client's initiative, understanding, awareness, and effort (Beck et al., 1979; Weishaar, 1993). This makes cognitive therapy, like REBT, an integrative form of psychotherapy.

Cognitive therapists aim to teach clients how to be their own therapist. Typically, a therapist will educate clients about the nature and course of their problem, about the process of cognitive therapy, and how thoughts influence their emotions and behaviors. The educative process includes providing clients with information about their presenting problems and about relapse prevention.

Homework and bibliotherapy are often used as a part of cognitive therapy. The homework is tailored to the client's specific problem and arises out of the collaborative therapeutic relationship. The purpose of homework in cognitive therapy is not merely to teach clients new skills but also to enable them to test their beliefs in daily-life situations. Emphasis is placed on self-help assignments that serve as a continuation of issues addressed in a therapy session.

Clients may be asked to complete readings dealing with the philosophy of cognitive therapy. According to Dattilio and Freeman (1992), these readings are assigned as an adjunct to therapy and are designed to enhance the therapeutic process by providing an educational focus. Some popular books often recommended are *Love Is Never Enough* (Beck, 1988); *Feeling Good* (Burns, 1988); *The Feeling Good Handbook* (Burns, 1989); *Own Your Own Life* (Emery, 1984); *Woulda, Coulda, Shoulda* (Freeman & DeWolf, 1990); and *Choosing to Live* (Ellis & Newman, 1996). Through self-help books such as these, cognitive therapy has become known to the general public.

Applications of Cognitive Therapy

Cognitive therapy initially gained recognition as an approach to treating depression, but extensive research has also been devoted to the study and treatment of anxiety disorders. Cognitive behavioral methods have been applied to children and families, parent training, child abusers, individuals recovering from substance abuse, marital distress, divorce counseling, anxiety disorders, skill training, stress management, and health care problems (see Granvold, 1994; Reineke, Dattilio, & Freeman, 1995; Dattilio, 1998). Freeman and Dattilio (1992) and Dattilio and Freeman (1994) illustrate the scope of treating clinical problems with cognitive therapy. These conditions include generalized anxiety disorder, performance anxiety, social phobia, panic attacks, chronic pain, posttraumatic stress disorder, adjustment disorder, suicidal behavior, eating disorders, borderline personality disorders, narcissistic personality disorders, marital and family dysfunction, and schizophrenic disorders. Clearly, cognitive behavioral programs have been designed for all ages and for a variety of client populations.

APPLYING COGNITIVE TECHNIQUES   Regardless of the nature of the specific problem, the cognitive therapist is mainly interested in applying procedures that will assist individuals in making alternative interpretations of events in their daily living. Think about how you might apply the principles of CT to yourself in the classroom situation outlined here, thus changing your feelings surrounding the situation (Beck, 1976).

The *situation* is that your professor does not call on you during a particular class session. Your *feelings* include depression. *Cognitively,* you are telling yourself: "My professor thinks I'm stupid and that I really don't have much of value to offer the class. Furthermore, she's right, because everyone else is brighter and more articulate than I am. It's been this way most of my life!" Some possible *alternative interpretations* are that the professor wants to include others in the discussion, that she is short on time and wants to move ahead, that she already knows your views, or that you are self-conscious about being singled out or called on.

The therapist would have you become aware of the distortions in your thinking patterns by examining your automatic thoughts. The therapist would ask you to look at your inferences, which may be faulty, and then trace them back to earlier experiences in your life. Then the therapist would help you see how you sometimes come to a conclusion (your decision that you are stupid, with little of value to offer) when evidence for such a conclusion is either lacking or based on distorted information from the past.

As a client in cognitive therapy, you would also learn about the process of magnification or minimization of thinking, which involves either exaggerating the meaning of an event (you believe the professor thinks you are stupid because she did not acknowledge you on this one occasion) or minimizing it (you belittle your value as a student in the class). The therapist would assist you in learning about how you disregard important aspects of a situation, engage in overly simplified and rigid thinking, and generalize from a single incident of failure. Can you think of other situations where you could apply CT procedures?

TREATMENT OF DEPRESSION   Beck challenged the notion that depression results from anger turned inward. Instead, he focuses on the content of the depressive's negative thinking and biased interpretation of events (DeRubeis & Beck, 1988). In an earlier study that provided much of the backbone of his theory, Beck (1963) even found cognitive errors in the dream content of depressed clients.

Beck (1987) writes about the *cognitive triad* as a pattern that triggers depression. In the first component of the triad, clients hold a negative view of themselves. They blame their setbacks on personal inadequacies without considering circumstantial explanations. They are convinced that they lack the qualities essential to bring them happiness. The second component of the triad consists of the tendency to interpret experiences in a negative manner. It almost seems as if depressed people select certain facts that conform to their negative conclusions, a process Beck refers to as selective abstraction. The third component of the triad pertains to depressed clients' gloomy vision and projections about the future. They expect their present difficulties to continue, and they anticipate only failure in the future.

Depression-prone people often set rigid, perfectionistic goals for themselves that are impossible to attain. Their negative expectations are so strong that even if they experience success in specific tasks they anticipate failure the next time. They screen out successful experiences that are not consistent with their negative self-concept. The thought content of depressed individuals centers on a sense of irreversible loss, which results in emotional states of sadness, disappointment, and apathy.

The Beck Depression Inventory (BDI) was designed as a standardized device to assess the depth of depression. The items are based on observations of the symptoms and basic beliefs of depressed people. The inventory contains 21 symptoms and attitudes: (1) sadness, (2) pessimism, (3) sense of failure, (4) dissatisfaction, (5) guilt, (6) sense of punishment, (7) self-dislike, (8) self-accusations, (9) suicidal ideation, (10) crying spells, (11) irritability, (12) social withdrawal, (13) indecision, (14) distorted body image, (15) work inhibition, (16) sleep disturbance, (17) tendency to become fatigued, (18) loss of appetite, (19) weight loss, (20) somatic preoccupations, and (21) loss of libido (Beck, 1967).

Beck's therapeutic approach to treating depressed clients focuses on specific problem areas and the reasons clients give for their symptoms. Some of the behavioral symptoms of depression are inactivity, withdrawal, and avoidance. Clients report that they are too tired to do anything, that they will feel even worse if they become active, and that they will fail at anything they try. The therapist is likely to probe with Socratic questioning such as: "What would be lost by trying? Will you feel worse if you are passive? How do you know that it is pointless to try?" Therapy procedures include setting up an activity schedule with graded tasks to be completed. Clients are asked to complete easy tasks first, so that they will meet with some success and become slightly more optimistic. The point is to enlist the client's cooperation with the therapist on the assumption that *doing something* is more likely to lead to feeling better than *doing nothing*.

Some depressed clients may harbor suicidal wishes. Cognitive therapy strategies may include exposing the client's ambivalence, generating alternatives, and reducing problems to manageable proportions. For example, the therapist may ask the client to list the reasons for living and for dying. Further, if the client can develop alternative views of a problem, then alternative courses of action can be developed. This can result not only in a client feeling better but also behaving in more effective ways.

A central characteristic of most depressive people is self-criticism. Underneath the person's self-hate are attitudes of weakness, inadequacy, and lack of responsibility. A number of therapeutic strategies can be used. Clients can be asked to identify and provide reasons for their excessively self-critical behavior. The therapist may ask the client, "If I were to make a mistake the way you do, would you despise me as much as you do yourself?" A skillful therapist may play the role of the depressed client, portraying the client as inadequate, inept, and weak. This technique can be effective in demonstrating the client's cognitive distortions and arbitrary inferences. The therapist can then discuss with the client how the "tyranny of shoulds" can lead to self-hate and depression.

Depressed clients typically experience painful emotions. They may say that they cannot stand the pain or that nothing can make them feel better. One procedure to counteract painful affect is humor. A therapist can demonstrate the ironic aspects of a situation. If clients can even briefly experience some lightheartedness, it can serve as an antidote to their sadness. Such a shift in their cognitive set is simply not compatible with their self-critical attitude.

Another specific characteristic of depressed people is an exaggeration of external demands, problems, and pressures. Such people often exclaim that they feel overwhelmed and that there is so much to accomplish that they can never do it. A cognitive therapist might ask clients to list things that need to be done, set priorities, check off tasks that have been accomplished, and break down an external problem into manageable units. When problems are discussed, clients often become aware of how they are magnifying the importance of these difficulties. Through rational exploration, clients are able to regain a perspective on defining and accomplishing tasks.

The therapist typically has to take the lead in helping clients make a list of their responsibilities, set priorities, and develop a realistic plan of action. Because carrying out such a plan is often inhibited by self-defeating thoughts, it is well for therapists to use cognitive rehearsal techniques in both identifying and changing negative thoughts. If clients can learn to combat their self-doubts in the therapy session, they may be able to apply their newly acquired cognitive and behavioral skills in real-life situations.

APPLICATION TO FAMILY THERAPY   The cognitive behavioral approach focuses on family interaction patterns, and family relationships, cognitions, emotions, and behavior are viewed as exerting a mutual influence on one another. A cognitive inference can evoke emotion and behavior, and emotion and behavior can likewise influence cognition in a reciprocal process that sometimes serves to maintain the dysfunction of the family unit.

Cognitive therapy, as set forth by Beck (1976), places a heavy emphasis on *schema,* or what have otherwise been defined as core beliefs (Beck, Rush, Shaw, & Emery, 1979; DeRubeis & Beck, 1988). A key aspect of the therapeutic process involves restructuring distorted beliefs (or schema), which has a pivotal impact on changing dysfunctional behaviors. Some cognitive behavior therapists place a heavy emphasis on examining cognitions among individual family members as well as on what may be termed the "family schemata" (Dattilio, 1993, 1998). These are jointly held beliefs about the family that have formed as a result of years of integrated interaction among members of the family unit. Dattilio (1993, 1994) suggests that individuals basically maintain two separate sets of schemata about families. These are family schemata related to the parents' family of origin and schemata related to families in general. It is the experiences and perceptions from the family of origin that shape the schema about both the immediate family and families in general. These schemata have a major impact on how the individual thinks, feels, and behaves in the family system.

For a concrete illustration of how Dattilio applies cognitive principles and works with family schemata, see his cognitive behavioral approach to family therapy with Ruth, in *Case Approach to Counseling and Psychotherapy* (Corey, 2001, Chapter 11). Also, for an expanded treatment of applications of cognitive behavioral approaches to working with couples and families, see Dattilio (1998), which includes the integration of cognitive behavioral strategies with more than 16 different modalities of couples and family therapy. This seminal work allows practitioners and theorists to appreciate the integrative nature that is characteristic of cognitive behavior therapy.

DONALD MEICHENBAUM'S COGNITIVE BEHAVIOR MODIFICATION

Introduction

Another major alternative to rational emotive behavior therapy is Donald Meichenbaum's *cognitive behavior modification* (CBM), which focuses on changing the client's self-verbalizations. According to Meichenbaum (1977), self-statements affect a person's behavior in much the same way as statements made by another person. A basic premise of CBM is that clients, as a prerequisite to behavior change, must notice how they think, feel, and behave and the impact they have on others. For change to occur, clients need to interrupt the scripted nature of their behavior so that they can evaluate their behavior in various situations (Meichenbaum, 1986).

This approach shares with REBT and Beck's cognitive therapy the assumption that distressing emotions are typically the result of maladaptive thoughts. There are differences, however. Whereas REBT is more direct and confrontational in uncovering and disputing irrational thoughts, Meichenbaum's self-instructional therapy focuses more on helping clients become aware of their self-talk. The therapeutic process consists of training clients to modify the instructions they give to themselves so that they can cope more effectively with the problems they encounter. The emphasis is on acquiring practical coping skills for problematic situations such as impulsive and aggressive behavior, fear of taking tests, and fear of public speaking.

Cognitive restructuring plays a central role in Meichenbaum's approach. He describes *cognitive structure* as the organizing aspect of thinking, which seems to monitor and direct the choice of thoughts (1977). Cognitive structure implies an "executive processor," which "holds the blueprints of thinking" that determine when to continue, interrupt, or change thinking.

How Behavior Changes

Meichenbaum (1977) proposes that "behavior change occurs through a sequence of mediating processes involving the interaction of inner speech, cognitive structures, and behaviors and their resultant outcomes" (p. 218). He describes a three-phase process of change in which those three aspects are interwoven. According to him, focusing on only one aspect will probably prove insufficient.

Phase 1: self-observation. The beginning step in the change process consists of clients learning how to observe their own behavior. When they begin therapy, their internal dialogue is characterized by negative self-statements and imagery. A critical factor is their willingness and ability to *listen* to themselves. This process involves an increased sensitivity to their thoughts, feelings, actions, physiological reactions, and ways of reacting to others. If depressed clients hope to make constructive changes, for example, they must first realize that they are not "victims" of negative thoughts and feelings. Rather, they are actually contributing to their depression through the things they tell themselves. Although self-observation is seen as a necessary process if change is to occur, it is not sufficient, per se, for change. As therapy progresses, clients acquire new cognitive structures that enable them to view their problems in a new light. This reconceptualization process comes about through a collaborative effort between client and therapist.

Phase 2: starting a new internal dialogue. As a result of the early client/ therapist contacts, clients learn to notice their maladaptive behaviors, and they begin to see opportunities for adaptive behavioral alternatives. If clients hope to change, what they say to themselves must initiate a new behavioral chain, one that is incompatible with their maladaptive behaviors. Clients learn to change their internal dialogue through therapy. Their new internal dialogue serves as a guide to new behavior. In turn, this process has an impact on clients' cognitive structures.

Phase 3: learning new skills. The third phase of the modification process consists of teaching clients more effective coping skills, which are practiced in real-life situations. (For example, clients who can't cope with failure may avoid appealing activities for fear of not succeeding at them. Cognitive restructuring can help them change their negative view, thus making them more willing to engage in desired activities.) At the same time, clients continue to focus on telling themselves new sentences and observing and assessing the outcomes. As they behave differently in situations, they typically get different reactions from others. The stability of what they learn is greatly influenced by what they say to themselves about their newly acquired behavior and its consequences.

Coping Skills Programs

The rationale for coping skills programs is that we can acquire more effective strategies in dealing with stressful situations by learning how to modify our cognitive "set." The following procedures are designed to teach coping skills:

- Exposing clients to anxiety-provoking situations by means of role playing and imagery

- Requiring clients to evaluate their anxiety level
- Teaching clients to become aware of the anxiety-provoking cognitions they experience in stressful situations
- Helping clients examine these thoughts by reevaluating their self-statements
- Having clients note the level of anxiety following this reevaluation

Research studies have demonstrated the success of coping skills programs when applied to problems such as speech anxiety, test anxiety, phobias, anger, social incompetence, addictions, alcoholism, sexual dysfunctions, and social withdrawal in children (Meichenbaum, 1977, 1986).

A particular application of a coping skills program is teaching clients stress-management techniques by way of a strategy known as *stress inoculation*. Using cognitive techniques, Meichenbaum (1985) has developed stress-inoculation procedures that are a psychological and behavioral analog to immunization on a biological level. Individuals are given opportunities to deal with relatively mild stress stimuli in successful ways, so that they gradually develop a tolerance for stronger stimuli. This training is based on the assumption that we can affect our ability to cope with stress by modifying our beliefs and self-statements about our performance in stressful situations. Meichenbaum's stress-inoculation training is concerned with more than merely teaching people specific coping skills. His program is designed to prepare clients for intervention and motivate them to change, and it deals with issues such as resistance and relapse. Stress-inoculation training (SIT) consists of a combination of information giving, Socratic discussion, cognitive restructuring, problem solving, relaxation training, behavioral rehearsals, self-monitoring, self-instruction, self-reinforcement, and modifying environmental situations. This approach is designed to teach coping skills that can be applied to both present problems and future difficulties.

Meichenbaum (1985) has designed a three-stage model for stress-inoculation training: (1) the conceptual phase, (2) the skills acquisition and rehearsal phase, and (3) the application and follow-through phase.

During the *conceptual phase,* the primary focus is on creating a working relationship with clients. This is mainly done by helping them gain a better understanding of the nature of stress and reconceptualizing it in social-interactive terms. The therapist enlists client collaboration during this early phase. Together they rethink the nature of the problem(s). Initially, clients are provided with a conceptual framework in simple terms designed to help them understand how they are responding to a variety of stressful situations. They learn about the role that cognitions and emotions play in creating and maintaining stress. They are taught this by didactic presentations, through Socratic questioning, and by a process of guided self-discovery.

Clients often begin treatment feeling that they are the victims of external circumstances, thoughts, feelings, and behaviors over which they have no control. Training includes teaching clients to become aware of their own role in creating their stress. They acquire this awareness by systematically observing the statements they make internally as well as monitoring the maladaptive behaviors that flow from this inner dialogue. Such self-monitoring continues throughout all the phases. As is true in cognitive therapy, clients typically keep an open-ended diary in which they systematically record their specific thoughts, feelings, and behaviors. In teaching these coping skills, therapists strive to be flexible in their use of techniques and to be sensitive to the individual, cultural, and situational circumstances of their clients.

During the *skills acquisition and rehearsal phase,* the focus is on giving clients a variety of behavioral and cognitive coping techniques to apply to stressful situations. This phase involves direct actions, such as gathering information about their fears, learning specifically what situations bring about stress, arranging for ways to lessen the stress by doing something different, and learning methods of physical and psychological relaxation. The training involves cognitive coping; clients are taught that adaptive and maladaptive behaviors are linked to their inner dialogue. They acquire and rehearse a new set of self-statements. Meichenbaum (1986) provides some examples of coping statements that are rehearsed in this phase of SIT:

- "How can I prepare for a stressor?" ("What do I have to do? Can I develop a plan to deal with the stress?")
- "How can I confront and deal with what is stressing me?" ("What are some ways I can handle a stressor? How can I meet this challenge?")
- "How can I cope with feeling overwhelmed?" ("What can I do right now? How can I keep my fears in check?")
- "How can I make reinforcing self-statements?" ("How can I give myself credit?")

As a part of the stress-management program, clients are also exposed to various behavioral interventions, some of which are relaxation training, social skills training, time-management instruction, and self-instructional training. They are helped to make lifestyle changes such as reevaluating priorities, developing support systems, and taking direct action to alter stressful situations. Clients are introduced to a variety of methods of relaxation and are taught to use these skills to decrease arousal due to stress. Through teaching, demonstration, and guided practice, clients learn the skills of progressive relaxation, which are to be practiced regularly. Other approaches that are recommended for learning to relax include meditation, yoga, tensing and relaxing muscle groups, and breath-control techniques. Relaxation also includes activities such as walking, jogging, gardening, knitting, or other physical activities. Meichenbaum stresses that relaxation is as much a state of mind as it is a physical state.

During the *application and follow-through phase,* the focus is on carefully arranging for transfer and maintenance of change from the therapeutic situation to the real world. It is clear that teaching coping skills is a complex procedure that relies on varied treatment programs. For clients to merely say new things to themselves is generally not sufficient to produce change. They need to practice these self-statements and apply their new skills in real-life situations. Once they have become proficient in cognitive and behavioral coping skills, clients practice behavioral assignments, which become increasingly demanding. Clients are asked to write down the homework assignments they are willing to complete. The outcomes of these assignments are carefully checked at subsequent meetings, and if clients do not follow through with them, the therapist and the client collaboratively consider the reasons for the failure. Follow-up and booster sessions typically take place at 3-, 6-, and 12-month periods as an incentive for clients to continue practicing and refining their coping skills. SIT can be considered part of an ongoing stress-management program that extends the benefits of training into the future.

Stress-management training has potentially useful applications for a wide variety of problems and clients, both for remediation and prevention. Some of these applications include anger control, anxiety management, assertion training, improving creative thinking, treating depression, and dealing with health problems. The approach has also been used in treating obese people, hyperactive children, social isolates, posttraumatic stress, and schizophrenics (Meichenbaum, 1977, 1985, 1994).

Constructivism as a Trend in Cognitive Behavior Therapy

In recent years cognitive behavior therapy has increasingly viewed the subjective framework and interpretations of the client as more important than the objective bases of faulty beliefs. The constructivist perspective focuses on the capacity of humans for creative and imaginative thought. At the core of constructivist theory is a view of people as active agents who are able to derive meaning out of their experiential world. Thus, the process of change can be facilitated, but not directed, by a therapist. Like cognitive therapists, constructivist practitioners work with clients collaboratively by helping them construct more coherent and comprehensive stories that they live by (Neimeyer, 1993a).

Constructivism stresses the client's reality without disputing whether it is accurate or rational (Weishaar, 1993). Lindsley (1994) emphasizes that therapists can encourage their clients to reconsider absolutist judgments by moving toward seeing both "good" and "bad" elements in situations. By using a constructivist perspective, therapists can enable clients to modify painful beliefs, values, and interpretations without imposing their value system and interpretations.

Meichenbaum (1997) discusses his personal evolution as a cognitive behavioral therapist. As of 1997 he was immersed in the constructivist narrative perspective (CNP), which focuses on the stories people tell about themselves and others about significant events in their lives. Meichenbaum operates on the assumption that there are multiple realities and one of the therapeutic tasks is to help clients appreciate how they construct their realities and how they author their own stories.

Meichenbaum (1997) states that the constructivist approach to cognitive behavior therapy is less structured and more discovery-oriented than standard cognitive therapy. The constructivist approach gives more emphasis to past development, tends to target deeper core beliefs, and explores the behavioral impact and emotional toll a client pays for clinging to certain root metaphors. REBT challenges the irrationality of clients' thoughts and beliefs, whereas constructivist therapists are concerned with helping clients explore how they create their realities and the consequences that follow from such constructions. Meichenbaum uses these questions to evaluate the outcomes of therapy:

- As a result of therapy, to what degree are clients able to tell a new story about themselves and the world?
- Do clients now use more positive metaphors to describe themselves?
- Are clients able to predict high-risk situations and employ coping skills in dealing with emerging problems?
- To what degree are clients able to take credit for the changes they have been able to bring about?

Successful therapy involves clients being able to develop their own voices, take pride in what they have accomplished, and take ownership of the changes they are bringing about.

Because constructivist philosophy serves as an overarching framework for understanding human knowing and change, it shows promise as a force contributing to a systematic integration of divergent therapeutic approaches (Neimeyer, 1993b; Neimeyer & Lyddon, 1993). Constructivism has begun to permeate numerous fields of contemporary psychology. Family therapy is one of the areas in which it has had a profound impact, a topic that is considered in more detail in Chapter 13.

 # COGNITIVE BEHAVIOR THERAPY APPLIED TO THE CASE OF STAN

The cognitive behavior therapist has as her broad objective minimizing Stan's self-defeating attitudes and helping him acquire a more realistic outlook on life. Stan's therapist is goal-oriented and problem-focused. She will ask Stan, from the initial session, to identify his problems and formulate specific goals. Furthermore, she will help him reconceptualize his problems in a way that will increase his chances of finding solutions.

Stan's therapist will follow a clear structure for every session. The basic procedural sequence of Stan's therapy includes (1) preparing Stan by providing a cognitive rationale for treatment and demystifying treatment; (2) encouraging Stan to monitor his thoughts that accompany his distress; (3) implementing behavioral and cognitive techniques; (4) working with Stan to assist him in identifying and challenging some basic beliefs and ideas;

(5) teaching Stan ways to examine his beliefs and assumptions by testing them in reality; and (6) teaching Stan basic coping skills that will enable him to avoid relapsing into old patterns.

As a part of the structure of Stan's therapy sessions, the therapist will ask Stan for a brief review of the week, elicit feedback from the previous session, review homework assignments, collaboratively create an agenda for the session, discuss topics on the agenda, and set new homework for the week. Stan will be encouraged to perform personal experiments and practice coping skills *in vivo*. It is not enough to learn about his problems in the therapy sessions; Stan will be expected to apply what he is learning in his everyday life.

Although the role of insight is not a central concept in cognitive behavior therapy, three levels of awareness can contribute to Stan's improvement, provided he is willing to put his insights into action. He tells his therapist that he would like to work on his fear of women and would hope to feel far less intimidated by them. He reports that he feels threatened by most women, but especially by women he perceives as powerful.

In the first level of insight, he becomes aware that there is some antecedent cause of his fear of women. This cause is not that his mother tried, for example, to dominate him. Rather, it is his self-defeating beliefs that she should not have tried to dominate him and that it was, and still is, awful that she did try and that other women may dominate him too.

On the second level of insight, Stan recognizes that he is still threatened by women and feels uncomfortable in their presence because he still believes in, and keeps repeating endlessly to himself, the faulty beliefs he once accepted. He sees that he keeps himself in a state of panic with women because he continues to tell himself "Women can castrate me!" or

"They'll expect me to be a superman!" or some other dysfunctional notion.

The third level of insight consists of Stan's acceptance that he will not improve unless he works diligently and practices changing his self-defeating beliefs by actively examining them and engaging in behavior that allows him to confront his fears. Once he clearly identifies some of his faulty or distorted beliefs, he can examine them in his therapy sessions.

First, Stan's therapist educates him about the importance of examining his automatic thoughts, his self-talk, and the many "shoulds," "oughts," and "musts" he has accepted without questioning. Working with Stan as a collaborative partner in his therapy, the therapist guides Stan in discovering some basic cognitions that influence what he tells himself and how he feels and acts. This is some of Stan's self-talk:

- "I always have to be strong, tough, and perfect."
- "I'm not a man if I show any signs of weakness."
- "If everyone didn't love me and approve of me, things would be catastrophic."
- "If a woman rejected me, I really would be diminished to a 'nothing.'"
- "If I fail, I am then a failure as a person."
- "I'm apologetic for my existence, because I don't feel equal to others."

Second, the therapist assists Stan in monitoring and evaluating the ways in which he keeps telling himself these self-defeating sentences. She challenges specific problems and confronts the core of his faulty thinking:

You're not your father. I wonder why you continue telling yourself that you're just like him? Do you think you need to continue accepting without question your parents' value judgments about your worth? Where is the evidence that they were right in their assessment of you? You say you're such a failure and that you feel inferior. Do your present activities support this? If you were not so hard on yourself, how might your life be different? Does having been the scapegoat in your family mean that you need to continue making yourself the scapegoat?

Third, once Stan comes to more fully understand the nature of his cognitive distortions and his self-defeating beliefs, his therapist will draw on a variety of cognitive, emotive, and behavioral techniques to help Stan make the changes he is most interested in making. Stan learns to identify, evaluate, and respond to his dysfunctional beliefs. The therapist uses both didactic and Socratic educational methods to assist him in examining the evidence that seems to support or contradict his core beliefs. Through this process Stan will be able to unfreeze his beliefs about himself and the world. The therapist works with Stan so he will view his basic beliefs and automatic thinking as hypotheses to be tested. In a way, Stan will become a personal scientist by checking out the validity of many of the conclusions and basic assumptions that contribute to his personal difficulties. By the use of guided discovery, Stan learns to evaluate the validity and functionality of his beliefs and conclusions.

Stan's counselor gives him specific homework assignments to help him deal with his fears. At one point, for instance, she asks him to explore his fears of powerful women and his reasons for continuing to tell himself: "They can castrate me. They expect me to be strong and perfect. If I'm not careful, they'll dominate me." His homework includes approaching a woman for a date. If he succeeds in getting the date, he can challenge his catastrophic expectations of what might happen. What would be so terrible if she did not like him or if she refused the date? Why does he have to get all his confirmation from one woman? Stan tells himself over and over that he must be *approved of* by women

and that if any woman rebuffs him the consequences are more than he can bear. With awareness of the unrealistic demands he is accepting, he eventually begins to tell himself that although he prefers acceptance to rejection it is not the end of the world if he does not get what he wants. He learns to substitute preferences and desires for "musts" and "shoulds."

In addition to homework assignments, the therapist may employ many other behavioral techniques, such as role playing, humor, modeling, behavior rehearsal, and desensitization. She asks Stan to read some cognitive behavioral self-help books. He can use the ideas he learns from them as he practices changing. Basically, she works in an active manner and focuses on cognitive and behavioral dimensions. She pays little attention to Stan's past. Instead, she highlights his present functioning and his faulty thinking and teaches him to rethink and reverbalize in a more constructive way. Thus, he can learn how to be different by telling himself a new set of statements, which might include:

- "I can be lovable."
- "I'm able to succeed as well as fail at times."
- "I need not make all women into my mother."
- "I don't have to punish myself by making myself feel guilty over past failures, because it is not essential to always be perfect."

Stan can benefit from the range of cognitive behavioral procedures aimed at helping him learn to make constructive self-statements. He can profit from cognitive restructuring, which proceeds as follows: First, the therapist assists him in learning ways to observe his own behavior in various situations. During the week he can take a particular situation that is problematic for him, paying particular attention to his automatic thoughts and internal dialogue. What is he telling himself as he approaches a difficult situation? How is he setting himself up for failure with his self-talk? Second, as he learns to attend to his maladaptive behaviors, he begins to see that what he tells himself has as much impact as others' statements about him. He also sees the connections between his thinking and his behavioral problems. With this awareness he is in an ideal place to begin to learn a new, more functional internal dialogue. Third, he can also learn new coping skills, which he can practice first in the sessions and then in daily-life situations. It will not be enough for him to merely say new things to himself, for to become proficient in new cognitive and behavioral coping skills he needs to apply them in various daily situations. As he experiences success with his assignments, these tasks can become increasingly demanding.

Follow-Up: You Continue as Stan's Cognitive Behavior Therapist

Use these questions to help you think about how to counsel Stan:

- In the work with Stan in this section, the therapist's style is characterized as an integrative form of cognitive behavioral therapy. She borrows concepts and techniques from the approaches of Ellis, Beck, and Meichenbaum. In your work with Stan, what specific concepts would you borrow from each of these approaches? What techniques would you draw from each of the cognitive behavioral approaches? What possible advantages do you see, if any, in applying an integrative cognitive behavioral approach in your work with Stan?

- What are some things you would most want to teach Stan about how cognitive behavior therapy works? What would you tell him about the therapeutic alliance and the collaborative therapeutic relationship?

- What are some of Stan's most prominent faulty beliefs that are getting in the way of his living fully? What cognitive, emotive, and behavioral techniques might you use in helping him examine his core beliefs?

- Stan lives by many "shoulds" and "oughts." His automatic thoughts seem to get in his way of getting what he wants. What techniques would you use to encourage guided discovery on his part?

- What are some homework assignments that might be useful for Stan to carry out? In what ways could you collaboratively design homework with Stan? How would you encourage him to develop action plans whereby he could test the validity of his thinking and his conclusions? ■

SUMMARY AND EVALUATION

Summary

REBT has evolved into a comprehensive and integrative approach that emphasizes thinking, judging, deciding, and doing. Therapy begins with clients' problematic behaviors and emotions and disputes the thoughts that directly create them. To block the self-defeating beliefs that are reinforced by a process of self-indoctrination, REBT therapists employ active and directive techniques such as teaching, suggestion, persuasion, and homework assignments, and they challenge clients to substitute a rational belief system for an irrational one. They demonstrate how and why dysfunctional beliefs lead to negative emotional and behavioral results. They teach clients how to dispute self-defeating beliefs and behaviors that might occur in the future. REBT stresses action—doing something about the insights one gains in therapy. Change comes about mainly by a commitment to consistently practice new behaviors that replace old and ineffective ones.

Rational emotive behavior therapists are typically eclectic in selecting therapeutic strategies. They draw heavily on cognitive and behavioral techniques that are geared to uprooting the irrational beliefs that lead to self-defeating feelings and behaviors and to teaching clients how to replace this negative process with a rational philosophy of life. Therapists have the latitude to develop their own personal style and to exercise creativity; they are not bound by fixed techniques for particular problems.

As we have seen, REBT is the forerunner of other cognitive behavioral approaches. Two therapies that are considered modifications and, in some ways, extensions of REBT are Beck's cognitive therapy and Meichenbaum's cognitive behavior modification. These therapies stress the importance of cognitive processes as determinants of behavior. They maintain that how people feel and what they actually do is largely influenced by their subjective assessment of situations. Because this appraisal of life situations is influenced by beliefs, attitudes, assumptions, and internal dialogue, such cognitions become the major focus of therapy.

Contributions of the Cognitive Behavioral Approaches

Most of the therapies discussed in this book can be considered "cognitive," in a general sense, because they have the aim of changing clients' subjective views of themselves and the world. But the cognitive behavioral approaches explored in this chapter differ in their major focus on both undermining faulty assumptions and beliefs and teaching clients the coping skills needed to deal with their problems.

ELLIS'S REBT   I find aspects of REBT very valuable in my work because I believe we are responsible for maintaining self-destructive ideas and attitudes that influence our daily transactions. I see value in confronting clients with questions such as: "What are your assumptions and basic beliefs? Have you really examined some of the core ideas you live by to determine if they are your own values or merely introjects?" REBT has built on the Adlerian notion that events themselves do not have the power to determine us; rather, it is our interpretation of these events that is crucial. The A-B-C model simply and clearly illustrates how human disturbances occur and the ways in which problematic behavior can be changed. Rather than focusing on events themselves, therapy stresses how clients interpret and react to what happens to them.

Another contribution of the cognitive behavioral approaches is the emphasis on putting newly acquired insights into action. Homework assignments are well suited to enabling clients to practice new behaviors and assisting them in the process of their reconditioning. Adlerian therapy, reality therapy, and behavior therapy all share with the cognitive behavioral approaches this action orientation.

One of the strengths of REBT is the focus on teaching clients ways to carry on their own therapy without the direct intervention of a therapist. I particularly like the emphasis that REBT puts on supplementary approaches such as listening to tapes, reading self-help books, keeping a record of what they are doing and thinking, and attending workshops. In this way clients can further the process of change in themselves without becoming excessively dependent on a therapist.

A major contribution of REBT is its emphasis on a comprehensive and eclectic therapeutic practice. Numerous cognitive, emotive, and behavioral techniques can be employed in changing one's emotions and behaviors by changing the structure of one's cognitions. Further, REBT is open to using therapeutic procedures derived from other schools, especially from behavior therapy.

BECK'S COGNITIVE THERAPY   Beck's key concepts are very similar to Ellis's, though there are some differences in underlying philosophy and the process by which therapy proceeds. Beck made pioneering efforts in the treatment of anxiety, phobias, and depression. He developed specific cognitive procedures that are useful in challenging a depressive client's assumptions and beliefs and in providing a new cognitive perspective that can lead to optimism and changed behavior. His approach has received a great deal of attention from clinical researchers, and a number of experiments support its efficacy for depressed clients (Haaga & Davison, 1986). The effects of cognitive therapy on depression and hopelessness seem to be maintained for at least one year after treatment.

Weishaar (1993) writes that when Beck developed cognitive therapy it served as a bridge between psychoanalytic therapy and behavior therapy. Cognitive therapy provided a structured, focused, active approach that focused on the client's inner world. Further, according to Weishaar, Beck demonstrated that a structured therapy that is present-centered and problem-oriented can be very effective in treating depression and anxiety in a relatively short time. In fact, Beck considers cognitive therapy to be *the* integrative psychotherapy because it draws from so many different modalities of psychotherapy (Alford & Beck, 1997).

One of the contributions of cognitive therapy is that it focuses on developing a detailed case conceptualization as a way to understand how clients view their world. Thus, cognitive therapy shares the phenomenological perspective with the Adlerian, existential, person-centered, and Gestalt approaches. According to Weishaar (1993), one of Beck's major theoretical contributions has been bringing private experience back into the realm of legitimate scientific inquiry.

In commenting on current and future trends in cognitive therapy, Beck (1993) cites its application to a range of disorders such as chronic pain, social phobia, HIV-related distress, guilt, and shame. Regarding the future of cognitive therapy, Beck (1991b) states that during the early years of its development it was pitted against the giants in the field, psychoanalysis and behavior therapy. It is now one of the more popular approaches. "At this point in time," he comments, "cognitive therapy is no longer a fledgling and has demonstrated its capacity to fly under its own power. How far it will fly remains to be seen" (p. 374).

MEICHENBAUM'S COGNITIVE BEHAVIOR MODIFICATION   Meichenbaum's work in self-instruction therapy and stress-inoculation training has been applied successfully to a variety of client populations and specific problems. Of special note is his contribution to understanding how stress is largely self-induced through inner dialogue. He has gone beyond simply adding a few cognitive techniques to behavior therapy and has actually broadened its theoretical base through his demonstration of the importance of self-talk (Patterson & Watkins, 1996). Meichenbaum (1986) cautions cognitive behavioral practitioners against the tendency to become overly preoccupied with techniques. If progress is to be made, he suggests that cognitive behavior therapy must develop a testable theory of behavior change. He reports that some attempts have been made to formulate a cognitive social learning theory that will explain behavior change and specify the best methods of intervention.

A major contribution made by both Beck and Meichenbaum is the demystification of the therapy process. Both of these cognitive behavioral approaches are based on an educational model that stresses a working alliance between therapist and client. The models encourage self-help, provide for continuous feedback from the client on how well treatment strategies are working, and provide a structure and direction to the therapy process that allows for evaluation of outcomes. Clients are active, informed, and responsible for the direction of therapy because they are partners in the enterprise. The cognitive behavioral approaches may well be the treatment of choice in the current managed-care environment.

Limitations and Criticisms of the Cognitive Behavioral Approaches

ELLIS'S REBT   My major criticisms of REBT involve aspects of the client's life that it ignores or tends to discount. Rational emotive behavior therapists do not encourage clients to recount "long tales of woes." They make little use of unconscious dynamics, free association, dream work, and the transference relationship. Although most REBT practitioners emphasize building rapport and a collaborative relationship between therapist and client, Ellis maintains that dimensions such as personal warmth, liking for the client, empathy, and a personal interest or caring are not essential ingredients for effective therapy. As is clear by now, I view the client/therapist relationship as the central factor accounting for client change. It is difficult for me to imagine effective therapy taking place in the absence of empathy, understanding, and caring. Therapy is more than simply challenging and modifying an individual's faulty thinking.

REBT is a confrontational therapy, which provides both advantages and disadvantages. Some clients will have trouble with a confrontive therapist before he or she has earned their respect and trust. If clients feel they are not being listened to and cared about, there is a good chance they will terminate therapy. One area where Ellis will confront clients relates to transference. Ellis attacks transference on the ground that the client is inventing a false connection between the therapist and some significant other in the client's past. I think that such feelings can teach clients about areas in their life that they still need to explore and resolve. Attacking these feelings does not build trust nor does it help the client work effectively with the therapist.

My view of therapeutic practice places value on paying attention to a client's past without getting lost in this past and without assuming a fatalistic stance about earlier traumatic experiences. I question the view of most cognitive behavioral therapists that exploring the past is ineffective in helping clients change faulty thinking and behavior. In some cases not enough emphasis is given to encouraging clients to express and explore their feelings. I believe the cognitive behavioral approaches can work best once clients have expressed their feelings, which often occurs when they relive and work through earlier emotional issues.

All the cognitive behavioral approaches, including REBT, are less concerned with unconscious factors and ego defenses than I would like. I do not see how clients can truly choose or make changes without awareness of influential factors in their development. Likewise, past unfinished business and childhood experiences have a great deal of therapeutic power if they are connected to our present functioning. From my perspective, some painful early experiences need to be recognized, felt fully, reexperienced, and worked through in therapy before people can free themselves of restrictive influences.

REBT therapists can misuse their power by imposing their ideas of what constitutes rational thinking. Due to the directive nature of this approach, it is particularly important for practitioners to know themselves well and to take care not to impose their own philosophy of life on their clients. Because the therapist has a large amount of power by virtue of persuasion, psychological harm is more possible in REBT than in less directive approaches. The therapist's level of training, knowledge, skill, perceptiveness, and judgment is particularly important. It is essential that the therapist be aware of when and how much to confront clients. An untrained therapist who uses REBT might view therapy as wearing down a client's resistance with persuasion, indoctrination, logic, and advice. Thus, a practitioner can misuse REBT by reducing it to dispensing quick-cure procedures—that is, by telling clients what is wrong with them and how they can best change.

It is well to underscore that REBT can be effective when practiced in a style different from Ellis's. Because Ellis has so much visibility, it is worth distinguishing between the principles and techniques of REBT and his very confrontational tactics. Indeed, a therapist can be soft-spoken and gentle and still use REBT concepts and methods. At times inexperienced REBT practitioners may assume that they must follow the fast pace of Ellis. Therapists who employ REBT techniques can use different degrees of directiveness, can vary the amount of activity, and can be themselves by developing a style that is consistent with their own personality.

BECK'S COGNITIVE THERAPY   Cognitive therapy has been criticized as focusing too much on the power of positive thinking; as being too superficial and simplistic; as denying the importance of the client's past; as being too technique-oriented; as failing to use the therapeutic relationship; as working only on eliminating symptoms, but failing to explore the underlying causes of difficulties; as ignoring the role of unconscious factors; and as neglecting the role of feelings (Freeman & Dattilio, 1992b; Weishaar, 1993).

Freeman and Dattilio (1992b, 1994) do a good job of debunking the myths and misconceptions about cognitive therapy, and Weishaar (1993) concisely addresses a number of criticisms leveled at the approach. Although the cognitive therapist is straightforward and looks for simple rather than complex solutions, this does not imply that the practice of cognitive therapy is simple. Cognitive therapists do not explore the unconscious or underlying conflicts but work with clients in the present to bring about schematic changes. However, they do recognize that clients' current problems are often a product of earlier life experiences. A criticism of cognitive therapy, like REBT, is that emotions are played down in treatment. Both approaches draw on emotional techniques, along with cognitive and behavioral strategies, to bring about client change, but neither encourages emotional ventilation or emotionally reexperiencing painful events. In my view, this criticism of underplaying the role of emotions in therapy has validity for all the cognitive behavioral therapies. One way of minimizing this shortcoming would be for practitioners to incorporate techniques from Gestalt therapy into their repertoire. If you are interested in a further discussion of criticisms and rebuttals of cognitive therapy, consult Weishaar (1993) and Freeman and Dattilio (1992b).

MEICHENBAUM'S COGNITIVE BEHAVIOR MODIFICATION   In his critique of Meichenbaum's approach, Patterson and Watkins (1996) raise some excellent questions that can apply to most cognitive behavioral approaches. The basic issue is discovering the best way to change a client's internal dialogue. Is directly teaching the client the most effective approach? Is the client's failure to think rationally or logically always due to a lack of understanding of reasoning or problem solving? Is learning by self-discovery more effective and longer lasting than being taught by a therapist? Although we don't have definitive answers to these questions yet, we cannot assume that learning occurs *only* by teaching. It is a mistake to conclude that therapy is mainly a cognitive process. Experiential therapies stress that learning also involves emotions and self-discovery.

 COGNITIVE BEHAVIOR THERAPY
FROM A MULTICULTURAL PERSPECTIVE

Contributions to Multicultural Counseling

The cognitive behavioral approaches have certain advantages in multicultural counseling situations. If therapists understand the core values of their culturally diverse clients, they can help clients explore these values and gain a full awareness of their conflicting feelings. Then client and therapist can work together to modify selected beliefs and practices.

Because counselors with a cognitive behavioral orientation function as teachers, clients' focus on learning skills to deal with the problems of living. In speaking with colleagues who work with culturally diverse populations, I have learned that their clients tend to appreciate the emphasis on cognition and action, as well as the stress on relationship issues. Beck's collaborative approach offers clients the structure they often feel they need, yet the therapist still makes every effort to enlist their active cooperation and participation.

The constructivist dimension of cognitive therapy provides clients with a framework to think about their thinking and to determine the impact their beliefs have on what they do. Within the framework of their cultural values and worldview, clients can explore their beliefs and provide their own reinterpretations of significant life events. The cognitive behavioral practitioner can guide clients in a manner that respects their underlying values. This dimension is especially important in those cases where counselors are from a different cultural background or do not share the same worldview as their clients.

Limitations for Multicultural Counseling

Exploring values plays an important role in all of the cognitive behavioral approaches, and it is crucial for therapists to have some understanding of the cultural background of clients and to be sensitive to their struggles. Therapists would do well to use caution in challenging clients about their beliefs and behaviors until they clearly understand their cultural context.

Consider an Asian American client, Sung, from a culture that stresses values such as doing one's best, cooperation, interdependence, and working hard. It is likely that Sung is struggling with feelings of shame and guilt if she perceives that she is not living up to the expectations and standards set for her by her family and her community. She may feel that she is bringing shame to her family if she is going through a divorce. If a counselor confronts Sung too quickly on living by the expectations of others, or on her "dependency," the results are likely to be counterproductive. In fact, she may leave counseling because she feels misunderstood.

One of the shortcomings of applying cognitive behavior therapy to diverse cultures pertains to the hesitation of some clients to question their basic cultural values. Dattilio (1995a) notes that some Mediterranean and Middle Eastern cultures have strict rules with regard to religion, marriage and family, and child-rearing practices. These rules are often in conflict with the cognitive behavioral suggestions of disputation. For example, a therapist might suggest to a woman that she question her husband's motive. Clearly, in some Middle Eastern or other Asian cultures, such questioning is forbidden. Thus, modifications in a therapist's style need to be made.

One limitation of REBT in multicultural settings stems from its negative view of dependency. Many cultures view interdependence as necessary to good mental health. According to Ellis (1994), REBT is aimed at inducing people to examine and change some of their most basic values. Clients with certain long-cherished cultural values pertaining to interdependence are not likely to respond favorably to forceful methods of persuasion toward independence.

A potential limitation of the cognitive behavioral approaches is that culturally different clients could become dependent on the counselor to make decisions about what constitutes rationality and about the appropriate ways to solve problems. Cognitive behavior therapists walk a fine line between being directive and promoting dependence. Such practitioners may be directive, yet it is important that they teach their clients to question and to assume an active role in the therapeutic process.

 # WHERE TO GO FROM HERE

The Journal of Rational-Emotive and Cognitive-Behavior Therapy is published by Human Sciences Press, 72 Fifth Avenue, New York, NY 10011-8004. This quarterly journal is an excellent way to keep informed of the developments of REBT. Subscriptions are $55 a year for individuals.

The Albert Ellis Institute in New York City offers a variety of professional training involving a primary (3-day) certificate, an advanced (5-day) certificate, an associate fellowship, and a fellowship program. The institute also offers a "home-study" primary certificate program. Students get direct hands-on training supervision in REBT disputing and assessment techniques. Each of these programs has requirements in the areas of clinical experience, supervision, and personal experience in therapy. Therapists who wish to practice REBT are encouraged to participate in some form of directly supervised training.

Several affiliated branches of REBT around the world offer official programs of study. You can get a catalog describing REBT training programs, workshops, books, cassette tapes, films, self-help forms, software items, and an order form for publications from:

Albert Ellis Institute
45 East 65th Street
New York, NY 10021-6593
Telephone: (212) 535-0822 or (800) 323-4738
Fax: (212) 249-3582
E-mail: info@rebt.org
Website: http:// www.rebt.org

The institute and many affiliated centers throughout the country provide official training programs that qualify for the Primary Training Certificate in REBT for professionals. Some of the places where this training is available are Riverside, California; Denver, Colorado; Tampa, Florida;

Jamesville, Iowa; Lake Oswego, Oregon; Wilkes-Barre, Pennsylvania; and Charlottesville, Virginia. For information regarding international affiliated training centers and for a list of training institutes in the United States, contact the Albert Ellis Institute. Training outside the United States is available through the affiliated centers in Australia, Canada, England, Germany, France, India, Israel, Italy, Mexico, and the Netherlands.

As a way of keeping up with the theory, practice, and research in cognitive therapy, consult the *Journal of Cognitive Psychotherapy: An International Quarterly,* edited by Dr. Robert Leahy.

> *American Institute for Cognitive Therapy*
> 136 East 57th Street, Suite 1101
> New York, NY 10022
> E-mail: AICT@aol.com
> Website: *www.CognitiveTherapyNYC.com*

The International Association for Cognitive Psychotherapy (*http://iacp.asu. edu*) provides information about the journal as well as other cognitive therapy resources.

The Center for Cognitive Therapy, Newport Beach, California, maintains a Website (*http://www.padesky.com*) for mental health professionals. They list cognitive therapy books, audio and video training tapes, current advanced training workshops, and other cognitive therapy resources and information. E-mail: *mooney@padesky.com*

For more information about a one-year, full-time postdoctoral fellowship and for shorter term clinical institutes, contact:

> *Beck Institute for Cognitive Therapy and Research*
> GSB Building
> City Line and Belmont Avenues, Suite 700
> Bala Cynwyd, PA 19004-1610
> Telephone: (610) 664-3020
> Fax: (610) 664-4437
> E-mail: *beckinst@gim.net*
> Website: *http://www.beckinstitute.org*

For information regarding ongoing training and supervision in cognitive therapy, contact:

> *Department of Clinical Psychology*
> Philadelphia College of Osteopathic Medicine
> 4190 City Avenue
> Philadelphia, PA 19131-1693
> Website: *www.pcom.edu/academicprograms/psyd/index.html*

Recommended Supplementary Readings

Better, Deeper, and More Enduring Brief Therapy: The Rational Emotive Behavior Therapy Approach (Ellis, 1996) applies REBT to brief therapy and shows how it helps clients *get* better rather than merely *feel* better.

The Practice of Rational-Emotive Behavior Therapy, 2nd ed. (Ellis & Dryden, 1997) is the most up-to-date and comprehensive summary of REBT practice.

A Guide to Rational Living (Ellis & Harper, 1997) is a revised and updated self-help book that presents a straightforward approach to REBT, based on homework assignments and self-questioning.

Rational Emotive Behavior Therapy: A Therapist's Guide (Ellis & MacLaren, 1998) is an excellent comprehensive guidebook that gives clear descriptions of cognitive, emotive/experiential, and behavioral techniques. A useful chapter describes the integration of REBT with other therapeutic approaches.

How to Make Yourself Happy and Remarkably Less Disturbable (Ellis, 1999) presents a wide range of techniques for challenging self-defeating beliefs and trying on new behaviors. It is a user-friendly self-help book that is fun to read.

Cognitive Therapy: Basics and Beyond (J. Beck, 1995) covers the nuts and bolts of cognitive therapy with all populations and cites important research on cognitive therapy since its inception.

Cognitive Therapy of Depression (Beck et al., 1979) is a classic text describing techniques used with depressed clients. The wide range of cognitive techniques is a useful handbook for practitioners.

Comprehensive Casebook of Cognitive Therapy (Freeman & Dattilio, 1992b) provides a good introduction to cognitive therapy. This edited book presents an array of treatment approaches for specific clinical problems.

Mind Over Mood: Change How You Feel by Changing the Way You Think (Greenberger & Padesky, 1995) provides step-by-step worksheets to identify moods, solve problems, and test thoughts related to depression, anxiety, anger, guilt, and shame. This is a popular self-help workbook and a valuable tool for therapists and clients learning cognitive therapy skills.

Clinician's Guide to Mind Over Mood (Padesky & Greenberger, 1995) shows therapists how to integrate *Mind Over Mood* in therapy and use cognitive therapy treatment protocols for specific diagnoses. This succinct overview of cognitive therapy has troubleshooting guides, reviews cultural issues, and offers guidelines for individual, couples, and group therapy.

Frontiers of Cognitive Therapy (Salkovskis, 1996) is an excellent edited text that describes the present status of cognitive therapy and applies cognitive therapy to a wide range of psychological problems.

Cognitive Behavior Modification: An Integrative Approach (Meichenbaum, 1977) integrates the techniques of behavior therapy with the clinical concerns of the cognitive approaches. The author summarizes both empirical studies and clinical techniques and offers a number of innovative procedures, such as self-instructional training.

References and Suggested Readings*

*ALFORD, B. A., & BECK, A. T. (1997). *The integrative power of cognitive therapy.* New York: Guilford Press.

ARNKOFF, D. B., & GLASS, C. R. (1992). Cognitive therapy and psychotherapy integration. In D. K. Freedheim (Ed.), *History of psychotherapy: A century of change* (pp. 657–694). Washington, DC: American Psychological Association.

BECK, A. T. (1963). Thinking and depression: Idiosyncratic content and cognitive distortions. *Archives of General Psychiatry, 9,* 324–333.

---

*Books and articles marked with an asterisk are suggested for further study.

BECK, A. T. (1967). *Depression: Clinical, experimental, and theoretical aspects.* New York: Harper & Row. (Republished as *Depression: Causes and treatment.* Philadelphia: University of Pennsylvania Press, 1972.)

*BECK, A. T. (1976). *Cognitive therapy and emotional disorders.* New York: International Universities Press.

BECK, A. T. (1987). Cognitive therapy. In J. K. Zeig (Ed.), *The evolution of psychotherapy* (pp. 149–178). New York: Brunner/Mazel.

*BECK, A. T. (1988). *Love is never enough.* New York: Harper & Row.

BECK, A. T. (1991a). Cognitive therapy as the integrative therapy: A reply to Alford and Norcross [Commentary]. *Journal of Psychotherapy Integration, 1*(3), 191–198.

BECK, A. T. (1991b). Cognitive therapy: A 30-year retrospective. *American Psychologist, 46*(4), 368–375.

BECK, A. T. (1993). Cognitive therapy: Past, present, and future. *Journal of Consulting and Clinical Psychology, 61*(2), 194–198.

BECK, A. T., & HAAGA, D. A. F. (1992). The future of cognitive therapy. *Psychotherapy, 29*(1), 34–38.

*BECK, A. T., RUSH, A., SHAW, B., & EMERY, G. (1979). *Cognitive therapy of depression.* New York: Guilford Press.

BECK, A. T., & WEISHAAR, M. E. (1995). In R. J. Corsini & D. Wedding (Eds.), *Current psychotherapies* (5th ed., pp. 229–261). Itasca, IL: F. E. Peacock.

BECK, A., WRIGHT, E. D., NEWMAN, C. E., & LIESE, B. (1993). *Cognitive therapy of substance abuse.* New York: Guilford Press.

*BECK, J. S. (1995). *Cognitive therapy: Basics and beyond.* New York: Guilford Press.

*BURNS, D. (1988). *Feeling good: The new mood therapy.* New York: Signet.

BURNS, D. (1989). *The feeling good handbook.* New York: Morrow.

COREY, G. (2000). *Theory and practice of group counseling* (5th ed.). Pacific Grove, CA: Brooks-Cole/Wadsworth.

*COREY, G. (2001). *Case approach to counseling and psychotherapy* (5th ed.). Pacific Grove, CA: Brooks-Cole/Wadsworth.

*COREY, G., ELLIS, A., & COOKER, P. (1998). Challenging the internal dialogue of group counselors. *Journal of the Mississippi Counseling Association, 6*(1), 36–44.

DATTILIO, F. M. (1993). Cognitive techniques with couples and families. *The Family Journal, 1*(1), 51–65.

DATTILIO, F. M. (1994). Families in crisis. In F. M. Dattilio & A. Freeman (Eds.), *Cognitive-behavioral strategies in crisis intervention* (pp. 278–301). New York: Guilford Press.

DATTILIO, F. M. (1995a). Cognitive therapy in Egypt. *Journal of Cognitive Psychotherapy, 9*(4), Winter, 285–286.

DATTILIO, F. M. (1995b). Nonpharmacological alternatives to the treatment of panic in crises and emergency settings. *Current Psychiatry, 2*(2), 236–253.

*DATTILIO, F. M. (1998). (Ed.). *Case studies in couple and family therapy: Systemic and cognitive perspectives.* New York: Guilford Press.

*DATTILIO, F. M., & FREEMAN, A. (1992). Introduction to cognitive therapy. In A. Freeman & E. M. Dattilio (Eds.), *Comprehensive casebook of cognitive therapy* (pp. 3–11). New York: Plenum.

*DATTILIO, F. M., & FREEMAN, A. (Eds.). (1994). *Cognitive-behavioral strategies in crisis intervention.* New York: Guilford Press.

*DATTILIO, F. M., & PADESKY, C. A. (1990). *Cognitive therapy with couples.* Sarasota, FL: Professional Resources Exchange.

DATTILIO, F. M., & SALAS-AUVERT, J. A. (1998). *Panic disorders: Multiple treatment perspectives.* Phoenix, AZ: Zeig/Tucker & Company.

DeRUBEIS, R. J., & BECK, A. T. (1988). Cognitive therapy. In K. S. Dobson (Ed.), *Handbook of cognitive-behavioral therapies* (pp. 273–306). New York: Guilford Press.

DOBSON, K. S., & BLOCK, L. (1988). Historical and philosophical bases of the cognitive-behavioral therapies. In K. S. Dobson (Ed.), *Handbook of cognitive-behavioral therapies* (pp. 3–38). New York: Guilford Press.

DRYDEN, W. (1989). Albert Ellis: An efficient and passionate life. *Journal of Counseling and Development, 67*(10), 539–546.

DRYDEN, W. (1995a). *Brief rational emotive behaviour therapy.* London: Wiley.

DRYDEN, W. (1995b). *Rational emotive behaviour therapy: A Reader.* London: Sage.

DRYDEN, W., & ELLIS, A. (1988). Rational-emotive therapy. In K. S. Dobson (Ed.), *Handbook of cognitive-behavioral therapies* (pp. 214–272). New York: Guilford Press.

ELLIS, A. (1973). *Humanistic psychotherapy: The rational-emotive approach.* New York: Julian Press.

ELLIS, A. (1979a). The practice of rational-emotive therapy. In A. Ellis & J. Whiteley (Eds.), *Theoretical and empirical foundations of rational-emotive therapy* (pp. 61–100). Pacific Grove, CA: Brooks/Cole.

ELLIS, A. (1979b). Rational-emotive therapy. In A. Ellis & J. M. Whiteley (Eds.), *Theoretical and empirical foundations of rational-emotive therapy* (pp. 1–6). Pacific Grove, CA: Brooks/Cole.

ELLIS, A. (1979c). Rational-emotive therapy: Research data that support the clinical and personality hypotheses of RET and other modes of cognitive-behavior therapy. In A. Ellis & J. M. Whiteley (Eds.), *Theoretical and empirical foundations of rational-emotive therapy* (pp. 101–173). Pacific Grove, CA: Brooks/Cole.

ELLIS, A. (1979d). The theory of rational-emotive therapy. In A. Ellis & J. Whiteley (Eds.), *Theoretical and empirical foundations of rational-emotive therapy* (pp. 33–60). Pacific Grove, CA: Brooks/Cole.

ELLIS, A. (1979e). Toward a new theory of personality. In A. Ellis & J. Whiteley (Eds.), *Theoretical and empirical foundations of rational-emotive therapy* (pp. 7–32). Pacific Grove, CA: Brooks/Cole.

ELLIS, A. (1985). *Overcoming resistance: Rational-emotive therapy with difficult clients.* New York: Springer.

ELLIS, A. (1986). Rational-emotive therapy. In I. L. Kutash & A. Wolf (Eds.), *Psychotherapist's casebook* (pp. 277–287). San Francisco: Jossey-Bass.

ELLIS, A. (1987a). The evolution of rational-emotive therapy (RET) and cognitive behavior therapy (CBT). In J. K. Zeig (Ed)., *The evolution of psychotherapy* (pp. 107–132). New York: Brunner/Mazel.

ELLIS, A. (1987b). The impossibility of achieving consistently good mental health. *American Psychologist, 42*(4), 364–375.

ELLIS, A. (1988). *How to stubbornly refuse to make yourself miserable about anything—Yes, anything!* Secaucus, NJ: Lyle Stuart.

ELLIS, A. (1991a). Achieving self-actualization. In A. Jones & R. Crandall (Eds.), *Handbook of self-actualization.* Corte Madera, CA: Select Press.

ELLIS, A. (1991b). The revised ABC's of rational-emotive therapy. In J. Zeig (Ed.), *The evolution of psychotherapy: The second conference.* New York: Brunner/Mazel. (Expanded version: *Journal of Rational-Emotive and Cognitive-Behavior Therapy, 9,* 139–172.)

ELLIS, A. (1991c). Using RET effectively: Reflections and interview. In M. E. Bernard (Ed.), *Using rational-emotive therapy effectively* (pp. 1–33). New York: Plenum.

*ELLIS, A. (1994). *Reason and emotion in psychotherapy revised.* Secaucus, NJ: Birch Lane.

ELLIS, A. (1995). Rational emotive behavior therapy. In R. J. Corsini & D. Wedding (Eds.), *Current psychotherapies* (5th ed., pp. 162–196). Itasca, IL: F. E. Peacock.

*ELLIS, A. (1996). *Better, deeper, and more enduring brief therapy: The rational emotive behavior therapy approach.* New York: Brunner/Mazel.

*ELLIS, A. (1997). The evolution of Albert Ellis and rational emotive behavior therapy. In J. K. Zeig (Ed.), *The evolution of psychotherapy: The third conference* (pp. 69–82). New York: Brunner/Mazel.

*ELLIS, A. (1998). *How to control your anxiety before it controls you.* Secaucus, NJ: Carol Publishing Group.

*ELLIS, A. (1999). *How to make yourself happy and remarkably less disturbable.* San Luis Obispo, CA: Impact.

*ELLIS, A., & BLAU, S. (1998). *The Albert Ellis reader.* Secaucus, NJ: Carol Publishing Group.

*ELLIS, A., & DRYDEN, W. (1997). *The practice of rational-emotive therapy.* (rev. ed.). New York: Springer.

ELLIS, A., GORDON, J., NEENAN, M., & PALMER, S. (1997). *Stress counseling.* London: Cassell & New York: Springer.

*ELLIS, A., & HARPER, R. (1997). *A guide to rational living* (3rd ed). No. Hollywood, CA: Wilshire.

*ELLIS, A., & MACLAREN, C. (1998). *Rational emotive behavior therapy: A therapist's guide.* San Luis Obispo, CA: Impact.

ELLIS, A., & TAFRATE, R. C. (1997). *How to control your anger—before it controls you.* Secaucus, NJ: Birch Lane.

ELLIS, A., & VELTEN, E. (1992). *When AA doesn't work: Rational steps for quitting alcohol.* New York: Barricade Books.

*ELLIS, A., & VELTEN, E. (1998). *Optimal aging: How to get over growing older.* Chicago: Open Court.

ELLIS, A., & YEAGER, R. J. (1989). *Why some therapies don't work.* Buffalo, NY: Prometheus Books.

ELLIS, T. E., & NEWMAN, C. F. (1996). *Choosing to live: How to defeat suicide through cognitive therapy.* Oakland, CA: New Harbinger.

FREEMAN, A., & DATTILIO, F. M. (1992a). Cognitive therapy in the year 2000. In A. Freeman & F. M. Dattilio (Eds.), *Comprehensive casebook of cognitive therapy* (pp. 375–379). New York: Plenum.

FREEMAN, A., & DATTILIO, R. M. (Eds.). (1992b). *Comprehensive casebook of cognitive therapy.* New York: Plenum.

FREEMAN, A., & DATTILIO, R. M. (1994). Cognitive therapy. In J. L. Ronch, W. Van Ornum, & N. C. Stilwell, (Eds.), *The counseling sourcebook: A practical reference on contemporary issues* (pp. 60–71). New York: Continuum Press.

FREEMAN, A., & DEWOLF, R. (1990). *Woulda, coulda, shoulda.* New York: Morrow.

GRANVOLD, D. K. (Ed.). (1994). *Cognitive and behavioral treatment: Method and applications.* Pacific Grove, CA: Brooks/Cole.

GREENBERGER, D., & PADESKY, C. A. (1995). *Mind over mood: Change how you feel by changing the way you think.* New York: Guilford Press.

HAAGA, D. A., & DAVISON, G. C. (1986). Cognitive change methods. In F. H. Kanfer & A. P. Goldstein (Eds.), *Helping people change: A textbook of methods* (3rd ed., pp. 236–282). New York: Pergamon Press.

HORNEY, K. (1950). *Neurosis and human growth.* New York: Norton.

KWEE, M. G. T., & ELLIS, A. (1997). Can multimodal and rational emotive behavioral therapy be reconciled? *Journal of Rational-Emotive and Cognitive-Behavior Therapy, 15,* 95–132.

LINDSLEY, J. R. (1994). Rationalist therapy in a constructivistic frame. *The Behavior Therapist, 17*(7), 160–162.

MAHONEY, M. J. (1991). *Human change processes: The scientific foundations of psychotherapy.* New York: Basic Books.

MAHONEY, M. J., & LYDDON, W. (1988). Recent developments in cognitive approaches to counseling and psychotherapy. *Counseling Psychology, 16,* 190–234.

MAULTSBY, M. C. (1984). *Rational behavior therapy.* Englewood Cliffs, NJ: Prentice-Hall.

*MEICHENBAUM, D. (1977). *Cognitive behavior modification: An integrative approach.* New York: Plenum.

*MEICHENBAUM, D. (1985). *Stress inoculation training.* New York: Pergamon Press.

MEICHENBAUM, D. (1986). Cognitive behavior modification. In F. H. Kanfer & A. P. Goldstein (Eds.), *Helping people change: A textbook of methods* (pp. 346–380). New York: Pergamon Press.

MEICHENBAUM, D. (1994). *A clinical handbook/practical therapist manual: For assessing and treating adults with post-traumatic stress disorder (PTSD).* Waterloo, Ontario: Institute Press.

*MEICHENBAUM, D. (1997). The evolution of a cognitive-behavior therapist. In J. K. Zeig (Ed.), *The evolution of psychotherapy: The third conference* (pp. 96–104). New York: Brunner/Mazel.

NEIMEYER, R. A. (1993a). An appraisal of constructivist psychotherapies. *Journal of Consulting and Clinical Psychology, 61*(2), 221–234.

NEIMEYER, R. A. (1993b). Constructivism and the cognitive psychotherapies: Some conceptual and strategic contrasts. *Journal of Cognitive Psychotherapy, 7*(3), 159–171.

NEIMEYER, R. A., & LYDDON, W. J. (1993). Constructivist psychotherapy: Principles into practice. *Journal of Cognitive Psychotherapy, 7*(3), 155–157.

PADESKY, C. A., & GREENBERGER, D. (1995). *Clinician's guide to* Mind Over Mood. New York: Guilford Press.

PATTERSON, C. H., & WATKINS, C. E. (1996). *Theories of psychotherapy* (5th ed.). New York: Harper/Collins.

REINEKE, M., DATTILIO, E. M., & FREEMAN, A. (Eds.). (1995). *Casebook of cognitive behavior therapy with children and adolescents.* New York: Guilford Press.

*SALKOVSKIS, P. M. G. (1996). *Frontiers of cognitive therapy.* New York: Guilford Press.

WALEN, S., DIGIUSEPPE, R., & DRYDEN, W. (1992). *A practitioner's guide to rational-emotive therapy.* New York: Oxford University Press.

WARREN, R., & MCLELLARN, R. W. (1987). What do RET therapists think they are doing? An international survey. *Journal of Rational-Emotive Therapy, 5*(2), 92–107.

WEISHAAR, M. E. (1993). *Aaron T. Beck.* London: Sage.

WESSLER, R. L. (1986). Varieties of cognitions in the cognitively oriented psychotherapies. In A. Ellis & R. Grieger (Eds.), *Handbook of rational-emotive therapy: Vol. 2* (pp. 46–58). New York: Springer.

YANKURA, J., & DRYDEN, W. (1994). *Albert Ellis.* Thousand Oaks, CA: Sage.

CHAPTER

12

Feminist Therapy

Co-authored by Barbara Herlihy and Gerald Corey

INTRODUCTION
   History and Development
KEY CONCEPTS
   View of Human Nature
   Feminist Perspective on Personality Development
   Challenging Traditional Roles for Women
   Principles of Feminist Psychology
THE THERAPEUTIC PROCESS
   Therapeutic Goals
   Therapist's Function and Role
   Client's Experience in Therapy
   Relationship Between Therapist and Client
APPLICATION: Therapeutic Techniques and Procedures
   The Role of Assessment and Diagnosis
   Techniques and Strategies
   The Role of Men in Feminist Therapy
FEMINIST THERAPY APPLIED TO THE CASE OF STAN
SUMMARY AND EVALUATION
   Summary
   Contributions of Feminist Therapy
   Limitations and Criticisms of Feminist Therapy
FEMINIST THEORY FROM A MULTICULTURAL PERSPECTIVE
   Contributions to Multicultural Counseling
   Limitations for Multicultural Counseling
WHERE TO GO FROM HERE
RECOMMENDED SUPPLEMENTARY READINGS
REFERENCES AND SUGGESTED READINGS

SOME CONTEMPORARY FEMINIST THERAPISTS

Feminist therapy does not have a single founder. Rather, it has been a collective effort by many. We have selected a few individuals who have made significant contributions to feminist therapy for inclusion here, recognizing full well that many others equally influential could have appeared in this space, Feminist therapy is truly founded on a theory of inclusion.

J EAN BAKER MILLER is a Clinical Professor of Psychiatry at Boston University School of Medicine and Director of the Jean Baker Miller Training Institute at the Stone Center, Wellesley College. She has written *Toward a New Psychology of Women* and co-authored *The Healing Connection: How Women Form Relationships in Therapy and in Life* and *Women's Growth in Connection.* A practicing psychiatrist and psychoanalyst, Dr. Miller is a fellow of the American Psychiatric Association, the American College of Psychiatrists, American Orthopsychiatric Association, American Academy of Psychoanalysis, and has been a member of the board of trustees of the last two. In recent decades, Dr. Miller has been collaborating with diverse groups of scholars and colleagues to continue development of relational/cultural theory. She has been expanding this theory and exploring new applications to complex issues in psychotherapy and beyond, including issues of diversity, social action, and workplace change.

C AROLYN ZERBE ENNS is Associate Professor of Psychology at Cornell College in Mt. Vernon, Iowa. She also maintains a part-time appointment at the University Counseling Service, University of Iowa. Dr. Enns became interested in feminist therapy while she was completing her Ph.D. in Counseling Psychology at the University of California, Santa Barbara. She has devoted much of her work to exploring the diversity of feminist theories that inform the work of feminist therapists. It is Dr. Enn's conviction that therapists' feminist theoretical orientations can have a profound impact on the manner in which therapists implement feminist therapy values, and she discusses these themes in her book, *Feminist Theories and Feminist Psychotherapies: Origins, Themes, and Variations.* As an extension of her commitment to social change, Dr. Enns served from 1994 to 1998 as Chair of the

American Psychological Association's Division 17 (Counseling Psychology) Committee on Women Task Force on Memories of Childhood Sexual Abuse. Her most recent efforts are directed toward articulating the importance of multicultural feminist therapy and understanding the practice of feminist therapy around the world.

Latina Healers: Lives of Power and Tradition and *Latina Realities: Essays on Healing, Sexuality, and Migration* have recently appeared. *Women Crossing Boundaries: A Psychology of Immigration and the Transformation of Sexuality,* based on a study of women immigrants from all over the world, was published by Routledge in 1999.

OLIVA M. ESPIN, Ph.D., is Professor of Women's Studies at San Diego State University and core faculty at the California School of Professional Psychology, San Diego. She is a pioneer in the theory and practice of feminist therapy with women from different cultural backgrounds and has done extensive research, teaching, and training on multicultural issues in psychology. Professor Espin has published on psychotherapy with Latinas, women immigrants and refugees, the sexuality of Latinas, language in therapy with fluent bilinguals, and training clinicians to work with multicultural populations. A native of Cuba, she did her undergraduate work in psychology at the Universidad de Costa Rica and her doctorate in Counselor Education and Latin American Studies at the University of Florida. Dr. Espin has co-edited *Refugee Women and Their Mental Health: Shattered Societies, Shattered Lives.* Her books

LAURA S. BROWN, Ph.D., is a founding member of the Feminist Therapy Institute, an organization dedicated to the support of advanced practice in feminist therapy, and a member of the theory workgroup at the National Conference on Education and Training in Feminist Practice. She has written several books considered core to feminist practice in psychotherapy and counseling. Her text, *Subversive Dialogues: Theory in Feminist Therapy* is considered by many to be the foundation book addressing how theory informs practice in feminist therapy. She has made particular contributions to thinking about ethics and boundaries, and the complexities of ethical practice in small communities. Her current interests include feminist forensic psychology and the application of feminist priniciples to treatment of trauma survivors. ■

INTRODUCTION

This chapter provides an alternative perspective to many of the models considered thus far in this book. As you will see, feminist therapy puts gender and power at the core of the therapeutic process. It is built on the premise that it is essential to consider the social and cultural context that contributes to a person's problems in order to understand that person. My (Jerry Corey's) own training did not include a feminist perspective—or, for that matter, a systemic or a multicultural perspective—yet I have become convinced that the feminist perspective offers a unique approach to understanding the roles that both women and men have been socialized to accept.*

The majority of clients in counseling are women, and the majority of psychotherapy practitioners at the master's level are women. Thus, the need for a theory that evolves from the thinking and experiencing of women seems self-evident. When we introduce our students to feminist therapy, we often ask them what all the following theories have in common: psychoanalysis, Adlerian therapy, Gestalt therapy, rational emotive behavior therapy, reality therapy, and person-centered therapy. Students are usually quick to come up with the answer: all of these theories were founded by White males from Western (American or European) cultures. Prochaska and Norcross (1999) make the point that contemporary counseling and psychotherapy were created by Western, White men in their own image and that psychotherapy based on a White, male definition of mental health and mental illness ignores the needs of the diverse populations it professes to serve.

Feminist therapists have helped us to question some of the basic assumptions of our profession: Are women more prone to depression, for example, or are they more likely to be *diagnosed* with depression in our society? Can theories developed by White males from Western cultures appropriately serve the needs of women clients in counseling? The needs of women of color?

Culture entails the sociopolitical reality of people's lives, including how the privileged dominant group (White males) treats those who are different from them. Feminist therapists believe psychotherapy is inextricably bound to culture, and increasingly they are being joined by thoughtful leaders in the field. Allen Ivey, for instance, has stated that he has become increasingly aware of the contradictions and limitations of our Eurocentric, male construction of the helping process and that he now believes all helping practice is based on a set of cultural assumptions (Ivey, 1993).

A central concept in feminist therapy is the psychological oppression of women and the constraints imposed by the sociopolitical status to which women have been relegated. The socialization of women inevitably affects

---

*I invited a colleague and friend, Dr. Barbara Herlihy, who is a professor of counselor education at the University of New Orleans, to take the leading role in co-authoring this chapter. We have presented at national conferences and co-authored three books (Herlihy & Corey, 1992; Herlihy & Corey, 1996; Herlihy & Corey, 1997). It seemed like a natural basis for collaboration on a project that we both considered valuable.

their identity development, self-concept, goals and aspirations, and emotional well-being. Our society reinforces dependent, submissive, and self-sacrificing behaviors in women. As Miriam Polster has stated, growing up female in our society "leaves a psychological residue that cripples and deforms all but the most exceptional women" (as cited in Franks & Burtle, 1974, p. 257).

History and Development

Feminist therapy has developed in a grassroots manner, responding to challenges and to the emerging needs of women (Brabeck & Brown, 1997). No single individual can be identified as the founder of this approach, and its history is relatively brief. The beginnings of feminist therapy can be traced to the women's movement of the 1960s, a time when women began uniting their voices to express their dissatisfaction with the limiting and confining nature of traditional female roles. Consciousness-raising groups, in which small groups of women came together to share their experiences and perceptions, helped individual women become aware that they were not alone in their views. A sisterhood developed, and some of the services that evolved from women's collective desires to improve society included shelters for battered women, rape crisis centers, and women's health and reproductive health centers.

Consciousness-raising groups had a significant impact on women, but these groups did not aim to change psychotherapy as it was traditionally practiced. Self-help, rather than "professional" help, was considered the most efficacious mode for helping women break free from role constraints and attitudes resulting from their early socialization. Because the therapeutic relationship is hierarchical, with the therapist in the power position, psychotherapy was viewed as a means of maintaining the oppressive status quo. Chesler (1972) compared psychotherapy to the relationship between a patient and a patriarch in which adjustment or mental health was equated with submission to the will of the therapist. It was said that "feminists do not practice *therapy* on their sisters" (Tennov, 1973, p. 110).

Changes in psychotherapy occurred only when women therapists participated in consciousness-raising groups and were changed by their experiences. They formed feminist therapy groups that operated from the same norms as the consciousness-raising groups, including nonhierarchical structures, equal sharing of resources and power, and empowerment of women that could be achieved by practicing new skills and ways of being in a safe environment.

Feminist principles also began to find their way into the work that many women therapists were doing with their individual clients. Believing that personal counseling was also a legitimate means to effect change, they viewed therapy as a partnership between equals. As therapists became sensitive to the potentially destructive power dynamics in therapy, they began building mutuality into the therapeutic process. They took the stance that therapy needed to move away from reliance on an intrapsychic psychopathology perspective (in which the sources of a woman's unhappiness or mental illness reside within her) to a focus on understanding the pathological forces in the culture that damage and constrain women. This focus forms the basis for one of the basic tenets of feminist therapy—that *the personal is political.*

Other forces that emerged in the 1970s that helped further feminist therapy were a profusion of research on sex and gender bias; the support of the Association for Women in Psychology (AWP); and various efforts by the American Psychological Association (APA) such as the Task Force on Sex Bias and Sex Role Stereotyping (APA, 1975) and APA's Division 35 (Psychology of Women), the publication of several special issues of journals, and the "Principles Concerning the Counseling and Therapy of Women" (APA, 1979). As the decade ended, however, feminist therapists had yet to develop a distinct theory and tended instead to pick and choose from mainstream theoretical perspectives (Enns, 1993).

The 1980s were marked by efforts to define feminist therapy as an entity in its own right (Enns, 1993). Gilligan's (1977, 1982) work on the different voice of women and the morality of care and the work of Miller (1976) and the Stone Center scholars on the self-in-relation model of women's development were influential in the development of a feminist personality theory. New theories emerged that honored the relational and cooperative nature of women's experiencing (Enns, 1991, 1997). Feminist therapists began to examine the relationship of feminist theory to traditional psychotherapy systems, and integrations with various existing systems were proposed. These efforts were particularly directed toward development of a feminist psychoanalysis (Chodorow, 1989; Lerner, 1988), feminist family therapy, and feminist career counseling.

By the 1980s feminist group therapy had changed dramatically, becoming more diverse as it focused increasingly on specific problems and issues such as body image, abusive relationships, eating disorders, and incest and sexual abuse (Enns, 1993). But by this time individual therapy was the most frequently practiced form of feminist therapy (Kaschak, 1981).

In the 1980s the feminist philosophies that guided the practice of therapy became more diverse. Enns (1993, 1997) identified four enduring feminist philosophies: liberal, cultural, radical, and socialist feminism. These philosophies all advocate activism as a goal but have differing views on the sources of oppression and the most effective methods of effecting changes in society. They are best seen as existing along a continuum rather than as completely separate philosophical stances. Practitioners interpret the basic tenets of feminist therapy in different ways depending on the feminist philosophy they espouse and their theoretical orientation.

Liberal feminists focus on helping individual women overcome the limits and constraints of their socialization patterns. These feminists tend to believe the differences between women and men will be less problematic as work and social environments become more bias-free. For liberal feminists, the major goals of therapy include personal empowerment of individual women, dignity, self-fulfillment, and equality.

Cultural feminists believe oppression stems from society's devaluation of women's strengths. They emphasize the differences between women and men and believe the solution to oppression lies in feminization of the culture so that society becomes more nurturing, cooperative, and relational. For cultural feminists, the major goal of therapy is the infusion of society with values based on cooperation.

Radical feminists focus on the oppression of women that is embedded in patriarchy and seek to change society through activism. Therapy is viewed as a political enterprise with the goal of transformation of society. The major goals are to transform gender relationships, to transform societal institutions, and to increase women's sexual and procreative self-determination.

Socialist feminists share with radical feminists the goal of societal change. Their emphasis differs, however, in that they focus on multiple oppressions and believe solutions to society's problems must include considerations of class, race, and other forms of discrimination. For socialist feminists, the major goal of therapy is to transform social relationships and institutions.

Since the early 1970s, several important critiques of the classic feminist theories have been offered by feminist women of color and postmodern feminists. Each of these new theoretical perspectives has focused on issues of diversity, the complexity of sexism, and the centrality of context to understanding gender issues. These newer developments are a primary focus of attention in feminist theory in the late 1990s.

In 1993 the National Conference on Education and Training in Feminist Practice drew over 75 psychologists who embraced a diversity of feminist perspectives. They met to discuss the principles of feminist psychological practice and reached consensus on a series of basic themes and premises underlying feminist practice. This conference represented a significant step toward integration of diverse feminist perspectives.

An ongoing challenge for feminist therapists will be to continue to work to integrate the disparate themes of past decades into a cohesive theory and to define the principles and practices that unify the various approaches to feminist therapy. According to Enns (1993), a goal for feminism in the future is to "search for balance between appreciating diversity between women, self-discovery, and self-determination while also maintaining some common framework that focuses on the collective transformation of society" (p. 48). Feminist therapy is not static, but is continually evolving.

Given the diversity of philosophies, and the fact that there is no set definition of feminist therapy, is it possible to determine just who is a feminist therapist? Many therapists, both male and female, support the ideals of the feminist movement. However, if they do not incorporate feminist methods of therapy in their practice, they would be erroneous in calling themselves feminist therapists (Brown, 1992). Feminist therapists, regardless of their philosophical orientation, believe gender is at the core of therapeutic practice, that understanding a client's problems requires adopting a sociocultural perspective, and that empowerment of the individual and societal changes are crucial goals in therapy.

KEY CONCEPTS

View of Human Nature

Worell and Remer (1992) indicate a number of salient characteristics that differentiate feminist theory from many of the traditional models. One fundamental difference is the view of human nature, which includes many of the assumptions underlying therapeutic practice. Many of the traditional theories grew out of a historical period in which social arrangements were assumed to be rooted in one's gender. Women and men were viewed as possessing different personality characteristics. It was assumed that women and men, because of biological gender differences, would pursue different directions in life. Worell and Remer describe six characteristics of traditional theories that reflect outdated assumptions about the role gender plays in behavior:

- An *androcentric theory* uses male-oriented constructs to draw conclusions about human nature.
- *Gendercentric theories* propose two separate paths of development for women and men.
- *Ethnocentric theories* assume that the facts pertaining to human development and interaction are similar across races, cultures, and nations.
- *Heterosexism* views a heterosexual orientation as normative and desirable, and devalues same-sex relationships.
- An *intrapsychic orientation* attributes behavior to intrapsychic causes, which often results in blaming the victim.
- *Determinism* assumes that present personality patterns and behavior are fixed at an early stage of development.

To the degree that traditional theories contain these gender-biased elements, they have clear limitations when it comes to counseling.

Worell and Remer (1992) describe the constructs of feminist theory, in contrast to traditional theories, as being gender-free, flexible, interactionist, and life-span-oriented. *Gender-free theories* explain differences in the behavior of women and men in terms of socialization processes, as opposed to explaining gender differences on the basis of "true" natures. These theories avoid stereotypes in social roles and interpersonal behavior. A *flexible theory* has concepts and strategies that apply equally to both individuals and groups regardless of age, race, culture, gender, or sexual orientation. *Interactionist theories* contain concepts specific to the thinking, feeling, and behaving dimensions of human experience, and include concepts that account for contextual and environmental factors. A *life-span perspective* assumes that human development is a lifelong process and that personality patterns and behavioral changes can occur at any time, rather than being fixed during early childhood. Worell and Remer provide procedures for evaluating the suitability of any theory for counseling women based on these criteria, and they offer suggestions for transforming a theory to conform to a feminist perspective.

Feminist Perspective on Personality Development

Feminist therapists emphasize that societal gender-role expectations profoundly influence a person's identity from the moment of birth and become deeply ingrained in adult personality. Because gender politics are imbedded in the fabric of American society, they influence how we see ourselves as girls and boys and as women and men throughout the course of our lives. "Girls are typically expected to be sweet, sensitive, and docile, while boys are expected to be strong, stoic, and brave" (Prochaska & Norcross, 1999, p. 403).

Chodorow (1978, 1989) has theorized that psychological differences between men and women are due to the fact that women are the primary caretakers who raise the children. The identity of girls is based on a sense of continuity in their relationship with their mothers, whereas boys form their identity by defining themselves as different from their mothers and by developing an identification with their fathers. Thus, girls learn from their mothers to be affiliative and nurturing and to place a high priority on relatedness and caring for others. At the same time, by identifying with mothers who sacrifice their own desires and goals to serve the family, girls reduce their capacity for autonomy and independence. Boys model the aggressive, power-seeking nature of adult males and thus reduce their capacity for the expression of empathy and certain emotions.

Recognizing that theories of human development were based almost exclusively on research with boys and men, Gilligan (1977) undertook a series of studies on women's moral and psychosocial development. As a result of her work, Gilligan came to believe women's sense of self and morality is based in issues of responsibility for and care of other people and is embedded in a cultural context. She posited that the concepts of connectedness and interdependence—virtually ignored in male-dominated developmental theories—are central to women's development. According to Gilligan (1982), women tend toward relationship, whereas men tend toward separation. In later years Gilligan expanded her work to explore crises faced by girls at adolescence. She asserts that it is difficult for girls to maintain a strong sense of identity and inner "voice" when to do so would be to risk disconnection in a society that does not honor their relational needs and desires. She was concerned that traits such as caring and compassion, which define the "goodness" of women, were seen as a deficit in their moral development and that their nurturing and caretaking roles were devalued in comparison to the values placed on independence and achievement.

Most models of human growth and development emphasize a struggle toward independence and autonomy, but feminists recognize that women are searching for a connectedness with others. In feminist therapy women's relational qualities are seen as strengths and as pathways for healthy growth and development instead of being identified as weaknesses or defects.

A number of writers, including Miller (1976, 1991), Miller and Stiver (1997), Jordan and her colleagues (1991), and Surrey (1991), have elaborated on the vital role that relationships and connectedness with others play in the lives of women. According to the *self-in-relation theory,* a woman's sense of self depends largely on how she connects with others. Surrey (1991), like Gilligan, believes women's identity and self-concept develop in the context of relationships. She sees the core self of women as including an interest in and an ability to form emotional connections with others. Women expect that a mutual and empathic relationship will enhance the development, empowerment, and self-knowledge of the parties involved in the relationship. Surrey, like Chodorow, believes the mother-daughter relationship is a crucially significant model for other relationships.

Sandra Bem's (1981, 1983, 1993) *gender schema theory* provides another perspective on the development of women. A schema is an organized set of mental associations people use to interpret what they see. For example, consider the varying interpretations that could be given by individuals watching a group of children at play. One person, using a leadership schema, might think, "How interesting that the youngest child is making up all the rules of the game." Another, using a health concerns schema, might think, "Those kids should not be out in the sun at noon." A third person might think, "The girls in the group are getting their clothes all dirty and sweaty—their mothers will be upset." This last person is using a gender schema to interpret the situation.

According to Bem (1981), children learn society's view of gender and apply it to themselves. They learn, for instance, that girls wear makeup and boys do not, that petite girls and tall boys are attractive, and that certain behaviors are desirable for girls to be considered "feminine" and for boys to be considered "masculine." Bem (1983, 1993) argues that gender schema is one of the strongest perceptual sets we use when looking at society and our place within it and that the ingrained gender schemas of American society are extremely limiting for *both* sexes. Sharf (2000) has noted that therapists who pay attention to their own gender schemas and those of their clients can become aware of patterns and interpretations that may be hampering progress in therapy.

Kaschak (1992) used the term *engendered lives* to describe her belief that gender is the organizing principle in people's lives. She has studied the role gender plays in shaping the identities of women and men and believes the masculine defines the feminine. For instance, because men pay great attention to women's bodies, women's appearance is given tremendous importance in Western society. Men, as the dominant group, determine the roles that women play. Men are not expected to control their sexual impulses, but women are expected both to remain chaste and to have sexually appealing bodies. Because women occupy a subordinate position, they must be able to interpret the needs and behaviors of the dominant group. To that end, women have developed "women's intuition" and have included in their gender schema the belief that women are less important than men. Women's roles include service to others, passivity, dependency, and lack of initiative.

Although most of the early research focused on women's development, the self-in-relation model and other feminist views on development have been expanded to include men. Feminist researchers have demonstrated that when all human development is seen through the lens of male gender, important qualities of both women and men are overlooked. Through the work of Gilligan, Miller, and others, we have new models of development to understand women and a new perspective that recognizes that both women and men have been misunderstood.

Challenging Traditional Roles for Women

Basow (1992) cites considerable research evidence that supports the existence of gender stereotypes, but there are signs that women increasingly recognize the price they have been paying for staying within the limited boundaries set for them by their culture. Basow emphasizes that gender stereotypes are powerful forces of social control but that women can choose either to be socially acceptable and conform or to rebel and deal with the consequences of being socially unacceptable.

Feminist therapists remind us that traditional gender stereotypes of women are still prevalent in our culture. Corey and Corey (1997) summarize some characteristics that are often associated with traditional roles:

- To a greater degree than men, women are expected to exhibit the qualities of warmth, expressiveness, and nurturance. They are expected to be kind, thoughtful, and caring. Many women have difficulty asking for these very qualities from others and do not allow themselves to receive nurturance.
- Women should not display an independent spirit. If women are assertive, they might well be viewed as being hostile and aggressive. If they display independence, men may accuse them of trying to "prove themselves" by taking on masculine roles.
- Rather than being rational and logical, women are traditionally viewed as being emotional and intuitive.
- Traditionally, traits such as passivity and submissiveness, a home orientation, being prone to tears and excitability in minor crises, indecisiveness, religiosity, and tactfulness are expected of the female role. If women deviate from these behavior patterns, they run the risk of being labeled "unfeminine."
- Women are viewed as being "naturally" interested in relationships more than in accomplishments. Rather than competing or striving to get ahead, women are expected to maintain relationships.

Feminist therapists teach their clients that uncritical acceptance of traditional roles can greatly restrict their range of freedom to define the kind of person they want to be. Today many women and men are resisting being so narrowly defined. Women and men in therapy learn that, if they choose to, they can experience mutual behavioral characteristics such as being both dependent and independent, giving to others and being open to receiving, thinking and feeling, and being tender and tough. Rather than being cemented to a single behavioral style, women and men who reject traditional roles are saying that they are entitled to express the complex range of characteristics that are appropriate for different situations.

SUMMARY   Chodorow's (1989) work on identity development, Gilligan's (1977, 1982) research into women's moral and psychosocial development, the self-in-relation concept, gender schema theory, the notion of engendered lives, and the permission to challenge gender stereotypes all have contributed to our understanding of women's development. Although each of these approaches emphasizes different aspects of development, they have much in common. According to Lerman (1986), they all view women in a positive light, encompass the diversity and complexity of women's lives, arise out of women's experience, and acknowledge the political and social oppression of women. Each has made a unique contribution and has had an impact on the practice of feminist therapy.

Principles of Feminist Psychology

A number of feminist writers have articulated core principles that form the foundation for the practice of feminist therapy. These principles are interrelated and have a great deal of overlap.

   1. *The personal is political.* A fundamental goal of feminist practice is social transformation: that is, to change the status quo and to improve the status and well-being of all women. Clients' individual problems have societal and political roots. Feminist therapy aims not only for individual change but for social change. Feminists view their therapy practice as existing not only to help individual clients in their struggles but also as a strategy for advancing a transformation in society. Direct action for social change is part of their responsibility as therapists. It is important that women who engage in the therapy process—clients and therapists alike—recognize that they have suffered from oppression as members of a subordinate group and that they can join with other women to right these wrongs. Identifying external sources of problems often results in anger, which can be harnessed as energy to take action for change. If the environment is a major source of pathology in the lives of women and men, then the toxic aspects of the environment must be changed if individual change is to occur. The goal is to advance a different vision of societal organization that frees both women and men from the constraints imposed by gender-role expectations.
   2. *The counseling relationship is egalitarian.* Attention to power is central in feminist therapy, and the therapeutic relationship is an egalitarian one. In feminist therapy the voices of the oppressed are acknowledged as authoritative and valuable sources of knowledge (Worell & Johnson, 1997). The person in the "client" role is seen as having the capacity to change and to produce change. Clients are active participants in defining themselves,

and the therapist is viewed as simply another source of information rather than as the best or "expert" source. Finding ways to share power with the client and to demystify therapy is essential because feminist therapists do not want to replicate in the therapy relationship society's power disparity and because they believe all relationships should strive for equality. Other elements essential to an egalitarian relationship are therapist self-disclosure when appropriate and clients' informed consent.

3. *Women's experiences are honored.* Women's experiences are considered central in understanding their distress. Traditional therapies that operate on androcentric norms compare women to the male norm and find them deviant. Our society has tended to devalue subjective experience in favor of the objective. A goal of feminist therapy is to replace patriarchal "objective truth" with feminist consciousness, which acknowledges a diversity of ways of knowing. Women are encouraged to express their emotions and their intuition and to use their personal experience as a touchstone for determining what is "reality." Theories of feminist therapy evolve from and reflect lived experiences that emerge from the relationships among the participants. Women's experiences include a number of gender-based phenomena such as rape, sexual assault, sexual harassment, childhood sexual abuse, eating disorders, and domestic violence. It is essential that therapists are aware of these phenomena.

4. *Definitions of distress and "mental illness" are reformulated.* Feminist therapy rejects the "disease model" of mental illness. Instead, feminist therapists consider intrapsychic and interpersonal factors as only partial explanations for the pain that brings people to therapy. External factors are also highly influential. Psychological distress is reframed, not as disease but as a communication about unjust systems. Pain is defined not as evidence of deficit or defect but as evidence of resistance and the skill and will to survive (Worell & Johnson, 1997). Resistance is seen as an indicator that the person is able to remain alive and powerful in the face of oppression (Brown, 1994).

Furthermore, by considering contextual variables, symptoms are reframed as survival strategies. Women's responses to pathological environmental forces are not viewed as symptoms but rather as creative strategies for coping with society's oppression (Worell & Remer, 1992). Finally, Enns (1993) makes the important point that learning to identify sources of pain and to express pain are crucial for the healing process. Enns suggests that learning to directly express this internalized pain (and anger, grief, and sorrow) represents a basic aspect of healing because it enables clients to productively redirect emotions they have introjected, or swallowed.

5. *Feminist therapists use an integrated analysis of oppression.* Gender is an essential consideration in feminist therapy, both in terms of oppression and in terms of differences that may influence one's understanding (Hill & Rothblum, 1996). Feminist therapists recognize that both women and men are affected by being raised in a culture where the sexes are differentially privileged. Men who have learned that vulnerability is a weakness may have difficulty expressing emotions in and outside the therapeutic relationship. Women who have learned to subordinate their own wishes to

care for their families may have difficulty identifying and honoring what they want out of therapy.

The therapist has a gender too, and the therapist's perceptions will always be filtered through the lens of her or his own experiences, which may be vastly different from those of the client. Although gender is emphasized, feminist therapists recognize that all forms of oppression profoundly influence beliefs, options, and perceptions, and they are equally committed to working against oppression on the basis of race, class, culture, religious beliefs, affectional or sexual orientation, age, or disability. Thus, feminists challenge all forms of oppression, not just oppression of women.

THE THERAPEUTIC PROCESS

Therapeutic Goals

The primary goal of feminist therapy is transformation, for both the individual client and society as a whole. At the individual level feminist therapists work to help women and men recognize, claim, and embrace their personal power. Through this empowerment, clients are able to free themselves from the constraints of their gender-role socialization and to expand their alternatives, options, and choices for living. Therapists help clients become interdependent, strong, resilient, and trusting of self and others. Women clients often are helped to rethink their relationship with their body. By examining the devastating effects of unrealistic societal expectations communicated by the media, women can assign less importance to appearance and focus more on pleasing themselves rather than conforming to a societal ideal.

Feminist therapy is a consciously political enterprise. The aim is to replace the current patriarchy with a feminist consciousness, creating a society in which relationships are interdependent, cooperative, and mutually supportive. Feminist therapists work to help women and men alike recognize that how they define themselves and how they relate to others are inevitably influenced by gender-role expectations. Furthermore, feminists confront all forms of institutional policies that discriminate on the basis of gender. Although some steps are being taken to change institutionalized sexism, there are still far too many examples of inequity between men and women in matters such as promotions and salaries.

Thus, transcendence rather than adjustment is the goal. Helping clients adjust to a sexist society would only perpetuate the status quo. By achieving personal power, women are able to exercise that power to help others. The full meaning of "the personal is political" is that women learn to free not only themselves but all people from the bonds of oppression and stereotypes. According to Worell and Remer (1992), feminist therapists help clients:

- Become aware of their own gender-role socialization process
- Identify their internalized gender-role messages and replace them with their own constructive beliefs

- Understand how sexist and oppressive societal beliefs and practices influence them in negative ways
- Acquire skills to bring about change in the environment
- Develop a wide range of behaviors that are freely chosen

Recognizing the power of relationships and connectedness is also important to feminist therapists. Therapists help clients break down the isolation that women feel regarding their experiencing and help them gain a sense of their unity and commonality with other women.

Feminist therapists also work toward reinterpreting women's mental health. Their aim is to depathologize women's experiencing and to change society so that women's voices are honored and women's relational qualities are valued. Women's experiences are examined without the bias of patriarchal values, and women's life skills and accomplishments are acknowledged. Among specific counseling goals defined by Worell and Remer (1992) are the therapist's efforts to:

- Help women and men to trust their own experience and their intuition
- Enable clients to appreciate female-related values
- Assist women in taking care of themselves
- Help women accept and like their own bodies
- Define and act in accordance with their own sexual needs rather than another's sexual needs

Therapist's Function and Role

Feminist therapists hold many beliefs in common with humanistic or person-centered therapists. Feminist therapists trust in the client's ability to move forward in a positive and constructive manner. They believe the therapeutic relationship should be a nonhierarchical, person-to-person relationship, and they aim to empower clients to live according to their own values and rely on an internal (rather than external or societal) locus of control in determining what is right for them. Like person-centered therapists, feminist therapists convey their genuineness rather than hiding behind an "expert" role. They offer their clients unconditional positive regard and acceptance and strive to empathically understand their clients' feelings and experiences.

Unlike person-centered therapists, however, feminist therapists do not see the therapeutic relationship as being, in and of itself, sufficient to produce change. Insight, introspection, or self-awareness is only a springboard to action. To free women (and men) of roles that have prohibited them from realizing their potential, an egalitarian counseling relationship is established. Therapy must not replicate the societal power imbalance and foster dependency in the client. The therapist and client take active and equal roles, working together to determine goals and procedures. Throughout this process, the therapist is appropriately self-disclosing and consciously works to serve as a positive role model. As feminist therapy has evolved, there has been discussion about the role and function of self-disclosure. The "Feminist Therapy Institute Code of Ethics" (1990) directly addresses this issue and notes the importance of using self-disclosure "with purpose and discretion."

Feminist therapy rests on a set of philosophical assumptions that can be applied to various theoretical orientations. Any theory can be evaluated against the criteria of being gender-free, flexible, interactionist, and life-span-oriented. Thus, with some transformation, it is possible for feminist therapists to incorporate contemporary forms of psychoanalytic therapy, Gestalt therapy, and cognitive behavior therapy in the fabric of their work. The therapist's role and functions will vary to some extent depending on what theory is combined with feminist principles and concepts.

Although feminist therapists have been critical of psychoanalysis as a sexist orientation, a number of feminist therapists believe psychoanalysis can be an appropriate approach to helping women. A psychodynamically oriented feminist therapist might examine Oedipal issues with the client to help her understand the development of her gender identity and male domination in society. Therapy might include an examination of the power of the unconscious and of the roles of mother and daughter to provide insights into why gender roles are so deeply ingrained and difficult to change.

Gestalt therapy and feminist therapy share the goal of increasing the client's awareness of personal power. A Gestalt-oriented feminist therapist functions as a facilitator of the client's active experimentation with new roles and behaviors. The client might be encouraged to directly express previously "disallowed" feelings in an empty-chair dialogue or to experiment with changing her language to feel her power and become aware of options she had not considered. Contemporary Gestalt therapy stresses dialogue between client and therapist rather than the techniques popularized by Perls. In this dialogic attitude the therapist has no agenda, no desire to get anywhere, and understands that the essential nature of the individual's relationship with the environment is interdependent, not independent. This approach creates a basis for genuine contact between client and counselor, and it also establishes the groundwork for contact and experiments that are spontaneous in the moment-to-moment experience of the therapeutic engagement. In many ways the dialogic and collaborative model of Gestalt therapy fits well with the philosophy of a feminist perspective (Enns, 1987, 1997).

A key concept in Gestalt therapy that applies well to feminist therapy is introjection. Societal gender-role messages are introjected, or swallowed whole, by most people. In therapy, gender-role introjects can be identified so that clients can "chew" on them, spitting out what does not fit and swallowing and digesting that which does fit.

Cognitive behavioral therapies and feminist therapy are compatible in that they view the therapeutic relationship as a collaboration and the client as being in charge of setting goals and selecting strategies for change. They both aim to help clients take charge of their own lives. Another commonality of both approaches is the commitment to demystifying therapy. Both the cognitive behavior therapist and the feminist therapist assume a range of information-giving functions and teaching functions so clients can become active partners in the therapy process.

A cognitive behavioral feminist therapist would likely employ action-oriented techniques such as assertiveness training and behavioral rehearsal and give homework assignments for clients to practice in their everyday lives. Like Albert Ellis and A. T. Beck, the therapist might explore with clients how their thoughts about women's roles and women's experiencing (e.g., "women shouldn't be strong") are limiting their choices. Rather than label clients' cognitions as "faulty" or "irrational," however, the feminist therapist would help clients explore how their gender-role socialization has engendered these beliefs. Clients then decide which of these beliefs to change or reconstruct. Three useful sources for further discussion of feminist cognitive behavior therapy are Worell and Remer (1992), Fodor (1988), and Kantrowitz and Ballou (1992).

As Prochaska and Norcross (1999) have noted, psychoanalysis, Gestalt therapy, and cognitive behavioral therapy are not the only therapeutic approaches that can be integrated with feminist principles. In essence, therapists of any orientation can infuse feminist practices in their work if they conduct therapy with a positive attitude toward women, value what is feminine, and are willing to confront patriarchal systems, empower women, and help them find their voice. Additionally, it is important that therapists pay attention to women's and men's development and gender-role socialization, power issues in the therapeutic relationship, and their own gender biases and stereotypes. Therapists need to identify any sources of bias in a given theory and work toward restructuring or eliminating sexist aspects. Finally, therapists view their role as being facilitators of the transformation of society with respect to gender equity.

A therapist of another orientation who uses feminist principles and practices is not the same as a feminist therapist. Feminist therapists have integrated feminism in their therapeutic style. Their actions and beliefs and their personal and professional lives are congruent. As Thomas (1977) has stated, feminist therapy is not merely an approach to alleviating occasional stress or resolving problems, it is a way of life for the therapist. The role of feminist therapists cannot be separated from certain personal characteristics that determine their effectiveness in carrying out their therapeutic functions. Feminist therapists are committed to monitoring their own biases and distortions, especially the social and cultural dimensions of women's experiences. They value being emotionally present for their clients, being willing to share themselves during the therapy hour, modeling proactive behaviors, and being committed to their own consciousness-raising process. Feminists share common ground with existential therapists who emphasize therapy as a shared journey—one that is life changing for both client and therapist.

Client's Experience in Therapy

Clients are active participants in the therapeutic process. Feminist therapists are committed to ensuring that this does not become another arena in which women remain passive and dependent. It is important that clients tell their stories and give voice to their experiencing. Initially, clients may look to the therapist for answers or advice. As the therapist continues to place the responsibility back on clients and to relate to clients more as a person than as an "expert," clients come to trust more in their own power. As clients realize they are really understood, they begin to get in touch with a range of feelings, including anger and other "prohibited" emotions that they may have learned to deny to themselves.

The female therapist may share some of her own struggles with sex-role oppression, and as an analysis of gender-role stereotyping is conducted, the client's consciousness is raised. For example, a female client will come to recognize her unity with other women and to realize that she is not alone. As she becomes more aware of ways she has been limited with respect to the development of her identity, her self-concept, and her goals and aspirations, she will begin to take on new roles. She may negotiate equality in her relationships with others in her life, be more assertive when needed, and identify her own needs and take the actions necessary to meet them. She will move from the safe environment of individual therapy sessions out into the larger support system of women. Perhaps she will join a women's self-help group. She may become an activist and participate in groups that are working to foster social change.

Feminist therapists do not restrict their practice to women clients; they also work with men, couples, families, and children. The experiences of a male client in therapy will in many ways parallel those of the female client just described. The therapeutic relationship is a partnership, and the client will be the expert in determining what he needs and wants from therapy. He will explore ways in which he has been limited by his gender-role socialization. He may become more aware of how he is constrained in his ability to express a range of emotions, and in the safe environment of the therapeutic sessions he may be able to fully experience such feelings as sadness, tenderness, uncertainty, and empathy. As he takes his new learnings out into his daily existence, he will find that relationships change in his family, his social world, and at work.

The experience of clients in feminist therapy will, of course, vary depending on a number of factors including the client and her or his needs and the particular orientation of the therapist. Nonetheless, here are some themes that clients are likely to deal with in their therapy:

- Exploring anxiety and defenses
- Understanding power and control issues
- Examining external forces that influence behavior
- Identifying messages received in growing up
- Learning to accept appropriate responsibility
- Critically examining social dictates and expectations
- Exploring one's values
- Reflecting on the meaning of life

The major goal of feminist therapy is empowerment, which involves acquiring a sense of self-acceptance, self-confidence, joy, and self-actualization. Worell and Remer (1992) write that feminist therapy clients acquire a whole new way of looking at and responding to their world. They add that the shared journey of empowerment can be one that is frightening and exciting—for both client and therapist. Clients can expect more than adjustment or simple problem-solving strategies; they need to be prepared for major shifts in their way of viewing the world around them, changes in the way they perceive themselves, and transformed interpersonal relationships.

Relationship Between Therapist and Client

The therapeutic relationship is based on empowerment and egalitarianism. Women are entitled to power, and the very structure of the client/therapist relationship models how to identify and use this power. Feminist therapists clearly state their values to reduce the chance of value imposition. This allows clients to make a choice regarding whether or not to work with the therapist. Another key characteristic of the therapeutic relationship is egalitarianism, or an equalizing of the power base between client and therapist.

Although there is an inherent power differential in the therapy relationship, feminist therapists work actively to break down the hierarchy of power and reduce artificial barriers to an egalitarian relationship by employing a number of strategies (Thomas, 1977). First, they are acutely sensitive to ways they might abuse their own power in the relationship, such as by diagnosing unnecessarily, by interpreting or giving advice, by staying aloof behind an "expert" role, or by discounting the impact the power imbalance between therapist and client has on the relationship. Counselor self-disclosure tends to reduce the power differential between client and counselor and aids in identifying their common issues as women.

Second, therapists actively focus on the power clients have in the therapeutic relationship. They give clients responsibility for themselves and encourage them to get in touch with their feelings and to honor their experiencing, to become aware of the ways they relinquish power in relationships with others, and to take charge of their lives.

Third, feminist therapists work to demystify the counseling relationship. They do this by sharing with the client their own perceptions about what is going on in the relationship, by making the client an active partner in determining any diagnosis, and by self-disclosing. If the therapist suggests a particular technique, she fully explains what its possible effects may be and her rationale for suggesting it, and she fully respects the client's decision to proceed or not to proceed. Some feminist therapists use contracts as a way to make the goals and processes of therapy overt rather than covert and mysterious.

To free women and men of roles that have prohibited them from realizing their potential, an egalitarian counseling relationship is established. The counselor is not the all-knowing expert but strives to develop a collaborative relationship in which clients can become experts on themselves. Worell and Remer (1992) identify several counseling goals that flow from the egalitarian relationship principle, some of which are:

- Striving for equal relationships
- Developing interdependence in relationships
- Developing a full range of interpersonal and life skills
- Learning appropriate assertive behavior
- Identifying personal strengths and assets

A further defining theme of the client/counselor relationship is the inclusion of clients in both the assessment and the treatment process. This commitment to including clients from the initial through the final session helps to keep the therapeutic relationship egalitarian. Walden (1997) has written about the inclusion of the clients' perspective in ethical practice. Her points about ethics apply directly to the relationship between client and therapist. Walden emphasizes the value of educating and empowering clients. She states that if counselors keep their clients uninformed about the nature of the therapeutic process, they deny them the potential for active participation in their therapy. Important therapeutic benefits can result from including clients as active partners in the therapeutic venture (Walden, 1997):

- When counselors make decisions about a client *for* the client rather than *with* the client, they rob the client of power in the therapeutic relationship. Collaboration with the client in all aspects of therapy leads to a genuine partnership and empowerment of the client.
- Bringing the client into ongoing dialogue regarding decisions about the therapy demonstrates a true respect for the client's views. This dialogue increases the chances that the client's therapy will be guided by self-determined goals, drawing on the client's successes and strengths.
- Including the client in the therapeutic process increases the chances that the interventions will be more culturally appropriate. Through the exchange of views, client empowerment and solutions consistent with the client's cultural values are possible.

 ## APPLICATION: Therapeutic Techniques and Procedures

The Role of Assessment and Diagnosis

Feminist therapists have been sharply critical of the DSM classification system. They have challenged sexism in diagnostic categories and proposed alternative classifications that reflect women's experiences. According to Enns (1993), many feminist therapists do not use diagnostic labels, or they use them reluctantly, because: (a) they focus on the individual's symptoms and not the social factors that cause dysfunctional behavior, (b) as part of a system developed mainly by White male psychiatrists, they represent an instrument of oppression, (c) they (especially the personality disorders) reinforce gender-role stereotypes and encourage adjustment to the norms of the status quo, (d) they reflect the inappropriate application of power in the therapeutic relationship, (e) they lead to an overemphasis on individual solutions rather than social change, and (f) they reduce one's respect for clients.

A part of the feminist critique of assessment and diagnosis is that these procedures are often based on sexist assumptions. To the degree that this is true, it is impossible to obtain an accurate assessment or to arrive at an appropriate diagnosis. Sources of gender bias include disregarding or minimizing the effect of environmental factors influencing behavior; providing different treatments to women and men who display similar symptoms; inappropriately selecting diagnostic labels due to gender-role stereotypical beliefs; and operating from a gender-biased theoretical orientation (Worell & Remer, 1992).

Sharf (2000) discusses feminist therapy perspectives on certain "mental disorders" that are identified in the DSM-IV as being particularly common in women, such as depression, posttraumatic stress disorder, borderline personality disorder, generalized anxiety disorder, and eating disorders. To take just a couple of examples, feminist therapists believe women have many more reasons to experience depression than do men. Their gender-role socialization has taught them to be dependent, submissive, and self-sacrificing to please others. Thus, depression may result from a woman's perception that she is not in control of her life or that she is less valuable than a man. Similarly, with eating disorders feminist therapists focus on messages given by society, and by the mass media in particular, about women's bodies and the importance of being thin. The therapist uses a gender-role analysis to help clients who suffer from anorexia or bulimia examine these societal injunctions and how they have come to accept them. Therapist and client work together on ways to challenge and change these messages. Common threads are an emphasis on gender-role socialization and the power differences between women and men, and an attention to societal as opposed to intrapsychic origins of problems.

Feminist therapists do not refuse to use the DSM-IV in this age of managed care and the prevalence of the medical model of mental health, but diagnosis results from a shared dialogue between client and therapist. The therapist is careful to review with the client any implications of assigning a diagnosis so the client can make an informed choice, and discussion focuses on helping the client understand the role of socialization and culture in the etiology of her problems.

An alternative form of assessment preferred by feminist therapists is gender-role analysis, which involves a cooperative exploration by client and therapist of the impact of gender on the client's distress. Santos De Barona and Dutton (1997) stress the importance for feminist therapy practice of incorporating other contextual variables (such as racism and heterosexism), not just gender, in assessment procedures in ways that are meaningful for the client. Whatever approach to assessment is used, the client is included in each of the stages of the process and participates in shaping the strategies, which build on the client's individual strengths.

Techniques and Strategies

Several techniques have been developed by feminist therapists, and others have been borrowed from traditional approaches and adapted to the feminist therapy model. Particularly important are consciousness-raising techniques that help women differentiate between what they have been taught is socially acceptable or desirable and what is actually healthy for them. Some of the techniques described by Sharf (2000), Worell and Remer (1992), and Enns (1993) are discussed in this section, using the case example of Susan to illustrate how these techniques might be applied.

> Susan, age 27, comes to therapy stating that she is depressed. She says she "hates herself" for having gained so much weight since she left college, and she is certain she is doomed to be alone for the rest of her life. She says, "I missed my chance. I was popular and attractive when I was in college, but no man would ever look twice at me the way I am now."

GENDER-ROLE ANALYSIS   This technique is used to help the client understand the impact of gender-role expectations in her life. The therapist begins by asking Susan to recall parental messages she received related to weight and appearance. Susan remembers that her mother struggled with weight gain and often made remarks to Susan like, "It's a good thing I captured your father when I still had a figure" and "You'll have your choice of men if you stay a perfect size 10." Susan struggles to identify some positive consequences of these messages. She states that she *did* feel attractive through her adolescence and college years and her self-confidence helped her develop a winning personality, make friends, and enjoy social activities. The negative consequences are easier to see and are evident when the therapist asks Susan to repeat the statements she made at the beginning of the session. Together the therapist and Susan decide which messages she wants to change and develop and implement a plan for creating those changes.

GENDER-ROLE INTERVENTION   Using this technique the therapist responds to Susan's concern by placing it in the context of society's role expectations for women. The aim is to provide Susan with insight into the ways that social issues are affecting her problem. Susan's therapist responds to her statement with, "Our society really is obsessed with thinness. The media bombards women with the message that they need to be rail-thin to be attractive. The reality is, most women don't look like models and those who try to often end up with eating disorders like anorexia." By placing Susan's concern in the context of societal expectations, the therapist gives Susan insight into how these expectations have effected her psychological condition and have led to her depression. The therapist's statement also paves the way for Susan to think more positively about her unity with other women who are not rail-thin.

POWER ANALYSIS AND POWER INTERVENTION   These techniques are similar to the analysis and intervention with gender roles. The emphasis here, however, is on helping Susan become aware of the power difference between men and women in our society and empowering Susan to take charge of herself and her life. Worell and Remer (1992) define power as "the ability to access personal and environmental resources in order to effect personal and/or external change" (p. 100). Power analysis includes recognizing different kinds of power that clients possess or to which they have access. In Susan's case the power analysis may focus on helping Susan identify alternate kinds of power she may exercise and to challenge the gender-role messages that prohibit the exercise of that kind of power. The power analysis helps Susan recognize that in this society women often gain power through their association with a powerful male and are perceived as powerless if they do not have a man in their lives. Interventions are aimed at helping Susan learn to like herself as she is, regain her self-confidence based on the personality attributes she possesses, and set goals that will be fulfilling to her and do not depend on whether she "finds a man."

BIBLIOTHERAPY   This technique is a useful tool in feminist therapy. The therapist describes a number of books that address the consequences of society's obsession with thinness, and Susan selects one to read over the next few weeks. Providing Susan with reading material increases her expertise and decreases the power difference between Susan and her therapist. Reading can supplement what is learned in the therapy sessions, and Susan can enhance her therapy by exploring her reactions to what she is reading. Nonfiction books, psychology and counseling textbooks, autobiographies, self-help books, educational videos, and films can all be used as bibliotherapy resources. At times, a novel may be extremely therapeutic and provide rich material for discussions in therapy sessions. Through well-timed reading assignments, Susan can learn valuable lessons about the influence of gender-role stereotypes, ways sexism is promoted, the power differential between women and men, and gender inequality. She can also learn specific coping skills that she can add to her behavioral repertoire.

SELF-DISCLOSURE   Therapist self-disclosure not only helps to demystify the therapy process, it helps to equalize the relationship by showing Susan that the therapist is a real person with her own struggles. Susan's therapist discloses her own difficulties in learning to accept that her body is different now, after her pregnancy and childbirth, and that she is not a size 10 either. Susan benefits from this modeling by a woman who does not meet society's standards for thinness and is comfortable with her body.

The therapist will also discuss with Susan how therapy works and will enlist Susan as an active partner in the therapeutic venture. Feminist therapists emphasize the importance of *informed consent,* which involves a discussion of ways of getting the most from the therapy session, clarifying expectations, identifying goals, and working toward a contract that will guide the therapeutic process. The therapist clearly states her relevant values and beliefs about society to allow Susan to make an informed choice about whether or not to work with this therapist. Susan's therapist explains to her the therapeutic interventions that are likely to be employed. Susan, as an informed consumer, can be involved in evaluating how well these strategies are working and the degree to which her personal goals in therapy are being met.

ASSERTIVENESS TRAINING   This technique helps women become aware of their interpersonal rights, transcend stereotypical sex roles, change negative beliefs, and implement changes in their daily lives. It is important that teaching and promoting assertive behavior be done in a manner that is culturally appropriate for each client. Becoming assertive is not a command, and some clients may choose not to behave assertively in certain situations.

Through learning and practicing assertive behaviors and communication, Susan may increase her own power, thus alleviating the depression she feels as a result of having measured herself against societal expectations rather than her own self-evaluations. Susan will learn about some important distinctions between being assertive and being aggressive. She will learn that it is her right to ask for what she wants and needs. The therapist helps Susan to evaluate and anticipate the possible negative consequences of behaving assertively. They talk about the possibility of being viewed as aggressive and how to best deal with this situation. The therapist recommends that Susan read Mary Crawford's (1995) book, *Talking Difference. On Gender and Language.*

REFRAMING AND RELABELING   Like bibliotherapy, therapist self-disclosure, and assertiveness training, reframing is not unique to feminist therapy. Reframing implies a shift from "blaming the victim" to a consideration of social factors in the environment that contribute to a client's problem. In reframing, rather than dwelling on intrapsychic factors, the focus is on examining societal or political dimensions. Thus, Susan may come to understand her depression as being linked to social pressures to have the "ideal body" rather than as stemming from some deficiency in her.

Relabeling is an intervention that changes the label or evaluation applied to some behavioral characteristic. Susan can change certain labels she has attached to herself, such as being inadequate or unattractive because she is not thin. She might relabel her depression and concerns about her weight as reactions to externally derived standards of how she should be.

GROUP WORK   An important adjunct to individual feminist therapy, group work alone is often the preferred modality for some issues that women experience in our culture. Women's groups, including self-help groups and advocacy groups, help women experience their connectedness and unity with other women. Susan and her therapist will likely discuss the possibility of Susan joining a women's support group or other type of group as a part of the process of terminating individual therapy. By joining a group Susan will have opportunities to discover that she is not alone in her struggles.

Other women can provide her with nurturance and support, and Susan will have the chance to be significant to other women as they engage in their healing process.

SOCIAL ACTION Susan might decide to join and participate in organizations that are working to change societal stereotypes about women's bodies. Taking this kind of social action is another way for Susan to feel more empowered.

The Role of Men in Feminist Therapy

Can a man be a feminist therapist? Feminist therapists are divided on this issue. Our own belief is that it is possible for men to be feminist therapists. We also make the assumption that men can be nonsexist therapists. We hope that all therapists strive to incorporate awareness of gender bias in their thinking and their practices with clients. It seems to us that men can be pro-feminist therapists when they embrace the principles and incorporate the practices of feminism in their work. This entails being willing to confront sexist behavior in themselves and others, redefining masculinity and femininity according to other than traditional values, working toward establishing egalitarian relationships, and actively supporting women's efforts to create a just society.

Feminist therapy can be an effective method for working with men as clients. Men, as well as women, are oppressed by a patriarchal system and can work for social change (Brown, 1994). Feminist therapists routinely work with men, especially with abusive men and in battering groups. According to Ganley (1988), issues that men can deal with productively in feminist therapy include learning how to increase their capacity for intimacy, expressing their emotions and learning self-disclosure, balancing achievement and relationship needs, and creating collaborative relationships at work and with significant others that are not based on power. Some of these themes emerge in the therapist's work with Stan, which is presented in the next section.

 # FEMINIST THERAPY APPLIED TO THE CASE OF STAN

Stan's fear of women and his gender role socialization experiences make him an excellent candidate to benefit from feminist therapy. A therapeutic relationship that is egalitarian, with a strong woman who respects and empowers him and does not demean him, will be a new kind of experience for Stan.

Stan has clearly indicated that he is willing and even eager to change. Despite his low self-esteem and negative self-evaluations, Stan is able to identify some positive attributes. These include his determination, his ability to feel his feelings, and his gift for working with children. Stan knows what he wants out of therapy and has clear goals: to stop drinking, to feel better about himself, to relate to women on an equal basis, and to learn to love and trust himself and others. His feminist therapist will build on these strengths.

In the first session Stan's therapist focuses on establishing an egalitarian working relationship to help Stan begin to regain his personal power. Stan may hold the assumption that because his therapist is a woman she will take a dominant role and *tell* him what he needs to do to accomplish his goals. It is important that the therapeutic relationship does not replicate other relationships Stan has had with women in his life, especially his mother and his ex-wife. The therapist consciously works to demystify the therapeutic process and equalize the relationship, conveying to Stan that he is in charge of the direction his therapy will take. She spends considerable time explaining her view of the therapy process and how it works. She lets Stan know that *he* is in charge of not only the direction but also the duration of therapy and that she will not abandon him.

A gender-role analysis is conducted to help Stan become aware of the influence of gender-role expectations in the development of his problems. The first step in a gender-role analysis is for the client to identify gender-role messages that were received while growing up from a variety of societal sources including parents, teachers, and peers. In his autobiography Stan has already written about some of the messages his parents gave him, and this provides a natural starting point for his analysis. He remembers his father calling him "dumb" and his mother saying, "Why can't you grow up and be a man?" Stan wrote about his mother "continually bitching at" his father and telling Stan that he did many things to hurt her and that she wished she hadn't had him. Stan describes his father as weak, passive, and mousy in relating to his mother and remembers that his father compared him unfavorably with his siblings. Stan internalized these messages, often crying himself to sleep and feeling·disgusted with himself.

The therapist asks Stan to identify the self-statements he makes now that are based on these early messages. As they review his writings, Stan sees how his parental messages have been translated into how he sees himself today—"not much of a man" and "someone who lets people down a lot." He and the therapist explore how his autobiography illuminates some societal messages he appears to have introjected, or swallowed whole. For instance, he wrote that he feels sexually inadequate and worries that he won't be able to perform. It appears that he has introjected the societal notion that men should always initiate sex, be ready for sex, and be able to achieve and sustain an erection. Stan also sees that he has already identified and written about how he wants to change those messages, as exemplified in his statements that he wants to "feel equal with others" and not "feel apologetic" for his existence and develop a loving relationship with a woman. Stan begins to feel capable and empowered as his therapist acknowledges the important work he has already done, even before he entered therapy.

The therapist follows this gender-role analysis with a gender-role intervention to place Stan's concerns in the context of societal role expectations. She says, "Indeed, it is a burden to try to live up to society's notion of what it means to be a man, always having to be strong and tough. Those aspects of yourself that you would like to value—your ability to feel your feelings, being good with children—are qualities society tends to label as 'feminine.'" Stan replies wistfully, "Yeah, it would be a better world if women could be strong without being seen as domineering and if men could be sensitive and nurturing without being seen as weak." The therapist gently challenges this statement by asking, "Are you sure that's not possible? Have you ever met a woman or a man who was like that?" Stan ponders for a minute and then with some animation describes the college professor who taught his Psychology of Adjustment class. Stan saw her as very accomplished and strong but also as someone who empowered him by encouraging him to find his own voice through writing his autobiography. He also remembers a male counselor at the youth rehabilitation facility where he spent part of his adolescence as a man who was strong as well as sensitive and nurturing.

As the first session draws to a close, the therapist asks Stan to say what he has gotten out of their time together. Stan says that two things stand out for him. First, he is beginning to believe he doesn't need to keep blaming himself. He realizes that many of the messages he has received from his parents and from society about what it means to be a man have been unrealistic and one-dimensional. He acknowledges that he has been limited and constrained by his gender-role socialization. Second, he feels hopeful because there *are* alternatives to those parental and societal definitions—people he admires have been able to successfully combine "masculine" and "feminine" traits. If they can do it, maybe he can too. The therapist asks Stan whether he chooses to return for another session. When he answers in the affirmative, she gives him a copy of Carl Rogers's (1977) book, *On Personal Power*, and suggests that he try reading some of it before their next session.

Stan comes to the second session eager to talk about his bibliotherapy homework assignment. He tells the therapist that he finds it affirming that a man can write about personal power in a way he had never thought of before. He says he is coming to realize that being powerful doesn't necessarily mean exerting power over someone else to dominate them. He adds, "I just wish my mother had read Rogers's book!" This leads to a further exploration of Stan's

relationship with his mother. He becomes tearful as he expresses the terrible bind he felt he was placed in as a child. On one hand he became very angry when she belittled him and told him he was a "mistake." On the other hand he was terrified to express his anger because he so desperately wanted her love and approval. When the therapist asks him about his feelings toward his father, Stan realizes that he is again both angry and afraid. He is angry not only that his father allowed himself to be pushed around by his mother but also that his father didn't seem to value Stan as he was, instead wanting him to be more like his siblings. He says he would like to be closer to his father but is afraid to try.

The therapist asks Stan whether he has been able, as an adult, to express either his anger or his fear to his parents. Stan seems startled at the very idea but says he sure *wishes* he could tell them how he feels. The therapist then explains to Stan what an empty-chair dialogue is like and how he might use it to "talk" to his parents in the safe environment of the therapy session. Stan says he would like to try that but finds it pretty scary. The therapist assures him that he is fully in charge of what he decides to say, he can stop at any time, and that his parents are not really there and can't actually hear him. She adds that this experiment is entirely his decision, and he can try it another time if not now.

Stan decides to go ahead and puts his parents in two empty chairs that are arranged facing him. He sits silently for several minutes, and then turns to the therapist saying, "I keep picturing how my father reacted when my mother went after him. He was just passive, a real mouse. I can be like that, but I don't know how else to be." The therapist suggests that maybe they can have some fun with this experiment instead of making it into a "perfect performance." She asks Stan if he is willing to be a mouse.

Stan says he thinks this will be easy, turns and faces the empty chairs, and begins talking to his "father" in a timid way with a squeaky voice. Tears well up as he says, "You were supposed to teach me how to be a man. But you weren't interested in me, except to compare me with my brother and sister." He turns to his "mother," and in an almost inaudible voice asks, "Why did you keep telling me I was a mistake? I tried so hard to please you, but it was never good enough." Speaking to both of them, he says in a stronger voice, "It wasn't fair!" As he continues to express his feelings, his voice gradually becomes louder and louder. He ends by yelling, "I don't care *how* miserable your lives were, you had no right to take it out on a helpless child!" He stops, takes a deep breath, and shoves his chair back. Turning to face the therapist, he starts to grin and says, "Wow, I guess I am the mouse that roared!"

The remainder of the session is spent in processing this Gestalt exercise from a feminist therapy perspective. His therapist helps him to understand his family from a feminist perspective that does not take his father or mother out of context. For example, the therapist and Stan discuss one possible explanation for his mother's behavior. Stan's mother may have been doing what she believed was best for Stan, trying to encourage masculine behaviors so that he would not suffer societal consequences for not being "manly" enough. His father may have had much the same goal; believing he had failed to be a "strong man," he may have hoped to spare Stan the same kind of failure. Stan finds that he still has mixed feelings toward his parents, but those feelings are different now. He is still angry but finds that his anger is tempered by compassion for how trapped they felt in a life that was not fulfilling to them. He is still afraid of them, but he no longer feels immobilized by his fear.

Understanding his parents' perspective may be Stan's first step on the road toward tolerance, healing, and forgiveness. He finds it helpful to understand their behavior in the context of societal expectations and stereotypes rather than continuing to blame them. He notes that he felt powerful when he was doing the empty-chairs experiment but that he didn't hurt anyone by doing it. He thinks of the saying, "Are you a man or a mouse?" This provides a springboard for further discussion of societal stereotypes about manliness and how he has been limited by his unquestioning acceptance of them.

Stan continues to work at learning to value the "feminine" parts of himself as well as the "masculine" or strong aspects of the women with whom he is interacting. He also continues to monitor and make changes in his self-talk about what it means to be a man.

Throughout the therapeutic relationship, Stan and the therapist discuss with immediacy how they are communicating and relating to each other during the sessions. The therapist is self-disclosing and treats Stan as an equal, continually acknowledging that he is the "expert" in knowing and getting what he wants out of life.

Follow-Up: You Continue as Stan's Feminist Therapist

Use these questions to help you think about how you would counsel Stan:

- What unique values do you see in working with Stan from a feminist perspective as opposed to working with Stan from the other therapeutic approaches you've studied thus far?
- If you were to continue working with Stan, what self-statements regarding his view of himself as a man might you focus on and how might you challenge his beliefs?

- In what ways could you integrate cognitive behavior therapy with feminist therapy in Stan's case? What possibilities do you see for integrating Gestalt therapy methods with feminist therapy? What other therapies might you combine with a feminist approach?
- Stan's feminist therapist used biblio-

therapy as a form of homework assignment. Would you suggest books for Stan to read? If so, what books do you think would be useful for him? What other homework might you suggest to Stan? What other feminist therapy strategies would you utilize in counseling Stan? ■

SUMMARY AND EVALUATION

Summary

The origins of feminist therapy are connected with the women's movement of the 1960s, when women united in vocalizing their dissatisfaction over the restrictive nature of traditional female roles. Eventually, feminist principles became part of the fabric of therapy for many women practicing both individual and group counseling. Feminist therapy largely grew out of the recognition by women that the traditional models of therapy suffer from basic limitations due to the inherent bias of earlier theoreticians. Feminist therapy emphasizes these concepts:

- Viewing problems in a sociopolitical and cultural context rather than on an individual level
- Recognizing that the client knows what is best for his or her life and is an expert on his or her own life
- Creating a therapeutic relationship that is egalitarian through the process of self-disclosure and informed consent
- Demystifying the therapeutic process by including the client as much as possible in all phases of assessment and treatment
- Emphasizing connectedness and unity among women and that healing comes from sharing concerns
- Viewing the nature of women's experiences from a unique perspective
- Challenging traditional ways of assessing the psychological health of women
- Understanding that individual change will best occur through social change
- Emphasizing the role of the therapist as advocate as well as facilitator of change within the individual
- Encouraging clients to take social action to address oppressive aspects of the environment

Feminist therapy is generally a relatively short-term therapy aimed at both individual and social change. The model is not static but is continually evolving. The major goal is to replace the current patriarchal system with feminist consciousness and thus create a society that values equality in relationships, that stresses interdependence rather than dependence, and that encourages women to define themselves rather than being defined by societal demands.

Instead of being a singular and unified approach to psychotherapy, feminist practice tends to be diverse. As feminist therapy has matured, it has become more self-critical and varied. Emerging feminisms of color and postmodern perspectives are helping feminists consider issues of diversity among women in new ways.

Each of the four basic philosophies underlying feminist practice—liberal, cultural, radical, and socialist—has a different view on the sources of oppression and what is needed to bring about substantial social transformation. Regardless of their particular approach, feminist therapists share a number of roles: they engage in appropriate self-disclosure; they make their values and beliefs explicit so that the therapy process is clearly understood; they establish egalitarian roles with clients; they work toward client empowerment; and they emphasize the commonalities among women.

Feminist therapists are committed to actively breaking down the hierarchy of power in the therapeutic relationship through the use of various interventions. Some of these strategies are unique to feminist therapy, such as gender-role analysis and intervention, power analysis and intervention, assuming a stance of advocate in challenging conventional attitudes toward appropriate roles for women, and encouraging clients to take social action. Many other therapeutic strategies are borrowed from various therapy models. A few of these interventions include bibliotherapy, assertiveness training, cognitive restructuring, role playing, psychodramatic techniques, identifying and challenging untested beliefs, and journal writing. Feminist therapy principles and techniques can be applied to a range of therapeutic modalities such as individual therapy, couples counseling, family therapy, group counseling, and community intervention. Regardless of the specific techniques used, the overriding goals are client empowerment and social transformation.

Contributions of Feminist Therapy

One of the major contributions feminists have made to the field of counseling and psychotherapy is paving the way for gender-sensitive practice. No other theoretical orientation has placed gender at the center of practice. This focus on gender is the heart of feminist therapy in much the same way as culture is central to the practice of multicultural counseling. Gender-sensitive principles can be applied to counseling individuals, couples, and families as well as to group work and community intervention. Therapists with a feminist orientation understand how important it is to become fully aware of typical gender-role messages clients have grown up with, and they are skilled in helping clients identify and challenge these messages (Philpot, Brooks, Lusterman, & Nutt, 1997).

A related contribution of the feminist model is the commitment to applying gender-fair principles in the therapy endeavor. Nutt (1991) has identified a set of principles for gender-fair counseling, which she applied to family therapists who work with couples and families. In many ways, her guidelines apply equally well to the practice of feminist therapy with individuals and groups. These guidelines for practitioners include the following:

- Therapists are knowledgeable concerning gender-role socialization and the impact these standards have on what it means to be a woman or a man.
- Therapists are aware of the impact of the distribution of power within the family and power differentials between women and men in terms of decision making, child rearing, career options, and division of labor.
- Therapists understand the sexist context of the larger social system and its impact on both individuals and the family unit.
- Therapists are committed to promoting roles for both women and men that are not limited by cultural and gender stereotypes.
- Therapists acquire intervention skills that assist clients in their gender-role journey.
- Therapists are committed to work toward the elimination of gender-role bias as a source of pathology in all societal institutions.

Feminism has done a good deal to make therapists sensitive to the gendered uses of power in relationships. For example, in writing about feminist couples therapy, Rampage (1998) claims that therapists should identify and challenge the distribution of power in relationships where it is unequal and this inequality is preventing the problem from being solved. Doing this often results in empowering women to claim what they want for themselves in their relationships. Examining the power differential in their relationship often helps partners demystify and depathologize the gendered differences between them.

Nichols and Schwartz (1998) credit feminist therapists with helping families reorganize so that neither the woman nor the man remains stuck in destructive patterns. Family therapists with a feminist orientation assist the family in critically examining and changing the rules and roles that have kept the mother down and the father out. According to Nichols and Schwartz, it is only when therapists look through the lens of gender that they will be able to interrupt the cycle of mother-blaming and will stop looking to mothers to do all the changing.

Feminist therapists have also made important contributions in questioning traditional counseling theories, especially the assumptions that traditional therapies make concerning women's experiences. Most theories place the cause of problems within individuals rather than with external circumstances and the environment. This has led to holding women and men responsible for their problems and not giving full recognition to social and political realities that create problems for women and men. A key contribution feminists continue to make is reminding all of us that the proper focus of therapy needs to address changing any oppressive factors in society rather than expecting women to merely adapt to expected role behaviors.

A major contribution of the feminist movement has been removing the blinders so that everyone can see certain realities more clearly. The unified feminist voice called attention to the extent and implications of child abuse, incest, rape, sexual harassment, and domestic violence. It was the feminists who pointed out the consequences of failing to recognize and take action in cases where children and women were victims of physical, sexual, and psychological abuse. Feminist therapists work with male clients who are abusive. For example, there are increasing numbers of groups composed of male batterers that are led or co-led by feminist therapists.

Feminist therapists demanded action in cases of sexual misconduct, whereas male therapists misused the trust placed in them by their female clients. Not too long ago the codes of ethics of all the major professional organizations were silent on the matter of therapist and client sexual liaisons. Now, virtually all of the professional codes of ethics prohibit sexual intimacies with current clients and prohibit sexual relationships between therapists and former clients for a specified time period. Furthermore, many of the professions agree that a sexual relationship cannot later be converted into a therapeutic relationship. Largely due to the efforts and input of women on ethics committees, the existing codes are explicit with respect to sexual harassment and sexual relationships with clients, students, and supervisees (Herlihy & Corey, 1997).

The strength of feminist therapy is that many of its principles and techniques can be incorporated in most of the other therapy models, including humanistic and relationship-oriented therapies, the cognitive behavioral models, the psychodynamic approaches, the family systems perspective, and the multicultural perspective. Adlerians and feminists are united in viewing the therapeutic relationship as egalitarian. Both feminist and person-centered therapists agree on the importance of therapist authenticity, modeling, and self-disclosure; empowerment is the basic goal of both orientations. When it comes to making choices about one's destiny, existential and feminist therapists are speaking the same language—both emphasize choosing for oneself instead of living life determined by societal dictates. Both cognitive behavioral therapy and feminist therapy share the importance of the collaborative relationship, learning coping skills, establishing mutually agreed on counseling goals, the value of educating clients about how therapy works, and including clients in evaluating how well the process is working for them.

Feminist therapy suggests that a counseling theory should be gender-free, flexible, interactionist, and life-span-oriented. A feminist therapy approach can contribute to broadening the theoretical base of other therapy models as well as enriching all of our lives by encouraging positive social activism in our communities and throughout the world.

Limitations and Criticisms of Feminist Therapy

One potential limitation of the feminist approach rests with therapists whose militance and over-zealousness might result in the imposition of their values on clients. Although a useful role of feminist therapists is to teach women about options for change, this role should not include persuading clients to move in a specific direction. The therapist's function is to offer a blend of support and challenge to examine what clients have in their lives. It is clients' responsibility to weigh the potential benefits and risks involved in remaining as they are or changing.

Feminist therapists do not take a neutral stance. They advocate for definite change in the social structure, especially in the area of equality, power in relationships, the right to self-determination, freedom to pursue a career outside the home, and the right to an education. What if a woman chooses to make her primary commitment to her children and decides she does not want to get professionally involved outside the home? What about the woman who realizes she is both financially and emotionally dependent on her husband but does not want to change this aspect of her relationship, or who feels she cannot realistically change her relationship? And how about a woman who recognizes she is sacrificing some of her personal educational or career ambitions for the sake of others? What if a woman clearly recognizes the hierarchy in her family, yet does not choose to risk upsetting her husband? Feminist therapists need to be cautious to avoid pushing their own agenda on their clients. The critical questions are, "Why is this client seeing me? What does the client want in life? How can I help the client sort her or his values and assist the client in deciding what to do?" The client is ultimately responsible for answering these questions. Feminist therapists believe all therapists have values and that it is important to be clear with clients about values. This is different, however, from imposing values on clients. An imposition of values is inconsistent with viewing clients as their own best experts.

A facet of feminist therapy that can be both a strength and a limitation is the focus on looking at environmental factors that contribute to a woman's problems. Moving away from exploring the intrapsychic domain as the source of a woman's problems does a great deal to illuminate a woman's perspective. Instead of being blamed for her depression, the client is able to come to an understanding of external realities that are indeed oppressive. However, viewing the source of a client's problem in the environment may actually contribute to not taking personal responsibility to act in the face of an unfair world. Therapists must balance an exploration of the outer and inner worlds of the client if the client is to find a way to take action in her own life. Although a woman may not be responsible for creating many of her problems, she will find empowerment by learning what she can do to assume responsibility for changing in the direction she chooses—whether or not certain facets of the environment change. Another choice would be to decide to leave an oppressive environment.

Two other criticisms of feminist therapy deserve a brief mention. There is some disagreement as to whether feminist therapy is a philosophical orientation or a theory. Recent writings and research have begun to clarify this debate. Some assert that feminist therapy is a theory and not just an orientation (Brown, 1994; Worell & Johnson, 1997). Another criticism is that feminist therapy was developed by White, middle class, heterosexual women (Brown, 1994). It was not until the late 1980s that developers of feminist theory acknowledged that they had overlooked women of color as if they were invisible or didn't matter. The fact that many women of color preferred to call themselves "womanists" is a testament to their feeling excluded from feminism. Feminist therapy has responded to this criticism and has made progress in being more inclusive (Brown & Ballou, 1990).

 # FEMINIST THERAPY FROM A MULTICULTURAL PERSPECTIVE

Contributions to Multicultural Counseling

Of all the theoretical approaches to counseling and psychotherapy in this book, feminist therapy and multicultural perspectives of therapy practice have the most in common. Feminist therapy recognizes the role that oppressive environmental forces have in keeping women subjugated to men. Likewise, multicultural approaches point to oppression, discrimination, and racism as the source of many of the problems faced by people of color. The feminist perspective of understanding the use of power in relationships has application for understanding power inequities due to racial and cultural factors as well. The "personal is political" principle has equal value when applied to counseling women and counseling culturally diverse client groups. Neither feminist nor multicultural therapists are willing to settle for adjustment to the status quo. Nor does either approach rest solely on individual change; both demand direct action for social change as a part of the role of therapists. Many of the social action and political strategies that call attention to oppressed groups have equal relevance for women and for ethnic minorities.

It is possible to incorporate the principles of feminist therapy with a multicultural perspective. Comas-Diaz (1987) describes a feminist model that empowers minority women by helping them to:

- Acknowledge the negative effects of sexism and racism
- Identify and deal with their feelings pertaining to their status as ethnic minority women
- View themselves as able to find solutions to their problems
- Understand the interplay between the external environment and their reality
- Integrate ethnic, gender, and racial components into their identity

Both the women's movement and the multicultural movement have called to our attention the negative effects discrimination and oppression have on its targets and also on those doing the discriminating and oppressing. Peggy McIntosh, a professor at Wellesley College, has described the concept of *White privilege* as an invisible package of unearned assets White people enjoy but that are not extended to people of color. Adapting her notion of White privilege to both race and gender, we would like to suggest that *White male privilege* is operating in our society. The reality is that both racism and sexism still favor one group of citizens—White males—while excluding other groups of citizens from the same opportunities. Therapy should free individuals and increase their range of choices. It is to the credit of both feminist and multicultural therapists that policies have been established to lessen the opportunities for discrimination based on gender, race, culture, sexual orientation, ability, and age.

Limitations for Multicultural Counseling

If feminist therapists are not aware of the consequences of certain choices their clients make, they are likely to increase their clients' dissatisfaction with life. Being aware of the cultural context is especially important when feminist therapists work with women from cultures that endorse culturally prescribed roles that keep women in a subservient place or from cultures that are based on patriarchy.

One of us (Jerry Corey) did a workshop in Hong Kong about 10 years ago, and some of the women who provided mental health services for women in that country made an important cultural point. They mentioned how careful they had to be in encouraging a woman to get a divorce, even if she was miserable in her marriage and even if it did not appear that her relationship would change. If a woman were to divorce, she would not find support from her family or community members in her country. In fact, she might pay the price of being cut off from family members and friends for disgracing the family for bringing about a divorce.

Consider that you are a feminist therapist and you are working with a Vietnamese woman who is struggling to find a way to be true to her culture and also to follow her own educational and career aspirations. Your client is a student in a helping profession who is being subjected to extreme pressure from her father to return home and take care of her family. Although she wants to complete a degree and eventually help others in the Vietnamese community, she feels a great deal of guilt when she considers "selfishly" pursuing her education when her family at home needs her. If you were counseling this woman, would you challenge her to take care of herself and do what is right for her? Might you persuade her to tell her father that she is going to follow her own path? The price may be very high if this woman chooses to go against what is culturally expected of her. Also, persuading the client would violate the feminist principle of egalitarian relationships in therapy. We see the therapist's job as helping the client balance the potential costs associated with any action she might choose. Indeed, it is likely that this client will experience pain no matter what her choice. The therapist's job is not to take away any of her pain or struggle, nor to choose for her client, but to be present in such a way that the client will truly be empowered to decide for herself. The core values of equality and individuality in feminist therapy may limit the effectiveness of the therapist in working with clients from culturally different backgrounds.

WHERE TO GO FROM HERE

The Jean Baker Miller Training Institute offers workshops, courses, professional training, publications, and ongoing projects that explore applications of the relational cultural approach and integrate research, psychological theory, and social action. This relational cultural model is based on the assumption that growth-fostering relationships and disconnections are constructed within specific cultural contexts. For more information contact:

> *Jean Baker Miller Training Institute*
> Stone Center, Wellesley College
> 106 Central Street
> Wellesley, MA 02481
> Telephone: (781) 283-3007
> Fax: (781) 283-3646
> Website: *www.wellesley.edu / JBMTI*

The Stone Center Work in Progress Series lists over 100 papers and books describing various applications of the relational cultural model. For a list of publications contact:

> *Stone Center Publications*
> The Wellesley Centers for Women
> Wellesley College
> Wellesley, MA 02481
> Telephone: (781) 283-2510
> Fax: (781) 283-2504
> Website: *www.wellesley.edu / WCW / infopub.html*

The American Psychological Association has two divisions devoted to special interests in women's issues: Division 17 (Counseling Psychology's Section on Women) Website: *http://www.div17.org*, and Division 35 (Psychology of Women) Website: *http://www.apa.org/divisons/div35*. For further information about these divisions contact:

> *American Psychological Association*
> 750 First Street, N.E.
> Washington, DC 20002-4242
> Telephone: (202) 336-5500 or (800) 374-2721
> Fax: (202) 336-5568
> Website: *http://www.apa.org*

The Association for Women in Psychology (AWP) sponsors an annual conference dealing with feminist contributions to the understanding of life experiences of women. AWP is a scientific and educational feminist organization devoted to reevaluating and reformulating the role that psychology and the mental health field generally play in women's lives. For more information about this organization and its annual conference contact the AWP at:

Website: *www.theworks.baka.com / awp*

POWR on line, or Psychology of Women Resource List, is co-sponsored by APA Division 35, Psychology of Women and the Association for Women in Psychology. This public electronic network facilitates discussion of current topics, research, teaching strategies, and practice issues among people interested in the discipline of psychology of women. Most people with computer access to Bitnet or the Internet can subscribe to POWR-L at no cost. Individuals with one of the private services (Compuserve, America Online, Genie, or Prodigy) can now access the Internet by following their instructions. To subscribe, send the command below via e-mail to *LISTSERV@ URIACC* (Binet) or *LISTSERV@URIACC.URI.EDU*

Subscribe POWR-L Your name (Use first and last name)

The University of Kentucky offers a minor specialty area in counseling women and feminist therapy within Counseling Psychology M.S. and Ph.D. programs. For information contact Dr. Pam Remer at:

University of Kentucky
Department of Educational and Counseling Psychology
251-C Dickey Hall
Lexington, KY 40506-0017
Telephone: (606) 257-4158
E-mail: *CPD412@ukcc.uky.edu*
Website: *www.uky.edu/Education/edphead.html*

Texas Women's University offers a training program with emphasis in women's issues, gender issues, and family psychology. For information contact Dr. Roberta Nutt at:

Texas Women's University
Counseling Psychology Program
P. O. Box 425470
Denton, Texas 76204
Telephone: (940) 898-2313
E-mail: *F_Nutt@twu.edu*
Website: *www.twu.edu/as/psyphil/cppc*

Other resources pertaining to women's issues include those listed here.

National Organization for Women (NOW)
1000 16th St. NW, Suite 700
Washington, DC 20036
Telephone: (202) 331-0066
Website: *www.now.org*

National Women's Health Network
514 10th Street NW, Suite 400
Washington, DC 20004
Telephone: (202) 347-1140
Fax: (202) 347-1168
Website: *www.womenshealthnetwork.org*

National Abortion and Reproductive Rights Action League (NARAL)
1156 15th St. NW, Suite 700
Washington, DC 20005
Telephone: (202) 973-3000
Fax: (202) 973-3096
E-mail: naral-comments@client-mail.com
Website: *http://www.naral.org*

Newcomb College Center for Research on Women
20 Caroline Richardson Building
Tulane University
New Orleans, LA 70118-5683
Telephone: (504) 865-5238
Fax: (504) 862-8948
E-mail: *willing@mailhost.tcs.tulane.edu*
Website: *http://www.tulane.edu/wc*

Recommended Supplementary Readings

The Healing Connection: How Women Form Relationships in Therapy and Life (Miller & Stiver, 1997) describes how connections are formed between people and how this leads to strong, healthy individuals. The authors also deal with disconnections between people that lead to anxiety, isolation, and depression.

Women's Growth in Connection: Writings From the Stone Center (Jordan, Kaplan, Miller, Stiver, & Surrey, 1991) grows out of the Stone Center's influential work on women's development. This book is both a critique of traditional psychodynamic training and a major theoretical contribution to the study of development.

Women's Growth in Diversity: More Writings From the Stone Center (Jordan, 1997) builds on the foundations laid by *Women's Growth in Connection.* This work offers insights on issues such as sexuality, shame, anger, depression, power relations between women, and women's experiences in therapy.

Feminist Theories and Feminist Psychotherapies (Enns, 1997) describes the wide range of feminist theories that inform feminist therapies, including women of color feminism, liberal feminism, radical feminism, cultural feminism, socialist feminism, and postmodern perspectives. The book discusses the manner in which each of these feminisms is likely to influence feminist practice and includes short self-assessment questionnaires designed to help readers clarify their feminist theoretical perspective. A series of chapters discuss the compatibility of various psychotherapy theories with diverse feminist theories.

Subversive Dialogues: Theory in Feminist Therapy (Brown, 1994) is a significant work that brings feminist theory and therapy together. The author illustrates the application of feminist principles using case examples.

Feminist Perspectives in Therapy: An Empowerment Model for Women (Worell & Remer, 1992) is an outstanding text that clearly outlines the foundations of feminist therapy. The book covers a range of topics such as changing roles for women, feminist views of counseling practice, feminist transformation of counseling theories, and a feminist approach to assessment and diagnosis. There are also excellent chapters dealing with depression, surviving sexual assault, confronting abuse, choosing a career path, and lesbian and ethnic minority women.

Shaping the Future of Feminist Psychology: Education, Research, and Practice (Worell & Johnson, 1997) is an up-to-date resource on feminist perspectives on research, education, and practice. There is a detailed treatment of topics including feminist perspectives on assessment, feminist theory and psychological practice, training in feminist therapy, and supervision issues.

Bridging Separate Gender Worlds: Why Men and Women Clash and How Therapists Can Bring Them Together (Philpot, Brooks, Lusterman, & Nutt, 1997) provides therapists with a framework for creating gender-fair interventions for working with women and men. The authors provide therapists and students with a very useful resource for exploring gender issues within the therapeutic relationship.

References and Suggested Readings*

AMERICAN PSYCHIATRIC ASSOCIATION. (1994). *Diagnostic and statistical manual of mental disorders* (4th ed.). Washington, DC: Author.

AMERICAN PSYCHOLOGICAL ASSOCIATION. (1975). Report on the task force on sex bias and sex role stereotyping in psychotherapeutic practice. *American Psychologist, 30,* 1169–1175.

AMERICAN PSYCHOLOGICAL ASSOCIATION. (1979). Principles concerning the counseling and psychotherapy of women. *The Counseling Psychologist, 8,* 21.

BALLOU, M. (1996). Multicultural counseling and therapy theory and women. In D. W. Sue, A. E. Ivey, & P. B. Pedersen (Eds.), *A theory of multicultural counseling and therapy* (pp. 236–246). Pacific Grove, CA: Brooks/Cole.

BANKART, C. P. (1997). *Talking cures: A history of western and eastern psychotherapies.* Pacific Grove, CA: Brooks/Cole.

BASOW, S. A. (1992). *Gender: Stereotypes and roles* (3rd ed.). Pacific Grove, CA: Brooks/Cole.

BEM, S. L. (1981). Gender schema theory: A cognitive account of sex typing. *Psychological Review, 88,* 354–364.

BEM, S. L. (1983). Gender schema theory and its implications for child development. *Signs, 8,* 598–616.

*BEM, S. L. (1993). *The lenses of gender.* New Haven, CT: Yale University Press.

BRABECK, M., & BROWN, L. (1997). Feminist theory and psychological practice. In J. Worell & N. G. Johnson (Eds.), *Shaping the future of feminist psychology: Education, research, and practice* (pp. 15–35). Washington, DC: American Psychological Association.

BROWN, L. S. (1986). Gender-role analysis: A neglected component of psychological assessment. *Psychotherapy: Theory, Research, and Practice, 23*(2), 243–248.

BROWN, L. S. (1990). Taking account of gender in the clinical assessment interview. *Professional Psychology: Research and Practice, 21*(1), 12–17.

---

*Books and articles marked with an asterisk are suggested for further study.

BROWN, L. S. (1992). A feminist critique of the personality disorders. In L. S. Brown & M. Ballou (Eds.), *Personality and psychopathology: Feminist reappraisals* (pp. 206–228). New York: Guilford Press.

*BROWN, L. S. (1994). *Subversive dialogues: Theory in feminist therapy.* New York: Basic Books.

BROWN, L. S., & BALLOU, M. (Eds.). (1990). *Diversity and complexity in feminist therapy.* New York: Guilford Press.

BROWN, L. S., & BALLOU, M. (Eds.). (1992). *Personality and psychopathology: Feminist reappraisals.* New York: Guilford Press.

BROWN, L. S., & BRODSKY, A. M. (1992). The future of feminist therapy. *Psychotherapy, 29,* 51–57.

*CAPLAN, P. J. (1989). *Don't blame mother.* New York: Harper & Row.

CHESLER, P. (1972). *Women and madness.* New York: Doubleday.

CHODOROW, N. J. (1978). *The reproduction of mothering.* Berkeley: University of California Press.

CHODOROW, N. J. (1989). *Feminism and psychoanalytic theory.* New Haven, CT: Yale University Press.

CHRISLER, J. C., & HOWARD, D. (1992). *New directions in feminist psychology.* New York: Springer.

COMAS-DIAZ, L. (1987). Feminist therapy wth mainland Puerto Rican women. *Psychology of Women Quarterly, 11,* 461–474.

COREY, G., & COREY, M. (1997). *I never knew I had a choice* (6th ed.). Pacific Grove, CA: Brooks/Cole.

*CRAWFORD, M. (1995). *Talking difference. On gender and language.* Newbury Park, CA: Sage.

*ENNS, C. Z. (1987). Gestalt therapy and feminist therapy: A proposed integration. *Journal of Counseling and Development, 66,* 93–95.

ENNS, C. Z. (1991). The "new" relationship models of women's identity: A review and critique for counselors. *Journal of Counseling and Development, 69,* 209–217.

ENNS, C. Z. (1992a). Self-esteem groups: A synthesis of consciousness-raising and assertiveness training. *Journal of Counseling and Development, 71,* 7–13.

*ENNS, C. Z. (1992b). Toward integrating feminist psychotherapy and feminist philosophy. *Professional Psychology: Research and Practice, 23*(6), 453–466.

*ENNS, C. Z. (1993). Twenty years of feminist counseling and therapy: From naming biases to implementing multifaceted practice. *The Counseling Psychologist, 21*(1), 3–87.

*ENNS, C. Z. (1997). *Feminist theories and feminist psychotherapies: Origins, themes, and variations.* New York: Haworth.

*ESPIN, O. M. (1993). Feminist therapy: Not for White women only. *The Counseling Psychologist, 21*(1), 103–108.

ESPIN, O. M. (1999). *Women crossing boundaries: A psychology of immigration and transformation of sexuality.* New York: Routledge.

FEMINIST THERAPY INSTITUTE. (1990). Feminist Therapy Institute code of ethics. In H. Lerman & N. Porter (Eds.), *Feminist ethics in psychotherapy* (pp. 37–40). New York: Springer.

FODOR, I. G. (1988). Cognitive behavior therapy: Evaluation of theory and practice for addressing women's issues. In M. A. Dutton-Douglas & L. E. Walker (Eds.), *Feminist psychotherapies: Integration of therapeutic and feminist systems* (pp. 91–117). Norwood, NJ: Ablex.

FRANKS, V., & BURTLE, V. (Eds.). (1974). *Women in therapy: New psychotherapies for a changing society.* New York: Brunner/Mazel.

GANLEY, A. L. (1988). Feminist therapy with male clients. In M. A. Dutton-Douglas & L. E. Walker (Eds.), *Feminist psychotherapies: Integration of therapeutic and feminist systems* (pp. 186–205). Norwood, NJ: Ablex.

GILLIGAN, C. (1977). In a different voice: Women's conception of self and morality. *Harvard Educational Review, 47,* 481–517.

*GILLIGAN, C. (1982). *In a different voice.* Cambridge, MA: Harvard University Press.

GOLDEN, C. (1996). Relational theories of White women's development. In J. C. Chrisler, C. Golden, & P. D. Rozee (Eds.), *Lectures on the psychology of women* (pp. 229–244). New York: McGraw Hill.

GREENE, B., & SANCHEZ-HUGHES, J. (1997). Diversity: Advancing an inclusive feminist psychology. In J. Worell & N. G. Johnson (Eds.), *Shaping the future of feminist psychology: Education, research, and practice* (pp. 173–202). Washington, DC: American Psychological Association.

GREENSPAN, M. (1993). *A new approach to women and therapy* (2nd ed.). Bradenton, FL: Human Services Institute.

HERLIHY, B., & COREY, G. (1992). *Dual relationships in counseling.* Alexandria, VA: American Counseling Association.

HERLIHY, B., & COREY, G. (1996). *ACA ethical standards casebook* (5th ed.). Alexandria, VA: American Counseling Association.

HERLIHY, B., & COREY, G. (1997). *Boundary issues in counseling: Multiple roles and responsibilities.* Alexandria, VA: American Counseling Association.

HILL, M., GLASER, K., & HARDEN, J. (1995). A feminist model for ethical decision making. In E. J. Rave & C. C. Larsen (Eds.), *Ethical decision making in therapy: Feminist perspectives* (pp. 18–37). New York: Guilford Press.

HILL, M., & ROTHBLUM, E. (Eds.). (1996). *Couples therapy: Feminist perspectives.* New York: Haworth Press.

IVEY, A. E. (1993). On the need for reconstruction of our present practice of counseling and psychotherapy. *The Counseling Psychologist, 21,* 225–228.

*JORDAN, J. V. (Ed.). (1997). *Women's growth in diversity: More writings from the Stone Center.* New York: Guilford Press.

*JORDAN, J. V., KAPLAN, A. G., MILLER, J. B., STIVER, I. P., & SURREY, J. L. (Eds.). (1991). *Women's growth in connection: Writings from the Stone Center.* New York: Guilford Press.

KANTROWITZ, R. E., & BALLOU, M. (1992). A feminist critique of cognitive-behavioral therapy. In L. S. Brown & M. Ballou (Eds.), *Personality and psychopathology: Feminist reappraisals* (pp. 70–87). New York: Guilford Press.

KASCHAK, E. (1981). Feminist psychotherapy: The first decade. In S. Cox (Ed.), *Female psychology: The emerging self* (pp. 387–400). New York: St. Martins.

KASCHAK, E. (1992). *Engendered lives.* New York: Basic Books.

*KIMMEL, E., & WORELL, J. (1997). Preaching what we practice: Principles and strategies of feminist pedagogy. In J. Worell & N. G. Johnson (Eds.), *Shaping the future of feminist psychology: Education, research, and practice* (pp. 121–153). Washington, DC: American Psychological Association.

*LANDRINE, H. (Ed.). (1995). *Bringing cultural diversity to feminist psychology: Theory, research and practice.* Washington, DC: American Psychological Association.

LERMAN, H. (1986). From Freud to feminist personality theory: Getting there from here. *Psychology of Women Quarterly, 10,* 1–8.

LERNER, H. G. (1988). *Women in therapy.* New York: Harper & Row.

*LOTT, B. (1994). *Women's lives: Themes and variations in gender learning* (2nd ed.). Pacific Grove, CA: Brooks/Cole.

*MILLER, J. B. (1976). *Toward a new psychology of women.* Boston: Beacon.

*MILLER, J. B. (1991). The development of women's sense of self. In J. V. Jordan, A. G. Kaplan, J. B. Miller, I. P. Stiver, & J. L. Surrey (Eds.), *Women's growth in connection* (pp. 11–26). New York: Guilford Press.

MILLER, J. B., & STIVER, I. P. (1993). A relational approach to understanding women's lives and problems. *Psychiatric Annals, 23*(8) 424–431.

*MILLER, J. B., & STIVER, I. P. (1997). *The healing connection: How women form relationships in therapy and in life.* Boston: Beacon Press.

NICHOLS, M. P., & SCHWARTZ, R. C. (1998). *Family therapy: Concepts and methods* (4th ed.). Boston: Allyn & Bacon.

NUTT, R. (1991). Ethical principles for gender-fair family therapy. *The Family Psychologist, 7*(3), 32–33.

*PHILPOT, C. L., BROOKS, G. R., LUSTERMAN, D. D., & NUTT, R. L. (1997). *Bridging separate gender worlds: Why men and women clash and how therapists can bring them together.* Washington, DC: American Psychological Association.

*POLSTER, M. (1992). *Eve's daughters: The forbidden heroism of women.* San Francisco: Jossey-Bass.

PROCHASKA, J. O., & NORCROSS, J. C. (1999). *Systems of psychotherapy: A transtheoretical analysis* (4th ed.). Pacific Grove, CA: Brooks/Cole.

RAMPAGE, C. (1998). Feminist couple therapy. In F. M. Dattilio (Ed.), *Case studies in couple and family therapy: Systemic and cognitive perspectives* (pp. 353–370). New York: Guilford Press.

RAVE, E. J., & LARSEN, C. C. (Eds.). (1995). *Ethical decision making in therapy: Feminist perspectives.* New York: Guilford Press.

ROGERS, C. (1977). *Carl Rogers on personal power: Inner strength and its revolutionary impact.* New York: Delacorte Press.

SANTOS DE BARONA, M., & DUTTON, M. A. (1997). Feminist perspectives on assessment. In J. Worell & N. G. Johnson (Eds.), *Shaping the future of feminist psychology: Education, research, and practice* (pp. 37–56). Washington, DC: American Psychological Association.

SHARF, R. S. (2000). *Theories of psychotherapy and counseling: Concepts and cases* (2nd ed.). Pacific Grove, CA: Brooks-Cole/Wadsworth.

*SURREY, J. L. (1991). The "self-in-relation": A theory of women's development. In J. V. Jordan, A. G. Kaplan, J. B. Miller, I. P. Stiver, & J. L. Surrey (Eds.), *Women's growth in connection* (pp. 51–66). New York: Guilford Press.

TENNOV, D. (1973). Feminism, psychotherapy, and professionalism. *Journal of Contemporary Psychotherapy, 5,* 107–111.

THOMAS, S. A. (1977). Theory and practice in feminist therapy. *Social Work, 22,* 447–454.

WALDEN, S. L. (1997). Inclusion of the client perspective in ethical practice. In B. Herlihy & G. Corey, *Boundary issues in counseling: Multiple roles and responsibilities* (pp. 40–47). Alexandria, VA: American Counseling Association.

WASTELL, C. A. (1996). Feminist developmental theory: Implications for counseling. *Journal of Counseling and Development, 74,* 575–581.

*WORDEN, M., & WORDEN, B. D. (1998). *The gender dance in couples therapy.* Pacific Grove, CA: Brooks/Cole.

*WORELL, J., & JOHNSON, N. G. (Eds.). (1997). *Shaping the future of feminist psychology: Education, research, and practice.* Washington, DC: American Psychological Association.

*WORELL, J., & REMER, P. (1992). *Feminist perspectives in therapy: An empowerment model for women.* New York: Wiley.

CHAPTER

13

Family Systems Therapy

Co-authored by James Robert Bitter and Gerald Corey

INTRODUCTION
  The Family Systems Perspective
  Differences Between Systemic and Individual Approaches
  Overview of This Chapter
ADLERIAN FAMILY THERAPY
  Introduction
  Key Concepts
  Therapy Goals
  Therapist's Function and Role
  Techniques
  Concluding Comments
MULTIGENERATIONAL FAMILY THERAPY
  Introduction
  Key Concepts
  Therapy Goals
  Therapist's Function and Role
  Techniques
  Concluding Comments
HUMAN VALIDATION PROCESS MODEL
  Introduction
  Key Concepts
  Therapy Goals
  Therapist's Function and Role
  Techniques
  Concluding Comments
EXPERIENTIAL FAMILY THERAPY
  Introduction
  Key Concepts
  Therapy Goals
  Therapist's Function and Role
  Techniques
  Concluding Comments

STRUCTURAL FAMILY THERAPY
Introduction
Key Concepts
Therapy Goals
Therapist's Function and Role
Techniques
Concluding Comments

STRATEGIC FAMILY THERAPY
Introduction
Key Concepts
Therapy Goals
Therapist's Function and Role
Techniques
Concluding Comments

SOCIAL CONSTRUCTIONISM AND FAMILY THERAPY
Introduction
Key Concepts
Therapy Goals
Therapist's Function and Role
Techniques
Concluding Comments

INTEGRATION OF FAMILY THERAPY MODELS

FAMILY THERAPY APPLIED TO THE CASE OF STAN

SUMMARY AND EVALUATION
Summary
Contributions of Family Systems Approaches
Limitations and Criticisms of Family Systems Approaches

FAMILY SYSTEMS THERAPY FROM A MULTICULTURAL PERSPECTIVE
Contributions to Multicultural Counseling
Limitations for Multicultural Counseling

WHERE TO GO FROM HERE

RECOMMENDED SUPPLEMENTARY READINGS

REFERENCES AND SUGGESTED READINGS

CONTRIBUTORS TO FAMILY SYSTEMS THEORY

Family systems therapy is represented by a number of divergent theories and approaches, six of which along with the individuals most closely associated with their development are discussed in this chapter. In addition to these six, social constructionism is beginning to play a significant role in family systems therapy; however, this emerging field cannot yet be identified with any one individual.

MURRAY BOWEN was one of the original developers of mainstream family therapy. Much of his theory and practice grew out of his work with schizophrenic individuals in families. He believed families could best be understood when analyzed from a three-generation perspective because patterns of interpersonal relationships connect family members across generations. His major contributions include the core concepts of differentiation of the self and triangulation.

ALFRED ADLER was the first psychologist of the modern era to do family therapy using a systemic approach. He set up more than 30 child guidance clinics in Vienna after World War I and later Rudolf Driekurs brought this concept to the United States in the form of family education centers. Adler conducted family counseling sessions in an open public forum to educate parents in greater numbers; he believed the problems of any one family are common to all others in the community.

VIRGINIA SATIR developed conjoint family therapy, a human validation process model that emphasizes communication and emotional experiencing. Like Bowen, she used an intergenerational model, but she worked to bring family patterns to life in the present. Claiming that techniques were secondary to relationship, she concentrated on the personal relationship between therapist and family to achieve change.

C ARL WHITAKER is the best known proponent of experiential family therapy, a freewheeling, intuitive approach to help families open channels of interaction. His goal was to facilitate individual autonomy while retaining a sense of belonging in the family. He saw the therapist as an active participant and coach who enters the family process with creativity, putting enough pressure on this process to produce change in the status quo.

S ALVADOR MINUCHIN began to develop structural family therapy in the 1960s through his work with delinquent boys from poor families at the Wiltwyck School in New York. Working with colleagues at the Philadelphia Child Guidance Clinic in the 1970s, Minuchin refined the theory and practice of structural family therapy. Focusing on the structure, or organization, of the family, the therapist helps the family modify its stereotyped patterns and redefine relationships among family members. He believed structural changes must occur before individual members' symptoms could be reduced or eliminated.

JAY HALEY, a prolific writer, has had a significant impact on the development of strategic family therapy, which blends structural family therapy with the concepts of hierarchy, power, and strategic interventions. Strategic family therapy is a pragmatic approach that focuses on solving problems in the present; understanding and insight are neither required nor sought.

CLOÉ MADANES, along with her then-husband Jay Haley, established the Family Institute in Washington, D.C. in the 1970s. Through their combined therapy practice, writings, and training of family therapists, strategic family therapy became the most popular family therapy approach by the 1980s. This is a brief, solution-oriented therapy approach. The problem brought by the family to therapy is treated as "real"—not a symptom of underlying issues—and is solved.

INTRODUCTION

You will discover as you read this chapter that family systems therapy is a complex and developing field that includes many approaches to understanding and working with families.* Although Adler started working with families and systems in Vienna in the 1920s (Dreikurs, 1957), the seeds of a North American family therapy movement were not planted until the 1940s. By the 1950s systemic family therapy began to take root (Becvar & Becvar, 1996), but it was still considered a revolutionary approach to treatment. In the 1960s and 1970s, psychodynamic, behavioral, and humanistic approaches (called the first, second, and third force, respectively) dominated counseling and psychotherapy. Today, the various approaches to family systems represent a paradigm shift that we might even call the "fourth force." They are becoming the major theoretical orientations of many practitioners.

The Family Systems Perspective

The family systems perspective holds that individuals are best understood within the context of relationships and through assessing the interactions within an entire family. Symptoms are often viewed as an expression of a dysfunction within a family; these dysfunctional patterns are often thought to be passed across several generations. It is revolutionary to conclude that the identified client's problem might be a symptom of how the system functions, not just a symptom of the individual's maladjustment, history, and psychosocial development. This perspective is grounded on the assumptions that a client's problematic behavior may (1) serve a function or purpose for the family; (2) be a function of the family's inability to operate productively, especially during developmental transitions; or (3) be a symptom of dysfunctional patterns handed down across generations. All these assumptions challenge the more traditional intrapsychic frameworks for conceptualizing human problems and their formation.

The one central principle agreed upon by family therapy practitioners, regardless of their particular approach, is that the client is connected to living systems and that change in one part of the unit reverberates throughout other parts. Therefore, a treatment approach that comprehensively addresses the other family members and the larger context as well as an "identified" client is required. Because a family is an interactional unit, it has its own set of unique traits. It is not possible to accurately assess an individual's concerns without observing the interaction with and mutual influence between

---

*My (Jerry Corey's) own training did not include a systemic perspective, and thus I have had to rely on reading and attending workshops to learn about this vast field. I invited a friend and colleague, Dr. Jim Bitter, who is a professor at East Tennessee State University and who teaches courses in family systems, to co-author this chapter. His scholarly activities include publications in the areas of family mapping and family constellation, couples counseling, and family reconstruction.

the other family members, as well as the broader contexts in which the person and the family live. To focus on the internal dynamics of an individual without adequately considering interpersonal dynamics yields an incomplete picture. Because the focus is on interpersonal relationships, Becvar and Becvar (1996) maintain that family therapy is a misnomer and that "relationship therapy" might be a more appropriate label.

The family therapy perspective calls for a conceptual shift, for the family is viewed as a functioning unit that is more than the sum of the roles of its various members. The family provides a primary context for understanding how individuals function in relationship to others and how they behave. Actions by any individual family member will influence all the others in the family, and their reactions will have a reciprocal effect on the individual. Goldenberg and Goldenberg (2000) point to the need for therapists to view all behavior, including all symptoms expressed by the individual, within the context of the family and society. They add that a systems orientation does not preclude dealing with the dynamics within the individual but that this approach broadens the traditional emphasis.

Differences Between Systemic and Individual Approaches

There are significant differences between individual therapeutic approaches and systemic approaches. An example may help to illustrate these differences. Ann, age 22, sees a counselor because she is suffering from a depression that has lasted for more than 2 years and has impaired her ability to maintain friendships and work productively. She wants to feel better, but she is pessimistic about her chances. How will a therapist choose to help her?

Both the individual therapist and the systemic therapist are interested in Ann's current living situation and life experiences. Both discover that she is still living at home with her parents, who are in their 60s. They note that she has a very successful older sister, who is a prominent lawyer in the small town in which the two live. The therapists are impressed by Ann's loss of friends who have married and left town over the years while she stayed behind, often lonely and isolated. Finally, both therapists note that Ann's depression affects others as well as herself. It is here, however, that the similarities end:

The individual therapist may:	*The systemic therapist may:*
Focus on obtaining an accurate diagnosis, perhaps using the DSM-IV	Explore the system for family process and rules, perhaps using a genogram
Begin therapy with Ann immediately	Invite Ann's mother, father, and sister into therapy with her
Focus on the causes, purposes, and cognitive, emotional, and behavioral processes involved in Ann's depression and coping	Focus on the family relationships within which the continuation of Ann's depression "makes sense"

Be concerned with Ann's individual experiences and perspectives	Be concerned with transgenerational meanings, rules, cultural and gender perspectives within the system, and even community and larger systems affecting the family
Intervene in ways designed to help Ann cope	Intervene in ways designed to help change the context

Systemic therapists do not deny the importance of the individual in the family system, but they believe an individual's affiliations and interactions have more power in the person's life than a single therapist could ever hope to have. By working with the whole family—or even the community—system, the therapist has a chance to observe how the individual acts within the system and serves its needs; how the system influences (and is influenced by) the individual; and what interventions might lead to changes that help the couple, family, or larger system as well as the individual expressing pain. *[handwritten: 3 elements]*

Ann's depression may have organic, genetic, or hormonal causes. It may be the result of cognitive, experiential, or behavioral patterns that interfere with effective coping. Even if her depression can be explained in this manner, however, the systemic therapist will be very interested in how her depression affects the family and is integrated into and being maintained by family relationship patterns. Indeed, many family systems approaches would investigate how the depression serves other family members; distracts from problems in the intimate relationships of others; or reflects her need to adjust to family rules, to cultural injunctions, or to processes influenced by gender or family life-cycle development. Rather than losing sight of the individual, family therapists understand the person as specifically embedded in larger systems.

From the systemic perspective, an individual may carry a symptom for the entire family. An individual's level of functioning is a manifestation of the way the family is functioning. For example, a young girl who develops ulcers may be signaling not only her own pain but also unexpressed pain somewhere else in the family. Thus, if individual change is a goal of therapy with the daughter, it is essential to understand how the family has a continuing influence on her and how any changes she makes are likely to affect the other members of her family.

An individual can have a symptom or disorder that exists independently of the family structure. As noted, Ann's clinical depression could be caused by a biochemical imbalance rather than some family dynamic. However, a symptom always has ramifications for members of the family. Even if Ann's depression is biochemical, her family participated in the creation of the context in which it emerged and will have to react to it and make systemic adjustments to the problem.

We have examined nine contemporary theories of individual counseling in Part Two, most of which have made some contributions to the development of family systems thinking and practice. The main goal of these orientations is to bring about changes within an autonomous individual in the realms of thinking, feeling, and behaving. It is true that these changes often have repercussions on the system of which the client is part, but with the exception of feminist therapy they generally do not aim at changing that system.

In contrast, the goal of most approaches to family therapy is change in the system, which is assumed to produce change in the individual members. Family, or relationship, therapy aims at helping family members change dysfunctional patterns of relating and create functional ways of interacting. From a pure family systems perspective, families have a tendency to remain static and to resist change. Even in clearly dysfunctional families, members tend to prefer known and practiced patterns to new and unknown processes. Family therapists are all too familiar with abusive systems in which victims of violence return to what is painfully "known" rather than risk a potentially healthier but "thoroughly unknown" change in living. The process of systemic change may be slow, requiring patience, understanding, and often carefully planned interventions. The family therapist may function as a teacher, a coach, a model, or a director. When therapy is successful, the family may learn about patterns that have been transmitted from generation to generation or learn ways to detect and solve problems that keep members stuck in dysfunctional relational patterns.

Overview of This Chapter

Guerin and Chabot (1992) make a critical point: "Forty years into its lifecycle, the family therapy movement has not yet developed a single comprehensive integrated theory" (p. 257). Some practitioners would not consider such an integration of approaches an appropriate goal anyway, noting that it has been 100 years since the birth of modern psychotherapy and there is still no comprehensive model for counseling individuals or groups. Indeed, we are entering a period in the helping professions when multiple perspectives are needed and valued. It is not possible in one chapter to integrate the diverse therapy perspectives that fall under the family systems umbrella. Rather, this chapter presents a brief overview of the major systemic theories and describes some of their common denominators.

Several excellent survey books deal with the major systems of contemporary family therapy: *Family Therapy: Concepts and Methods* (Nichols & Schwartz, 1998); *Family Therapy: A Systemic Integration* (Becvar & Becvar, 1996); *Family Counseling and Therapy* (Horne, 2000); *Family Therapy: An Overview* (Goldenberg & Goldenberg, 2000); *The Practice of Family Therapy: Key Elements Across Models* (Hanna & Brown, 1999); *Systems of Family Therapy: An Adlerian Integration* (Sherman & Dinkmeyer, 1987); *Case Studies in Couple and Family Therapy: Systemic and Cognitive Perspectives* (Dattilio, 1998); *The Family Interpreted: Feminist Theory in Clinical Practice* (Luepnitz, 1988); and *Ethnicity and Family Therapy* (McGoldrick, Pearce, & Giordano, 1996). If you are interested in gaining a more in-depth understanding of the theory and practice of family therapy, we highly recommend that you begin by reading one or more of these books.

This chapter deals with seven models of family therapy: (1) the open forum model of Alfred Adler, Rudolf Dreikurs, and their associates; (2) the multigenerational family systems model of Murray Bowen; (3) the human validation process model of Virginia Satir; (4) the experiential/symbolic approach of Carl Whitaker; (5) the structural approach of Salvador Minuchin; (6) the strategic approach of Jay Haley and Cloé Madanes; and (7) recent innovations in family therapy, labeled as second-order family therapy (Hoffman, 1993). A systemic therapist of the new century may practice by utilizing any one of these approaches or may creatively employ various perspectives when dealing with a particular case. Six of these approaches are briefly compared in Table 13-1.

Because there is no unified theory of family therapy, this chapter deviates from the usual format. Each of the seven models of family therapy is described by attending to a set of common themes: (1) key concepts, (2) therapy goals, (3) the therapist's function and role, and (4) techniques. Following this relatively brief overview, we discuss the trend toward integration of approaches to family therapy. As with the preceding chapters, the case of Stan illustrates how a family systems therapist might work with his presenting problems.

ADLERIAN FAMILY THERAPY

Introduction

Alfred Adler was the first psychologist of the modern era to do family therapy. His approach was systemic long before systems theory had been applied to psychotherapy. After World War I, Adler set up more than 30 child guidance clinics in Vienna where he conducted therapy sessions in an "open forum" before parents, teachers, and members of the local community. All of these clinics were eliminated by Hitler's Nazi Party by 1934 (Christensen, 1993). Rudolf Dreikurs brought the process to the United States in the form of family education centers. He systematized and refined Adler's early work with family constellation and purposeful behavior, delineating the goals of children's misbehavior and developing an interview and goal-disclosure process that produced a "recognition reflex" in children (Terner & Pew, 1978).

A basic assumption in Adlerian family therapy is that both parents and children often become locked in repetitive, negative interactions based on mistaken goals that motivate all parties involved. Further, these negative interactional patterns are a reflection of the autocratic/permissive dialectic that has permeated much of our social heritage. In most cases, therefore, the problems of any one family are common to all others in the community. Although much of Adlerian family therapy is conducted in private sessions, Adlerians also use an educational model to counsel families

TABLE 13-1 ■ A Comparison of Six Systemic Viewpoints in Family Therapy

	ADLERIAN FAMILY THERAPY	MULTI-GENERATIONAL FAMILY THERAPY	HUMAN VALIDATION PROCESS MODEL	EXPERIENTIAL/ SYMBOLIC FAMILY THERAPY	STRUCTURAL FAMILY THERAPY	STRATEGIC FAMILY THERAPY
Key figures	Alfred Adler, Rudolf Dreikurs, Oscar Christensen & Manford Sonstegard	Murray Bowen	Virginia Satir	Carl Whitaker	Salvador Minuchin	Jay Haley & Cloé Madanes
Time focus	Present with some reference to the past	Present and past: family of origin; three generations	Here and now	Present	Present and past	Present and future
Therapy goals	Enable parents as leaders; unlock mistaken goals and interactional patterns in family; promotion of effective parenting	Differentiate the self; change the individual within the context of the system; decrease anxiety	Promote growth, self-esteem, and connection; help family reach congruent communication and interaction	Promote spontaneity, creativity, autonomy, and ability to play	Restructure family organization; change dysfunctional transactional patterns	Eliminate presenting problem; change dysfunctional patterns; interrupt sequence

TABLE 13-1 ■ (continued)

	ADLERIAN FAMILY THERAPY	MULTI-GENERATIONAL FAMILY THERAPY	HUMAN VALIDATION PROCESS MODEL	EXPERIENTIAL/ SYMBOLIC FAMILY THERAPY	STRUCTURAL FAMILY THERAPY	STRATEGIC FAMILY THERAPY
Role and function of the therapist	Educator; motivational investigator; collaborator	Guide, objective researcher, teacher; monitor of own reactivity	Active facilitator; resource person; detective; model for congruence	Family coach; challenger; model for change through play	"Friendly uncle"; stage manager; promoter of change in family structure	Active director of change; problem solver
Process of change	Formation of relationship based on mutual respect; investigation of birth order and mistaken goals, re-education	Questions and cognitive processes lead to differentiation and understanding of family of origin	Family is helped to move from status quo through chaos to new possibilities and new integrations	Awareness and seeds of change are planted in therapy confrontations	Therapist joins the family in a leadership role; changes structure; sets boundaries	Change occurs through action-oriented directives and paradoxical interventions
Techniques and innovations	Family constellation; typical day; goal disclosure; natural/logical consequences	Genograms; dealing with family-of-origin issues; detriangulating relationships	Empathy; touch; communication; sculpting; role playing; family-life chronology	Co-therapy; self-disclosure; confrontation; use of self as change agent	Joining & accommodating; unbalancing; tracking; boundary making; enactments	Reframing; directives and paradox; amplifying; pretending; enactments

in public in an open forum at schools, community agencies, and specially designed family education centers. At these centers the therapist engages both a family-in-focus and the audience in an exploration of motivations and a reorientation of the family based on encouragement and the use of natural and logical consequences.

Key Concepts

As noted in Chapter 5, Adlerians believe human beings are essentially social, purposeful, subjective, and interpretive in their approach to life. These attributes are no accident; they are required, at least in part, from the moment of birth. Without the social, physical, and emotional nurturing provided in the family, no infant would survive. Within the family, children quickly become active agents, defining and redefining the family constellation or system; striving for growth, significance, and meaning; and acting in line with their subjective—and too often mistaken—interpretations of life.

Parents should be the natural leaders of families. They are older, more experienced, and carry the societal mandate for rearing the next generation. Too often, however, children in Western cultures have a far greater impact on the development and interactions of the family than do the parents. Even in functional families, children seem more capable of influencing adult behavior than the other way around. In part this is because most adults have very little effective preparation for parenting. When push comes to shove, most parents reenact the autocratic or permissive upbringings they experienced themselves.

FAMILY ATMOSPHERE   "The conjunction of all the family forces—the climate of relationships that exist between people—is termed family atmosphere" (Sherman & Dinkmeyer, 1987, p. 9). Because the family is a system, each member exerts an influence on every other member. In each family an atmosphere or climate develops that can be said to characterize how the family members relate to each other. Both autocratic and permissive atmospheres are common in Western culture and easily become incorporated in family life as a need for power and control.

Family atmosphere, however, is unique to each family. The relationship between the parents is often the clearest indication of what will constitute the family's way of being and interacting. Parents are the models for how one gender relates to the other, how to work and participate in the world, and how to get along with other people. Children may experience these models as joyful, angry, loving, frightening, strict, easygoing, involved, indulgent, protective/overprotective, hostile, nurturing, challenging, or respectful, to name a few.

What the family comes to value plays a significant role in the development of children and family life. When both parents maintain and support the same value, Adlerians call it a *family value:* it is a value that cannot be ignored and that will require each child to take a stand in relation to it. Common family values emerge around education, religion, money, achievement, and right and wrong.

Each person in the system learns to negotiate within the limitations of the climate established. With rare exceptions, the atmosphere in which we are raised tends to become the model for how we expect life and the world to be.

FAMILY CONSTELLATION   Adler (1930, 1931, 1938) often noted that the family system or constellation consisted of the parents, children, and even extended family members, but then he would immediately shift to a discussion of birth order. Adler identified five birth positions: oldest, second of only two, middle, youngest, and only (see Chapter 5). These five positions represent vantage points from which children view the world. It is not the position that counts, however, but rather the meaning and interpretation the child gives to that position. In this sense every person's birth position is unique and uniquely defined.

Adlerian family therapists approach family constellation as a description of how each person finds a place within the system. How does each child relate to the parents, guardians, or extended family members? How does each child relate to and define "self" in relation to the other children? Who is most different from whom? Which children have aligned with each other? Against whom? Which parents have aligned with which children? Toward what end? How does each child address family values; negotiate within and influence the family atmosphere; or handle the impact of culture, age and gender differences, and the demands of school and society?

A typical investigation of family constellation may start by asking the parents to describe each of the children. These descriptions often reveal both the effects of birth order and the unique ways each child has adapted to engage or challenge what is important to the parents. Many Adlerians use genograms (a three-generation family map) to develop a graphic picture of the family system (Sherman & Dinkmeyer, 1987; Bitter, 1988, 1991a). A phenomenological perspective can be gained by asking family members, especially the index person or a child the family identifies as having difficulties, to provide three adjectives for each person in the genogram. In the Adlerian model a genogram says nothing in and of itself; it is a starting point from which clients communicate the meaning in their lives. When whole families construct a genogram, there are often as many interpretations as there are family members.

MISTAKEN GOALS: AN INTERACTIONAL VIEW   Adlerians make a distinction between the life goals that account for the development of lifestyles and the more immediate goals that account for everyday behavior. Dreikurs (1940a, 1940b) first delineated four goals of children's misbehavior as a motivational typology for the everyday behaviors of children. These goals are attention getting, power struggle, revenge, and a demonstration of inadequacy (also called an assumed disability). They act as "shorthand explanations/descriptions of consistent patterns of misbehavior in children" (Bitter, 1991b, p. 210).

Dreikurs (1950; Dreikurs & Soltz, 1964) developed a systematic approach to goal recognition based on (a) descriptions of the child's misbehavior,

(b) the parents' reactions to the misbehavior, and (c) the child's reaction to the parents' attempts at discipline. Using these four goals as tentative hypotheses, Dreikurs found that he could suggest mistaken goals to children and that a *recognition reflex* (a smile or a twinkle in the eyes) would indicate which goals the children sought. Bitter (1991b) added three additional goals to this Adlerian conceptualization that he believed acted as conscious motivations for some behaviors in young children: these goals were self-elevation, getting, and avoidance.

By keeping these interactive goal patterns in mind, Adlerians are able to make sense of both children's behaviors and parental actions and reactions reported in family process. Goal recognition and disclosure are central to Adlerian family counseling (Bitter, Christensen, Hawes, & Nicoll, 1998; Christensen, 1993). It systematizes the interviewing process and allows parents and children to back away from mistaken behaviors in favor of more functional and effective approaches.

Therapy Goals

Adlerian family therapists want to engage parents in a learning experience and a collaborative assessment. Part of this assessment includes an investigation of the multiple ways parents function as family leaders—or lose the ability to do so. Under most conditions, a goal of therapy is to establish and support parents as effective leaders of the family.

Using the information gathered during assessment, Adlerians explicate the systemic process in the family by describing the place each person has assumed and the interactive processes that are repeated in daily living. Goal disclosure is also used to facilitate an understanding of the motivations involved. These interventions serve another goal of therapy: to replace automatic, often nonconscious, negative interactions with a conscious understanding of family process.

Adlerian family therapists characterize their approach as motivation modification rather than behavior modification. The therapist develops with families specific changes in process that are designed to replace mistaken goals with those that favor functional family interactions. Over the last half of the 20th century, Adlerians developed a wide range of parenting skills and interventions that constitute what is now called authoritative-responsive parenting or "democratic" child rearing (Dinkmeyer, McKay, & Dinkmeyer, 1997; Popkin, 1993). Based on an understanding of the family's specific motivational patterns, parents often leave the therapy session with suggestions designed to initiate a reorientation of the family.

Therapist's Function and Role

Adlerian family therapists function as collaborators who seek to join the family from a position of mutual respect. Within this collaborative role, Bitter et al. (1998) stress the functions of systemic investigation and education. The systemic investigation focuses on (a) the family constellation or system, (b) the motivations behind problematic interactions, and (c) the family process throughout a typical day. The results of this investigation are used to develop interventions and recommendations designed to correct mistaken goals and provide parents with an understanding of parenting skills associated with more effective and harmonious living.

Adlerian family therapists often use a public therapy process they call "open forum" family counseling (Bitter et al., 1998; Christensen, 1993). Similar to the process first used by Adler in Vienna, the therapist counsels a family in front of a group of parents, teachers, and other community members. The counselor in these sessions has two clients: the family-in-focus and the audience. The process emphasizes interactions within the family. Very little is disclosed that could not be observed by anyone watching the family in public. By working with the commonalities between the family and the audience, the therapist educates many families through one. It is not uncommon for families in the audience to get more out of the session than the family-in-focus.

Techniques

The open forum process has been incorporated as part of Adlerian brief therapy (Bitter et al., 1998). In this model the parents are generally interviewed initially without the children, a process that supports the establishment of parents-as-leaders in the family. The therapist joins with the parents and the audience through an exploration of the family constellation. The experience of parent/child relationships held in common between the family and the audience links the two, allowing members of each system to have a therapeutic influence on the other.

PROBLEM DESCRIPTIONS AND GOAL IDENTIFICATION   Adlerian therapists use specific examples to understand the concerns parents present. While listening to a description of specific problem incidents, the counselor often asks the parent(s) "What did you do about it?" This question helps to establish the negative interaction pattern that is likely to be repeated many times during the day. The therapist also asks the parent(s) "How did you feel (or react) when . . . ?" Parents' feelings and reactions are often the most reliable clue to mistaken goals in both children and adults. (See Bitter et al., 1998, or Dreikurs and Soltz, 1964, for the relationship between motivation and parental response.)

TYPICAL DAY   Adlerians often assess the family atmosphere and family interactional patterns by asking the family to describe a typical day. An exploration of a typical day will reveal repeated patterns of interaction and the ways children meet their immediate goals—as well as the atmosphere and family values supported by the parents' approach to each other and to child rearing. An investigation of a typical day is especially useful when parents are unable to present specific incidents of concern. Adlerians expect that the same parent/child interactions reported while trying to get the children up will be repeated at or before bedtime.

THE CHILD INTERVIEW AND GOAL DISCLOSURE   Parent interviews generally yield tentative hypotheses about the goals of children's misbehavior. These guesses are shared with the parents, but they remain only *possibilities* until they are confirmed in an interview with the child(ren). Goal disclosure with children works best in relation to a specific event or misbehavior rather than a general discussion. When such an event or misbehavior has been clarified with the child, goals are suggested tentatively. Adlerians often ask, "Do you know why you do . . . ?" Children's answers are neither accepted nor rejected but are acknowledged as a transition to disclosure: "That's a possibility. I have another idea. Would you like to hear it?" As much as possible, goals are suggested in language that has meaning for the child. For example, using Dreikurs's four goals with a child who skips school:

- Could it be that you skip school to keep dad busy with you (attention)?
- Could it be that you skip school to show mom that you're the boss and that no one can make you go (a power struggle)?
- Could it be that you skip school to get even with dad (revenge)?
- Could it be that you skip school because you want to be left alone (an assumed disability)?

If the therapist is correct with any of these guesses, the child will often exhibit a recognition reflex. This reflex is a confirmation of the motivational diagnosis. Without a recognition response, the counselor's original assessment of the purposes for misbehavior is suspect, and a reevaluation must be considered based on the development of new data.

Concluding Comments

Open forum family counseling usually ends with the therapist asking the parents and the audience to generate new approaches that will end mistaken interactions and lead to more democratic, harmonious, and effective family living. Recommendations that come from the audience are often more easily received by the family-in-focus than those that come from the counselor because families-in-focus experience the audience as peers in the therapy process. In the final phase of counseling, therefore, the therapist serves as a leader and educator, helping the family and the audience make the best use of the ideas generated. Adlerian family therapists use a lot of encouragement to strengthen parents in their resolve and help children find new purpose in life.

Confidentiality is impossible in an open forum setting, and the therapist cannot guarantee it. The process relies on families to be somewhat self-monitoring of what they say and what they present. Christensen (1993) suggests that what is lost in confidentiality is gained in accountability because every part of the change process must "make common sense" to the members of the audience. Based on Dreikurs's (1971) original formulations, most Adlerians seek to develop *social equality*—the sense that everyone has an equal right to be valued and respected—in the family. This is a development welcomed by feminists and much needed at a time when abuse of power in families is at such high levels.

If you are interested in a more in-depth study of this approach, we recommend Bitter et al. (1998), Christensen (1993), and Sherman and Dinkmeyer (1987).

 # MULTIGENERATIONAL FAMILY THERAPY

Introduction

Murray Bowen was one of the original developers of mainstream family therapy. His family systems theory, which is a theoretical/clinical model that evolved from psychoanalytic principles and practices, is sometimes referred to as multigenerational (or transgenerational or intergenerational) family therapy. In fairness, Bowen would have seen his approach as a departure from psychoanalytic therapy. His approach operates on the premise that a family can best be understood when it is analyzed from at least a three-generation perspective, because a predictable pattern of interpersonal relationships connects the functioning of family members across generations. According to Bowen, the cause of an individual's problems can be understood only by viewing the role of the family as an emotional unit. A basic assumption in Bowenian family therapy is that unresolved emotional fusion to one's family must be addressed if one hopes to achieve a mature and unique personality.

Key Concepts

Bowen emphasizes the role of theory as a guide in practicing family therapy. For him a well-articulated theory is essential in remaining emotionally detached as a family therapist. Bowen (1976) believes the absence of a clearly articulated theory had resulted in an unstructured state of chaos in family therapy. According to Becvar and Becvar (1996), Bowenian therapeutic practice is built on a solid theoretical base, and the practices are consistent with that conceptual foundation. This approach offers a method for organizing data, explaining past events, and predicting future events. It contributes to an understanding of both the causes of and how to control events.

Bowen's theory and practice of family therapy grew out of his work with schizophrenic individuals in families. He was much more interested in developing a theory of family systems therapy than in designing techniques for working with families. In two major articles Bowen (1966, 1976) identifies eight key concepts as being central to his theory: differentiation of the self, triangulation, the nuclear family emotional system, the family-projection process, emotional cutoff, the multigenerational transmission process, sibling position, and societal regression. Of these, the major contributions of Bowen's theory are the core concepts of differentiation of the self and triangulation. In this section we also deal with the importance of self-awareness on the part of the family therapist, especially with reference to understanding how experiences in the family of origin are likely to affect clinical practice.

DIFFERENTIATION OF THE SELF   The cornerstone of Bowen's theory is differentiation of the self, which involves both the psychological separation of intellect and emotion and independence of the self from others. Differentiated individuals are able to choose between being guided by their feelings or by their thoughts. Undifferentiated people have difficulty separating themselves from others and tend to fuse with dominant emotional patterns in the family. These people have a low degree of autonomy, react emotionally, and are unable to take a clear position on issues. People who are fused to their family of origin tend to marry others to whom they can become fused. Two undifferentiated individuals seek and find each other and become a couple. Unproductive family dynamics of the previous generation are transmitted from one generation to the next through such a marriage (Becvar & Becvar, 1996). In family systems theory the key to being a healthy person encompasses both a sense of belonging to one's family and a sense of separateness and individuality.

Similar to psychoanalytic theory, the process of individuation involves a differentiation whereby individuals acquire a sense of self-identity. This differentiation from the family of origin allows one to accept personal responsibility for one's thoughts, feelings, perceptions, and actions. Simply leaving one's family of origin, however, does not mean that one has differentiated. Individuation, or psychological maturity, is not a fixed destination that is reached once and for all; rather, it is a lifelong developmental process that is achieved relative to the family of origin through reexamination and resolution of conflicts within individual and relational contexts.

The distinction between emotional reactivity and thinking can be difficult to discern at times. Those who are not emotionally reactive experience themselves as having a choice of possible responses; their reactions are not automatic but involve a reasoned and balanced assessment of self and others. Emotional reactivity, in contrast, is easily seen in clients who present themselves as paranoid, intensely anxious, panic stricken, or even "head over heels in love." In these cases feelings have overwhelmed thinking and reason, and people experience themselves as being unable to choose a different reaction. Clarity of response, in Bowen's theory, is marked by a broad perspective, a focus on facts and knowledge, an appreciation of complexity, and a recognition of feelings rather than being dominated by them (Papero, 2000).

TRIANGULATION   Bowen (1976) notes that anxiety can easily develop within intimate relationships. In stressful situations two people may recruit a third person into the relationship to reduce the anxiety and gain stability. This is called triangulation. Although triangulation may lessen the emotional tension between the original pair, the underlying conflict is not addressed and in the long run the situation worsens. If a couple has unresolved and intense conflicts, for instance, they may focus their attention on a problematic son. Instead of fighting with each other, they are temporarily distracted by riveting their attention on their son. Yet their basic conflict remains unsolved. Once the child's problem is resolved or he leaves home, they no longer have him to balance their system. The couple often resumes fighting and may even file for divorce because their differences and conflicts were never resolved. Because the family is not a static entity, a change in one part of the system affects the actions of all others involved.

Bowen sometimes worked with both members of a conflictual dyad (the couple), and he did not require that every family member be involved in the therapy sessions. Bowen tended to work from the inside out: Starting with the spousal relationship, he helped the two adults establish their own differentiation. He often worked with the strongest individual while the rest of the family was present, coaching each person through his or her conflictual relationships. As a therapist, he attempted to maintain a stance of neutrality. If the therapist becomes emotionally entangled with any one family member, the therapist loses effectiveness and becomes part of a triangulated relationship. Bowen maintains that to be effective family therapists have to have a very high level of differentiation. If therapists still have unresolved family issues and are emotionally reactive, they are likely to revisit those difficulties in every family they see.

Therapy Goals

Although all family therapists are interested in resolving problems presented by a family and decreasing symptoms, Bowenians are mainly interested in changing the individuals within the context of the system. They contend that problems manifested in one's current family will not significantly change until relationship patterns in one's family of origin are understood and directly challenged. Emotional problems will be transmitted from generation to generation until unresolved emotional attachments are dealt with effectively. Change must occur with other family members and cannot be done by an individual in a counseling room.

The practice of Bowenian family therapy is governed by the following two goals: (1) lessening anxiety and symptom relief and (2) an increase in each family member's level of differentiation of the self (Kerr & Bowen, 1988). To bring about significant change in a family system, it is necessary to open closed family ties and to engage actively in a detriangulation process. Although problems are seen as residing in the system rather than in the individual, the route to changing oneself is through changing in relationship to others in the family of origin (Nichols & Schwartz, 1998).

Therapist's Function and Role

Bowen viewed himself as an objective researcher who aimed to help individuals in the family assess and understand their relational styles within the family system. Bowenian therapists function as teachers, coaches, and neutral observers who are responsible for establishing the tone of family therapy. Bowen taught individuals or couples about triangulation and then expected them to go back to their family of origin to emotionally extricate themselves from these triangular patterns. The purpose of going home again is not to confront family members or even to establish peace and harmony but to encourage clients to come to know others in their family as they are (Bowen, 1976).

Let us say that an adult only child of aging parents returns home to help her parents decide whether to sell the home they have had for 35 years. The minute Alice walks in the door, her parents begin to bicker about little things. This is a pattern she knows all too well, and in the past it has left her stomach in knots. Today, however, she is prepared. Rather than getting caught up in the content of their arguments, she carefully observes how they handle their disagreements. She notices that her parents seem to argue about things that don't really matter, and she wonders if it helps them avoid the bigger issue of possibly leaving their home. When Alice's father turns to her and says, "You're a banker; will you please tell your mother that we can't be wasting money all the time?", she does not take the bait this time. Rather, she says: "Mom, Dad, please sit down. I want you to know that I love you both. I know a decision about moving is a very big decision and that's why I want to be here to support you. But it's your decision to make, not mine. The two of you have been working things out together a long time, and you can work this out too. I want to be here with you, but I won't be part of the decision-making team."

In his role as expert, Bowen helped individuals or couples gather information, and he coached or guided them into new behaviors by demonstrating how individuals might change their relationships with their parents, siblings, and extended family members. He instructed them how to be better observers and also how to move from emotional reactivity to increased objectivity. He did not tell clients what to do but asked a series of questions designed to help clients figure out their own role in their family emotional process. Although he provided guidance for how they could free themselves from fused emotional relationships, he saw it as their responsibility to take the steps necessary to bring about self-differentiation. According to Bowenians, this occurs through a rational understanding of the nuclear family emotional system, the family-projection process, and the transmission process over several generations. Bowenians maintain that therapy sessions can be viewed as rehearsals for becoming differentiated; the main therapeutic work is relating to members of their family in new ways. Clients learn through the work they do outside the therapy session. It should be mentioned that extended family systems work cannot be completed in a few visits to one's family; it is an ongoing process.

THERAPIST SELF-AWARENESS   As a prerequisite to practicing effectively with families, therapists must be aware of how they have been influenced by their own family of origin. If a family therapist overly identifies with one family member in the therapeutic encounter, it is likely that his or her own childhood issues will be triggered. Without self-awareness, perceptions will be colored and distorted by one's personal history. The therapist will probably not be objective or open to understanding certain clients. It is inevitable that we will encounter aspects of our family in the families with whom we work. The premise underlying the significance of understanding our family of origin is that the patterns of interpersonal behavior we learned in our family of origin will be repeated with clients.

Techniques

Bowen's theory describes how individuals function within a family system, how they develop dysfunctional patterns, and how they can repair and enhance their relationships with members of their family. The transgenerational approach focuses on emotional sequences with one's family of origin, spouse, and children. Bowenians believe understanding how a family system operates is far more important than using a particular technique. They tend to use interventions such as questions, tracking sequences, teaching, and directives to a family. They value information about past relationships as a significant context from which they design interventions in the present.

GENOGRAM WORK   Bowen assumes that multigenerational patterns and influences are central in understanding present nuclear family functioning. What occurs in one generation will probably occur in the next because key unresolved emotional issues tend to be played out over generations. He devised a "family diagram," or genogram, as a way of collecting and organizing important data over at least three generations. A family genogram consists of a pictorial layout of each partner's three-generational extended family. It is a tool for both the therapist and family members to understand critical turning points in the family's emotional processes and to note dates of births, deaths, marriages, and divorces. The genogram also gives information about some of these characteristics of a family: cultural and ethnic origins, religious affiliation, socioeconomic status, type of contact among family members, and proximity of family members. By providing an evolutionary picture of the nuclear family, a genogram becomes a tool for assessing each partner's degree of fusion to extended families and to each other. Bowen also integrates the perspective of Walter Toman (1994) on birth order and family constellation, so that these family maps have a structural consistency. Unlike Adlerians, who approach the family constellation more phenomenologically, Toman and Bowen tend to present birth order as fixed and ordinal with more or less constant characteristics. Thus, siblings are presented in genograms horizontally, oldest to youngest, each with more of a relationship to the parents than to one another. Genograms are used by family therapists of various orientations, not simply Bowenians, and many adaptations in form have been made. For a comprehensive guide to working with genograms, see McGoldrick, Gerson, and Shellenberger's (1999) book, *Genograms: Assessment and Intervention*.

ASKING QUESTIONS   Another Bowenian technique consists of asking questions that are designed to get clients to think about the role they play in relating with members of their family. Bowen's style tended to be controlled, somewhat detached, and cerebral. In working with a couple, for example, he expected each partner to talk to him rather than to talk directly to each other in the session. This calm style of questioning was aimed at helping each partner think about particular issues that are problematic with his or her family of origin. The attempt is to resolve the fusion that exists between the partners and to maximize each person's self-differentiation from both the family of origin and the nuclear family system.

Bowenian therapists are more concerned with managing their neutrality than with having the "right" question at the right time. Still, questions that emphasize personal choice are very important. A therapist attempting to help a woman who has been divorced by her husband may ask:

- "Do you want to continue to react to him in ways that keep the conflict going, or would you rather feel more in charge of your life?"
- "What other ways could you consider responding if the present way isn't very satisfying to you and is not changing him?"
- "Given what has happened recently, how do you want to react when you're with your children and the subject of their father comes up?"

Notice that these questions are all asked of the person as part of a relational unit. This type of questioning is called *circular* (or is said to have circularity) because the focus of change is in relation to others who are recognized as having an effect on the person's functioning.

Concluding Comments

Bowen's approach to family therapy can be characterized as the application of rational thinking in emotionally saturated systems. His emphasis on the separation of thought and feeling as well as therapeutic detachment has been criticized by some feminists as another case of elevating "rationality" and "autonomy" over connectedness, integration, and interdependence (Luepnitz, 1988). And indeed Bowen's model, although claiming to support personal presence and involvement, tends to put greater emphasis on emotional neutrality and objective observation than on personal connection and conjoint family process. The current feminist emphasis on collaboration, involvement, and connection places most feminist therapists at the opposite end of the continuum from Bowen's detachment theory.

If you are interested in a more in-depth study of this approach, we recommend Papero (2000), Kerr and Bowen (1988), and Bowen (1966, 1972, 1976, 1978). In addition to Bowen, James Framo (1992) has made significant contributions to multigenerational family therapy, integrating perspectives from object-relations theory.

 HUMAN VALIDATION PROCESS MODEL

Introduction

At the same time that Bowen was developing his approach, Virginia Satir (1983) began emphasizing family connection in a model called conjoint family therapy. The human validation process model grew out of Satir's mission to release the potential that she saw in every family (Satir & Baldwin, 1983; Satir & Bitter, 2000). Her approach emphasizes communication as well as emotional experiencing. She was highly intuitive and believed spontaneity, creativity, self-disclosure, and risk taking were central to family therapy. In her view, techniques are secondary to the relationship the therapist is able to establish with the family. The personal involvement of the therapist with a family is what makes a difference.

Key Concepts

Satir's human validation process stresses enhancement and validation of self-esteem, family rules, congruence versus defensive communication patterns, sculpting, nurturing triads and family mapping, and family life-fact chronologies. It emphasizes factors such as making contact, metaphor, reframing, emotional honesty, clear communication, creating new possibilities, drama, humor, and personal touch in the therapy process. Like Bowen, Satir believed in looking at three generations of family life. Unlike him, she worked to bring those patterns to life *in the present,* either by having families develop maps (her word for genograms) and life-fact chronologies or by creating a group process in which family patterns and experiences could be simulated in a reconstruction.

FAMILY LIFE   Children always enter the world as part of preexisting systems, with the family being the most common and central one. Their early experience is a constant transition from what is known and familiar to what is unknown and unfamiliar, the movement from the womb to the outside world being but the first of many such transitions. These transitions often leave children with feelings of fear, helplessness, and even anger as they struggle for competence and security in a challenging and often difficult new environment.

Children enter families that are already loaded with rules, and as they grow, more rules are developed to help the system function and prosper. Rules can pertain to any part of human living and interaction, but the most important rules, according to Satir, are the ones that govern communication: who says what to whom under what conditions. Rules may be spoken or unspoken and are embedded in the behavioral responses and interactions of the system. These rules, which are often couched in terms of "shoulds" or "should nots," become strong messages that govern interactions within a family. When parents feel worried or helpless, they tend to set rules in an attempt to control a situation. These family rules may initially assist children in handling anger, helplessness, and fear. They are intended to provide a safety net as children venture into the world (Satir, Bitter, & Krestensen, 1988).

It is impossible for children to escape growing up without such rules. Unfortunately, they often receive these rules in forms that quickly lose their effectiveness; that is, the rules are perceived to be *absolute* and too often *impossible.* Examples are: "Never be angry with your father." "Always keep a smile on your face." "Don't bring attention to yourself." "Never let people see your weaknesses; show neither affection nor anger." "Don't confront your parents; always try to please them." "Don't talk to outsiders about your family." "Children are to be seen but not heard." "Have fun only when all the work is finished." "Don't be different from other family members." Children have to make early decisions about these rules, whether to accept them or to fight against them.

As children, we learn rules by observing the behavior of our parents. When rules are presented without choice as absolutes, they typically pose problems for us. As small children, we may have decided to accept a rule and live by it for reasons of both physical and psychological survival. When we carry such a pattern into our adult interactions, however, it can become self-defeating and dysfunctional.

Rather than trying to get people to give up these survival rules in their lives, Satir would assist them in transforming those that are extreme into something useful and functional. For example, if she were working with a person's rule "You must never get angry!", Satir would broaden the range of choice and transform the impossibility of living up to "always" and "never" standards. To make the element of choice more salient, she would ask clients to think of three times that they could imagine getting angry and list these situations. Through this process, a dysfunctional survival rule can be transformed rather than being attacked (Satir & Baldwin, 1983).

In healthy families rules are few and are consistently applied. They are humanly possible, relevant, and flexible, depending on changing situations (Bitter, 1987). According to Satir and Baldwin (1983), the most important family rules are the ones that govern individuation (being unique) and the sharing of information (communication). These rules influence the ability of a family to function openly, allowing all members the possibility to change. Satir notes that many people develop a range of styles as a means for coping with the stress that results from such change and the inability of family rules to meet the demands of change.

FUNCTIONAL VERSUS DYSFUNCTIONAL COMMUNICATION IN FAMILIES
Satir's approach to family therapy distinguishes between functional and dysfunctional communication patterns. Bitter (1987) contrasts a functional family structure with one that is dysfunctional. In families that are functioning relatively well, each member is allowed to have a separate life as well as a shared life with the family group. Different relationships are allowed and are nurtured. Change is expected and invited, not viewed as a threat. When differentness leads to disagreements, the situation is viewed as an opportunity for growth rather than an attack on the family system. The structure of this family system is characterized by freedom and flexibility and by open communication. All the members within the family have a voice and can speak for themselves. In this atmosphere individuals feel support for taking risks and venturing into the world. A healthy family encourages sharing experiences; the members are secure enough to be themselves and to allow others to be who they are.

In contrast, a dysfunctional family is characterized by closed communication, poor self-esteem of one or both parents, and rigid patterns. This kind of family resists awareness and blunts responsiveness. There is little support for individuality, and relationships are strained. In a family that exhibits dysfunctional patterns, the members are incapable of autonomy or genuine intimacy. Rules serve the function of masking fears over differences. Rules are rigid, many, and frequently inappropriate in meeting given situations. The members are expected to think, feel, and act in the same way. Parents attempt to control the family by using fear, punishment, guilt, or dominance. Eventually, the system breaks down because the rules are no longer able to keep the family structure intact.

DEFENSIVE STANCES IN COPING WITH STRESS When stress increases, threatening a breakdown of the family system, members tend to resort to defensive stances. Satir (1983, 1988; Satir & Baldwin, 1983) identifies four universal communication patterns that express these defensive postures, or stress positions: placating, blaming, being super-reasonable, and being irrelevant.

1. Family members who use *placating* behaviors as a style for dealing with stress pay the price of sacrificing themselves in their attempt to please others. They are weak, tentative, and self-effacing. Because they do not feel an inner sense of value and feel helpless without others, they say and do what they think others expect of them. Out of their fear of being rejected, they strive to be too many things to too many significant others.

2. People who adopt a *blaming* posture will sacrifice others to maintain their view of themselves. They assume a dominating style and find fault with others. As they point the finger of blame at others, they avoid responsibility for mistaken actions and the perceived loss of self-worth and meaning. They frequently say, "If it weren't for you . . ." They attribute responsibility to others for the way they are.

3. People who become *super-reasonable* tend to function much like a computer. They strive for complete control over themselves, others, and their environment by living a life governed by principle. In their attempt to avoid humiliation and embarrassment, they keep their emotions tightly in check. Of course, the price they pay for being overly controlled and rigid is distance and isolation from others.

4. *Irrelevant behavior* is manifested by a pattern of distractions in the mistaken hope that hurt, pain, or stress will diminish. The irrelevant person is unable to relate to what is going on. He or she appears to be in constant motion, with everything going in different directions at the same time. Because people who rely on this style of behavior are frightened of stress, they avoid taking a clear position lest they offend others.

Is there an alternative to dealing with family life other than taking one of the four defensive postures described here? How does a healthy person deal with the stress of meeting family rules? Satir and Bitter (2000) describe how congruent people cope with this stress. They do not sacrifice themselves to a singular style in dealing with it. Instead, they transform it into a challenge that is met in a useful way. Such people are centered, and they avoid changing their colors like a chameleon. Their words match their inner experience, and they are able to make direct and clear statements. They are congruent; they face stress with confidence and courage because they know they have the inner resources to cope effectively and to make sound choices. The congruent communicator is alert, balanced, sensitive, and real and sends clear messages.

It is a mistake to assume that once decisions have been made they are cemented forever. Even as children, people are not completely helpless with respect to how they will respond to the messages sent to them. If there are two children in a family, for example, each may react very differently to the same message of working hard that is modeled by their parents. The son decides to have more fun in his life than his parents and work even harder, becoming a workaholic. Children are not passively programmed, although they frequently develop patterns in reaction to what they see their parents doing. On some level children cooperate in making the early decisions that direct their lives, which means that they have the capacity to make new decisions that are appropriate to changing life circumstances.

FAMILY ROLES AND FAMILY TRIADS   Various members also assume roles that influence family interaction. For instance, a youngest brother may assume the role of victim, whereby he typically feels picked on and is constantly seeking protection. His sister may assume the role of keeping peace within the family. Even at an early age, other members may look to her as their counselor or expect her to take care of family difficulties. Father may take on the role of the stern taskmaster and disciplinarian, and mother may assume a hard-working caregiver role. In this family, each member has learned a role that characterizes his or her behavior.

The roles the parents play in relation to each child is especially important, because children always see their parents as essential to their survival. Like Bowen, Satir acknowledges that a child can be brought into the parents' relationship and that the resulting triadic process will be dysfunctional for everyone involved. Unlike Bowen, however, Satir also sees the possibility of parents forming a *nurturing triad* with each of the children. In such a triad, roles become flexible and open to change. Children are encouraged to make a place for themselves that fits the various situations they are in; they are supported, allowed to make mistakes, and engaged in congruent communication. Most important, each child's self-esteem is tended and enhanced. They are heard, acknowledged, appreciated, allowed to complain, and given the information they need to handle life both within and outside of the family. Rather than the "two against one" that Bowen noted in triangulation, Satir's nurturing triad can be characterized as "two for one."

Therapy Goals

The key goals of Satir's approach to family therapy are communicating clearly, expanding awareness, enhancing potentials for growth, especially in self-esteem, and coping with the demands and process of change. Satir believes families, like all systems, tend to establish a relatively constant state that she calls the *status quo*. Each family's status quo is familiar and known; as such, it is maintained by the family even if there are problems because it is less threatening than what is unknown and unfamiliar. When a *foreign element*, or outside stressor, is introduced into the system, change is required, and the family system is thrown into *chaos* while the members try to adapt. To the extent that the family can be helped to identify *new possibilities* and practice them, it is possible for it to change and integrate the change in a new way in family life. This model of family therapy is concerned with the growth of individuals and the family rather than with merely stabilizing the family. The aim is for individual members of the family to become more sensitive to one another, to share their experiences, and to interact in new and genuine ways. The task of therapy is to transform defenses and dysfunctional rules, opening people to new possibilities and integration of nurturing family-life experiences.

The general goal and process of therapy is facilitation of desired change in the family system. The specific goals, which are related to this change process, are:

- Generating hope and courage in the family members to formulate new options
- Accessing, strengthening, enhancing, or generating coping skills in family members
- Encouraging members to exercise options that will result in health as opposed to the mere elimination of symptoms (Satir & Bitter, 2000)

Satir (1988) identifies three goals of family therapy: (1) each individual within a family should be able to report honestly about what he or she sees, hears, feels, and thinks; (2) decisions in a family are best made by exploring individual needs and negotiating rather than through power; and (3) differences should be openly acknowledged and used for growth within the family.

Therapist's Function and Role

The therapist's function and role are to guide family members through the change process. Who the therapist is as a person is far more important than specific intervention techniques. Therapists are best conceived of as facilitators in charge of the therapeutic process; they do not have the task of making change happen or curing individuals. The therapist's faith in the ability of family members to move toward growth and actualization is central to this approach. This attitude infuses the therapy experience with nurturing support, safety, and human validation (Satir & Bitter, 2000).

Satir (1983) views the therapist as a resource person who has a special advantage in being able to observe the family situation. She uses the analogy of a camera with a wide-angle lens, which allows the counselor to see things from each person's vantage point. As an official observer, the therapist is able to report on what the family cannot see. Satir describes many roles and techniques that family therapists employ in helping a family achieve its goals. For example, the therapist:

- Creates a setting in which people can risk looking clearly and objectively at themselves and their actions
- Assists family members in building self-esteem
- Helps clients identify their assets
- Takes the family's history and notes past achievements
- Decreases threats by setting boundaries and reducing the need for defenses
- Shows that pain and the forbidden are acceptable to explore
- Uses certain techniques for restoring the client's feeling of accountability
- Helps family members see how past models influence their expectations and behavior and looks for change in these expectations
- Delineates roles and functions
- Completes gaps in communication and interprets messages
- Points out significant discrepancies in communication
- Identifies nonverbal communication

Although Satir's therapeutic style was quite different from Carl Whitaker's approach, which we will examine next, both emphasize the role of the therapist as a person. Whereas Whitaker developed his methods out of existential and psychoanalytic roots, Satir was influenced by the thinking of Carl Rogers and studied with him. Along with Rogers, she based her practice on the notion that we have an inner striving toward fulfillment and that we have the resources to reach our full potential. As you will remember from the person-centered perspective, it is the quality of the relationship between therapist and client that stimulates growth and change in the client. In Satir's view, the therapist is a model of effective communication and a resource person for developing it in a family. Regardless of the theoretical orientation of the therapist, it is possible to utilize many of the concepts of Satir's model in working with families.

Techniques

Change occurs in the session and healing occurs in the family's relationships, largely as a function of the relationship and climate created by the therapist. It is the individual family member, not the therapist, who is responsible for change. Within the therapy session the focus of techniques is on emotional honesty, congruence, and systemic understanding. Although Satir developed a number of techniques aimed at facilitating the change process, most of her interventions grew out of her intuitions about what a given family or member needed. Some of the techniques for assessment and intervention that she developed or employed in a special way are family maps (similar to genograms), family life-fact chronology (a listing of a family's three-generation history), family sculpting, drama, reframing, humor, touch, and family reconstruction (Satir & Bitter, 2000). Techniques from Gestalt therapy, psychodrama, and person-centered therapy were often incorporated in her work with a family.

FAMILY SCULPTING   Family sculpting may be used to increase members' awareness of how they function and how they are viewed by others in the system. Satir would actually physically position each family member in relation to the whole, often using her communication stances when she wanted to emphasize how members were coping. Through the use of this technique, the family process, boundaries, and interactions became evident, yielding significant information about each member. Family sculpting gives members an opportunity to express how they view one another in the family structure and also to express how they would like relationships to be different.

FAMILY RECONSTRUCTION   As a form of psychodramatic reenactment, family reconstruction enables clients to explore significant events in three generations of family life. This technique guides clients in unlocking dysfunctional patterns that stem from their family of origin. Family reconstruction, which takes members through different stages of their lives, has three goals: (1) to enable family members to identify the roots of old learning, (2) to help them formulate a more realistic picture of their parents, and (3) to assist them in discovering their unique personality (Satir & Baldwin, 1983; Satir, Bitter, & Krestensen, 1988).

 Although Satir would occasionally use reconstruction with whole families who were stuck in a closed system, the real advantage of this approach is for individuals who have family issues but little or no access to their family of origin. By using a group to simulate three generations of family life, clients are able to make sense out of past experiences that would otherwise continue to mystify them. Satir tended to build family reconstruction around the person's family maps, family life-fact chronology, wheel of influence (a spatial diagram of all the significant people in one's life), or some combination of the three. The experience of reenacting and observing significant life events in a focused group process often gives the protagonist a new starting point and the opportunity to interrupt old and entrenched family patterns in favor of more useful processes.

Concluding Comments

For many years Satir was the only woman to have developed a complete model of family therapy. To be sure, much of her approach and emphasis on relationship will be welcomed by people who sense too much detachment or use of power in other systems of family therapy. Although feminists have often acknowledged Satir's courageous stand in favor of nurturing connection, personal involvement, and even touch in therapy, they also recognized that Satir was not primarily a feminist in her approach. Satir was concerned with the *personhood* of everyone—men, women, and children alike. She tended to play down the importance of political struggles and believed change starts within, extends to relationships, and eventually changes the world (Satir & Baldwin, 1983).

Satir devoted a great deal of time to giving workshops and conducting training for family therapists. To her credit, she demonstrated her work with families before large audiences of mental health workers. It was in these public demonstrations that her concepts came alive. During her career she worked with more than 5,000 families, representing a wide range of diversity.

If you are interested in a more in-depth study of this approach, we recommend Satir and Bitter (2000), Satir (1983, 1988), Bitter (1987), and Satir and Baldwin (1983).

 ## EXPERIENTIAL FAMILY THERAPY

Introduction

Experiential family therapy, sometimes known as the experiential/symbolic approach, has a strong relationship to other existential, humanistic, and phenomenological orientations. The experiential approach stresses choice, freedom, self-determination, growth, and actualization. It is an interactive process involving a family with a therapist who is willing to be real. The focus is on here-and-now interaction between the family and the therapist rather than on exploring past experiences.

Carl Whitaker, who died in April 1995, was the best known exponent of this freewheeling, intuitive approach. His aim was to unmask pretense and create new meaning while liberating family members to be themselves. As in the other existential approaches, techniques are secondary to the relationship the therapist is able to establish with the family. Whitaker did not propose a set of methods; rather, it is the personal involvement of the therapist with a family that makes a difference. When techniques are employed, they arise from the therapist's intuitive and spontaneous reactions to the present situation and are designed to increase clients' awareness of their inner potential and to open channels of family interaction.

Key Concepts

SUBJECTIVE FOCUS   Experiential family therapists focus on the subjective needs of the individual in the family as they attempt to facilitate family interaction that will result in the individuality of each member (Hanna & Brown, 1999). They operate on the assumption that all members have the right to be themselves but that the needs of the family may suppress this individuation and self-expression. In this sense, there is no right or wrong—or even preferred—way for a family to be: the goal is member authenticity.

ATHEORETICAL STANCE   Whitaker's approach to family therapy is pragmatic and atheoretical, to the point of being antitheoretical. He believes theory can be a hindrance to clinical practice (Whitaker, 1976), maintaining that clinicians may use their theory to create distance in the name of being objective or that unseasoned therapists may use theory as a way of controlling their anxiety over dealing with a family (Guerin & Chabot, 1992). This highly intuitive form of therapy is aimed at intensifying present experiencing. Indeed, his personal style was unconventional and provocative, and he valued his capacity for "craziness"—an ability to reach into his own unconscious to understand what is going on in the family. Through his own spontaneous reactions, he was able to tap material a family keeps secret. Although the family members may view secret material as crazy, it is the process of keeping secrets that drives family members crazy.

Therapy Goals

In Whitaker's view, the goal of family therapy is to promote the feeling dimension: spontaneity, creativity, the ability to play, and the willingness to be "crazy." Keith (2000) writes that "we seek to increase the creativity (what we call craziness or right-brained living) of the family and of the individual members" (p. 113). The central goal is to facilitate individual autonomy *and* a sense of belonging in the family. Experiential family therapists operate on the assumption that if individual members increase their awareness and capacity for experiencing, more genuine intimacy will result within the family circle. According to Whitaker, it is experience, not education, that changes families. They assume that most of human experience occurs on the unconscious level, which can best be reached symbolically. For both Keith and Whitaker, "symbolic" refers to finding multiple meanings for the same process.

A central tenet of Whitaker's approach is that therapists need to be aware of their own responses to families to be therapeutic. The therapist functions best as an instigator of family openness, realness, and spontaneity. Experiential therapists place value on their own responses as a measure of healthy interaction. Furthermore, their personal experience determines their work in family therapy. Experiential therapy is a way for therapists to be actively engaged in their own personal development. Thus, therapy is a process that helps the therapist as much as the family.

Therapist's Function and Role

Experiential therapists tend to create family turmoil and then coach the members through the experience. They are primarily interested in the interaction between themselves and the family. The therapist's role requires immediacy, a willingness to be oneself, vitality, a degree of transparency, and a willingness to use personal reactions during the family sessions. Although these therapists are willing to act as temporary experts and issue directives to the family, they are just as likely to maintain long periods of silence to augment the member's anxiety. Whitaker liked to think of himself as a coach or a surrogate grandparent. His enactment of these roles required structure, discipline, creativity, and presence (Keith, 2000). The relationship between the active and vital therapist and the family is the catalyst for growth and movement.

Therapeutic interventions are aimed at intensifying what is going on in the here and now of the family session. The focus of therapy is on the process of what is unfolding during the session, a time when the seeds of change are planted. Instead of giving interpretations, the therapist provides an opportunity for family members to be themselves by freely expressing what they are thinking and feeling. Whitaker did not treat families. Instead, he saw his role as creating, with the family, a context in which change can occur through a process of reorganization and reintegration (Becvar & Becvar, 1996).

As a therapist, Whitaker grasped the complex world of a family by focusing on impulses and symbols. He was interested in going beyond the surface level of interactions by dealing with symbolic meanings of what evolved between the family and himself. In his sometimes outrageous style, he gave voice to his own impulses and fantasies, and in doing so he encouraged family members to become more accepting of their moment-by-moment experiencing (Goldenberg & Goldenberg, 2000).

Family therapy occurs in three phases: engagement, involvement, and disentanglement. According to Keith (2000), the counselor's role changes throughout therapy. During the early phase, the therapist assumes an all-powerful position. Initially, the therapist increases the anxiety a family is experiencing so that members are challenged to recognize intersectional patterns. In this context, families are almost forced to come up with alternative ways of operating. At different times in therapy the counselor shifts from being a dominant and parental figure to being an adviser and a resource person. Eventually, family members are expected to assume responsibility for their own living and changing. As the family assumes more independence, the therapist generally becomes more personal and less involved in the family system. The therapist respects the family's initiative as it moves toward termination.

Because this approach emphasizes the counselor's personal characteristics over the use of techniques, therapy for the therapist is viewed as being essential. This therapy may include marital and family counseling as well as personal counseling to increase the therapist's access to his or her own creativity. The reason behind recommending family therapy for therapists— coupled with the study of their own family—is not only to assist them in the process of individuation from their family but also to help them establish a greater sense of belongingness to their family (Keith, 2000).

Techniques

In Whitaker's model change must be experienced rather than understood or designed. Families will tend to stay the same unless the therapist can disturb or frustrate family process. Keith (2000) puts this notion as follows: "Whether they change or not has to do with their level of desperation, which must outweigh the pressure for homeostasis, or remaining the same" (p. 118). Within the experiential therapy session, the focus of techniques is on expressing blocked affect.

Whitaker believes the person of the therapist is the main therapeutic factor that facilitates change within a family. He did not use planned techniques or structured exercises but placed emphasis on *being with* a family. His interventions were aimed at challenging the symbolic meaning people give to events. In his view, the ability to be caring, vital, firm, and unpredictable is a more effective therapeutic instrument than any technical strategies (Nichols & Schwartz, 1998).

Whitaker liked to be part of a co-therapy team. He felt that having a co-therapist freed him to act in whatever manner seemed to fit the situation; he knew that his co-therapists would be available to help the family deal with what happened. Over the years, Whitaker teamed with some of the most sensitive and innovative family therapists in the field, including Thomas Malone, Gus Napier, and David Keith. This co-therapy arrangement allowed for a sharing of the emotional involvement of the therapeutic process. Furthermore, the practice afforded both therapists opportunities to have fun together, to disagree, to embellish on each other's interventions, and to model creative and productive interaction (Goldenberg & Goldenberg, 2000).

Keith (2000) maintains that practicing family therapy stirs up emotional reactions in the therapist. Because countertransference tends to be unconscious, the use of a co-therapist lessens the danger of acting out such feelings with a family. Each therapist can use his or her subjectivity more freely, for the colleague can function as a counterbalancing force. For example, Napier and Whitaker (1978) would express their thoughts and consult about the family during the therapy session.

Concluding Comments

In some ways Whitaker's experiential approach to family therapy is not unlike other approaches that focus on the therapist/client relationship. Individual approaches such as existential therapy, person-centered therapy, and Gestalt therapy all assign a central role to the importance of the therapist as a person and view the quality of the therapeutic relationship as significantly affecting the process and outcomes of therapy. Experiential family therapy applies many of the processes of these relationship-oriented therapies to working with families. Relying on empathy, interactions, joining, enactments, and experiments, the experiential therapist attempts to understand the family's dynamics and create experiences that will lead to family vitality and change. It is clear that this approach places primary value on therapist self-awareness and the full use of the therapist's self in encountering a family.

If you are interested in a more in-depth study of this approach, we recommend Keith (2000), Napier and Whitaker (1978), Whitaker (1976), and Whitaker and Malone (1981).

STRUCTURAL FAMILY THERAPY

Introduction

The origins of structural family therapy can be traced to the early 1960s when Salvador Minuchin was conducting therapy, training, and research with delinquent boys from poor families at the Wiltwyck School in New York. This approach to family therapy flourished in the 1970s, when Minuchin and his colleagues at the Philadelphia Child Guidance Clinic more fully developed the theory and practice of structural therapy. In his book *Families and Family Therapy* (1974), Minuchin focuses on the interactions of family members as a way of understanding the *structure,* or organization, of a family. Structural family therapists concentrate on how, when, and to whom family members relate. Through this information, the structure of a family and the problems that bring the family into therapy can be assessed.

This orientation is based on the notion that most symptoms are a by-product of structural failings within the family organization (Guerin & Chabot, 1992). Therapeutic change consists of helping the family modify its stereotyped patterns and redefine relationships (Colapinto, 2000). Minuchin's central idea is that an individual's symptoms are best understood from the vantage point of interactional patterns within a family and that structural changes must occur in a family before an individual's symptoms can be reduced or eliminated.

Key Concepts

Structural family therapy is an approach to understanding the nature of the family, the presenting problem, and the process of change. In this perspective the key concepts are family structure, family subsystems, and boundaries, each of which is briefly described here.

FAMILY STRUCTURE   According to Minuchin (1974), a family's structure is the invisible set of functional demands or rules that organize the way family members relate to one another. The structure that governs a family's transactions can be understood by observing the family in action or by seeing interactions unfold among family members in the therapy sessions. To understand a family's structure, it is useful to pay attention to who says what to whom and in what way with what result. By noting family process, rather than listening for mere content, the therapist can detect problematic transactions. Repeated sequences that emerge in a therapy session reveal the structural patterns of a family. Of particular interest is the appropriateness of hierarchical structure in the family.

For example, if every time a woman complains about her husband he hangs his head and says nothing, the theme of the process is *avoidance of conflict.* If a father's expression of anger leads almost inevitably to an asthma attack in his daughter, the sequence is *complementary* (an exchange of opposite kinds of behaviors) and reveals problems in the power structure between parent and child. In violent families therapists often find a *symmetrical* sequence (an exchange of similar behaviors) in which each person assumes an absolute position in argument from which neither can withdraw. Each part of the symmetrical sequence happens at once, leading to an almost automatic escalation of the fight (Fishman, 1993). Here is an example of such an argument:

HUSBAND: Where are you going?

WIFE: Out.

HUSBAND: Did I say you could go out?!

WIFE: You don't tell me what to do!

HUSBAND [*shouting*]:   The hell I don't!

WIFE [*shouting back*]:   The hell you *do!*

FAMILY SUBSYSTEMS   The family is considered a basic human system, which is composed of a variety of subsystems. The term *subsystems* encompasses various categories: *spousal* (wife and husband), *parental* (mother and father), *sibling* (children), and *extended* (grandparents, other relatives, and even reaching into the church and school). Members who join together do so to perform tasks that are essential for the functioning of the subsystems as well as the overall family system. Determining that the parent subsystem is appropriately separate from the child subsystem is central to structural therapy.

Each family member plays a different role in different subgroups. For example, Tom is a father in the parental subsystem, a husband in the spousal subsystem, and the third brother in the sibling subsystem of his own family of origin. Ann is the daughter of Tom, but she is also the sister of Julie in her sibling subsystem, the wife of Hank in her spousal subsystem, and a member of her church choir in her extended community subsystem. Subsystems are typically determined by factors such as gender, age, common interests, and role function. These subsystems are also defined by rules and boundaries.

In structural family therapy subsystems have appropriate tasks and functions. When family members of one subsystem take over or intrude on another subsystem in which they do not belong, the result is usually some form of structural difficulty. For example, the sex life of the adults in the family belongs to the spousal subsystem; when children are allowed to witness, comment on, or investigate their parent's sexual activity, they are inappropriately involved in the spousal subsystem. This extreme example may be easier to understand than noting that parents ought to allow their children to form their own relationships. This second example, however, is just as important; working out brother and sister relationships is a task for the sibling subsystem, not the parental subsystem. Parents have their own activities and functions to address.

BOUNDARIES   The emotional barriers that protect and enhance the integrity of individuals, subsystems, and families are referred to as boundaries. The demarcation of boundaries governs the amount of contact with others. These interpersonal boundaries can best be conceptualized on a continuum ranging from rigid (*disengagement*) to diffuse (*enmeshment*).

Rigid boundaries lead to impermeable barriers between subsystems and with subsystems outside the family. In some cases, because of a generational gap, parent and child may be unable to understand or relate to each other. In this process of disengagement, individuals or subsystems become isolated, and relationships suffer or even deteriorate. Family members become isolated not only from one another but also from systems in the community. In a case where a teacher notified the police that a student in her sixth-grade class had been missing for several days and that she had been unable to contact his parents in spite of repeated tries, police officers went to the house to investigate. Finding the father at home and engaged in personal projects, they asked about his son. They discovered that both parents were unaware that the boy had also been missing from home for three days. Again, this is an extreme form of disengagement that illustrates a physical as well as an emotional cutoff.

At the other end of the spectrum are diffuse interpersonal boundaries, which are blurred to the extent that others can intrude into them. A diffuse boundary leads to enmeshment, which is characterized by family members' over-involvement in one another's lives. There is an extreme of giving support, and there is too much accommodation. Although overly concerned parents invest a great deal of interest in their children, they often foster dependency and make it difficult for the children to form relationships with people outside of the family. This results in a loss of independence for both the children and the parents.

In working with a psychosomatic family Minuchin once demonstrated enmeshment in the therapy session by pinching a 12-year-old diabetic daughter and asking the father if he felt the pain of the pinch. The father responded that he did. When Minuchin asked the same question of the mother, she said that she did not feel the pain but that she had "poor circulation" (Fishman, 1993, p. 43).

In the middle of the continuum between rigid and diffuse boundaries are clear or healthy boundaries, which consist of an appropriate blending of rigid and diffuse characteristics. Healthy boundaries help individuals attain a sense of their own identity yet allow for a sense of belongingness within the overall family system. Healthy families have an ability to cope effectively with the various stresses of living by maintaining a sense of family unity; at the same time, there is flexibility that allows for restructuring the family and meeting individual development needs of its members.

Therapy Goals

The goals of structural family therapy are twofold: (1) to reduce symptoms of dysfunction and (2) to bring about structural change within the system by modifying the family's transactional rules and developing more appropriate boundaries. Colapinto (2000) points out that by releasing family members from their stereotyped roles and functions the family system is able to mobilize resources and to improve members' ability to cope with stress and conflict.

In general, the goal for families is creation of an effective hierarchical structure. Parents are in charge of their children and give them increasing independence and freedom as they mature. The family attempts to change the rules governing interactional patterns so that individual members have clear boundaries. In working with enmeshed families, the aim is to assist individuals in achieving greater individuation. In the case of disengaged families, the goal is to increase interaction between members by loosening up rigid boundaries and moving toward clear ones.

Structural family therapy provides a context for viewing a family, offering a clear description of how a family should operate. Minuchin's approach is a therapy of action rather than insight. Action changes behavior without the need for insight. It also provides opportunities that lead to new experiences and to a transformed family organization. Family therapy aims to modify the present organization of that family, not to explore and interpret the past.

Therapist's Function and Role

Minuchin (1974) identifies three interactive functions of the therapist: (1) joining the family in a position of leadership, (2) mapping its underlying structure, and (3) intervening in ways designed to transform an ineffective structure. Structural therapists assume that individual change will result from modifying a family's organization and from changing its transactional patterns. The therapist's basic task is to actively engage the family as a unit for the purpose of initiating a restructuring process.

Structural therapists are active in challenging rigid transactional patterns that characterize certain families as they attempt to organize themselves to cope with stressful situations. The therapeutic endeavor involves pushing for clearer boundaries, increasing the degree of flexibility in family interactions, and modifying a dysfunctional family structure (Goldenberg & Goldenberg, 2000). It is the job of structural therapists to join with the family, to block stereotyped interactional patterns, and to facilitate the development of more flexible transactions.

Colapinto (2000) writes that structural therapists play a number of different roles with families, depending on the phase of therapy. From the initial session therapists are engaged in a dance with the family. Soon after this dance they become stage directors who create scenarios in which problems are played out according to different scripts. Therapists lay the groundwork for a particular situation, create a scenario, assign roles and tasks to a family, and issue directives to members. Then they sit back as spectators and observe the family in action. Therapists must offer a combination of support and challenge. They need to sustain certain patterns and undermine other patterns. They must learn the appropriate balance between accommodating and negotiating with a family.

Techniques

Therapists join the family system they are helping, and they make interventions designed to transform the organization of that family. *Joining* is the process of building and maintaining a therapeutic alliance. As the family accepts the leadership of the therapist, it becomes possible for the therapist to intervene actively. The therapist joins the family for the purpose of modifying its functioning, not to solve the family's problem. The therapist establishes rapport by being sensitive to each of the members. Through the process of joining, the family learns that the therapist understands the members and is working with and for each of them.

The family and the therapist form a therapeutic partnership to achieve a common goal: "to free the family symptom bearer of symptoms, to reduce conflict and stress for the whole family, and to learn new ways of coping" (Minuchin & Fishman, 1981, p. 29). By joining the family and accommodating to its style, the therapist gains a picture of how members cope with problems and with one another. The aim is to change dysfunctional patterns as they occur in the session; there is a focus on realigning faulty hierarchies and correcting family structure.

In their book *Family Therapy Techniques* (1981), Minuchin and Fishman emphasize the importance of the therapist's use of self. They believe therapists need to be comfortable with different levels of involvement. A wide range of techniques may be employed, depending on what fits the situation, the family, and the therapist. At times, therapists may want to disengage from a family by prescribing a course of action. At other times, they may engage and operate as a coach. Sometimes they may align with one member of the family, a process called *unbalancing,* lending their authority and weight to one family member to break a stalemate maintained by the family system.

Minuchin's techniques are active, directive, and well thought out. His style is typically assertive and even blunt. At times he manipulates the system toward the end of changing inappropriate structures. For example, he may ask the children in the family to solve a sibling problem by discussing it without the parents interfering. Therapists can use whatever strategy is appropriate for meeting a therapeutic goal. These therapeutic techniques need to be suited to the personal characteristics of the family. Minuchin draws from many other approaches and combines strategies. Although his basic theory has remained relatively constant, he has moved toward eclecticism in techniques (Nichols & Schwartz, 1998). Techniques include joining, accommodation, working with family interactions, tracking sequences, enactments, intensifying, boundary making, restructuring (strengthening diffuse boundaries and softening rigid one), reframing, issuing directives, and family mapping. Three of these will be briefly outlined.

FAMILY MAPPING   Minuchin (1974) employs a method for mapping the structure of the family. In drawing a family map, the therapist identifies boundaries as rigid, diffuse, or clear; transactional styles are identified as enmeshed or disengaged. A variety of maps can highlight the functioning and nature of interpersonal relationships within the family and can be used fruitfully in the therapy sessions. Most of Minuchin's mapping processes are incorporated in McGoldrick, Gerson, and Shellenberger's (1999) book on genograms.

ENACTMENTS   In enactments the therapist asks family members to engage in some conflict situation that would happen at home. This allows the therapist to observe how family members interact and to draw conclusions about the structure of the family. The therapist also blocks existing patterns, determines the family's ability to accommodate to different rules, and encourages members to experiment with more functional rules. Change occurs as a result of enacting and dealing with problems rather than merely talking about these problems (Colapinto, 2000).

REFRAMING   Sometimes therapists cast a new light and provide a different interpretation to a problem situation in a family. This is called reframing. The presenting problem can then be explored in ways that allow the family to understand an original complaint from many angles. Through reframing it becomes possible to grasp the underlying family structure that is contributing to an individual's problem. In this way one member does not bear the full burden of blame for a problem or the total responsibility for solving it.

Concluding Comments

The basic processes of structural family therapy have been delineated by Becvar and Becvar (1996). The focus is on the structure, or organization, within a family. Therapists observe transactions and patterns and are involved in joining, accepting, and respecting the family in its efforts to reorganize and to achieve its goals. A structural map is formed, which provides the therapist with a basis for intervening firmly and directly so that the family will move toward health. Family members are both supported and challenged as they try new behaviors in the session.

Although feminists would join Minuchin in his consideration of larger systems affecting the family, he has not been favorably disposed to feminist interventions designed to save the woman at the expense of the family unit. Feminists, in turn, note that he will often join with the father in the family structure, reinforcing the patriarchy and male authority in the system. Indeed, the process of unbalancing, whether used by Bowenian, structural, strategic, or other therapists, has all too often been used in favor of men and at the expense of women—even in potentially abusive and dangerous situations.

Minuchin's extension of systemic process into larger systems is to be applauded. He was one of the first to work actively with poor families in slums, and he has applied his approach to homosexual couples, seeing no difference in the processes observed. Because of his ability to join successfully with fathers in family systems, his approach is particularly well suited for cultures that place a high value on the authority of the father.

If you are interested in more in-depth study of this approach, we recommend Minuchin (1974), Minuchin and Fishman (1981), Colapinto (2000), and Fishman (1993).

 # STRATEGIC FAMILY THERAPY

Introduction

Strategic therapy—called that because the therapist designs strategies for change—has its foundation in communications theory. The key contributors to the communication model included Gregory Bateson, Don Jackson, Paul Watzlawick, and Jay Haley, all of whom were associated with the Mental Research Institute (MRI) in Palo Alto, California. Satir was associated with the MRI in its early stages of development, but she eventually left to develop her own approach. In the 1960s Bateson first proposed blending general systems theory with metaphor. At the same time, Milton Erickson was carving out a professional reputation for being particularly skilled at dealing with resistance through unconventional techniques such as hypnosis and paradoxical directives. Strategic family therapy received its impetus from his therapy (Haley, 1973). Haley, a key strategic therapist, was affiliated with Erickson and with Minuchin's structural therapy. He was influenced by all of these approaches, and because he is a prolific writer, he was able to have a significant impact on the development of strategic family therapy.

Watzlawick (1978), Segal (1991), and others stayed with the MRI and developed a similar strategic approach called brief family therapy, but Haley left to work with Minuchin at the Philadelphia Child Guidance Clinic. In the 1970s he and Cloé Madanes (who was his wife at the time) established their own Family Institute in Washington, D.C. They focused on working with hierarchy, power, and strategic interventions; they contributed to the development of this approach through their therapy practice, writings, and training of family therapists. At that time, structural family therapy enjoyed the status of being the most popular therapeutic approach; during the 1980s, the strategic approach (or a blend of strategic and structural) was clearly receiving top billing in the field of family therapy.

Key Concepts

In strategic family therapy the problem is not addressed as a symptom of some other systemic dysfunction (as in Bowenian or structural family therapy). The problem brought by the family is treated as "real" and is solved. It is understood, however, that the behaviors the client has identified as the problem represent the client's attempted solutions.

Strategic therapy is a pragmatic approach based on the notion that change occurs through a family carrying out a therapist's directives and changing its transactions. Understanding and insight are not required or sought. No value is placed on therapist interpretation. The focus of therapy is not on growth or resolving issues from the past; rather, it is on solving problems in the present. Therapy tends to be brief, focused on process rather than content, and solution-oriented. The process orientation deals with who is doing what to whom under what conditions. The presenting problem is seen as both the real problem and a metaphor for the system functioning. Considerable emphasis is given to power, control, and hierarchies in families and in the therapy sessions.

In a court-ordered referral of a teenager who attempted suicide, for example, the strategic family therapist assumes that the court is now operating in executive control of the family, because the potential suicide indicates that the family is not handling the problem adequately. Based on an understanding of structural requirements in functional families, the therapist works immediately to join the family and assist in putting the parents back in charge, reestablishing the appropriate hierarchy. The therapist seeks to engage the parents in a discussion about their concern for this suicidal situation rather than attempting to establish rules or consequences for behavior. Why would this teenager in this family be taking such a desperate measure? This frames the problem as a system problem that is real and must be solved. The therapist does not let the session end without a plan that will guarantee the child's safety. The therapist may help the family hospitalize the adolescent or establish a 24-hour watch that involves responsible adult members of the family.

Haley and Madanes are far more interested in the practical applications of strategic interventions to ameliorate a family's problems than they are in formulating a theory of therapy. Strategic family therapy stresses some of the same key concepts as the structural approach to family therapy. In addition, Haley and Madanes maintain a primary concern with how power is distributed in a family, how members communicate with one another, and how the family is organized.

Therapy Goals

The goal of strategic therapy is to resolve a presenting problem by focusing on behavioral sequences. Being rather behavioral at heart, Haley has little use for insight as a goal of therapy. He is concerned about getting people to behave differently, and he is unconcerned with helping people figure out why they act as they do. It is his view that behavior change is the main goal of therapy, for if there is a change in behavior, feelings will change as a result. He hopes to prevent repetition of maladaptive sequences and attempts to introduce a greater number of alternatives. The intent of strategic interventions is to shift the family organization so that a presenting problem is no longer functional. Strategic therapists have short-range goals that guide their interventions.

Therapist's Function and Role

The therapist's role is that of a consultant, an expert, and a stage director. Clearly, the therapist is in charge of the session. There is very little focus on the client/therapist relationship; instead, the therapist is directive and authoritarian. Because Haley (1976) believes direct educational methods are of little value, he tends to be unwilling to explain himself to his clients; instead, he operates covertly. The therapist is primarily interested in control of power within the therapy relationship. Haley believes the responsibility for initiating change rests with the therapist, not with the client. Because he views his task as assuming the responsibility for changing the organization of a family and resolving the problems that it brings to therapy, he operates directively, giving the members specific instruction on what they are to do, both inside and outside of the therapy sessions. These instructions are aimed at changing the manner in which clients behave with other family members and with the therapist and guides both overt and covert interventions that may follow.

A basic feature of Haley's approach is that it is the therapist's responsibility to plan a strategy for solving the client's problems (Haley, 1973). At the initial phase of therapy, clear goals are established, a plan is developed, and specific therapeutic strategies are carefully designed to address problems. Because therapy focuses on the social context of human dilemmas, the therapist's task is to design interventions aimed at the client's social situation (Madanes, 1981).

Techniques

Like structural family therapists, strategic therapists track sequences, use reframing techniques, and issue directives. Key techniques are paradoxical interventions, joining, reframing, amplifying, pretending, asking about attempted solutions, and enactments. Haley and Madanes developed ordeal therapy, which is a clinical method for working strategically with marital or family dysfunction (Haley, 1984). Strategic ordeals provide rituals of penance and absolution, and they facilitate bonding among family members who go through the ordeal together. Madanes (1991) applied this approach to families in which an older child had sexually molested a younger one; she required the family to insist that the perpetrator kneel down in front of the molested child, confess the crime, and beg for forgiveness. The ordeal was not complete unless the confession and begging were sincerely enacted.

The strategic therapy that is taught and practiced by Haley and Madanes views symptoms as some form of communication aimed at gaining control over other family members. For instance, a child's acting-out behavior may symbolize a way to communicate his or her fear of an impending divorce. Madanes and Haley are likely to use indirect methods of provoking the parents and the child to interact and communicate in a way that would make the symptoms unnecessary.

In writing about the elements of strategic family therapy, Madanes (1981) describes employing strategic interventions. Each problem is defined as involving at least two people. It is the therapist's job to figure out who is involved in the problem and in what way. The therapist then decides on what interventions will most effectively reorganize the family so that the presenting problem will no longer serve the same function. Interventions are designed to involve certain family members with one another or to disengage other members of a family.

USE OF DIRECTIVES   Interventions usually take the form of a directive, which may be either straightforward or paradoxical. Straightforward directives include giving advice, making suggestions, coaching, and giving ordeal-therapy assignments (Haley, 1984). The clearer the formulation of the problem and the goals of therapy, the easier it becomes to design and implement directives. Therapists intervene to change a dysfunctional family structure by assigning homework. Directives may be simple, involving one or two people, or complex, involving an entire family. For example, when Haley (1976) discovers that a father is indirectly siding with his daughter (who was wetting her bed) against his wife, he directs the father "to wash the sheets when the daughter wets the bed. The task will tend to disengage daughter and father or cure the bedwetting" (p. 60). This is a simple, straightforward directive designed to change the system and end the problem.

PARADOXICAL INTERVENTIONS   Strategic therapists rely on paradoxical interventions to cut through a client's resistance and to bring about change. They devote a great deal of effort to devising paradoxical assignments that fit a problem situation or an individual's symptom. Haley (1976) assumes that families who seek his help will typically resist help from a therapist, often resulting in a power play between family members and the therapist. By using indirect procedures such as paradox, the counselor can deal with an individual's resistance to change creatively and therapeutically. Haley believes paradoxical strategies force the family to change. In taking control, the therapist upsets the power balance in the family.

Paradoxical techniques place clients in a double bind, so that therapeutic change occurs regardless of the paradoxical directives. Clients may be asked to exaggerate and even perfect a problematic behavior; these directives are designed to move the person and a family relationship in the direction of a solution. For example, a mother who is overly involved with her daughter, watching everything she does, may be asked to increase this activity and "hover" over the daughter every waking minute. The paradoxical intervention is designed to get the mother to protest that the daughter is not taking enough responsibility for herself.

Similarly, a client who complains that he or she cannot sleep is directed to stay awake. A client who is depressed is told: "Maybe you should not give up this symptom too quickly. It gets you the attention that you say you want. If you got rid of your depression, your family might not notice you." By accepting the therapist's directives and maintaining the symptom, the client demonstrates control over it and is no longer helpless to change it. If clients choose to resist the directives and let go of a particular symptom, the problem is not merely controlled but eliminated. For a more detailed review of current schools of paradoxical interventions and a compilation of paradoxical techniques, see Weeks and L'Abate (1982).

Strategic therapists monitor the outcomes of their directives. If a strategy is not working after a short time, they will design a new one. In working with a family, strategic therapists freely borrow techniques from other approaches if they prove to be useful in dealing with a presenting problem.

Haley maintains that his methods, including the use of paradoxical interventions, are not overly manipulative, because all forms of therapy utilize interpersonal influence and depend on the therapist's expertise in solving a family problem. It should be pointed out that all forms of paradoxical intervention do not have to rely so heavily on the power base, authority, and confrontational style of the therapist. For example, Madanes (1981, 1984) has designed techniques for working with a family that are less confrontational than Haley's. Her approach tends to be gentler; she uses humor, fantasy, and playfulness, all of which are a part of her "pretend" techniques. She might ask a child to pretend to have symptoms and the family to pretend to help the child. Madanes views the problem from a metaphorical standpoint. Her goal is to open up possibilities for creating more adaptive behavioral patterns and for the families to abandon dysfunctional or symptomatic patterns of behaving.

REFRAMING   Problematic behavior patterns often become entrenched. Reframing consists of reinterpreting such problematic behavior. If a husband devotes most of his time to work and if his preoccupation interferes with the family's functioning, his behavior can be given a new interpretation. Rather than labeling him a "workaholic," the therapist interprets his behavior as his way of showing his concern for his family. The underlying assumption is that giving new meaning to a behavior pattern may produce new behaviors that fit the interpretation. Not only does reframing change the meaning, but frequently it results in understanding other levels of meaning that exist in a transaction. The ultimate objective of a reframing technique is to help family members view problematic behaviors from a different vantage point. From the new vantage point, an intractable problem may become solvable.

Concluding Comments

Strategic family therapy gained much of its popularity by focusing on problems and solutions. By accepting that the presenting problem really was the problem, it avoided the appearance of ignoring the problem in favor of system correction. And by concentrating on solutions, strategic therapists were able to use the same planning and measurement of effectiveness that are inherent in behavioral models. It is the refusal of most strategic therapists to address insight or even an understanding of family processes, however, that generates the most criticism.

Without insight and understanding, strategic interventions fall easily into "the ends justify the means" approaches to therapy. Although strategic therapists would say that "common sense" is required in designing interventions, common sense is always common sense *to someone or some group* but may not reach the level of universal acceptance (Luepnitz, 1988). There are plenty of examples in the strategic reports of the 1970s and early 1980s of interventions that maintained sexism within families. For example, a depressed man was congratulated for getting his wife to have sex with him the way he desired "by demanding what you have coming to you" (Madanes, 1981, p. 192). To be fair, other strategic interventions involved empowerment of women and broadening men's useful participation in the family, but there is nothing in strategic therapy that requires or seeks the integration of an ethical, social, or political value system.

It is interesting to note that practitioners and students of strategic therapy often have more insight into the case presented than the people or families involved. Haley would argue that just as a person does not need a degree in auto mechanics to get a car repaired at a service station and moving down the road, a family does not need to understand the metaphor expressed by a symptom, the family organizational pattern that maintains a problem, or the way an intervention works to change their behavior. There is a significant difference, however, between seeking a one-time service for an object (as from an auto mechanic for your car) and seeking guidance for an ongoing change in family functioning. If discovering the use and purpose of a symptom or a problematic organizational problem helps the therapist make a difference, why would this information not be useful for the family members too? Would such information not reduce confusion? Is the mother who was directed paradoxically to "hover over her daughter" going to use this technique with all of her other children? Or does the family have to return to the therapeutic mechanic for a new prescription each time a problem develops? It is difficult to see how even a focus on "brief" therapy would be harmed by a session devoted to "debriefing" the therapeutic process and helping clients understand what processes made a real difference.

If you are interested in a more in-depth study of this approach, we recommend Haley (1963, 1973, 1976, 1984), Homrich and Horne (2000), Keim (2000), Madanes (1981, 1984, 1991), and Watzlawick, Weakland, and Fisch (1974).

SOCIAL CONSTRUCTIONISM AND FAMILY THERAPY

Introduction

Each of the family therapy approaches we have studied so far has its own version of "reality." Adlerians want to unlock negative interactions dominated by mistaken notions and to help families adopt more functional approaches based on social equality and democratic living. Bowen emphasizes the need for differentiation of self, the power of families to transmit problems over generations, and the difficulties caused by triangulation. Satir stresses congruent communication, nurturance, connection, and support through the process of change. Even Whitaker's atheoretical approach consistently aims at enlarging a family's ability to experience by creating interpersonal stress and coaching members in alternative ways of relating. Both Minuchin and Haley believe to varying degrees in the foundational nature of family structure and the use of problems within family systems to maintain structure as well as more or less fixed family problems.

Each of these approaches to family therapy rests on the assumption that there is something essential about a system that can be discovered and, if discovered, that will reveal the universal principles that explain all human behavior in the system. In this sense, most family therapies share with medicine, economics, the sciences, and even religion the search for universal truth that we associate with a modernist perspective. The simultaneous existence of multiple and often antithetic "truths" has led to increasing skepticism in the possibility that a singular, universal truth will one day explain human beings and the systems in which they live. We have entered a postmodern world in which truth and reality are understood as conceptualizations, points of view bound by history and context.

To differentiate a modern from a postmodern perspective, it is helpful to look at their differing views of reality. Modernists believe in objective reality that can be observed and systematically known. They further believe reality exists independent of any attempt to observe it. A modernist believes people seek therapy for a problem when they have deviated too far from some objective norm. For example, clients are depressed when the range of their mood is below that of what we would consider normal, everyday blues. Postmodernists, in contrast, believe in subjective realities that cannot exist independent of observational processes. To postmodernist social constructionists, reality is based on the use of language and is largely a function of the situations in which people live. A problem exists when people agree there is a problem that needs to be addressed: A person is depressed when he or she has internalized a definition of self as depressed. Once a definition of self is internalized, it is hard to recognize behaviors that are counter to the definition; that is, it is hard for someone who is suffering from depression to distinguish a good mood from a bad mood even when he or she is in it.

In postmodern thinking, language and the use of language in stories create meaning. There may be as many stories of meaning as there are people to tell the stories, and each of these stories is true for the person telling it. Further, every person involved in a situation has a perspective on the "reality" of that situation. When Kenneth Gergen (1985, 1991), among others, began to emphasize the ways in which people make meaning in social relationships, the field of *social constructionism* was born. It signaled a shift in emphasis in both individual and family therapy.

In social constructionism, points of view about families are pluralistic (Breunlin, Schwartz, & MacKune-Karrer, 1997). Gender awareness, cultural outlooks, developmental processes, and even an interest in the impact of mental illness on families are all entertained as important perspectives in understanding how individuals and families construct their lives. In social constructionism, the therapist disavows the role of expert, preferring a more collaborative or consultative stance. Empathy and therapeutic process are more important than assessment or technique. Narratives and language processes (linguistics) have become the focus for both understanding families and helping them construct desired change. We will now examine four of these newer approaches.

THE REFLECTING TEAM: TOM ANDERSEN   Tom Andersen (1987, 1991) practices family therapy in northern Norway. He is a psychiatrist who has both pioneered community-based mental health programs and initiated a "reflecting team" approach to systemic family therapy. Norwegian health programs have been nationalized, and everyone has equal access to both physical and mental health services. When Andersen started to visit the smaller communities in the north, he immediately recognized that "help" would often include work with extended families. Starting in the mid-1970s, he and his colleagues began to study the structural and strategic approaches used in the United States, incorporating some of the behind-the-mirror processes that Haley had popularized. This process involved a therapist who interviewed a family in one room while a team of consulting therapists watched through a two-way mirror in another room. Occasionally, strategic interventions were sent into the therapy session from the observing team. In the early 1980s the use of circular questions and longer interviews replaced much of the strategic interventions the team had used for some time. Still, the therapy team remained detached from the family, continuing to work behind the observation mirrors as they had for many years.

Andersen (1991) reports that it was a family mired in misery that pulled the therapy team out of the darkness and into the light. One day when the team was getting nowhere with its interventions, a therapist knocked on the door of the interview room and asked the family members if they would like to watch and listen to the team's conversation about the family. When the family agreed, the lights in the observation room were turned on, and the family and their interviewer listened to the team process their session. This was the birth of the *reflecting team,* an approach that has quickly gained wide acceptance in family therapy.

Over time, an interviewing process that Andersen (1991) calls "dialogues and dialogues about the dialogues" has been developed to facilitate the use of a reflecting team. An initial interview with a family involves development of an extensive picture of the clients, the therapist, and "the history of the idea of coming for therapy" (pp. 131–133). A second level of dialogue is about the family members' stories of how their family picture and history came to be; each person in the family may have a different story. A third level of dialogue is about the future, about how the family members would like the picture of themselves to change and what alternative stories about their lives might be developed.

When the reflecting team responds to the family, the team members are expected to let their imaginations flow, subject only to a respect for the system and a sensitivity about what the family can handle. Reflections are most often offered as tentative ideas directly connected to the verbal and nonverbal information in the preceding dialogue. The team remains positive in reflecting, reframing stories and parts of stories, looking for alternative stories, and wondering out loud about the possibility and impact of implementing these alternative stories. The family and the initial interviewer listen, and the interviewer notes family reactions, looking for ways in which the reflecting team may be expanding the family's ideas. The session ends with the initial interviewer seeking the family members' reactions to what they have experienced (Becvar & Becvar, 1996).

THE LINGUISTIC APPROACH: HARLENE ANDERSON AND HAROLD GOOL-ISHIAN   A less structured social-constructionist dialogue has been suggested by Harlene Anderson and the late Harold Goolishian (1992) of the Houston Galveston Institute. Rejecting the more therapist-controlled and theory-based interventions of North American family therapy, Anderson and Goolishian developed a therapy of *caring* and *being with* the client. Informed by and contributing to the field of social constructionism, they came to believe human life is constructed in personal and family narratives that maintain both process and meaning in people's lives. These narratives are constructed in social interaction over time. The sociocultural systems in which people live are a product of social interaction, not the other way around. In this sense, therapy is also a system process created in the therapeutic conversations of the client and the listener/facilitator.

When people or families come for therapy, they are often "stuck" in a dialogic system that has a unique language, meaning, and process related to "the problem." Therapy is another conversational system that becomes therapeutic through its "problem-organizing, problem-dis-solving" nature (Anderson & Goolishian, 1992, p. 27). It is the therapist's willingness to enter the therapeutic conversation from a "not-knowing" position that facilitates this caring relationship with the client. In the *not-knowing position,* therapists still retain all of the knowledge and personal, experiential capacities they have gained over years of living, but they allow themselves to enter the conversation in *curiosity* and with intense interest in discovery. Clients become the experts who are informing and sharing with the therapist the significant narratives of their lives. The not-knowing position is empathic and is most often characterized by questions that "come from an honest, continuous therapeutic posture of not understanding too quickly" (Anderson, 1993, p. 331).

In this approach the questions the therapist asks are always informed by the answers the client/expert has provided. The therapist enters the session with some sense from referral or intake of what the client or family wishes to address. Their answers provide information that stimulates the interest of the therapist, still in a posture of inquiry, and another question proceeds from each answer given. The process is similar to the Socratic method without any preconceived idea about how or in which direction the development of the stories should go. The intent of the conversation is not to confront or challenge the narrative of the clients but to facilitate the telling and retelling of the story until opportunities for new meaning and new stories develop: "Telling one's story is a representation of experience; it is constructing history in the present" (Anderson & Goolishian, 1992, p. 37). By staying with the story, the therapist/client conversation evolves into dialogues of new meaning, constructing new narrative possibilities.

THE NARRATIVE APPROACH: MICHAEL WHITE AND DAVID EPSTON Of all the social constructionists, Michael White and David Epston (1990) are best known for their use of narrative in therapy. Because of the power of dominant culture narratives, individuals and families tend to integrate these positions as if they are the only possible ones to take—even if those positions are not useful to the individual or the family. Like those who identify themselves with feminist therapy, White (1992) believes a dominant culture is designed to perpetuate viewpoints, processes, and stories that serve those who benefit from that culture but that may work against the freedom and functionality of the individual and the family.

Societal narratives in most countries perpetuate a strong preference for men, often discriminate against diversity, and may be designed to exclude gay men and lesbians from being full members of a given community. These narratives are so strong that even the people who suffer within these stories believe them. Hence, many women *accept* their inequality with men; members of minority cultures discriminate against one another and against other cultures; and gay men and lesbians, like the heterosexual community, may also be homophobic, if to a lesser extent.

Families, too, incorporate the dominant culture narratives about what a family "should" be, and to the extent that problems can be met and handled within that narrative structure, life seems to go smoothly. When the dominant story loses its power to meet the needs and demands of family life, the family has a problem. Within the family, narratives are maintained that allow each individual as well as the system to construct meaning in the lives and relationships of the members. These stories become dominant culture for a given family unit and are given the same power that a societal narrative often has.

According to White, individuals construct the meaning of life in interpretive stories, which are then treated as "truth." The construction of meaning can happen monologically (by oneself) or dialogically (with others), with the latter having the greater power in our lives because we are social beings. In this sense, an individual is most often a socially constructed narrative system. The process of *living our story* is not simply metaphorical; it is very real, with real effects and real consequences in family and societal systems. Families are small social systems with communal narratives that express their values and meanings, which are embedded in larger systems, such as culture and society. Because people are systems within systems within still other systems, they can easily lose freedom. Therapy is, in part, a reestablishment of individual and family freedom from the oppression of external problems and the dominant stories of larger systems.

Like Anderson and Goolishian, White and Epston (1990) have developed a therapeutic process based on questions. Their questions are purposeful and politically organized to deconstruct oppressive narrative. Their therapy starts with an exploration of the family in relation to the present-ing problem. It is not uncommon for clients to present initial stories in which they and the problem are fused, as if one and the same. White uses externalizing questions to separate the problem from the people affected by the problem. This shift in language begins the deconstruction of the origi-nal narrative in which the people and the problem were fused; now the problem is objectified as external to them.

Jim starts by saying that he gets angry far too much, especially when he feels that his wife is criticizing him unjustly: "I just flare! I pop off, get upset, fight back. Later, I wish I hadn't, but it's too late. I've messed up again." Although questions about how his anger occurs, complete with spe-cific examples and events, will help chart the influence of the problem, it is really the following kinds of questions that *externalize* the problem: "What is the mission of the anger, and how does it recruit you into this mission?" "How does the anger get you, and what are you doing to let it become so powerful?" "What does the anger require of you, and what happens to you when you meet its requirements?"

In this narrative approach, externalizing questions are followed by questions searching for unique outcomes: "Was there ever a time in which anger wanted to take you over, and you resisted? What was that like for you? How did you do it?" Unique outcomes can often be found in the past or the present, but they can also be hypothesized for the future: "What form would standing up against your anger take?" It is within the account of unique events that alternative narratives are facilitated and developed.

Following the description of a unique event, White (1992) suggests questions that lead to more clearly declared narratives:

■ What do you think this tells me about what you have wanted for your life and about what you have been trying for in your life?
■ How do you think knowing this has affected my view of you as a person?
■ Of all those people who have known you, who would be least sur-prised that you have been able to take this step in challenging the problem's influence in your life? (p. 133)

The development of unique outcome stories into solution stories is fa-cilitated by what Epston and White (1992) call "circulation questions":

■ Now that you have reached this point in life, who else should know about it?
■ I guess there are a number of people who have an outdated view of who you are as a person. What ideas do you have about updating these views?
■ If other people seek therapy for the same reasons you did, can I share with them any of the important discoveries you have made? (p. 23)

In a review of White and Epston's work, O'Hanlon (1994) describes their narrative therapeutic process in the following steps:

- Collaborate with the person or the family to come up with a mutually acceptable name for the problem
- Personify the problem and attribute oppressive intentions and tactics to it
- Investigate how the problem has been disrupting, dominating, or discouraging the person and the family
- Discover moments when the clients haven't been dominated or discouraged by the problem or their lives have not been disrupted by the problem
- Find historical evidence to bolster a new view of the person as competent enough to have stood up to, defeated, or escaped from the dominance or oppression of the problem
- Evoke speculation from the person and the family about what kind of future is to be expected from the strong, competent person that has emerged from the interview so far
- Find or create an audience for perceiving the new story (pp. 25–26)

Epston has developed a special facility for carrying on therapeutic dialogues between sessions through the use of letters (White & Epston, 1990). His letters may be long, chronicling the process of the interview and the agreements reached, or short, highlighting a meaning or understanding reached in the session and asking a question that has occurred to him since the end of the previous therapy visit. These letters are also used to encourage clients, noting their strengths and accomplishments in relation to handling problems or noting the meaning of their accomplishments for others in their community.

SOLUTION-ORIENTED THERAPY: WILLIAM O'HANLON, MICHELLE WEINER-DAVIS, INSOO KIM BERG, AND STEVE DE SHAZER   Similar in many ways to White's re-authoring process, but growing out of the strategic therapy orientation at the Mental Research Institute, solution-oriented therapy finds its place in social constructionism by shifting the MRI focus on problem solving to a complete focus on solutions. Steve de Shazer (with Insoo Kim Berg) initiated this shift at the Brief Therapy Center in Milwaukee in the late 1970s. He had trained with the MRI people but had grown dissatisfied with the constraints of their strategic model. In the 1980s he collaborated with a number of therapists, including Michelle Weiner-Davis, who started her own solution-focused center. Weiner-Davis later joined O'Hanlon, who had been trained by Milton Erickson, and together they have expanded the foundation originated by de Shazer (Nichols & Schwartz, 1998).

Solution-oriented therapy differs from both strategic models and traditional therapies by eschewing the past—and even the present—in favor of the future. It is so focused on what is possible that it has little or no interest in understanding the problem. De Shazer (1991), who is often the most radical of the group, has suggested that therapists do not need to know a problem to solve it and that there is no necessary relationship between problems and their solutions. If knowing and understanding problems is unimportant, so is searching for "right" solutions. O'Hanlon and Weiner-Davis (1989) believe any person or family might consider multiple solutions and that what is right for one person or family may not be right for others. Unlike the MRI strategic therapy approach, in this model clients choose the goals they wish to accomplish in therapy.

Because clients often come to therapy in a "problem-oriented" state, even the few solutions they have considered are wrapped in the power of the problem orientation. Solution-oriented therapists counter this client presentation with optimistic conversations that highlight their belief in achievable, usable goals that are just around the corner. These goals are developed by using what de Shazer (1985, 1988) calls the *miracle question:* Essentially, if a miracle happened and the problem you have was solved overnight, how would you know it was solved, *and what would be different*? Clients are then encouraged to enact "what would be different" in spite of perceived problems. This process reflects O'Hanlon and Weiner-Davis's (1989) belief that changing the *doing* and *viewing* of the perceived problem changes the problem.

Similar to White's process of eliciting "unique events," solution-oriented therapists ask *exception questions* that direct clients to times in their lives when the problem didn't exist. This exploration reminds clients that problems are not all-powerful and have not existed forever; it also provides a field of opportunity for evoking resources, engaging strengths, and positing possible solutions. Solution-oriented therapists focus on small, achievable changes that may lead to additional positive outcomes. Their language joins with the client's, using similar words, pacing, and tone, but also involves questions that presuppose change, posit multiple answers, and remain goal-directed and future-oriented.

Solution-oriented therapists also use *scaling questions* when change is required in human experiences not easily observed, such as feelings, moods, or communication. For example, a woman reporting feelings of panic or anxiety might be asked: "On a scale of zero to 10, with zero being how you felt when you first came to therapy and 10 being how you feel the day after your miracle occurs and your problem is gone, how would you rate your anxiety right now?" Even if the client has only moved away from zero to one, she has improved. How did she do that? What does she need to do to move another number up the scale?

Individuals and families bring narratives to therapy. Some are used to justify their belief that life can't be changed or, worse, that life is moving them further and further away from their goals. De Shazer (1991) prefers to engage clients in conversations that lead to progressive narratives whereby people create situations in which they can make steady gains toward their goals: for example, "Tell me about times when you feel good, when things are going your way, and when you enjoy your family and friends." It is in these stories of life worth living that the power of problems is deconstructed and new solutions are manifest and made possible. Like other social constructionists, solution-oriented therapists believe nothing is ever the same. Life is *change,* and change is inevitable. Solution-oriented therapists seek only to guide the changer and the changed in a self-chosen direction.

TABLE 13-2 ■ A Comparison of Four Approaches to Social Construction in Family Therapy

	THE REFLECTING TEAM	THE LINGUISTIC APPROACH	THE NARRATIVE APPROACH	SOLUTION-ORIENTED THERAPY
Key figures	Tom Andersen	Harlene Anderson & Harold Goolishian	Michael White & David Epston	William O'Hanlon, Michelle Weiner-Davis, Steve de Shazer, & Insoo Kim Berg
Therapy goals	Share reflections; create new life stories for family	Create alternative narratives	Deconstruct dominant narratives; re-author lives	Stop problem focus; co-create new solutions and life stories
Role and function of the therapist	Actively facilitates; investigates life stories of family; reflects and conducts dialogue	Reflects empathetic responses; co-evolves new alternative stories; displays compassion and "not knowing"	Questions clients to develop life narrative; facilitates deconstruction and re-authoring	Co-develops new solutions with family
Process of change	Develop family life story; use reflecting team dialogue; help family reflect	Adopt not-knowing position; follow stories; evolve alternative stories	Develop narrative; deconstruct story; re-author new narrative	Focus on the positive; develop solutions; support progress; celebrate change
Techniques and innovations	Reflections and dialogues; open teams	Listening from a not-knowing position	Externalizing and developing unique events	Miracle questions; exception questions; scaling questions

The four social constructionist approaches to family therapy we have considered are compared in Table 13-2.

Key Concepts

COLLABORATION AND EMPOWERMENT   In social constructionist theory the therapist-as-expert is replaced by the client-as-expert. The therapist enters into dialogues in an effort to elicit the perspectives, resources, and unique experiences of clients. A heavy emphasis is placed on the use of questions, often relational in nature, that empower the people in families to speak, to give voice to their diverse positions, and to own their capabilities in the presence of others. The past is history, but it sometimes provides a foundation for understanding and discovering differences that will make a difference. It is the present and the future, however, in which life will be lived. The therapist supplies the optimism and sometimes a process, but the client generates what is possible and contributes the movement that actualizes it.

STORIED LIVES AND NARRATIVES   Social constructionists believe real people live in families and that each person is living the "story of his or her life." Each person contributes to the "story of family life," and all of the stories are in constant co-construction. Human beings "make meaning" expressed in language and narratives; in this sense, families are meaningful systems. When the narratives of meaning become saturated with problems and overwhelming to those who live with and through them, social constructionists enter the personal and familial searches for alternative stories.

Therapy Goals

Social constructionists share an interest in the generation of new meaning in the lives of the people and families they serve. They seek to enlarge perspective and focus, facilitate the discovery or creation of new options, and co-develop solutions that are unique to the people and families they see. Social constructionism almost always includes an awareness of the impact of various aspects of dominant culture on human life, and therapists in this model seek to develop alternative ways of being, acting, knowing, and living.

Therapist's Function and Role

Therapists using the social constructionist model are active facilitators. The concepts of care, interest, empathy, contact, and even fascination that are essential to the person-centered therapists, the existentialists, the Gestalt therapists, and other humanists reemerge here as a relational necessity. The not-knowing position, which allows therapists to follow, affirm, and be guided by the stories of their clients, creates participant/observer and process-facilitator roles for the therapist and integrates therapy with a postmodern science of human inquiry. Collaboration, compassion, reflection, and discovery characterize the interactions of therapist and client.

Techniques

LISTENING WITH AN OPEN MIND   Whether the therapist is part of a reflecting team or is a single interviewer, all social constructionist theories place a strong emphasis on listening to clients without judgment or blame, affirming and valuing them. Social constructionists want to create meaning and new possibilities out of the stories they share rather than out of a preconceived and ultimately imposed theory of importance and value.

QUESTIONS THAT MAKE A DIFFERENCE   Depending on the approach, the questions therapists ask may seem embedded in a unique conversation, part of a dialogue about earlier dialogues, a discovery of unique events, a search for miracle solutions, or an exploration of dominant culture processes and imperatives. Whatever the purpose, the questions are often circular, or relational, and they seek to empower clients and families in new ways. To use Bateson's famous phrase, they are questions in search of a difference that will make a difference.

DECONSTRUCTION AND EXTERNALIZATION   Human beings and families come to therapy when their lives are overwhelmed by the problems they face. Both people and systems of people express their concerns in problem-saturated stories to which they are fused. Social constructionists differ from many early family therapists in believing it is neither the person nor the family that is the problem. Living life means coping with problems, not being fused with them. Problems and problem-saturated stories have real impacts on real people and dominate living in extremely negative ways. Externalization is one process for deconstructing the power of a narrative and separating the person or family from identifying with the problem. The separation facilitates hope by allowing clients to take a stand against that which is not useful in their storied lives. Deconstructions seek to empower the person and the family as competent to handle the problems they face.

ALTERNATIVE STORIES AND RE-AUTHORING   Whether involved in a free-flowing conversation or engaged in a series of questions in a relatively consistent process, social constructionists seek to elicit new possibilities and embed them in the life narratives and processes of the people they serve. White and Epston's inquiry into unique events is similar to the exception questions of solution-oriented therapists. Both seek to build on the competence already present in the person or the family. The development of alternative stories, or narratives, is an enactment of ultimate hope: Today is the first day of the rest of your life.

Concluding Comments

A mere hundred years ago, Freud, Adler, and Jung were part of a major paradigm shift that transformed psychology as well as philosophy, science, medicine, and even the arts. In the 21st century, postmodern constructions of alternative knowledge sources seem to be one of the paradigm shifts most likely to affect family counseling and psychotherapy. The creation of the self, which so dominated the modernist search for human essence and truth, is being replaced with the concept of *storied lives*. Diversity, multiple frameworks, and an integration/collaboration of the knower with the known are all part of this new social movement to enlarge perspectives and options. For some social constructionists the process of "knowing" includes a distrust of the dominant culture positions that permeate families and society today. For these people change starts with deconstructing the power of cultural narratives and then proceeds to the co-construction of a new life of meaning.

If you are interested in more in-depth study of social constructionism, we recommend Andersen (1991), White and Epston (1990), O'Hanlon and Weiner-Davis (1989), de Shazer (1991), Freedman and Combs (1996), McNamee and Gergen (1992), West, Bubenzer, and Bitter (1998), Becvar and Becvar (1996), Goldenberg and Goldenberg (2000), Kogan and Gale (2000), and Nichols and Schwartz (1998, Part III).

 INTEGRATION OF FAMILY THERAPY MODELS

Satir (1983) suggests that although most family therapists agree on some basic points about how family systems operate they have wide differences regarding the best ways of modifying these systems. She calls for family practitioners to be open to drawing from the best of what the schools of family therapy offer.

In predicting the future of marital and family therapy, Gurman and Kniskern (1992) say that the field will be characterized by more permeable boundaries both among the various orientations within the field and between family therapy and other therapies. Even today treatment techniques and strategies from seemingly incompatible systems of family therapy are being combined. Gurman and Kniskern emphasize the importance of a basic theoretical foundation to serve as a guide for integrating concepts and techniques from the various approaches, which will lead to improved practice. As you will see in Chapter 14, there is a similar trend toward integration for individual counseling models.

Hanna and Brown (1999) assert that rigidly adhering to a theoretical orientation is likely to limit therapeutic effectiveness. They acknowledge that the majority of family therapists do not limit themselves to a single approach; rather, they integrate their own blend of methods based on their training, personality, and the population of families they serve. They believe the integrative approach, which can begin at an early stage of training, is developed by focusing on similarities among approaches and identifying common elements of how families change. These elements include the role of the therapist and theories explaining how change comes about in a family. Hanna and Brown maintain that the practice of family therapy can be based on a synthesis of key principles across multiple models.

Nichols and Schwartz (1998) also maintain that family therapy is moving toward integration. They believe it does not make sense to study one and only one model and to neglect the insights of others. In their recommendations to students about how to select a theoretical position, they make these points:

- During training concentrate on learning one approach well by becoming immersed in that particular model.
- Because the therapy techniques are never separate from the person using them, choose an approach that is congruent with your style as a person.
- The ability to integrate various theoretical orientations with your personal style requires knowledge of the major approaches to family therapy and a thorough background of training and supervision in some form of family therapy.

For a comparative analysis of the major models of family therapy and an excellent discussion of an integrative perspective, see Nichols and Schwartz (1998, Chapter 14).

FAMILY THERAPY APPLIED TO THE CASE OF STAN

Although it is impossible to provide an example of each family systems approach to the case of Stan, we want to demonstrate at various points in the session the uses of genograms, engaging a multigenerational family, joining, reframing, congruent communication, boundary setting in therapy, and creating new possibilities. We have tried to provide an integrative example, but we want to emphasize that this is not the only way to do family therapy.

A therapist with a family systems orientation begins working with Stan by conducting an assessment of his family of origin (Figure 13-1). In addition to considering relationships with his parents, grandparents, and siblings, a systemic therapist is interested in finding out about his interactions at his school, place of work, church, and any friendship networks. Stan's problems cannot be fully understood or fruitfully explored in therapy without addressing his relationships within his family and other key systems of which he is a

part. Many of Stan's presenting complaints are best understood as symptoms of power struggles and dysfunctional communication patterns within his family of origin. The family therapist approaches Stan as part of an ongoing, living unit. Most of Stan's problems have familial roots, and he is still very much engaged with his parents and siblings, no matter how difficult their relationships may be.

Stan's genogram is really a family picture, or map of his family-of-origin system. In this genogram, Stan is the index person (IP) whose problems are the purpose for the family session. The index person is indicated on the genogram with either a double square (for a man or boy) or a double circle (for a woman or girl). All other men are designated with a single square, and women with a single circle. In each square or circle, the name of the person is noted along with the year the person was born. In Stan's family, his grandparents tend to have fairly long lives. One

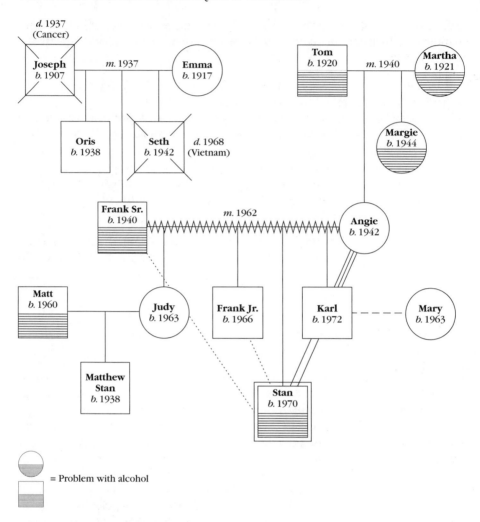

FIGURE 13-1
Three-Generation Genogram of Stan's Family

grandparent (Joseph) died at the age of 69; the rest are still alive in their late 70s and early 80s. Death in a genogram is indicated by an X through a person's name and square or circle. Next to the person we indicate the year and cause of death. Stan's Uncle Seth died in Vietnam in 1968 at 26 years of age. He wanted to be a career soldier, but his career was all too short. Stan's paternal grandfather died of cancer in 1976.

Stan's maternal grandparents are both alive. The shaded lower half of their square and circle indicates that each had some problem with alcohol. In the case of Tom, Stan reports that he was an admitted alcoholic who recommitted himself to Christ and found help through Alcoholics Anonymous. Stan's maternal grandmother always drank a little socially and with her husband, but she never considered herself to have a problem. In her later years, however, she seems to sneak alcohol more and more, and it is a source of distress in her marriage. Stan also knows that Margie drinks a lot because he has been drinking with his aunt for years. She is the one who gave him his first drink.

Angie, Stan's mother, married Frank Sr. after he had stopped drinking, also with the help of AA. He still goes to meetings. Angie is suspicious of all men around alcohol. She is especially upset with Stan and with Judy's husband, Matt, who "also drinks too much." The genogram makes it easy to see the pattern of alcohol problems in this family.

Solid lines between people indicate a formal and direct relationship. The solid lines between Joseph and Emma, Tom and Martha, Frank Sr. and Angie, and Matt and Judy all indicate a marriage, and the year of the marriage is shown above the line. The dashes between Karl and Mary indicate a relationship that is not formalized; they are living together but are not married. The jagged lines between Frank Sr. and Angie indicate conflict in the relationship. The three solid lines between Frank Sr. and Frank Jr. and between Angie and Karl indicate a very close or even fused relationship. The double lines between Karl and Stan are used to note a close relationship only. As you will see, Karl actually looks up to Stan in this family. The dotted lines between Frank Sr. and Stan and between Frank Jr. and Stan indicate a distant or even disengaged relationship.

Frank Sr. was a middle child who took orders and was criticized by his mother, a very strong woman. He married an oldest child, who was also a strong, critical woman. Although Angie has never had a personal problem with alcohol, it has been an issue in her family life for three generations now. She is surrounded by people who have problems or have had problems with drinking. In Stan's family of origin, there are two psychologically "oldest" children (the oldest girl, Judy, and the oldest boy, Frankie); both are very good. Stan is a middle child who never quite lives up to his parents' expectations, and Karl is the baby who was spoiled when he was young and now gets to do things his own way. This is the beginning picture of Stan's family system. This genogram serves as a map to guide the family therapist through the initial interviews.

The family therapist starts by helping Stan invite his family into the therapeutic process:

THERAPIST: What will it be like for you to invite your parents, your brothers, and your sister into therapy with you?

STAN: It will be very difficult. I don't really think my dad and mom will come.

THERAPIST: Who do you think will come? Who in your family genogram here can you really count on?

STAN: I think my sister Judy would come, and my brother Karl. We haven't been all that close—any of us—but I think they would want to help if they could.

This brief sample of dialogue illustrates the therapist's attempt to get the entire family involved in the counseling process. To a family therapist, Stan is part of a system that is part of still larger systems. Whereas counselors and therapists who see individuals may already have enough information to begin work with him, the family therapist often prefers to work with the whole system or as much of it as Stan can get into therapy. The family of origin is essential in his case, because he still lives much of his life in relation to these people. His extended family is also important, because these members can help him understand familial patterns over many generations, find new resources in the system, and perhaps even humanize his parents. Realizing that his family has lived in the same community for many years, it may be important for the therapist to encourage Stan to consider including people from his work, his school, or his neighborhood.

Stan may have many difficulties, but at the moment his difficulty with alcohol is the primary focus. Alcohol is a negative part of his life, and as such it has systemic meaning. It may have started out as a symptom of other problems, but now the alcohol is a problem in itself. From a systemic perspective, the question is, "How does this problem affect the family?" or "Is the family using this problem to serve some other purpose?"

The early phase of working with the family would be devoted to meeting the family, joining with various family members, and reframing Stan's problem into a family problem in which everyone has a stake. The chances are great that Stan's problem has a multigenerational context. If this context is explored, family processes that support and maintain alcohol as a problem may be identified. It is possible to track the interactions of the family members and to transform communication patterns into more useful possibilities. Alliances and resources in this family might be explored as a means of creating new possibilities in the life of the family. If the therapist were just listening to Stan, only one point of view would be evident. In a family session multiple perspectives and the entire interactive process will become clear in a very short time.

One goal of therapy is to assist Stan in individuating from his parents and help everyone in the family establish clearer boundaries and more useful interactions. Stan has revealed how much resentment he feels toward his mother, the emotional distance he experiences from his father, and his tendency to compare himself unfavorably with his older sister and brother. One intervention the therapist is likely to use to help change the family's interactive process with Stan is to ask the siblings to talk among themselves without the interference of their parents.

Much more may happen in these sessions; many relationships still need attention. Some family therapists might decide what the clients need to do to address Stan's presenting problem and intervene with directives designed to make a difference. What is clear, however, is that *this* therapist views the presenting problem as a crack in the family vase. By working to strengthen the vase (the coping mechanisms and interactive processes of everyone involved), she hopes to transform the system and activate solutions that the family designs.

Follow-Up: You Continue as Stan's Family Therapist

Use these questions to help you think about how you would counsel Stan:

- What unique values do you see in working with Stan from a systemic perspective as opposed to doing individual therapy?
- If you were Stan's therapist and he resisted the idea of bringing his family to therapy, what direction might you take with him?
- Assume that Stan was successful in getting at least some of his family members to another session. Where would you want to begin? How do you expect that you'd get everyone involved in the sessions?
- What are some specific ways in which you might keep a systemic focus, even if you were seeing Stan individually? ■

SUMMARY AND EVALUATION

Summary

In this section we review the themes that unite the many schools of family therapy and also look at some of the variations among these theoretical orientations.

VIEW OF THE FAMILY If we hope to work therapeutically with an individual, it is critical to consider him or her within the family system. An individual's dysfunctional behavior grows out of the interactional unit of the family as well as the larger community and societal systems. With the exception of some social constructionist perspectives, virtually all other orientations accept the notion that families are systems.

FOCUS OF FAMILY THERAPY Most of the family therapies tend to be brief, because families who seek professional help typically want resolution of some problematic symptom. In addition to being short-term, solution-focused, and action-oriented, family therapy tends to deal with present interactions. One way in which family therapy differs from many individual therapies is its emphasis on how current family relationships contribute to the development and maintenance of symptoms.

Almost all of the family therapies are concerned with here-and-now interactions in the family system. The role of history is handled in different ways. Some approaches assume that family history is crucial in understanding present functioning, whereas other models treat the information phenomenologically or make no assumption about history at all. The Adlerian model gathers background information from a phenomenological perspective, knowing that each member's contribution is an interpretation. Bowen's multigenerational approach gives high priority to both current history and early history as a means of helping clients differentiate themselves from their family of origin. In a different way, Satir considers the past as a way to help members of a family realize that problems are the result of decisions that have been made by the family unit. Experiential therapists generally deal with past unresolved conflicts by treating their expression in current interactions.

Strategic and structural family therapists are less concerned with gathering family history. They focus on what maintains the current problem and how to solve it in the present. The past does have a bearing from a developmental perspective on the structural problems within a family. Haley's strategic therapy, however, deals mainly with here-and-now power struggles and control issues in a family, and it does not attempt to educate clients about the origin or development of these problems.

Another focus that characterizes family therapy is the attention all approaches pay to both verbal and nonverbal communication. Structural and strategic therapy, both of which are derivatives of the communications model, focus on various aspects of how family members communicate. Structural therapists focus on the family organization as it is expressed in repeated patterns of communication. They identify the underlying organization of a family by noting who speaks to whom and in what manner with what results. Strategic therapy, as practiced by Haley and Madanes, assumes that the central aim of communication is to attain power in interpersonal relationships. Symptoms are seen as ways of communicating with the aim of controlling other family members. For instance, a child's fears of going to school may express his or her insecurity in dealing with the world alone. The strategic therapist would try to provoke the child's parents to communicate with the child in a different way, which would make the symptom unnecessary (Nichols & Schwartz, 1998).

Satir's approach is an example of a humanistically oriented communications model of therapy. This model strives to teach all the members of a family how to express what they want for themselves and with others. Satir (1983) holds that communication is a process of giving and getting information. In conducting family sessions, the therapist attends to both the verbal and nonverbal process of making requests. People who communicate in a functional way are able to be firm in their position, yet they can ask for feedback and be open to it when they get it. People who communicate dysfunctionally leave others guessing what is in their heart or head.

ROLE OF THE THERAPIST   In most of the models considered, the therapist functions as a teacher, model, or coach. These approaches have in common a commitment to helping family members learn new and more effective ways of interacting. Bowenians block triangulation and encourage members of a family to move toward differentiation; structural therapists realign psychological boundaries and strengthen hierarchical organization; strategic therapists identify interactional sequences that maintain a problem; and experiential therapists attempt to reduce defensiveness and facilitate open and honest expression of feelings and thoughts (Nichols & Schwartz, 1998).

GOALS OF FAMILY THERAPY   There are some general goals that most family therapists adhere to; specific goals are determined by the practitioner's orientation or by a collaborative process between family and therapist. Global goals include intervening in ways that enable individuals and the family to change to relieve their distress. Tied to the question of what goals should guide a therapist's interventions is the question of the therapist's values. As you have seen, each of the seven approaches to family therapy is grounded on a set of values and theoretical assumptions. Ultimately, every intervention a therapist makes is an expression of a value judgment. It is critical for therapists, regardless of their theoretical orientation, to be aware of their values and monitor how these values influence their practice with families.

HOW FAMILIES CHANGE   An integrative approach to the practice of family therapy must include guiding principles that help the therapist organize goals, interactions, observations, and ways to promote change. In reviewing the theories of family therapy, it is evident that they can be grouped into two categories: (1) those that focus on change within the therapy sessions and (2) those that deal with the occurrence of change outside the therapeutic context, in the natural world (Hanna & Brown, 1999). Some theories focus on perceptual and cognitive change, others deal mainly with changing feelings, and still other theories emphasize behavioral change. Change needs to happen relationally, not just intrapsychically, in all family therapy models.

TECHNIQUES OF FAMILY THERAPY   The intervention strategies therapists employ are best considered in conjunction with their personal characteristics. Writers such as Goldenberg and Goldenberg (2000) and Nichols and Schwartz (1998) emphasize that techniques are tools for achieving therapeutic goals but that these intervention strategies do not make a family therapist. Personal characteristics such as respect for clients, compassion, empathy, and sensitivity are human qualities that influence the manner in which techniques are delivered. It is also essential to have a rationale for the techniques that are used, with some sense of the expected outcomes. Faced with meeting the demands of clinical practice, practitioners will need to be flexible in selecting intervention strategies. The central consideration is what is in the best interests of the family. Many therapy procedures can be borrowed from various models, depending on what is likely to work best with a given family. As we have seen, there is a great deal of overlap among the techniques used by family therapists, irrespective of their theoretical base.

Contributions of Family Systems Approaches

One of the key contributions of most systemic approaches is that neither the individual nor the family is blamed for a particular dysfunction. The family is empowered through the process of identifying and exploring interactional patterns. If change is to come about in a family or with individual members of a family, there is a need to be aware of as many of the systems of influence as possible.

Most of the individual therapies that have been considered in this textbook have not given a primary focus to the role of systemic factors in influencing the individual. All of the contemporary approaches to family therapy give major emphasis to understanding individuals in their systems, which sheds an entirely different perspective on assessing and treating individuals and families. An advantage to this viewpoint is that an individual is not scapegoated as the "bad person" in the family. Rather than blaming either an individual "identified patient" or a family, the entire family has an opportunity to examine the interactional patterns that characterize the unit and participate in finding solutions.

Limitations and Criticisms of Family Systems Approaches

In the early days of family therapy, it appeared that people all too often got lost in the consideration of system. In adopting the language of systems, therapists began to describe and think of families as being made up of "dyads" and "triads"; as being "functional" or "dysfunctional," "stuck" or "unstuck," and "enmeshed" or "disengaged"; and as displaying "positive" and "negative" outcomes and "feedback loops." It was as if the family was a well-oiled machine or perhaps a computer that occasionally broke down. Just as it was easy to fix a machine without an emotional consideration of the parts involved, some therapists approach family systems work with little concern for the individuals as long as the "whole" of the family "functioned" better. Feminists were perhaps the first, but not the only, group to lament the loss of a personal perspective within a systemic framework. As the field moves now toward an integration of individual and systemic frameworks, it is important to reinvest the language of therapy with human emotional terminology that honors the place real people have always held in families. Satir's model is one approach that offers a fully human and emotionally respectful language.

FAMILY SYSTEMS THERAPY FROM A MULTICULTURAL PERSPECTIVE

Contributions to Multicultural Counseling

One of the contributions of the systemic perspective in working from a multicultural framework is that many ethnic and cultural groups place great value on the extended family. If therapists are working with an individual from a cultural background that gives special value to including grandparents, aunts, and uncles in the treatment, it is easy to see that family approaches have a distinct advantage over individual therapy. Family therapists can do some excellent networking with members of the extended family.

In many ways family therapists are like anthropologists. They approach each family as a unique culture whose particular characteristics must be understood. Like larger cultural systems, families have a unique language that governs behavior, communication, and even how to feel about and experience life. Families have celebrations and rituals that mark transitions, protect them against outside interference, and connect them to their past as well as a projected future.

Although each family has a discrete culture, it is also connected to the larger culture from which it emanates. The larger experience of culture and ethnicity permeates relationships in families stretching back generations, often to other lands and other periods of time and history. Our children may ask us why we always throw rice on the bride and groom when they leave a wedding, and we are so far removed from the origin of the ritual that we can only say: "I don't know. We've always done it, that's why." Yet even without understanding the ritual, we feel compelled to honor it.

Just as differentiation means coming to understand our family well enough to be a part of it—to belong—and also to be separate and our own person, understanding the cultural system allows therapists and the families they serve to appreciate diversity and to contextualize family experiences in relation to the larger culture. As fundamental as culture is to family life, it has only been in the last 20 years that the field of family therapy has significantly addressed this relationship. McGoldrick, Pearce, and Giordano (1996) are largely responsible for elevating an awareness of and sensitivity to culture in family systems therapy.

Today, family therapists explore both the individual culture of the family and the larger culture to which the family belongs. They look for ways in which culture can both inform and modify family work. Interventions are no longer applied universally, regardless of the culture involved. Rather, they are adapted and designed to join with the cultural system. Just as society can exact standards and practices from families that may not fit the needs of that family system, so do cultural imperatives. Sensitivity to culture in family therapy means knowing when cultural meaning can enlarge and contextualize family experience and when it needs to be faced as an external stress on the system.

Limitations for Multicultural Counseling

Some approaches to family therapy are heavily loaded with value orientations that are not congruent with the value system of clients from other ethnic and cultural backgrounds. The notions of independence, autonomy, and self-determination mirror Western values, and not all cultures pay homage to such values. Asian American, Native American, and Latino families may be in conflict with these concepts and how they are addressed in family therapy. The Western emphasis on the nuclear family and independence tends to reduce the importance of the family of origin. For example, Sue and Sue (1991) note that in Chinese American families the notion of filial piety is a strong determinant of how children behave, even as they move to adulthood. Obedience, respect, obligation to parents, and duty leave little room for self-determination. Allegiance to one's parents is expected from a man even after he marries and has his own family. The concept of separation from his family can easily lead to conflicts in his family relationships.

The process of differentiation occurs in most cultures, but it takes on a different shape because of cultural norms. For instance, a young person may become separate from her parents yet not move out of the house. When families immigrate to North America, the children often adapt more quickly to a Western concept of differentiation. In such cases, the intergenerational process of therapy is appropriate if the therapist is sensitive to the family of origin's cultural roots. Bowen believes there needs to be a balance between what is beneficial for the individual and what is beneficial for the group.

WHERE TO GO FROM HERE

A good place to begin is by doing some of the supplementary reading listed in the next section. It is also a good idea to join the American Association for Marriage and Family Therapy, which has a student membership category. You must obtain an official application, including the names of at least two Clinical Members from whom the association can request official endorsements. Members receive either the *Journal of Marital and Family Therapy*, which is published four times a year, or *Practice Strategies*, and a subscription to *The Family Therapy News.* For a copy of the AAMFT Code of Ethics, membership applications, and further information, write to:

American Association for Marriage and Family Therapy
1133 15th Street NW, Suite 300
Washington, DC 20005-2710
Telephone: (202) 452-0109
Fax: (202) 223-2329
E-mail: *Ethics@aamft.org*
Website: *www.aamft.org*

An excellent journal is *The Family Therapy Networker.* For information about subscriptions write to:

The Family Therapy Networker
7705 13th Street NW
Washington, DC 20012
Telephone: (202) 829-2452
E-mail: *FTNetwork@aol.com*
Website: *www.familytherapynetwork.com*

Another option is for students to join the International Association of Marital and Family Counselors (IAMFC), which is a division of the ACA. Student membership is available. For membership applications and further information, write to:

ACA Membership Division
5999 Stevenson Avenue
Alexandria, VA 22304
Telephone: (800) 347-6647, ext. 222
E-mail: *Ipeele@counseling.org*
Website: *www.counseling.org*

Virignia Satir developed a group known as the Avanta Network for implementing her approach to family therapy. The network is made up of mental health professionals from various disciplines who worked and trained with her. Information about training programs offered through this group is available by contacting:

The Avanta Network
2104 S.W. 152nd Street, Suite 2
Burien, WA 98166

Telephone: (206) 241-7566
Fax: (206) 241-7527
E-mail: *avanta@foxinternet.net*
Website: *www.avanta.net*

Recommended Supplementary Readings

Family Therapy: Concepts and Methods (Nichols & Schwartz, 1998) is an excellent
    text written in a clear manner. The authors provide a historical and conceptual
    context for family therapy as well as covering the major contemporary systems.
Family Counseling and Therapy (Horne, 2000) is a comprehensive overview of the
    major models of family therapy, each written by an expert in the field. The
    format of the book allows for comparisons among the models.
Family Therapy: A Systemic Integration (Becvar & Becvar, 1996) provides a clear
    and comprehensive discussion of the contemporary models of family therapy.
    Emphasis is placed on understanding and integrating a systemic perspective.
The Practice of Family Therapy: Key Elements Across Models (Hanna & Brown, 1999)
    focuses on the diversity of family therapy and integrating common elements
    of the field. It also deals with family therapy assessment and treatment skills.
Ethnicity and Family Therapy (McGoldrick, Pearce, & Giordano, 1996) is the semi-
    nal work on culture in family therapy. The authors review the importance of
    cultural considerations in relation to family therapy and provide chapters on
    the background, research, and therapy issues of more than 15 cultures.
Family Therapy: An Overview (Goldenberg & Goldenberg, 2000) provides an excel-
    lent basic overview of contemporary perspectives on family therapy that are
    briefly described in this chapter.

References and Suggested Readings*

ADLER, A. (1930). *The education of children*. New York: Greenberg.
ADLER, A. (1931). *What life should mean to you*. Boston: Little, Brown.
ADLER, A. (1938). *Social interest: A challenge to mankind*. London: Faber & Faber.
ANDERSEN, T. (1987). The reflecting team: Dialogue and metadialogue in clinical
    work. *Family Process, 26*(4), 415–428.
ANDERSEN, T. (1991*). The reflecting team: Dialogues and dialogues about the dia-
    logues*. New York: Norton.
ANDERSON, H. (1993). On a roller coaster: A collaborative language system approach
    to therapy. In S. Friedman (Ed.), *The new language of change* (pp. 324–344).
    New York: Guilford Press.
ANDERSON, H., & GOOLISHIAN, H. (1992). The client is the expert: A not-knowing
    approach to therapy. In S. McNamee & K. J. Gergen (Eds.), *Therapy as social
    construction* (pp. 25–39). Newbury Park, CA: Sage.
BECVAR, D. S., & BECVAR, R. J. (1996). *Family therapy: A systemic integration* (3rd
    ed.). Needham Heights, MA: Allyn & Bacon.
BITTER, J. R. (1987). Communication and meaning: Satir in Adlerian context. In
    R. Sherman & D. Dinkmeyer (Eds.), *Systems of family therapy: An Adlerian
    integration* (pp. 109–142). New York: Brunner/Mazel.

---

*Books and articles marked with an asterisk are suggested for further study.

BITTER, J. R. (1988). Family mapping and family constellation: Satir in Adlerian context. *Individual Psychology, 44*(1), 106–111.

BITTER, J. R. (1989). The mistaken goals of adults with children. In B. L. Bettner (Ed.), *An Adlerian resource book* (pp. 54–55). Chicago: NASAP.

BITTER, J. R. (Speaker). (1991a). *Adlerian family mapping* (Video VHS Cassette Recording #TRT:105:00). Villa Park, IL: Copymaster Video Inc.

BITTER, J. R. (1991b). Conscious motivations: An enhancement to Dreikurs' goals of children's misbehavior. *Individual Psychology, 47*(2), 210–221.

BITTER, J. R., CHRISTENSEN, O. C., HAWES, C., & NICOLL, W. G. (1998). Adlerian brief therapy with individuals, couples, and families. *Directions in Clinical and Counseling Psychology, 8*(8), 95–112.

BOWEN, M. (1966). The use of family theory in clinical practice. *Comprehensive Psychiatry, 7,* 345–374.

*BOWEN, M. (1972). On the differentiation of self. In J. Framo (Ed.), *Family interaction: A dialogue between family researchers and family therapists* (pp. 111–173). New York: Springer.

*BOWEN, M. (1976). Theory in the practice of psychotherapy. In P. J. Guerin Jr. (Ed.), *Family Therapy: Theory and practice* (pp. 42–90). New York: Gardner Press.

*BOWEN, M. (1978). *Family therapy in clinical practice.* New York: Aronson.

BREUNLIN, D. C., SCHWARTZ, R. C., & MACKUNE-KARRER, B. (1997). *Metaframeworks: Transcending the models of family therapy.* San Francisco: Jossey-Bass. (Original work published 1992)

*BROWN, J. H., & CHRISTENSEN, D. N. (1999). *Family therapy: Theory and practice* (2nd ed.). Pacific Grove, CA: Brooks/Cole.

CHRISTENSEN, O. C. (Ed.). (1993). *Adlerian family counseling* (rev. ed.). Minneapolis, MN: Educational Media Corp. (Original work published 1983)

COLAPINTO, J. (2000). Structural family therapy. In A. M. Horne (Ed.), *Family counseling and therapy* (3rd ed., pp. 140-169). Itasca, IL: F. E. Peacock.

COREY, G. (2001). *Case approach to counseling and psychotherapy* (5th ed.). Pacific Grove, CA: Brooks-Cole/Wadsworth.

*DATTILIO, F. M. (Ed.). (1998). *Case studies in couple and family therapy: Systemic and cognitive perspectives.* New York: Guilford Press.

DE SHAZER, S. (1985). *Keys to solutions in brief therapy.* New York: Norton.

DE SHAZER, S. (1988). *Clues: Investigating solutions in brief therapy.* New York: Norton.

DE SHAZER, S. (1991). *Putting difference to work.* New York: Norton.

DINKMEYER, D. C., MCKAY, G. D., & DINKMEYER, D. C. (1997). *STEP: Systematic training for effective parenting* (rev. ed.). Circle Pines, MN: American Guidance Service.

DREIKURS, R. (1940a, November). The importance of group life. *Camping Magazine, 3–4,* 27.

DREIKURS, R. (1940b, December). The child in the group. *Camping Magazine, 7–9.*

DREIKURS, R. (1950). The immediate purpose of children's misbehavior, its recognition and correction. *Internationale Zeitschrift fur Individual-psychologie, 19,* 70–87.

DREIKURS, R. (1957). Our child guidance clinics in Chicago. *Collected papers of Rudolf Dreikurs.* Eugene, OR: University of Oregon Press.

DREIKURS, R. (1971). *Social equality: The challenge of today.* Chicago: Regnery.

DREIKURS, R., & SOLTZ, V. (1964). *Children: The challenge.* New York: Hawthorn.

EPSTON, D., & WHITE, M. (1992). Consulting your consultants: The documentation of alternative knowledges. In *Experience, contradiction, narrative and imagination: Selected papers of David Epston and Michael White, 1989–1991* (pp. 11–26). Adelaide, South Australia: Dulwich Centre Publications.

FISHMAN, H. C. (1993). *Intensive structural therapy: Treating families in their social context.* New York: Basic Books.

FREEDMAN, J., & COMBS, G. (1996). *Narrative therapy: The social construction of preferred realities.* New York: Norton.

*FRAMO, J. L. (1992). *Family-of-origin therapy: An intergenerational approach.* New York: Brunner/Mazel.

GERGEN, K. (1985). The social constructionist movement in modern psychology. *American Psychologist, 40,* 266–275.

GERGEN, K. (1991). *The saturated self.* New York: Basic Books.

GOLDENBERG, H., & GOLDENBERG, I. (1998). *Counseling today's families* (3rd ed.). Pacific Grove, CA: Brooks-Cole/Wadsworth.

*GOLDENBERG, I., & GOLDENBERG, H. (2000). *Family therapy: An overview* (5th ed.). Pacific Grove, CA: Brooks-Cole/Wadsworth.

*GUERIN, P. J., & CHABOT, D. R. (1992). Development of family systems theory. In D. K. Freedheim (Ed.), *History of psychotherapy: A century of change* (pp. 225–260). Washington, DC: American Psychological Association.

GURMAN, A. S., & KNISKERN, D. P. (1992). The future of marital and family therapy. *Psychotherapy, 29*(1), 65–71.

HALEY, J. (1963). *Strategies of psychotherapy.* New York: Grune & Stratton.

HALEY, J. (1973). *Uncommon therapy: The psychiatric techniques of Milton H. Erickson, M.D.* New York: Norton.

*HALEY, J. (1976). *Problem-solving therapy: New strategies for effective family therapy.* San Francisco: Jossey-Bass.

*HALEY, J. (1984). *Ordeal therapy: Unusual ways to change behavior.* San Francisco: Jossey-Bass.

*HANNA, S. M., & BROWN, J. H. (1999). *The practice of family therapy: Key elements across models* (2nd ed.). Pacific Grove, CA: Brooks/Cole.

HOFFMAN, L. (1993). *Exchanging voices.* London: Karnak.

HOMRICH, A. M., & HORNE, A. M. (2000). Brief family therapy. In A. M. Horne (Ed.), *Family counseling and therapy* (3rd ed.) (pp. 243–271). Itasca, IL: F. E. Peacock.

*HORNE, A. M. (2000). *Family counseling and therapy* (3rd ed.). Itasca, IL: F. E. Peacock.

KEIM, J. (2000). Strategic family therapy: The Washington school. In A. M. Horne (Ed.), *Family counseling and therapy* (3rd ed.) (pp. 170–207). Itasca, IL: F. E. Peacock.

*KEITH, D. V. (2000). Symbolic experiential family therapy. In A. M. Horne (Ed.), *Family counseling and therapy* (3rd. ed., pp. 102–139). Itasca, IL: F. E. Peacock.

*KERR, M. E., & BOWEN, M. (1988). *Family evaluation.* New York: Norton.

KOGAN, S. M., & GALE, J. E. (2000). Taking a narrative turn: Social constructionism and family therapy. In A. M. Horne (Ed.), *Family counseling and therapy* (3rd ed.) (pp. 208–242). Itasca, IL: F. E. Peacock.

*LUEPNITZ, D. A. (1988). *The family interpreted: Feminist theory in clinical practice.* New York: Basic Books.

*MADANES, C. (1981). *Strategic family therapy.* San Francisco: Jossey-Bass.

*MADANES, C. (1984). *Behind the one-way mirror: Advances in the practice of strategic therapy.* San Francisco: Jossey-Bass.

MADANES, C. (1991). *Sex, love, and violence: Strategies for transformation.* New York: Norton.

*MCGOLDRICK, M., GERSON, R., & SHELLENBERGER, S. (1999). *Genograms: Assessment and Intervention* (2nd ed.). New York: Norton.

*MCGOLDRICK, M., & GIORDANO, J. (1996). Overview: Ethnicity and family therapy. In M. McGoldrick, J. K. Pearce, & J. Giordano (Eds.), *Ethnicity and family therapy* (2nd ed., pp. 1–27). New York: Guilford Press.

*MCGOLDRICK, M., PEARCE, J. K., & GIORDANO, J. (Eds.). (1996). *Ethnicity and family therapy* (2nd ed.). New York: Guilford Press.

*MCNAMEE, S., & GERGEN, K. J. (Eds.). (1992). *Therapy as social construction.* Newbury Park, CA: Sage.

*MINUCHIN, S. (1974). *Families and family therapy.* Cambridge, MA: Harvard University Press.

*MINUCHIN, S., & FISHMAN, H. C. (1981). *Family therapy techniques.* Cambridge, MA: Harvard University Press.

*NAPIER, A. Y., & WHITAKER, C. A. (1978). *The family crucible.* New York: Harper & Row.

*NICHOLS, M. P., & SCHWARTZ, R. C. (1998). *Family therapy: Concepts and methods* (4th ed.). Boston: Allyn & Bacon.

O'HANLON, W. H. (1994). The third wave: The promise of narrative. *The Family Therapy Networker, 18*(6), 18–29.

O'HANLON, W. H., & WEINER-DAVIS, M. (1989). *In search of solutions: A new direction in psychotherapy.* New York: Norton.

PAPERO, D. V. (2000). The Bowen theory. In A. M. Horne (Ed.), *Family counseling and therapy* (3rd ed., pp. 272–299). Itasca, IL: F. E. Peacock.

POPKIN, M. (1993). *Active parenting today.* Atlanta, GA: Active Parenting Publications.

*SATIR, V. (1983). *Conjoint family therapy* (3rd ed.). Palo Alto, CA: Science and Behavior Books.

*SATIR, V. (1988). *The new peoplemaking.* Palo Alto, CA: Science and Behavior Books.

SATIR, V., & BALDWIN, M. (1983). *Satir: Step by step.* Palo Alto, CA: Science and Behavior Books.

SATIR, V. M., & BITTER, J. R. (2000). The therapist and family therapy: Satir's human validation process model. In A. M. Horne (Ed.), *Family counseling and therapy* (3rd ed., pp. 62–101). Itasca, IL: F. E. Peacock.

SATIR, V., BITTER, J. R., & KRESTENSEN, K. K. (1988). Family reconstruction: The family within—a group experience. *Journal for Specialists in Group Work, 13*(4), 200–208.

SCHILSON, L. (1991). Strategic therapy. In A. M. Horne & J. L. Passmore (Eds.), *Family counseling and therapy* (2nd ed., pp. 141–178). Itasca, IL: F. E. Peacock.

SEGAL, L. (1991). Brief family therapy. In A. M. Horne & J. L. Passmore (Eds.), *Family counseling and therapy* (2nd ed., pp. 179–205). Itasca, IL: F. E. Peacock.

SHERMAN, R., & DINKMEYER, D. C. (Eds.). (1987). *Systems of family therapy: An Adlerian integration.* New York: Brunner/Mazel.

SUE, D., & SUE, D. W. (1991). Counseling strategies for Chinese Americans. In C. C. Lee & B. L. Richardson (Eds.), *Multicultural issues in counseling: New approaches to diversity* (pp. 79–90). Alexandria, VA: American Counseling Association.

TERNER, J., & PEW, W. L. (1978). *The courage to be imperfect: The life and work of Rudolf Dreikurs.* New York: Hawthorn Books.

TOMAN, W. (1994). *Family constellation: Its effects on personality and social behavior* (4th ed.). Northvale, NJ: Aronson.

WATZLAWICK, P. (1978). *The language of change.* New York: Basic Books.

*WATZLAWICK, P., WEAKLAND, J. H., & FISCH, R. (1974). *Change: Principles of problem formation and problem resolution.* New York: Norton.

WEEKS, G. R., & L'ABATE, L. (1982). *Paradoxical psychotherapy: Theory and practice with individuals, couples, and families.* New York: Brunner/Mazel.

WEST, J. D., BUBENZER, D. L., & BITTER, J. R. (Eds.). (1998). *Social construction in couple and family counseling.* Alexandria, VA: ACA/IAMFC.

WHITAKER, C. A. (1976). The hindrance of theory in clinical work. In P. J. Guerin Jr. (Ed.), *Family therapy: Theory and practice* (pp. 154–164). New York: Gardner Press.

WHITAKER, C. A., & MALONE, T. P. (1981). *The roots of psychotherapy.* New York: Brunner/Mazel.

WHITE, M. (1992). Deconstruction and therapy. In *Experience, contradiction, narrative, and imagination: Selected papers of David Epston and Michael White, 1989–1991* (pp. 109–151). Adelaide, South Australia: Dulwich Centre Publications.

*WHITE, M., & EPSTON, D. (1990). *Narrative means to therapeutic ends.* New York: Norton. (Original title *Linguistic means to therapeutic ends*)

PART

3

Integration and Application

14   *An Integrative Perspective*

15   *Case Illustration: An Integrative Approach in Working With Stan*

CHAPTER

14

An Integrative Perspective

INTRODUCTION

THE TREND TOWARD PSYCHOTHERAPY INTEGRATION

The Future of Psychotherapy: Some Predictions
Integration of Multicultural Issues in Counseling
Integration of Spiritual/Religious Issues in Counseling
The Challenge of Developing an Integrative Perspective

ISSUES RELATED TO THE THERAPEUTIC PROCESS

Therapeutic Goals
Therapist's Function and Role
Client's Experience in Therapy
Relationship Between Therapist and Client

THE PLACE OF TECHNIQUES AND EVALUATION IN COUNSELING

Drawing on Techniques From Various Approaches
Evaluating the Effectiveness of Counseling and Therapy

SUMMARY

RECOMMENDED SUPPLEMENTARY READINGS

REFERENCES AND SUGGESTED READINGS

INTRODUCTION

This chapter will help you think about areas of convergence and divergence among the 10 therapeutic systems. Although the approaches all have some goals in common, they have many differences when it comes to the best route to achieve these goals. Some therapies call for an active and directive stance on the therapist's part, and others place value on clients being the active agent. Some therapies focus on bringing out feelings, whereas others stress identifying cognitive patterns, and still others concentrate on actual behavior. The key challenge is to find ways to integrate certain features of each of these therapies so that you can work with clients on all three levels of human experience.

The field of psychotherapy is characterized by a diverse range of specialized models. With all this diversity, is there any hope that a practitioner can develop skills in all of the existing techniques? How does a student decide which theories are most relevant to practice? In addressing these questions, it is well to consider the competitive strife and theoretical "cold war" that dominated the field of counseling and psychotherapy for decades. The rivalry among theoretical orientations, dating back to Freud, has been characterized by various practitioners battling over who has the "best" way to bring about personality change. According to Norcross (1986a), the proliferation of therapy systems has been accompanied by a deafening cacophony of rival claims. He pleads for networks of practitioners who are willing to work toward rapprochement and integration.

Since the early 1980s, psychotherapy has been characterized by a rapidly developing movement toward integration and eclecticism. This movement is based on combining the best of differing orientations so that more complete theoretical models can be articulated and more efficient treatments developed (Goldfried & Castonguay, 1992). The Society for the Exploration of Psychotherapy Integration is an international organization that was formed in 1983. Its members are professionals who are working toward development of therapeutic approaches that transcend single theoretical orientations.

In this chapter I consider the advantages of developing an integrated perspective for counseling and deal briefly with some of the potential problems. I also present a framework for helping you begin to integrate concepts and techniques from various approaches. As you read, begin to formulate your personal perspective for counseling. Rather than merely reviewing the basic issues, look for ways to synthesize diverse elements from different theoretical perspectives. As much as possible, be alert to how these systems can function in harmony.

THE TREND TOWARD PSYCHOTHERAPY INTEGRATION

Integrative counseling and psychotherapy is the process of selecting concepts and methods from a variety of systems. Surveys of clinical and counseling psychologists consistently reveal that 30% to 50% of the respondents consider themselves to be eclectic or integrative in their therapeutic practice (Norcross & Newman, 1992). Psychologists generally believe the best hope for a truly comprehensive therapeutic approach lies with eclecticism (Norcross & Prochaska, 1988; Kelly, 1991; Smith, 1982). This trend toward integrating perspectives has both promises and pitfalls. Goldfried and Safran (1986) caution that if integration is carried to its extreme there is a danger of constructing too many eclectic models. They are concerned that the growing interest in integration could result in competition to determine who can formulate the best eclectic system.

A large number of therapists identify themselves as "eclectic," and this category covers a broad range of practice. Perhaps at its worst eclectic practice consists of haphazardly picking techniques without any overall theoretical rationale. This is known as *syncretism,* wherein the practitioner grabs for anything that seems to work, often making no attempt to determine whether the therapeutic procedures are indeed effective. This unsystematic approach is eclecticism "by default," as these practitioners lack the knowledge and skill to select interventions meaningfully (Norcross, 1986a). Such a hodgepodge is no better than a narrow and dogmatic orthodoxy. Pulling techniques from many sources without a sound rationale can only result in syncretistic confusion (Lazarus, 1986, 1996b; Lazarus, Beutler, & Norcross, 1992).

Psychotherapy integration is best characterized by attempts to look beyond and across the confines of single-school approaches to see what can be learned from—and how clients can benefit from—other perspectives. The integrative approach is characterized by an openness to various ways of integrating diverse theories and techniques.

There are multiple pathways to achieving this integration; three of the most common are technical eclecticism, theoretical integration, and common factors (Arkowitz, 1997). *Technical eclecticism* tends to focus on differences, chooses from many approaches, and is a collection of techniques. This path calls for using techniques from different schools without necessarily subscribing to the theoretical positions that spawned them. In contrast, *theoretical integration* refers to a conceptual or theoretical creation beyond a mere blending of techniques. This path has the goal of producing a conceptual framework that synthesizes the best of two or more theoretical approaches under the assumption that the outcome will be richer than either of the theories alone (Norcross & Newman, 1992). The *common factors* approach attempts to look across different theoretical systems in search of common elements. Although there are differences among the theories, there is a recognizable core of counseling composed of nonspecific variables common to all therapies. This perspective on integration is based on the premise that these common factors are at least as important in accounting for therapeutic outcomes as the unique factors that differentiate one theory from another.

Norcross and Newman (1992) identify eight interacting and mutually reinforcing motives that have fostered the trend toward psychotherapy integration:

1. A proliferation of therapies
2. The inadequacy of a single theory that is relevant to all clients and all problems
3. External socioeconomic realities, such as restrictions for insurance reimbursement and the prospect of national health insurance
4. The growing popularity of short-term, prescriptive, and problem-focused therapies
5. Opportunities to observe and experiment with various therapies
6. A paucity of differential effectiveness among therapies
7. Recognition that therapeutic commonalities play a major role in determining therapy outcome
8. Development of professional societies aimed at the integration of psychotherapies

One reason for the trend toward psychotherapy integration is the recognition that no single theory is comprehensive enough to account for the complexities of human behavior, especially when the range of client types and their specific problems are taken into consideration. Because no one theory has a patent on the truth, and because no single set of counseling techniques is always effective in working with diverse client populations, Kelly (1988, 1991) does not think it makes sense to follow a single theory. Instead, he calls for theoretical integration as the basis for future counseling practice. Lazarus (1996b) states that because no single theory is able to provide all theoretical and practical answers it may be sensible to cross boundaries. He adds, however, that "there are numerous booby traps that lie in wait for the unsuspecting" who attempt to combine theories (p. 59). Lazarus (1995) is eclectic in that he borrows techniques from many models (such as psychodrama and Gestalt therapy), but he operates from a consistent framework based on social and cognitive learning theory.

Practitioners who are open to an integrative perspective will find that several theories play a crucial role in their personal counseling approach. Each theory has its unique contributions and its own domain of expertise. By accepting that each theory has strengths and weaknesses and is, by definition, "different" from the others, practitioners have some basis to begin developing a theory that fits for them. Developing an integrative perspective is a lifelong endeavor that is refined with experience.

The Future of Psychotherapy: Some Predictions

The 10 systems discussed in this book have evolved in the direction of broadening their theoretical and practical bases, becoming less restrictive in their focus. Thus, many practitioners who claim allegiance to a particular system of therapy are expanding their theoretical outlook and developing a wider range of therapeutic techniques to fit a more diverse population of clients. Lazarus and his colleagues (1992) predict that "technical eclecticism will represent the psychotherapeutic *Zeitgeist* well into the 21st century" (p. 13).

They also suggest a trend toward matching clients not only to specific treatment techniques but also to therapists' interpersonal styles. What this means is that we will be better able to prescribe therapeutic relationships of choice for individual clients. Goldfried, Castonguay, and Safran (1992) predict that although the traditional theoretical orientations are likely to continue in the future, these systems will increasingly incorporate contributions from other approaches. They express concerns about delineating "integrative psychotherapy" as yet another system, because there is no consensus on what should be integrated. Arkowitz (1997) views current integrative approaches as an attempt to build a coherent framework for understanding or predicting change and for determining the choices of therapy techniques. Prochaska and Norcross (1999) agree with these earlier predictions and also foresee enormous pressure toward intertheoretical cooperation and short-term, integrative, and cost-effective treatments.

Integration of Multicultural Issues in Counseling

Because of the increased diversity of client problems and client populations, psychotherapy integration must include cultural factors in the assessment and treatment process. Multiculturalism is a reality that cannot be ignored by practitioners if they hope to meet the needs of their diverse client groups. There is a growing movement toward creating a separate multicultural theory of counseling and therapy (Sue, Ivey, & Pedersen, 1996; Sue & Sue, 1999), but I believe current theories can be expanded to incorporate a multicultural component. If current theories are not modified, however, they will have limited applicability in working with culturally diverse client populations.

Technical eclecticism seems especially necessary in working with a diverse range of cultural backgrounds. Harm can come to clients who are expected to fit all the specifications of a given theory, whether or not the values espoused by the theory are consistent with their own cultural values. Rather than stretching the client to fit the dimensions of a single theory, practitioners must make their theory and practice fit the unique needs of the client. This requirement calls for counselors to possess knowledge of various cultures, be aware of their own cultural heritage, and have skills to assist diverse clients in meeting their needs within the realities of their culture.

In your role as a counselor, you must be able to assess the special needs of clients. Depending on the individual client's ethnicity and culture and on the concerns that bring this person to counseling, you will need to show flexibility in utilizing diverse therapeutic strategies. Some clients will need more direction, and even advice. Others will be very hesitant in talking about themselves in personal ways, especially during the early phase of the counseling process. You need to recognize that what may appear to be resistance is very likely to be the client's response to years of cultural conditioning and respect for certain values and traditions. What the matter comes down to is your familiarity with a variety of theoretical approaches and the ability to employ and adapt your techniques to fit the person-in-the-environment. It is not enough to merely assist your clients in gaining insight, expressing suppressed emotions, or making certain behavioral changes. The challenge is to find practical strategies for adapting the techniques you have developed to enable clients to question the impact their culture continues to have on their lives and to make decisions about what they want to change. Being an effective counselor involves reflecting on how your own culture influences you and your interventions in your counseling practice. This awareness will be a critical factor in your becoming more sensitive to the cultural backgrounds of the clients who seek your help. An integrative perspective favors broadening the base of the contemporary theories to encompass social, spiritual, and political dimensions.

Integration of Spiritual/Religious Issues in Counseling

The field of counseling and psychotherapy has been slow to recognize the need to address spiritual/religious concerns. During the past decade, more attention has been given to this topic, and there has been increasing debate in psychology over the role spiritual and religious issues should play in psychotherapy (Younggren, 1993). There is now widespread interest in the topic of spiritual and religious beliefs—both the counselor's and the client's—and how such beliefs might be incorporated in therapeutic relationships (Miller, 1999). Evidence for this interest is found in the increased number of articles in this area in professional journals and in presentations at professional conferences.

Spirituality is an intensely personal and subjective concept. Psychotherapy has recognized that a broad definition of this concept best serves both counselors and clients. Here is one definition that fits these criteria:

> Spirituality is described as a capacity and tendency that is innate and unique to all persons. This spiritual tendency moves the individual towards knowledge, love, meaning, hope, transcendence, connectedness, and compassion. Spirituality includes one's capacity for creativity, growth, and the development of a values system. Spirituality encompasses the religious, spiritual, and transpersonal. (Summit on Spirituality, 1995, p. 30)

Bergin (1991) is one of the many researchers who believes being open to spiritual/religious values will result in a change in the focus of treatment away from symptom relief and toward more general changes in lifestyle. Spirituality is an important component for mental health, and its inclusion in counseling practice renders the therapeutic process more effective. Spiritual/religious beliefs need not be feared in a counseling setting and should be used to the client's benefit to enhance the therapeutic process (Mattson, 1994).

From my perspective, spirituality is a factor that should be addressed if it is a concern of the client. Whatever one's particular view of spirituality, it is a force that can help the individual make sense of the universe and find a purpose (or purposes) for living. For some clients spirituality entails embracing a religion, which can have many different meanings. Other clients value spirituality yet do not have any ties to a formal religion. There are many paths toward fulfilling spiritual needs, and it is not your task as a counselor to prescribe any particular pathway. If clients give an indication that they are concerned about any of their beliefs or practices, this is a useful focal point for exploration. The key here is that you remain finely tuned to clients' stories and to the purpose for which they sought therapy.

COMMON GOALS   In some ways a spiritual/religious perspective and a counseling perspective have similar goals. Both perspectives emphasize learning to accept oneself, forgiving others and oneself, admitting one's shortcomings, accepting personal responsibility, letting go of hurts and resentments, dealing with guilt, and learning to let go of self-destructive patterns of thinking, feeling, and acting.

Spiritual/religious values have a major part to play in human life and struggles, which means that exploring these values has a great deal to do with providing solutions for clients' struggles. Because spiritual and therapeutic paths converge in some ways, integration is possible, and dealing with a client's spirituality will often actually enhance the therapy process.

Religion and spirituality can be sources of healing, and both can give strength in critical times by helping people find purpose in life. Themes that have healing influences include loving, caring, learning to listen with compassion, challenging clients' basic life assumptions, accepting human imperfection, and going outside of self-oriented interests (social interest). Both religion and counseling help people ponder questions of "Who am I?" and "What is the meaning of my life?" At their best, both counseling and religion are able to foster healing through an exploration of the role of shame and guilt in human behavior, understanding the differences between blame and responsibility, healthy and unhealthy guilt, and the power of sharing deeply human concerns.

IMPLICATIONS FOR ASSESSMENT AND TREATMENT   Traditionally, when clients come to a therapist with a problem, the therapist explores all the factors that contributed to the development of the problem. Even though clients may no longer consider themselves to be religious or spiritual, a background of involvement in religion should be explored as part of clients' history. These beliefs may have been factors in the development of the problem, and thus could be part of the problem.

Faiver and O'Brien (1993) and Kelly (1995) believe it is essential to understand and respect clients' religious beliefs and to include such beliefs in their assessment and treatment practice. The first step is to include spiritual and religious dimensions as a regular part of the intake procedure and the early phase of the counseling process. Faiver and O'Brien devised a form to assess the religious beliefs of clients, which they use to glean relevant information on clients' belief systems for diagnostic, treatment, and referral purposes. They recommend assessing clients' problems from a holistic perspective. They add that the assessment process should include questions pertaining to spiritual and religious issues as they are relevant to clients' presenting problems, questions about the roles religion and spirituality have played or currently play in clients' lives, and questions about how religious and spiritual beliefs might be related to clients' cognitive, affective, and behavioral processes. For example, is guilt an issue? What is the source of guilt, and does it serve any functional purpose?

Kelly (1995) endorses the notion of including items pertaining to general information about clients' spirituality and religion that serve the purposes of (a) obtaining a preliminary indication about the relevance of spirituality and religion for clients, (b) gathering information that the helper might refer to at a later point in the helping process, and (c) indicating to clients that it is acceptable to talk about religious and spiritual concerns.

YOUR ROLE AS A COUNSELOR   How people handle guilt feelings, authority, and moral questions are just a few of the issues clients bring to counseling. Miranti and Burke (1995) maintain that counselors must be prepared to deal with spiritual issues that lie at the very core and essence of the clients' being. For many clients in crisis, the spiritual domain offers solace, comfort, and is a major sustaining power that keeps them going when all else seems to fail. The guilt, anger, and sadness that clients experience often results from a misinterpretation of the spiritual and religious realm, which can lead to depression and a sense of worthlessness.

Personal beliefs have been shown to directly and indirectly affect the course of therapy (Younggren, 1993). Therapists must be careful not to make decisions for clients but to let clients choose how their own values will guide their behavior. There is always a danger that counselors may inadvertently or purposely impose their own values, in any direction. Therapists must guard against indoctrinating clients with a particular set of spiritual/religious values (Grimm, 1994).

It is my opinion that the emphasis on spirituality will continue to be important in counseling practice. My hope is that you prepare yourself to work effectively with clients' spiritual/religious concerns. If you are interested in integrating a spiritual orientation in your counseling style, I recommend Faiver and O'Brien (1993), Georgia (1994), Grimm (1994), Hinterkopf (1994, 1998), Ingersoll (1994), Kelly (1994), Mattson (1994), Miller (1999), Miranti and Burke (1995), Pate and Bondi (1992), Peck (1978), Richards and Bergin (1997), and Younggren (1993).

The Challenge of Developing an Integrative Perspective

In addressing the proper degree of integration to introduce into counseling practice, Messer (1986, 1992) concludes that the debate will continue between adherents of a single theoretical system and those who favor moving toward some form of integration. A survey of approaches to counseling and psychotherapy reveals that no common philosophy unifies them. Many of the theories have different basic philosophies and views of human nature (Table 14-1). Your philosophical assumptions are important because they influence which "reality" you perceive, and they direct your attention to the variables that you are "set" to see. A word of caution, then: Beware of subscribing exclusively to any one view of human nature; remain open and selectively incorporate a framework for counseling that is consistent with your own personality and your belief system.

TABLE 14-1   ■   The Basic Philosophies

Psychoanalytic therapy	Human beings are basically determined by psychic energy and by early experiences. Unconscious motives and conflicts are central in present behavior. Irrational forces are strong; the person is driven by sexual and aggressive impulses. Early development is of critical importance because later personality problems have their roots in repressed childhood conflicts.
Adlerian therapy	Humans are motivated by social interest, by striving toward goals, and by dealing with the tasks of life. Emphasis is on the individual's positive capacities to live in society cooperatively. People have the capacity to interpret, influence, and create events. Each person at an early age creates a unique style of life, which tends to remain relatively constant throughout life.
Existential therapy	The central focus is on the nature of the human condition, which includes a capacity for self-awareness, freedom of choice to decide one's fate, responsibility, anxiety, the search for a unique meaning in a meaningless world, being alone and being in relation with others, and facing the reality of death.
Person-centered therapy	The view of humans is positive; we have an inclination toward becoming fully functioning. In the context of the therapeutic relationship, the client experiences feelings that were previously denied to awareness. The client actualizes potential and moves toward increased awareness, spontaneity, trust in self, and inner-directedness.
Gestalt therapy	The person strives for wholeness and integration of thinking, feeling, and behaving. The view is antideterministic in that the person is viewed as having the capacity to recognize how earlier influences are related to present difficulties. As an experiential approach, it is grounded in the here and now and emphasizes personal choice and responsibility.
Reality therapy	Based on choice theory, this approach assumes that we are by nature social creatures and we need quality relationships to be happy. Psychological problems are the result of our resisting the control by others or of our attempt to control others. Choice theory is an explanation of human nature and how to best achieve good relationships.
Behavior therapy	Behavior is the product of learning. We are both the product and the producer of the environment. No set of unifying assumptions about behavior can incorporate all the existing procedures in the behavioral field.
Cognitive behavior therapy	Individuals tend to incorporate faulty thinking, which leads to emotional and behavioral disturbances. Cognitions are the major determinants of how we feel and act. Therapy is primarily oriented toward cognition and behavior, and it stresses the role of thinking, deciding, questioning, doing, and redeciding. This is a psychoeducational model, which emphasizes therapy as a learning process, including ac-

TABLE 14-1   ■   (*continued*)

	quiring and practicing new skills, learning new ways of thinking, and acquiring more effective ways of coping with problems.
Feminist therapy	Feminists criticize many traditional theories to the degree that they are based on gender-biased concepts and practices of being: androcentric, gendercentric, ethnocentric, heterosexist, and intrapsychic. The constructs of feminist therapy include being gender-free, flexible, interactionist, and life-span-oriented.
Family systems therapy	The family is viewed from an interactive and systemic perspective. Clients are connected to a living system; a change in one part of the system will result in a change in other parts. The family provides the context for understanding how individuals function in relationship to others and how they behave. Treatment is best focused on the family unit. An individual's dysfunctional behavior grows out of the interactional unit of the family and out of larger systems as well.

Despite the divergences in the various theories, there are possibilities for a creative synthesis among some models. For example, an existential orientation does not necessarily preclude using techniques drawn from behavior therapy or from some of the cognitive theories. All these theories represent different vantage points from which to look at human behavior, but no one theorist has "the truth" with the others all in error. Each point of view offers a perspective for helping clients in their search for self. I encourage you to study all the major theories, to resist being converted to any single point of view, and to remain open to what you might take from the various orientations as a basis for an integrative perspective that will guide your practice.

In developing a personal integrative perspective, it is important to be alert to the problem of attempting to mix theories with incompatible underlying assumptions. Lazarus (1995) raises the question: "How is it possible to blend two systems that rest on totally different assumptions about the meaning, origins, development, maintenance, significance, and management of problems" (p. 156)? Lazarus (1995), who is an advocate of technical eclecticism, has consistently emphasized over the years that a blend of different theories is likely to result in confusion. He adds that basic concepts that may seem compatible are, upon closer scrutiny, quite often irreconcilable (Table 14-2). Although Lazarus is not aware of any instances where blending different theories resulted in a more powerful technique, he states there are numerous cases where techniques drawn from different theoretical systems have enriched a practitioner's therapeutic style. Lazarus stresses that psychotherapy integration does not have to rely on a theoretical amalgamation. Clinicians can select techniques from any discipline without necessarily endorsing any of the theories that spawned them.

TABLE 14-2   ■   Key Concepts

Psychoanalytic therapy	Normal personality development is based on successful resolution and integration of psychosexual stages of development. Faulty personality development is the result of inadequate resolution of some specific stage. Id, ego, and superego constitute the basis of personality structure. Anxiety is a result of repression of basic conflicts. Unconscious processes are centrally related to current behavior.
Adlerian therapy	It stresses the unity of personality, the need to view people from their subjective perspective, and the importance of life goals that give direction to behavior. People are motivated by social interest and by finding goals to give life meaning. Other key concepts are striving for significance and superiority, developing a unique lifestyle, and understanding the family constellation. Therapy is a matter of providing encouragement and assisting clients in changing their cognitive perspective.
Existential therapy	It is an experiential therapy. Essentially an approach to counseling rather than a firm theoretical model, it stresses core human conditions. Normally, personality development is based on the uniqueness of each individual. Sense of self develops from infancy. Self-determination and a tendency toward growth are central ideas. Focus is on the present and on what one is becoming; that is, the approach has a future orientation. It stresses self-awareness before action.
Person-centered therapy	The client has the potential to become aware of problems and the means to resolve them. Faith is placed in the client's capacity for self-direction. Mental health is a congruence of ideal self and real self. Maladjustment is the result of a discrepancy between what one wants to be and what one is. Focus is on the present moment and on experiencing and expressing feelings.
Gestalt therapy	Emphasis is on the "what" and "how" of experiencing in the here and now to help clients accept their polarities. Key concepts include holism, figure-formation process, awareness, unfinished business and avoidance, contact, and energy.
Reality therapy	The basic focus is on what clients are doing and how to get them to evaluate whether their present actions are working for them. People create their feelings by the choices they make and by what they do. The approach rejects the medical model, the notion of transference, the unconscious, and dwelling on one's past.
Behavior therapy	Focus is on overt behavior, precision in specifying goals of treatment, development of specific treatment plans, and objective evaluation of therapy outcomes. Therapy is based on the principles of learning theory. Normal behavior is learned through reinforcement and imitation. Abnormal behavior is the result of faulty learning. This approach stresses present behavior.

TABLE 14-2   ■   (continued)

Cognitive behavior therapy	Although psychological problems may be rooted in childhood, they are perpetuated through reindoctrination in the now. A person's belief system is the primary cause of disorders. Internal dialogue plays a central role in one's behavior. Clients focus on examining faulty assumptions and misconceptions and on replacing these with effective beliefs.
Feminist therapy	Core principles that form the foundation for practice of feminist therapy are the personal is political, the counseling relationship is egalitarian, women's experiences are honored, definitions of distress and mental illness are reformulated, emphasis on gender equality, and commitment to confronting oppression on any grounds.
Family systems therapy	Focus is on communication patterns within a family, both verbal and nonverbal. Problems in relationships are likely to be passed on from generation to generation. Symptoms are viewed as ways of communicating with the aim of controlling other family members. Key concepts vary depending on specific orientation but include differentiation, triangles, power coalitions, family-of-origin dynamics, functional versus dysfunctional interaction patterns, family rules governing communication, and dealing with here-and-now interactions. The present is more important than exploring past experiences.

According to Lazarus (1986, 1989, 1992, 1995, 1996a, 1996b, 1997a, 1997b), therapists who hope to be effective with a wide range of problems and with different client populations must be flexible and versatile. The basic questions they ask are: What works for whom under which particular circumstances? Why are some procedures helpful and others unhelpful? What can be done to ensure long-term success and positive follow-ups? Lazarus believes some clients respond to warm, informal counselors but that others want more formal counselors. Whereas some clients work well with therapists who are quiet and nonforceful, others work best with directive and outgoing therapists. Further, the same client may respond favorably to various therapeutic techniques and styles at different times.

Lazarus (1996a) mentions the value of a therapist assuming an active role in blending a flexible repertoire of *relationship styles* with a wide range of techniques as a way to enhance therapeutic outcomes. He maintains that a skilled therapist is able to determine when and when not to be confrontational, when to be directive and when to allow the client to struggle, when to be formal or informal, when to self-disclose or remain anonymous, and when to be gentle or tough. Lazarus asserts that *relationships* of choice are at least as important as *techniques* of choice. (For a review of multimodal procedures and their rationale, see Chapter 10.)

One of the challenges you will face as a counselor is to deliver therapeutic services in a brief, comprehensive, effective, and flexible way. Many of the theoretical orientations addressed in this book can be applied to brief forms of therapy. According to Prochaska and Norcross (1999), the clinical realities of brief therapy demand a flexible and eclectic orientation. Most forms of short-term psychotherapy are active in nature, collaborative in relationship, and eclectic in orientation. One of the driving forces of the psychotherapy integration movement has been the increase of brief therapies and the pressures to do more for a variety of client populations within the limitations of 6 to 20 sessions. Prochaska and Norcross (1999) make an excellent point in stating that effective brief therapy depends less on the hours counselors put in than on what they put into those hours. The challenge is for eclectic practitioners to learn how to rapidly and systematically identify problems, create a collaborative relationship with clients, and intervene with a range of specific methods. In his excellent book, *Brief But Comprehensive Psychotherapy: The Multimodal Way* (1997a), Lazarus shows how to provide short-term and comprehensive psychotherapy.

An integrative perspective at its best entails a *systematic integration* of underlying principles and methods common to a range of therapeutic approaches. To develop this kind of integration, you will eventually need to be thoroughly conversant with a number of theories, be open to the idea that these theories can be unified in some ways, and be willing to continually test your hypotheses to determine how well they are working. An integrative perspective is the product of a great deal of study, clinical practice, research, and theorizing.

If you are interested in developing an eclectic approach or in the movement toward the integration of psychotherapies, a great deal has been written. Consult some of these resources in the suggested readings at the end of this chapter: Abernethy (1992), Alford and Beck (1997), Arkowitz (1997), Garfield (1992a), Goldfried and Newman (1992), Lazarus (1995, 1996a, 1996b, 1997a, 1997b), Lazarus and Beutler (1993), Lazarus, Beutler, and Norcross (1992), Norcross (1986a, 1986b), Norcross and Goldfried (1992), Norcross and Newman (1992), Prochaska and Norcross (1999), and Young (1992).

 ## ISSUES RELATED TO THE THERAPEUTIC PROCESS

Therapeutic Goals

The goals of counseling are almost as diverse as are the theoretical approaches. Goals include restructuring the personality, uncovering the unconscious, creating social interest, finding meaning in life, curing an emotional disturbance, examining old decisions and making new ones, developing trust in oneself, becoming more self-actualizing, reducing anxiety, shedding maladaptive behavior and learning adaptive patterns, and gaining more effective control of one's life (Table 14-3). Is there a common denominator in this range of goals?

TABLE 14-3   ■   Goals of Therapy

Psychoanalytic therapy	To make the unconscious conscious. To reconstruct the basic personality. To assist clients in reliving earlier experiences and working through repressed conflicts. To achieve intellectual awareness.
Adlerian therapy	To challenge clients' basic premises and life goals. To offer encouragement so individuals can develop socially useful goals. To develop the client's sense of belonging.
Existential therapy	To help people see that they are free and become aware of their possibilities. To challenge them to recognize that they are responsible for events that they formerly thought were happening to them. To identify factors that block freedom.
Person-centered therapy	To provide a safe climate conducive to clients' self-exploration, so that they can recognize blocks to growth and can experience aspects of self that were formerly denied or distorted. To enable them to move toward openness, greater trust in self, willingness to be a process, and increased spontaneity and aliveness.
Gestalt therapy	To assist clients in gaining awareness of moment-to-moment experiencing and to expand the capacity to make choices. Aims not at analysis but at integration.
Reality therapy	To help people become more effective in meeting their needs. To enable clients to get reconnected with the people they have chosen to put into their quality worlds and teach clients choice theory.
Behavior therapy	Generally, to eliminate maladaptive behaviors and learn more effective behaviors. To focus on factors influencing behavior and find what can be done about problematic behavior. Clients have an active role in setting treatment goals and evaluating how well these goals are being met.
Cognitive behavior therapy	To challenge clients to confront faulty beliefs with contradictory evidence that they gather and evaluate. Helping clients seek out their dogmatic beliefs and vigorously minimize them. To become aware of automatic thoughts and to change them.
Feminist therapy	To bring about transformation both in the individual client and in society. For individual clients the goal is to assist them in recognizing, claiming, and using their personal power to free themselves from the limitations of gender-role socialization. To confront all forms of institutional policies that discriminate on the basis of gender.
Family systems therapy	Most approaches are aimed at helping family members gain awareness of patterns of relationships that are not working well and create new ways of interacting to relieve their distress. Some approaches focus on resolving the specific problem that brings the family to therapy.

This diversity can be simplified by considering the degree of generality or specificity of goals. Goals exist on a continuum from specific, concrete, and short term, on one end, to general, global, and long term, on the other. The cognitive behavioral approaches stress the former; the relationship-oriented therapies tend to stress the latter. The goals at opposite ends of the continuum are not necessarily contradictory; it is a matter of how specifically they are defined.

Therapist's Function and Role

Just as the various theories are guided by different goals, so, too, do the therapist's functions vary among the models. In working toward an integrative perspective, we need to address a number of questions about the counselor's behaviors: How do the counselor's functions change depending on the stage of the counseling process? Does the therapist maintain a basic role, or does this role vary in accordance with the characteristics of the client? How does the counselor determine how active and directive to be? How is structuring handled as the course of therapy progresses? What is the optimum balance of responsibility in the client/therapist relationship? When and how much does the counselor self-disclose?

As you saw through your study of the 10 therapeutic approaches, a central issue of each system is the degree to which the therapist exercises control over clients' behavior both during and outside the session. Cognitive behavior therapists and reality therapists, for example, operate within a directive and didactic structure. They frequently suggest homework assignments that are designed to get clients to practice new behavior outside therapy sessions. In contrast, person-centered therapists operate with a much looser and less defined structure.

Structuring depends on the particular client and the specific circumstances he or she brings to the therapy situation. From my perspective, clear structure is most essential during the early phase of counseling. It helps encourage clients to talk about the problems that led them to seek therapy. In a collaborative way, it is useful for both counselor and client to make some initial assessment that can provide a focus for the therapy process. As soon as possible, clients should be given a significant share of the responsibility for deciding on the content of the sessions. From early in the therapy process clients can be empowered if the counselor expects that they will become active participants in the process.

Client's Experience in Therapy

What expectations do clients have as they approach therapy? What are their responsibilities in the process? Is therapy only for the "disturbed"? Can the relatively healthy person benefit from therapy? Are there any commonalities among the grand diversity of clients?

Most clients share some degree of suffering, pain, or at least discontent. There is a discrepancy between how they would like to be and how they are. Some initiate therapy because they hope to cure a specific symptom or set of symptoms: They want to get rid of migraine headaches, free themselves of chronic anxiety attacks, lose weight, or get relief from depression. They may have conflicting feelings and reactions, may struggle with low self-esteem, or may have limited information and skills. Many seek to resolve conflicts with a marital partner. Increasingly, people are entering therapy with existential problems; their complaints are less defined but relate to the experiences of emptiness, meaninglessness in life, boredom, dead personal relationships, a lack of intense feelings, and a loss of their sense of self.

The initial expectations of many clients are expert help and a fast result. They often have great hope for major changes in their lives with little effort on their part. As therapy progresses, clients discover that they must be active in the process, selecting their own goals and working toward them, both in the sessions and in daily living.

In thinking about your integrative perspective on counseling practice, consider the characteristics of each client who seeks your help. Some clients can benefit from recognizing and expressing pent-up feelings, others will need to examine their beliefs and thoughts, others will most need to begin behaving in different ways, and others will benefit from talking with you about their relationships with the significant people in their lives. In deciding what interventions are most likely to be helpful, take into account the client's cultural, ethnic, and socioeconomic background. Moreover, the focus of counseling may change with each of these clients at different phases in the counseling process. Although some clients initially feel a need to be listened to and allowed to express deep feelings, they can profit later from examining the thought patterns that are contributing to their psychological pain. And certainly at some point in therapy it is essential that clients translate what they are learning about themselves into concrete action. The client's given situation in the environment provides a framework for selecting interventions that are most appropriate.

Relationship Between Therapist and Client

Most approaches share common ground in accepting the importance of the therapeutic relationship. The existential, person-centered, and Gestalt views are based on the personal relationship as the crucial determinant of treatment outcomes. It is clear that some other approaches—such as rational emotive behavior therapy, cognitive behavior therapy, and behavior therapy—do not ignore the relationship factor, even though they do not give it a place of central importance (Table 14-4).

Counseling is a personal matter that involves a personal relationship, and evidence indicates that honesty, sincerity, acceptance, understanding, and spontaneity are basic ingredients of successful outcomes. Therapists' degree of caring, their interest and ability in helping their clients, and their genuineness are factors that influence the relationship. Lazarus (1986) describes what he considers to be the common characteristics of "highly successful therapists": a genuine respect for people, flexibility, a nonjudgmental attitude, a good sense of humor, warmth, authenticity, and the willingness to recognize and reveal their shortcomings. Lazarus (1996b) views the

TABLE 14-4 ■ The Therapeutic Relationship

Psychoanalytic therapy	The analyst remains anonymous, and clients develop projections toward him or her. Focus is on reducing the resistances that develop in working with transference and on establishing more rational control. Clients undergo long-term analysis, engage in free association to uncover conflicts, and gain insight by talking. The analyst makes interpretations to teach them the meaning of current behavior as related to the past.
Adlerian therapy	The emphasis is on joint responsibility, on mutually determining goals, on mutual trust and respect, and on equality. A cooperative relationship is manifested by a therapeutic contract. Focus is on identifying, exploring, and disclosing mistaken goals and faulty assumptions within the person's lifestyle.
Existential therapy	The therapist's main tasks are to accurately grasp clients' being in the world and to establish a personal and authentic encounter with them. The relationship is seen as critically important. Clients discover their own uniqueness in the relationship with the therapist. The immediacy of the client/therapist relationship and the authenticity of the here-and-now encounter are stressed. Both client and therapist can be changed by the encounter.
Person-centered therapy	The relationship is of primary importance. The qualities of the therapist, including genuineness, warmth, accurate empathy, respect, and nonjudgmentalness—and communication of these attitudes to clients—are stressed. Clients use this real relationship with the therapist to help them transfer their learning to other relationships.
Gestalt therapy	Central importance is given to the I/Thou relationship and the quality of the therapist's presence. The therapist's attitudes and behavior counts more than the techniques used. The therapist does not interpret for clients but assists them in developing the means to make their own interpretations. Clients identify and work on unfinished business from the past that interferes with current functioning.
Reality therapy	A therapist's main function is to create a good relationship with the client. Therapists are then able to engage clients in an evaluation of all their relationships with respect to what they want and how effective they are in getting this. Therapists find out what clients want, ask what they are choosing to do, invite them to evaluate present behavior, help them make plans for change, and get them to make a commitment. The therapist is a client's advocate, as long as the client is willing to attempt to behave responsibly.
Behavior therapy	The therapist is active and directive and functions as a teacher or trainer in helping clients learn more effective behavior. Clients must be active in the process and experiment with new behaviors. Although a quality client/therapist relationship is not viewed as sufficient to bring about

TABLE 14-4 ■ (continued)

	change, a good working relationship is essential for implementing behavioral procedures.
Cognitive behavior therapy	In REBT the therapist functions as a teacher and the client as a student. The therapist is highly directive and teaches clients an A-B-C model of changing their cognitions. In CT the focus is on a collaborative relationship. Using a Socratic dialogue, the therapist assists clients in identifying dysfunctional beliefs and discovering alternative rules for living. The therapist promotes corrective experience that lead to learning new skills. Clients gain insight into their problems and then must actively practice changing self-defeating thinking and acting.
Feminist therapy	The therapeutic relationship is based on empowerment and egalitarianism. Therapists actively break down the hierarchy of power and reduce artificial barriers by engaging in appropriate self-disclosure and teaching clients about the therapy process. Therapists strive to create a collaborative relationship in which clients can become their own expert.
Family systems therapy	The family therapist functions as a teacher, coach, model, and consultant. The family learns ways to detect and solve problems that are keeping members stuck, and it learns about patterns that have been transmitted from generation to generation. Some approaches focus on the role of therapist as expert; others concentrate on intensifying what is going on in the here and now of the family session. All family therapists are concerned with the process of family interaction and teaching patterns of communication.

client/therapist relationship as the soil that enables the therapist's techniques to take root. Within the context of a warm, caring, therapeutic relationship, it is also necessary to remedy faulty cognitions and maladaptive behaviors. To bring about these changes, effective therapy often requires that therapists teach clients a range of coping skills that they can use in solving their problems. Clients also contribute to the relationship with variables such as their motivation, cooperation, interest, concern, and expectations.

As you think about developing your personal counseling perspective, give consideration to the issue of the match between client and counselor. I certainly do not advocate changing your personality to fit your perception of what each client is expecting; it is important that you *be yourself* as you meet clients. You also need to consider the reality that you will probably not be able to work effectively with every client. Some clients will work better with counselors who have another type of personal and therapeutic style than yours. Thus, I recommend sensitivity in assessing what your clients need, along with good judgment about the appropriateness of the match between you and a potential client.

Although you do not have to be like your clients or have experienced the same problems to be effective with them, it is critical that you be able to understand their world and respect them. The matter of matching client and therapist has implications for multicultural counseling. You might ask yourself how well prepared you are to counsel clients from a different cultural background. To what degree do you think you can successfully establish a therapeutic relationship with a client of a different race? Ethnic group? Gender? Age? Sexual orientation? Spiritual/religious orientation? Socioeconomic group? Do you see any potential barriers that would make it difficult for you to form a working relationship with certain clients? (This would be a good time to review the discussion of the culturally skilled counselor in Chapter 2 and to consult Tables 14-7 and 14-8, which appear later in this chapter.)

THE PLACE OF TECHNIQUES AND EVALUATION IN COUNSELING

Drawing on Techniques From Various Approaches

Effective therapists incorporate a wide range of procedures into their therapeutic style. Much depends on the purpose of therapy, the setting, the personality and style of the therapist, the qualities of the particular client, and the problems selected for intervention.

Beutler (1983) addresses the question "What therapy activities are most appropriate for what type of problem, by which therapist, for what kind of client?" Regardless of what model you may be working with, you must decide *what* techniques, procedures, or intervention methods to use, *when* to use them, and with *which* clients. Take time to review Tables 14-5 and 14-6 on therapeutic techniques and applications of techniques. Pay careful attention to the focus of each type of therapy and how that focus might be useful in your practice.

TABLE 14-5   ■   Techniques of Therapy

Psychoanalytic therapy	The key techniques are interpretation, dream analysis, free association, analysis of resistance, and analysis of transference. All are designed to help clients gain access to their unconscious conflicts, which leads to insight and eventual assimilation of new material by the ego. Diagnosis and testing are often used. Questions are used to develop a case history.
Adlerian therapy	Adlerians pay more attention to the subjective experiences of clients than to using techniques. Some techniques include gathering life-history data (family constellation, early recollections, personal priorities), sharing interpretations with clients, offering encouragement, and assisting clients in searching for new possibilities.

(continued)

TABLE 14-5 ■ (continued)

Existential therapy	Few techniques flow from this approach, because it stresses understanding first and technique second. The therapist can borrow techniques from other approaches and incorporate them in an existential framework. Diagnosis, testing, and external measurements are not deemed important. The approach can be very confrontive.
Person-centered therapy	This approach uses few techniques but stresses the attitudes of the therapist. Basic techniques include active listening and hearing, reflection of feelings, clarification, and "being there" for the client. This model does not include diagnostic testing, interpretation, taking a case history, or questioning or probing for information.
Gestalt therapy	A wide range of experiments are designed to intensify experiencing and to integrate conflicting feelings. Experiments are co-created by therapist and client through an I/Thou dialogue. Therapists have latitude to invent their own experiments. Formal diagnosis and testing are not a required part of therapy.
Reality therapy	An active, directive, and didactic therapy. Various techniques may be used to get clients to evaluate what they are presently doing to see if they are willing to change. If they decide that their present behavior is not effective, they develop a specific plan for change and make a commitment to follow through.
Behavior therapy	The main techniques are systematic desensitization, relaxation methods, flooding, eye movement and desensitization reprocessing, reinforcement techniques, modeling, cognitive restructuring, assertion and social skills training, self-management programs, behavioral rehearsal, coaching, and various multimodal therapy techniques. Diagnosis or assessment is done at the outset to determine a treatment plan. Questions are used, such as "what," "how," and "when" (but not "why"). Contracts and homework assignments are also typically used.
Cognitive behavior therapy	Therapists use a variety of cognitive, emotive, and behavioral techniques; diverse methods are tailored to suit individual clients. An active, directive, time-limited, present-centered, structured therapy. Some techniques include engaging in Socratic dialogue, debating irrational beliefs, carrying out homework assignments, gathering data on assumptions one has made, keeping a record of activities, forming alternative interpretations, learning new coping skills, changing one's language and thinking patterns, role playing, imagery, and confronting faulty beliefs.
Feminist therapy	Although techniques from traditional approaches are used, feminist practitioners tend to employ consciousness-raising techniques aimed at helping clients recognize the impact of gender-role socialization on their lives. Other

(continued)

TABLE 14-5 ■ (continued)

	techniques frequently used include gender-role analysis and intervention, power analysis and intervention, bibliotherapy, journal writing, therapist self-disclosure, assertiveness training, reframing and relabeling, cognitive restructuring, identifying and challenging untested beliefs, role playing, psychodramatic methods, group work, and social action.
Family systems therapy	There is a diversity of techniques, depending on the particular theoretical orientation. Interventions may target behavior change, perceptual change, or both. Techniques include using genograms, teaching, asking questions, family sculpting, joining the family, tracking sequences, issuing directives, anchoring, use of countertransference, family mapping, refraining, paradoxical interventions, restructuring, enactments, and setting boundaries. Techniques may be experiential, cognitive, or behavioral in nature. Most are designed to bring about change in a short time.

TABLE 14-6 ■ Applications of the Approaches

Psychoanalytic therapy	Candidates for analytic therapy include professionals who want to become therapists, people who have had intensive therapy and want to go further, and those who are in pain. Analytic therapy is not recommended for self-centered and impulsive clients or for severely impaired psychotics. Techniques can be applied to individual and group therapy.
Adlerian therapy	Because the approach is based on a growth model, it is applicable to such varied spheres of life as child guidance, parent/child counseling, marital and family therapy, individual counseling with all age groups, correctional and rehabilitation counseling, group counseling, substance abuse programs, and brief counseling. It is ideally suited to preventive care and alleviating a broad range of conditions that interfere with growth.
Existential therapy	Can be especially suited to people facing a developmental crisis or a transition in life. Useful for clients with existential concerns (making choices, dealing with freedom and responsibility, coping with guilt and anxiety, making sense of life, and finding values). Appropriate for those seeking personal enhancement. Can be applied to both individual and group counseling, marital and family therapy, crisis intervention, and community mental health work.
Person-centered therapy	Has wide applicability to individual and group counseling. It is especially well suited for the initial phases of crisis intervention work. Its principles have been applied to marital and family therapy, community programs, administration and management, and human relations training. It is

(continued)

TABLE 14-6 ■ (continued)

	a useful approach for teaching, parent/child relations, and working with groups composed of people from diverse cultural backgrounds.
Gestalt therapy	Addresses a wide range of problems and populations: crisis intervention, treatment of a range of psychosomatic disorders, marital and family therapy, awareness training of mental health professionals, behavior problems in children, and teaching and learning. It is well suited to both individual and group counseling. The methods are powerful catalysts for opening up feelings and getting clients into contact with their present-centered experience.
Reality therapy	Geared to teaching people ways of using choice theory in everyday living to increase effective behaviors. It has been applied to individual counseling with a wide range of clients, group counseling, working with youthful law offenders, and marital and family therapy. In some instances it is well suited to brief therapy and crisis intervention.
Behavior therapy	A pragmatic approach based on empirical validation of results. Enjoys wide applicability to individual, group, marital, and family counseling. Some problems to which the approach is well suited are phobic disorders, depression, sexual disorders, children's behavioral disorders, stuttering, and prevention of cardiovascular disease. Beyond clinical practice, its principles are applied in fields such as pediatrics, stress management, behavioral medicine, education, and geriatrics.
Cognitive behavior therapy	Has been widely applied to treatment of depression, anxiety, marital problems, stress management, skill training, substance abuse, assertion training, eating disorders, panic attacks, performance anxiety, and social phobia. The approach is especially useful for assisting people in modifying their cognitions. Many self-help approaches utilize its principles. Can be applied to a wide range of client populations with a variety of specific problems.
Feminist therapy	Principles and techniques can be applied to a range of therapeutic modalities such as individual therapy, relationship counseling, family therapy, group counseling, and community intervention. The approach can be applied to both women and men with the goal of bringing about empowerment.
Family systems therapy	Applications vary depending on the particular approach to family therapy. Useful for dealing with marital distress, problems of communicating among family members, power struggles, crisis situations in the family, helping individuals attain their potential, and enhancing the overall functioning of the family.

It is critical to be aware of how clients' cultural backgrounds contribute to their perceptions of their problems. Each of the 10 therapeutic approaches has both strengths and limitations when applied to culturally diverse client populations (Tables 14-7 and 14-8). Although it is unwise to stereotype clients because of their cultural heritage, it is useful to assess how the cultural context has a bearing on their concerns. Some techniques are contraindicated because of a client's socialization. Thus, the client's responsiveness (or lack of it) to certain techniques is a critical barometer in judging the effectiveness of these methods.

It is a mistake to equate counselor effectiveness with proficiency in a single technique or even a set of techniques. For example, some counselors become specialists in confrontational techniques. They develop a style of relating to clients geared to provoking them, goading them to "get their anger expressed," or merely focusing on techniques to deal with anger. These therapists derive a sense of power from becoming "confrontation specialists."

TABLE 14-7   ■   Contributions to Multicultural Counseling

Psychoanalytic therapy	Its focus on family dynamics is appropriate for working with many minority groups. The therapist's formality appeals to clients who expect professional distance. Notion of ego defense is helpful in understanding inner dynamics and dealing with environmental stresses.
Adlerian therapy	Its focus on social interest, collectivism, pursuing meaning in life, importance of family, goal orientation, and belonging is congruent with many cultures. Focus on person-in-environment allows for cultural factors to be explored.
Existential therapy	Focus is on understanding client's phenomenological world, including cultural background. This approach leads to empowerment in an oppressive society. It can help clients examine their options for change within the context of their cultural realities.
Person-centered therapy	Focus is on breaking cultural barriers and facilitating open dialogue among diverse cultural populations. Main strengths are respect for clients' values, active listening, welcoming of differences, nonjudgmental attitude, understanding, willingness to allow clients to determine what will be explored in sessions, and prizing of cultural pluralism.
Gestalt therapy	Its focus on expressing oneself nonverbally is congruent with those cultures that look beyond words for messages. Provides many experiments in working with clients who have cultural injunctions against freely expressing feelings. Can help to overcome language barrier with bilingual clients. Focus on bodily expressions is a subtle way to help clients recognize their conflicts.
Reality therapy	Focus is on members' making own evaluation of behavior (including how they respond to their culture). Through personal assessment they can determine the degree to which their needs and wants are being satisfied. They can

TABLE 14-7   ■   *(continued)*

	find a balance between retaining their own ethnic identity and integrating some of the values and practices of the dominant society.
Behavior therapy	Its focus on behavior, rather than on feelings, is compatible with many cultures. Strengths include a collaborative relationship between counselor and client in working toward mutually agreed-on goals, continual assessment to determine if the techniques are suited to clients' unique situation, assisting clients in learning practical skills, an educational focus, and stress on self-management strategies.
Cognitive behavior therapy	The collaborative approach offers clients opportunities to express their areas of concern. The psychoeducational dimensions are often useful in exploring cultural conflicts and teaching new behavior. The emphasis on thinking (as opposed to identifying and expressing feelings) is likely to be acceptable to many clients. The focus on teaching and learning tends to avoid the stigma of mental illness. Clients may value active and directive stance of therapist.
Feminist therapy	This approach is not willing to settle for adjustment to the status quo. Both individual change and social transformation are the ultimate goals of therapy. A key contribution is that both the women's movement and the multicultural movement have called attention to the negative impact of discrimination and oppression for both women and men.
Family systems therapy	Many ethnic and cultural groups place value on the role of the extended family. Many family therapies deal with extended family members and with support systems. Networking is a part of the process, which is congruent with the values of many clients. There is a greater chance for individual change if other family members are supportive. This approach offers ways of working toward the health of the family unit and the welfare of each member.

TABLE 14-8   ■   Limitations in Multicultural Counseling

Psychoanalytic therapy	Its focus on insight, intrapsychic dynamics, and long-term treatment is often not valued by clients who prefer to learn coping skills for dealing with pressing daily concerns. Internal focus is often in conflict with cultural values that stress an interpersonal and environmental focus.
Adlerian therapy	This approach's detailed interview about one's family background can conflict with cultures that have injunctions against disclosing family matters. Some clients may view the counselor as an authority who will provide answers to problems, which conflicts with the egalitarian, person-to-person spirit as a way to reduce social distance.

(continued)

TABLE 14-8   ■   (continued)

Existential therapy	Values of individuality, freedom, autonomy, and self-realization often conflict with cultural values of collectivism, respect for tradition, deference to authority, and interdependence. Some may be deterred by the absence of specific techniques. Others will expect more focus on surviving in their world.
Person-centered therapy	Some of the core values of this approach may not be congruent with the client's culture. Lack of counselor direction and structure are unacceptable for clients who are seeking help and immediate answers from a knowledgeable professional.
Gestalt therapy	Clients who have been culturally conditioned to be emotionally reserved may not embrace Gestalt experiments. Some may not see how "being aware of present experiencing" will lead to solving their problems.
Reality therapy	This approach stresses taking charge of one's own life, yet some clients hope to change their external environment. Counselor needs to appreciate the role of discrimination and racism and help clients deal with social and political realities.
Behavior therapy	Counselors need to help clients assess the possible consequences of making behavioral changes. Family members may not value clients' newly acquired assertive style, so clients must be taught how to cope with resistance by others.
Cognitive behavior therapy	Before too quickly attempting to change the beliefs and actions of clients, it is essential for the therapists to understand and respect their world. Some clients may have serious reservations about questioning their basic cultural values and beliefs. Clients could become dependent on the therapist for deciding what are appropriate ways to solve problems. There may be a fine line between being directive and promoting dependence.
Feminist therapy	One criticism is that feminist therapy was developed by White, middle class, heterosexual women. Based on the feminist notions of collaborative relationships, self-determination, and empowerment, therapists need to assess with their clients the price of making significant personal change. If this assessment is not made, clients in certain cultures may experience isolation as a result of making life changes or of assuming a new role.
Family systems therapy	Some approaches are based on value assumptions that are not congruent with the values of clients from other cultures. Concepts such as individuation, self-actualization, self-determination, independence, and self-expression may be foreign to some clients. In some cultures, admitting problems within the family is shameful. The value of "keeping problems within the family" may make it difficult to explore conflicts openly.

For a different set of motives, other counselors limit themselves to techniques of reflection and clarification. Perhaps they are fearful of getting involved with clients on more than the empathic and supportive level; thus, they continue to reflect because there are few risks involved.

Effective counseling involves proficiency in a combination of cognitive, affective, and behavioral techniques. Such a combination is necessary to help clients *think* about their beliefs and assumptions, to experience on a *feeling* level their conflicts and struggles, and to translate their insights into *action* programs by behaving in new ways in day-to-day living. Tables 14-9 and 14-10 outline the contributions and limitations of the various therapeutic approaches. These tables will help you identify elements from the various approaches that you may want to incorporate in your own counseling perspective.

TABLE 14-9   ■   Contributions of the Approaches

Psychoanalytic therapy	More than any other system, this approach has generated controversy as well as exploration and has stimulated further thinking and development of therapy. It has provided a detailed and comprehensive description of personality structure and functioning. It has brought into prominence factors such as the unconscious as a determinant of behavior and the role of trauma during the first 6 years of life. It has developed several techniques for tapping the unconscious. It has shed light on the dynamics of transference and countertransference, resistance, anxiety, and the mechanisms of ego defense.
Adlerian therapy	One of the first approaches to therapy that was humanistic, unified, holistic, and goal-oriented and that put an emphasis on social and psychological factors. A key contribution is the influence that Adlerian concepts have had on other systems and the integration of these concepts into various contemporary therapies.
Existential therapy	Its major contribution is a recognition of the need for a subjective approach based on a complete view of the human condition. It calls attention to the need for a philosophical statement on what it means to be a person. Stress on the I/Thou relationship lessens the chances of dehumanizing therapy. It provides a perspective for understanding anxiety, guilt, freedom, death, isolation, and commitment.
Person-centered therapy	Unique contribution is having the client take an active stance and assume responsibility for the direction of therapy. The approach has been subjected to empirical testing, and as a result both theory and methods have been modified. It is an open system. People without advanced training can benefit by translating the therapeutic conditions to both their personal and professional lives. Basic concepts are straightforward and easy to grasp and apply. It is a foundation for building a trusting relationship, applicable to all therapies.

(continued)

TABLE 14-9 ■ (continued)

Gestalt therapy	Main contribution is an emphasis on direct experiencing and doing rather than on merely talking about feelings. It provides a perspective on growth and enhancement, not merely a treatment of disorders. It uses clients' behavior as the basis for making them aware of inner creative potential. The approach to dreams is a unique, creative tool to help clients discover basic conflicts. Therapy is viewed as an existential encounter; it is process-oriented, not technique-oriented. It recognizes nonverbal behavior as a key to understanding.
Reality therapy	Consists of simple and clear concepts that are easily grasped in many helping professions; thus, it can be used by teachers, nurses, ministers, educators, social workers, and counselors. It is a positive approach, with an action orientation. Due to the direct methods, it appeals to many clients who are often seen as resistant to therapy. It is a short-term approach that can be applied to a diverse population, and it has been a significant force in challenging the medical model of therapy.
Behavior therapy	Emphasis is on assessment and evaluation techniques, thus providing a basis for accountable practice. Specific problems are identified, and clients are kept informed about progress toward their goals. The approach has demonstrated effectiveness in many areas of human functioning. The roles of the therapist as reinforcer, model, teacher, and consultant are explicit. The approach has undergone extensive expansion, and research literature abounds. No longer is it a mechanistic approach, for it now makes room for cognitive factors and encourages self-directed programs for behavioral change.
Cognitive behavior therapy	Major contributions include emphasis on a comprehensive and eclectic therapeutic practice; numerous cognitive, emotive, and behavioral techniques; an openness to incorporating techniques from other approaches; and a methodology for challenging and changing faulty thinking. Most forms can be integrated into other mainstream therapies. REBT makes full use of action-oriented homework, listening to tapes, and keeping records of progress. CT is a structured therapy that has a good track record for treating depression and anxiety in a short time.
Feminist therapy	Major contributions are paving the way for gender-sensitive practice and bringing attention to the gendered uses of power in relationships. The feminist perspective is responsible for encouraging increasing numbers of women to question gender stereotypes and to reject limited views of what a woman is expected to be. The unified feminist voice brought attention to the extent and implications of child abuse, incest, rape, sexual harassment, and domestic violence. Feminist principles and interventions can be incorporated in other therapy approaches.

(continued)

TABLE 14-9   ■   (continued)

Family systems therapy	In all of the systemic approaches, neither the individual nor the family is blamed for a particular dysfunction. The family is empowered through the process of identifying and exploring interactional patterns. Working with an entire unit provides a new perspective on understanding and working through both individual problems and relationship concerns. By exploring one's family of origin, there are increased opportunities to resolve other relationship conflicts outside of the family

TABLE 14-10   ■   Limitations of the Approaches

Psychoanalytic therapy	Requires lengthy training for therapists and much time and expense for clients. The model stresses biological and instinctual factors to the neglect of social, cultural, and interpersonal ones. Its methods are not applicable for solving specific problems of clients in lower socioeconomic classes and are not appropriate for many ethnic and cultural groups. Many clients lack the degree of ego strength needed for regressive and reconstructive therapy. It is inappropriate for the typical counseling setting.
Adlerian therapy	Weak in terms of precision, testability, and empirical validity. Few attempts have been made to validate the basic concepts by scientific methods. Tends to oversimplify some complex human problems and is based heavily on common sense.
Existential therapy	Many basic concepts are fuzzy and ill-defined, making its general framework abstract at times. Lacks a systematic statement of principles and practices of therapy. Has limited applicability to lower functioning and nonverbal clients and to clients in extreme crisis who need direction.
Person-centered therapy	Possible danger from the therapist who remains passive and inactive, limiting responses to reflection. Many clients feel a need for greater direction, more structure, and more techniques. Clients in crisis may need more directive measures. Applied to individual counseling, some cultural groups will expect more counselor activity. The theory needs to be reassessed in light of current knowledge and thought if rigidity is to be avoided.
Gestalt therapy	Techniques lead to intense emotional expression; if these feelings are not explored and if cognitive work is not done, clients are likely to be left unfinished and will not have a sense of integration of their learning. Clients who have difficulty using imagination may not profit from experiments.

(continued)

TABLE 14-10   ■   (continued)

Reality therapy	Discounts the therapeutic value of exploration of the client's past, dreams, the unconscious, early childhood experiences, and transference. The approach is limited to less complex problems. It is a problem-solving therapy that tends to discourage exploration of deeper emotional issues. It is vulnerable to practitioners who want to "fix" clients quickly.
Behavior therapy	Major criticisms are that it may change behavior but not feelings; that it ignores the relational factors in therapy; that it does not provide insight; that it ignores historical causes of present behavior; that it involves control and manipulation by the therapist; and that it is limited in its capacity to address certain aspects of the human condition. Many of these assertions are based on misconceptions, and behavior therapists have addressed these charges. A basic limitation is that behavior change cannot always be objectively assessed because of the difficulty in controlling environmental variables.
Cognitive behavior therapy	Tends to play down emotions, does not focus on exploring the unconscious or underlying conflicts, and sometimes does not give enough weight to client's past. REBT, being a confrontational therapy, might lead to premature termination. CT might be too structured for some clients.
Feminist therapy	A possible limitation is the potential for therapists to impose a new set of values on clients—such as striving for equality, power in relationships, defining oneself, freedom to pursue a career outside the home, and the right to an education. Therapists need to keep in mind that clients are their own best experts, which means it is up to them to decide which values to live by.
Family systems therapy	Limitations include problems in being able to involve all the members of a family in the therapy. Members may be resistant to changing the structure of the system. Therapists' self-knowledge and willingness to work on their own family-of-origin issues is crucial, for the potential for countertransference is high. It is essential that the therapist be well trained, receive quality supervision, and be competent in assessing and treating individuals in a family context.

Evaluating the Effectiveness of Counseling and Therapy

Research in psychotherapy gained little momentum until the 1950s. Since the late 1950s and the early 1960s researchers have mainly addressed the process and outcomes of therapy to gain a clearer understanding of what constitutes therapeutic change and how it comes about (Strupp, 1986; Vanden-Bos, 1986).

The acceleration of public funding for all types of human services programs during the 1960s also stirred a keen interest in evaluation research. In essence, if government funds were to continue to be allocated to human services agencies, the burden of proof rested on researchers and practitioners to demonstrate the effectiveness of psychotherapy by using scientific methods. The central question raised was "Of what value is psychotherapy to the individual and society?" (Strupp, 1986). Mental health providers are still faced with accountability. In the era of managed care, it becomes even more essential for practitioners to demonstrate the degree to which their interventions are both clinically sound and cost-effective.

Does therapy make a significant difference? Are people substantially better after therapy than they were without it? Can therapy actually be more harmful than helpful? A thorough discussion of these questions is beyond the scope of this book, but I will address a few basic issues related to evaluating the effectiveness of counseling. If you are interested in a more in-depth review of psychotherapy research, I suggest Garfield (1987, 1992b); Imber, Glanz, Elkin, Sotsky, Boyer, and Leber (1986); Lambert (1992); Lambert and Bergin (1992); Smith, Glass, and Miller (1980); Strupp (1986); Strupp and Howard (1992); and VandenBos (1986).

There are problems in lumping together many research efforts to answer the general question "Does psychotherapy work?" A basic difficulty is that each of the multitude of therapeutic systems is applied by a practitioner with individual characteristics that are difficult to measure. Further, clients themselves have much to do with therapeutic outcomes. If clients choose to engage in activities that are self-destructive, this behavior will cancel out the positive effects of therapy. To add to the problem, effects resulting from unexpected and uncontrollable events in the environment can destroy gains made in psychotherapy. As Garfield (1992b) has pointed out, the basic variables that influence therapy research are extremely difficult to control and evaluate. Clinical research cannot exert the degree of control that is true for controlled laboratory experiments but can only strive for approximations. Evaluating how well psychotherapy works is far from simple.

One of the first issues is how much outcome research has been conducted on the therapeutic approaches presented in this book. Most of the studies have been done by two divergent groups: (1) the behavior and cognitive therapists, who have based their therapeutic practice on empirical studies, and (2) the person-centered researchers, who have made significant contributions to understanding both process and outcome variables. Most of the other models covered in this book have not produced significant empirical research dealing with how well their therapy works.

By about 1980 a consensus had emerged that psychotherapy was demonstrably more effective than no treatment (VandenBos, 1986). Smith et al. (1980) presented a meta-analysis of psychotherapy outcome literature and concluded that psychotherapy was highly effective. Despite this general support of the value of psychotherapy, hard data that supports the concepts and procedures of most of the therapeutic approaches is sparse at best. One reason is that one approach's "cure" is another approach's "resistance." In other words, because each approach works toward different outcomes, it is almost impossible to compare them. Despite the wide range of purportedly distinct psychotherapeutic treatments, most reviews of outcome research show little differential effectiveness of the tested psychotherapies (Stiles, Shapiro, & Elliott, 1986). Factors other than scientific data must be considered if we are to determine the validity and usefulness of most of the therapeutic approaches.

Lambert (1992) writes that because of the wide variability of techniques employed by integrative practitioners, it is extremely difficult to assess the effectiveness of standard eclectic approaches. His discussion of the implications of therapy outcome research for integrative therapists is quite involved, but four of his conclusions are worth noting here:

1. A substantial number of outpatients improve without formal psychotherapy. One implication for eclectic therapists is that they should draw on the natural helping systems in the client's environment.
2. In general, psychological treatments are beneficial. However, there is little evidence to support the superiority of one school or technique over another.
3. Various factors common across therapy systems account for a substantial degree of the improvement found in clients. They include *support factors* (therapist warmth, respect, empathy, acceptance, feedback, and other factors associated with a positive relationship); *learning factors* (insight, cognitive learning, and self-acceptance); and *action factors* (expectations for improvement, facing one's fears, reality testing, modeling, practice, and working through). Research suggests that these common factors may be more important than specific techniques as a catalyst for facilitating positive changes in clients.
4. Specific techniques can be selected for dealing with specific problems on the basis of their effectiveness. This provides a framework to assess the direction and outcomes of therapy.

One of Lambert's key points is the lack of clear research evidence to support the therapeutic value of many eclectic practices. He concludes that until empirical investigations are conducted integrative therapists would do well to be more modest in their claims of being superior to the single-school models.

The general question "Does psychotherapy work?" is often raised, but such a global question is very difficult to answer meaningfully (Strupp &

Howard, 1992). Garfield (1980) argues that psychotherapy is not a clearly defined and uniform process and that there is thus no basis for any objective answer to the question. As VandenBos (1986) concludes, it appears that outcome research aimed at proving the efficacy of therapy should be a thing of the past. He contends that future research should be focused on exploring the relative advantages and disadvantages of alternative treatment strategies for clients with different psychological and behavioral problems. Included in this research should be factors such as the relative cost, the length of time necessary to effect change, and the nature and extent of change. Whatever form it takes, research will apparently play an increasingly important role in determining the future of psychotherapy (Strupp, 1986).

A guideline for improving on the global question regarding the effectiveness of therapy is provided by Paul (1967): *"What* treatment, by *whom,* is the most effective *for this* individual with *that* specific problem, and under what set of circumstances?" It is clear that greater precision and specificity are needed in research (Stiles et al., 1986). Thus, the question of the effectiveness of psychotherapy needs to be narrowed to a specific type of therapy and usually narrowed further to a certain technique. Moreover, practitioners who adhere to the same approach are likely to use techniques in various ways and to relate to clients in diverse fashions, functioning differently with different clients and in different clinical settings.

 ## SUMMARY

Creating an integrative stance is truly a challenge. Therapists cannot simply pick bits and pieces from theories in a random and fragmented manner. In forming an integrated perspective, it is important to ask: Which theories provide a basis for understanding the *cognitive* dimensions? What about the *feeling* aspects? And how about the *behavioral* dimension? Most of the 10 therapeutic orientations discussed here focus on one of these dimensions of human experience. Although the other dimensions are not necessarily ignored, they are often given short shrift.

Developing an integrated theoretical perspective requires much reading, thinking, and actual counseling experience. Unless you have an accurate, in-depth knowledge of these theories, you cannot formulate a true synthesis. Simply put, you cannot integrate what you do not know (Norcross & Newman, 1992). A central message of this book has been to remain open to each theory, to do further reading, and to reflect on how the key concepts of each approach fit your personality. Building your personalized orientation to counseling, which is based on what you consider to be the best features of several theories, is a long-term venture.

Besides considering your own personality, think about what concepts and techniques work best with a range of clients. It requires knowledge, skill, art, and experience to be able to determine what techniques are suitable for particular problems. It is also an art to know when and how to use a particular therapeutic intervention. Although reflecting on your personal preferences is important, I would hope that you also balance your preferences with scientific evidence. Developing a personal approach to counseling practice does not imply that anything goes. Indeed, in this era of managed care and cost-effectiveness, your personal preferences may not always be the sole determinant of your psychotherapy practice. In counseling clients with certain problems, specific techniques have demonstrated their effectiveness. For instance, behavior therapy, cognitive therapy, interpersonal therapy, and short-term psychodynamic therapy have repeatedly proved successful in treating depression. Although I am not suggesting that you adopt a theory with which you are uncomfortable, ethical practice implies that you employ efficacious procedures in dealing with clients and their problems. You might ask yourself these questions: "Under what circumstances is it appropriate, or ethical, for me to bypass a scientifically proved treatment for a treatment that I personally prefer?" "What relative weight do I give to my personal preferences and to scientific evidence?"

Think about the theories that seem to have the most practical application in helping you understand your present life situation. Consider what changes you are interested in making and which approaches could provide you with strategies to modify specific thoughts, feelings, and behaviors. This is a good time to review what you may have learned about your ability to establish effective relationships with other people. Especially important is a review of any personal characteristics that could either help or hinder you in developing solid working relationships with clients. Ask yourself these questions:

- What have I learned about my personal needs, and how they are likely to operate in a counseling relationship?
- What did I learn about my values and how my attitudes and beliefs could work either for or against establishing effective relationships with clients?
- What steps can I take now to increase the chances of becoming an effective person and counselor?

After you make this review of significant personal learning, ponder what you have learned about the counseling process. Identify a particular theory that you might adopt as a foundation for establishing your own perspective on counseling theory and practice. Consider from which therapies you would be most inclined to draw (1) underlying assumptions, (2) major concepts, (3) therapeutic goals, (4) therapeutic relationship, and (5) techniques and procedures. Also, consider the major applications of each of the therapies as well as their basic limitations and major contributions.

Recommended Supplementary Readings

Handbook of Psychotherapy Integration (Norcross & Goldfried, 1992) is a superb resource for conceptual and historical perspectives on therapy integration. This edited volume gives a comprehensive overview of the major current approaches, such as theoretical integration and technical eclecticism.

Systematic Treatment Selection: Toward Target Therapeutic Interventions (Beutler & Clarkin, 1990) is an excellent source on an integrated approach. The book describes a systematic eclectic therapy that can be applied in a relatively consistent and reliable fashion. It attempts to define the ingredients of good therapy and to maximize their effective use by matching clients to both therapists and techniques.

The Art of Integrative Counseling (Corey, 2001a) is designed to assist students in developing their own integrative approach to counseling. This book is geared very closely to the videotape described next.

Student Video and Workbook for the Art of Integrative Counseling (Corey, 2001b) illustrates my own integrative perspective in working with a hypothetical client, Ruth. This video brings together most of the therapies that are discussed in this book. Information about this video can be obtained from Brooks-Cole/Wadsworth Publishing Company, Pacific Grove, CA, 93950.

Case Approach to Counseling and Psychotherapy (Corey, 2001c) illustrates each of the 10 contemporary theories as they can be applied to the single case of Ruth. I also demonstrate my integrative approach in counseling Ruth in the final chapter.

References and Suggested Readings*

*ABERNETHY, R. (1992). The integration of therapies. In J. S. Rutan (Ed.), *Psychotherapy for the 1990s* (pp. 19–34). New York: Guilford Press.

*ALFORD, B. A., & BECK, A. T. (1997). *The integrative power of cognitive therapy.* New York: Guilford Press.

*ARKOWITZ, H. (1997). Integrative theories of therapy. In P. L. Wachtel & S. B. Messer (Eds.), *Theories of psychotherapy: Origins and evolution* (pp. 227–288). Washington, DC: American Psychological Association.

BERGIN, A. E. (1991). Values and religious issues in psychotherapy and mental health. *American Psychologist, 46*(4), 393–403.

BEUTLER, L. E. (1983). *Eclectic psychotherapy: A systematic approach.* New York: Pergamon Press.

BEUTLER, L. E., & CLARKIN, J. (1990). *Selective treatment selection: Toward targeted therapeutic interventions.* New York: Brunner/Mazel.

*COREY, G. (2001a). *The art of integrative counseling.* Pacific Grove, CA: Brooks-Cole/Wadsworth.

*COREY, G. (2001b). *Student video and workbook for the art of integrative counseling.* Pacific Grove, CA: Brooks-Cole/Wadsworth.

*COREY, G. (2001c). *Case approach to counseling and psychotherapy* (5th ed). Pacific Grove, CA: Brooks-Cole/Wadsworth.

FAIVER, C. M., & O'BRIEN, E. M. (1993). Assessment of religious beliefs form. *Counseling and Values, 37*(3), 176–178.

GARFIELD, S. L. (1980). *Psychotherapy: An eclectic approach.* New York: Wiley.

GARFIELD, S. L. (1987). Ethical issues in research on psychotherapy. *Counseling and Values, 31*(2), 115–125.

GARFIELD, S. L. (1992a). Eclectic psychotherapy: A common factors approach. In J. C. Norcross & M. R. Goldfried (Eds.), *Handbook of psychotherapy integration* (pp. 169–201). New York: Basic Books.

---

*Books and articles marked with an asterisk are recommended for further study.

GARFIELD, S. L. (1992b). Major issues in psychotherapy research. In D. K. Freed-heim (Ed.), *History of psychotherapy: A century of change* (pp. 335–359). Washington, DC: American Psychological Association.

GEORGIA, R. T. (1994). Preparing to counsel clients of different religious backgrounds: A phenomenological approach. *Counseling and Values, 38*(2), 143–151.

GOLDFRIED, M. R., & CASTONGUAY, L. G. (1992). The future of psychotherapy integration. *Psychotherapy, 29*(1), 4–10.

*GOLDFRIED, M. R., CASTONGUAY, L. G., & SAFRAN, J. D. (1992). Core issues and future directions in psychotherapy. In J. C. Norcross & M. R. Goldfried (Eds.), *Handbook of psychotherapy integration* (pp. 593–616). New York: Basic Books.

*GOLDFRIED, M. R., & NEWMAN, C. (1992). A history of psychotherapy integration. In J. C. Norcross & M. R. Goldfried (Eds.), *Handbook of psychotherapy integration* (pp. 46–93). New York: Basic Books.

*GOLDFRIED, M. R., & SAFRAN, J. D. (1986). Future directions in psychotherapy integration. In J. C. Norcross (Ed.), *Handbook of eclectic psychotherapy* (pp. 463–483). New York: Brunner/Mazel.

GRIMM, D. W. (1994). Therapist spiritual and religious values in psychotherapy. *Counseling and Values, 38*(3), 154–164.

HINTERKOPF, E. (1994). Integrating spiritual experiences in counseling. *Counseling and Values, 38*(3), 165–175.

HINTERKOPF, E. (1998). *Integrating spirituality in counseling: A manual for using the experiential focusing method.* Alexandria, VA: American Counseling Association.

IMBER, S. D., GLANZ, L. M., ELKIN, I., SOTSKY, S. M., BOYER, J. L., & LEBER, W. R. (1986). Ethical issues in psychotherapy research. *American Psychologist, 41*(2), 137–146.

INGERSOLL, R. E. (1994). Spirituality, religion, and counseling: Dimensions and relationships. *Counseling and Values, 38*(2), 98–111.

KELLY, E. W. (1994). The role of religion and spirituality in counselor education: A national survey. *Counselor Education and Supervision, 33*(4), 227–237.

KELLY, E. W. (1995). *Spirituality and religion in counseling and psychotherapy.* Alexandria, VA: American Counseling Association.

KELLY, K. R. (1988). Defending eclecticism: The utility of informed choice. *Journal of Mental Health Counseling, 10*(4), 210–213.

KELLY, K. R. (1991). Theoretical integration is the future for mental health counseling. *Journal of Mental Health Counseling, 13*(1), 106–111.

LAMBERT, M. J. (1992). Psychotherapy outcome research: Implications for integrative and eclectic therapists. In J. C. Norcross & M. R. Goldfried (Eds.), *Handbook of psychotherapy integration* (pp. 94–129). New York: Basic Books.

LAMBERT, M. J., & BERGIN, A. E. (1992). Achievements and limitations of psychotherapy research. In D. K. Freedheim (Ed.), *History of psychotherapy: A century of change* (pp. 360–390). Washington, DC: American Psychological Association.

LAZARUS, A. A. (1986). Multimodal therapy. In J. C. Norcross (Ed.), *Handbook of eclectic psychotherapy* (pp. 65–93). New York: Brunner/Mazel.

*LAZARUS, A. A. (1989). *The practice of multimodal therapy.* Baltimore: Johns Hopkins University Press.

LAZARUS, A. A. (1992). Multimodal therapy: Technical eclecticism with minimal integration. In J. C. Norcross & M. R. Goldfried (Eds.), *Handbook of psychotherapy integration* (pp. 231–263). New York: Basic Books.

*LAZARUS, A. A. (1995). Different types of eclecticism and integration: Let's be aware of the dangers. *Journal of Psychotherapy Integration, 5*(1), 27–39.

LAZARUS, A. A. (1996a). Some reflections after 40 years of trying to be an effective psychotherapist. *Psychotherapy, 33*(1), 142–145.

*LAZARUS, A. A. (1996b). The utility and futility of combining treatments in psychotherapy. *Clinical Psychology: Science and Practice, 3*(1), 59–68.

*LAZARUS, A. A. (1997a). *Brief but comprehensive psychotherapy: The multimodal way.* New York: Springer.

LAZARUS, A. A. (1997b). Can psychotherapy be brief, focused, solution-oriented, and yet comprehensive? A personal evolutionary perspective. In J. K. Zeig (Ed.), *The evolution of psychotherapy: The third conference* (pp. 83–94). New York: Brunner/Mazel.

*LAZARUS, A. A., & BEUTLER, L. E. (1993). On technical eclecticism. *Journal of Counseling and Development, 71*(4), 381–385.

*LAZARUS, A. A., BEUTLER, L. E., & NORCROSS, J. C. (1992). The future of technical eclecticism. *Psychotherapy, 29*(1), 11–20.

MATTSON, D. L. (1994). Religious counseling: To be used, not feared. *Counseling and Values, 38*(3), 187–192.

MESSER, S. B. (1986). Eclecticism in psychotherapy: Underlying assumptions, problems, and trade-offs. In J. C. Norcross (Ed.), *Handbook of eclectic psychotherapy* (pp. 379–397). New York: Brunner/Mazel.

MESSER, S. B. (1992). A critical examination of belief structures in integrative and eclectic psychotherapy In J. C. Norcross & M. R. Goldfried (Eds.), *Handbook of psychotherapy integration* (pp. 130–165). New York: Basic Books.

*MILLER, W. R. (Ed.). (1999). *Integrating spirituality into treatment: Resources for practitioners.* Washington, DC: American Psychological Association.

MIRANTI, J., & BURKE, M. T. (1995). Spirituality: An integrated component of the counseling process. In M. T. Burke & J. G. Miranti (Eds.), *Counseling: The spiritual dimension* (pp. 1–3). Alexandria, VA: American Counseling Association.

NORCROSS, J. C. (1986a). Eclectic psychotherapy: An introduction and overview. In J. C. Norcross (Ed.), *Handbook of eclectic psychotherapy* (pp. 3–24). New York: Brunner/Mazel.

NORCROSS, J. C. (Ed.). (1986b). *Handbook of eclectic psychotherapy.* New York: Brunner/Mazel.

*NORCROSS, J. C., & GOLDFRIED, M. R. (Eds.). (1992). *Handbook of psychotherapy integration.* New York: Basic Books.

NORCROSS, J. C., & NEWMAN, C. F. (1992). Psychotherapy integration: Setting the context. In J. C. Norcross & M. R. Goldfried (Eds.), *Handbook of psychotherapy integration* (pp. 3–45). New York: Basic Books.

NORCROSS, J. C., & PROCHASKA, J. O. (1988). A study of eclectic (and integrative) views revisited. *Professional Psychology: Research and Practice, 19*(2), 170–174.

PATE, R. H., & BONDI, A. M. (1992). Religious beliefs and practice: An integral aspect of multicultural awareness. *Counselor Education and Supervision, 32*(2), 108–115.

PAUL, G. L. (1967). Outcome research in psychotherapy. *Journal of Consulting Psychology, 31,* 109–188.

PECK, M. S. (1978). *The road less traveled: A new psychology of love, traditional values and spiritual growth.* New York: Simon & Schuster (Touchstone).

*PRESTON, J. (1998). *Integrative brief therapy: Cognitive, psychodynamic, humanistic and neurobehavioral approaches.* San Luis Obispo, CA: Impact.

*PROCHASKA, J. O., & NORCROSS, J. C. (1999). *Systems of psychotherapy: A transtheoretical analysis* (4th ed.). Pacific Grove, CA: Brooks-Cole/Wadsworth.

*RICHARDS, P. S., & BERGIN, A. E. (1997). *A spiritual strategy for counseling and psychotherapy.* Washington, DC: American Psychological Association.

SHARF, R. S. (2000). Theories of psychotherapy and counseling: Concepts and cases. Pacific Grove, CA: Brooks-Cole/Wadsworth.

SMITH, D. (1982). Trends in counseling and psychotherapy. *American Psychologist, 37,* 802–809.

SMITH, M. L., GLASS, G. V., & MILLER, T. I. (1980). *The benefits of psychotherapy.* Baltimore: Johns Hopkins University Press.

STILES, W. B., SHAPIRO, D. A., & ELLIOTT, R. (1986). Are all psychotherapies equivalent? *American Psychologist, 41*(2), 165–180.

STRUPP, H. H. (1986). Psychotherapy: Research, practice, and public policy (How to avoid dead ends). *American Psychologist, 41*(2), 120–130.

STRUPP, H. H., & HOWARD, K. I. (1992). A brief history of psychotherapy research. In D. K. Freedheim (Ed.), *History of psychotherapy: A century of change* (pp. 309–334). Washington, DC: American Psychological Association.

SUE, D. W., IVEY, A., & PEDERSEN, P. (1996). *A theory of multicultural counseling and therapy.* Pacific Grove, CA: Brooks/Cole.

*SUE, D. W., & SUE, D. (1999). *Counseling the culturally different: Theory and practice* (3rd ed.). New York: Wiley.

SUMMIT ON SPIRITUALITY. (1995, December). *Counseling Today,* p. 30.

VANDENBOS, G. R. (1986). Psychotherapy research: A special issue. *American Psychologist, 41*(2), 111–112.

YOUNG, M. E. (1992). *Counseling methods and techniques: An eclectic approach.* New York: Macmillan.

YOUNGGREN, J. N. (1993). Ethical issues in religious psychotherapy. *Register Report, 19*(4), 1–8.

CHAPTER

15

Case Illustration: An Integrative Approach in Working With Stan

INTRODUCTION
>   *Some Themes in Stan's Life*

WORKING WITH STAN: Integration of Therapies
>   *A Place to Begin*
>   *Clarifying the Therapeutic Relationship*
>   *Clarifying the Goals of Therapy*
>   *Identifying Feelings*
>   *Expressing and Exploring Feelings*
>   *Working With Stan's Past, Present, and Future*
>   *The Thinking Dimension in Therapy*
>   *Doing: Another Essential Component of Therapy*
>   *Working Toward Revised Decisions*
>   *Encouraging Stan to Work With His Family of Origin*
>   *The Spiritual Dimension*
>   *Working With Stan's Drinking Problem*
>   *Moving Toward Termination of Therapy*
>   *Encouraging Stan to Join a Therapy Group*
>   *Commentary on the Thinking, Feeling, and Doing Perspective*
>   *Follow-Up: You Continue Working With Stan in an Integrative Style*

WHERE TO GO FROM HERE

INTRODUCTION

The purpose of this chapter is to bring together in an integrative fashion the 10 approaches you have studied by using a thinking, feeling, and acting model in counseling Stan. At this point I recommend that you think concretely about how to blend the concepts and techniques of various theories in a way that makes the most sense to you so that you can move toward developing your own integrative approach. As a reference point, the chapter begins with an overview of some of the themes in Stan's life that have emerged from his intake interview, his autobiography, and his work with the therapists representing each of the models covered in this book.

Some Themes in Stan's Life

A number of themes appear to represent core struggles in Stan's life. Here are some of the statements he has made at various points in his therapy:

- "Although I'd like to have people in my life, I just don't seem to know how to go about making friends or getting close to people."
- "When I'm with other people, I feel stupid much of the time."
- "I'd like to turn my life around, but I don't know where to start."
- "I'd like to find a career working with people so that I can make a difference in their lives. I want to return a favor to a person who really helped me."
- "I worry about whether I'm smart enough to complete my studies and do what's needed to become a counselor."
- "Sometimes, when I feel alone, scared, and overwhelmed, I drink heavily to feel better."
- "When I'm around a woman, I generally feel sweaty and terribly uptight. I'm sure she's judging me and will think I'm not a real man."
- "I'm so afraid of getting close to a woman. If I were to get close, my fear is that she would swallow me up."
- "My divorce made me wonder what kind of man I am."
- "Sometimes at night I feel a terrible anxiety and feel as if I'm dying."
- "There have been times when I've fantasized committing suicide, and I wondered who would care."
- "I often feel guilty that I've wasted my life, that I've failed, and that I've let people down. At times like this, I get really depressed."
- "I like it that I have determination and that I really want to change. I hate being a quitter."
- "I remember hearing from my parents that I couldn't do much of anything right."
- "My parents compared me unfavorably with my older sister and brother. I've never felt that I could measure up!"
- "I've never really felt loved or wanted by my parents."
- "I'd like to feel equal with others and not always have to feel apologetic for my existence."

- "I'd like to get rid of my self-destructive tendencies and learn to trust people more."
- "Although I put myself down a lot, I'd like to feel better about myself."

If I were Stan's therapist, we would explore many of these themes in our sessions. He will lead the way in therapy by the concerns he identifies. My job is to intervene in ways that will enable Stan to work through places where he is stuck. Many of these personal issues are connected, which will give some continuity to the work.

Table 15-1 provides a concise overview of the major emphasis of each theoretical orientation. The table illustrates how I am likely to work with Stan by selecting goals, key concepts, and techniques from the various approaches.

TABLE 15-1   ■   Major Areas of Focus in Stan's Therapy

Psychoanalytic therapy	My focus is on the ways in which Stan is repeating his early childhood in his present relationships. I am particularly interested in how he brings his experiences with his father into the sessions with me. As it is relevant, I will focus on his feelings for me, because working with transference is one path toward insight. I am interested in his dreams, any resistance that he reveals in the sessions, and other clues to his unconscious processes. One of my main goals is to assist him in bringing to awareness buried memories and experiences, which I assume have a current influence on him.
Adlerian therapy	My focus is on determining what Stan's lifestyle is. As a part of conducting a lifestyle assessment, I will examine his early childhood experiences through his recollections and family constellation. My main interest is in identifying what his goals and priorities in life are. I assume that what he is striving toward is equally as valid as his past dynamics. Therapy will consist of doing a comprehensive assessment, helping him understand his dynamics, and then helping him define new goals and translate them into action.
Existential therapy	My aim is to be as fully present and available for Stan as possible, for I assume that the relationship I am able to establish with him will be the source of our work together. An area that I am likely to concentrate on is how he finds meaning in life. He says he feels anxious a great deal, and this is an avenue to explore. Because Stan mentioned a fear of dying, and even entertained suicide as an option, I will certainly encourage him to explore his thoughts and feelings in these areas. I want to find out more about the nature of his fear of death and what keeps him alive, and I will assess the risk of suicide at the outset. We will also explore what quality of life he is striving for. I am interested in how Stan is dealing with freedom and the responsibility that accompanies it. Therapy is a venture that can

(continued)

TABLE 15-1 ■ *(continued)*

	help him expand his awareness of the way he is in his world, which will give him the potential to make changes.
Person-centered therapy	Because I trust Stan to find his own direction for therapy, I will avoid planning and structuring the sessions. My main focus is on being real, on accepting his feelings and thoughts, on demonstrating my unconditional positive regard for him, and on respecting him as a person. If I am able to listen carefully and reflect what I am hearing, and if I am able to deeply empathize with his life situation, he will be able to clarify his struggles and work out his own solutions to his problems. Although Stan is only dimly aware of his feelings at the initial phase of therapy, he will move toward increased clarity as I accept him fully, without conditions and without judgments. My main aim is to create a climate of openness, trust, caring, understanding, and acceptance. Then Stan can use this relationship to move forward and grow.
Gestalt therapy	My focus is on noticing signs of Stan's unfinished business, as evidenced by the ways in which he reaches a stuck point in his therapy. If he has never worked through his feelings of not being accepted, for example, these issues will appear in his therapy. I will ask Stan to bring them into the present by reliving them rather than merely talking about past events. I hope to help him experience his feelings fully, instead of simply gaining insight into his problems or speculating about why he feels the way he does. I'll encourage Stan to pay attention to his moment-by-moment awareness, especially to what he is aware of in his body. We will concentrate on *how* he is behaving and *what* he is experiencing.
Reality therapy	Counseling will be guided by the principles of choice theory. First, I will do my best to demonstrate my personal involvement with Stan by listening to his story. The emphasis is on his total behavior, including his doing, thinking, feeling, and physiology. If we concentrate on what he is actually doing and thinking and if change occurs on these levels, I assume Stan will automatically change on the feeling and physiological levels. After he evaluates his present behavior, it is up to him to decide the degree to which it is working for him. We will explore those areas of his behavior that he identifies as not meeting his needs. Much of therapy will consist of creating specific, realistic, and attainable plans. Once Stan agrees to a plan of action, it is essential that he make a commitment to following through with it.
Behavior therapy	Initially, I'll conduct a thorough assessment of Stan's current behavior. I'll ask him to monitor what he is doing so that we can create baseline data to evaluate any changes. We will continue our work by collaboratively developing concrete goals to guide our work, and I will draw on a wide range of cognitive and behavioral techniques to help Stan achieve his goals. We may use techniques such as role play-

TABLE 15-1   ■   (*continued*)

	ing, modeling, coaching, assertion training, carrying out homework assignments, and relaxation methods. I will stress learning new coping skills that Stan can use in everyday situations. He will practice what he learns in therapy sessions in his daily life.
Cognitive behavior therapy	My focus is on how Stan's internal dialogue and thinking processes are affecting his behavior. I will use an active and directive therapeutic style. Therapy will be time-limited, present-centered, and structured. My task is to create a form of collaborative working relationship in which Stan will learn to recognize and change self-defeating thoughts and maladaptive beliefs. We will concentrate on the content and process of his thinking by looking for ways to restructure some of his beliefs. Rather than merely telling Stan what faulty beliefs he has, I will emphasize his gathering data and weighing the evidence in support of certain beliefs. By the use of Socratic dialogue, I will assist Stan in detecting his faulty thinking, in learning ways of correcting his distortions, and in substituting more effective self-talk and beliefs. We will be using a wide range of cognitive, emotive, and behavioral techniques to accomplish our goals.
Feminist therapy	Stan comes to therapy with clear goals: to stop drinking, to feel better about himself, to relate to women on an equal basis, and to learn to love and trust himself and others. I build on these strengths. I focus on establishing an egalitarian working relationship to help Stan begin to regain his personal power. It is important that the therapeutic relationship does not replicate other negative relationships Stan has experienced. I spend considerable time explaining my view of the therapy process and how it works. By demystifying the therapeutic process, I am conveying to Stan that he is in charge of the direction his therapy will take. Our therapy might include a gender-role analysis so that Stan can come to a fuller understanding of the limiting roles he has uncritically accepted.
Family systems therapy	Stan has identified a number of strained relationships with his mother, father, and siblings. Ideally, we will have at least one session with all of the members of his family. The focus will be on his gaining greater clarity on how his interpersonal style is largely the result of his interactions with his family of origin. I am likely to focus on the degree to which Stan has developed his uniqueness rather than seeing him as merely his parents' son. If I work individually with Stan, the emphasis can still be on the many ways in which his current struggles are related to the system of which he is a part. Through our therapy, Stan will learn to recognize the rules that governed his family of origin and the decisions he made about himself. Rather than trying to change the members of his family, we will largely work on discovering what Stan most wants to change about himself in relation to how he interacts with them.

WORKING WITH STAN: Integration of Therapies

In this section I work toward integrating therapeutic concepts and techniques from the 10 theoretical perspectives. As I describe how I would counsel Stan on the levels of *thinking, feeling,* and *doing,* based on information presented in his autobiography, I will indicate from what orientations I am borrowing ideas at the various stages of his therapy. As you read, think about interventions you might make with Stan that would be either similar to or different from mine. Questions at the end of the chapter will guide you as you reflect about being Stan's counselor and working with him from your own integrative perspective.

A Place to Begin

I start by giving Stan a chance to say how he feels about coming to the initial session. Questions that I might explore with him are:

- "What brings you here? What has been going on in your life recently that gave you the impetus to seek professional help?"
- "What expectations do you have of therapy? Of me? What are your hopes, fears, and any reservations? What goals do you have for yourself through therapy?"
- "Could you give me a picture of some significant turning points in your life? Who have been the important people in your life? What significant decisions have you made? What are some of the struggles you've dealt with, and what are some of these issues that are current for you?"
- "What was it like for you to be in your family? How did you view your parents? How did they react to you? What about your early development?" (It would be useful to administer the Adlerian lifestyle questionnaire.)

Clarifying the Therapeutic Relationship

I will work with Stan to develop a contract, which involves a discussion of our mutual responsibilities and a clear statement of what he wants from these sessions and what he is willing to do to obtain it. I believe it is important to discuss any factors that might perpetuate a client's dependency on the therapist, so I invite Stan's questions about this therapeutic relationship. One goal is to demystify the therapy process; another is to get some focus for the direction of our sessions.

In establishing the therapeutic relationship, I am influenced by the person-centered, existential, Gestalt, feminist, and Adlerian approaches. They do not view therapy as something that the therapist *does* to a passive client. I will apply my knowledge of these therapies to establish a working relationship with Stan that is characterized by mutual trust and respect. I will ask myself these questions: "To what degree am I able to listen to and hear Stan in a nonjudgmental way? Am I able to respect and care for him? Do I have the capacity to enter his subjective world without losing my own identity? Am I able to share with him my own thoughts and reactions as they pertain to our relationship?" This relationship is critical at the initial stages of therapy, but it must be maintained during all stages if therapy is to be effective.

My contract with Stan specifies his rights and responsibilities as a client and my role as his therapist. Expectations are explored, goals are defined, and there is a basis for therapy as a collaborative effort. This emphasis is consistent with Adlerian therapy, the behavior therapies, the cognitive therapies, feminist therapy, and reality therapy. An excellent foundation for building a working partnership is openness by the counselor about the process of therapy. I think it is a mistake to hide behind "professionalism" as a way of keeping distance from the client. Therefore, I begin by being as honest as I can be with Stan as the basis for creating this relationship.

Clarifying the Goals of Therapy

It is not enough simply to ask clients what they hope they will leave with at the conclusion of therapy. Typically, I find that clients are vague, global, and unfocused about what they want. From behavior therapy, cognitive behavior therapy, Adlerian therapy, and reality therapy I borrow the necessity of getting Stan to be specific in defining his goals. Thus, Stan says: "I want to stop playing all these games with myself and others. I'd hope to stop putting myself down. I want to get rid of the terrible feelings I have. I want to feel OK with myself and begin living." I strive to get more concrete responses by asking questions such as: "Let's see if we can narrow down some of these broad goals into terms specific enough that both you and I will know what you're talking about. What exactly are these games you talk about? In what ways do you put yourself down? What are some of these terrible feelings that bother you? In what specific ways do you feel that you're not living now? What would it take for you to begin to feel alive?"

I do not ask all these questions at once; they are merely illustrations of ways in which I would work with Stan toward greater precision and clarity. If we merely talked about lofty goals such as self-actualization, I fear we would have directionless sessions. Thus, I focus on concrete language and specific goals that both of us can observe and understand. Once we have identified some goals, Stan can begin to observe his own behavior, both in the sessions and in his daily life. This self-monitoring is a vital step in any effort to bring about change.

My main aim is to encourage Stan to assume responsibility for what he wants to accomplish from the onset of our relationship. A large part of our early work together consists of helping Stan get a clear sense of concrete changes he would most like to make and how he can make them happen. Here are a few interchanges that focus on the process of defining goals that will give direction to Stan's therapy:

JERRY: What would you most hope for, through our work together?

STAN: Well, I know I put myself down all the time. I'd really like to feel better about myself.

JERRY: You put yourself down all of the time? Is what you've just said an example of how you are being hard on yourself right now?

STAN: Well, once in a great while I don't put myself down.

JERRY: If you had what you want in your life today, what would that be like? What would it take for you to feel good about yourself?

STAN: For one thing, I'd have people in my life, and I wouldn't run from intimacy.

JERRY: So this might be an area you'd be willing to explore in your sessions.

STAN: Sure, but I wouldn't know where to begin.

JERRY: I'll be glad to provide suggestions of ways to begin, if I know what you want.

STAN: Well, for sure I'd like to get over my fears of being with people. All my dumb fears really get in my way.

JERRY: I like it that you're willing to challenge your fears. Are you aware that you also just put yourself down again in labeling your fears as dumb?

STAN: It just comes as second nature to me. But I really would like to be able to feel more comfortable when I'm with others.

JERRY: How is it for you to be here with me now?

STAN: It's really not like me to do something like this, but it feels good. At least I'm talking, and I'm saying what's on my mind.

JERRY: It's good to see you give yourself credit for being different in our interchange right now.

This process of formulating goals is not accomplished in a single session. Throughout our time together, I ask Stan to decide time and again what he wants from his therapy and to assess the degree to which our work together is resulting in his meeting his goals. As his therapist, I expect to be active, yet it is important that Stan provides the direction in which he wants to travel on his journey. If Stan has clear, specific, and concrete goals for each therapy session, he will be the one who determines what we explore in our sessions. Once I have a clear sense of the specific ways Stan wants to change how he is thinking, feeling, and acting, I am likely to become quite active and directive in suggesting experiments that can be done both in the therapy sessions and on his own outside of our sessions.

Identifying Feelings

The person-centered approach stresses that one of the first stages in the therapy process involves identifying, clarifying, and learning how to express feelings. Because of the therapeutic relationship I have built with Stan, I expect him to feel increasingly free to mention feelings that he has kept to himself. In some cases these feelings are out of his awareness. Thus, I encourage Stan to talk about any feelings that are a source of difficulty. Again drawing on the person-centered model, I expect these feelings to be vague and difficult to identify at first.

During the early stages of our sessions, I rely on empathic listening. If I can really hear Stan's verbal and nonverbal messages, some of which may not be fully clear to him, I can respond to him in a way that lets him know that I have some appreciation for what it is like in his world. I need to do more than merely reflect what I hear him saying; I need to share with him my reactions as I listen to him. As I communicate to Stan that he is being deeply understood and accepted for the feelings he has, he has less need to deny or distort his feelings. His capacity for clearly identifying what he is feeling at any moment gradually increases.

There is a great deal of value in letting Stan tell his story in a way he chooses. The way he walks into the office, his gestures, his style of speech, the details he chooses to go into, and what he decides to relate and not to relate—to mention just a few elements—provide me with clues to his world. If I do too much structuring too soon and if I am too directive, I will interfere with his typical style of presenting himself. At this stage I agree with the Adlerians, who stress attending and listening on the counselor's part and who focus on the productive use of silence. Although I am not inclined to promote long silences early in counseling, there is value in not jumping in too soon when silences occur. Instead of coming to the rescue, it is better to explore the meanings of the silence.

Expressing and Exploring Feelings

My belief is that it is my authenticity as a person that encourages Stan to begin to identify and share with me a range of feelings. But I do not believe an open and trusting relationship between us is sufficient to change Stan's personality and behavior. I am convinced that I must also use my knowledge, skills, and experiences.

As a way of helping Stan express and explore his feelings, I draw heavily on Gestalt experiments. Eventually, I ask Stan to avoid merely talking about situations and about feelings. Rather, I encourage him to bring whatever reactions he is having into the present. For instance, if Stan reports feeling tense, I ask him *how* he experiences this tension and *where* it is located in his body. One of the best ways I have found to encourage clients to make contact with their feelings is to ask them to "be that feeling." Thus, if Stan has a knot in his stomach, he can intensify his feeling of tension by "becoming the knot, giving it voice and personality." If I notice that he has moist eyes, I may direct him to "be his tears now." By putting words to his tears, he avoids merely abstractly intellectualizing about all the reasons *why* he is sad or tense. Before he can change his feelings, Stan must allow himself to *fully experience* these feelings. The experiential therapies give me valuable tools for guiding Stan to the expression of his feelings.

Here are some segments of our dialogue in a session where Stan becomes quite aware of what he is feeling as he talks about his relationship with his father:

JERRY: You mentioned that your father often compared you with your brother Frank and your sister Judy. What was that like for you?

STAN: I hated it! He told me that I'd never amount to a hill of beans.

JERRY: And when he said that, how did that affect you?

STAN: It made me feel that I could never measure up to all the great things that Judy and Frank were accomplishing. I felt like a failure. [*As he says this, he begins welling up with tears, and his voice changes.*]

JERRY: Stan, what are you experiencing now?

STAN: All of a sudden a wave of sadness is coming over me. I'm getting all choked up. Wow—this is heavy!

JERRY: Stay with what you're feeling in your body. What's going on?

STAN: My chest is tight, and something wants to come out.

JERRY: And what's there?

STAN: I'm feeling very sad and hurt.

JERRY: Would you be willing to try something? I'd like you to talk to me as though I were your father. Are you willing?

STAN: Well, you're not mean the way he was to me, but I can try.

JERRY: How old are you feeling now?

STAN: Oh, about 12 years old—just like when I had to be around him and listen to all the stuff he told me about how rotten I was.

JERRY: Let yourself be 12 again, and tell me what it's like for you to be you—speaking to me as your father.

STAN: There was nothing that I could ever do that was good enough for you. No matter how hard I tried, I just couldn't get you to notice me. [*crying*] Why didn't I count, and why did you ignore me?

JERRY: Stan, I'll just let you talk for a while, and I'll listen. So keep on, telling me all the things you may be feeling as that 12-year-old now.

STAN: All I ever wanted was to know that I mattered to you. But no matter how hard I tried, all you'd do was put me down. Nothing I ever did was worth anything. All you ever told me was that I could never do anything right. I just wanted you to love me. Why didn't you ever do anything with me? [*Stan stops talking and just cries for a while.*]

JERRY: What's happening with you now?

STAN: I'm just feeling so damn sad. As if it's hopeless. Nothing I can do will ever get his approval. And that hurts!

JERRY: At 12 it was important for you to get his acceptance and his love. There is still that part in you that wants his love.

STAN: Yeah, and I don't think there's much I can do now to get it.

JERRY: So, tell him more of what that's like.

Stan continues talking to his "father" and recounts some of the ways in which he tried to live up to his expectations. Stan lets him know that no matter what he did there was no way to get the acceptance that Frank and Judy got from him.

JERRY: Having said all that, what are you aware of now?

STAN: I'm feeling kind of embarrassed. I shouldn't have gotten so emotional and worked up over such a dumb thing.

JERRY: You say you're embarrassed. Whom are you aware of?

STAN: Well, right now of you. I'm such a wimp. You're probably thinking that I'm really weak and dumb for letting this get to me.

JERRY: Tell me more about feeling weak and dumb.

Stan expresses that he should be stronger and that he is afraid I'll think he is hopeless. He goes into some detail about putting himself down for what he has just experienced and expressed. I do not too quickly reassure him that he "shouldn't feel that way." Instead, I let him talk, for this is what he so often feels. After expressing many of the ways in which he is feeling embarrassed, he wonders if I still want to work with him. At this point I let him know that I respect his struggle and hope that he can eventually learn to avoid judging himself so harshly. Because this session is coming to an end, I talk with Stan about the value of releasing feelings that he has been carrying around for a long time, suggesting that this work is a good beginning. I am also interested in getting him to do some homework before the next session.

JERRY: Stan, I'd like to suggest that you write a letter to your father . . .

STAN [*interrupting*]:   Oh no! I'm not going to give that guy the satisfaction of knowing that I need anything from him!

JERRY: Wait. I was about to say that I hope you'll write him a letter that you don't mail.

STAN: What's the point of a letter that won't be sent?

JERRY: Writing him a letter is an opportunity for further release and to gain some new insights. I hope you'll let yourself write about all the ways you tried to live up to his expectations. Let him know what it felt like to be you when you were around him. Tell him more about you, especially how you felt in not getting those things that you so much wanted.

STAN: OK, I'll do it if you think it might help.

In this session I might have made many different interventions. For the moment, I chose to let him "borrow my eyes" and talk to me as his father while he was 12 years old. I asked him to stay with whatever he was experiencing, paying particular attention to his body and to the emotions that were welling up in him. I see therapeutic value in letting Stan identify and express his feelings. It is premature to suggest problem-solving strategies or to attempt to figure everything out. My intent in offering him the homework assignment of writing a letter was to promote further work during the week. Writing the letter may trigger memories, and he may experience further emotional release. I hope this will help Stan begin thinking about the influence his father had on him then and also now. At our next session I will ask Stan if he wrote the letter and, if he did, what it was like for him to do so. What was he feeling and thinking as he was writing to his father? How was he affected when he read the letter later? Is there anything that he wants to share with me? The direction of our next session could depend on his response. Again, Stan will provide clues to where we need to go next.

Working With Stan's Past, Present, and Future

DEALING WITH THE PAST   Reality therapy, behavior therapy, and rational emotive behavior therapy do not place much emphasis on the client's history. Their rationale is that early childhood experiences do not necessarily have much to do with the maintenance of present ineffective behavior. My inclination, in contrast, is to give weight to understanding, exploring, and working with Stan's early history and to connect his past with what he is doing today. My view is that themes running through our life can become evident if we come to terms with significant turning points in our childhood. The use of an Adlerian lifestyle questionnaire would indicate some of these themes that originate from Stan's childhood. The psychoanalytic approach, of course, emphasizes uncovering and reexperiencing traumas in early childhood, working through the places where we have become "stuck," and resolving unconscious conflicts.

Although I agree that Stan's childhood experiences were influential in contributing to his present personality (including his ways of thinking, feeling, and behaving), it does not make sense to me to assume that these factors have *determined* him. I favor the Gestalt approach of having Stan bring his "toxic introjects" to the surface by dealing in the here and now with people in his life with whom he feels unfinished. This can be accomplished by fantasy exercises and a variety of role-playing techniques. In these ways Stan's past comes intensely to life in the present moment of our sessions.

DEALING WITH THE PRESENT   Being interested in Stan's past does not mean that we get lost in history or that we dwell on reliving traumatic situations. In fact, by paying attention to what is going on in the here and now of the counseling session, I get excellent clues to what is unfinished for him in his past. There is no need to go on digging expeditions, because the present is rich with material. He and I can direct attention to his immediate feelings as well as to his thoughts and actions. It seems essential to me that we work with all three dimensions—what he is thinking, what he is actually doing, and how his thoughts and behaviors affect his feeling states. Again, by directing Stan's attention to what is going on with him during our sessions, I can show him how he interacts in his world apart from therapy.

DEALING WITH THE FUTURE   Adlerians are especially interested in where the client is heading. Humans are pulled by goals, strivings, and aspirations. It would help to know what Stan's goals in life are. What are his intentions? What does he want for himself? If he decides that his present behavior is not getting him what he wants, he is in a good position to think ahead about the changes he would like and what he can do *now* to actualize his aspirations. The present-oriented behavioral focus of reality therapy is a good reference point for getting Stan to dream about what he would like to say about his life 5 years hence. Connecting present behavior with future plans is an excellent device for helping Stan formulate a concrete plan of action. He will have to actually *create* his future.

The Thinking Dimension in Therapy

Once Stan has gotten in touch with some intense feelings and perhaps experienced catharsis (release of pent-up feelings), some cognitive work is essential. Stan needs to be able to experience his feelings fully, and he may need to express them in symbolic ways. This may include getting out his anger toward women by hitting a pillow and by saying angry things that he has never allowed himself to say. Eventually Stan needs to begin to make sense of the emotional range of material that is surfacing.

To bring in this cognitive dimension, I focus Stan's attention on messages he incorporated as a child and on the decisions he made. I get him to think about the reason he made certain early decisions. Finally, I challenge Stan to look at these decisions about life, about himself, and about others and to make necessary revisions that can lead him to getting on with his living.

After getting basic information about Stan's life history (by means of the Adlerian lifestyle assessment form), I summarize and interpret it. For example, I find some connections between his present fears of developing intimate relationships and his history of rejection by his siblings and his parents. Thus, I am interested in his family constellation and his early recollections. Rather than working exclusively with his feelings, I want Stan to begin to understand (cognitively) how these early experiences affected him then and how they still influence him today. I concur with the Adlerians in their therapeutic interest in identifying and exploring basic mistakes. Here my emphasis is on having Stan begin to question the conclusions he came to about himself, others, and life. What is his private logic? What are some of his mistaken, self-defeating perceptions that grew out of his family experiences? An Adlerian perspective provides tools for doing some productive cognitive work both in and out of the therapy sessions.

From rational emotive behavior therapy I especially value the emphasis on learning to think rationally. I look for the ways in which Stan contributes to his negative feelings by the process of self-indoctrination with irrational beliefs. I get him to really test the validity of the dire consequences he predicts. I value the stress put on doing hard work in demolishing beliefs that have no validity and replacing them with sound and rational beliefs. I do not think Stan can merely think his way through life or that examining his faulty logic is enough by itself for personality change. But I do see this process as an essential component of therapy.

The cognitive behavioral therapies have a range of cognitive techniques that can help Stan recognize connections between his cognitions and his behaviors. He should also learn about his inner dialogue and the impact it has on his day-to-day behavior. Eventually, our goal is some cognitive restructuring work by which Stan can learn new ways to think, new things to tell himself, and new assumptions about life. This provides a basis for change in his behavior.

I have given Stan a number of homework assignments aimed at helping him identify a range of feelings and thoughts that may be problematic for him. In several of our sessions Stan has talked about messages he picked up about himself through his family. We have explored some specific beliefs he holds about himself, and he is beginning to recognize how his thinking processes are influencing the way he feels and what he is doing. Here are some sample pieces of a session in which we focus on his cognitions:

JERRY: Several times now you've brought up how you're sure you'd be judged critically if you allowed yourself to get close to a woman. Is this a topic you want to explore in more depth?

STAN: For sure. I'm tired of avoiding women, but I'm still too scared of approaching a woman. Part of me wants to meet a woman, and the other part of me wants to run. I'm convinced that if any woman gets to know me, she'll eventually reject me.

JERRY: Really, any woman will reject you? Have you checked out this assumption? How many women have you approached, and how many of them have actually rejected you?

STAN: Well, it's not that bad! They never tell me these things. But in my head I keep telling myself that if they get to know the real me they'll be turned off by my weakness and then they wouldn't want anything to do with me.

JERRY: How about telling me some of the things you tell yourself when you think of meeting a woman? Just let yourself go for a while, listing out loud some of the statements you make to yourself internally. Ready?

STAN: So often I say to myself that I'm not worth knowing. [*pause*]

JERRY: Just rattle off as many of these self-statements as you can. Don't worry about how it sounds. Rehearse out loud some of the familiar self-talk that keeps you from doing what you want.

STAN: What a nerd! Every time you open your mouth, you put your foot in
it. Why don't you just shut up and hide in the corner? When you do
talk to people, you always freeze up. They're judging you, and if you
say much of anything, they'll find out what a jerk you are! You're a
complete and utter failure. Anything you try, you fail in. There's not
much in you that anybody would find interesting. You're stupid, boring,
weak, and a scared kid. Why don't you keep to yourself so that others
won't have a chance to reject you?

Stan continues with this list, and I listen. After he seems finished, I tell
him how I'm affected by hearing his typical self-talk. I let him know that it
saddens me to see how hard he is on himself. Although I like Stan, I don't
have the sense that he will emotionally believe that I care about him. I let
him know that I respect the way he doesn't run from his fears and that I
like his willingness to talk openly about his troubles.

Stan has acquired a wide range of critical internal dialogues that he
has practiced for many years. My hope is that he will begin to challenge
those thoughts that are unfounded, that he will discover the nature of his
faulty thinking, and that eventually he will restructure some of his beliefs.
Along this line, I work with him to pinpoint specific beliefs and then do my
best to get him to come up with evidence to support or refute them. I am influenced by the constructivist trend in cognitive behavior therapy. Applied
to Stan, constructivism holds that his subjective framework and interpretations are far more important than the objective bases that may be at the
origin of his faulty beliefs. Thus, rather than imposing my version of what
may constitute faulty, irrational, and dysfunctional beliefs on his part, I
pursue a line of Socratic questioning whereby I get Stan to evaluate his own
thinking processes and his conclusions:

JERRY: Let's take one statement that you've made a number of times:
"When I'm with other people, I feel stupid most of the time." What goes
on within you when you say this?

STAN: It's like I hear critical voices, almost like people are in my head or
are sitting on my shoulder.

JERRY: Name one person who often sits on your shoulder and tells you
you're stupid.

STAN: My dad, for one. I hear his voice in my head a lot.

JERRY: Let me be Stan for a moment, and you be your dad, saying to me
some of those critical things that you hear him saying inside your head.

STAN: Why are you going to college? Why don't you quit and give your seat
to someone who deserves it? You always were a bad student. You're
just wasting your time and the taxpayers' money by pretending to be a
college student. Do yourself a favor and wake up to the fact that you'll
always be a dumb kid.

JERRY: How much truth is there in what you just said as your dad?

STAN: You know, it sounds stupid that I let that old guy convince me that I'm totally stupid.

JERRY: Instead of saying that you're stupid for letting him tell you that you're stupid, can you give yourself credit for being smart enough to come to this realization?

STAN: OK, but he's right that I've failed at most of the things I've tried.

JERRY: Does failing at a task mean that you're right holding to the label of being a failure in life? I'd like to hear you produce the evidence that supports your interpretation of being stupid and of being a failure.

STAN: How about the failure in my marriage? I couldn't make it work, and I was responsible for the divorce. That's a pretty big failure.

JERRY: And were you totally responsible for the divorce? Did your wife have any part in it?

STAN: She always told me that no woman could ever live with me. She convinced me that I couldn't have a satisfying relationship with her or any other woman.

JERRY: Although she could speak for herself, I'm wondering what qualifies her to determine your future with all women. Tell me what study was conducted that proves that Stan is utterly destined to be allergic to all women forever.

STAN: I suppose I just bought into what she told me. After all, if I couldn't live with her, what makes me think I could have a satisfying life with any woman?

At this point, there are many directions in which I could go with Stan to explore the origin of his beliefs and to assess the validity of his interpretations about life situations and his conclusions about his basic worth. In this and other sessions, we explore what cognitive therapists call "cognitive distortions," some of which are:

- *Arbitrary inferences.* Stan makes conclusions without supporting and relevant evidence. He often engages in "catastrophizing," or thinking about the worst possible scenario for a given situation.
- *Overgeneralization.* Stan holds extreme beliefs based on a single incident and applies them inappropriately to other dissimilar events or settings. For instance, because he and his wife divorced, he is convinced he is destined to be a failure with any woman.
- *Personalization.* Stan has a tendency to relate external events to himself, even when there is no basis for making this connection. He relates an incident in which a female classmate did not show up for a lunch date. He agonized over this event and convinced himself that she would have been humiliated to be seen in his presence. He did not consider any other possible explanations for her absence.
- *Labeling and mislabeling.* Stan presents himself in light of his imperfections and mistakes. He allows his past failures to define his total being.

■ *Polarized thinking.* Stan frequently engages in thinking and interpreting in all-or-nothing terms. Through this process of dichotomous
thinking, he has created self-defeating labels and boxes that keep
him restricted.

Over a number of sessions we work on specific beliefs. The aim is for
Stan to critically evaluate the evidence for many of his conclusions. My role
is to promote corrective experiences that will lead to changes in his thinking. I am striving to create a collaborative relationship, one in which he will
discover for himself how to distinguish between functional and dysfunctional beliefs. He can learn this by testing his conclusions.

Doing: Another Essential Component of Therapy

Stan can spend countless hours gathering interesting insights about why
he is the way he is. He can learn to express feelings that he kept inside for
many years. And he can think about the things he tells himself that lead to
defeat. Yet in my view feeling and thinking are not a complete therapy
process. *Doing* is a way of bringing these feelings and thoughts together by
applying them to real-life situations in various action programs. I am in-
debted to Adlerian therapy, behavior therapy, reality therapy, and rational
emotive behavior therapy, all of which give central emphasis to the role of
action as a prerequisite for change.

Behavior therapy offers a multitude of techniques for behavioral change.
In Stan's case I am especially inclined to work with him in developing self-
management programs. For example, Stan complains of often feeling tense
and anxious. Daily relaxation procedures are one way Stan can gain more
control of his physical and psychological tension. Perhaps by a combination
of meditation and relaxation procedures he can get himself centered before
he goes to his classes, meets women, or talks to friends. He can also begin
to monitor his behavior in everyday situations to gain increased awareness
of what he tells himself, what he does, and then how he feels. When Stan
gets depressed, he tends to drink to alleviate his symptoms. He can carry a
small notebook with him and actually record events that lead up to his feeling depressed (or anxious or hurt). He might also record what he actually
did in these situations and what he might have done differently. By paying
attention to what he is doing in daily life, he is already beginning to gain
more control of his behavior.

This behavioral monitoring can be coupled with both Adlerian and cognitive approaches. My guess is that Stan gets depressed, engages in self-
destructive behavior (drinking, for one), and then feels even worse. I work
very much on both his behaviors and cognitions and show him how many of
his actions are influenced by what he is telling himself. For example, Stan
wants to go out and apply for a job but is afraid that he might "mess up" in
the interview and not get the job. This is an ideal time to use behavioral rehearsal. Together we work on how he is setting himself up for failure by his
self-defeating expectations. True to the spirit of rational emotive behavior
therapy, we explore his faulty assumptions that he *must* be perfect and that

if he does not get the job, life will be unbearable. There are many opportunities to help Stan see connections between his cognitive processes and his daily behavior. I encourage Stan to begin to behave differently and then look for changes in his feeling states and his thinking.

With this in mind I ask Stan to think of as many ways as possible of actually bringing into his daily living the new learning he is acquiring in our sessions. Practice is essential. Homework assignments (preferably ones that he could give himself) are an excellent way for Stan to become an active agent in his therapy. He must do something himself for change to occur. I hope that he sees that the degree to which he will change is directly proportional to his willingness to get out in life and experiment. I want Stan to learn from his new behavior in life. Thus, each week we discuss his progress toward meeting his goals and review how well he is completing his assignments. If he fails in some of them, we can use this as an opportunity to learn how he can adjust his behavior. I insist on a commitment from him that he have an action plan for change and that he continually look at how well his plan is working.

I am very interested in what Stan is doing and how his thoughts and emotions are affecting this behavior. In the following dialogue, our interchanges deal primarily with Stan learning a more assertive style of behavior with one of his professors. Although this session focuses on Stan's behavior, we are also dealing with what he is thinking and feeling. These three dimensions are interactive.

JERRY: Last week we role-played different ways you could approach a professor with whom you were having difficulty. You learned several assertive skills that you used quite effectively when I assumed the role of the critical professor. Before you left last week, you agreed to set up a time to meet with your professor and let her know how she affects you. When we did the role playing, you were very clear about what you wanted to say and strong in staying with your feelings. Did you carry out your plan?

STAN: The next day I tried to talk to her before class. She said she didn't have time to talk but that we could talk after class.

JERRY: And how did that go?

STAN: After class all I wanted to do was make an appointment with her so that I could talk in private and without feeling hurried. When I tried to make the appointment, she very brusquely said that she had to go to a meeting and that I should see her during her office hours.

JERRY: How did that affect you?

STAN: I was mad. All I wanted to do was make an appointment.

JERRY: Did you go to her office hours?

STAN: I did, that very afternoon. She was 20 minutes late for her office hours, and then a bunch of students were waiting to ask her questions. All I got to do was make an appointment with her in a couple of days.

JERRY: Did that appointment actually take place?

STAN: Yes, but she was 10 minutes late and seemed preoccupied. I had a hard time at the beginning.

JERRY: How so? Tell me more.

STAN: I feel stupid in her class, and I wanted to talk to her about it. When I ask questions, she gets a funny look on her face—as if she's impatient and hopes I'll shut up.

JERRY: Did you check out these assumptions with her?

STAN: Yes I did, and I feel proud of myself. She told me that at times she does get a bit impatient because I seem to need a lot of her time and reassurance. Then I let her know how much I was studying for her class and how serious I was about doing well in my major. It was good for me to challenge my fears, instead of avoiding her because I felt she was judgmental.

JERRY: It's good to hear you give yourself credit for the steps you took. Even though it was tough, you hung in there and said what you wanted to say. Is there anything about this exchange with her that you wish you could have changed?

STAN: For the most part, I was pretty assertive. Generally, I blame people in authority like her for making me feel stupid. I give them a lot of power in judging me. But this time I remembered what we worked on in our session, and I stayed focused on myself rather than telling her what she was doing or not doing.

JERRY: How did that go?

STAN: The more I talked about myself, the less defensive she became. I learned that I don't need to give all my power away and that I can still feel good about myself, even if the other person doesn't change.

JERRY: Great! Did you notice any difference in how you felt in her class after you had this talk?

STAN: For a change, I didn't feel so self-conscious, especially when I asked questions or took part in class discussions. I was not so concerned about what she might think about me.

JERRY: What did your meeting with her teach you about yourself?

STAN: For one thing, I'm learning to check out my assumptions. That frees me up to act much more spontaneously. Also, I learned that I could be clear, direct, and assertive without getting nasty. It was possible for me to take care of myself without being critical of her. Normally, I'd just swallow all my feelings and walk away feeling dumb. This time I could be assertive and was able to let her know that I needed some unhurried time from her.

Practicing assertive behavior is associated with working with the feeling and thinking domains. Had Stan not done as well as he did in engaging his professor, we could have examined what had gone wrong from his vantage point. We could have continued role-playing various approaches in our sessions, and then with new knowledge and skills and more practice, he could have tried again. If Stan hopes to make the changes he desires, it is essential that he be willing to experiment with new ways of acting, especially outside of the therapy sessions. In a sense, counseling is like a dress rehearsal for living. Stan exhibited courage and determination in carrying out a specific action plan, which is a catalyst for change.

Working Toward Revised Decisions

When Stan has identified and explored both his feelings and his faulty beliefs and thinking processes, it does not mean that therapy is over. Becoming aware of early decisions, including some of his basic mistakes and his self-defeating ideas, is the starting point for change. It is essential that Stan find ways to translate his emotional and cognitive insights into new ways of thinking, feeling, and behaving. Therefore, as much as possible I structure situations in the therapy sessions that will facilitate new decisions on his part on both the emotional and cognitive levels. In encouraging Stan to make these new decisions, I draw on cognitive, emotive, and behavioral techniques. A few techniques I might employ are role playing, fantasy and imagery, assertion training procedures, and behavioral rehearsals. Both reality therapy and Adlerian therapy have a lot to offer on getting clients to decide on a plan of action and then make a commitment to carry out their program for change.

Here are some examples of experiments I suggest for Stan during the therapy sessions and homework assignments. They are geared to helping him apply what he is learning to situations in everyday life.

- I engage in a number of reverse role-playing situations in which I "become" Stan and have Stan assume the role of his mother, father, former wife, sister, older brother, and a professor. Through this process Stan gets a clearer picture of ways in which he allowed others to define him, and he acquires some skills in arguing back to self-defeating voices.
- To help Stan deal with his anxiety, I teach him relaxation methods and encourage him to practice them daily. Stan learns to employ these relaxation strategies in anxiety-arousing situations. I also teach him a range of coping skills, such as assertiveness and disputing irrational beliefs. Stan is able to apply these skills in several life situations.
- Stan agrees to keep a journal in which he records impressions and experiences. After encountering difficult situations, he writes about his reactions, both on a thinking and a feeling level. He also records how he behaved in these situations, how he felt about his actions, and how he might have behaved differently. He also agrees to read a few self-help books in areas that are particularly problematic for him.
- As a homework assignment, I urge Stan to meet with people whom he would typically avoid. For instance, he is highly anxious over his performance in a couple of his classes. He accepts my nudging to

make an appointment with each professor to discuss his progress. In one case, a professor takes an increased interest in him, and he does very well in her class. In the other case, the professor is rather abrupt and not too helpful. Stan is able to recognize that this is more the professor's problem than anything he is doing wrong.

- Stan wants to put himself in situations where he can make new friends. We work on a clear plan of action that involves joining a club, going to social events on campus, and asking a woman in his class for a date. Although he is anxious in each of these situations, he follows through with his plans. In our sessions we explore some of his self-talk and actions at these events.

Encouraging Stan to Work With His Family of Origin

After working with Stan for a short time, I suggest that he take the initiative to invite his entire family for a session. My assumption is that many of his problems stem from his family-of-origin experiences and that he is still being affected by these experiences. I think it will be useful to have at least one session with the family so that I can get a better idea of the broader context. The following dialogue illustrates my attempt to introduce this idea to Stan:

JERRY: Our sessions are certainly revealing a good deal of unfinished business with several members of your family. I think it would be useful to bring in as many of them as you can for a session.

STAN: No way! I'm not going to jump in that snake pit.

JERRY: Are you willing to talk with me more about this idea?

STAN: I'll talk, but it won't do any good.

JERRY: What stops you from asking them?

STAN: They already think I'm nutty as a fruitcake, and if they find out I'm seeing a psychologist, that's just one more thing they can throw in my face.

JERRY: You think they'd use this against you?

STAN: Yep. Besides, I can't see how getting my family together is going to help much. My mother and father don't think they have any problems. I don't see them wanting to change much.

JERRY: I wasn't thinking of their changing but more of giving you a chance to say directly some of the things you've said about them in your sessions with me. It might help you gain clarity about how you are with them.

STAN: Maybe, but I'm not ready for that one yet!

JERRY: OK, I can respect that you don't feel ready yet. I hope you'll remain open to this idea, and if you change your mind, let me know.

My rationale for including at least some of Stan's family members is to provide him with a context for understanding how his behavior is being influenced by what he learned as a child. He is a part of this system, and as he changes, it is bound to influence others in his family with whom he has contact. From what he has told me, I am assuming that he has unclear boundaries with his mother that have an impact on his relationships with other women. He is convinced that if he gets close to a woman she will swallow him up. If he can gain a clearer understanding of his relationship with his mother, he may be able to apply some of these insights with other women. In many ways Stan has allowed himself to be intimidated by his father, and he still hears Dad's voice in his head. In much of his present behavior, Stan compares himself unfavorably with others, which is a pattern he established in early childhood with his siblings. If he is able to begin dealing with the members of his family about some of his past and present pain, there is a good chance that he will be able to free himself of emotional barriers that are preventing him from forming those intimate relationships that he says he would like to have in his life. (For a more complete description of working with Stan from a family systems perspective, see Stan's case in Chapter 13.)

The Spiritual Dimension

Although I do not have an agenda to impose religious or spiritual values on Stan, I want to assess the role spirituality plays, if any, in his life currently—and to assess beliefs, attitudes, and practices from his earlier years. When I ask Stan if religion was a factor in his childhood or adolescence, he informs me that his mother was a practicing Lutheran and his father was rather indifferent to religion. His mother made sure that Stan went to church each week. Stan lets me know that mainly what he remembers from his church experiences is feeling a sense of guilt that he was not good enough and that he was always missing the mark of being a decent person. Stan recalls that his attitudes about religion fit in with his low self-esteem. Not only was he not good enough in the eyes of his parents, but he was also not good enough for God. Stan also adds that when he went to college he developed a new interest in spirituality as a result of a course he took in world religion.

Although formal religion does not seem to play a key role for Stan now, he is struggling to find his place in the universe. He reports that he would like to find a spiritual core as this is a missing dimension in his life. Stan also lets me know that he is pleasantly surprised that I am even mentioning religion and spirituality. He was under the impression that counselors would not be too interested in these areas. Stan would like to find meaning in life, and he indicates that he wants to have a clearer sense of the role of spirituality in his life. Upon further discussion of this area, Stan informs me of his intention to bring up his concerns about his spiritual life at a future session.

Working With Stan's Drinking Problem

Although each of the 10 therapeutic approaches would address drug and alcohol abuse in different ways, all probably agree that it would be imperative at some point in Stan's therapy to confront him on the probability that he is a chemically dependent person. In this section I describe my approach to working with his dependence as well as giving some brief background information on the alcoholic personality and on treatment approaches.

SOME BASIC ASSUMPTIONS   Stan has given me a number of significant clues suggesting that he may be a chemically dependent person. From the information he has provided, it is clear that Stan has many of the personality traits typically found in alcoholics, including low self-concept, anxiety, sexual dysfunctions, underachievement, feelings of social isolation, inability to love himself or to receive love from others, hypersensitivity, impulsivity, dependence, fear of failure, feelings of guilt, self-pity, and suicidal impulses. In addition, he has used drugs and alcohol as a way of blunting anxiety and attempting to control what he perceives as a painful reality. He has switched from drugs to alcohol, which is a common attempt to control the disastrous effects of addiction.

　　Once our therapeutic relationship is firmly established, I confront Stan (in a caring and concerned manner) on his self-deception that he is doing something positive by not getting loaded with drugs but is merely getting drunk. He needs to see that alcohol *is* a drug, and I want him to make an honest evaluation of his behavior so that he can recognize the degree to which his drinking is interfering in his living. Although Stan resorts to excuses, rationalizations, denials, distortions, and minimizations about his drinking patterns, I provide some information he can use to examine his confused system of beliefs. Johns Hopkins University Hospital in Baltimore has designed a questionnaire that is useful in assessing the preliminary signs of alcohol addiction. A few questions are:

- Have you lost time from work due to drinking?
- Do you drink to escape from worries?
- Do you drink to build up your self-confidence?
- Have you ever felt remorse after drinking?
- Do you drink because you're shy with other people?
- Does drinking cause you to have difficulty sleeping?

From what I already know of Stan, it is likely that he will answer yes to several of these questions if he responded honestly. "Yes" answers to even one or two of these questions indicate enough of a problem to warrant further assessment for chemical dependency.

A SUPPLEMENTARY TREATMENT PROGRAM   Stan eventually recognizes and acknowledges that he does indeed have a problem with alcoholism, and he says he is willing to do something about this problem. I tell him that alcoholism is considered by most substance abuse experts to be a disease in itself, rather than a symptom of another underlying disorder. It is a chronic condition that can be treated, and it is a progressive disorder that eventually results in death if it is not arrested. It will be helpful for Stan to know that long-term recovery is based on the principle of total abstinence from all drugs and alcohol and that such abstinence is a prerequisite to effective counseling. In addition to his weekly individual therapy sessions with me, I provide Stan with a referral to deal with his chemical dependence.

I encourage Stan to join Alcoholics Anonymous and attend their meetings. The 12-step program of AA has worked very well for many alcoholics. It is not a substitute for therapy, but it can be an ideal supplement. Once Stan understands the nature of his chemical dependence and no longer uses drugs, the chances are greatly increased that we can focus on the other aspects of his life that he sees as problematic and would like to change. In short, it is possible to treat his alcoholism and at the same time carry out a program of individual therapy geared to changing Stan's ways of thinking, feeling, and behaving.

Moving Toward Termination of Therapy

The process I have been describing will probably take months. During this time, I will continue to draw simultaneously on a variety of therapeutic systems in working with Stan's thoughts, feelings, and behaviors. Although I have described these three dimensions separately in the examples, I tend to work in an integrated fashion among the dimensions as well. Eventually this process will lead to a time when Stan can continue what he has learned in therapy without my assistance.

Termination of therapy is as important as the initial phase, for now the challenge is to put into practice what he has learned in the sessions by applying new skills and attitudes to daily social situations. When Stan brings up a desire to "go it alone," we talk about his readiness to end therapy and his reasons for thinking about termination. I also share with him my perceptions of the directions I have seen him take. This is a good time to talk about where he can go from here. Together we spend a few sessions developing an action plan and talking about how he can best maintain his new learning. He may want to join a therapeutic group. He could find support in a variety of social networks. In essence, he can continue to challenge himself by doing things that are difficult for him yet at the same time broaden his range of choices. Stan might take some dancing classes, an activity he has previously avoided out of a fear of failing. Now he can take the risk and be his own therapist, dealing with feelings as they arise in new situations.

In a behavioral spirit, evaluating the process and outcomes of therapy seems essential. This evaluation can take the form of devoting a session or two to discussing Stan's specific changes in therapy. A few questions for focus are: "What stands out the most for you, Stan? What did you learn that you consider the most valuable? How did you learn these lessons? What can you do now to keep practicing new behaviors that work better for you than the old patterns? What will you do if you experience setbacks? How will you handle any regression to old ways or temporary defeats?" With this last question it is helpful for Stan to know that his termination of formal therapy does not mean that he cannot return for a visit or session when he considers it appropriate. Rather than coming for weekly sessions, Stan might well decide to come in at irregular intervals for a "checkup." Of course, he will be the person to decide what new areas to explore in these follow-up sessions.

Encouraging Stan to Join a Therapy Group

As Stan and I talk about termination, he gives me clear indications that he has learned a great deal about himself through individual counseling. Although Stan has been applying his learning to difficult situations that he encounters, I believe he would benefit from a group experience. I suggest that Stan consider joining a 16-week therapy group that will begin in two months.

To me, progressing from individual therapy to a group seems useful for a client like Stan. Because many of his problems are interpersonal, a group is an ideal place for him to deal with them. The group will give Stan a context for practicing the very behaviors he says he wants to acquire. Stan wants to feel freer in being himself, to feel easier in approaching people, and to be able to trust people more fully. He realizes that he has made gains in these areas, yet he has some distance to travel. In addition to a group experience, I will be working with Stan in the final phases of his therapy to find some other steps he can take to continue his growth. Together we will make plans for putting him into situations that will foster change. He might take skiing lessons, attend more parties, engage in volunteer work with children, or continue writing in his journal.

Commentary on the Thinking, Feeling, and Doing Perspective

In applying my integrated perspective to Stan, I've dealt separately with the cognitive, affective, and behavioral dimensions of human experience. Although the steps I outlined may appear relatively structured and even simple, actually working with clients is more complex and less predictable. If you are practicing from an integrative perspective, it would be a mistake to assume that it is best to always begin working with what clients are thinking (or feeling or doing). Effective counseling begins where the client is, not where a theory indicates a client should be.

Applied to Stan, a person-centered focus takes into account factors such as his cultural background, his presenting problem, what he says he needs and wants at the initial session, and the clues he gives both verbally and nonverbally. I began by exploring his feelings because as he was talking he teared up, and it was evident that he had a need to express feelings that had been bottled up for years. Some clients might leave counseling never to return if I attempted to call attention to their feelings at the initial session. Feelings might be too threatening for them, and in such situations it might be more appropriate to focus on underlying assumptions or thoughts. For others, a proper launching point might be what they are actually doing, with a discussion of how well it is working for them. By paying attention to the client's energy (or blocked energy), therapists have many clues about where to begin. If the client resists, dealing with the resistance in a respectful way could open other doors.

In summary, depending on what clients need at the moment, I may focus initially on what they are thinking and how this is affecting them, or I may focus on how they feel, or I may choose to direct them to pay attention to what they are doing. Because these facets of human experience are interrelated, one route generally leads to exploring the other dimensions. Thus, I frequently ask a client: "What are you aware of now?" or "What are you experiencing now?" If they say "I'm thinking that . . .", I may follow that path and ask them to say more about what they are thinking. If they say "I'm feeling a tightness in my chest and . . .", I am likely to ask them to stay with their bodily sensations for a bit longer and see where that leads them. If they say "What I'm doing is . . .", I generally encourage them to tell me more about how well their actions are serving them. If they say "I'm feeling lonely and frightened . . .", I may encourage them to stay with their feelings and talk more about what it is like to experience these feelings.

A person-centered focus respects the wisdom within the client and uses it as a lead for where to go next. My guess is that counselors often make the mistake of getting too far ahead of their clients, thinking, "What should I do next?" By staying with our clients and asking them what they want, we do not need to assume too much responsibility by deciding for them the direction in which they should be heading. Instead, we can learn to pay attention to our own reactions to our clients and to our own energy. By doing so we can engage in a therapeutic dance that is exciting for both parties in the relationship.

Follow-Up: You Continue Working With Stan in an Integrative Style

Think about these questions to help you decide how to counsel Stan:

- What themes in Stan's life do you find most significant, and how might you draw on these themes during the initial phase of counseling?
- What specific concepts from the various theoretical orientations would you be most inclined to utilize in your work with Stan?
- Identify some key techniques from the various therapies that you are most likely to employ in your therapy with Stan. What are a few cognitive techniques you'd probably use? Emotive techniques? Behavioral techniques? What are some interventions you would draw from feminist therapy? Family therapy?
- How might you invent experiments for Stan to carry out both inside and outside the therapy sessions? How are you likely to present these experiments to him?
- As you were reading about the integrative perspective, what ideas did you have about continuing as Stan's counselor?
- Knowing what you do about Stan, what do you imagine it would be like to be his therapist? What problems, if any, might you expect to encounter in your counseling relationship with him?

■ What are your thoughts about ways in which you could pay attention to working with Stan from a thinking, feeling, and behaving perspective? What modalities might you emphasize?

 WHERE TO GO FROM HERE

At the beginning of the introductory course in counseling, my students typically express two reactions: "How will I ever be able to learn all these theories?" and "How can I make sense out of this mass of knowledge?" By the end of the course, these students are often surprised by how much work they have done *and* by how much they have learned. Although an introductory survey course will not turn students into accomplished counselors, it generally provides the basis for selecting from among the many models to which they are exposed.

At this point you may be able to begin putting the theories together in some meaningful way for yourself. This book will have served its central purpose if it has encouraged you to read further and to expand your knowledge of the theories that most caught your interest. I hope you have made friends with some theories that were unknown to you before and that you have seen something of value that you can use from each of the approaches described. You will not be in a position to conceptualize a completely developed integrative perspective after your first course in counseling theory, but you now have the tools to begin the process of integration. With additional study and practical experience, you will be able to expand and refine your emerging personal philosophy of counseling.

Finally, the book will have been put to good use if it has stimulated and challenged you to think about the ways in which your philosophy of life, your values, your life experiences, and the person you are becoming are vitally related to the caliber of counselor you can become and to the impact you can have on those who establish a relationship with you personally and professionally. This book and your course may have raised questions for you regarding your decision to become a counselor. If this is the case, I encourage you to seek out at least one of your professors to explore these questions.

If you have read the chapters in the order presented in the book, I suggest that you take time to reread Chapters 2 and 3, as they can help you put some of the personal and professional issues in perspective. Compare your current thinking on the issues examined in these early chapters with your views when you began the course.

Now that you have finished this book, I would be very interested in hearing about your experience with it and with your course. The comments readers have sent me over the years have been helpful in revising each edition, and I welcome your feedback. You can write to me in care of Brooks-Cole/Wadsworth Publishing Company, Pacific Grove, CA 93950-5098, or you can complete the reaction sheet at the end of the book and mail it to me.

AUTHOR INDEX

Adler, A., 7, 8, 67, 81, 107, 108, 109, 110, 112, 119, 123, 126, 127, 134, 142, 298, 384, 387, 437, 391, 392, 395
Agras, W. S., 259
Albert, L., 126
Alberti, R. E., 274, 275
Alford, B. A., 328, 468
Alperin, R. M., 101
Andersen, T., 429, 430, 435, 438
Anderson, H., 430, 431, 435
Angel, E., 144
Ansbacher, H. L., 110, 111, 112, 131
Ansbacher, R. R., 110, 111, 112
Arkowitz, H., 458, 460, 468
Arnkoff, D. B., 256, 259, 297
Arredondo, P., 26
Atkinson, D. R., 103

Baldwin, D. C., 157, 405, 406, 407, 411, 412
Ballou, M., 356, 373
Bandura, A. A., 8, 248, 255, 256, 258, 259, 263
Barker, S. B., 273
Barlow, D. H., 265
Basow, S. A., 350
Bateson, G., 422, 437
Beck, A. T., 8, 256, 259, 296, 309, 310, 311, 312, 313, 314, 315, 316, 317, 324, 328, 329, 356, 468
Beck, J. S., 313
Becker, L. A., 273
Becvar, D. S., 387, 388, 390, 399, 400, 414, 421, 430, 438
Becvar, R. J., 387, 388, 390, 399, 400, 414, 421, 430, 438
Beisser, A. R., 196, 203
Bem, S. L., 349
Berg, I. K., 433, 435
Bergin, A. E., 461, 463, 485

Beutler, L. E., 258, 277, 468, 474
Bitter, J. R., 108, 118, 119, 121, 123, 124, 127, 387, 395, 396, 397, 399, 405, 406, 407, 409, 411, 412, 438
Blanchard, W., 127
Blau, W., 68, 299, 304, 309
Block, L., 297
Bondi, A. M., 463
Bowen, M., 384, 391, 392, 399, 400, 401, 402, 403, 404, 427–428, 447
Boyer, J. L., 485
Brabeck, M., 344
Bracke, P. E., 161, 162
Breshgold, E., 196, 211, 219
Breunlin, D. C., 428
Brickell, J., 237
Brink, D. C., 184
Brooks, G. R., 369
Brown, L. S., 342, 344, 346, 352, 364, 372, 373, 390, 412, 438, 445
Bubenzer, D. L., 438
Buber, M., 156, 208
Bugental, J. F. T., 144, 154, 156, 161, 162
Burke, M. T., 463
Burns, D., 314
Burtle, V., 257, 344

Cain, D. J., 169, 172, 179, 183, 185, 186, 187
Callanan, P., 52
Campos, P. E., 287
Carlson, J., 125, 126
Castonguay, L. G., 457, 460
Chabot, D. R., 390, 413, 416
Chambless, D. L., 272
Chesler, P., 344
Chodorow, N. J., 345, 348, 349, 351
Christensen, O. C., 391, 392, 396, 397, 398, 399
Coates, T. J., 260

Colapinto, J., 416, 419, 421, 422
Comas-Diaz, L., 102, 373
Combs, A. W., 173, 184, 186, 438
Corey, G., 52, 55, 123, 131, 307, 318, 350
Corey, M., 52, 350
Cormier, W. H., 262, 268, 269, 275
Cormier, L. S., 262, 268, 269, 275
Corsini, R. J., 115, 125
Crawford, M., 363
Cristol, A. H., 285

Dattilio, F. M., 297, 310, 312, 314, 317, 318,
    331, 332, 390
Davison, G. C., 259, 328
De Shazer, S., 433, 434, 435, 438
DeAngelis, T., 102
DeRubeis, R. J., 310, 315, 317
DeWolf, R., 314
Dinkmeyer, D., 110, 116, 117, 122, 126, 390,
    394, 395, 396, 399
Dobson, K. S., 297
Dreikurs, R., 8, 108, 112, 114, 118, 119, 126,
    127, 128, 384, 387, 391, 392, 395, 397,
    398
Dryden, W., 295, 297, 298, 299, 300, 302, 307,
    309
Dutton, M. A., 360

Elkin, I., 485
Ellenberger, H. F., 144
Ellis, A., 8, 131, 256, 259, 295, 297, 298, 299,
    300, 301, 302, 303, 304, 305, 306, 307,
    309, 313, 314, 330, 333, 356, 395
Emery, G., 309, 314, 317
Emmons, M. L., 274, 275
Enns, C. Z., 101, 341–342, 345, 346, 352, 355,
    359, 361
Epp, L. R., 154–155
Epston, D., 431, 432, 433, 435, 437, 438
Erickson, M., 422, 433
Erikson, E. H., 68, 73, 74, 77, 78, 79, 80, 83,
    97
Espin, O. M., Ph.D., 342
Evans, I. M., 266
Eysenck, H., 257, 258

Faiver, C. M., 462, 463
Farber, B. A., 184
Farha, B., 149
Fisch, R., 427
Fishman, D. B., 257, 258
Fishman, H. C., 417, 418, 420, 422
Fodor, I. G., 356
Framo, J. L., 404
Frankl, V., 8, 131, 141, 144, 145, 147, 151
Franks, C. M., 257, 258, 259, 344
Freeman, A., 310, 312, 314, 331, 438
Freud, S., 8, 67, 68, 70, 74, 76, 79, 81, 82, 93,
    97, 108, 106, 144, 195, 216, 234, 437,
    457
Frew, J. E., 197, 201, 212
Fromm, E., 108

Ganley, A. L., 364
Garfield, S. L., 468, 485, 487
Georgia, R. T., 463
Gergen, K. J., 428, 438
Gerson, R., 403, 421
Gillette, C. S., 273
Gilligan, C., 345, 348, 350, 351
Giordano, J., 390, 447
Glanz, L. M., 485
Glass, C. R., 256, 259, 297, 485
Glasser, W., 8, 229, 230, 231, 236, 238, 240,
    246, 247, 248, 251
Goldenberg, H., 388, 390, 414, 415, 438, 445
Goldenberg, I., 388, 390, 414, 415, 438, 445
Goldfried, M. R., 259, 457, 458, 460, 468
Goldstein, A. P., 275, 283, 287
Goldstein, K., 193
Goodman, R., 203, 211
Goolishian, H., 430, 431, 435
Gordon, J., 298, 300, 303, 309
Grant, S. K., 103
Granvold, D. K., 264, 314
Griffith, J., 115, 122–123, 124
Grimm, D. W., 463
Guerin, P. J., 390, 413, 416
Guevremont, D. C., 256, 260, 262, 263, 264,
    266, 267, 268, 270, 272, 284, 286, 287
Gurman, A. S., 438

Haaga, D. A. F., 313, 328
Haley, J., 386, 391, 392, 422, 423, 424, 425,
    427, 429, 444
Hamachek, D. F., 99
Hanna, S. M., 390, 412, 438, 445
Harper, R., 299, 300, 304
Harris, A. S., 83
Hawes, C., 126, 127, 273, 396
Hedges, L. E., 84, 85, 87
Hefferline, R., 203, 211
Heppner, R. R., 169
Herlihy, B., 55, 56, 57, 343, 371
Hill, M., 352
Hinterkopf, E., 463
Hoffman, L., 391
Horne, A. M., 390
Horney, K., 108, 193, 298
Howard, K. I., 482, 486, 487
Humphrey, K., 194

Imber, S. D., 485
Ingersoll, R. E., 463
Ivey, A. E., 343, 460
Iwamasa, G. Y., 287

Jackson, D., 422
Jacobs, L., 203, 207, 208
Jacobson, E., 266
Johnson, J. A., 154–155, 351, 352, 372
Jung, C. G., 67, 68, 81, 82, 83, 108, 437

Kanfer, E. H., 275, 283, 287
Kantrowitz, R. E., 356

Kaplan, L., 87
Kaschak, E., 345, 349
Kazdin, A. E., 257, 259, 260, 263, 266, 283, 286
Kefir, N., 111, 121, 122
Keith, D. V., 413, 414, 415
Kelly, E. W., 458, 459, 462, 463
Kernberg, O. F., 84–85
Kerr, M. E., 401, 404
Klein, M., 84
Kniskern, D. P., 438
Kohut, H., 85
Kovel, J., 68
Krestensen, K. K., 405, 411
Kwee, M. G. T., 304

Laing, R. D., 162, 167
Lambert, M. J., 45, 485, 486
Latner, J., 197
Lazarus, A. A., 8, 255, 257, 258, 259, 265, 266, 268, 276, 277, 278, 279, 280, 285, 458, 459, 465, 467, 468, 471, 472
Lazarus, C. N., 279
Lazrove, S., 273
Lee, L. A., 169
Lerman, H., 351
Lerner, H. G., 345
Leupnitz, D. A., 390
Levitsky, A., 213
Liese, B., 310
Lindsley, J. R., 322
Losoncy, L. E., 118
Luepnitz, D. A., 404, 427
Lusterman, D. D., 369
Lyddon, W., 297, 323

MacKune-Karrer, B., 428
MacLaren, C., 302, 303, 305
MacMillan, P., 86
Madanes, C., 386, 391, 392, 422, 423, 424, 426, 427, 444
Mahler, M. S., 83, 84, 85, 90
Mahoney, M. J., 259, 297
Malone, T. P., 415
Manaster, G. J., 115, 125
Maniacci, M. P., 126
Marcus, S. V., 273
Marmor, J., 100
Marquis, P., 273
Mash, E. J., 265
Maslow, A., 131
Masterson, J. F., 85
Mattson, D. L., 461, 463
Maultsby, M. C., 307
May, R., 8, 131, 142, 143, 144, 145, 152, 154, 155, 161
McDavis, R. J., 26
McGoldrick, M., 390, 403, 421, 447
McIntosh, P., 373
McKay, G., 396
McLellarn, R. W., 305
McNamee, S., 438

Meichenbaum, D., 256, 259, 260, 297, 313, 318–323, 329
Messer, S. B., 463
Miller, J. B., 341, 345, 349, 350, 461, 463, 485
Minrath, M., 102
Minuchin, S., 385, 391, 392, 416, 419, 420, 422
Miranti, J., 463
Morgan, B., 86
Morris, R. J., 268
Mosak, H. H., 112, 114, 116, 119, 125, 126
Mozdzierz, G. J., 119, 132–133

Napier, A. Y., 415
Napier, G., 415
Neenan, M., 298, 300, 303, 309
Neimeyer, R. A., 322, 323
Newman, C. E., 310, 314, 458, 468, 487
Nichols, M. P., 370, 390, 401, 415, 420, 433, 438, 439, 444, 445
Nicoll, W. G., 396
Nietzsche, F., 144
Nira, K., 121
Norcross, J. C., 277, 343, 348, 356, 358, 457, 458, 460, 468, 487
Nutt, R. L., 369
Nystul, M. S., 131

O'Brien, E. M., 462, 463
O'Hanlon, W. H., 432, 433, 434, 435, 438

Padesky, C. A., 297
Palmer, S., 298, 300, 303, 309
Papero, D. V., 400, 404
Passmore, J. L., 390
Pate, R. H., 463
Patterson, C. H., 329, 331
Paul, G. L., 261, 487
Pearch, J. K., 390, 447
Peck, M. S., 463
Pedersen, P., 52, 134, 460
Perilla, J. L., 287
Perls, F., 8, 171, 193, 194, 195, 199, 200, 203, 206, 208, 211, 213, 216, 220, 221
Perls, L., 8, 194, 195, 206, 207
Pew, W. L., 391
Philpot, C. L., 369
Polster, E., 198, 199, 200, 205, 207, 208, 209, 211
Polster, M., 198, 199, 200, 206, 207, 208, 209, 211, 344
Popkin, M., 126, 396
Powers, W., 115, 119, 122–123, 124, 229
Prochaska, J. O., 343, 348, 356, 458, 460, 468
Purcell, D. W., 287

Rampage, C., 370
Raskin, P. M., 170, 184
Reich, W., 193
Reik, T., 92
Reineke, M., 314
Remer, P., 336, 347, 352, 353, 354, 356, 357, 358, 361, 362

Richards, P. S., 463
Ridley, C. R., 287
Rogers, C. R., 8, 169, 170, 171, 172, 173, 174, 176, 178, 179, 184, 185, 186, 187, 180, 313, 366
Rogers, M. E., 169
Rothbaum, B. O., 273
Rothblum, E., 352
Rush, A., 309, 317
Russell, J. M., 147

Safran, J. D., 458, 460
Sakai, C., 273
Salas-Auvert, J. A., 310
Sanford, R., 174
Santos De Barona, M., 360
Saretsky, T., 89, 93
Sartre, J. P., 147, 158
Satir, V. M., 384–385, 391, 392, 404, 405, 406, 407, 409, 411, 412, 422, 428, 438, 443, 444
Schaeffer, J. A., 273
Scheck, M. M. 273
Schilson, L., 427
Schultz, D., 81, 82, 109
Schultz, S. E., 81, 82, 109
Schwartz, R. C., 370, 390, 401, 415, 420, 428, 433, 438, 439, 444, 445
Searles, H. F., 90, 91
Segal, L., 422
Shapiro, F., 270, 271, 273
Sharf, R. S., 349, 360, 361
Shaw, B., 309, 317
Sherman, R., 110, 111, 390, 394, 395, 399
Shulman, B. H., 119
Skinner, B. F., 256, 258, 259
Slavik, S. 125
Sloane, R. B., 285, 286
Smith, S. K., 287, 458, 485, 486
Soltz, V., 126, 395, 397
Sonstegard, M. A., 128, 392
Sperry, L., 116, 122, 125, 126
Spiegler, M. D., 256, 260, 262, 263, 264, 266, 267, 268, 270, 272, 284, 286, 287
St. Clair, M., 83, 84, 85, 87
Staples, E. R., 285
Stiver, I. P., 349
Stosky, S. M., 485
Strupp, H. H., 100, 482, 485, 486, 487
Sue, D., 26, 52, 447, 460
Sue, D. W., 26, 52, 447, 460
Sullivan, H. S., 108
Surrey, J. L., 349
Sweeney, T. J., 115

Tafrate, R. C., 299
Tennov, D., 344

Terdal, L. G., 265
Terner, J., 391
Tharp, R. G., 260, 276
Thomas, S. A., 356, 358
Thoresen, C. E., 260
Thorne, B., 179, 180
Tillich, P., 142, 148
Tinker, R. H., 273
Toman, W., 403

Vaihinger, H., 110
Van Deurzen-Smith, E., 143, 152, 153, 157, 161
Van Etten, M. L., 273
VandenBos, G. R., 485, 486, 487
Velten, E., 302, 305
Voltz, L. M., 266
Vontess, C. E., 154–155, 156, 160, 163

Walden, S. L., 359
Ward, F. L., 180
Warren, R., 305
Watkins, C. E., 329, 331
Watson, D. L., 260, 276
Watts, R. E., 131, 132
Watzlawick, P., 422, 427
Weakland, J. H., 427
Weiner-Davis, M., 433, 438, 434, 435
Weishaar, M. E., 259, 296, 297, 310, 313, 314, 322, 328, 331
Wessler, R. L., 308
West, J. D., 438
Whipple, K., 285
Whitaker, C. A., 385, 391, 392, 410, 412, 413, 414, 415
White, M., 431, 432, 433, 435, 437, 438
Wilson, G. T., 259, 261, 286
Wilson, S. A., 273
Wodarski, J. S., 264
Wolpe, J., 257, 258, 267, 268
Wood, J., 173
Worell, J., 336, 347, 351, 352, 353, 354, 356, 357, 358, 361, 362, 372
Wright, E. D., 310
Wubbolding, R. E., 237, 238, 240, 241, 242, 243, 249, 251

Yalom, I., 8, 143, 144, 145, 151, 152, 153, 154, 161
Yankura, J., 298
Yeager, R. J., 298, 307
Yontef, G. M., 203, 207, 212, 221
Yorkston, N. J., 285
Young, M. E., 468
Younggren, J. N., 461, 463

Zimring, F. M., 170
Zinker, J., 200, 202, 203, 208, 209, 211

SUBJECT INDEX

A-B-C approach, 309
A-B-C model, 327, 473
A-B-C theory, 300–301, 305
Acceptance, 126, 160, 172, 177, 178, 215,
    354, 471, 496
  of client, 177
  of feelings, 176
  parental, 77
  therapist's, 178
  unconditional full, 304
Accommodation, 206, 418, 420
Accountability, 485
  ethical, 284
  societal pressures for, 100–101
Accurate empathic understanding, 172,
    178–179, 284
Achievement, 151, 394
  values placed on, 348
Act, freedom to, 36
Acting, 232, 245
  alternative ways of, 436
  commitment to, 161
  new ways of, 512
  and thinking, focus on, 249
Acting "as if," 125
Action, 9, 10, 20, 125, 130, 151, 257, 388,
    419, 466
  alternative, 130, 316
  conscious, 9
  constricting, 162
  courses of, 125, 164, 243
  developing, 516
  future, 271
  parental, 396
  quality of, 242
  role of, as prerequisite for change, 509
Action orientation, 328, 482
Action plan, 69, 131, 242, 247, 286, 512, 513

Action-oriented phase, 86
  of Adlerian therapy, 125
  of therapeutic process, 124
Active listening, 284, 478
Activism, 346
  as a goal, 345
Activities:
  experiential, 10
  meaningful, 234, 246
  process-centered, 243
  record of, 476
Actualization, 172, 412
  and growth, tendency toward, 299
Actualizing tendency, 170
Adler, contributions of, 131
Adlerian approach, 112, 131, 132, 133, 134,
    298, 328, 396, 498, 509
  contributions of, 131–132
  goal of, 130
  strength of, 131
Adlerian counselors, 125, 126, 134
Adlerian family therapists, 395, 396, 397
Adlerian family therapy, 127, 391–394
  assumption in, 391
  goals, 392–393
  key figures, 392–393
  process of change, 392–393
  role and function of therapist,
    392–393
  techniques and innovations, 392–393
  time focus, 392–393
Adlerian *Individual Psychology,* 273
Adlerian interpretations, 123
Adlerian lifestyle assessment form, 505
Adlerian lifestyle questionnaire, 504
Adlerian theory, 133
  writing and research on, 132
Adlerian therapists, 128, 130

Adlerian therapy, 8, 9, 106–139, 113, 116,
      328, 343, 499, 509, 512
   application: therapeutic techniques and
         procedures, 117–128
   areas of focus in Stan's therapy, 495
   assessment, 120
   basic philosophies, 464
   brief therapy, 126, 397
   contributions of, 481
   contributions to multicultural counseling,
         478
   goals of therapy, 469
   key concepts of, 108–117, 131, 466
   limitations of, 134, 483
   limitations in multicultural counseling,
         479
   from multicultural perspective, 132–134
   therapeutic relationship, 472
   view of human nature, 108–109
Adolescence, 75, 79, 97
Adolescent conflicts, 80
Adolescent development, 74, 79
Adulthood:
   later, 74
   mature, 79
   mid-, 74
   phases of, 79
   young, 76, 80
Advice, 5, 36, 125, 170, 425
Affect, 278, 280
   blocked, 415
   conflicting, 92
   inappropriate, 90
   role of, 257
Affectional orientation, 353
African Americans, 51, 53
Age, 26, 353, 417
Aged:
   neglect of, 43
   problems of, 126
Aggression, 274
Aggressive impulses, 464
Aging parents, adult only child of, 402
Agoraphobia, behavioral treatment for, 270
Alcohol abuse, 513
Alcoholics Anonymous, 516
Alcoholism, 296, 515
Alienation, 76, 143, 148, 156
   from others, 159
   understanding, 160
Alliances, 22, 156, 442
Aloneness, 158
   experience of, 149, 159
Alternatives, 125
   awareness of, 146
   for choice and action, 162
Alternative stories, 435
   and re-authoring, 437
   development of, 437
Ambiguity, 33–34, 102–103
   learning to tolerate, 153
Anal stage, 74, 79, 97, 100

tasks of, 77
Analysis:
   of basic mistakes, 122
   central functions of, 87
   experimental, 257
   gender-role, 360, 361, 365
   long-term, 103, 472
   successful, 87, 89
Analytic framework, maintaining the, 92,
      98
Analytic therapy, 87
   candidates for, 476
   Jungian, 97
Androcentric norms, 352
Androcentric theory, 347
Anger, 18, 73, 95, 305, 505
   expression of, 416
   feelings of, 405
   retroflected, 310
   techniques to deal with, 481
Anorexia nervosa, 269, 360
Antecedents, 265, 276, 324
Antitheoretical approach, 412
Anxiety, 6, 9, 12, 18, 24, 32, 33, 35, 36,
      70–71, 72, 87, 95, 112, 143, 150, 154,
      155, 156, 161, 163, 267, 305, 464, 466,
      481, 512, 515
   assessment scales for, 296
   castration, 98
   as a condition of living, 145, 151–153
   coping with, 29, 477
   disorder, 360
   existential, 146, 152, 159
   exploring, 357
   healthy, 158
   hierarchy, 268
   nature of, 142
   neurotic, 71, 151, 152
   normal, 151, 152, 158
   reactions to, 98
   reducing, 468
   role of, 97
   as source of growth, 151
   sources of, 152
   treatment of, 267, 268–269, 270, 328, 477,
         483
   understanding, 160, 482
Anxiety-management training, 277
Arbitrary inferences, 310–311, 316, 508
Archetypes, 82
Argument, absolute position in, 417
Asian Americans, 53, 103, 447
Asian perspective, 51
"As if," acting, 125
Aspirational ethics, definition, 45
Aspirations, 8, 505
   actualize, 505
   unrealistic, 95
Assertion skills training, 475
Assertion training, 266, 497
   in behavior therapy, 274
   goal of, 274

procedures, 512
Assertive behavior, learning and practicing, 363, 511
Assertive language, 249
Assertiveness training, 274, 277, 281, 308, 355, 363, 369, 476
Assessment, 35, 133, 158, 180, 181, 257, 271, 274, 287, 429, 470, 475, 480
    Adlerian, 120
    alternative form of, 360
    behavioral, 265
    for chemical dependency, 515
    of client's functioning, 114
    of client's personality, 93
    collaborative, 396
    comprehensive, 278, 280, 495
    continual, 262, 479
    and diagnosis, 52, 53, 54, 360
    of ego strength, 13
    of family of origin, 439
    initial, 119
    lifestyle, 115, 119, 123, 128, 129, 495
    methods, 287
    personal, 478
    procedures, 54, 120, 122, 180, 260, 360
    process, 52–55, 86, 120, 180, 462
    role of, 52, 180
    techniques for, 180, 410, 482
    and treatment, 262, 462–463
    of treatment outcomes, 283
Assignments, 36
    homework, 4, 6
    outcomes of, 322
Assimilation, 206, 475
Assumed disability, 395, 398
Assumptions, 51, 157, 297
    basic, 28, 195
    about behavior, 464
    culturally learned, 134
    faulty, 9, 114,
    about human nature, 145
    philosophical, 355
    self-defeating, 9
    self-limiting, 125
    underlying, 517
Attachments, 85
    dependent, 149
    emotional, unresolved, 401
Attachment theory, and object-relations, 86
Attitudes, 58, 115, 130, 131, 157, 172, 513
    awareness of, 26
    change in, 173
    counselor's, 243
    dialogic, 206
    nonjudgmental, 478
    parental, 74
    therapist's, 9, 156, 175, 185, 207, 472
    toward women, 356
Attunement, emotional, 84, 91
Authenticity, 162, 177, 412, 471
    as a person, 501
    therapist, 185, 371

Autogenic training, 266
Automatic thoughts, 9, 310, 315, 324, 325, 326, 469
Autonomy, 73, 77, 153, 154, 171, 392, 447, 480
    and independence, capacity for, 348
    individual, 385, 413
    sense of, 98
    versus shame and doubt, 74
    versus shame and guilt, 89
    steps toward, 148
Autosuggestion, processes of, 299
Avoidance, 216, 244, 248, 268, 466
Avoiding the traps, 125
Awareness, 4, 8, 9, 69, 71, 91, 127, 151, 152, 195, 198, 205, 218, 247, 320, 325, 326, 461, 466, 509
    client, 37, 207, 264
    concept of, 208
    constricting, 162
    creating, 123
    of death and nonbeing, 145, 153
    expanding, 161, 408
    increased, 147, 206, 220, 413, 464
    of inner potential, 412
    levels of, 324
    limited, 155
    moment-by-moment, 496
    of others, 83
    out of, 70, 201, 501
    of personal power, 355
    present-centered, 219, 220
    resistance to, 211
    self-, 17
    therapist's, 207
    training, 477

Barriers:
    artificial, 473
    dealing with, 52
    emotional, 418, 513
    impermeable, between subsystems, 418
    institutional, 27
Basic assumptions, 170, 261, 274, 515
BASIC I.D., 277, 278
    diagnosis, 280
    framework, 279
Basic mistakes, 114, 115, 116, 120, 122, 131, 512
    analysis of, 122
    identifying, 129
    identifying and exploring, 505
    summary of, 122
    ways to prevent and correct, 126
Basic needs, 83, 112, 231, 239, 246, 250
Battering groups, 364
Beck Depression Inventory (BDI), 316
Behaving:
    as if, 199
    patterns of, 426
    ways of, 115
    wholeness and integration of, 464

Behavior, 9, 35, 37, 53, 69, 91, 109, 123, 131,
    172, 232, 236, 240, 277, 278, 280, 317,
    464, 466, 472, 496, 515
  adaptive and maladaptive, 321
  Adlerian principles of, 126
  authentic, 156
  change, 58, 126, 173, 246, 247, 258, 259,
    318–319, 329, 330, 423, 476
  in children, 477
  choice theory explanation of, 232–233
  consequence of, 126, 237, 242, 258, 423
  dysfunctional, 443, 465
  effective, 245, 472
  ethical, 46
  evaluation of, 472, 478, 515
  goals of, 123
  here-and-now, 123
  historical causes of, 286
  human, 15, 50, 67, 109, 110
  impulsive, 87
  inauthentic, 157
  incongruent, 16
  ineffective, 233, 504
  insights into, 130
  irrational, 87
  irrelevant, 407
  maladaptive, 269, 279, 319, 321, 326, 468,
    469, 473
  medical model of, 256
  modification, 259, 262, 285, 304, 369
  overt, 178, 466
  passive, 274
  pathological, 132
  patterns, 149, 426
  problematic, 239, 387, 425, 426, 469
  purposeful, 9, 108, 391
  rehearsal, 277, 281, 325
  responsible, 248
  rules for, 423
  self-destructive, 20, 509
  stimulus/response model of, 259
  symptomatic, 239
  therapists', 90, 185, 207, 256–257, 283,
    287, 472
  total, 232, 233, 238, 239, 241, 245, 496
  understanding, 70, 96
  verbal and nonverbal, 186, 222, 482
Behavioral approach, 51, 256
  alternative to, 171
  procedures drawn from, 277
  related strength of, 284
  strength of, 265
Behavioral changes, 286
  consequences of, 480
  making, 461
Behavioral methods, 275, 301, 303
Behavioral rehearsals, 274, 320, 355, 405,
    475, 509, 512
Behavioral treatment:
  for agoraphobia, 270
  for anxiety-related disorders, 267, 270
  for obsessive-compulsive disorder, 270
  phobias, 270

  for posttraumatic stress disorder, 270
Behaviorism, 256, 282
Behavior therapy, 8, 9, 254–293, 308, 328,
    329, 471, 488, 499, 504, 509
  application: therapeutic techniques and
    procedures, 265–280
  applied to case of Stan, 280–282, 496–497
  assertion training, 274
  basic characteristics and assumptions,
    260–261, 282
  contemporary, 256, 257, 258, 259, 262,
    266, 282
  contributions of, 264, 282–283, 481
  contributions to multicultural counseling,
    479
  definition of, 256
  goals of therapy, 261–263, 469
  historical background, 256–257
  homework assignments, 303, 308
  interventions, 273, 288, 321
  key concepts of, 259–261, 466
  limitations and criticisms of, 284–286,
    484
  limitations in multicultural counseling,
    480
  from a multicultural perspective, 286–288
  rational-emotive, 8
  summary and evaluation, 282–286
  therapeutic process, 261–265
  therapeutic relationship, 472
  therapeutic techniques and procedures,
    256, 265–280, 283, 284, 287, 308,
    325, 473, 476, 482, 496, 512
  view of human nature, 259–260
Being:
  alternative ways of, 156
  and interacting, way of, 394
  experience of, 149
  problems of, 142
  ways of, 5, 148, 150, 175, 436
  in the world, 162, 472
Beliefs, 26, 131, 298
  absolute, 25, 305
  basic, 298, 325
  clarification of, 179
  clients', 309
  counselor's, 19
  disputing, 305, 512
  dogmatic, 469
  dysfunctional, 9, 296, 313, 327, 473, 507
  empirically testing, 312
  faulty, 324, 469, 497, 507
  functional, 308
  irrational, 278, 298, 299, 301, 506, 507
  maladaptive, 497
  rational, 301, 302
  religious, 23, 26
  restructure, 507
  self-defeating, 30, 274, 299, 302, 324, 325,
    326
  spiritual, 26
  untested, 369, 476
Belief systems, 58, 467

rational, 326
role of, 8
self-defeating, 300
Belonging, 231, 236, 250, 478
sense of, 112, 114, 128, 385, 400, 413, 469
and significance, goal of, 273
Bereavement, 161
Biases, 26, 102, 115, 356, 360
Bibliotherapy, 277, 304, 314, 362, 363, 366, 369, 476
Bilingual clients, language barriers with, 478
Biochemical imbalances, 278, 389
Biofeedback, 277
Biofeedback-induced relaxation, 266
Biological drives, 68
Biological dysfunctions, 279
Birth order, 112–113, 120, 134, 395, 403
Birth position, 395
psychological, 112
Blame, 38–39, 98, 155, 233, 239, 244, 299, 363, 407, 436, 445, 462
Body image, 269, 345
distorted, 316
Body language, 215
client's, 203
Borderline clients, from ethnic minorities, 102
Borderline conditions, 100
Borderline disorders, treating, 85
Borderline personality disorder, 85, 360
Boundaries, 17, 32, 56, 416, 417, 418, 419, 420, 421, 438, 439, 444, 476, 513
Bowenian family therapy,
assumptions in, 399
goals, 401
practice, 399
Bowenian therapists, 404
Bowen's detachment theory, 404
Brief counseling, 161, 476
Brief therapy, 87, 279, 309, 427, 468, 477
Adlerian, 126, 397
comprehensive, 278
treatment, 284
Bulimia, 360
Burnout, 35, 38, 39–40

Caretaking roles, 348
Catastrophizing, 310, 508
Catching oneself, 125
Catharsis, 91, 92, 221, 223, 286, 505
Challenges, developmental, 161
Change:
paradoxical theory of, 196, 203, 208
personality, 91, 92, 175, 176, 177, 303, 506
plan for, 276
social, 51, 360, 364
therapeutic, 173, 175, 257, 416, 485
Child abuse, 48, 483
implications of, 371
victim of, 49
Child beating, cycle of, 72
Child guidance, 126, 476

Childhood, 74, 77, 513
experiences, 9, 98, 108, 247, 330, 484, 495, 504
Child interview, and goal disclosure, 398
Child rearing, democratic, 396
Children, 84, 395
inhumane practices against, 43
leaving home, 161
misbehavior, 395, 398
Choice, 15, 68, 70, 109, 171, 172, 202, 412
freedom of, 4
informed, 360, 363
personal, 464
Choices, 15, 73, 125, 144, 145, 148, 151, 153, 239, 371, 466
behavioral, 230, 248
consequences of, 36, 146, 374
effective, 230, 242, 246
informed, 47, 196
self-destructive, 231, 246
Choice theory, 228–253, 469, 477
in action, 238
existential underpinnings of, 247
principles of, 249, 496
Chronologies, family life-fact, 405
Class, 346, 353
diversity in, 28
social, 17
Classical conditioning, 257, 258, 267, 282
Client-as-expert, 119, 435
Client-centered therapy, 170
Clients:
characteristics of, 6, 471
cultural background of, 28
cultural context of, 26
culturally diverse, 163, 222, 250, 333
ethnic minority, 102, 103, 164, 188, 249, 288, 350
experience in therapy, 88–89, 155–156, 356–358
gay, 23
identified, 387
lesbian, 23
Native American, 133
non-Western, 250
phenomenological world of, 170, 173
suicidal, 49, 50
women, 343
Client/therapist relationship (*See also* Relationships), 5, 9
Clinical research, 485
Coaching, 425, 428, 475, 497
Codes of ethics, 45, 46, 53, 55, 57, 371
Coercion:
by client, 238
by therapist, 238
Coercion-free atmosphere, 238
Cognitions, 116, 256, 277, 278, 280, 317, 327, 464
anxiety-provoking, 320
changing, 297, 473
client's, 297
distorted and dysfunctional, 311

Cognitions *(continued)*
  effective and rational, 298
  faulty, 356, 473
  focus on, 506
  modifying, 477
  negative, 271, 272
  positive, 271, 272
Cognitive approaches, 509
Cognitive behavioral approaches, 51, 86, 109,
    185, 256, 274, 317, 328, 329, 330, 332,
    333, 356, 366, 470, 506
  contributions of, 327–329
  limitations and criticisms of, 329–331
Cognitive behavioral feminist therapist, 355
Cognitive behavioral strategies, integration
    of, 318
Cognitive behavior modification (CBM), 318
  Meichenbaum's, 297, 318–323, 327, 329,
    331
Cognitive behavior therapy, 4, 8, 256, 258,
    294–339, 295, 355, 471, 499
  application: therapeutic techniques and
    procedures, 304–309
  applied to case of Stan, 323–326, 497
  basic philosophies, 464–465
  constructivism as a trend in, 322–323,
    507
  contributions of, 481
  contributions to multicultural counseling,
    479
  goals of, 301–302, 469
  key concepts, 298, 299–304, 467
  limitations in multicultural counseling,
    480
  limitations of, 484
  multicultural perspective, 331–333
  summary and evaluation, 326–331
  therapeutic process, 301–304
  therapeutic techniques and procedures,
    86–87, 304–309
  therapist's function and role, 302–303
  view of emotional disturbance, 299–300
  view of human nature, 299
Cognitive distortions, 296, 310, 316, 325, 508
Cognitive factors, 9, 10, 221, 282, 482
  as determinant of behavior, 9
  focusing on, 310
  influencing behavior, 282
  of personality, 221
Cognitive homework, 305
Cognitive inference, 317
Cognitive learning theory, 459
Cognitive map, 114, 278
Cognitive methods, 275, 301, 303, 305, 308
Cognitive perspective, changing, 466
Cognitive processes, 256, 259, 510
  as determinants of behavior, 327
  disturbances in, 297
Cognitive restructuring, 86, 272, 303, 318,
    320, 325, 369, 476
Cognitive set, 319
Cognitive social learning theory, 329
Cognitive strategies, 297, 331

Cognitive structure, 318, 319
Cognitive techniques, 305, 314–315, 476,
    482, 496, 506, 512
Cognitive theories, 465
Cognitive therapy (CT), 8, 9, 256, 296, 297,
    309, 310, 328, 473, 488, 499
  applications of, 314–318
  basic principles of, 310–313
  Beck's, 309–318, 327, 328–329, 331, 332
  constructivist dimension of, 332
  contributions of, 328
  criticism of, 331
  effects of, 328
  myths and misconceptions about, 331
  and REBT, differences between, 312–313
  theoretical assumptions of, 309
Cognitive triad, 315
Collaboration, 4, 320, 332, 359, 435, 479
  feminist emphasis on, 404
Collaborative empiricism, 312
Collaborative relationship, 262, 329, 479
Collective unconscious, 82, 97
Collectivism, 478, 480
Commitment, 125, 151, 243, 510, 512
  lack of, 32, 33
Communal narratives, 431
Communication, 127, 249, 406, 408, 442, 467
  aim of, 444
  congruent, 392, 428, 439
  cross-cultural, 187
  defensive, 405
  dysfunctional, 439
  in families, 406–407, 467
  functional and dysfunctional, 406
  learning and practicing, 363
  model, 422
  modeling, 116
  patterns of, 444, 473
  theory, 422
  training, 277
  universal, 407
  verbal and nonverbal, 32, 170, 222, 443,
    467
Compassion, 5, 18, 435, 445
Compensation:
  definition, 73
  ideas of, 110
Competence, 31, 75
  striving for, 74, 111
  struggle for, 405
Conditioning, 4
  classical and operant, 256, 258, 308
  of client, 26
  cultural, 25, 26
Confidentiality, 35, 48, 58, 101, 398
  dimensions of, 48–49
  exceptions to, 47
  guidelines on, 49–50
  issues of, 49
  limitations of, 32, 47, 48, 49, 50
  nature and purpose of, 48
Conflicts, 18, 19, 28, 29, 71, 73, 92, 220, 464,
    472

of adolescent years, 79–80
avoidance of, 416
cultural, 28, 126
intrapsychic, 73, 74, 83, 195, 286
repressed, 247, 464
resolution of, 91, 101, 171, 400
unconscious, 74, 90, 475, 504
unresolved, 34, 90
value, 20, 22, 25
Confluence, 161, 200, 201
Confrontation, 125, 212, 220, 250
Confrontational therapy, 329, 484
Congruence, 172, 177, 178, 237, 405, 410
  or genuineness, 177
  therapist, 185
Conjoint family therapy, 384, 404–405
Connectedness:
  concept of, 348
  with others, 148, 348
  power of, 354
Connection, 236, 392, 428
  feminist emphasis on, 404
  with others, 247
Consciousness, 70, 109, 146
  feminist, 352
Consciousness-raising groups, 344
Consciousness-raising techniques, 476
Consequences, 45, 125, 164, 257, 265, 276,
      287, 288, 323, 325
  for behavior, 258, 300, 423
  of choices, 146
  emotional, 300
  of freedom, 152
  negative, 268, 303
Constructivism, as a trend in cognitive
      behavior therapy, 322–323
Constructivist:
  approach, 109
  perspective, 322
  philosophy, 323
  theory, 322
Constructivist narrative perspective (CNP),
      322
Consultation, 26, 57, 58
Contact, 221, 466
  between client and therapist, 195
  between individual and environment, 219
  concept of, 208
  and resistances to contact, 200–202
Contemporary counseling:
  theories, 50
  values implicit in, 51
Contemporary psychoanalytic practice, 100
Contingency contracting, 277
Contracts, 4, 36, 116, 262, 358, 498
  client-initiated, 36
  formulating, 36
  therapeutic, 472
Control, 87, 88, 121, 129, 423, 484
  effective, 246
  executive, 423
  and freedom, 284
  issues, 357

of one's life, 468
and power, position of, 212
of psychic energy, 71
rational, 472
theory, 229
Coping model, 265
Coping skills, 275, 312, 318, 320, 362, 473,
      479, 497, 512
  cognitive and behavioral, 322, 326
  effective, 319
  in vivo, 324
  learning, 261, 371, 476
  programs, 259, 319–322
Coping techniques, behavioral and cognitive,
      321
Counseling:
  Adlerian, 113, 117
  with adolescents, 126
  with adults, 126
  aim of, 146–147
  brief, 161, 476
  with children, 126
  for the counselor, 17
  couples, 126, 309
  cross-cultural, 163
  culturally biased, 51
  culture-bound, 50–51
  cycle of, 237, 238, 242, 249
  early phase of, 462
  effective, 26, 54, 481, 516, 517
  environment, 237, 238–239, 247
  evaluating, 485
  existential, 143, 156, 157, 158
  experiential aspects of, 10
  family, 477
  gender-fair, principles for, 369
  global approach to, 282
  goals of, 172, 345, 371
  group, 126, 130, 171, 476, 477
  individual, 130, 171, 476, 477
  initial phase of, 118
  integrated model, 86
  lack of progress in, 33
  marital, 126, 127, 477
  multicultural, 132–134, 288. See Multi-
      cultural counseling.
  multicultural, contributions to, 249
  multicultural, limitations for, 134–135,
      164–165, 250
  parent/child, 126, 476
  personal, 19, 457
  personalized theory of, 487
  phases in, 471
  problem-oriented approach to, 103, 164
  process and outcomes of, 34, 36, 114, 117,
      162, 184
  and psychotherapy, theories of, 68
  relationship, egalitarian, 351, 354, 358
  reorientation phase of, 125
  risks involved in, 47
  Roger's contribution to, 179
  structured approach to, 164
  style, 37–38, 185

Counseling *(continued)*
   techniques, 27
   testing in, 54
   theories of, 6, 50, 68, 371
   Western models of, 50
Counselors, 29, 49, 180
   Adlerian, 114, 117, 118, 125, 126, 131, 134
   beginning, 29, 37
   behavior of, 5
   Christian, 23
   concerns of, 29
   culturally skilled, 26, 27
   effective, 16, 19, 25, 26, 37
   existential, 148, 160
   intervention strategies of, 26
   nondirective, 170
   personal characteristics of, 16
   person-centered, 181, 188
   skills of, 26
   student, 18
Countertransference, 19, 90, 91, 98, 100, 162, 415, 481
   definition of, 34
   outcomes to, 90
   potential for, 484
   sources of, 102
   use of, 476
Courage, 6, 18, 29, 114, 124, 148, 156, 160
Crisis, 73, 74, 85, 97
   clients in, 242
   developmental, 161
   intervention, 181, 244, 477
   situational, 161
Crooked thinking, tendency toward, 299
Cross-cultural:
   activity, 171
   communication, 187
   counseling, 163
   therapy, 249
Cues, nonverbal, 203
Cultural awareness. *See* Multicultural awareness.
Cultural backgrounds, 28, 133, 217, 286, 446, 471, 478, 517
   diverse, 477
   of clients, 210, 332, 461, 474
Cultural conditioning, 25, 26, 163
Cultural conflicts, 28, 126, 479
Cultural differences, 25, 26, 27, 133
Cultural diversity, 26, 163, 287
   person-centered approach to, 187
Cultural expectations, 217
Cultural factors, 51, 53, 108, 373
   in assessment and treatment process, 460
Cultural feminists, 346
Cultural groups, 133, 187, 479, 483
Cultural heritage, 26, 27, 134, 460, 481
Cultural injunctions, 210, 223, 389, 478
Culturally diverse client populations, 4, 26, 50, 102, 163, 222, 332, 373, 460, 474
   values of, 331–332
   working with, 250
Cultural norms, 210, 250, 447

Cultural sensitivity, 163
Cultural stereotypes, 370
Cultural values, 27, 133, 188, 249, 250, 332, 359, 479, 480
Culture, 10, 17, 28, 120, 133, 134, 249, 343, 353, 374, 431, 446, 460
   awareness of and sensitivity to, 26, 447
   definition, 26
   dominant, 53, 431, 437
   Euro-American, 51
   evaluation of, 134
   feminization of, 346
   perception of, 134
   role of, 360
   sensitivity to, 447
   understanding of, 28
Culture-centered approach, 134

Death, 18, 23, 142, 145, 151, 153, 156, 163
   awareness of, 145, 153
   facing, 142
   fear of, 160, 495
   and nonbeing, awareness of, 153
   physical, 153
   as a positive force, 160
Death and dying, 146
Death instincts, 69
Debating, 301, 305, 476
Debriefing, therapeutic process, 427
Deception, self-, 23
Decision making, 127, 247
Decision-making model, 57
Decision-making process, 47
Decisions, 4, 25, 36, 37, 96, 146, 175, 180, 468, 497, 512–513
Deconstruction, 437
Defenses, 18, 23, 30, 33, 44, 71, 89, 94, 200, 357
Defensiveness, 176, 444
Defensive stances, in coping with stress, 407–408
Denial, 515
   definition, 71
   of one's basic worth, 122
Dependence, 84, 96, 153, 333, 349, 369, 418, 498, 515
   fostering, 36, 304
   promoting, 480
   security of, 144, 146
   versus independence, 89, 99
Depression, 18, 33, 95, 116, 230, 232, 239, 245, 269, 296, 305, 316, 317, 343, 360, 477
   treatment of, 315, 328, 477, 483, 488
Desensitization, 267, 268, 269, 308, 325
   phase, of EMDR, 271
Despair, 18, 76, 118, 151, 158
   versus integrity, 80
Detachment theory, Bowen's, 404
Determinism, 68, 347
   Freudian, 82, 144
Development, 69, 120, 257–259
   adolescent, 79

deficiencies and distortions in, 101
ego's place in, 74
Erikson's view of, 79
feminist view on, 350
human, 50, 348
identity, 344, 351
Jung's perspective, 81–83
personal, 73, 131, 413
personality, 73, 86, 100, 466
psychoanalytic view of, 73
psychosexual, 4, 73, 79, 466
psychosocial, 4, 73, 83
social, 73, 78
stages of, 74, 83–85, 98, 99, 102, 145, 170
women's, 345, 350, 351
Developmental perspective, 81, 97, 102
on structural problems, 443
Developmental task, 73, 74, 76, 97, 99
Diagnosis, 43, 54, 170, 181, 230, 278, 360,
475
and assessment, 53, 54
BASIC I.D., 280
commentary on, 53–54
cultural implications of, 53
differential, 119
DSM–IV, 53
erroneous, 53
forming, 180
implications of assigning, 360
psychological, 177
purpose of, 52
role of, in counseling, 52–54
and testing, 475
Diagnostic procedures, 52, 53, 170
Dialogic attitude, 206, 355
Dialogic encounter, 162
Dialogic system, 430
Dialogue, 5, 206, 213, 216, 513
between client and therapist, 196, 221,
355
exercise, 213
internal, 319, 321, 329, 331, 433, 446,
497, 506, 507
I/Thou, 203, 475
social-constructionist, 430
Didactic therapy, 475
Differentiation, 100, 201, 384, 392, 399, 400,
428, 447, 467
Direction, 164, 170, 240–241, 329, 480
Directive approaches, 184
Directives, 242, 424, 425, 426, 480, 501
issuing, 420, 476
outcomes of, 426
paradoxical, 425
therapist's, 423
use of, 425
Directive structure, 470
Directive therapy, 475, 476
Disclosure, 123, 396
Adlerian, 123
client, 49
counselor, 30
excessive, 30

self-, 16, 18
therapist, 30
uncensored, 157
Discouragement, 114, 118, 124, 125
Discrimination, 27, 43, 164, 250, 255, 301,
373, 374, 479
Disengagement, 418
Disentanglement, 414
Disorders:
behavioral, 8
cause of, 467
neurotic, 71
severe and multifaceted, 270
specific, treatment for, 100
Displacement, definition, 72
Disputations, 332
Disputing, 300, 301, 305
Disturbances, 269, 271
A-B-C approach to changing, 309
cognitive hypothesis of, 303
emotional and behavioral, 300, 303, 464
Diversity, 25, 26, 28, 341, 346, 369, 431, 437
Divorce, 12, 21, 22, 23, 374
Dogmas, irrational, 299
Dogmatic beliefs, 173, 469
Doing, 10, 149, 297, 496, 509
component of therapy, 509–512
role of, 464
Domestic violence, 352, 371, 483
Dominant culture,
narratives, 431
processes and imperatives, exploration of,
437
Dominant group, 343, 349
Dream analysis, 92, 93, 98, 101, 475
Dream content, of depressed clients, 310
Dreams, 70, 76, 82, 83, 88, 93, 216, 248, 304,
482, 484, 495
analyzing, 180, 247
Gestalt approach to, 215–216, 220
meaning of, 67, 94, 215
purpose of, 82
therapeutic value of, 247
Dream work, 93, 329
Drives, 172
aggressive, 69
biological, 68
Freudian emphasis on, 100
instinctual, 68
irrational, 143
Drug abuse, 296, 513
Drugs, 11, 277, 281
Drugs/biology, 279, 281
DSM–IV, 53, 230, 248, 359, 360, 388
Dual relationships, 43, 55, 56
in counseling practice, 55–57
examples of, 55
nonsexual, 57
working through, 57
Duty to report, 48
Dyad, conflictual, 401
Dyads, and triads, 446
Dying, fear of, 495

Dysfunction:
  family, 387, 424
  marital, 424
  systemic, 422
Dysfunctional behavior:
  changing, 317
  social factors, 359
Dysfunctional beliefs, 9, 301, 313, 327, 507
Dysfunctional patterns, 387, 390, 403, 407,
    411, 420
Dysfunctional rules, 409

Early childhood, 77, 97, 99, 134, 464, 484, 495
Early decisions, 406, 505, 512
Early development:
  influence of, 100
  patterns of, hypothesis about, 101
Early recollections, 115, 120, 125, 127, 128,
    129, 475, 505
  clinical use of, 131
Eating disorders, 296, 305, 345, 352, 360
Eclectic approach, 3, 486
Eclectic orientation, 468
Eclectic practitioners, 468
Eclectic therapeutic practice, 482
Eclecticism, 277, 420, 458
Education, 26, 43, 126, 171, 244, 372, 394,
    477, 484
Educational methods, 325, 424
Educational model, 329, 391
Egalitarianism, 184, 473
Egalitarian spirit, 479
Ego, 69, 71, 79, 93, 100, 466, 475
  defenses, 71–73, 98, 330, 478, 481
  integrity, 76, 80, 102
  psychology, 74, 83
  strength, 13, 101, 483
Elderly, 50, 80
Electra complex, 75, 78, 101
Emotional disturbance, cognitive behavior
    therapy, view of, 299–300
Emotional system, nuclear family, 399, 402
Emotions, 116, 131, 317
  associated with traumatic event, 271
  distressing, 318
  expressing, 364, 461
  painful, 317
  role of, 331
Emotive techniques, 306–307, 476, 482, 512
Empathy, 6, 34, 178, 179, 184, 237, 284, 415,
    429, 445, 472
Empowerment, 357, 358, 369, 371, 435, 473,
    478, 480
  of client, 359
  of individual, 346
  in oppressive society, 478
  of women, 344, 345, 427
Empty-chair, 277
  dialogue, 355, 366
  experiment, 367
  technique, 213
Enactments, 413, 415, 420, 421, 424, 476

Encounter, 208
  authentic, 472
  existential, 203, 482
  genuine, 159
  groups, 169, 171, 187
  here-and-now, 472
  I/Thou, 157
  personal, 472
  person-to-person, 156
  therapeutic, 15, 195
Encouragement, 114, 116, 118, 124, 131, 125,
    126, 398, 466, 469, 475
Energy, 237, 466
  blocks to, 202, 517
  client's, 517
  personal, 39
  sexual, 68, 69, 72, 75
Engagement, 151, 196, 203, 414
Enmeshment, 418
Environment, 109
  counseling, 238–239, 247
  external, 480
  knowledge of, 195
  oppressive, 103
  product and producer of, 464
  social, 4
Environmental forces, 250, 373
  pathological, 352
Equality, 345, 372, 472
  core values of, 374
  gender, 4
  in relationships, 368–369
  sense of, 114
  striving for, 484
  for women, 134
Ethical decisions, 43, 45, 46–47
Ethical dilemmas, 46, 47, 54, 48
Ethical issue, 19, 22, 43, 44, 47, 48, 52, 55,
    221, 273, 284
  in assessment process, 52–55
  in counseling practice, 42–59
  in multicultural perspective, 50–52
Ethical practice, 25, 45, 50, 57–58, 222, 284,
    488
Ethical principles, 43, 46
Ethics, 359
  aspirational, 45
  codes of, 45, 46, 47, 48, 55–56, 57, 371
  mandatory, 45
Ethnic diversity, 287, 288
Ethnic groups, 132, 479, 483
Ethnic identity:
  retaining, 479
  and values, retaining, 249
Ethnicity, 26, 28, 287, 446
Ethnic minority clients, 53, 102, 103, 164,
    188, 249, 250, 373
Ethnocentric theories, 347
Evaluation, 53, 240, 241, 257, 278
  of the client, 271
  empirical, 256
  external locus of, 188

internal locus of, 170, 188
of life circumstances, 287
objective, 466
process of, 311
self-, 15
techniques, 482
Exaggeration exercise, 215, 425
Exception questions, 434, 435
Exercises, 209, 277
assertiveness-training, 281
relaxation, 6
shame-attacking, 307–308
Existence:
inauthentic mode of, 147
meaningful, 196
paradoxes of, 152
present, 155
purposeful, 158
restricted, 148
significance of, 145
Existential anxiety, 146, 152, 159
Existential approach, 3, 93, 51, 141, 143,
145, 157, 164, 172, 328, 498
contributions of, 160
limitations and criticisms of, 162–163, 164
strength of, 163
Existential counseling, 143, 156
final phase of, 158
middle phase of, 157
Existential encounter, 203
Existential guilt, 147, 151
Existentialism, 144
Existentialism and humanism, 171
Existential isolation, 145
Existential neurosis, of modern life, 151
Existential orientation, 54, 153, 155, 161,
412, 465
Existential/phenomenological approach, 195
Existential philosophy, 141, 144, 151, 196
Existential psychodynamics, 145
Existential psychotherapy, 145
Existential questions, 144, 150
Existential themes, 145
Existential therapists, 143, 144, 145, 148,
149, 151, 153, 156, 164, 356
Existential therapy, 8, 51, 109, 140–167, 171,
265, 415
aim of, 152
applied to case of Stan, 157–159, 495
basic philosophies, 464
contributions of, 481
contributions to multicultural counseling,
478
goals of therapy, 154, 469
historical background of, 143–145
key concepts of, 145–157, 466
limitations of, 483
limitations in multicultural counseling,
480
from a multicultural perspective, 163–164
process or outcomes of, 162
task of, 154

techniques and procedures, therapeutic,
157–158
therapeutic relationship, 472
therapist's function and role, 154–155
Existential thinking, 144, 171
Existential vacuum, 144, 151
Expectations, 27, 32, 115, 123, 148, 499
client's, 24, 471
gender-role, 361, 365
imposing, 27
of others, 215
role, 30
self-defeating, 509
societal, 161, 188, 361, 363, 367
unrealistic, 30
Experiential approach, 219, 464
Experiential family therapists, 413
Experiential family therapy, 385, 412–415
goals, 413
techniques, 414
therapist's function and role, 413–414
Experiential/symbolic approach, 391, 412
Experiential/symbolic family therapy,
392–393
Experiential techniques, 476
Experiential therapies, 8, 9, 52, 265, 331,
443, 444, 466, 502
Experiments, 195, 208, 209, 210, 213, 220,
221, 324, 415, 475, 478, 500, 512
controlled laboratory, 485
with ethnic minority clients, 223
Gestalt, 210, 211, 220, 222
groundwork for, 355
Exposure therapies, 266, 267, 269, 272
Exposure therapy, prolonged/intense, 270
Extended families, 120, 479
fusion to, 403
networking with, 446
three-generational, 403
value of, 446, 479
work with, 429
Eye movement desensitization and reprocessing (EMDR), 266, 270–273, 475
as applied to Adlerian theory, 273
studies, 272–273
training in, 273

Faith, 12, 118, 156, 169
Familial patterns, over many generations,
441
Family, 8, 10, 49, 111, 396, 423, 424, 443, 465
atmosphere, 120, 127, 394, 397
characteristics of, 403
development and interactions of, 113, 394
dynamics within, 134
dysfunctional, 407
functional, 394
extended, 120
importance of, 478
men in, 427
organization of, 444
role of, 130, 132, 399

Family *(continued)*
  structure and dynamics within, 133, 421, 423
  violent, 417
Family constellation, 112, 114, 119, 120, 127, 129, 387, 391, 394, 395, 397, 403, 475, 495, 505
Family counseling, 390, 477
  Adlerian approach to, 127, 396
  open forum, 397, 398
Family diagram, 403
Family dynamics, 113, 389, 478
  of previous generation, 400
Family-in-focus, 394, 397
Family life, 171, 405–406
  life-fact chronologies, 405, 410, 411
  three generations of, 405, 411
Family mapping, 387, 395, 405, 410, 411, 420, 421, 476
Family members:
  contact among, 403
  extended, 395
  functioning of, 399
  interaction with, 387–388
  liberating, 412
  mutual influence between, 387–388
  proximity of, 403
Family of origin, 392, 401, 439, 441, 443
  assessment of, 439
  dynamics, 467
  exploring, 483
  importance of, 447
  issues, 484
  map of, 439
  self-differentiation from, 404
  understanding, 403
Family-projection process, 399, 402
Family reconstruction, 387, 411
Family roles, 408
Family rules, 388, 389, 405
Family schemata, 317, 318
Family sculpting, 410, 411, 476
Family structure, 416
  correcting, 420
  dysfunctional, 406
  functional, 406
Family subsystems, 416, 417
Family systems approaches,
  contributions to, 445
  limitations and criticisms of, 446
Family systems model, multigenerational, 391
Family systems perspective, 371, 387–388
Family systems theory, 98, 384–386, 399
  key concepts, 467
Family systems therapy, 4, 8, 10, 52, 126, 309, 382–453, 476, 477, 478
  action-oriented, 443
  Adlerian, 127, 391–394
  application to, 317–318
  applied to case of Stan, 439–442, 497
  Bowenian, 422–423
  brief, 422

comparative analysis of, 439
conjoint, 384
contributions of, 483
contributions to multicultural counseling, 479
experiential, 385
focus of, 443–444
goals of, 390, 391, 396, 408, 409, 413, 444, 469
integration of, 438–439
key concepts, 391, 394, 467
limitations in multicultural counseling, 480
limitations of, 484
from multicultural perspective, 446–448
multigenerational, 392–393, 399–404
North American, 430
short-term, 443
social construction, comparison of four approaches to, 435
social constructionism, 427–438
solution-focused, 443
summary and evaluation, 443–446
techniques, 391, 397, 445
theory and practice of, 391, 445
therapeutic relationship, 473
therapist's function and role, 391, 396–397
Whitaker's approach to, 412
Family therapists, 4, 390, 396, 473
  Adlerian, 395, 396, 397
  effective, 401
Family therapy, experiential/symbolic, 392–393
  goals, 392–393
  key figures, 392–393
  process of change, 392–393
  role and function of therapist, 392–393
  techniques and innovations, 392–393
Family therapy, strategic, 386, 392–393
  key figures, 392–393
  process of change, 392–393
  role and function of therapist, 392–393
  techniques and innovations, 392–393
  therapy goals, 392–393
  time focus, 392–393
Family therapy, structural, 385, 386, 392–393
  key figures, 392–393
  process of change, 392–393
  role and function of therapist, 392–393
  techniques and innovations, 392–393
  therapy goals, 392–393
  time focus, 392–393
Family triads, 408
Family values, 120, 394
Fantasies, 92, 414, 426, 512
Faulty assumptions, 310, 467, 472, 509
  and beliefs, undermining, 327
Faulty beliefs, 324, 469, 473, 507, 512
  confronting, 312, 476
  objective bases of, 322
  origin of, 507

Faulty lifestyles, 126
Faulty thinking, 274, 279, 310, 329, 464, 482, 497, 506, 507
Fears, 11, 29, 71, 73, 76, 93, 114, 182, 145, 364, 405, 515
Feedback, 127, 207, 265, 281, 324, 329, 446
Feelings, 4, 10, 12, 19, 20, 70, 88, 89, 130, 198, 199, 209, 232, 245, 278, 301, 464, 496, 500, 501, 502, 505, 516, 517
    ambivalent, 29, 133, 279, 475
    denied to awareness, 464
    experiencing and expressing, 286, 304, 444, 466, 478, 501–504
    of hopelessness, 39
    identifying, 249, 479, 500–501, 504, 506, 512
    incestuous, 78, 98
    past, 217
    of powerlessness, 39
    reflection of, 179, 475
    sexual, 67, 73
    suicidal, 13
Female development, Freudian view of, 78
Female roles, traditional, 344, 368
Femininity, redefining, 364
Feminism:
    cultural, 345
    liberal, 345
    radical, 345
    socialist, 345
Feminist cognitive behavior therapy, 356
Feminist consciousness, 352, 368
Feminist couples therapy, 370
Feminist family therapy, 345
Feminist group therapy, 345
Feminist movement, contribution of, 371
Feminist personality theory, development of, 345
Feminist perspective, 53, 101, 343, 346
Feminist philosophies, 345
    philosophies underlying, 369
    themes and premises underlying, 346
Feminist psychoanalysis, 345
Feminist psychology, principles of, 351
Feminist researchers, 350
Feminists, 421, 446
    cultural, 346
    liberal, 345
    radical, 346
    socialist, 346
Feminist theories, 341, 342, 352
    classic, 346
    constructs of, 347
    diversity of, 341
    relationship of, to traditional psychotherapy systems, 345
Feminist therapists, 4, 51, 164, 343, 352, 354, 358, 369, 370
    challenge for, 346
    contemporary, 341–342
    Gestalt-oriented, 355
    psychodynamically oriented, 355
    role of, 356

Feminist therapy groups, 344
Feminist therapy, 4, 8, 10, 52, 340–381, 431, 465, 499
    adjunct to individual, 363
    applied to case of Stan, 364–368, 497
    contributions of, 369–371, 483
    contributions to multicultural counseling, 479
    criticisms of, 372
    definition of, 346
    goal of, 351, 352, 353–354, 357, 469
    history and development, 344–346, 368
    key concepts, 347–353, 467
    limitations and criticisms, 371–373, 484
    limitations in multicultural counseling, 480
    from a multicultural perspective, 342, 373–375
    philosophies, 465
    principles and techniques, 54, 344, 355, 356, 368, 369, 373
    role of men in, 364
    strength of, 371
    summary and evaluation, 368–373
    theories of, 352
    therapeutic process, 353–359
    therapeutic relationship, 473
    therapeutic techniques and procedures, 359–364
    therapist's function and role, 354–356
Fictional finalism, 110
Field theory, 196, 197
Figure-formation process, 196, 197, 209, 220, 466
Filial piety, 447
Flooding, 269, 272, 475
    imaginal, 270
    in vivo, 269
Frame of reference, 313
    client's subjective, 109
    experiential, 18
    internal, 170, 173, 181
Free association, 70, 88, 92, 93, 96, 101, 215, 304, 329, 472, 475
Freedom, 8, 9, 75, 143, 144, 145, 147, 149, 152, 154, 156, 159, 160, 171, 176, 250, 259, 372, 406, 412, 469, 480, 495
    to act, 153
    avoiding, 147
    awareness of, 159
    to choose, 4, 143, 464
    consciousness of, 146
    emphasis on, 160
    escape from, 153
    to explore, 175
    to play, 87
    possibilities for, 145–146
    and responsibility, 142, 145, 147
    spiritual, 141
    to work, 87
Freudian position, orthodox, 99
Freudian revisionists, 108
Freudian theory, 78, 97

Freudian view, of phallic stage, 77
Full acceptance, REBT's concept of, 304
Fusion, 84, 404
Future, 17, 74, 110, 128, 130, 392, 466
    dealing with, 505
    planning for, 146

Gay, clients, 23
Gay men, 431
Gender, 17, 26, 28, 134, 343, 417
    awareness, 428
    biases, 356, 360, 364
    consideration, in feminist therapy, 352
    differences, biological, 347
    equity, 4, 356, 467
    focus on, 369
    identity, development of, 355
    inequalities, 362
    issues, 134, 346
    perspectives, 389
    politics, 348
    role socialization, 4, 10, 364
    schema theory, 349, 351
    stereotypes, 350, 351, 356, 370, 483
    society's view of, 349
Gender-based oppression, 342
Gender-biased concepts, 465
Gender-biased practices of being, 465
Gendercentric theories, 347
Gender-fair counseling, principles for, 369
Gender-fair principles, 369
Gender-free criteria, 355
Gender-free theories, 347
Gender-role:
    analysis, 360, 361, 365, 369, 476, 497
    bias, elimination of, 370
    expectations, 348, 351, 353, 361, 365
    identity, 75
    intervention, 361, 365, 369
    introjects, 355
    messages, 353, 355, 362, 365
    socialization, 353, 356, 357, 360, 366, 370, 469, 476
    stereotypes, 357, 362
Gender-sensitive practice, 369, 483
Gender-sensitive principles, 369
Generativity, 76, 80
Genital stage, 75, 76, 79, 97
Genograms, 388, 395, 403, 405, 410, 421, 438, 439, 476
    Adlerian model, 395
Genuineness, 15, 172, 177, 181, 185, 284, 354, 472
Geriatrics, 477
Gestalt approach, 297, 328, 498
Gestalt therapist, 200
    concepts essential to, 436
    concern of, 201
    role of, 219
Gestalt therapy, 8, 9, 51, 109, 171, 192–227, 331, 343, 355, 356, 415, 459
    application: therapeutic techniques and procedures, 208–217

applied to case of Stan, 217–219, 496
basic assumption of, 196
collaborative model of, 355
contemporary, 196, 212, 220, 221, 355, 481
contributions to multicultural counseling, 478
dialogic model of, 355
experiment in, 208–209, 210, 211, 220, 222, 223, 480, 501
goal of, 202–203, 213, 469
interventions, 220
key concepts, 195–202, 355, 466
limitations and criticisms of, 220–222, 484
limitations in multicultural counseling, 480
from a multicultural perspective, 222–223
philosophies, 464
principles underlying, 196
summary and evaluation of, 219–222
techniques of, 213–217
therapeutic process, 202
therapeutic relationship, 472
Gestalt therapy theory, principles of, 196–197
Goal disclosure, 396, 398
    with children, 398
    purposes, 123
Goals, 4, 8, 9, 23, 25, 27, 75, 101, 114, 116, 121, 123, 130, 131, 152, 174, 277, 298, 302, 310, 323, 368, 395, 462, 466, 478, 495, 499, 505
    in Adlerian therapy, 113–114
    advantages and disadvantages of, 262
    alignment of, 117
    and aspirations, 344
    in behavior therapy, 261–263
    of cognitive behavior therapy, 301–302
    of counseling, 24, 116, 128, 172
    determining, 262
    developing, 496
    establishing, 86
    of existential therapy, 153–154
    exploring, 128
    of feminist therapy, 353–354
    formulating, 262, 500
    fictional, 110
    general, 24, 35, 262, 281, 470
    of Gestalt therapy, 202–203
    identification, 282, 397, 495
    interactive, focus on, 127
    of Jungian analytical therapy, 97
    mistaken, 114, 395–396, 472
    mutually agreed-on, 131, 472, 479
    outcome, identifying and evaluating, 271
    perfectionistic, 95, 316
    personal, 24, 75, 111, 146
    of person-centered therapy, 174
    of psychoanalytic therapy, 87
    purpose of, 262
    rationale for, 262
    in reality therapy and choice theory, 235–236

recognition, 395, 396
search for, 145
setting, 24, 86, 355
societal, 262
specific, 470, 499
striving for, 111, 464
of therapy, 37, 160, 262, 284, 345, 346, 499
of treatment, specifying, 466
Group counseling, 126, 476, 477, 478
Group experience, 517
Group psychotherapy, 127
Groups, 171
advocacy, 363
assertion training, 274
battering, 364
characteristics of, 127
encounter, 169, 171, 187
rationale for, 127
self-help, 363
therapeutic, 516
women's, 363
Group supervision, 49
Group therapy, 127, 309, 476
psychodynamic, 101
Group work, 363, 476
Adlerian therapy, application to, 127–128
Growth, 5, 15, 34, 69, 144, 154, 174, 183, 195, 412, 469
and actualization, tendency toward, 299
conditions for fostering, 172
emotional, 95
focus on, 220
personal, 17, 125, 161, 196
psychosexual, 73
psychosocial, 73
self-directed, 170
stages of, 74
therapeutic, 173
Growth and development, views of, 97
Growth model, 8, 126, 476
Guilt, 75, 78, 95, 146, 151, 155, 158, 160, 182, 316
coping with, 477
existential, 147, 151
feelings of, 515
healthy and unhealthy, 462
sense of, 513
understanding of, 160, 482

Health care, 171, 259
Helpers, ineffective, 41
Helping process, Eurocentric, male construction of, 343
Helplessness, 18, 155, 175, 306, 405
Here-and-now:
experiences, 195, 204, 303
focus on, 392, 464, 466, 473
framework, 203
interaction, 412
Heredity, 109
rejection of, in determining behavior, 132

Heritage:
cultural, 26, 27
ethnic, 26
racial, 26, 27
Heterosexism, 347, 360
Hierarchy, 386, 416, 419, 420, 422, 423, 444
History, 99
clients', 304, 462
current, 443
early, 98, 119, 303, 443, 504
life, 505
personal, 402
social, 119
three-generation, 410
HIV-positive, 23
Homeostasis, pressure for, 415
Homework, 4, 6, 86, 127, 130, 206, 261, 268, 303, 305, 306, 308, 312, 314, 322, 324, 325, 326, 327, 356, 366, 425, 470, 476, 497, 502, 504, 506, 510, 512
action-oriented, 482
cognitive, 305
role of, 297
Homophobic, 431
Homosexual couples, 422
Homosexuality, 23
Honesty, 31, 156, 471
achieving, 87
emotional, 410
Hope, 437
ultimate, enactment of, 437
Hopelessness, 39
Human behavior, 50, 67, 99, 109, 110, 145, 259, 260
Human condition, 9, 149, 151, 466
basic, 145, 153
complete view of, 481
nature of, 464
Human development, 81
eight stages of, 97
Human existence, 160, 437
conditions of, 8
meanings in, 298
nature of, 157
Human experience, 8, 145
cognitive, affective, and behavioral dimensions, 517
interrelated facets of, 518
nature of, 142
understanding, 143
Human growth, 146
and development, models of, 348
Humanism, and existentialism, 171
Humanistically oriented communications model of therapy, 444
Humanistic approach, third force, 387
Humanistic orientation, 173, 412
Humanistic philosophy, 9, 171, 172
Humanistic psychology, 169, 170
Humanistic therapies, 282, 285, 371
Humanists, 171, 436
Human nature:
assumptions about, 145

Human nature *(continued)*
   behavior therapy view of, 259–260
   cognitive behavior therapy view of, 299
   conception of, 195, 196
   constructive side of, 173
   deterministic view of, 143
   environmental view of, 259
   existential view of, 145
   feminist therapy view of, 347–348
   Freudian view of, 68
   Gestalt view of, 195–196
   person-centered therapy, view of, 172–173
   philosophy of, 8, 68, 183
   positive view of, 173, 237
   reality therapy and choice theory, view of, 231–235
   Roger's view of, 183
   view of, 68–69, 463
   social-psychological view of, 108
   teleological (or goal-oriented) view of, 108
Human personality, 81, 110
Human validation process model, 384, 391, 392–393, 404–412
   goals, 392–393, 408–409
   key concepts, 405–408
   key figures, 392–393
   process of change, 392–393
   techniques and innovations, 392–393, 410–411
   therapist's function and role, 392–393, 409–410
   time focus, 392–393
Humor, 35, 125, 302, 317, 325, 410, 426
   overuse of, 201
   sense of, 35, 471
   use of, 16, 306
Hypnosis, 266, 277, 422

Id, 69, 70, 71, 79, 466
Id psychology, 73
Identification, 72, 78, 348
Identified patient, 445
Identity, 16, 75, 80, 99, 102, 142, 145, 148, 149
   confusion, 80
   development, 8, 27, 344, 351
   gender-role, 75
   lack of, 85
   sense of, 34, 161
   striving for, 148–150
   struggle for, in adolescence, 161
   struggling with, 149–150
   versus role confusion, 75
   women's, 349
Imagery, 278, 280, 319, 476, 512
   guided, 272
   positive, 277
   rational-emotive, 306, 307
Images, 69, 267, 277, 278
Imaginal desensitization procedures, 269
Imaginal flooding, 270
Imitation, 263, 466
Impulses, 70, 72, 214, 414, 464
Inauthenticity, 147, 154, 208

Incest, 345, 483
   implications of, 371
   victim of, 49
Inclusion, theory of, 341
Incongruence, 175, 176, 178, 212
Independence, 26, 36, 84, 85, 141, 174, 348, 400, 414, 418, 447, 480
Individual and family therapy, 342
Individual and system approaches, 388–391
Individual counseling, 476, 477
Individualism, ethos of rugged, 212
Individuality, 85, 480
   core values of, 374
Individual Psychology, 107, 112, 126, 130, 132, 273
   Adlerian, 110
   basic assumption of, 110
Individual therapy, 345, 476, 478
Individuation, 83–84, 96, 400, 419
Indulgence therapy, 304
Industry, 75, 79, 171
Inequality, 353, 362, 373, 431
Infancy, 74, 97
Infantile conflicts, 90
Infantile stage, 84
Infantile strivings, 89
Inferences, 315
   arbitrary, 316
   cognitive, 317
   incorrect, 310
Inferiority, 75, 110
   complex, 13
   coping with, 110
   feelings of, 107, 127, 128, 131
   and industry, 79
   sense of, 109
Influences, 110, 403, 426, 445, 464
   cultural and social, 83
   social and political, 287
   social, 74
Informed choice, 360, 363
Informed consent, 35, 48, 57, 58, 352, 362
   document, 48
   process of, 47
   right of, 47–48
Informed decisions, 270
Initiative, 75, 78
   lack of, 349
   versus guilt, 75
Injunctions, 217
   cultural, 210, 223, 389
   societal, 360
Injustice, social, 51
Inner dialogue, 321, 329
Insight, 4, 7, 32, 51, 67, 70, 86, 87, 88, 91, 92, 93, 94, 95, 123, 124, 125, 130, 155, 158, 162, 170, 195, 215, 247, 285, 303, 312, 324, 354, 361, 419, 423, 460, 472, 473, 475, 479, 484, 495, 513
Insight-focused therapy, 309
Instincts, 68, 69, 71, 73
   death, 69
   life, 68, 69

Instinctual drives, 68
Instinctual factors, 483
Institutionalized sexism, 353
Intake, 11, 24, 117, 430, 462
Integrated perspective, 457, 458, 487
Integration, 8, 83, 97, 457, 469
    in Adlerian therapy, 122
    and application, 455–519
    emphasis on, 197
    of feelings, 176
    of individual and systemic frameworks,
        446
    of learning, 484
    movement toward, 457
    multicultural issues, 460–461
    pathways to achieving, 458
    between polarities and conflicts, 214
    psychotherapy, 458
    spiritual/religious issues, 461–463
    theoretical, 459
    trend toward, 391, 438
Integrative counseling and psychotherapy,
    457
Integrative perspective, 7, 297, 438, 439, 445,
    456–492, 494
    Adlerian therapy, 475
    applied to Stan, 493–519
    behavior therapy, 475
    client's experience in therapy, 470–471
    cognitive behavior therapy, 476
    developing an, 459, 463–468
    existential therapy, 475
    family systems therapy, 476
    feminist therapy, 476
    Gestalt therapy, 475
    goals, 468–470
    personal, 465
    person-centered therapy, 475
    psychoanalytic therapy, 475
    reality therapy, 475
    summary, 487–488
    techniques and evaluation, 474–484
    therapeutic process, issues related to,
        468–474
Integrative psychotherapy, 328
    concerns about delineating, 460
Integrative treatments, 460
Integrity, 76, 156
    maintaining, 161
    versus despair, 76, 80
Interactional patterns, 390, 391, 392, 430,
    445, 467
    family, 392, 397, 416
    identifying and exploring, 483
Interactional sequences, 444
Interactional unit, of the family, 443
Interactionist criteria, 355
Interactionist theories, 347
Intergenerational family therapy, 385, 399,
    447
Internal dialogue, 213, 319, 326, 331, 467
International relations, 171
Interns, counseling, 29, 31, 49

Interpersonal therapy, 488
Interpretations, 87, 88, 89, 92, 93, 94, 95, 98,
    109, 123, 124, 129, 131, 133, 170, 180,
    298, 305, 394, 395, 414, 423, 443, 475,
    472, 507
    Adlerian, 123
    alternative, 312, 476
    ill-timed, 88
    imposing, 322
Interpretive stories, 431
Interpsychic dimensions, 4
Interventions, 6, 19, 20, 24, 25, 27, 157, 160,
    213, 266, 272, 362, 365, 369, 403, 447,
    471
    behavioral, 288, 321
    with clients, 157
    confrontational, 6
    congruent, 25
    counseling, 86
    culturally appropriate, 359
    feminist, 421
    framework for, 471
    gender-role, 361
    Gestalt, 220
    medical, 119
    methods of, 329
    overt and covert, 424
    self-management, 275
    strategic, 386, 423–424, 425, 529
    supportive, 6
    techniques for, 410
    theory-based, 34, 430
    therapeutic, 185, 363, 414
    therapist-controlled, 430
Interview process, 11, 41, 118, 119, 122, 123,
    391, 398, 429, 479
Intimacy, 76, 80, 99, 142, 413
    achieving, 112
    capacity for, 364
    versus isolation, 76, 80
Intrapsychic analysis, 103
Intrapsychic conflicts, 73, 74, 83, 195, 286
Intrapsychic domain, exploring the, 372
Intrapsychic dynamics, 479
Intrapsychic factors, 352
Intrapsychic frameworks, traditional, 387
Intrapsychic orientation, 347
Intrapsychic psychopathology perspective,
    344–345
Introjection, 200–201, 213, 355
    definition, 72
    of parents, 148
    of parent substitutes, 148–149
    positive forms of, 72
    toxic, 213
In vivo desensitization, 269
In vivo exposure, 270
In vivo flooding, 269
Irrational beliefs, 300, 301, 302, 303, 305,
    306, 307, 308, 312, 313, 318, 506, 507
Isolation, 76, 143, 145, 146, 149, 156, 159,
    480
    existential, 145

Isolation (continued)
  feelings of, 159
  sense of, 149
  understanding, 482
  versus intimacy, 80

Joining, 415, 420, 424, 439
  the family, 476
Judgment, 21, 46, 131, 436

Labeling and mislabeling, 311, 508, 509
Language, 249, 306, 355, 428, 430, 436, 446
  awareness of, 92
  barrier, with bilingual clients, 478
  body, 215
  that denies power, 204
  emotionally respectful, 446
  focusing on, 204
  global and impersonal, 204
  listening for, 205
  nonverbal, 204
  processes, 429
  shift in, 432
  of therapy, 446
Language patterns, 306, 476
  effects of, 204
  and personality, relationship between, 204
Latency stage, 75, 79, 97
Latent content, of dreams, 93
Later life, 76, 80, 97
Latinos, 51, 53, 447
Laughter, 35
Learning, 4, 8, 221, 464, 477
  conditions for, 261
  emphasis on, 257
  experiential, 209
  faulty, 466
  lifelong, 231
  observational, 256
  principles of, 8
  stages of, 29
Learning theory, 256, 266, 297
Legal rights, 27
Lesbians, 23, 431
Liberal feminists, 345
Liberal philosophy, 369
Libido:
  definition of, 68–69
  loss of, 316
Life:
  and death, 152
  goals, 75, 131, 395, 466
  narrative, 435
  skills, 359
  span, 73, 74
  stages, 81, 97
  tasks, 112, 115, 116, 119, 127, 464
Life-cycle development, gender or family, 389
Life-fact chronologies, 405, 410, 411
Life-history data, gathering, 475
Lifelong learning, 231
Life-span-oriented criteria, 355
Life-span perspective, 347

Lifestyle assessment, 115, 128, 129, 495
Linguistic approach, 430–431
  key figures, 435
  process of change, 435
  role and function of therapist, 435
  techniques and innovations, 435
  therapy goals, 435
Listening, 92, 118, 127, 177, 179
  active, 119, 284, 475, 478
  empathic, 119, 501
  for language that uncovers a story, 205
  nonjudgmental, 169
Locus of control, internal, 354
Logical errors, 296, 301, 310
Loneliness, 18, 146, 148, 159
  and isolation, 182
  understanding of, 160
Long-term treatment, 479
Loss, 161
Love, 163, 231, 236, 250
  versus hate, 89
Love object, 78

Magnification and minimization, 311, 315
Maintaining the symptom, 425
Making the rounds, 214
Maladaptive behaviors, 326
Maladjustment, 173, 466
  symptom of individual's, 387
Male authority, reinforcing, 421
Male client, in therapy, experiences of, 357
Male domination, in society, 355
Malpractice, 45, 46
Managed care, 100, 101, 360, 485, 488
  philosophy of, 101
  environment, 329
Managed care therapy, short-term, 102
Mandatory ethics, definition, 45
Manifest content, 205
  of dreams, 93
Marital and family therapy, 130, 438, 477
Marital therapy, 476, 477
  Adlerian, 126
Marriage conferences, 127
Marriage counseling, 127
  Adlerian therapy application to, 126–127
Masculinity, redefining, 364
Maturity, 79
  professional, 47
  psychological, 199
Meaning and purpose, searching for, 141
Meaning, 8, 9, 75, 82, 109, 128, 144, 145,
  146, 151, 158, 159, 171, 206, 357, 412,
  414, 431, 436, 438, 468, 478, 495, 513
Meaninglessness, 143, 144, 145, 146,
  150–151
Mechanistic approach, 482
Mediational concepts, 258
Medical history, 119
Medical intervention, 119
Medical model of therapy, 126, 143, 466, 482
Meditation, 266, 272, 277
Memories, 67, 70, 96

dysfunctional, 271
earliest, 120
early, 119
exploring, 86
recalling, 86
traumatic, 271
Mental disorders, feminist therapy perspectives on, 360
Mental health, 50, 126, 354, 466
  and mental illness, White male definition of, 343
  medical model of, 360
  movement, 131
  programs, community-based, 429
  providers, 43, 49, 126, 180, 485
  services, 27, 51, 429
Mental illness, 231
  definition, 352, 467
  disease model of, 352
  impact of, 428
  stigma of, 479
Messages:
  gender-role, 362, 365
  identifying, 357
  nonverbal, 27, 118
  verbal and nonverbal, 27, 118, 501
Metaphors, 205, 237, 427
Middle age, 76, 80, 81, 97, 161
Middle childhood, tasks of, 79
Mid-life crisis, Jung, 81
Mid-life period, tasks, 81
Minimizations, 515
Minority:
  ethnic, 53, 164
  groups, 50–51, 478
  racial, 164
  treatment of, 27
  women, 373
  youth, 102
Miracle question, 434, 435
Miracle solutions, search for, 437
Mistaken behaviors, 396
Mistaken beliefs, 130
Mistaken concepts, 127
Mistaken goals, 391, 392, 396
  an interactional view, 395–396
Mistaken interactions, 398
Mistaken notions, 427
Modeling, 277, 281, 304, 306, 308, 325, 362, 371, 497
Models:
  positive, 41
  synthesis among, 465
Modernist perspective, 428
Modernists, 428
Moment-by-moment experiencing, 355, 414, 469
Moment-to-moment contacting process, 209
Moral anxiety, definition, 71
Moral development, deficit in, 348
Mother-blaming, cycle of, 370
Mother, dependency on, 84
Mother/infant partnership, 90–91

Motivational model, Freud's, 296
Motivation modification, 396
  focus on, 126
Motivations, 7, 15, 17, 47, 68, 69, 70, 89, 92, 93, 110, 114, 123, 128, 146, 151, 396
Multicultural approaches, 134, 373
Multicultural awareness, 29
Multicultural competence, 29
Multicultural counseling, 27, 288, 473
  Adlerian therapy, contributions to, 132–134
  advantages in, 331
  competencies in, 26–27
  contributions to, 163–164, 187, 249, 286–287, 331–332, 373–374, 446–447
  effective, 25–29
  limitations for, 134–135, 187
  theory of, 50
Multicultural counselor, 25–29
Multicultural experiences, 187, 249
Multicultural feminist therapy, 342
Multiculturalism, 134, 460
Multicultural issues, in psychology, 342
Multicultural movement, 479
Multicultural perspective, 29, 50, 343, 371, 446–448
  Adlerian therapy, 132–134
  behavior therapy, 286–288
  of cognitive behavior therapy, 331–333
  ethical issues in, 50–52
  existential therapy, 163–164
  feminist therapy, 373–375
  Gestalt therapy, 222–223
  person-centered therapy, 187–188
  psychoanalytic therapy, 102–103
  reality therapy, 249
Multicultural theory, of counseling and therapy, 50, 460
Multi-generational family therapy, 391, 392–393, 399–404
  goals, 392–393, 401–403
  key concepts, 399
  key figures, 392–393
  process of change, 392–393
  role and function of therapist, 392–393
  techniques and innovations, 392–393, 403
  therapist's function and role, 401–403
  time focus, 392–393
Multi-generational patterns, 399, 403
Multimodal approach, 280, 297
  life-history inventory, 279
  perspective, principles of, 278
  techniques, 475
  therapy, 266, 276–280, 282
Multimodal therapists, 276, 277, 278, 280
Multiple, and dual relationships, perspectives on, 55, 56–57

Narcissistic disorders, 79, 84, 85, 100
Narrative approach, 431–433
  goals, 435
  key figures, 435

Narrative approach *(continued)*
   process of change, 435
   role and function of therapist, 435
   techniques and innovations, 435
Narratives, 429, 430, 431, 434, 435, 436, 437
Narrative structure, 431
Narrative system, socially constructed, 431
Narrative therapeutic process, 432
National health programs, 259
Native Americans, 51, 53, 133, 447
Needs, 15, 17, 19, 30, 43, 44–45, 57, 69, 70, 74,
      83, 90, 93, 97, 99, 103, 112, 197, 231,
      239, 240, 245, 247, 250, 354, 364, 412
Neo-Adlerians, 108
Neo-Freudians, 108
Neo-Freudian school, 83
Neuroses:
   clients', 34
   existential, 151
   five layers of, 199
Neurotic anxiety, 151, 152
   definition, 71
Nonbeing:
   awareness of, 145
   fear of, 160
   threat of, 153
Nondirective counseling, 170
Nonsexist therapists, 364
Nonverbal clients, 483
Nonverbal cues, 203
Nonverbal language, 27, 204
Nonverbal process, 444
Normal infantile autism, 84
Norms:
   cultural, 210, 250
   objective, 428
Nuclear family:
   evolutionary picture of, 403
   self-differentiation from, 404
   Western emphasis on, 447
Nurturing triad, 408

Object-relations theory, 68, 83, 84, 85, 97, 99,
     101
   assessment process, 86
   and attachment theory, 86
   central influence on, 83
   contemporary trends, 83–87
   integration with cognitive behavioral
      techniques, 86–87
   perspectives from, 404
   relationship-building process, 86
Observational learning, 256
Observational processes, 428
Obsessions, 269
Obsessive-compulsive disorders, 305
   behavioral therapy for, 270
Oedipal issues, 355
Oedipus complex, 75, 78, 98, 101
   resolution of, 83
Open forum family counseling, 391, 397, 398
Open forum setting, 398
Operant behaviors, examples of, 257

Operant conditioning, 257, 282, 308
   models, 258
   principles of, 258
Oppression, 27, 164, 353, 373
   commitment to confronting, 467
   gender-based, 342
   integrated analysis of, 352
   for men and women, 479
   multiple, 346
   negative effects of, 373, 479
   political and social, of women, 351
   psychological, 8
   sources of, 345, 369
Oppressive forces, 370, 373
Oral fixation, 74, 95
Oral gratification, 74
Oral stage, 74, 76, 79, 97
Ordeal therapy, 424
   assignments, 425
Organismic self-regulation, 197, 221
Organization, within a family, 416, 421
Outcomes:
   counseling, 184
   to countertransference, 90
   evaluation of, 272, 329
   generalizations and maintenance of, 275
   global, 283
   positive, and negative, 90, 434, 446
   questions, 432
   research, 308, 485, 486, 487
   successful, 264–265, 471
   therapeutic, 323, 458, 466, 467, 485
   treatment, 266, 272, 283
   unique, 432

Pacific Islanders, 51
Paradox, 237, 425
Paradoxical assignments, 425
Paradoxical directives, 422, 425
Paradoxical intention, 125
Paradoxical interventions, 424, 425–426, 476
Paradoxical strategies, 277, 425
Paradoxical techniques, 425
Paradoxical theory, of change, 196, 203, 208
Paraphrasing, 127
Parental influence, 79
Parental messages, 361, 365
Parental relationship, 120
Parental subsystem, 417
Parental values, introjecting, 95
Parent, critical, 213
Parent/child counseling, 476
Parent education, 126
   Adlerian therapy, application to, 126
Parenting:
   authoritative-responsive, 396
   effective, 392
   preparation for, 394
Parenting failures, 305
Parenting skills, 396, 397
Parents, 18, 126, 395
   as leaders, 392
   as models, 394

standards of, 70
Parents-as-leaders, 397
Parent study groups, Adlerian, 126
Past, 17, 19, 74, 82, 98, 128, 130, 143, 146,
    155, 220, 234, 240
    client's, 89, 93, 484
    conditioning, victim of, 158
    experiences, 91, 96, 467, 495
    exploration of, 4, 96, 98, 235, 330, 484
    influences, 95, 110
    power of, 247
    understand our, 234
    victims of , 4, 235
Patriarchy, 346, 354, 356, 364, 368, 421
Pavlovian (or classical) conditioning, 257
Penis envy, 78, 98
People of color, 102, 373
Perception, 109, 129, 133, 474, 505
    clients, 120, 172, 175
    exploration of, 240
    field of visual, 197
    individual's, 109
    mistaken, self-defeating, 505
    of others, 248
    of self and world, 173
    therapist's, 207
Perceptual change, 445, 476
Perfection, 30, 70, 109
    image of, 31
    striving for, 110, 111
Performance anxiety, treatment of, 477
Personal identity, formation of, 80
Personal is political, 345, 351, 353, 373, 467
Personality, 69, 70, 82, 85, 110, 199
    A-B-C theory of, 300–301
    alcoholic, 515
    assessment scales for, 296
    change, 91, 92, 96, 303
    cognitive factors of, 221
    determinants of, 8
    development of, 8, 67, 68, 73–87, 97, 99,
        100, 348, 466
    disorders, 100, 296, 305, 360
    formation of, 74
    holistic approach to, 110, 195
    human, 81, 110
    integration, 213
    and language patterns, relationship
        between, 204
    narcissistic, 84
    poles in, 213
    reconstruction of, 7, 103, 469
    restructuring, 468
    splits in, 213
    structure of, 69–70, 79, 88, 466, 481
    theories of, 6, 8, 67, 81
    transformation of, 97
    unity of, 108, 132, 466
Personality and psychotherapy, theory of, 67
Personal narratives, 430
Personal power, 164, 353, 469
    awareness of, 355
Person-centered counselor, 181, 188

Person-centered philosophy, 187
Person-centered theory, 51, 172, 173, 174
    evolution of concepts or methods of, 187
Person-centered therapists, 180, 354, 470
    concepts essential to, 436
Person-centered therapy, 8, 9, 109, 168–191,
        178, 183, 265, 296, 328, 343, 415, 498,
        500
    application of, 179–182
    applied to case of Stan, 181–182, 496
    basic characteristics of, 173–174
    basic concepts, 181
    contemporary, 179
    contributions of, 183–184, 481
    contributions to multicultural counseling,
        478
    goal of, 174, 469
    historical background, 170–171
    hypothesis of, 176
    key concepts, 172–174, 466
    limitations in multicultural counseling,
        480
    limitations and criticisms of, 185–186,
        483–484
    methods, 179–180
    from multicultural perspective, 187–188
    philosophies, 464
    research on, 175, 184
    role of assessment in, 180
    summary and evaluation, 183–187
    therapeutic process, 174–179
    therapeutic relationship, 472
    therapeutic techniques and procedures,
        179–182
    therapist's function and role, 175
    view of human nature, 172–173
Person-in-environment:
    focus, 50, 478
    perspective, 52
    techniques to fit, 460
Phallic stage, 75, 77, 78, 79, 97
    conflict of, 78
Phenomenological orientation, 109, 412
Phenomenological perspective, 109, 328, 395
Phenomenological world, 144, 156, 478
Phenomenology, 172, 196
Philosophical restructuring, 301
Philosophy of dialogue, 208
Philosophy of life:
    "musturbatory," 306
    rational, 302
Phobias, 257, 477
    treatment of, 268, 270, 328
Physical abuse, victims of, 371
Physiology, 232, 245, 496
Plans, 116, 243
    of action, 496, 505, 512
    for change, 276, 472, 475
    process of carrying out, 242
    process of creating, 242
Pleasure principle, 69
Pluralism, 26
    theoretical, 3

Polarities, 219, 222, 466
Positive reinforcement, 258, 277
Postmodern perspective, 428
Postmodernists, 428
Posttraumatic stress disorder (PTSD), 270,
    272, 273, 360
Poverty, 126
Power, 16, 18, 204, 231, 250, 343, 351, 362,
    423
    abuse of, 221, 398
    analysis, 362, 369, 476
    and control, 212, 394, 424
    concepts of, 386
    denial of, 73
    differentials, 358, 360, 362, 370
    hierarchy of, 358, 473
    inequities, 373
    personal, 39, 164, 204, 353, 355, 469, 497
    recognizing and dealing with, 142
    in relationships, 358, 360, 372, 444, 484
    sense of, 481
    struggle, 395, 398, 439, 443, 478
    of the unconscious, 355
    working with, 422
Powerlessness, 39, 155, 164, 175
Practitioners:
    behaviorally oriented, 263
    existentially oriented, 144
    mental health, 49
    multicultural, 51
Pregenital period, 79
Prejudice, recognizing areas of, 44
Preschool phase, 75, 78, 97
Presence:
    lack of, 156
    quality of, 5
    of therapist and client, 161
    therapist's, 156, 207, 472
Present (See also Here-and-now, focus on), 8,
    17, 197, 198, 219, 220, 234, 236, 241,
    495, 504
Present-centered experience, 477
Present-centered focus, 312
Present-centered therapy, 476
Prevention, focus on, 134
Preventive care, 476
Private logic, 115, 116, 123, 129, 505
Privilege, white male, 374
Problem-solving:
    skills, 286, 312
    strategies, 358, 504
    therapy, 484
Process, 25, 33, 466
    to be in, 170
    counseling, 34, 37, 184
    and outcomes of counseling, 162
    therapeutic, 23, 27
    unification, 196
Professional distance, 160, 478
Projection, 70, 72, 87, 88, 200, 201, 216, 220,
    248, 472
Psychiatric disorders, 259
Psychic energy, 71, 464

Psychoanalysis, 95, 215, 329, 343, 356
    alternative to, 184
    approach, 95
    classical, 73, 88
    modifications of, 100
    reaction against, 8, 9
    as a sexist orientation, 355
    theory of, 67
    traditional, 91
Psychoanalytic approach, 51, 68, 70, 73, 89,
    91, 99, 297 504
    alternative to, 171
    concepts, classical, 68
    contemporary, 86, 100
    contributions of, 98–99
    directive and traditional, 170
    limitations and criticisms of, 101–102
    perspective, 256
    principles, 68
    process, 92
    techniques, 68, 101
    traditional, 102
Psychoanalytic orientation, contemporary, 96
Psychoanalytic psychotherapy, 8
Psychoanalytic system, Freud's, 68
Psychoanalytic theories, 83, 400
    contemporary, 68, 100
    concepts of, 97
    newer formulations of, 87
Psychoanalytic therapy (See also Psychother-
        apy; Psychoanalysis), 7, 66–105
    aim of, 70
    application: therapeutic techniques and
            procedures, 91–95
    applied to case of Stan, 95–97, 495
    clients in, 88
    conceptual foundation of, 86–87
    contemporary forms of, 86, 355
    contributions of, 481
    contributions to multicultural counseling,
            478
    counseling implications of, 80–81
    departure from, 399
    goals of, 87, 92, 469
    key concepts, 466
    limitations in multicultural counseling,
            479
    limitations of, 101, 483
    from multicultural perspective, 102–103
    philosophies, 464
    summary and evaluation, 97–102
    techniques of, 91, 92
    therapeutic process, 87–91
    therapeutic relationship, 472
    therapist's role and function, 87–88
Psychoanalytic view, 69, 73
    Freudian, 73
    contemporary, 73
Psychodiagnosis, definition, 52
Psychodrama, 459
Psychodramatic methods, 476
Psychodramatic techniques, 369
Psychodynamic approaches, 108, 371

diversity of, 68
existential, 145
insight-oriented, 258
principles of, 101
Psychodynamic factors, 68
Psychodynamic group therapy, 101
Psychodynamic problems, 102
Psychodynamic psychotherapy, 100
Psychodynamics, 88, 91, 110
Psychodynamic theory, 86
    and practice, current trends and
        directions in, 100
    brief, 100
    long-term, 100
Psychoeducational dimensions, 479
Psychoeducational model, 297, 464
Psychological abuse, victims of, 371
Psychological disorders, 248
    role of biological factors in, 257
Psychological theory, 41
Psychologists, clinical and counseling,
        surveys of, 457
Psychology:
    experimental, 261
    humanistic, 169
    multicultural issues in, 342
    subjective approach to, 109, 131
Psychopathology, 5, 50
Psychosexual concepts, Freud's, 99
Psychosexual development, 4, 78, 79, 466
    Freudian view of, 99
    growth, 73
    stages of, 68, 73, 74–76, 85
    throughout life, 99
Psychosexual perspective, 80
Psychosis, profound, 230
Psychosocial theory:
    development, 4, 68, 73, 83, 387
    factors, 74, 99
    growth, 73
    perspective, Erikson's, 73–74, 76, 78, 80,
        102
    stages, 74–76, 85
    strength of, 99
    trends, 97
Psychosomatic disorders, 305, 477
Psychosomatic family, 418
Psychosomatic symptoms, 244
Psychotherapeutic practice, 144
Psychotherapy (See also Psychoanalytic
        therapy; Psychoanalysis), 7, 15, 19,
        153, 343, 457
    existential, 144, 161–162
    future of, 459–460, 487
    group, 127
    humanistic approaches to, 142
    humanistic movements in, 169
    individual, techniques in, 277
    integrative, 314, 328, 457–468
    method of, 8, 68
    principles and practices of, 162
    process and outcomes of, 170
    psychoanalytic, 8

psychodynamic, 100
purpose of, 154
REBT, school of, 298
as reeducative process, 303
research in, 485
short-term, 468
spiritual and religious issues in, 461
theories of, 50, 67, 68
theory and practice of, 144
traditional, alternative to, 256
value of, 161, 486
work of, 156
Psychotic disorders, 305
Psychotic symptoms, 70
Punishments, psychological, 70
Purpose, 117, 123, 128, 130, 144, 145, 146,
    150, 159, 171, 298, 388

Qualifiers, 204, 205
Quality world, 231, 232, 236, 239, 240
Questionnaire, 114, 128, 267
    Adlerian lifestyle, 504
    in assessing signs of alcohol addiction, 515
    life-history, 279
Questions, 24, 29, 33, 53–54, 120, 121, 145,
    169, 201, 204, 240, 283, 298, 323,
    403–404, 431, 435, 437, 475, 476
    circular, 404, 437
    direct, 249
    exception, 434, 435, 437
    existential, 150
    externalizing, 432
    miracle, 434, 435
    open-ended, 312
    politically organized, 431
    reflective, 312
    relational, 437
    role of, 464
    scaling, 434
    skillful, 241, 249
    "what" and "how," 198
    "why," 198

Race, 17, 26, 28, 287, 346, 353
Racial heritage, 27
Racial minorities, 102, 164
Racial tension, 187
Racism, 27, 43, 164, 250, 255, 360, 373, 374
    effects of, 373
    role of, 480
Radical feminists, 346
Rape, 49, 344, 352, 371, 483
Rapport, building, 329
Rapprochement, 457
Rational beliefs, 302, 326
Rational disputation, 312
Rational emotive behavior self-help forms, 305
Rational emotive behavior therapists, 304, 327
Rational emotive behavior therapy (REBT),
        (See also Cognitive behavior therapy),
        8, 9, 256, 295, 297, 298, 301, 313, 318,
        326, 333, 343, 471, 473, 484, 504, 506,
        509

REBT (continued)
  applications of, to client populations,
    308–309
  assumptions, 297, 299
  contributions of, 328
  development of, 297–298
  Ellis's, 327–328, 329
  extensions of, 327
  hypothesis, 298
  limitation of, in multicultural settings,
    333
  practice of, 304–309
  strengths of, 328
  theory and applications of, 295
  theory and practice, 300
Rational-emotive imagery, 306, 307
Rational-emotive role-playing, 306
Rational-emotive therapy, 295
Rationalization, 72, 515
Rational thinking, application of, 404
Reaction formation, definition, 71
Reality anxiety, definition, 71
Reality principle, 69
Reality testing, 312
Reality therapists, 230, 233, 242, 246, 470
Reality therapy, 8, 109, 228–253, 328, 343,
    499, 504, 509
  advantages of, 247
  applications of, 244
  applied to case of Stan, 244, 496
  basic philosophies, 464
  characteristics of, 233
  and choice theory, 228–253
  contributions of, 247, 481
  contributions to multicultural counseling,
    478
  goals of, 244, 247, 469
  key concepts, 231–235, 466
  key procedures in the practice of, 240
  limitations and criticisms of, 247–248
  limitations in multicultural counseling,
    480
  limitations of, 484
  from a multicultural perspective, 249
  practice of, 237–238, 247
  present-oriented behavior focus of, 505
  summary, 246–247
  therapeutic relationship, 472
  therapeutic techniques and procedures,
    237–244
  summary and evaluation, 246–248
  therapeutic process in, 235–237
  view of human nature, 231–232
  WDEP system, 238, 240–244
Re-authoring, 125, 433, 435, 437
Recognition reflex, 391, 396
Recollections:
  early, 120, 121
  purposes for, 120, 495
Reconceptualization process, 272, 319
Reconstruction, 405
Reconstructive therapy, 483
Redeciding, role of, 464

Reeducation, 92, 109, 124
  of the client, 114
  and reorientation, 117
Reenactment, psychodramatic, 411
Referral, 22, 25, 27, 117, 430
  court-ordered, 423
Reflecting team, 429–430, 436
  approach to systemic family therapy, 429
  key figures, 435
  process of change, 435
  role and function of therapist, 435
  techniques and innovations, 435
  therapy goals, 435
Reflection, 6, 58, 430, 435, 481, 483
Reframing, 237, 363, 410, 420, 421, 424, 426,
    430, 439, 476
Regression, definition, 72
Regressive therapy, 483
Regressive transference, 88
Rehabilitation counseling, 476
Re-identification, with self, 220
Reindoctrination, 467
Reinforcement, 34, 258, 466
  external, 258
  negative, 258
  positive, 258, 277
  principles, 258
  social, 274
Reintegration, 196, 219
Rejection:
  history of, 505
  maternal, 85
Relabeling, 363, 476
  and reframing, 363
Relating, dysfunctional patterns of, 390
  I/Thou, 203
  to others, 112
  symbiotic forms of, 84
Relational/cultural theory, 341
Relational factors, 285, 484
Relational patterns, 86, 390, 401
Relations, parent/child, 477
Relationship-building process, of object-
    relations theory, 86
Relationship counseling, 478
Relationship-oriented therapies, 9, 51, 52,
    304, 371, 415, 470
Relationships, 12, 57, 73, 76, 95, 99, 117–118,
    127, 145, 155, 156, 160, 173, 175, 177,
    183, 230, 233, 234, 239, 244, 247, 285,
    287, 394, 400, 405, 430, 467, 472
  abusive, 345
  authentic, 9, 158
  with clients, 44, 156, 179, 210, 231, 285,
    320, 359, 472, 479
  collaborative, 4, 26, 100, 116, 131, 262,
    297, 329, 358, 364, 371, 473, 479,
    480, 497
  counseling, 24, 180, 354
  dependent, 90, 159
  dual, 43, 55, 56–57
  egalitarian, 128, 352, 358, 359, 364, 365,
    374, 467, 497

establishing, 498
evaluation of, 236, 472
family, 96, 101, 112, 128, 317, 348, 349,
    385, 388, 389, 402, 439
female/male, 96
freedom in, 180
fused, 402
gender, 346
growth-producing, 44
interdependent, 353, 355, 359
interpersonal, 74, 83, 110, 112, 277, 279,
    388, 399, 444
intimate, 76, 79, 80, 96, 127, 156, 389,
    505, 513
I/Thou, 156, 183, 207, 472, 482
life-affirming, 149
multiple, 55, 56
nonhierarchical, 354
open and trusting, 501
to others, 75, 79, 148–150
between parent and child, 120, 126, 394,
    397, 402, 439
personal, 183, 471
person-to-person, 15, 159, 183, 207, 354
power in, 210, 354, 358, 359, 370, 373
primacy of, 184
quality of, 117, 179, 313
role of, 208
sibling, 96, 111, 402, 417, 439
spousal, 401
symbiotic, 83, 149
therapeutic, 30, 34, 35, 37, 40, 47, 49,
    100, 117, 118, 156, 170, 174, 176,
    179, 185, 218, 264, 313, 314, 354,
    355, 364, 464, 473, 497, 515
therapist/client, 5, 9, 35, 48, 89–91,
    116–117, 156–157, 160, 171, 172,
    176–177, 180, 185, 207–208, 236,
    237, 264–265, 297, 304, 313–314,
    329, 358–359, 410, 415, 424,
    471–474
therapist/family, 414
transference, 87, 89, 95, 96, 98, 101, 304,
    329
trusting, 47, 482
understanding, 183, 237
unsatisfying, 230, 233, 234, 248
working, 5, 32, 87, 473
Relationship therapy, 390
Relaxation, 266, 268, 269, 267, 272, 321
techniques, 308, 475, 497, 509, 512
training, 259, 266, 267, 268, 277, 320, 321
Religion, 23, 26, 28, 126, 394
background of involvement in, 462
embracing, 461
formal, 461, 513
relevance of, for clients, 463
Religious affiliations, 403
Religious beliefs, 26, 353, 461
Reorganization, and reintegration, process
    of, 414
Reorientation, 117, 124–126, 130, 396
Repression, 70, 71, 91, 94, 95, 469

Reprocessing, 266
Research, 169, 170, 175, 184, 283, 285, 308,
    350
in behavioral therapies, 266
clinical, 485
controlled, 272, 308
criticisms of, 186
evidence, 351, 486
experimental, with animals, 257
methods, 260
outcome, 485, 486, 487
person-centered, 185, 485
practice based on, 162
precision and specificity in, 487
psychological, 256
in psychotherapy, 485
on sex and gender bias, 345
value of, 184
variables, 485
Researchers, feminist, 350
Resistance, 92, 93, 94, 98, 100, 210, 219, 352,
    460, 472, 480, 481, 486, 495
analysis of, 92, 94, 98, 475
to awareness, 211
channels of, 200, 201
client's, 87, 239, 425
conceptualizing, 211
to contact, 200, 201, 211
to counseling, 249
dealing with, 33, 422
emergence of, 210
forms of, 89, 202
Respect:
for client, 46, 178, 212, 360, 445
mutual, 128, 472
for the person, 145
for values and traditions, 460
Responsibility, 8, 9, 39, 44, 45, 109, 116, 127,
    128, 134, 144, 146, 147, 156, 158, 164,
    173, 195, 234, 260, 297, 357, 407, 464,
    470, 495, 498
to act, 153
for direction of therapy, 482
ethical, 48
freedom and, 147
joint, 33, 472
lack of, attitudes of, 316
professional and ethical, 57
sharing, with client, 35–36
Restricted existence, 148, 155
Restructuring, 158, 301, 310, 419, 420, 468,
    476
Results, empirical validation of, 477
Retroflection, 200, 201
Reversal technique, 214, 215
Rhythmic eye movements, 271
Rights:
of clients, 262
interpersonal, 363
legal, 27
and responsibilities, 47, 499
Risks, 12, 15, 33, 55, 56, 57, 209
Rituals, 446

Rivalry, sibling, 113
Role behaviors, expected, 370
Role confusion, 75, 80
Role constraints, and attitudes, 344
Role expectations, 30, 361
Role models, 127
Role-playing, 281, 306, 307, 308, 319, 325,
    369, 476, 496–497, 511, 512
Role-play technique, 3, 213
Rules, 115, 332, 389, 405, 406, 407, 409, 416,
    417, 419, 421, 423, 473, 497
Ruth, case of, diagnostic perspective on, 54

Schema:
    emphasis on, 317
    gender, 349
    health concerns, 349
    leadership, 349
Schema restructuring, 310, 317
Schemata, family, 318
Schizophrenic patients, treating, 162
Scientific method, 184, 265, 260, 282, 301,
    328, 483, 485, 488
Scripts, 216, 419
Sculpting, 405
Search for meaning, in meaningless world,
    464
Second force, behavioral approach, 387
Second-order family therapy, 391
Selective abstraction, 311, 315
Self psychology, 83–87, 96, 97
Self:
    authentic, 200
    creation of, 437
    definition of, 428
    differentiate, 392
    and object, constancy of, 85
    search for, 465
    sense of, 84, 348, 466
    stages of, 84
    trust in, 464
    view of, 132
Self-acceptance, 195, 357
Self-actualization, 82, 162, 183, 357, 468,
    480, 499
Self-assessment, 242, 272
Self-awareness, 15, 17, 44, 87, 145, 146, 158,
    159, 173, 195, 354, 466
    capacity for, 145–147, 464
    cultural, 26
    importance of, 399
    therapist, 402, 415
Self-confidence, 114, 357
Self-control approach, 261
Self-deception, 23, 72, 515
Self-defeating beliefs, 299, 323, 324, 327,
    512
Self-defeating patterns, tendency toward,
    299
Self-determination, 8, 164, 259, 346, 372,
    412, 447, 466, 480
Self-differentiation, 402, 404
Self-direction, 9, 183, 282, 276, 466, 482

Self-disclosure, 16, 18, 87, 177, 354, 362, 364,
    371
    therapist, 352, 362, 363, 476
Self-discovery, 156, 221, 320
Self-doubt, 29, 34, 74
Self-efficacy, theory of, 258
Self-esteem, 73, 76, 84, 85, 392, 405, 513
Self-evaluation, 15, 58, 242, 247, 248, 363
Self-exploration, 17, 18, 19, 30, 158, 173, 469
Self-hate, 316, 317
Self-image, 201, 241
Self-indoctrination, 298, 326, 506
Self-in-relation:
    concept, 351
    theory, 349
    model, 345, 350
Self-instruction therapy, 318, 329
Self-instructional training, 256, 277, 320,
    321
Self-management, 261, 275, 479
    principles, 308
    programs, 259, 266, 275–276, 475, 509
Self-monitoring, 272, 275, 276, 320, 499
Self-realization, 131, 480
Self-regulation, 219
    organismic, 196, 197, 221
Self-reinforcement, 275, 276, 320
Self-reliance, 74, 196
Self-respect, sense of, 118
Self-statements, 30, 274, 297, 306, 318, 319,
    320, 321, 324, 329, 365, 497, 507
Self-understanding, 87, 91, 117, 123–124,
    176, 179
Self-worth, 72, 118, 127, 182
Sensate-focus training, 277
Sensations, 197, 277, 278, 280
Sensitivity, 5, 29, 445
Separateness:
    feelings of, 159
    and individuality, sense of, 400
Separation, 83, 84
    and individuation, 83, 84, 85, 96, 99
Sequences, 424
    maladaptive, 423
    repeated, 416
    tracking, 476
Sex, 142
    extramarital, 21
    and gender bias, research on, 345
    premarital, 22, 23
Sexism, 346, 353, 362, 373, 374, 427
    in diagnostic categories, 359
Sexist society, 353
Sex-role identification, 96
Sex-role oppression, struggles with, 357
Sex roles, 112, 127, 363
Sexual abuse, 345
    childhood, 352
    victims of, 371
Sexual assault, 352
Sexual disorders, 477
Sexual energy, 68, 69, 75
Sexual harassment, 352, 371, 483

Sexual intimacy, 56
    with current clients, students, and super-
        visees, 371
Sexuality, 18, 73, 75, 78,
    theory of, 81
Sexual misconduct, 371
Sexual orientation, 22, 23, 25, 26, 28, 287,
    353
Sexual relationships, with clients, students,
    and supervisees, 371
Shame, 74, 77, 307, 462
Shame-attacking exercises, 306, 307–308
Short-term approach, 482
Short-term focus, 247
Short-term therapy, 368, 488
Short-term treatments, 100, 180, 460
Silence, 31–32, 125, 510
Skills, 5, 26, 27, 29, 75, 181, 516
    acquiring and practicing, 321, 465
    clinical, 54, 265
    communication, 181
    coping, 319, 473
    intervention, 370
    interviewing, 41
    learning, 319, 479
    problem-solving and coping, 312
    relationship, 181
    training, 308, 477
Slips of the tongue, 70, 92
Social action, 43, 51, 164, 341, 364, 476
Social activism, positive, 371
Social change, 51, 351, 360, 364, 373
Social class, 17
Social construction, in family therapy, com-
    parison of four approaches to, 435
Social constructionism, 384, 428, 429, 433
    family therapy, 427–438
    goals, 436
    key concepts, 435–436
    techniques, 436–437
    therapist's function and goals, 436
Social constructionists, 434, 437, 438
    dialogue, 430
    perspectives, 443
    postmodern, 428
    theories, 435, 436
Social equality, 398
    approaches based on, 427
Social expectations, examining, 357
Social factors, 51, 52, 73, 108, 130, 164
    Adlerian approach to, 131
    paying attention to, 100
Social influences, 83, 287
Social injustice, 51
Social interest, 9, 111–112, 114, 126, 132,
    133, 142, 144, 464, 466, 478
    Adlerian focus on, 132
    creating, 468
    role of, 298
Social isolation, feelings of, 515
Social justice perspective, 342
Social learning theory, 256, 257, 258, 259,
    282, 459

Social roles, 134
    stereotypes in, 347
Social skills training, 274, 277, 321, 475
Socialist feminists, 346
Socialist philosophy, 369
Socialization, 79, 210
    client's, 481
    gender-role, 4, 10, 353, 356, 360
    patterns, limits and constraints of, 345
    role of, 360
    of women, 343
Socially constructed narrative system, 431
Societal beliefs, sexist and oppressive, 354
Societal expectations, 188, 353, 361, 363, 367
Societal practices, sexist and oppressive, 354
Societal stereotypes, 367
Sociocultural conditioning, 143, 259
Sociocultural environment, client's, 287
Sociocultural factors, 99
Sociocultural perspective, 102, 346
Sociocultural systems, 430
Socioeconomic background, 471
Socioeconomic classes, lower, 483
Socioeconomic status, 26, 403
Sociopolitical forces, 27
Sociopolitical reality, 343
Sociopolitical status, 343
Sociopolitical system, 26
Socratic dialogue, 312, 316, 320, 476, 497,
    507
Solution-oriented therapists, 434
Solution-oriented therapy, 433–435
    approach, 386
    key figures, 435
    and function of therapist, 435
    process of change, 435
    techniques and innovations, 435
    therapy goals, 435
Somatic preoccupations, 316
Spirituality/religious, 127, 461
    approach, 81–82
    beliefs, 26, 461
    concerns, 461
    dimensions, 112, 461, 462, 513
    needs, 461
    perspective, 462
    relevance of, for clients, 463
    values, being open to, 461
Splitting, 85, 213
Spontaneity, 392, 413, 464, 469, 471
Stage of development, 102
    tasks and crises of, 99
    turning points at, 99
Stage directors, 419, 424
Stan, case of, 10–13, 391, 495–497
    Adlerian therapy applied to, 128–130
    areas of application, 160–161
    behavior therapy applied to, 280–282,
        323–326
    existential therapy applied to, 158–159
    family therapy applied to, 439–442
    feminist therapy applied to, 364–368
    Gestalt therapy applied to, 217–219

Stan, case of *(continued)*
    integrative approach in working with, 493–519
    person-centered therapy applied to, 181–182
    psychoanalytic therapy applied to, 95–97
    reality therapy applied to, 244
    working with, 128
Status:
    socioeconomic, 26
    sociopolitical, 8
Status quo, 353, 403
    adjustment to, 479
    norms of, 360
    oppressive, 344
Stereotyped patterns, 385, 416
Stereotypes, 353, 474
    cultural and gender, 370
    gender, 350, 356
    gender-role, 360, 362
    societal, 364, 367
Stimuli, aversive, 257
Stimulus control, 275
Stimulus event, 258
Stimulus, presentation of, 258
Storied lives and narratives, 436, 437
Stories, 205, 432, 435, 436
    alternative, 430, 436, 437
    interpretive, 431
    solution, 432
    use of, 125
Strategic approach, 391, 429
Strategic family therapists, 443, 444
Strategic family therapy, 386, 392–393, 422–427, 433, 443, 444
    development of, 422
    elements of, 425
    goals, 423–424
    key concepts, 422–423
    techniques, 424–426
    therapist's function and role, 424
Strategic interventions, 425, 429
    applications of, 423
    concepts of, 386
    working with, 422
Strategic models, 433
Stress, 329, 407
    coping with, 406
    external, 447
    inoculation, 256, 272, 320, 329
    interpersonal, 428
    management, 477
Stress-inoculation training (SIT), 320, 329
Stress-management program, 322
Stress-management training, 321, 322
Structural family therapists, 416, 419, 443, 444
Structural family therapy, 385, 386, 392–393, 416–422, 422–423, 443–444
    goals, 418–419
    key concepts, 416
    Minuchin's, 422
    process of, 421

subsystems, tasks and functions, 417
    techniques, 420–421
    therapist's function and role, 419–420
Structural map, 421
Structural patterns, of a family, 416
Structural requirements, in functional families, 423
Structured therapy, 328, 476
Structuring, 188, 470, 501
Stuttering, 269, 477
Subjective approach, need for, 481
Subjective experience, 155, 171, 178, 184, 352, 475
Subjective framework, 322, 507
Subjective interview, 118, 119, 122
Subjective unit of disturbance (SUD), 271
Sublimation, definition, 72
Subordinate group, oppression as members of, 351
Substance abuse, 126, 476, 477
Suicidal risk, 12, 13, 49, 50, 158, 316, 423, 495, 515
    assessment, 296, 495
Summary:
    in Adlerian therapy, 122, 130
    of coping strategies, 122
    of early recollections, 122
    of family constellation, 122
    narrative, 122
Superego, 69, 70, 71, 79, 95, 466
Superiority, 121, 129
    goal of, 110, 111
    striving for, 110–111, 129, 131, 466
Supervision, 19, 26, 57, 484
    group, 49
Support, 29, 37, 118, 125
    external, 199
    genuine, 181
    self-, 196
    in social networks, 516
    systems, 27, 38
Support groups, women's, 363
Survival, 103, 164, 231, 250, 352, 406
Symbiosis, 84, 85, 90
    normal, 97
Symbiotic phase, 96
Symbols, focusing on, 414
Symmetrical sequence, 417
Syncretism, 458
Systematic desensitization, 257, 266, 267–269, 281, 308, 475
Systematic eclecticism, 277
Systematic integration, 468
Systemic family therapy, 387
    reflecting team approach to, 429
Systemic perspective, 164, 343, 465
Systemic therapist, 388
Systems, language of, 446
Systems orientation, 388
Systems, within systems, 431

Taskmaster, role of, 408
Tasks:

basic, 75
counselor's, 124
and functions, of structural family
    therapy subsystems, 417
infant's, 76
life, 115, 119, 127
setting, 125
of therapeutic process, 150
therapist's, 147
Teaching, 170, 221, 298, 304, 305, 326, 476,
    477, 479
the client, 236
student-centered, 171
Teaching/learning process, foundation for, 126
Technical eclecticism, 131, 276, 277, 308,
    458, 459, 460, 465
Techniques, 3, 5, 6, 8, 37, 118, 123, 126, 127,
    131, 133, 154, 159, 162, 209, 221, 244,
    265, 282, 287, 326, 362, 405, 420, 429,
    459, 465, 467, 472, 474, 475, 481
absence of, 480
action-oriented, 133, 355
administering, 179
affective, 304
applications of, 474
assessment, 180
behavioral, 86, 131, 256, 304, 308, 325,
    497, 512
of behavioral approaches, 221
behavioral conditioning, 256
in behavior therapy, 265–280
of choice, 467
classical analytic, 100
cognitive, 86, 131, 133, 221, 304, 314–315,
    325, 497, 512
cognitive behavioral, 86, 304–309, 327
cognitive rehearsal, 317
confrontational, 481
consciousness-raising, 361
counseling, 5, 6, 27
culture-bound, 27
diagnostic, 15
diverse, 266
effective use of, 285
emotive, 306–307, 325, 497, 512
empirically tested, 284
experiential, 86, 131
of experiential family therapy, 414
in feminist therapy, 359–364
free-association, 70
in Gestalt therapy, 208–217, 411
of human validation process model,
    410–411
multigenerational family therapy, 403
openness to incorporating, 482
paradoxical, 425
person-centered, 179, 411
in psychoanalytic practice, 98
from psychodrama, 411
popularized by Perls, 355
and procedures, in existential therapy,
    157–158
and procedures, therapeutic, 91, 179–182

and procedures, therapeutic, in feminist
    therapy, 359–364
projective, 70
psychoanalytic, 68, 98, 101
psychodramatic, 369
push-button, 125
quick-fix, 102
reflection, 263
reframing, 424
reversal, 214, 215
role-play, 3, 213
of social constructionism family therapy,
    436–437
of structural family therapy, 420–421
summarizing, 263
therapeutic, 100, 157, 474
theoretical rationale for, 37
traditional, 27
treatment, 438
unconventional, 422
use of, 185, 414
variability of,486
from various approaches, 474–484
without theoretical rationale, 458
Techniques and procedures, therapeutic,
    117–128
Techniques and strategies, in feminist
    therapy, 361–364
Termination, 125, 363
of counseling, 86
premature, 484
talk about, 517
of therapy, moving toward, 516–517
Tests, 43, 54, 180, 475
as adjunct to counseling, 54
cautions and guidelines regarding use of,
    54–55
caution in using, 180
cultural implications of, 53
guidelines for use of, 54–55
Theoretical eclecticism, 277
Theoretical integration, 458, 459
Theoretical orientations, 36, 51, 438
diverse, 154
emphasis of each, 495
rivalry among, 457
Theoretical position, how to select, 439
Theories, 3, 465
contemporary, 50, 109
of counseling, 6
current, 50
of personality, 6, 15
of psychotherapy, 15
traditional, 26
Theorists:
behavior modification, 285
contributions of modern analytic, 99–101
modern analytic, contributions of, 99–101
newer psychoanalytic, 100
Theory:
choice, 228–253
control, 229
of change, paradoxical, 203, 208

Theory *(continued)*
  of inclusion, 341
  object-relations, 68
  of personality, 81
  person-centered, 172, 173, 174
  psychoanalysis, 67
  psychological, 41
  of sexuality, 81
  social learning, 256
Therapeutic alliance, establishing, 271
Therapeutic goals *(See also* Goals),152, 302
Therapeutic process, 5, 23, 25, 27, 113, 127,
      130, 144, 155, 303, 429
  in Adlerian therapy, 113–117
  behavior therapy, 261–265
  in cognitive behavior therapy, 301–304
  core of, 247
  demystifying, 237, 497
  in existential therapy, 153–158
  of feminist therapy, 353–359
  four phases of, 117
  gender and power at the core of, 343
  of Gestalt therapy, 208
  outcome of, 170
  in person-centered therapy, 174–179
  in reality therapy and choice theory,
      235–237
  task of, 150
Therapeutic relationship, 8, 15, 16, 23, 30,
      34, 35, 37, 40, 47, 49, 218, 355, 358
  Adlerian therapy, 472
  behavior therapy, 472
  cognitive behavior therapy, 473
  collaborative, 314
  egalitarian, 351, 359
  emphasis on, 313
  empowerment and egalitarianism, 358
  existential therapy, 472
  family systems therapy, 473
  feminist therapy, 473
  Gestalt therapy, 472
  hierarchical, 344
  person-centered therapy, 472
  psychoanalytic therapy, 472
  reality therapy, 472
Therapeutic strategies, 50, 369
  diverse, 460
  eclectic, 327
Therapeutic style, 237, 473
  active and directive, 497
  Satir's, 410
Therapist:
  as expert, 435
  as model, 410, 482
  rational emotive behavior, 327
Therapists, 4, 6
  active and directive stance of, 479
  Adlerian, 130
  analytic, 92
  attitude of, 9, 170, 175, 177, 475
  authentic, 208
  beginning, 29, 31
  behavior and cognitive, 256–257, 485

Bowenian, 404
  characteristics of, 313
  cognitive behavioral, 330
  collaborating with, 24
  confrontational style of, 426
  congruent, 183
  contemporary, 207
  culturally insensitive, 287
  effective, 6, 13, 91, 474
  existential and feminist, 371
  existential, 148, 149, 151, 153, 156, 158,
      164
  family, 4, 390
  feminist, 4, 51, 53, 164, 352, 371
  function of, 133, 151, 173, 203–206, 263,
      419
  Gestalt, 200, 201
  human qualities of, 6
  inexperienced, 30
  main tasks of, 178
  multimodal, 276, 277, 278, 280
  nonreligious, 23
  nonsexist, 364
  perceptions of, 352
  personal characteristics of, 170
  personality and style of, 474
  in person-centered therapy, 175, 180
  function in psychoanalytic therapy, 87–88
  psychoanalytically oriented, 102
  qualities of, 472
  reality, 233, 237, 246
  rational emotive behavior, 304
  of reality therapists, 230, 236, 242
  realness of, 177
  role, 36, 87–88, 101, 114–115, 173, 195,
      196, 208, 262, 264, 373, 413, 444,
      473, 499
  self-actualized, 178
  solution-oriented, 434
  task of, 147, 148
  as teacher, 231, 312, 313, 444, 472, 482
Therapy:
  action-oriented, 8, 9
  aim of, 143, 158, 162, 174
  analytic, 87
  assumptions about, 26
  basic work of, 203
  behavior, 9, 254–293
  brief, 102, 279, 427, 468
  client's experience in, 88–89, 206, 236,
      264, 303–304, 356–358
  cognitive behavioral and feminist, 371
  cognitive, 8, 9, 256
  confrontational, 329
  contemporary models of, 4, 130
  core of, 157
  culture-bound, 50–51
  didactic, 8
  direction of, 35, 164, 183
  effective, 155, 237, 264, 280, 473, 487
  existential, 150, 152, 153, 154, 159, 161,
      171, 207
  experiential, 8, 9, 52

family, 4, 8, 10, 52, 126, 130, 477
feminist, 4, 8, 10, 52, 353
Gestalt, 9, 171, 195
goals of, 160, 183, 235, 281, 346, 389, 396
group, 127
humanistic and behavioristic, 282
individual and family, 342
insight-focused, 309
intergeneratinoal process of, 447
key focus of, 162
marital, 130, 476, 477
nondirective, 180
outcome research, implications of, 486
person-centered, 168–191
present-centered, 497
problem-oriented, 328
process, 48, 88, 96, 149, 313, 470, 473, 485
psychoanalytic, 8
psychodynamic group, 101
purpose of, 474
rational-emotive behavior, 8, 9, 256
reality and choice theory, 8, 228–253
relationship-oriented, 9, 51, 52
self-instructional, 318
short-term, 101, 102
structured, 497
styles, 212
team, 429
termination, moving toward, 516–517
time-limited, 101, 497
third force in, 171
traditional, 51, 433
Thinking, 4, 10, 25, 232, 245, 297, 305, 496,
    497, 507, 512
and acting, 298, 473
diagnostic, 54
dichotomous, 311, 509
emotional, 400
emphasis on, 479
errors in, 115
existential, applied to psychotherapy, 142
and feeling, 494, 512, 517–518
illogical, 299, 302, 474
logical, 69
polarized, 509
rational, or straight, 299
realistic, 69
revising, 306
role of, 8, 464
scientific approach to, 303
self-defeating, 304
wholeness and integration of, 464
Third force, humanistic approach, 387
Thoughts, 20, 130, 506, 517
and actions, 505
automatic, 9, 310
and beliefs, irrationality of, 323
expression of, 444
maladaptive, 318
negative, 309
self-defeating, 497
suicidal, 13
Thought stopping, 277

Tolerance, REBT's concept of, 304
Total behaviors, 233, 241, 496
Tracking sequences, 420, 476
Traditional roles, 350, 351
Traditional theories, characteristics of, 347
Training, 27, 180
    counselor's level of, 37
    in EMDR, 273
    psychoanalytic, 91
Transactions, 392, 419, 421, 423
Transference, 19, 90, 98, 100, 162, 234, 247,
    304, 330, 466, 481, 484
    analysis of, 92, 94–95, 98, 475
    distortions, 70
    interpretation of, 94–95
    manifestations, 88
    negative, 89, 90
    positive, 89
    regressive, 88
    rejection of, 234
    relationships, 87, 96, 98, 101
    understanding value and role of, 98
    working through, 91
    working with, 472, 495
Transgenerational approach, 403
Transgenerational family therapy, 399
Transgenerational meanings, 389
Treatment, 54
    approaches, 387, 515
    brief, 284
    comprehensive, 270, 278
    cost of, 102, 460
    focus of, 461
    goals, 469
    integrative, 460
    outcomes, 266
    outpatient, 188
    plans, 466, 475
    procedures, 259, 260
    process, 52, 180
    program, supplementary, 515–516
    short-term, 100, 180, 279, 460
    strategies, 276, 279, 487
    successful, 264
    time-limited and educational, 297
Triadic process, 408
Triads, nurturing, 405
Triangles, 467
Triangular patterns, 401
Triangulation, 384, 399, 400, 401, 428, 444
Trust, 73, 76, 128, 150, 170, 172, 265, 468,
    472, 496, 498
    therapist's, 150
    versus mistrust, 74, 76, 89
Tyranny of "shoulds," 298, 317

Unconditional acceptance, 304, 306
Unconditional positive regard, 172, 177, 178,
    181, 304, 354, 496
Unconscious, 68, 69, 70, 81, 94, 97, 180, 466,
    468, 469, 481, 484
    as determinant of behavior, 481
    dynamics, 9, 329

Unconscious (continued)
  focus, 8, 96, 143
  Freudian concepts of, 100
  material, 88, 89, 91, 93
  motivations, 7, 68, 464
  power of, 247
  processes, 70, 466, 495
  role of, 68, 70
Underachievement, 515
Understanding, 86, 126, 133, 162, 179, 182,
    423, 471, 475, 478, 496
  emotional, 92
  empathic, 172, 177, 178–179, 181, 304
  emphasis on, 162
  intellectual, 92
  lack of, 33, 85
  of world, 75
Unethical practices, 45
Unfinished business, 34, 44, 89, 98, 198–199,
    202, 205, 213, 217, 330, 466, 472, 496
  effects of, 199

Value:
  adaptive, 71
  adjustive, 73
  assumptions, 51, 480
  conflicts, 20, 21–25
  imposition, 358
  judgments, 21, 444
  orientations, 447
Values, 5, 15, 17, 20, 22, 25, 29, 47, 58, 131,
    133, 142, 150, 163, 171, 298, 302
  and beliefs, about society, 362–363
  client, 25, 27, 447
  in contemporary counseling, 51
  cultural, 26, 27, 58, 250, 332
  exploring, 128, 332, 357
  faulty, 114, 122
  feminist therapy, 341
  imposing, 20, 27, 51, 150, 248, 322, 371–372
  integration of ethical, social, or political,
    427
  internally derived, 150
  parental, 72
  personal, 160

  respect for, 26, 460, 478
  retaining, 249
  role of, 19, 20, 24
  search for, 144, 145
  of society, 70
  source and authority of, 157–158
  spiritual/religious, 23, 26, 461, 513
  therapeutic, 24
  therapist's, 24, 72, 444
  traditional, 150
  upper- and middle-class, 102
Victims, 4, 130, 244, 319
  blaming, 248, 347
  of circumstances, 143, 164, 246
  of the past, 158, 235
  role of, 154, 213, 408
Violence, victims of, 390
Visualization techniques, use of, 272
Visual perception, field of, 197

Warmth, 304, 471, 472
  nonpossessive, 181
Western standards, 53
Western values, 447
Wheel of influence, 411
White privilege, 373, 374
Will to meaning, 144
Women, 53
  of color, 343, 373
  core self of, 349
  different voices of, 345
  equality for, 134
Womanists, 373
Women's intuition, 349
Women's movement, 479
  of the 1960s, 344, 368
Working through, 70, 89, 90, 91, 95, 98, 285,
    504
Worldviews, 50
  clarification of, 179
  client's subjective, 109
  differences in, 249

"You" talk, 204
Young adulthood, 76, 79, 80, 97

TO THE OWNER OF THIS BOOK:

I hope that you have found *Theory and Practice of Counseling and Psychotherapy,* Sixth Edition useful. So that this book can be improved in a future edition, would you take the time to complete this sheet and return it? Thank you.

School and address: _____

_____

Department: _____

Instructor's name: _____

1. What I like most about this book is: _____

_____

_____

2. What I like least about this book is: _____

_____

_____

3. My general reaction to this book is: _____

_____

_____

4. The name of the course in which I used this book is: _____

_____

5. Were all of the chapters of the book assigned for you to read? _____

   If not, which ones weren't? _____

6. In the space below, or on a separate sheet of paper, please write specific suggestions for improving this book and anything else you'd care to share about your experience in using this book.

_____

_____

_____

_____